SPORT AND SOCIAL SYSTEMS

SPORT AND SOCIAL SYSTEMS

A Guide to the Analysis, Problems, and Literature

John W. Loy
Barry D. McPherson
Gerald Kenyon

University of Waterloo

ADDISON-WESLEY PUBLISHING COMPANY
Reading, Massachusetts
Menlo Park, California
London • Amsterdam • Don Mills, Ontario • Sydney

This book is in the
Addison-Wesley series in the
Social Significance of Sport

ISBN 0-201-04143-X
ABCDEFGHIJK-MA-798

In memory of Donald W. Ball (1934–1976) and Pekka
Kiviaho (1938–1977), two sporting colleagues and
seminal sociologists, whose lives were tragically taken
in midcareer.

PREFACE

In recent years social scientists have given increased attention to the study of sport. One must frankly acknowledge, however, that while interest in sport from the perspective of the social sciences has prevailed for some time in Europe, North America, and other parts of the world, much of the scholarship has been short on theory, short on data, or both. Although there has been a noticeable increase in both the quantity and quality of research in sport sociology during the past few years, these conditions still persist to some degree. Nevertheless, sufficient work has accumulated to warrant bringing it together in one place: both to introduce the sociology of sport to the interested reader, and to encourage further work in the field by codifying and critiquing the body of knowledge as it presently exists.

Given that courses in the subject are being offered in increasing numbers through departments of physical education, sociology, sport studies, and kinesiology, *Sport and Social Systems* has been written largely for the undergraduate student who desires to become acquainted with the sociology of sport. In addition, the relatively large number of references cited makes the text a valuable source for both graduate students initially engaging in research in the area, and instructors who may be teaching a course on the subject for the first time.

The contents of the book are based not only on sociological perspectives, but to some extent on those of social psychology, anthropology, and the other social sciences. No single theoretical stance has been taken. To have done so would have been too limiting for a textbook, since important contributions to sport sociology would have had to be excluded, or subject to criticism as being out of context. Moreover, we believe that the sociology of sport is a multiparadigm specialty and thus we have attempted to expose the reader to a variety of sociological methods and theoretical perspectives.

In organizing the book we were confronted with the problem of how to steer the structure, as it were, between the Scylla of a too simple and trite topical outline and the Charybdis of a too complex and formal framework. A compromise was reached by organizing the material into logical units according to levels of sociological analysis within a social-system frame of reference. The concept of a social system is not employed in the particular Parsonian sense of the term, but rather is used in the generic sense of the term to refer to all social units—small or large, simple or complex—that are characterized by persons engaged in patterned social interaction by means of and according to shared normative expectations. Perhaps a more precise and appropriate construct would have been the term "psycho-socio-cultural system." However, the latter term is awkward to say the least, and the term social system has by now achieved consensus among most social scientists as a construct embracing a variety of social collectivities from small groups, to formal organizations, to social institutions, to total societies and nation-states.

In brief, the book is structured in four parts designed to move the reader from micro- to macrolevel sociological concerns as they relate to the social phenomenon of sport. Part 1 contains two chapters providing a general introduction to the field by addressing both the subject matter of inquiry, that is, sport; and the nature of a discipline-oriented approach to its study, that is, sociology. Part 2 contains three chapters viewing sport as a microsocial system, more particularly, small groups in sport, sport organizations, and sport subcultures. Part 3 contains four chapters, each addressed to sport as a macrosocial system, covering socializing institutions, regulative institutions, cultural institutions, and systems of social stratification. Part 4 concludes with a single chapter, "Sport as a Social Institution," which serves as a summary of the text.

Although the general outline of the text is seemingly static in nature with its focus on units of analysis (for example, groups, organizations, subcultures, institutions, etc.), the basic content of the text is dynamic in the sense that emphasis is placed on the analysis of psychosociological processes such as leadership, discrimination, socialization, communication, conflict, and cooperation. Moreover, while the text is somewhat flavored by a neopositivistic bias, we have attempted to address a number of social problems of humanistic concern such as the matters of agism, racism, sexism, and social inequality in general. Finally, throughout the text we have made an effort to highlight the processes underlying the socialization into and via sport, and to contrast the interpretation of sport-related phenomena from both the consensus and conflict perspectives of social reality.

The research and scholarship on which the material is based has emanated largely from North America and to some extent Western Europe—the two regions in which most of the literature in the field has been generated. Wherever possible we have tried to illustrate major concerns with examples drawn from American and Canadian sport. However, the last chapter of the text is restricted to the American case and the reader is referred to Gruneau and Albinson (1976) and Helmes (1977) for insight into the Canadian situation.*

---

*Richard S. Gruneau and John G. Albinson (eds.), *Canadian Sport-Sociological Perspectives.* Don Mills, Ontario: Addison-Wesley (Canada) Ltd., 1976; and Richard C. Helmes, *Canadian Sport as an Ideological Institution* (M.A. thesis, Queens University, Kingston, Ontario, April 1977).

As implied above, a large number of references are given for each chapter. This should facilitate concentration on a particular topic, should the reader desire, as well as accommodate the assignment of specific readings by the instructor. However, since no textbook can include material more recent than six months or so before its publication, the reader should regularly consult general sources such as *Current Contents* in the social and behavioral sciences and journals addressed to the sociology of sport, such as the *International Review of Sport Sociology* and the *Review of Sport and Leisure,* or SIRLS,* for references and documents relating directly to the field. In addition, a number of articles cited in the text have been reprinted in several recent readers or monographs that are referred to throughout the volume. Finally, the second edition of Loy and Kenyon (1978)† has been structured to include material closely paralleling the outline of this book.

Ontario, Canada   J.W.L.
January 1978   B.D.M.
                                                                                     G.K.

---

*Information Retrieval System for the Sociology of Leisure and Sport, University of Waterloo, Canada.

†J. W. Loy and G. S. Kenyon (eds.), *Sport, Culture and Society,* 2nd ed. Dubuque, Iowa: Gorsuch Scarisbrick Publishers, 1978.

ACKNOWLEDGMENTS

A text of this nature could not be written without the assistance of many friends and associates. First, the sources and documents required to write the text were retrieved by Ms. Susan Chang and her staff in the Information Retrieval System for the Sociology of Sport and Leisure at the University of Waterloo. Second, colleagues far and near provided intellectual stimulation and offered valuable critical comment. In particular, we express our thanks to Susan Birrell, James Curtis, Peter Donnelly, Richard Gruneau, Robert Faulkner, Alan Ingham, Erik Kjeldsen, Walter Kroll, Guy Lewis, Larry Locke, Charles Page, Gerald Redmond, John Roberts, Brian Sutton-Smith, Nancy Theberge, Judy Toyama, and Neil Widmeyer. Third, appreciation is extended to Mrs. Eleanor Fox, Ms. Ginger Loalbo, Mrs. L. MacDonald, and Mrs. T. Schuett, and others who performed a variety of arduous typing tasks.

Fourth, a special gratitude is due Ms. Christine Felstead, who sacrificed many evenings and weekends to prepare both early drafts and the final manuscript, always of the highest quality; her unswerving diligence, together with a fine sense of humor in the face of both rigid deadlines and a not-always cooperating computer, will not be forgotten. Fifth, the first author wishes to acknowledge his appreciation of the award of an Andrew Mellon Postdoctoral Fellowship in the Department of Anthropology at the University of Pittsburgh (1976), which afforded him much of the needed resources and stimulation required for the preparation of his part of the book. Finally, the first author gives special thanks to Quest for permission to reproduce a liberally revised version in Chapter 1 of an article titled "The Nature of Sport: A Definitional Effort" (1968), and to the Macmillan Publishing Company for granting permission to draw extensively in Chapter 2 from work previously published in Robert N. Singer et al., Physical Education: An Interdisciplinary Approach (1972).

The authors

CONTENTS

PART 1
INTRODUCTION
A Social-System Approach

Chapter 1
SPORT AS
A SOCIAL
PHENOMENON

During the present century sport has become a cultural phenomenon of great magnitude and complexity, having both positive and negative consequences for individuals and society at large. It has permeated most, if not all, of our social institutions, including education, economics, art, politics, law, mass communications, and international diplomacy. Its scope is awesome; nearly everyone has become involved in some way, albeit vicariously for most.

Despite the magnitude of the public's commitment to sport, it has, until recently, received little serious study as a social phenomenon. Rather, the ubiquitous presence of sport has largely been taken for granted by social scientists and a clear description, let alone explanation, of this important social force has been largely nonexistent.

Notwithstanding the limited study of sport, it is evident that the concept is a highly ambiguous term having different meanings for various people. Its ambiguity is attested to by the range of topics treated in the sport sections of daily newspapers. Here one can find accounts of various sport competitions, advertisements for the latest sport fashions, advice on how to improve one's skills in certain games, and essays on the state of organized sports, including such matters as the recruitment of athletes, financial success and failure, political interference, and even scandal.

Although this "broad, yet loose" view of sport is quite appropriate for the mass media, a complete understanding of various sport phenomena requires a more systematic conceptual approach. As a step in this direction, a consideration of sport in terms of four levels of analysis follows: sport as a *game occurrence*, as an *institutionalized game*, as a *social institution*, and as a form of *social involvement*. These four levels of analysis are schematically represented in Fig. 1.1.

1.1 SPORT AS A GAME OCCURRENCE

Perhaps most often when we think of the meaning of sport, we think of specific sports. From an analytical perspective, however, sports are considered as a

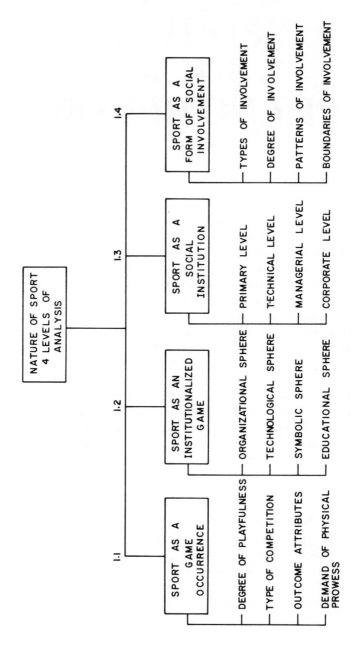

Fig. 1.1   *The nature of sport: Four levels of analysis.*

specialized type of game. That is, a single sport is viewed as an actual game occurrence or event. In succeeding paragraphs the basic characteristics of games are outlined briefly, and reference is continually made to sport as a special type of *game*. By way of definition, a game is any form of *playful competition* whose outcome is determined by *physical skill, strategy,* or *chance,* employed singly or in combination.[1]

1.1.1 Playful

A "playful competition" is any given contest that has one or more elements of play. A game has purposely not been considered as simply a subclass of play,[2] since sport would then logically become a subset of play and thus preclude professional sport being considered under this definition of the term. It must be recognized, however, that one or more aspects of play constitute basic components of games and that even the most highly organized forms of sport are not completely devoid of the characteristics of play.

The Dutch historian Johan Huizinga has probably made the most thorough effort to delineate the fundamental qualities of play. He describes play as follows:

> Summing up the formal characteristics of play we might call it a free activity standing quite consciously outside "ordinary" life as being "not serious," but at the same time absorbing the player intensely and utterly. It is an activity connected with no material interest, and no profit can be gained by it. It proceeds within its own proper boundaries of time and space according to fixed rules and in an orderly manner. It promotes the formation of social groupings which tend to surround themselves with secrecy and to stress their differences from the common world by disguise or other means. (Huizinga, 1955, p. 13)

Caillois (1961) subjected Huizinga's definition to a critical analysis and redefined play as an activity that is *free, separate, uncertain, unproductive, governed by rules and characterized by make-believe.* A brief discussion of these qualities ascribed to play by Huizinga and Caillois follows, including a suggestion as to how they relate to games in general and to sports in particular.

Free

This element suggests that play is a voluntary activity. That is, no one is ever strictly forced to play, playing is done in one's free time, and playing can be initiated and terminated at will. This characteristic of play is no doubt common to many games, including some forms of amateur sport.

Separate

By separate Huizinga and Caillois mean that play is spatially and temporally limited. This feature of play is certainly true of sport. For example, most forms of sport are conducted in a spatially circumscribed social milieu such as a bullring, football stadium, golf course, race track, or swimming pool. Furthermore, with few exceptions every form of sport has rules that precisely determine the duration of a given contest.

Uncertain

The course or result of play cannot be determined beforehand. Similarly, a chief characteristic of all games is that they are marked by an uncertain outcome. Perhaps it is this factor more than any other that lends excitement and tension to a contest. Strikingly uneven competition is routine for the contestants and boring for the spectators; hence efforts to ensure a semblance of equality between opposing sides are a notable feature of sport. These efforts typically focus on the matters of size, skill, and experience. Examples of attempts to establish equality based on size are the formation of athletic leagues and conferences composed of social organizations of similar size and the designation of weight classes for boxers and wrestlers. Illustrations of efforts to ensure equality among contestants on the basis of skill and experience are the establishment of handicaps for bowlers and golfers, the designation of various levels of competition within a given organization as evidenced by freshman, junior varsity, and varsity teams in scholastic athletics, and the drafting of players from established teams when a new team is admitted to a professional league.

Unproductive

Normally, playing does not in itself result in the creation of new material goods, although in certain games such as poker there may occur an exchange of money or property among players. Furthermore, in professional sport victory may result in substantial increases in wealth for given individuals. Nevertheless, a case can be made that a game per se is nonutilitarian;[3] that is, what is produced during any sport competition is a game, and the production of the game is generally carried out in a prescribed setting and conducted according to specific rules.

Governed by rules

All types of games have agreed-upon rules, be they formal or informal. It is suggested that sports can be distinguished from games in general by the fact that they usually have a greater variety of norms and a larger absolute number of formal norms (i.e., written prescribed and proscribed norms).[4] Similarly, sanctions are larger in number and more stringent in sports than in games. For example, a basketball player must leave the game after committing a fixed number of fouls, a hockey player must spend a certain amount of time in the penalty box after committing a foul, and a football player may be asked to leave the game for engaging in unsportsmanlike conduct.

With respect to the normative order of games and sports, one explicit feature is that they usually have definite criteria for determining the winner. Although it is true that some end in a tie, most contests do not permit an ambivalent termination since a means of breaking a deadlock and ascertaining the "final" victor is provided. The various means of determining the winner in sporting endeavors are beyond enumeration here. However, it is relevant to observe that in many sport competitions where the stakes are high, a series of contests is held (e.g., the

World Series) in an effort to rule out the element of chance and decide the winner on the basis of merit. A team may be called "lucky" if it beats an opponent once by a narrow margin (e.g., the Super Bowl), but if it does so repeatedly, then the appellations of "better" or "superior" are generally applied.

Make-believe

To Huizinga and Caillois the term make-believe signifies that play stands outside "ordinary" or "real" life and is distinguished by an "only pretending" quality. While some would deny that this characteristic of play applies to sport, it is interesting to note that at the turn of the century Veblen stated:

> Sports share this characteristic of make-believe with the games and exploits to which children, especially boys, are habitually inclined. Make-believe does not enter in the same proportion into all sports, but it is present in a very appreciable degree in all. (Veblen, 1934, p. 256)

Huizinga (1955) observes that the " 'only pretending' quality of play betrays a consciousness of the inferiority of play compared with 'seriousness'." For example, occasionally one reads of a retiring professional athlete who remarks that he or she is giving up the game to take "a real job."[5] Similarly, several writers have commented on the essential shallowness of sport.[6] Roger Kahn, for example, has written that:

> The most fascinating and least reported aspect of American sports is the silent and enduring search for a rationale. Stacked against the atomic bomb or even against a patrol in Algeria, the most exciting rally in history may not seem very important, and for the serious and semi-serious people who make their living through sports, triviality is a nagging, damnable thing. Their drive for self-justification has contributed much to the development of sports. (Kahn, 1957, p. 10)

On the other hand, Huizinga (1955) is careful to point out that " . . . the consciousness of play being 'only pretend' does not by any means prevent it from proceeding with the utmost seriousness." As examples, consider the seriousness with which duffers treat their game of golf, the seriousness that fans accord discussions of their home team, and the seriousness that national governments give to the Olympic Games or university alumni to collegiate football in the United States.[7,8]

Accepting the fact that the make-believe quality of play has some relevance for sport, it nevertheless remains difficult to empirically ground the "not-ordinary-or-real-life" characteristic of play. However, the "outside-of-real-life" dimension of a game is perhaps best seen in (1) its "as-if" quality, (2) its artificial obstacles, and (3) its potential resources for actualization or production. Thus:

"As-if" quality. In a game, the contestants act as if all were equal, and numerous aspects of "external reality" such as race, education, occupation, and financial status are excluded as relevant attributes for the duration of a given contest.[9]

Artificial obstacles.   The obstacles that individuals encounter in their workaday lives are not usually predetermined and are real in the sense that they must be adequately coped with if certain inherent and socially conditioned needs are to be met. On the other hand, in games, obstacles are artificially created to be overcome. Although these predetermined obstacles can sometimes attain "life-and-death" significance, as in a difficult Alpine climb, they are not usually essentially related to an individual's daily toil for existence.[10]

Potential resources.   Similarly, it is observed that in many real-life situations the structures and processes needed to cope with a given obstacle are often not at hand; however, in a play or game situation all the structures and processes necessary to deal with any deliberately created obstacle and to realize any possible alternative course of action are potentially available.[11]

In sum, then, games are *playful* in that they typically have one or more elements of play—freedom, separateness, uncertainty, unproductiveness, order, and make-believe. In addition to having elements of play, however, games are competitive.

1.1.2 Competition

Competition is defined as a struggle for supremacy between two or more opposing sides. The phrase "between two or more opposing sides" is interpreted rather broadly to encompass the competitive relationships between humans and other objects of nature, both animate and inanimate. Thus competitive relationships include:

1. Competition between one individual and another—e.g., a boxing match or a 100-meter dash.
2. Competition between one team and another—e.g., a hockey game or a yacht race.
3. Competition between an individual or a team and an animate object of nature—e.g., a bullfight or a deerhunt.
4. Competition between an individual or a team and an inanimate object of nature—e.g., white water canoeing or mountain climbing.
5. Competition between an individual or a team and an "ideal" standard—e.g., an individual attempting to establish a world record in the 1500-meter run or a basketball team trying to set an all-time scoring record. Competition against an "ideal" standard might also be conceptualized as man against time or space, or as man against himself.[12]

The preceding classification has been set forth to illustrate the meaning of the phrase "two or more opposing sides" and is not intended to be a classification of competition per se. Although the scheme may have some relevance for such a purpose, its value is limited by the fact that its categories are neither mutually exclusive nor mutually inclusive. For instance, an athlete competing in a cross-country race may be competitively involved in all of the following ways: as an individual against another individual, as a team member against members of an opposing team, and as an individual or team member against an "ideal" standard (e.g., an attempt to set an individual and/or team record for the course).[13]

1.1.3 Outcome Attributes: Physical Skill, Strategy, and Chance

Roberts and Sutton-Smith suggest that the various games of the world can be classified on the basis of outcome attributes such as:

> (1) games of physical skill, in which the outcome is determined by the players' motor activities; (2) games of strategy, in which the outcome is determined by rational choices among possible courses of action; and (3) games of chance, in which the outcome is determined by guesses or by some uncontrolled artifact such as a die or wheel. (Roberts and Sutton-Smith, 1962, p. 166)

Examples of relatively pure forms of competitive activities in each of these categories are weight-lifting contests, chess matches, and crap games, respectively. Most games are, however, of a mixed nature. Card and board games, for instance, generally illustrate a combination of strategy and chance. Although chance is also associated with sport, its role in determining the outcome of a contest is generally held to a minimum in order that the winning side can attribute its victory to merit rather than to a fluke of nature. Rather interestingly, it appears that a major role of chance in sport is to ensure equality. For example, the official's flip of a coin before the start of a football game randomly determines which team will receive the kickoff and from what side of the field, and, similarly, the drawing for lanes by competitors in track and swimming events is an attempt to assure equal opportunity of being assigned a given lane.

1.1.4 Physical Prowess

Although sports and games share a number of characteristics, the major attribute separating the two is *physical prowess*. Sports can be distinguished from games in that they require the use of *developed* physical skills and abilities (acquired through training) to conquer an opposing object of nature. Although many games require a minimum of physical skill, they do not usually demand the degree of physical skill required by sports. The idea of developed physical skills implies much practice and learning and suggests the attainment of a high level of proficiency in one or more general physical abilities relevant to sport competition (i.e., strength, speed, endurance, accuracy, etc.).

Although the concept of physical prowess permits sports to be generally differentiated from games, some borderline problems remain. For example, a dart game among friends, a horseshoe pitching contest between husband and wife, or a fishing contest between father and son might be considered a game occurrence but not necessarily sport. But, when games requiring physical prowess to determine their outcome become formally organized and sponsored contests such as dart, horseshoe, or fishing tournaments, they would be legitimately labeled sport.

An alternative approach to answering the aforementioned questions, however, is to define sport as an institutionalized game demanding the demonstration of physical prowess. If the latter approach is accepted, then a different set of answers to the above questions will be derived since this approach views a "game" as *a unique event* and "sport" as *an institutionalized pattern*. As Weiss has rather nicely put it:

> A game is an occurrence; a sport is a pattern. The one is in the present, the other primarily past, but instantiated in the present. A sport defines the conditions to which the participants must submit if there is to be a game; a game gives rootage to a set of rules and thereby enables a sport to be exhibited. (Weiss, 1967, p. 82)

1.2 SPORT AS AN INSTITUTIONALIZED GAME

To treat sport as an institutionalized game is to consider sport as an abstract entity. For example, the organization of a football team as described in a rule book can be discussed without reference to the members of any particular team, and the relationships among team members can be characterized without reference to unique personalities or to particular times and places. In treating sport as an institutionalized game it is conceived of as a distinctive, enduring pattern of culture and social structure combined into a single complex, the elements of which include values, norms, sanctions, knowledge, and social positions (i.e., roles and statuses).[14] A firm grasp of the meaning of the term institutionalization is necessary for understanding the idea of sport as an institutional pattern, or blueprint, guiding the organization and conduct of given games and sporting endeavors.

The formulation of a set of rules for a game or even their enactment on a particular occasion does not constitute a sport as conceptualized here. The institutionalization of a game implies that it has a tradition of past exemplifications and definite guidelines for future realizations. Moreover, in a concrete game situation the form of a particular sport need not reflect all the characteristics represented in its institutional pattern. The more organized a sport contest in a concrete setting, however, the more likely it will illustrate the institutionalized nature of a given sport. A professional baseball game, for example, is a better illustration of the institutionalized nature of baseball than is a sandlot baseball game, but both games are based on the same institutional pattern and thus both may be considered forms of sport. In brief, a sport may be treated analytically in terms of its degree of institutionalization and dealt with empirically in terms of its degree of organization. The latter is an empirical instance of the former.

In order to illustrate the institutionalized nature of sport more adequately, there follows a contrast of the *organizational, technological, symbolic*, and *educational* spheres of sport with those of games. Both games and sport are considered in their most formalized and organized state. Although there are nonsport institutionalized games that possess characteristics similar to the ones ascribed to sports (e.g., chess and bridge), such games are in the minority and, in any case, are excluded as sports because they do not demand the demonstration of developed physical prowess.

1.2.1 Organizational Sphere

The organizational aspects of sport are discussed, though somewhat arbitrarily, in terms of *teams, sponsorship*, and *government*.

Teams

Competing sides for most games are usually selected rather spontaneously and typically disband following a given contest. In sport, however, competing groups are generally selected with care and, once membership is established, maintain a stable social organization. Although individual persons may withdraw from such organizations after they are developed, their social positions are taken up by others and the group endures.[15]

Another differentiating feature is that sport shows a greater degree of role differentiation than that found in games. Although games often involve several contestants (e.g., poker), the contestants often perform identical activities and thus may be considered to have the same roles and statuses. On the other hand, in a sport involving a similar number of participants (e.g., basketball), each individual or combination of a few individuals performs specialized activities within the group and may be said to possess a distinct role. Moreover, to the extent that such specialized and differentiated activities can be ranked in terms of some criterion such as skill or prestige, they also possess different statuses.

Sponsorship

In addition to there being permanent social groups established for purposes of sport competition, there is usually found in the sport realm social organizations that act as sponsoring bodies for sport teams. These sponsoring bodies may be characterized as being direct or indirect. Direct sponsoring groups include municipalities that sponsor Little League baseball teams, universities that support intercollegiate teams, and business corporations that sponsor amateur teams. Indirect sponsoring organizations include sporting goods manufacturers, booster clubs, and sport magazines.

Government

While all types of games have at least a modicum of norms and sanctions associated with them, the various forms of sport are set apart from many games by the fact that they have more (and more formal and more institutionalized) sets of these cultural elements. In games, rules are often passed down by oral tradition or spontaneously established for a given contest and forgotten afterwards; even if codified, they are often simple and few. In sport, rules are usually many, and they are formally codified and typically enforced by a regulatory body. For example, there are international organizations governing most sports (e.g., the

International Olympic Committee, the Federation Internationale Natation, the International Gymnastics Union, etc.), while in North America there are relatively large organizations governing both amateur (e.g., the National Collegiate Athletic Association, the Amateur Athletic Union) and professional sport (e.g., the National Football League, the National Hockey League).

1.2.2 Technological Sphere

In a sport, technology denotes the material equipment, physical skills, and body of knowledge that are necessary for conducting competition and for providing technical improvements in the level of competition. While all types of games require a minimum of knowledge and often a minimum of physical skill and material equipment, the various sports are set apart from many games by the fact that typically they require greater knowledge, involve higher levels of physical skill, and necessitate more material equipment. The technological aspects of a sport may be classified as those that are *intrinsic* and those that are *extrinsic*. Intrinsic technological aspects of a sport consist of the physical skills, knowledge, and equipment required for the conduct of a given contest per se. For example, the intrinsic technology of football includes (a) the equipment (field, ball, uniform, etc.), (b) the repertoire of physical skills necessary (running, passing, kicking, blocking, tackling, etc.), and (c) the knowledge (rules, strategy, norms, etc.). Examples of extrinsic technological elements associated with football include (a) the physical equipment (the stadium, press facilities, dressing rooms, etc.), (b) the physical skills possessed by coaches, cheerleaders, and ground crews, and (c) the knowledge possessed by coaches, team physicians, and spectators.

1.2.3 Symbolic Sphere

The symbolic dimension of a sport includes elements of secrecy, display, and ritual. Huizinga (1955) contends that play " . . . promotes the formation of social groupings which tend to surround themselves with secrecy and to stress their difference from the common world by disguise or other means." Caillois (1961) criticizes this contention and states to the contrary that " . . . play tends to remove the very nature of the mysterious." He further observes that " . . . when the secret, the mask or the costume fulfills a sacramental function one can be sure that not play, but an institution is involved."

Albeit ambivalently, it is possible to agree with both writers. On the one hand, to the extent that Huizinga means by "secrecy" the act of making distinctions between "play life" and "ordinary life," his proposition that groups engaged in playful competition surround themselves with secrecy can be accepted. On the other hand, to the extent that he means by "secrecy" something hidden from others, Caillois's edict that an institution and not play is involved can be accepted also. The latter type of secrecy might well be called "sanctioned secrecy" in sport, for there is associated with many forms of sport competition rather clear norms regarding approved clandestine behavior. For example, football teams are permitted to set up enclosed practice fields, send out scouts to spy on opposing teams, and exchange a limited number of game films revealing the strategies of future opponents. Other kinds of clandestine action, such as "slush" funds established for coaches and gambling on games by players, are not always looked upon with such favor.[16]

A thorough reading of Huizinga (1955) leads one to conclude that what he means by secrecy is best discussed in terms of *display* and *ritual*. He points out, for example, that " . . . the 'differentness' and secrecy of play are most vividly expressed in 'dressing up' " and states that the higher forms of play are " . . . a contest for something or a representation of something," adding that " . . . representation means display." The "dressing-up" element of play noted by Huizinga is certainly characteristic of most sports. Perhaps it is carried to its greatest extreme in bullfighting, but it is not absent in some of the less overt forms of sport. Veblen writes:

> It is noticeable, for instance, that even very mild-mannered and matter-of-fact men who go out shooting are apt to carry an excess of arms and accoutrements in order to impress upon their own imagination the seriousness of their undertaking. These huntsmen are also prone to a histrionic, prancing gait and to an elaborate exaggeration of the motions, whether of stealth or of onslaught, involved in their deeds of exploit. (Veblen, 1934, p. 256)

A more modern and analytical account of "dressing-up" and display in sport has been given by Stone (1955), who treats display as spectacle and as a counterforce to play. Stone asserts that the tension between the forces of play and display constitute an essential component of sport. The following quotations give the essence of his account:

> Play and dis-play are precariously balanced in sport, and, once that balance is upset, the whole character of sport in society may be affected. Furthermore, the spectacular element of sport may, as in the case of American professional wrestling, destroy the game. The rules cease to apply, and the "cheat" and the "spoilsport" replace the players . . . .

> The point may be made in another way. The spectacle is predictable and certain; the game, unpredictable and uncertain. Thus spectacular display may be reckoned from the outset of the performance. It is announced by the appearance of the performers—their physiques, costumes, and gestures. On the other hand, the spectacular play is solely a function of the uncertainty of the game. (Stone, 1955, p. 98)

In a somewhat different manner another sociologist, Erving Goffman (1961), has analyzed the factors of the uncertainty of a game and display. Concerning the basis of "fun in games" he states that " . . . mere uncertainty of outcome is not enough to engross the players," and suggests that a successful game must combine "sanctioned display" with problematic outcome. By display Goffman means that " . . . games give the players an opportunity to exhibit attributes valued in the wider social world, such as dexterity, strength, knowledge, intelligence, courage, and self-control." Thus, for Stone, display signifies spectacular exhibition involving externally nonrelevant attributes with respect to the game situation; while for Goffman, display represents spectacular play involving externally relevant attributes. Moreover, display as viewed by Goffman often reflects tests of moral character (see Section 5.3).

Another concept related to display and spectacle which is relevant to sport is that of *ritual*. According to Leach (1964) " . . . ritual denotes those aspects of prescribed formal behavior which have no direct technological consequences." Ritual may be distinguished from spectacle by the fact that it generally has a greater element of drama and is less ostentatious and more serious. Leach states that "ritual actions are 'symbolic' in that they assert something about the state of affairs, but they are not necessarily purposive: i.e., the performer of ritual does not necessarily seek to alter the state of affairs." Empirically, ritual can be distinguished from spectacle by the fact that those engaged in ritual express an attitude of solemnity toward it, an attitude that they do not direct toward spectacle. Examples of rituals in sport are the shaking of hands between team captains before a game and between coaches after a game, and the singing of the national anthem before a game and the school song after a game.

1.2.4 Educational Sphere

The educational sphere focuses on those activities related to the transmission of skill and knowledge to those who lack them. Many if not most people learn to play the majority of socially preferred games in an informal manner. That is, they learn the required skills and knowledges associated with a given game through the casual instruction or observation of friends or associates. On the other hand, in sport, skills and knowledge enabling actual participation as players or athletes are often obtained only by means of formal instruction.

In short, the educational sphere of sport is institutionalized, whereas in most games it is not. One reason for this situation is the fact that sport requires highly developed physical skills (as games often do not) and to achieve proficiency requires long hours of practice and qualified instruction (i.e., systematized training). Finally, it should be pointed out that associated with the instructional personnel of sport programs are a number of auxiliary personnel such as managers, physicians, and trainers—a situation not commonly found in games.

1.3 SPORT AS A SOCIAL INSTITUTION

Extending the notion of sport as an institutional pattern still further, the term *sport* in its broadest sense supposes a social institution. Schneider writes that the term *institution*:

> . . . denotes an aspect of social life in which distinctive value-orientations and interests, centering upon large and important social concerns . . . generate or are accompanied by distinctive modes of social interaction. Its use emphasizes "important" social phenomena; relationships of "strategic structural significance." (Schneider, 1964, p. 338)

Thus it can be argued that the magnitude of sport in the Western world justifies its consideration as a social institution. As Boyle succinctly states:

> Sport permeates any number of levels of contemporary society, and it touches upon and deeply influences such disparate elements as status, race relations, business life, automotive design, clothing styles, the concept of the hero, language, and ethical values. For better or worse it gives form and substance to much in American life. (Boyle, 1963, pp. 3–4)

When considering sport as a social institution the term *sport order* is appropriate. The sport order is composed of all organizations in society that organize, facilitate, and regulate human action in sport situations. Hence, such organizations as sporting goods manufacturers, sport clubs, athletic teams, national governing bodies for amateur and professional sports, publishers of sport magazines, etc., are part of the sport order. For analytical purposes four levels of social organization within the sport order may be distinguished: the primary, technical, managerial, and corporate levels.[17]

Organizations at the *primary level* permit face-to-face relationships among all members and are characterized by the fact that administrative leadership is not formally delegated to one or more persons or positions. An example of a social organization associated with sport at the primary level is an informally organized (i.e., pick-up) team in a sandlot baseball game.

Organizations at the *technical level* are too large to permit simultaneous face-to-face relationships among their members but small enough so that every member knows of every other member. Moreover, unlike organizations at the primary level, organizations at the technical level officially designate administrative leadership positions and assign individuals to them. Thus most scholastic and university athletic teams, for example, would be classified as technical organizations with coaches and athletic directors functioning as administrative leaders.

At the *managerial level,* organizations are too large for every member to know every other member but small enough so that all members know one or more of the administrative leaders of the organization. Some of the large professional clubs (e.g., football, basketball, and baseball) represent social organizations at the managerial level.

Finally, organizations at the *corporate level* are characterized by bureaucracy; they have centralized authority, a hierarchy of personnel, protocol, and procedural emphases; and they stress the rationalization of operations and impersonal relationships. A number of the major national and international governing bodies of amateur and professional sport illustrate sport organizations of the corporate type (e.g., the International Olympic Committee).

In summary, the sport order is composed of the congeries of primary, technical, managerial, and corporate social organizations which arrange, facilitate, and regulate human action in sport situations. The value of the concept lies in its use in macroanalyses of the social significance of sport. It is also useful in a historical and/or comparative perspective. For example, the sport order of nineteenth-century England can be analyzed, or the sport order of Russia can be contrasted with that of the United States.

1.4 SPORT AS A FORM OF SOCIAL INVOLVEMENT

As noted above, the sport order is composed of all social organizations that organize, facilitate, and regulate human action in sport situations. Human "action consists of the structures and processes by which human beings form meaningful intentions and, more or less successfully, implement them in concrete situations" (Parsons, 1966). A sport situation then consists of any social context wherein individuals are involved with sport.

1.4.1 Definition of Situation and Involvement

Situation

The term *situation* denotes ". . . the total set of objects, whether persons, collectivities, culture objects, or himself to which an actor responds" (Friedsam, 1964). The set of objects related to a specific sport situation may be quite diverse, ranging from the elements of the social and physical environment of a football game to those associated with two avid fans in a neighborhood bar arguing the pros and cons of the strategy employed by the manager of the local baseball team.

Although there are many kinds of sport situations, most if not all may be conceptualized as a social system. A social system may be defined as ". . . a set of persons with an identifying characteristic plus a set of relationships established among those persons by interaction" (Caplow, 1964). Thus, each of the following situations constitutes a social system: (a) two teams contesting within the confines of a football field; (b) a father and son fishing from a boat; and (c) a golf pro giving a lesson to a novice.

Social systems of prime concern to the sport sociologist are those that directly or indirectly relate to a game occurrence. That is, a sport sociologist may be concerned with why and how persons become involved in sport and what effect this involvement has on other aspects of their social environment.

Involvement

Casual observation reveals that the word involvement enjoys widespread use in the English language. However, many of the common dictionary definitions are inadequate for the specific case of sport involvement, although some have merit, including "to combine inextricably," "to engage the interest or emotions or commitment of," and "to preoccupy or absorb fully." When we speak of being involved in sport, we are talking about a person's relationship with one or more manifestations of sport. Thus involvement becomes *social action related to some manifestation of sport.* Moreover, it consists of more than just active participation in sport situations as a participant (i.e., athlete).

1.4.2 Types of Sport Involvement

In addition to being *behaviorally* involved in sport, people can be *cognitively* and *affectively* (i.e., emotionally) involved with different aspects of sport situations.

Behavioral Involvement

Obviously, people can behave in many sport situations in different ways and at different times. However, most of the sport roles that are "acted out" or "played" can be classified in one of two *modes* of behavioral involvement: *primary* involvement and *secondary* involvement.

Primary involvement refers to actual participation in the game or sport as a player or contestant, not unlike the role of actors in the production of a film or play. More specific sport roles may include winners, losers, starters, substitutes, superstars, marginal or journeyman players, etc.

Secondary involvement refers to all other forms of participation, of which there are several, including participation via the *production* of sport and participation via the *consumption* of sport.

Producers are responsible for staging the event, i.e., bringing the spectacle up to expectations. Individuals involved with the actual production of a game or sporting event may be characterized as being direct or indirect producers, as follows. *Direct producers* are those individuals who, while not actually competing in a sport contest, nonetheless perform tasks that have direct consequences for the outcome of a game. Direct producers include instrumental leaders such as coaches, managers, and nonplaying captains, arbitrators such as judges, umpires, and referees, and health service personnel such as doctors, trainers, and water boys. *Indirect producers* are those persons who are actively involved in a sport situation but whose activities have no direct or immediate consequences for the outcome of a sport event. Indirect producers include entrepreneurs such as owners, promoters, and sporting goods manufacturers, expressive leaders such as cheerleaders, bandleaders, and mascots, technicians such as broadcasters, photographers, reporters, and scorekeepers, and service personnel such as concession workers, groundskeepers, program hawkers, and security guards.

Consumers are those who at any point in time consume sport either *directly*, through attendance at the performance of others (those who are primarily involved), or *indirectly*, by exposure to one of the several forms of mass media. Although it is not possible to delineate all of the role expectancies associated with the role of sport consumer, an individual who plays this role may be expected to (1) invest a varying amount of time and money in numerous forms of direct and indirect secondary sport involvement, (2) have varying degrees of knowledge concerning sport performers, sport statistics, and sport strategies, (3) have an affective (emotive) involvement with one or more individuals or groups in the sport system, (4) experience and either internalize or verbalize feelings and mood states while consuming a sport event, (5) use sport as a major topic of conversation with peers and strangers, and (6) arrange leisure-time life-styles around professional and amateur sport events.

The distinction between direct and indirect consumption may be appreciated better when we consider that the spectator is a part of the sport situation and may have some immediate and spontaneous effect on the event, while this is not the case for indirect sport consumers.

Table 1.1
Some social roles associated with the production and consumption of sport*

General sport roles	Primary sport involvement	Secondary sport involvement				
		Producers		Consumers		
		Direct	Indirect	Direct	Indirect	
	Athlete	*Instrumental Leaders*	*Entrepreneurs*			
	Contestant	Coaches Managers	Manufacturers Owners			
	Player	Nonplaying captains	Promoters Sponsors	Active spectators	Viewers	
Specific sport roles		*Arbitrators*	*Expressive Leaders*			
		Judges Umpires	Cheerleaders Bandleaders			
	Winner	Referees	Mascots		Listeners	
	Loser		*Technicians*			
	Starter	*Health Service Personnel*	Broadcasters Photographers Reporters Scorekeepers			
	Substitute					
	Superstar	Physicians Trainers Waterboys	*Service Personnel* Concession workers Grounds- keepers Program hawkers Security guards			

Adapted from Kenyon (1969, p. 79).

Table 1.1 shows the various roles associated with primary and secondary modes of sport involvement.

Cognitive Involvement

The amount of sport information made available to persons in most countries makes it almost impossible to avoid learning something about the world of sport. On the one hand, people acquire information about the history, structure, rules, strategies, and technical requirements of given sports and their environmental settings. On the other hand, knowledge about the success or failure of particular players, teams, and leagues and the outcome of particular sporting events is also acquired, retained, and perhaps even cited in encyclopedic fashion. At this time, little is known about the amount, variability, and source of such sport knowledge. Suffice it to say that this is a most fertile field for research, particularly in view of the attention paid today to the study of linguistics and mass communication. Despite this state of affairs, it seems that the learning and enactment of sport roles (whether they be primary or secondary, producer- or consumer-oriented) depends on the nature of the role players' cognitive systems pertaining to sport in general, and to the sport situations in which they find themselves in particular.

Affective Involvement

Whether a person is overtly involved in sport at a given point in time is not a necessary condition for harboring certain mood states or dispositions toward one or more manifestations of sport. Even without actually engaging in sport, people may become deeply involved in an emotional sense. This can be expressed by adhering to strong loyalties or identification with given players or teams or by experiencing emotional changes in mood states while consuming or producing sport. Extreme examples include the player who loses emotional control and attacks (verbally or physically) an official or spectator, or the consumer who yells "Kill the umpire" and then tries to do it. Similarly, the consumers who are emotionally or affectively involved in a game experience mood changes depending on whether their favorite team or player is successful. Many of these changes can be determined by physiological measurements (e.g., heart rate, blood pressure, galvanic skin response). Most members of society have selected perceptions of sport and hold positive or negative attitudes toward it. In short, just as sport becomes a part of most people's cognitive systems, it also becomes a part of most people's affective systems.

The affective or subjective meaning of sport involvement is multidimensional in nature. The work of Osgood and associates (Osgood et al., 1957, 1975) have shown that the connotative meaning or emotional dimensionality of any object (be it social, material, or ideal) has three underlying components or factors which they term (1) the *evaluative factor*, (2) the *potency factor*, and (3) the *activity factor*. They have identified these three factors as cross-cultural universals by using the semantic-differential rating instrument, an attitude assessment device consisting of a set of bipolar adjectival scales. Thus for any social object—for example, the role of "woman athlete"—(1) the evaluative factor is most prominently identified by such bipolar scales as good–bad, valuable–worthless, beautiful–ugly; (2) the potency factor is typically measured by such scales as weak–strong, soft–hard, and light–heavy; whereas (3) the activity factor is usually measured by such scales as active–passive, fast–slow, and static–dynamic. To illustrate, Griffin (1973) employed semantic differential scales to examine college students' perceptions of the three factors. She found that the woman athlete and woman professor were perceived to have active and potent roles (i.e., nonfeminine), while the highly evaluated roles were ideal woman, girlfriend, and mother. The former roles were valued less because they appeared to be inconsistent with the normative behavioral role for women.

In brief, then, one of the more frequently studied dispositions associated with sport is *attitude*, and any attitude held toward any particular manifestation of sport has three types of feeling states or subjective meanings associated with it, namely, an evaluative factor, a potency factor, and an activity factor. The precise nature of the subjective meaning and emotional dimensionality of sport for various groups in society will be discussed at various points in the text.

In summary, individuals, separately or simultaneously, may be behaviorally, cognitively, and affectively involved in sport through role enactment as producers or consumers. However, if the involvement behavior of a large group of persons identified with a specific sport were examined, different degrees and patterns of involvement over time might evolve.

1.4.3   Degree and Pattern of Sport Involvement

Degree of involvement can be assessed in terms of *frequency, duration,* and *intensity.* Frequency refers to the *rate* of participation—for example, bowling twice a week or watching football on television three or more times a week during the season. Duration refers to the *length* of participation at a given time—for example, playing three sets of tennis or listening to sport broadcasts for five or more hours on a Saturday. The combination of frequency and duration of involvement may be taken as an index of an individual's *investment* (in terms of time and perhaps expense) in a sport situation.

Intensity of involvement denotes what Goffman (1961) has labeled "engrossment," or what Sarbin and Allen (1968) refer to as "organismic involvement." The combination of frequency, duration, and intensity of involvement may be considered an index of an individual's *personal commitment* to a given sport situation.

Since not everyone participates with the same frequency, duration, or intensity over time, different *patterns* of sport involvement might be expected. Four discernable patterns (among many others) that might emerge are *normal* involvement, *cyclic* involvement, *divergent* involvement, and *withdrawal* or *noninvolvement* (Kenyon and Schutz, 1970). Normal involvement is characteristic of individuals who participate in sport on a regular basis and whose participation patterns are well integrated into their life-styles (e.g., the thrice-weekly set of tennis at noon hour). Cyclic involvement is characterized by sporadic participation in sport separated by periods of inactivity (e.g., the person who plays tennis only during his or her two-week vacation). Divergent secondary involvement is characteristic of "sport addicts" who become, in McPhee's (1963) terms, ". . . carried away toward consumption ever rising beyond any bounds and without return . . ." such as the practice of betting to bankruptcy at the racetrack. Divergent active involvement might be represented by middle-aged academic or business persons who quit their career to spend their lives surfing or skiing. Withdrawal is, of course, the extreme opposite of divergent involvement and is characteristic of "asportual" individuals who abhor any association (actual or vicarious) with sport. These individuals may never have been socialized into sport roles (see Chapter 6) or they may have been involved at one time and become desocialized because of a lack of opportunity, a declining interest, competing interests that take priority, or an unpleasant experience that led them to drop out of sport.

1.4.4 Boundaries of Sport Involvement

A chief interest of sport sociologists is to identify and explain *how* and *why* people become involved in sport phenomena. More specifically, the question is asked: *Who* came together to engage in *what* social acts *when* and *where* (see McCall and Simmons, 1966, p. 11). The sociologist interested in sport often focuses on these latter four W's as "dependent," "effect," "outcome," or "consequent" variables.

In examining the above four dependent variables associated with sport involvement, the objective is to discover the boundaries or constraints of social interaction in sport situations. These include intrinsic constraints, cultural boundaries, social boundaries, personal boundaries, and historical conditions (see McCall and Simmons, 1966, pp. 14–38). Chapter 2 suggests how these boundaries of social interaction in sport situations can be described and analyzed from a sociological perspective.

Before moving to the following chapter, it might be appropriate to review the definitions of the three major concepts treated so far:

1. *Play.*   Any activity that is free, separate, uncertain, spontaneous, unproductive, and governed by rules and make-believe.

2. *Games.*   Any form of playful competition in which the outcome is determined by physical skill, strategy, or chance, employed singly or in combination.

3. *Sport.*   Any institutionalized game demanding the demonstration of physical prowess.

The logical relationship of these three definitions is schematically illustrated in Fig. 1.2. Thus, all sports are games but not all games are sport, and all games are play but not all forms of play are games.[18]

Finally, it should be noted that thus far no reference has been made to the term *athletics* and the relationship between athletics and play, games, and sport. Although the term is not used very often in this text, the reader should be aware that athletics, as a concept in sport studies, has received considerable attention.[19] The conceptual concern of distinguishing sport from athletics and vice versa has arisen as a consequence of *work* and other instrumental orientations having found their way into sport (e.g., professional athletics). Accordingly, just as sport may be considered as a subset of games and games a subset of play (Fig. 1.2), *athletics* may be viewed as a subset of *occupations,* and *occupations* as a subset of *work* (Fig. 1.3). Thus, while the play-game-sport sequence portrays an "ideal" scale of expressive activities, by juxtaposing it with the work-occupation-athletics sequence reflecting a scale of instrumental activities, we acknowledge that modern sport may be best conceived as being located on a continuum be-

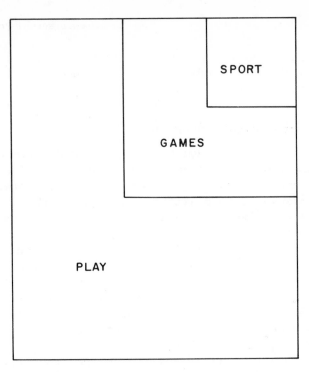

Fig. 1.2 *Play, games, and sport as a set and subsets.*

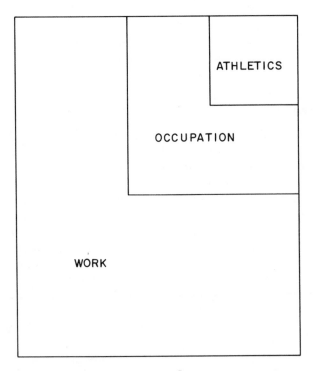

Fig. 1.3 *Work, occupation, and athletics as a set and subsets.*

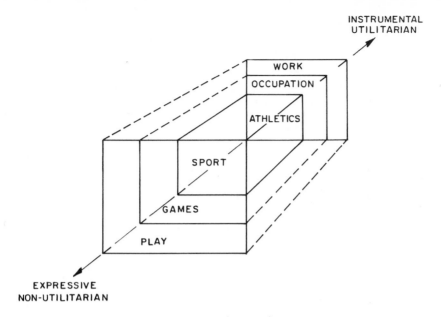

Fig. 1.4 *Sport on a play–work continuum.*

tween play and work[20] (Fig. 1.4). Moreover, we acknowledge that in our every-day world some degree of play permeates work and some elements of work are found in many forms of play (this is indicated by the dotted lines in Fig. 1.4).

NOTES

1. This definition is based largely on the work of Caillois (1961) and Roberts et al. (1959). Other definitions and classifications of games having social import are given in Ball (1972), Berne (1964), Glassford (1974), and Manning and Campbell (1973).

2. See similar definitions by Huizinga (1955), Stone (1955), and Caillois (1961).

3. See Goffman's discussion (1961, pp. 19–26) of "rules of irrelevance" as applied to games and social encounters in general.

4. For example, compare the rules given for games in any edition of Hoyle's *Book of Games* with the NCAA rule books for various collegiate sports.

5. There is, of course, the amateur who gives up the "game" to become a professional.

6. For an early discussion of the problem of legitimation in sport, see Veblen (1934, pp. 268–270).

7. An excellent philosophical account of play and seriousness is given by Kurt Riezler (1941, pp. 505–517).

8. A sociological treatment of how an individual engaged in an activity can become "caught up" in it is given by Goffman (1961, pp. 37–45) in his analysis of the concept of spontaneous involvement.

9. For a discussion of how certain aspects of reality are excluded from a game situation, see Goffman's treatment of "rules of irrelevance" (1961, pp. 29–34). Contrariwise, see his treatment of "rules of transformation" for a discussion of how certain aspects of reality are permitted to enter a game situation.

10. Professional sports provide an exception, of course, especially such a sport as professional bullfighting.

11. The use of the term "structures and processes" at this point is similar to Goffman's concept of realized resources (1961, pp. 16–19).

12. Other possible categories of competition are, of course, animals against animals as seen in horse racing, or animals against an artificial animal, as seen in dog racing. As noted by Weiss: "When animals or machines race, the speed offers indirect testimony to men's excellence as trainers, coaches, riders, drivers and the like—and thus primarily to an excellence in human leadership, judgment, strategy, and tactics" (1967, p. 22).

13. The interested reader can find examples of sport classifications in Edwards (1973), Gerber (1972), Hesseltine (1964), Kenyon (1969), McIntosh (1963), Petrie (1971), Sapora and Mitchell (1961), Vanek and Cratty (1970), and Worthy and Markle (1970).

14. This definition is patterned after one given by Smelser (1963, p. 28).

15. Huizinga states that the existence of permanent teams was, in fact, the starting point of modern sport (1955, p. 196).

16. This discussion of sanctioned secrecy closely parallels Johnson's discussion of official secrecy in bureaucracies (1960, pp. 295–296).

17. This discussion of the four levels is similar to Caplow's treatment of small, medium, large, and giant organizations (1964, pp. 26–27).

18. For a more thorough explication of the essential nature of play, games, and sport, the reader should consult the works of Gerber (1972), Pearson (1975), VanderZwaag (1972), and Weiss (1969).

19. Several scholars have contrasted the basic differences between sport and athletics, and at least one international conference has been devoted to the issue (Murray, 1973). For example, Keating states that:

> In essence, sport is a kind of diversion which has for its direct and immediate end, fun, pleasure and delight and which is dominated by a spirit of moderation and generosity. Athletics, on the other hand, is essentially a competitive activity, which has for its end, victory in the contest and which is characterized by a spirit of dedication, sacrifice and intensity. (Keating, 1964, p. 28)

> VanderZwaag (1972) has expanded on the distinction drawn between sport and athletics by Keating. In a related manner, Morford (1973) distinguishes between the triumph (i.e., athletics) and the struggle (i.e., sport). Pearson (1975) further suggests that there are three dimensions for discriminating between sport and athletics: competition, organizational complexity, and value on physical prowess.

20. As the noted sport sociologist Gunther Luschen has observed:

> Sport, sociologically speaking, is a competitive activity which is located on a continuum between work and play. The degree of reward, in the form of material gain as well as social recognition and status, determines where on the continuum a specific sport activity is located. (Luschen, 1975, p. 39)

REFERENCES

Ball, D. (1972). "The scaling of gaming." *Pacific Sociological Review* 15 (July): 277–293.

Berne, E. (1964). *Games People Play.* New York: Grove Press.

Boyle, R. (1963). *Sport—Mirror of American Life.* Boston: Little, Brown.

Caillois, R. (1961). *Man, Play and Games.* New York: Free Press.

Caplow, T. (1964). *Principles of Organization.* New York: Harcourt, Brace and World.

Edwards, H. (1973). *Sociology of Sport.* Homewood, Ill.: Dorsey Press.

Friedsam, H. (1964). "Social situation." In J. Gould and W. Kolb (eds.), *A Dictionary of the Social Sciences*, pp. 667–668. New York: Free Press.

Gerber, E. (ed.) (1972). *Sport and the Body: A Philosophical Symposium.* Philadelphia: Lea and Febiger.

Glassford, G. (1974). "A cultural-anthropological approach toward the understanding of the game phenomenon." *Katimavik* **1** (Spring): 2–5.

Goffman, E. (1961). *Encounters.* Indianapolis: Bobbs-Merrill.

Griffin, P. (1973). "What's a nice girl like you doing in a profession like this?" *Quest* **XIX** (January): 96–101.

Hesseltine, W. (1964). "Sports." *Collier's Encyclopedia.*

Huizinga, J. (1955). *Homo Ludens—A Study of the Play Element in Culture.* Boston: Beacon Press. Used with permission.

Johnson, H. (1960). *Sociology: A Systematic Introduction.* New York: Harcourt, Brace.

Kahn, R. (1957). "Money, muscles and myths." *Nation* **CLXXXV** (6 July): 9–11. Used with permission.

Keating, J. (1964). "Sportsmanship as a moral category." *Ethics* **75** (October): 25–35. Used with permission.

Kenyon, G. (1969). "Sport involvement: a conceptual go and some consequences thereof." In G. Kenyon (ed.), *Aspects of Contemporary Sport Sociology*, pp. 77–100. Chicago: Athletic Institute. Used with permission.

Kenyon, G., and R. Schutz (1970). "Patterns of involvement in sport: A stochastic view." In G. Kenyon and T. Grogg (eds.), *Contemporary Psychology of Sport*, pp. 781–798. Chicago: Athletic Institute.

Larrabee, E., and R. Meyersohn (eds.) (1958). *Mass Leisure.* Glencoe, Ill.: The Free Press.

Leach, E. (1964). "Ritual." In J. Gould and W. Kolb (eds.), *A Dictionary of the Social Sciences*, pp. 607–608. New York: The Free Press.

Luschen, G. (1975). "The development and scope of a sociology of sport." *American Corrective Therapy Journal* **29** (March–April): 39–43.

Manning, P., and B. Campbell (1973). "Pinball as game, fad and synedoche." *Youth and Society* **4** (March): 333–357.

McCall, G., and J. Simmons (1966). *Identities and Interactions.* New York: The Free Press.

McIntosh, P. (1963). *Sport in Society.* London: C.A. Watts.

McPhee, W. (1963). *Formal Theories of Mass Behavior.* New York: The Free Press.

Morford, R. (1973). "Is sport the struggle or the triumph?" *Quest* **XIX** (January): 83–87.

Murray, A. (ed.) (1973). *Sports or Athletics: A North-American Dilemma.* Windsor, Ontario: Canadian-American Seminar, University of Windsor.

Osgood, C., W. May, and M. Miron (1975). *Cross-Cultural Universals of Affective Meaning.* Urbana, Ill.: University of Illinois Press.

Osgood, C., G. Suci, and P. Tannenbaum (1957). *The Measurement of Meaning.* Urbana, Ill.: University of Illinois Press.

Parsons, T. (1966). *Societies—Evolutionary and Comparative Perspectives.* Englewood Cliffs, N.J.: Prentice-Hall.

Pearson, K. (1975). "The 'at leasts' of games and sport and a model for conceptualizing and locating games, sports and forms of athletics." Paper presented at the Conference on Sport, Society and Personality, La Trobe University, Melbourne, Australia.

Petrie, B. (1971). "Achievement orientations in adolescent attitudes toward play." *International Review of Sport Sociology* **6**: 89–99.

Riezler, K. (1941). "Play and seriousness." *Journal of Philosophy* **XXXVIII**: 505–517.

Roberts, J., et al. (1959). "Games in culture." *American Anthropologist* **61**: 597–605.

Roberts, J., and B. Sutton-Smith (1962). "Child training and game involvement." *Ethnology* **I**: 166–185. Used with permission.

Sapora, A., and E. Mitchell (1961). *The Theory of Play and Recreation.* New York: Ronald Press.

Sarbin, T., and V. Allen (1968). "Role theory." In G. Lindzey and E. Aronson (eds.), *Handbook of Social Psychology*, Vol. 1, pp. 488–567. Reading, Mass.: Addison-Wesley.

Schneider, T. (1964). "Institution." In J. Gould and W. Kolb (eds.), *A Dictionary of the Social Sciences*, p. 338. New York: The Free Press.

Smelser, N. (1963). *The Sociology of Economic Life.* Englewood Cliffs, N.J.: Prentice-Hall.

Stone, G. (1955). "American sports: Play and display." *Chicago Review* **IX** (Fall): 83–100. Copyright © 1955 by *Chicago Review.* Permission to reprint from *Chicago Review.*

VanderZwaag, H. (1972). *Toward a Philosophy of Sport.* Reading, Mass.: Addison-Wesley.

Vanek, M., and B. Cratty (1970). *Psychology of the Superior Athlete.* New York: Macmillan.

Veblen, T. (1934). *The Theory of the Leisure Class.* New York: Modern Library. Used with permission.

Weiss, P. (1967). "Sport: A philosophic study." Unpublished manuscript.

Weiss, P. (1969). *Sport: A Philosophic Inquiry.* Carbondale, Ill.: Southern Illinois Press. Used with permission.

Worthy, M., and A. Markle (1970). "Racial differences in reactive versus self-paced sports activities." *Journal of Personality and Social Psychology* **16**: 439–443.

Chapter 2
SOCIOLOGICAL
ANALYSIS
OF SPORT

The two-fold purpose of this chapter is to describe the nature of sociology and to illustrate how the sociological perspective is relevant and applicable to the study of sport. Broadly conceived, the focus of sociological inquiry is the study of human behavior as influenced by social organization. " 'Social organization' refers to the ways in which human conduct becomes socially organized, that is, to the observed regularities in the behavior of people that are due to the social conditions in which they find themselves rather than to their physiological or psychological characteristics as individuals" (Blau and Scott, 1962). Yet even though sociology is interested in socially organized behavior, the distinctive nature of the sociological perspective is not totally revealed since other social sciences are also concerned with the social dimensions of human action. Thus, the distinctive orientation of sociology to the study of human behavior is its focus on a special form of social organization: *the social system*.

It is this system to which the substantive concerns of sociology are directly related. First, sociologists are interested in the "structure and composition" of social systems; that is, they are concerned with the description and analysis of social systems in terms of their primary properties, including attributes, boundaries, components, elements, and environments. Second, sociologists are interested in the "functioning and change" of social systems; that is, they are concerned with the dynamic aspects of social systems such as their underlying processes of socialization, social change, conflict, control, communication, and stratification. Third, sociologists are interested in many different kinds of social systems: analytical and empirical, large and small, simple and complex. In sum, *sociology is the scientific study of the structure and composition, functioning and change of social systems and their relation to human behavior.*

The scientific nature of sociology is reflected in its theoretical and empirical modes of inquiry and in its emphasis on intellectual craftsmanship. Like any other science, sociology has three main tasks of inquiry: *description, discovery,* and *explanation.* Sociology as a particular form of scientific inquiry specifically seeks (1) to describe the nature of social systems, (2) to discover relationships between properties of social systems, and (3) to explain disclosed social systematic relationships.

Intrinsically associated with the tasks of inquiry is the development of *concepts, propositions,* and *theories.* These three terms comprise the basic linguistic elements of the *language of science* (see Brodbeck, 1963, pp. 45–47).[1] Concepts are the *words* of science and are used to label significant phenomena. Propositions are the *sentences* of science and are used to state relationships between concepts. Theories are the *paragraphs* of science and are used to explain the relationships among sentences; that is, a set of interrelated propositions.

Having presented an overview of the nature of sociology, the following sections present a detailed examination of each of the main tasks of sociological inquiry. The chapter is divided into four sections: Section 2.1 deals with the nature of sociological description, Section 2.2 describes the nature of sociological discovery, Section 2.3 discusses the nature of sociological explanation, and Section 2.4 explores the interaction of theory and research.

2.1 SOCIOLOGICAL DESCRIPTION (CONCEPTS AND CLASSIFICATIONS)

Sociologists are interested in first providing descriptive accounts of the structure, composition, functioning, and change of social systems. To do this requires *concepts, definitions,* and *classifications.* A sociological concept (e.g., social class) is a symbol for a social object or phenomenon. Concepts direct attention to what is to be observed and constitute definitions of what is described. A *typology* or *taxonomy* is a systematic classification of selected, but interrelated, concepts such as play, games, and sport.

Together concepts and taxonomies provide orientating statements about the locus, context, and methods of sociological inquiry. They outline a domain of study, give a perspective from which to view it, indicate its crucial variables, and suggest how these variables should be empirically treated. Last, but not least, concepts and taxonomies serve the overall function of providing a common means of communication among sociologists and other social scientists interested in similar phenomena.

The key construct of sociology is that of the *social system.* Moreover, the major concepts and taxonomies in sociology are chiefly associated with the nature of social systems, particularly their properties, problems, and processes. These concepts may be thought of as "sensitizing concepts" or "orientating statements"[2] which indicate social phenomena that need to be described and explained by sociologists.

The logical arrangement and ordering of sensitizing concepts provides *descriptive schemas.* As Zetterberg has observed:

> The researcher needs terms so arranged as to guide him to the phenomena to which he shall pay attention and presented in the order in which he shall pay attention to them. He needs a set of terms in the form of a check list for the observation he is supposed to record. Terms organized for this purpose constitute a *schema for routine description.* Such "shopping lists" tell him

what he must know to have a standard sociological account of a person, a social role, a group, an institutional realm, a society. (Zetterberg, 1965, p. 57)

Zetterberg further observes that: "In no case can we claim complete agreement among sociologists as to what constitutes the best descriptive schema for any given topic; however, there is usually enough consensus to warrant criticism when a sociologist has omitted a common item."

Thus, aware that all authors are subject to criticism, we present the following descriptive schemas for describing the nature of social systems. Not all sociologists will be in accord with these schemas, but they are representative of the present state of sociology and offer satisfactory "shopping lists" for the novice interested in the sociology of sport.

2.1.1 The Nature of Social Systems

Empirically considered, a social system consists of a set of ". . . (1) individuals who are (2) interacting with others on the basis of a minimal degree of complimentary expectations by means of, and according to (3) a shared system of beliefs, standards, and means of communication" (Wiseman, 1966). Conceptually considered, a social system is composed of (1) a *normative* subsystem called culture, (2) a *structural* subsystem termed social structure, and (3) a *behavioral* subsystem of persons in social interaction.

It follows from the preceding considerations that any given social system is a dynamic human collectivity based on the interaction between, among, and within specific sets of cultural, social, and personal variables. These three sets of variables, which constitute the primary properties of social systems, are outlined in Table 2.1 and are nominally defined in the following discussion. Because these properties are represented by relatively abstract sociological concepts, their meaning is concretely illustrated through continual reference to a hypothetical football team viewed as a social system.

Table 2.1
Basic components of social systems

A. Normative subsystem (Culture)
   1. Values
   2. Norms
   3. Sanctions

B. Structural subsystem (Social structure)
   1. Patterned interaction
   2. Social positions
   3. Roles, ranks, and statuses

C. Behavioral subsystem (Persons)
   1. Physical characteristics
   2. Social characteristics
   3. Psychological characteristics

Adapted from Loy (1972, p. 181).

Culture

The normative subsystem of culture is composed of many elements, including beliefs, folkways, ideologies, laws, mores, norms, and values. Simply defined, *culture* is a system of values, norms, and sanctions.[3] Abstractly viewed, (1) *values* constitute the goals of social systems, (2) *norms* indicate the preferred pattern of means for obtaining goals, (3a) *positive sanctions* reflect the rewards given for being committed to system goals and using proper means to obtain them, while (3b) *negative sanctions* represent the punishments given for not being committed to the goals of a system or for failing to use legitimate means in pursuit of them.

To illustrate these normative elements of culture, we consider a football team as a social system having a normative subsystem organized around a specific set of values, norms, and sanctions.

Values. Team values in football are reflected in the explicit emphasis on winning, personal achievement, and successful team performance. These values act as goals or guiding principles of behavior for members of the team (i.e., the social system).

Norms. Numerous norms exist regarding the expected standards of conduct among team members. These norms can be classified according to a taxonomy given by Mott (1965) as follows.

1. *Prescribed norms*, which specify what patterns of behavior are required of all members of the social system—for example, every team member must report daily to practice.

2. *Proscribed norms*, which specify what patterns of behavior are expressly forbidden members of the system—for example, players must not use drugs for nonmedical reasons.

3. *Permissive norms*, which specify what patterns of behavior are permitted but not required—for example, players may travel to and from practice in their own cars rather than on the team bus.

4. *Preference norms*, which specify what patterns are preferred but not required—for example, coaches may prefer that players wear short hair but do not demand that they get short haircuts.

Prescribed and proscribed norms may be thought of as "formal norms," for they tend to be very explicit and often are recorded as official rules of conduct. Permissive and preference norms may be thought of as "informal norms," for they are often tacitly assumed. Informal norms include the unwritten rules of the game, such as notions regarding sportsmanship and fair play.

Sanctions. Every football team invokes several sanctions to assure conformance to norms and commitment to values. Like norms, sanctions may be either formal or informal. Sanctions are also positive or negative in nature. Perhaps the greatest positive (informal) sanctions are the rewards of approval and praise that an athlete receives from teammates and coaches for successful performance. The most negative (formal) sanction is undoubtedly being "cut" from the team (i.e., being formally excluded from the social system).

Social Structure

The *social structure* of a social system consists of patterned interaction among a set of social positions. A *social position* designates an individual's place or specific location in the overall formal structure of a system. *Patterned interaction* refers to the recurrent and regulated reciprocal acts of behavior among occupants of a given set of positions. Three other important elements of social structure are role, status, and rank. A *social role* refers to the specific set of normatively defined duties, obligations, and responsibilities associated with the occupancy of a particular position. *Social status* signifies the prerequisites, privileges, rights, and symbolic rewards associated with the occupancy of a particular position. *Social rank* denotes the prestige of a person in a given position within the prestige hierarchy of a specific social system. As Catton (1964) observed: "The rank of a person in a position will depend partly on the adequacy of his performance of its role, partly on the nature of the duties or obligations incumbent on him and how these are socially evaluated, and partly on the value attached socially to the rights, privileges, and perquisites given him by the position."

To return to our analogy, in addition to culture, every football team has a well-defined social structure based on ordered, repetitive, and regulated interaction among team members.

Positions. The basic units of social structure are (1) social positions such as center, guard, tackle, end, quarterback, running back, fullback, manager, and coach; and (2) substructures consisting of the combination of several social positions into functional units such as linemen, backfielders, the offensive team, the defensive team, the coaching staff, etc.

Roles. Each position or substructure has a specific role or role complex associated with it. The role of quarterback or the role of guard can be identified and the particular functions each fulfills for the team can be compared. Similarly, role complexes associated with substructures can be analyzed, such as the offensive and defensive teams which have specialized tasks they are expected to perform.

Statuses. The occupants of particular positions on a football team have specific statuses resulting in different kinds of rights and privileges. For example, a starter or first-string player in contrast to a substitute or second-string player usually gets to wear newer and better equipment, is allowed into the training room first, and is always allowed to travel with the team to away games, whereas the marginal player gets "seconds."

Ranks. Finally, with respect to the elements of social structure, the occupant of every social position has a specific rank in the prestige hierarchy or stratification system of a football team. As we previously noted, a person's rank is dependent on both his or her role performance and the particular position he or she occupies. For example, a quarterback is usually accorded a higher social rank than a center, but an all-star center would be accorded a higher social rank than an average collegiate quarterback.

Persons

In sum, culture and social structure are highly abstract concepts representing two perspectives from which social systems may be conceptually viewed. A third perspective focuses on persons participating in a system. This perspective contains several alternatives. As Cotgrove (1968) observed: "When we look at the social system from the perspective of the individual, we can start either by locating his *position* . . . in the system . . . or we can examine the way he acts . . . out his *role*, or we can look at the characteristic personal qualities that he brings to his role."

The many kinds of personal qualities that influence an individual's role enactments may be broadly classified as physical characteristics, social characteristics, and psychological characteristics. Examples of physical characteristics are height, body type, oxygen diffusion capacity, and reaction time. Examples of social characteristics are the significant and relatively permanent social identities[4] of age, education, nationality, race, religion, sex, and socioeconomic status. Examples of psychological characteristics are attitudes, beliefs, perceptions, personality, and cognitive abilities. The totality of personal qualities characteristic of a given individual denotes the *self* of that individual.

When dealing with football teams in general as social systems, sociologists typically view persons occupying particular positions as role-actors. Players are thought of as performers acting out specific roles according to a prepared script. As an example, reference can be made to the role responsibilities of a tackler in general without referring to a certain individual who plays tackle.

On the other hand, when a particular team is treated as a social system, persons in given positions are viewed as social selves possessing unique physical, social, and psychological characteristics. For example, one may observe that Stan Williams, a black linebacker, has greater concentration and a better competitive attitude than Paul Bailey, a white defensive lineman. This latter view is usually of more interest to those who study sport from a psychological perspective. That is, whereas psychologists are interested in the person as an *individual*, sociologists are interested in the person as a *role*-actor in a social system.

Problems and Processes

In addition to the properties defined above and outlined in Table 2.1, social systems are characterized by numerous social problems and sociological processes. Every social system is confronted with the overall problem of "social survival." If a system is to persist as an ongoing social entity, certain organizational requirements must be met. As summarized by Olsen, these basic organizational requirements include:

1. Maintenance of the population through either reproduction or recruitment.

2. Provision for the training and/or socialization of members of the organization.

3. Promotion of communication and interaction among members and parts of the organization.

4. Establishment of a division of labor through specialization of tasks, activities, duties, and responsibilities.

5. Assignment of social actors to necessary roles, or tasks, activities, duties, and responsibilities.

6. Ordering relationships among the component parts of the organization.

7. Sharing of common social values among the members, including agreement on organization goals.

8. Establishment of a common, consistent, and adequate set of social norms and rules.

9. Procurement of necessary resources from the natural and social environments.

10. Development of methods for organizational decision making.

11. Coordination of organizational activities so as to achieve organizational goals.

12. Provision for the allocation to members of the benefits of organizational activities.

13. Protection of the organization against external threats and stresses.

14. Control of deviant and disruptive actions by organizational members.

15. Creation of procedures for managing or resolving conflicts within the organization.

16. Promotion of organizational unity or integration.

17. Development of procedures for changing the organization. (Olsen, 1968, pp. 74–75)

Social systems develop different institutional structures and utilize a variety of social processes in attempting to meet their organizational requirements. Examples of such processes are recruitment, acculturation, socialization, assimilation, communication, and social stratification. It should be made clear, however, that social systems are seldom, if ever, successful in fully satisfying their organizational requirements. Moreover, the patterned mechanisms developed by social systems to meet their organizational requirements usually engender varying degrees and various forms of social conflict. Such conflict is expressed by the social processes associated with the pattern behavior of deviance, discrimination, political protest, riots, rebellion, strikes, and war.

It should be evident from the above account that a football team, if it is to persist with some degree of permanency as a social organization, must meet certain basic organizational requirements. For example, it must maintain an adequate complement of players by means of recruitment; allocate members to

particular playing positions; provide for the training of players; ensure conformity to core values and norms by means of socialization; and maintain
economic viability by means of athletic fees, gate receipts, and television contracts.[5]

Having outlined the nature of social systems, we now consider the different
types of social systems.

2.1.2 Types of Social Systems

There is a multitude of social systems in society that influence human behavior.
Similarly, within that segment of the social order related to sport, there are many
kinds of social systems that organize, facilitate, and regulate human conduct
associated with sport involvement. Because of the great diversity of social
systems within society, it often becomes necessary for purposes of description
and analysis to classify them in terms of selected criteria. The basis of classification, however, depends on the purpose at hand.[6] In order to exemplify both the
abstract and the concrete dimensions of social systems, a general taxonomy of
types of social systems, based on level of analysis, is presented. This taxonomy in
turn is used as the basis of classification of different *analytical* and *empirical*
social systems. But first the general taxonomy.

Levels of Analysis

Sociologists when analyzing a social system seldom pay attention to all aspects of
it, but rather center their attention on selected dimensions of the system. For
example, in examining the family as a social system, one sociologist might focus
on its cultural elements, another might stress its structural dimensions, while a
third might emphasize its behavioral characteristics. These various emphases
imply different *levels of analysis*. At least four levels of sociological analysis may
be distinguished: the *aggregate*, the *group*, the *organization*, and the *institution*
(Caplow, 1953).[7]

1. At the *aggregate level* sociologists focus on individuals categorized according
to particular social identities (categories) such as age, sex, income, or religion. A
sociologist making an analysis of baseball teams at the aggregate level might be
interested in the relationship between leadership and educational status, and
might therefore be concerned with answering the question: "Are the highly educated players more often selected as team leaders than the less educated players?"

2. At the *group level* sociologists focus on individuals as personalities and often
are concerned with analyzing the relationships between personality and social
structure. A hypothetical research problem that might interest the sociologist
studying baseball teams as groups is the question: "Are teams with 'democratic
leaders' more successful than teams with authoritarian leaders'?"

3. At the *organizational level* of analysis sociologists treat persons as role
players (social actors) rather than as unique personalities. They are chiefly concerned with the patterned interaction among a set of social positions, regardless
of the behavioral dispositions of the people in them. A question that might be

asked by a sociologist viewing baseball teams as organizations is: "Are team managers more often recruited from positions of high interaction (infield) than low interaction (outfield)?"

4. At the *institutional level* sociologists direct their attention to enduring social patterns associated with a set of (abstract) social positions. The baseball team described in an official rule book reflects baseball as an institutional social system. The positions that constitute the social structure of a team are abstractly considered without reference to specific players or teams at particular times and places. Baseball as an institution may be regarded as a model or blueprint for the structuring of concrete empirical social systems (i.e., actual teams participating at particular times and places). A sociologist analyzing baseball at the institutional level might be interested in answering the question: "Are there fewer formal norms in professional baseball for managerial personnel than for player personnel?"

Given a general taxonomy of social system types, we now apply it to both analytical and empirical systems.

Analytical Systems

The four levels of sociological analysis may be treated as analytical social systems. However, the term social category is used in preference to the term aggregate in order to avoid confusion with the term aggregation, which is discussed below as a type of empirical social organization. Thus:

1. A *social category* is a social system organized around a set of persons categorized according to one or more social identities shared in common.

2. A *group* is a social system organized around a set of interacting personalities.

3. An *organization* is a social system organized around the patterned interaction of the occupants of a set of social positions.

4. An *institution* is a social system organized around enduring social patterns and practices developed about a set of values, norms, and sanctions.[8]

Each type of social system includes all of the basic components of social systems previously outlined (see Table 2.1), but each type places primary emphasis on one or more of these components, as shown in Table 2.2. It is important to bear in mind that the four kinds of analytical social systems represent levels of analysis and not discrete social phenomena. Moreover, one must keep in mind that a given social phenomenon may be analyzed at more than one level. For example, in the preceding discussion of levels of analysis we raised a sociological question at each level regarding the social phenomenon of leadership in organized baseball.

Empirical Systems

As shown in Table 2.3, certain kinds of empirical social systems *tend* to be associated with given types of analytical social systems.

Table 2.2
Basic types of analytical social systems

Type of social system	Fundamental focus
Social category	Social identities: social characteristics
Group	Personalities: psychological characteristics
Organization	Social structure: positions, roles, ranks, statuses
Institution	Culture: values, norms, sanctions

Table 2.3
Basic types of empirical social systems

I. Social categories
   A. Unidimensional
     1. Age (young-old)
     2. Sex (male-female)
     3. Residence (urban-rural)
   B. Multidimensional
     1. Social classes
     2. Ethnic groups
     3. Subcultures

II. Groups
   A. Primary groups
     1. Nuclear families
     2. Cliques
     3. Peer groups
   B. Secondary groups
     1. Work groups
     2. Creative groups
     3. Gratification groups
     4. Social-action groups

III. Organizations
   A. Aggregations
     1. Audiences
     2. Crowds
     3. Publics

   B. Associations
     1. Business associations
     2. Mutual-benefit associations
     3. Service associations
     4. Commonwealth associations
   C. Territorial collectivities
     1. Communities
     2. Societies
     3. Confederations

IV. Institutions
   A. Socializing institutions
     1. Kinship networks
     2. Educational networks
     3. Voluntary associations
   B. Regulative institutions
     1. Economic networks
     2. Legal networks
     3. Military networks
     4. Political networks
   C. Cultural institutions
     1. Artistic networks
     2. Mass media networks
     3. Religious networks
     4. Scientific networks

Adapted from Loy (1972, p. 189).

Social categories may be classified as unidimensional or multidimensional. As illustrated by the numerous survey polls reported in the press, social scientists often classify people according to selected unidimensional social categories such as age, sex, race, income, religion, marital status, and political preference. They also classify people according to certain multidimensional social categories, such as social classes, ethnic groups, and subcultures.

Groups may be classified as *primary* or *secondary*. "The *primary group* may be defined as a group in which each member interacts directly and regularly with every other member, often in the presence of all members. A *secondary group* is any group that does not meet these conditions" (Caplow, 1964). Examples of primary groups are nuclear families, friendship cliques, and peer groups. There exists a wide variety of secondary groups, which can be classified according to a number of diverse criteria. Following Krech et al. (1962), groups are classified somewhat arbitrarily according to their primary goal or purpose into work groups, creative groups, gratification groups, and social action groups.

Organizations may be classified as (a) *aggregations*, (b) *associations*, and (c) *territorial collectivities*.

"An *aggregation* is a social organization that is relatively spontaneous in origin, temporary in duration and minimally ordered" (Olsen, 1968). Examples of aggregations are audiences, crowds, and publics.

"An *association* is a social organization that is more or less purposefully created for the attainment of relatively specific and limited goals" (Olsen, 1968). Examples of associations are mutual-benefit associations, business concerns, service organizations, and "commonwealth" organizations (Blau and Scott, 1962).

Institutions may be classified according to three major institutional spheres: socializing institutions, regulative institutions, and cultural institutions (Eisenstadt, 1968).[9] *Socializing institutions* include family and kinship networks, school and educational networks, and clubs and voluntary associations. The school deals with the socialization of youth for adulthood, and voluntary associations act as agents of socialization for members of society throughout their life cycles. *Regulative institutions* include the economic, legal, political, and military networks of society. The economy " . . . regulates the production , distribution, and consumption of goods and services within any society"; while law, the polity, and the military deal " . . . with the control and use of force within a society and maintenance of internal and external peace of the boundaries of the society, as well as control of the mobilization of resources for the implementation of various goals and the articulation and setting up of certain goals for the collectivity." *Cultural institutions* include art, mass media, and religious and scientific networks, and deal with " . . . artifacts and with their differential distribution among the various groups of a society." Sometimes *systems of social stratification* are viewed as social institutions since they represent institutionalized means for dealing with " . . . the differential distribution of positions, rewards, and resources and the access to them by the various individuals and groups within a society" (Eisenstadt, 1968). Social stratification networks include classes and castes, age and sex categories, and race and ethnic categories.

Social institutions are usually viewed as analytical systems rather than as empirical systems. This distinction is clearly drawn by Bertrand, as follows:

> Institutions represent a higher order of abstraction than groups, organizations or other social systems. This fact may be illustrated as follows: When *the family* is thought of as a social institution, what is in mind is a set of behavioral patterns related solely to the basic function of "creating" a new member of society. This concept is quite distinct from a family considered as a social group which has essentially the same goals or objectives, but which includes in its make-up activity in support of several other institutions. All activity in a family is *not* related to the function of *the family*. In other words, all systems include some behavioral patterns which serve a number of different institutions, yet all systems are primarily devoted to one or another institution. (Bertrand, 1972, p. 162)

The empirical counterpart to the analytical system of institution is the *social network*. "A network is the functionally specialized social organization that links together numerous associations, groups and other types of organizations, throughout a society, all of which are interrelated through their concern with a common set of activities" (Olsen, 1968).

This section has presented the nature of sociological description and has outlined in detail the focus and concerns of sociological inquiry through the development of descriptive schemas dealing with the nature of social systems. The various taxonomies of the properties and types of social systems presented above are employed throughout the text in a sociological analysis of sport. Having examined the task of sociological description, we now consider the task of sociological discovery.

2.2 SOCIOLOGICAL DISCOVERY (PROPOSITIONS AND PROCEDURES)

The job of social description is an important one, but the two major tasks of sociology, as of any science, are discovery and explanation (Homans, 1967). In sociology discovery involves finding more or less general relationships between properties of social systems. In order to discover and test relationships there must be at least two concepts that can be operationally defined. A concept becomes known as a variable once it can be measured along a scale with two or more values (e.g., degree of success as measured by the number of wins or losses.) The discoveries resulting from sociological inquiry are stated as propositions. A proposition is an empirically testable assertion of the relationship between an independent and a dependent variable. As Kerlinger noted:

> An *independent variable* is the *presumed* cause of the *dependent variable*, the *presumed* effect. The independent variable is the antecedent; the dependent variable is the consequent. Whenever we say "If A, then B," whenever

we have an implication, A implies B, we have an independent variable (A) and a dependent variable (B). (Kerlinger, 1964, p. 39)

Sociological discovery, then, involves a never-ending search for relations between independent and dependent variables that can be stated as scientific generalizations.

2.2.1 Types of Propositions

Though sociological propositions take the logical form of "If A, then B," they may be verbally expressed in a number of ways, as illustrated in the following statements.

1. "If the population of a social organization increases, then the roles become more formalized" (Mott, 1965).
2. "For any member of a small group, the greater his centrality, the higher his rank" (Hopkins, 1964).
3. "The size of the nuclear family is an inverse function of position in the stratification system" (Smelser, 1969).
4. "Earlier adopters utilize a greater number of different information sources than do later adopters" (Rogers, 1962).
5. "In American cities there is an inverse relation between the incidence of reported crime and distance from the center of the city" (Bates, 1967).
6. "Organizations which have a high degree of division of labor are more likely to have a higher degree of effectiveness than organizations which have a low division of labor" (Price, 1968).

Sociological propositions can be classified according to their degree of explanatory power (i.e., informative value) and their degree of research support (i.e., empirical evidence). Table 2.4 presents a typology of propositions based on

Table 2.4
A typology of scientific propositions

	Low informative value	High informative value	
Empirical support wanting	Ordinary hypothesis	Theoretical hypothesis	Hypotheses
Empirical support sufficient	Ordinary invariance: Finding	Theoretical invariance: Law	Invariances
	Ordinary propositions	Theoretical propositions	

Adapted from Zetterberg (1965, p. 101).

these two criteria. As can be seen from the table, ". . . propositions supported by evidence are called *invariances,* and propositions for which more evidence is needed are called *hypotheses*" (Zetterberg, 1965). There are, as well, two kinds of hypotheses—ordinary and theoretical—and two kinds of invariances—findings and laws. An examination of the present state of knowledge of sociology shows that it has many ordinary hypotheses and empirical findings, but possesses relatively few theoretical hypotheses and virtually no laws. As a subdomain of sociology, the sociology of sport is at an even more impoverished level of knowledge, especially in comparison to more established subdisciplines within the field of sport studies, such as exercise physiology.

2.2.2 Methodological Perspectives

Specific relationships between properties of social systems are typically discovered, revealed, or confirmed in the course of research. Empirical investigation in sociology is conducted in a variety of social situations using a variety of observational methods. Notwithstanding such important pragmatic factors as time, cost, and accessibility, the choice of a given observational context and particular observational method is generally dependent on the theoretical questions being asked and the degree of empirical control desired (Festinger and Katz, 1965).

Since space does not permit a full description of the many situations and techniques associated with sociological inquiry (see Babbie, 1975), attention is focused on three general research settings and centered on four general research methods. Specifically, for purposes of discussion, situations for sociological study are divided into *library* settings, *field* settings, and *laboratory* settings, and mention is made of the four dominant research methods: secondary data analysis (including content analysis), surveys, participant observation, and controlled investigation (including field experiments, laboratory experiments, and game simulation).

Library Settings

Libraries and museums as well as many other kinds of public and private archives provide vast storehouses of readily available data for the interested investigator. These data include official statistical records, personal documents, and mass communications. The research uses of these materials are several. For example, sociologists may draw on them in order to gain insight into a specific situation, they may use them to formulate hypotheses, and they may use the available materials to test particular propositions (Kerlinger, 1964).

Archival materials are often examined by means of *secondary data analysis.* This form of analysis has been defined as "the study of specific problems through the analysis of existing data which were originally collected for other purposes" (Lipset and Bendix, 1953). The data used for secondary analysis include census and registration data at various government levels, official records of voluntary, public, and private organizations, and previously obtained survey materials (e.g., Harris or Gallup Poll findings).

A distinction may be made between pure secondary analysis based on special collections of published and unpublished materials contained in specific social science archives and semisecondary analysis based on published materials found in a variety of locations (see Hyman, 1972). A special form of secondary analysis is *content analysis,* which consists of "any technique for making inferences by systematically and objectively identifying specified characteristics of messages" (Holsti, 1969). General uses of content analysis include the following:

1. To describe trends in communication content.
2. To relate known characteristics of sources to the messages they produce.
3. To audit communication content against standards.
4. To analyze techniques of persuasion.
5. To analyze style.
6. To relate known characteristics of the audience to messages produced for them.
7. To describe patterns of communication.
8. To secure political and military intelligence.
9. To analyze psychological traits of individuals.
10. To infer aspects of culture and cultural change.
11. To provide legal evidence.
12. To identify authorship.
13. To measure readability.
14. To analyze the flow of information.
15. To assess responses to communication. (Holsti, 1969, pp.619–644)

Space does not permit a description of these many uses of content analysis, but in order that the technique may be better understood, let us consider its use in inferences of culture and cultural change (see item 10 above). A research example of the use of content analysis for this problem is Wolfenstein's study (1951) of the emergence of fun morality in American culture. She examined the contents of the 1914, 1942, and 1945 editions of the *Infant Care Bulletin* published by the United States Department of Labor Childrens' Bureau. She discovered striking differences in the themes of infant care from World War I to World War II. For example, she found that childrens' autotelic play activities, which were perceived as sinful and wicked in the earlier period, were viewed as harmless and good in the 1940s. Wolfenstein shows how the conception of parenthood also altered in keeping with the changed evaluation of play activities and speculates about the association between attitudes in child-training literature and changes in moral values in the culture at large. She suggests that various forms of amusements, fun, and play have increasingly become divested of their puritanical association of wickedness and it has now become a moral duty for Americans to have fun and seek enjoyment through a wide variety of means of self-gratification.

Field Settings

Most sociological research is conducted in real-life settings, which can vary widely in size. The geographical United States is an example of a large field setting, while a hospital ward exemplifies a small field setting. The forms of social research carried out in field settings may be broadly categorized as sample surveys, field studies, and field experiments.

Survey research. Kerlinger (1964) defines survey research as ". . . that branch of social scientific investigation that studies large and small populations (universes) by selecting and studying samples chosen from the populations to discover the relative incidence, distribution, and interrelations of sociological and psychological variables." Surveys can be roughly classified according to different levels of empirical complexity such as frequency counts, interrelationships of events, and quasi-experimental surveys. A study to determine how many adults attended civic concerts during a given season is an example of a frequency count survey, whereas an opinion poll to ascertain whether Catholics or Protestants are more likely to vote Republican illustrates an interrelationship of events survey. A quasi-experimental survey involves giving a "before" and "after" questionnaire to a given group of subjects. Thus, if a sociologist wished to determine the effects of a college education on certain political beliefs, he or she might administer a survey to a class of entering freshmen and reevaluate their responses during their senior year with a similar survey.

The two basic methods of collecting data in survey research are mailed questionnaires and interview schedules (see Babbie, 1973). Each method has its particular strengths and weaknesses. On the one hand, the advantages of mailed questionnaires over interview schedules is that they (1) are usually less expensive, (2) take less skill to administer, (3) generally permit the collection of data from a greater number of people, (4) usually permit the collection of data from wider geographical areas, (5) often provide subjects with greater anonymity, (6) give subjects more time to respond, and (7) are more standardized both in terms of questions asked and interviewer effects.

On the other hand, interview schedules have the following advantages over mailed questionnaires:

1. They can be used in one form or another with most segments of the population. Mailed questionnaires cannot be used with some people, such as those with little education, because they may not be able to read fluently or deal with abstract ideas. Interview schedules, however, can be adopted for such subjects.

2. They tend to give a more complete sample of subjects because people prefer speaking to writing. Mailed questionnaires are generally returned by only 10–50 percent of the subjects sampled, whereas 65–95 percent of a sample of respondents will give replies to an interviewer.

3. Interviews typically permit greater flexibility in that they provide an opportunity for misinterpretations to be cleared up, qualifications made, etc.

4. Interviews provide a better opportunity to appraise the validity of a respondent's report. For example, if a subject states that he or she owns two cars, the interviewer has a good possibility of checking the truth of the statement.

5. Interview schedules offer a better means of probing sentiments and feelings, whereas questionnaires best deal with factual materials.

6. Usually more information can be obtained in an interview than with a questionnaire (see Selltiz et al., 1963, pp. 238–243).

Overall, the major advantage of survey research is that a great deal of information can be obtained from samples representing large populations (see Sudman, 1976). The major disadvantages of survey research are two. First, information is usually obtained at the expense of much time and cost. Second, survey data often give only the most superficial kind of information because survey techniques do not allow the researcher to probe very deeply below the surface of things. Typically, surveys provide information about the static aspects of social systems, and seldom offer data about their dynamic dimensions.

Field studies. In field studies greater depth of insight is gained by focusing on the study of a single community or a single group. The major research method employed in field studies is participant observation.[10] This method entails the "conscious and systematic sharing insofar as circumstances permit, in the life activities and, on occasion, in the interests and affects of a group of persons" (Kluckhohn, 1940). Terms used synonymously or in conjunction with participant observation include direct observation, qualitative observation, field research, field study, field work, and ethnographic study. All these terms refer to a methodological strategy whereby data about human behavior are obtained through an investigator's direct involvement with his or her respondents and personal participation in a given social setting over a period of time.

A succinct example of participant observation is provided in Sullivan's (1958) study of a military training program. In this study an officer enlisted as a basic trainee and was a full-fledged member of the group studied. His role of researcher was unknown even to his commanding officer.

The advantages of the participant observation technique have been set forth by Doby, as follows.

1. It is not bound by prejudgment; it can reformulate the problems as it goes along.

2. Because of the closer contact with the field situation, the participant observer is better able to avoid misleading or meaningless questions.

3. The impressions of a participant field worker are often more reliable in classifying respondents than a rigid index based on one or two questions in a questionnaire.

4. The unstructured field inquiry usually uses the highest paid talent in direct contact with the data in the field.

5. The participant observer can ease himself into the field situation at the ap-

propriate pace and thus avoid rebuff by blundering into delicate situations or subject matter.

6. The participant field worker can constantly remodify his categories to provide more meaningful analysis of problems he is studying.

7. The field participant can generally impute motives more validly on the basis of interlocking aspersions and actual behavior, supplemented by occasional "feedback" reactions (i.e., the researcher's stating the motivational picture of a respondent for corroboration or modification by the respondent).

8. The participant field worker can select later informants in such a way as to throw additional light on emerging hypotheses.

9. The field participant absorbs a lot of information that at times seems irrelevant. Later when his perspective on the situation has changed, this information may turn out to be extremely valuable.

10. It is much easier for the field participant to make use of selected informant's skills and insights by giving these informants free rein to report the problem situation as they see it. (Doby, 1954, pp. 227–229)

In summary, the technique of participant observation permits one to obtain a greater range of information and often more relevant information than can be gained through other methods, such as a survey. The technique also affords a means of catching the "telling remarks" and thoughtless "giveaways," thus providing checks of reliability through observation of internal consistency. Furthermore, it can get at the more intimate kinds of information and there is not the danger that the informant will be aberrant.

On the negative side of the ledger, there are a number of disadvantages in using the participant observation method. The reliability and validity of field data are affected by a large number of factors. There are errors arising from sources of response. Some informants will intentionally give misinformation, some will offer invalid rationalizations for certain behavior patterns, and some will refuse to respond to selected subjects. The factors of recall, memory, personal likes or dislikes, inhibitions, etc., also make for errors. To the degree that investigators become a part of the social system they are studying, they narrow their range of experience; that is, as they take on a particular role and status in the system, they tend to follow a pattern of behavior characteristic of a given segment of the system and become less able to observe what is going on in other segments of the social system. There is also the danger that the participant observer will become overemotionally involved, and cease to be an objective observer. Still another danger is that observers may be misled by their first informants and direct their inquiry in the wrong direction. Perhaps the greatest limitation of participant observation is that it is a nonstandardized method of collecting data and not readily amenable to experimental control or statistical treatment.

Field experiments.   "A field experiment is a research study in a realistic situation in which one or more independent variables are manipulated by the experimenter under as carefully controlled conditions as the situation will permit" (Kerlinger,

1964). The basic difference between the field study and the field experiment lies in the design of the research and the degree of control imposed. "The field experiment involves the actual manipulation of conditions by the experimenter in order to determine causal relations, whereas in the field study the researcher uses the selection of subjects and the measurement of existing conditions in the field setting as a method of determining correlations" (French, 1965).

Lieberman's (1950) study of factory workers in a midwestern home appliance company is a good illustration of the nature of a field experiment. The purpose of his experiment was to test the proposition that an individual's attitudes are influenced by the role he or she occupies in a social system. At the beginning of the study attitude questionnaires dealing with management and union were administered to the rank-and-file factory workers. During the year following the administration of questionnaires, a number of the workers were promoted to foremen or were elected union stewards. The effects of these role changes were assessed by a readministration of the attitude questionnaires to the two groups of workers who had changed roles and to two matched groups of workers who had not changed roles. Findings supported the hypothesis that role changes influence attitudes. For example, workers who were promoted to foremen acquired more favorable attitudes toward their union.

The virtues of field experiments have been listed by Kerlinger as follows.

1. The variables in a field experiment usually have a stronger effect than those of laboratory experiments.
2. Field experiments are appropriate ". . . for studying complex social influences, processes, and changes in lifelike settings."
3. Field experiments are well suited both to the testing of theory and to the solution of practical problems.
4. Field experiments ". . . are suited to testing broad hypotheses."
5. Finally, "flexibility and applicability to a wide variety of problems are important characteristics of field experiments. . . ." (Kerlinger, 1964, pp. 383–385)

The research drawbacks of field experiments are associated with the fact that (1) many relevant variables cannot be manipulated in a field setting; (2) a field researcher must possess a number of highly developed personal attributes related to interpersonal rapport if he or she is going to be effective working with others in a field situation; (3) unlike the laboratory context, it is difficult to achieve complete randomization of subjects and conditions in a field setting; and (4) it is difficult to obtain a high degree of precision in the measurement of variables in a field setting (Kerlinger, 1964).

Laboratory Settings

Laboratories provide the ideal research setting for controlled investigation. In the laboratory setting the researcher can eliminate many extraneous factors that might influence the relationship between the variables he or she has under consideration. This is achieved by situation control, randomization of conditions, precise manipulation of variables, and accurate measurement of the effects resulting from this manipulation (Kerlinger, 1964).

An example of a laboratory experiment with sociological implications is Schachter and Heizelmann's investigation of ordinal position and pain tolerance (Schachter, 1959). In a laboratory setting they administered three series of electric shocks to two groups of female subjects. One group contained only first-born subjects, while the other group contained only later-born subjects. They found that ". . . first born and only children are considerably less willing or able to withstand pain than are later-born children" (Schachter, 1959). Although laboratory settings are often portrayed as the ideal research setting, one must recognize that like all research methods, laboratory experiments also have certain weaknesses. There are three major disadvantages of laboratory experiments. First, independent variables in a laboratory setting are usually not as strong as in a field setting. Second, the laboratory setting is a more artificial situation than a field setting. Third, laboratory experiments lack external validity (Kerlinger, 1964).

In summary, we note that: "The variety of observational techniques not only provide a wealth of data for the social sciences, but they also provide validity checks on one another. That is, if different techniques lead to similar conclusions, more confidence can be placed in each technique (and the conclusion) than if each is used alone"[11] (Labovitz and Hagedorn, 1971).

2.3 SOCIOLOGICAL EXPLANATION (THEORIES AND PARADIGMS)

Once relationships between properties of social systems are revealed, the most crucial task of sociological inquiry comes into play, namely, to account for the discovered relationships by means of scientific explanation. The explanation of a phenomenon is inherently associated with a theory of that phenomenon. "A *theory* is a systematically related set of statements, including some lawlike generalizations, that is empirically testable" (Rudner, 1966). An explanation consists of logically deriving (deducing) a proposition (i.e., a specific statement of relationship) from a theory. That is, ". . . specific statements are explained by general propositions under which they can be demonstrably subsumed" (Blau, 1969). Homans (1967) has rather forcefully stated the matter: ". . . a theory of a phenomenon is an explanation of the phenomenon, and nothing that is not an explanation is worthy of the name theory." Homans further notes that:

> If we like, we can look on theory as a game. The winner is the man who can deduce the largest variety of empirical findings from the smallest number of general propositions, with the help of a variety of given conditions. Not everyone need get into the game. A man can be an admirable scientist and stick to empirical discovery, but most scientists do find themselves playing it sooner or later. It is fascinating in itself, and it has a useful ulterior result. A science whose practitioners have been good at playing it has achieved a great economy of thought. No longer does it face just one damn finding after another. It has acquired an organization, a structure. (Homans, 1967, p. 27)

In short, ". . . all theory tends to be both a *tool* and a *goal*" (Marx, 1963), and thus serves several distinct scientific functions.

The "goal" function of theory is succinctly expressed in Stinchcombe's (1968) statement that "the reason for having theories of social phenomena is to explain the pattern in observations of the world." On the other hand, as Goode and Hatt have written:

> Theory is a tool of science in these ways: (1) it defines the major orientation of a science, by defining the kinds of data which are to be abstracted; (2) it offers a conceptual scheme by which the relevant phenomena are systematized, classified, and interrelated; (3) it summarizes facts into (a) empirical generalizations and (b) systems of generalizations; (4) it predicts facts; and (5) it points to gaps in our knowledge.*

With particular respect to empirical investigation, the virtues of theory for the researcher have been clearly set forth by Zetterberg (1965) as follows:

1. A theory can be used to provide the most parsimonious summary of actual or anticipated research findings (p. 161).

2. A theory can be used to coordinate research so that many separate findings support each other, giving the highest plausibility to the theory per finding (p. 163).

3. A theory can be used to locate the most strategic or manageable propositions for testing (p. 164).

4. A theory provides a limited area in which to locate false propositions when a hypothesis fails to meet an empirical test (p. 166).

These four virtues of theorizing are more characteristic of some types of theories than of other types, but all theories possess these virtues to some degree.

2.3.1 Types of Theories

Three generic classes of sociological theory seem to fit the definition of theory given above: (1) the set-of-laws form of theory, (2) the axiomatic form of theory, and (3) the causal process form of theory (see Reynolds, 1971, pp. 83–114). A hypothetical example of each form is provided at this point so that the reader will readily recognize a given form of theory when it is introduced later in the text.

The Set-of-Laws Form

The set-of-laws form of theory consists of general propositions expressing lawlike generalizations as relational statements in the logical form: "If *A*, then *B*."

An example of a lawlike generalization in sociology is the statement: "If *authority*, then *prestige*." For present purposes, "the authority of a person (denotes) the extent to which he issues directions to the group that are acceptable to

---

*From *Methods in Social Research* by W. Goode and P. Hatt. Copyright 1952 by McGraw-Hill Book Company. Used with permission of McGraw-Hill.

the group members"; while "the *prestige* of a person (denotes) the extent to which others give him a favorable evaluation" (Zetterberg, 1965). Thus this hypothetical law *predicts* that in any group persons who have high authority will have greater prestige than those who have low authority, and it *explains* the empirical finding that head coaches have higher prestige than assistant coaches and that owners or athletic directors have higher prestige than coaches.

The Axiomatic Form

General propositions systematically related in an axiomatic theory are termed *postulates.* Axiomatic theories are composed of two sets of postulates: a set of postulates called *axioms,* and a set of postulates derived from the axioms called *theorems.* A hypothetical example of sociological theory in axiomatic form is the following set of interrelated propositions:

> *Axiom I:*   If knowledge, then authority.
>
> *Axiom II:*   If authority, then prestige.
>
> *Theorem A:*   Therefore, if knowledge, then prestige.

The general proposition deduced from the set of two axioms predicts that in any group persons who possess a great deal of knowledge related to the function and membership of that group will have higher prestige than persons who possess more limited knowledge. This derived proposition may explain in part why managers, coaches, and captains in sport groups tend to have higher prestige than other group members.

The Causal Process Form

"The major difference between this form of theory and the axiomatic form is that all statements are considered to be of equal importance, they are not classified into axioms and theorems, and the statements are presented in a different fashion, as a causal process" (Reynolds, 1971). As an example of this form of theory we diagrammatically describe (see Fig. 2.1) the following propositional statements as a causal process:

> If centrality, then knowledge.
>
> If knowledge, then authority.
>
> If authority, then prestige.
>
> If prestige, then centrality.

Authority, knowledge, and prestige are defined above, while the *centrality* of a person in the group denotes the extent to which he or she maintains interaction with many other group members.

    The causal process illustrated in Fig. 2.1 implies that (1) an individual who has a high degree of interaction with other group members will tend to obtain knowledge about their needs and attitudes, and (2) this obtained knowledge permits him or her to exert greater influence and acquire more authority, which (3) accords the individual greater prestige and (4) results in his or her being placed in a position of centrality (see Zetterberg, 1965, pp. 91–92). This theory may

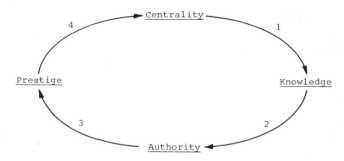

Fig. 2.1 *A schema of a causal process. (Adapted from Zetterberg, 1965, p. 92)*

explain in part why occupants of central positions in sport groups (e.g., quarterbacks, catchers, pitchers, and shortstops) tend to have greater knowledge about the game, more influence on other team members, and greater prestige within the group. Examples of each form of theory outlined above can be found within most of the dominant theoretical perspectives of modern sociology.

2.3.2 Theoretical Perspectives

There are a variety of competing schools of thought in present-day sociology (see Wallace, 1969). These include *conflict* theorists (e.g., Collins, 1975; Dahrendorf, 1959), *functional* theorists (e.g., Demerath and Peterson, 1967; Martindale, 1965; Merton, 1968; Parsons, 1966, 1971; Sztompka, 1974), modern *system* theorists (e.g., Buckley, 1967, 1968; Kuhn, 1974, 1975), social *exchange* theorists (e.g., Blau, 1964; Burns, 1973; Ekeh, 1974; Emerson, 1976; Homans, 1961; Thibault and Kelly, 1959), and *symbolic interaction* theorists (e.g., Blumer, 1969; Hewit, 1976; Kuhn, 1964; Manis and Meltzer, 1972; Rose, 1962; Shibutani, 1961, 1970; Stone and Farberman, 1970). For an overview, analysis, and critique of these dominant theoretical perspectives, the reader is referred to Turner (1974), Warshay (1975), and Zeitlin (1973).

The utility of several of the theoretical approaches noted above for explaining sport-related phenomena is exemplified throughout the text, since no particular theoretical perspective is endorsed. As Stinchcombe (1968) noted, "constructing theories of social phenomena is done best by those who have a variety of theoretical strategies to try out"; and "if one approach does not work for explaining a particular phenomenon, the theorist should try another." In short, sociology is both a multimethod and a multiple paradigm science (see Bottomore, 1975; Ritzer, 1975b).

The most persuasive proponent of the position that sociology is a multiple paradigm science is Ritzer (1975b). Drawing on the seminal work of Thomas Kuhn (1970b), Ritzer defines a paradigm as:

> . . . a fundamental image of the subject matter within a science. It serves to define what should be studied, what questions should be asked, how they should be asked, and what rules should be followed in interpreting the

answers obtained. The paradigm is the broadest unit of consensus within a science and serves to differentiate one scientific community (or sub-community) from another. (Ritzer, 1975b, p. 7)

Ritzer reasons that a paradigm has four basic components: (1) an exemplar, or piece of work that stands as a model for those who work within the paradigm; (2) an image of the subject matter; (3) theories; and (4) methods and instruments. Thus, theories are *not* paradigms in themselves but rather components of far broader paradigms in modern sociology: social facts, social definitions, and social behavior.

The Social Facts Paradigm

The work of Emile Durkheim (1951, 1954) is the classical exemplar of the social facts paradigm, and the work of Warriner (1956) offers a contemporary exemplar of this paradigm. As Ritzer has summarized the conceptual focus of the paradigm:

> . . . the contemporary social factist accepts the reality of such social facts as a group, a norm, an institution, or a social system. They focus on the study of these social facts and their coercive effect on the individual and they argue that a given social fact can only be explained by other social facts. (Ritzer, 1975a, p. 159)

According to Ritzer, the most closely identified sociological frames of reference associated with the social facts paradigm are structural functionalism (or system theory) and conflict theory.

Structural functionalism, characterized by the work of Parsons (1951, 1966, 1971) and Merton (1968), is oriented to the analysis of the relationships between social structures and social institutions and their resulting effect on human behavior. This sociological frame of reference represents an order or consensus model of society that views "society as a natural boundary-maintaining system of action" and that expresses a "positive attitude toward the maintenance of social institutions" (Horton, 1965).

Conflict theory is repressented by the work of Dahrendorf (1959). This sociological frame of reference views "society as a contested struggle between groups with opposed aims and perspectives" and expresses a "positive attitude toward change" (Horton, 1965). For conflict theorists, dissension and conflict are inevitable and stem from the differential allocation of authority and power among various positions in society.

The Social Definition Paradigm

The social definition paradigm is exemplified in the work of Weber who argued that:

> . . . action is social insofar as by virtue of the subjective meaning attached to it by the acting individual or individuals, it takes account of the behavior of others and is thereby oriented in its course. (Weber, 1947, p. 88)

Social definitionists adhere to the view that a person is an active creator of his or her own social reality, and thus they are interested in "the mental process as well as the resulting action and interaction" (Ritzer, 1975a). Although they cannot examine directly what takes place in the minds of people, they believe that something occurs in an individual's mind between the application of a stimulus and the response. Thus they refute the idea that social structure is a static set of social facts operating on and controlling the individual. Rather, they concentrate on the ways in which individuals define their social situations and how these definitions affect action. The theories most closely linked to this paradigm are action theory, symbolic interaction theory, and phenomenology (including ethnomethodology).

Action theory and symbolic interaction theory are somewhat similar in that both see the actor as attaching subjective meaning to social behavior. To illustrate, Mead (1934) stressed the importance of learning to take the role of the other in learning one's social position, while Berger and Luckman (1966) speak of the social construction of reality.

Phenomenology and ethnomethodology concentrate on "reconstructing the cognitive map in people's minds which enables them to make sense of their everyday activities and encounters" (Coser, 1975). This approach stresses that subjective meaning is crucial to interaction, both for the actor and for others who must interpret it and act accordingly. This perspective is reflected in the work of Schutz (1964), Garfinkel (1967), and Cicourel (1974), and their followers.

The Social Behavior Paradigm

The work of B. F. Skinner (1971) provides the exemplar for the social behavior paradigm. The most closely identified sociological perspectives associated with this paradigm are behavioral sociology (see Burgess and Bushell, 1969) and exchange theory (see Blau, 1964; Homans, 1961; Thibault and Kelly, 1959). These perspectives focus on the relationship between individuals and their environments and attempt to explain social interaction in terms of principles of behavioral psychology.

In summary, we note that just as any single research method or technique of data treatment is inadequate for the full empirical analysis of a social system, any particular paradigm is inadequate for a complete theoretical analysis of a social system. As Ritzer (1975b) forcefully concludes in his argument: "In fact, no aspect of social reality can be adequately explained without drawing on insights from all of the paradigms." Finally, it should be recognized that theory and method are intimately related and often certain methods are more appropriate for particular paradigms.[12]

2.4 INTERACTION OF SOCIAL THEORY AND EMPIRICAL RESEARCH

The overall aim of any science is the establishment of a systematic body of knowledge about a given aspect of social reality. As Lastrucci observed:

> The accumulated knowledge making up a systematic science is dynamic, not static. Science always seeks additional knowledge in the belief (borne out by history) that knowledge is never complete. "Truth" in science is always relative and temporal, never absolute or final. In contrast to many closed philosophical or ideological "systems" (e.g., political, aesthetic, moral, religious and other theories with which we are familiar), science may properly be defined as an "open" rather than as a "closed" system of ideas. Therefore, it grows constantly by discarding erroneous or useless notions and by substituting more correct or useful ones in the light of new evidence. (Lastrucci, 1967, p. 13)

Sociology in its present state seemingly lacks the "cumulative characteristic" of science in general.[13] One reason for this state is that sociology has overemphasized the processes and procedures required to confirm and verify hypotheses and theories and has given short shrift to the matters of hypothesis discovery and theory generation. However limited the interaction between theory and research in sociology, when it takes place it does result in a relatively "open system" of inquiry.

On the one hand, "theory increases the fruitfulness of research by providing significant leads for inquiry by means of similar underlying processes, and by providing an explanation of derived relationships" (Selltiz et al., 1963). On the other hand, research provides a means of testing theories.[14] It leads to the development of new theories by forcing the rejection of theories that do not confirm to empirical evidence, and by bringing about the reformulation of theories through classification and definition of central concepts contained in their propositions (Goode and Hatt, 1952).[15]

The interaction between theory and research is illustrated in more detail in the following discussion of the process of scientific sociology.

2.4.1 The Process of Scientific Sociology

By way of summarizing this introduction to the three scientific tasks of sociology—description, discovery, explanation—a schematic outline of the *processes* and *products* of sociological inquiry is presented in Fig. 2.2. The various components of the figure are described below.

Processes and Products of Sociological Inquiry

The theoretical products of sociological inquiry are concepts, propositions (hypotheses and empirical generalizations), and theories. The methodological processes of sociological inquiry include *logical processes* such as induction and deduction as well as *empirical processes* such as operationalization, instrumentation, scaling, and measurement.

Theory. Let us assume that we are interested in studying leadership on college baseball teams. In order to explain this phenomenon we begin our inquiry with the following propositions:

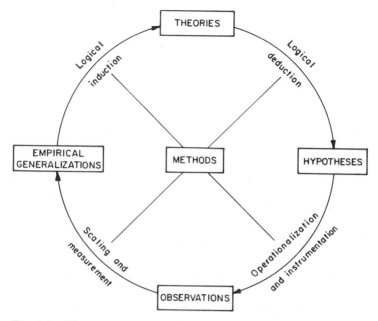

Fig. 2.2 *The components and process of scientific sociology. (Reprinted by permission from Walter L. Wallace,* Sociological Theory, *Chicago: Aldine. Copyright © 1969 by Walter L. Wallace.)*

1. Leadership is positively related to sentiment.
2. Sentiment is positively related to interaction.
3. Interaction is positively related to centrality.

These three propositions are based on the consideration of four concepts that must be theoretically (nominally) defined: leadership, interaction, sentiment, and centrality. Sentiment denotes the degree to which a member of a social system is liked by his or her fellow members. Centrality designates the degree to which a person occupies a central position in a social system.

The first proposition states that individuals who are well liked are more often selected as leaders than those who are less well liked. The second proposition states that persons who frequently interact with others tend to be more well liked than those persons who interact relatively infrequently. The third proposition states that occupants of central positions are more likely to have high rates of interaction than incumbents of peripheral positions within a social system.

Hypotheses. A hypothesis is a tentative statement of the relationship between concepts. A theoretical hypothesis is a hypothesis deduced from a theory. By means of *logical deduction*, we can derive the theoretical hypothesis that "leadership is directly related to centrality" (i.e., occupants of central positions are more often chosen as leaders than are occupants of peripheral positions).

Before a theoretical hypothesis can be tested and verified, it must be re-formulated as an empirical hypothesis. This is done by operationally defining each concept contained in the theoretical hypothesis. *Operationalization* consists of giving each concept an empirical referent or indicator. For the theoretical hypothesis presented here, team captaincy could be taken as an indicator of leadership, and occupancy of an infield position could be used as an indicator of centrality. Hence, the empirical hypothesis states that "infielders will be more often chosen as team captains than outfielders."

Observations. In order to test our empirical hypothesis, we must make a number of observations to determine the values of our empirical indicators. The preparation of materials for recording observations is called *instrumentation*. Data collection depends on a variety of observational techniques. For example, in terms of the problem treated herein, field observations could be made of a number of baseball teams to discover what positions team captains most often occupy, or the sport sections of college yearbooks in several university libraries might be examined (i.e., content analysis) to determine whether team captains are predominantly infielders or outfielders. Let us assume, however, that a short survey questionnaire was mailed to a sample of college baseball coaches, asking them to report what positions their team captains played last season.

Empirical generalizations. Assuming that a substantial number of returns were received from the sample of coaches, the degree of relationship between team captaincy and playing position could be determined by *measurement* procedures. If the results of the data analysis showed that the majority of team captains came from infield positions, there would be strong support for the empirical hypo-thesis. Moreover, if other investigators conducted similar studies with different samples of coaches (perhaps in different sports, assuming a common definition of centrality could be derived) and discovered the same relationship between team captaincy and field position, then it could be stated as an empirical generalization that "infielders are more often selected as team captains than are outfielders."

Theoretical generalization. Sociologists are most interested in propositions that can be generalized to a number of social phenomena; thus, the preceding empirical generalization by itself might not greatly interest a sociologist. How-ever, a combination of empirical generalizations indicating that in a variety of social situations (e.g., within sport and outside) occupants of central positions tend to assume positions of leadership would greatly interest a sociologist, since by logical induction the theoretical generalization (having a high level of general-ity) can be formulated that "leadership is directly related to centrality." The scientific process has now come full circle since this proposition was stated in the original theoretical hypothesis. The predicted relationship, however, now has been empirically verified in a variety of social situations, which greatly enhances its scientific status and utility. Finally, the theoretical generalization, by means of *ordering*, may be incorporated into a matrix of theoretical propositions, thus creating a new theory or causing the reformulation of an old one. For example:

1. Leadership is positively related to centrality.
2. Centrality is positively related to status.
3. Status is positively related to conformity.

In conclusion, it must be stressed that the process of inquiry schematically illustrated in Fig. 2.2 has no actual beginning or end and thus any given sociological investigation could begin with any component of the figure. For example, one's initial inquiry about a social phenomenon might start with simple observations of a certain human activity. The point at which a social scientist begins the process of inquiry largely depends on the philosophical position that an individual scientist holds regarding the "best" strategy for developing a scientific body of knowledge.

Strategies for Developing a Scientific Body of Knowledge

Throughout history there have been two general schools of thought concerning the basis for the development of scientific knowledge. One school of thought emphasizes induction and is represented in modern sociology by the "research-then-theory" strategy. The second school of thought emphasizes deduction and is represented in modern sociology by the "theory-then-research" strategy.

Research-then-theory.   This strategy is largely inductive in nature and reflects the philosophical position of Francis Bacon. In contemporary sociology this strategy is most clearly delineated and supported in the work of Glaser and Strauss. They state that:

> Theory based on data can usually not be completely refuted by more data or replaced by another theory. Since it is too intimately linked to data, it is destined to last despite its inevitable modification and reformulation. (Glaser and Strauss, 1967, p. 4)

On the other hand, the major limitations of this strategy are expressed by Reynolds as follows:

> . . . it is almost impossible to define all the variables that might be measured for any phenomenon; the list of things to measure is infinite. But even if this is overlooked, the problem of selecting the significant causal relationships from among the infinite number of possible relationships is insurmountable. (Reynolds, 1971, p. 149)

In sum, the research-then-theory strategy is represented by the bottom left-hand quadrant of Fig. 2.2 (i.e., observations and empirical generalizations) and " . . . reflects the assumption that there are 'real' patterns in nature and the task of scientists is to *discover* these patterns, the laws of nature" (Reynolds, 1971) (see section 2.2 above).

Theory-then-research.   This strategy is largely deductive in nature and reflects the philosophical position of Karl Popper (1959). In contemporary sociology this strategy is most clearly delineated in the work of Zetterberg (1965), and was illustrated in the earlier example of the processes and products of sociological inquiry. The strengths of this strategy are outlined in the discussion of the virtues of theory in Section 2.3 above. "The most fundamental problem with implementing the theory-then-research strategy is inventing the initial theory" (Reynolds, 1971).

The theory-then-research strategy is represented by the top right-hand quadrant of Fig. 2.2 (i.e., theories and hypotheses) and:

> . . . reflects the assumption that . . . Scientific activity is the process of inventing theories (formalizing an idea in axiomatic or causal process form) and then testing the usefulness of the invention. (Reynolds, 1971, p. 147)

A composite approach.   In many respects the two strategies just described represent the long-standing debate between empiricists and theorists in sociology. Some years ago Merton characterized the debate by observing that for theorists:

> . . . the identifying motto would at times seem to be: "We do not know whether what we say is true, but it is at least significant." And for the radical empiricist the motto may read: "This is demonstrably so, but we cannot indicate its significance." (Merton, 1968, p. 139)

Reynolds suggests that a combination of the research-then-theory and the theory-then-research strategies may provide the best means of sociological inquiry. His composite approach consists of three stages of inquiry:

1. *"Exploratory.* Research is designed to allow an investigator to just look around with respect to some phenomenon. The researcher should endeavor to develop suggestive ideas, and the research should be as flexible as possible. If possible, the research should be conducted in such a way as to provide guidance for procedures to be employed in research activity during stage two.

2. *"Descriptive.* The goal at this stage is to develop careful descriptions of patterns that were suspected in the exploratory research. The purpose may be seen as one of developing intersubjective descriptions (i.e., empirical generalizations). Once an empirical generalization is developed, it is then considered worth explaining (i.e., the development of a theory).

3. *"Explanatory.* The goal at this stage is to develop explicit theory that can be used to explain the empirical generalizations that evolve from the second stage. This is a continuous cycle of (a) theory construction; (b) theory testing, attempts to falsify with empirical research; and (c) theory reformulation (back to step 3a)."*

It is evident that the three stages of Reynolds's composite approach closely correspond to the discussion in this chapter of the three major tasks of sociological inquiry: description, discovery, and explanation.

---

*From *A Primer in Theory Construction,* copyright © 1971 by Paul D. Reynolds and The Bobbs-Merrill Company, Inc., reprinted by permission of the publisher.

2.4.2 Intellectual Craftsmanship: Science as Art and Play

The above overview of the nature of sociological analysis represents a highly formalized and a very idealized sketch of the theoretical approaches to and modes of sociological inquiry. In concluding this chapter, an attempt is made to mitigate the unbalanced treatment of sociological inquiry in terms of its formal qualities by stressing that sociological inquiry is a creative endeavor and is as much an art (Nisbet, 1976) as a science.

A sociologist is a craftsman as much as a scientist per se. Moreover, the craft is often a playful endeavor providing aesthetic pleasure and on occasion resulting in the creation of artistic artifacts (e.g., lucid social analyses, clear propositions, and elegant models and theories). As Ravetz has noted:

> To anyone with experience of the "art" of scientific inquiry, this may seem so obvious as to be banal. Yet this feature of science has generally been ignored in philosophical discussion, even in those that try to take into account the work by which scientific knowledge is achieved. Yet without an appreciation of the craft character of scientific work there is no possibility of resolving the paradox of the radical difference between the subjective, intensely personal activity of creative science, and the objective, impersonal knowledge which results from it. (Ravetz, 1971, p. 75)

Ravetz provides a detailed outline of the craft character of scientific inquiry in terms of data, information, tools, pitfalls, techniques, and style. With respect to the latter attribute he observes that:

> One of the reasons for the lack of awareness of the craft character of scientific work is the form in which the results of that work reach students and the lay public. There they are presented out of the context of their creation and in a simplified or vulgarized version. The fine structure of the argument by which the result was established, and its context in earlier and alternative approaches, cannot be conveyed except to a technically competent audience. It is just in these fine points of detail that the style of a scientist is revealed. (Ravetz, 1971, p. 104)

As C. Wright Mills (1959) expressed the matter in his essay on intellectual craftsmanship: "Only by conversations in which experienced thinkers exchange information about their actual ways of working can a useful sense of method and theory be imparted to the beginning student."

Unfortunately, students are seldom exposed to the working accounts of productive scientists and thus lack awareness of the craft character of scientific inquiry. Many teachers are not active scholars in their own right and accordingly cannot provide students with personal insights about intellectual inquiry, and scientists rarely offer their own descriptive accounts of the nature of their research activities. In view of this situation three procedures are recommended. First, a student should attempt to serve as a research assistant for an individual engaged in a scientific investigation so as to receive an apprenticeship in the craft of social inquiry. Second, a student should read the few accounts available of the personal nature of sociological inquiry. A good starting point is P. E. Hammond's book *Sociologists at Work: Essays on the Craft of Social Research* (1964), wherein leading sociologists give behind-the-scene accounts of classic sociological investigations. Third, students should read biographical essays of scientists that focus on their styles of inquiry, especially the "profiles" of scientists that are periodically presented in *The New Yorker*. These profiles present numerous insights into the "subjective, intensely personal activity of creative science."

One important kind of insight is the nature of personal experiences that have led given individuals to take up science as a career. For example, I. I. Rabi (a Noble prizewinning physicist) in response to the question of whether any particular experience had directed him toward science, replied:

> "Yes, . . . A very profound one. One time, I was walking along and looked down the street—looked right down the street, which faced east. The moon was just rising. And it scared the hell out of me. Absolutely scared the hell out of me. Another profound experience that I had revolved around the first verses of Genesis. The whole idea of the creation—the mystery and the philosophy of it. It sank in on me, and it's something I still feel. But, as a matter of fact, I got into science in a funny way. I read all the fairy stories and other stories in the children's section of the library. I started with Alcott and worked down through Trowbridge—all those children's books, all those writers. Then I came to the end of *those* shelves, and there was a science shelf. So I started with astronomy. That was what determined my later life more than anything else—reading a little book on astronomy. That's where I first heard of the Copernican system and the explanation of the changes of the seasons, the phases of the moon, and the idea that the stars were suns, very distant suns. Ours was such a fundamentalist family that my parents hadn't heard of the Copernical system, and for me it was a tremendous revelation. I was so impressed—the beauty of it all, and the simplicity." (Bernstein, 1975, pp. 49–50)

A second kind of insight concerns the demanding work of scientific inquiry. For example, in a profile on the noted sociologist Robert K. Merton, the following account was given of his early career:

> For all his sociability at Harvard, Merton was, as he has been ever since, an extremely hard worker, keeping long hours and sleeping little. He devoted one of his graduate-school summers to visiting all the Hoovervilles and hobo jungles of Boston, interviewing their homeless tenants to find out who they were and had been and where they came from. He spent four or five months immured in the cellar of Harvard's Widener Library classifying tens of thousands of patents issued in the United States between 1860 and 1930 in order to chart the fluctuations in the rate of invention within each industry and to relate these fluctuations to changing social conditions. And for his doctoral dissertation he doggedly read 6,034 biographies in the fine type of the Dictionary of National Biography—just as a starter. (Hunt, 1961, p. 53)

A third kind of insight concerns the pleasures and difficulties associated with scholarly pursuit. For example, a profile of Einstein suggests that:

> Einstein never fully belonged to any institution, any country, or any one person or group of people. He found great pleasure in the company of certain friends and he constantly carried on an enormous correspondence with people of all sorts, but those who knew him always had a sense that his thoughts were elsewhere. He needed absolute solitude for his work, but this need produced an inevitable loneliness. He was also aware, obviously, of his celebrity, which he had not sought and did not understand. In September, 1952, he wrote to a friend, "For my part, I have always tended to solitude, a trait that usually becomes more pronounced with age. It is strange to be known so universally and yet to be so lonely. The fact is that the kind of popularity which I am experiencing pushes the subject into a defensive attitude that leads him into isolation." (Bernstein, 1973, p. 45)

Yet another kind of insight concerns the playfulness of inquiry and the creative nature of the investigator. For example, a profile of Dr. Carl Sagan, a member of the planning team for the Viking landings on Mars, describes him as follows:

> . . . a man whose own childhood never seems very far behind him; he has remained close to it and seems to draw from it a rich and playful imagery.

> With his playfulness, his ability to bring science fiction to the aid of science, and his nimble way of turning a question inside out, so that an adverse circumstance suddenly becomes an asset, Sagan alternately delights and infuriates not only children, but his scientific colleagues as well. The latter don't know quite what to make of him, for although they regard him as a good, even brilliant scientist, they have trouble coming to grips with his most distinctive quality, his imagination. Sagan is a theorist—a type of scientist who traditionally irritates many of his fellows, because he necessarily deals with what might be instead of what is. Scientists can be quite tough on colleagues who they feel speculate too much, especially in public. (Cooper, 1976, pp. 39–83)

In summary, while this text hopes to convince the student that scientific inquiry in general and sociological inquiry in particular is serious work demanding a high degree of formal training and discipline, hopefully the student will be persuaded that such work is often a playful and enjoyable activity for those who become involved. As Schrodinger remarked in his essay on "Science, Art and Play":

> . . . science with all its consequences is not such a desperately serious affair and that, all things considered, it contributes less to material well-being than is generally assumed, while it contributes more than is generally assumed to purely ideal pleasures. True, its effect on the multitude is generally indirect and the occasions are rare when science can give joy to the many by laying before it immediate results: indeed, this happens only in those cases where it lays before the community a work of art. (Schrodinger, 1957, p. 33)

NOTES

1. Our linguistic analogy deviates slightly from Brodbeck's formulation. She states: "Language consists of words and sentences. To the *words* of ordinary speech correspond the *concepts* of science; to the *sentences* its *definitions*, its *statements of individual fact* and *laws.* Certain sets of sentences constitute the *theories* of science" (Brodbeck, 1963).

2. See Blumer (1969, pp. 140–152) and Homans (1967, pp. 10–18).

3. For a more complete and anthropological analysis of the scientific concept of culture the reader is referred to Weiss (1973). For a different analytical discrimination of the concepts of culture and of social system (society), the reader is referred to Kroeber and Parsons (1958). For a detailed discussion of norms, values, and sanctions the reader is referred to Blake and Davis (1964).

4. For a more thorough definition of social identity the reader is referred to Tumin (1973, pp. 27–30).

5. For related but different treatments of social system problems the reader is referred to Caplow (1964), Fallding (1968), and Parsons (1959).

6. Social systems, for example, have been classified according to such diverse criteria as type of tasks performed, organizational effectiveness, social homogeneity, technological complexity, system permanency, and primary beneficiary (see Blau and Scott, 1962; Caplow, 1964).

7. Rosenberg (1968) distinguishes seven levels of sociological analysis: the individual, the group, the organizational, the ecological, the institutional, the cultural, and the societal levels.

8. A related typology of analytical social systems is given in Phillips (1969, pp. 45–46). He defines three types of social systems: groups (focused on interaction patterns), social-category systems (focused on norms), and institutions (focused on values).

9. Eisenstadt (1968) views all institutions as regulative and although he uses the term "cultural institutions" he does not employ the terms "socializing" and "regulative" institutions as used in this text.

10. For a discussion of other kinds of research methods associated with field studies, the reader is referred to Webb et al. (1966).

11. The process of using several different research techniques to measure a given social phenomenon has been referred to as "triangulation" (see Webb et al., 1966, pp. 3, 174).

12. For example, Ritzer (1975b) contends that the observation technique is associated with the social definition paradigm, the experiment is associated with the social behavior paradigm, and interviews and questionnaires are associated with the social facts paradigm.

13. Kuhn's (1970) analysis of the structure of science suggests that no science is in fact cumulative in character in the direct, linear sense of scientific evolution.

14. It must be recognized that research strategies bearing on theory verification may at times be markedly different from those related to theory generation.

15. For a detailed treatment of "The Bearing of Sociological Theory on Empirical Research" and "The Bearing of Empirical Research on Sociological Theory," the reader is referred to Merton (1968, pp. 139–171).

REFERENCES

Babbie, E. (1973). *Survey Research Methods*. Belmont, Calif.: Wadsworth.

Babbie, E. (1975). *The Practice of Social Research*. Belmont, Calif.: Wadsworth.

Bates, S. (1967). *The Sociological Enterprise*. Boston: Houghton Mifflin.

Berger, P., and T. Luckman (1967). *The Social Construction of Reality*. New York: Anchor Books.

Bernstein, J. (1973). "The secrets of the old one—I." *The New Yorker* (March 10): 44–101.

Bernstein, J. (1975). "Physicist—I." *The New Yorker* (October 13): 47–110. Used with permission.

Bertrand, A. L. (1972). *Social Organization: A General Systems and Role Theory Perspective*. Arlington Heights, Ill.: AHM. Used with permission.

Blake, J., and K. Davis (1964). "Norms, values and sanctions." In Faris (ed.), *Handbook of Modern Sociology*, pp. 456–485. Chicago: Rand McNally.

Blau, P. (1964). *Exchange and Power in Social Life*. New York: Wiley.

Blau, P. (1969). "Objectives of sociology." In R. Bierstedt (ed.), *A Design for Sociology: Scope, Objectives and Methods*, pp. 43–71. Philadelphia: The American Academy of Political and Social Science.

Blau, P., and W. R. Scott (1962). *Formal Organizations*. San Francisco: Chandler.

Blumer, H. (1969). *Symbolic Interactionism: Perspective and Method*. Englewood Cliffs, N.J.: Prentice-Hall.

Bottomore, T. (1975). "Competing paradigms in macrosociology." In A. Inkeles (ed.), *Annual Review of Sociology*, Vol. 1, pp. 191–202. Palo Alto, Calif.: Annual Reviews, Inc.

Brodbeck, M. (1963). "Logic and scientific method in research and teaching." In N. L. Gage (ed.), *Handbook of Research on Teaching*, pp. 44–93. Chicago: Rand McNally.

Buckley, W. F. (1967). *Sociology and Modern Systems Theory*. Englewood Cliffs, N.J.: Prentice-Hall.

Buckley, W. F. (ed.) (1968). *Modern Systems Research for the Behavioral Scientist*. Chicago: Aldine.

Burgess, R., and D. Bushell (eds.) (1969). *Behavioral Sociology*. New York: Columbia University Press.

Burns, T. (1973). "A structural theory of social exchange." *Acta Sociologica* **16**: 188–207.

Caplow, T. (1953). "The criteria of organizational success." *Social Forces* **32**: 1–9. Used with permission.

Caplow. T. (1964). *Principles of Organization*. New York: Harcourt, Brace and World.

Catton, W. (1964). "The development of sociological thought." In R. Faris (ed.), *Handbook of Modern Sociology*, pp. 912–950. Chicago: Rand McNally.

Cicourel, A. V. (1974). *Cognitive Sociology: Language and Meaning in Social Interaction*. New York: The Free Press.

Collins, R. (1975). *Conflict Sociology. Toward An Explanatory Science*. New York: Academic Press.

Cooper, H. S. (1975). "A resonance with something alive—I." *The New Yorker* (June 21): 39–83. Used with permission.

Coser, L. (1975). "Two methods in search of a substance." *American Sociological Review* **40** (December): 691–700.

Cotgrove, S. (1968). *The Science of Society*. New York: Barnes and Noble.

Dahrendorf, R. (1959). *Class and Conflict In Industrial Society*. Stanford, Calif.: Stanford University Press.

Demerath, N. J., and R. Peterson (eds.) (1967). *System, Change and Conflict*. New York: The Free Press.

Doby, J. (1954). *An Introduction to Social Research*. Harrisburg, Pa.: Stackpole. Used with permission.

Durkheim, E. (1951). *Suicide*. New York: The Free Press.

Durkheim, E. (1954). *The Rules of Sociological Method*. New York: The Free Press.

Eisenstadt, S. N. (1968). "Social institutions: The concept." In D. E. Sills (ed.), *International Encyclopedia of the Social Sciences*, 2nd ed., Vol. 14, pp. 409–421. New York: Macmillan.

Ekeh, P. (1974). *Social Exchange Theory: The Two Traditions*. London: Heinemann Educational.

Emerson, R. M. (1976). "Social exchange theory." In A. Inkeles (ed.), *Annual Review of Sociology*, Vol. 2, pp. 335–362. Palo Alto, Calif.: Annual Reviews, Inc.

Fallding, H. (1968). *The Sociological Task*. Englewood Cliffs, N.J.: Prentice-Hall.

Festinger, L., and D. Katz (eds.) (1965). *Research Methods in the Behavioral Sciences*. New York: Holt, Rinehart and Winston.

French, J. (1965). "Experiments in field settings." In L. Festinger and D. Katz (eds.), *Research Methods in the Behavioral Sciences*, pp. 98–135. New York: Holt, Rinehart and Winston.

Garfinkel, H. (1967). *Studies in Ethnomethodology*. Englewood Cliffs, N. J.: Prentice-Hall.

Glaser, B., and A. Strauss (1967). *The Discovery of Grounded Theory*. Chicago: Aldine.

Goode, W., and P. Hatt (1952). *Methods in Social Research*. New York: McGraw-Hill.

Hammond, P. E. (1964). *Sociologists at Work: Essays on the Craft of Social Research*. New York: Basic Books.

Hewit, J. P. (1976). *Self and Society: A Symbolic Interactionist Social Psychology*. Boston: Allyn and Bacon.

Holsti, O. R. (1969). *Content Analysis and the Social Sciences and the Humanities*. Reading, Mass.: Addison-Wesley.

Homans, G. C. (1961). *Social Behavior: Its Elementary Forms*. New York: Harcourt, Brace and World.

Homans, G. C. (1964). "Contemporary theory in sociology." In R. Faris (ed.), *Handbook of Modern Sociology*, pp. 951–977. Chicago: Rand McNally.

Homans, G. C. (1967). *The Nature of Social Science*. New York: Harcourt, Brace and World. Used with permission.

Hopkins, T. (1964). *The Exercise of Influence in Small Groups*. Totowa, N.J.: The Bedminster Press.

Horowitz, I. L. (ed.) (1965). *The New Sociology*. New York: Oxford University Press.

Horton, J. (1965). "Order and conflict theories of social problems as competing ideologies." *American Journal of Sociology* 71: 701–713.

Hunt, M. M. (1961). "How does it come to be so?" *The New Yorker* (January 28): 39–63. Used with permission.

Hyman, H. (1972). *Secondary Analysis of Sample Surveys*. New York: John Wiley.

Kerlinger, F. (1964). *Foundations of Behavioral Research*. New York: Holt, Rinehart and Winston.

Kluckhohn, F. (1940). "The participant-observer technique in small communities." *American Journal of Sociology* 46: 331–343.

Krech, D., et al. (1962). *Individual in Society*. New York: McGraw-Hill.

Kroeber, A., and T. Parsons (1958). "The concepts of culture and of social system." *American Sociological Review* 23: 582–583.

Kuhn, A. (1974). *The Logic of Social Systems*. San Francisco: Jossey-Bass.

Kuhn, A. (1975). *Unified Social Science: A System-Based Introduction*. Homewood, Ill.: Dorsey Press.

Kuhn, M. H. (1964). "Major trends in symbolic interaction theory in the past twenty-five years." *Sociological Quarterly* 5: 61–84.

Kuhn, T. S. (1970). "The structure of scientific revolutions," In O. Neurath et al. (eds.), *Foundations of the Unity of Science*, 2nd ed., Vol. 2, No. 2. Chicago: University of Chicago Press.

Labovitz, S., and R. Hagedorn (1971). *Introduction to Social Research*. New York: McGraw-Hill.

Lastrucci, C. (1967). *The Scientific Approach*. Cambridge, Mass.: Schenkman. Used with permission.

Lieberman, S. (1950). "The effects of changes in roles on the attitudes of role occupants." *Human Relations* 9: 385–403.

Lipset, S., and R. Bendix (1953). *Social Mobility in Industrialized Society*. Berkeley: University of California Press.

Loy, J. W. (1972). "Sociology and physical education." In R. Singer et al., *Physical Education: An Interdisciplinary Approach*, pp. 168–236. New York: Macmillan. Used with permission.

Loy, J. W., and J. Segrave (1974). "Research methodology in the sociology of sport." In J. Wilmore (ed.), *Exercise and Sport Sciences Reviews*, Vol. 2, pp. 289–333. New York: Academic Press.

Manis, J. G., and B. N. Meltzer (eds.) (1972). *Symbolic Interactionism: A Reader in Social Psychology*, 2nd ed. Boston: Allyn and Bacon.

Martindale, D. (ed.) (1965). *Functionalism in the Social Sciences*. Philadelphia: American Academy of Political and Social Science.

Marx, M. (1963). *Theories in Contemporary Psychology*. New York: Macmillan.

Mead, G. H. (1934). *Mind, Self and Society*. Chicago: University of Chicago Press.

Merton, R. K. (1968). *Social Theory and Social Structure*, 3rd ed. New York: The Free Press.

Mills, C. W. (1959). *The Sociological Imagination*. New York: Grove Press.

Mott, P. E. (1965). *The Organization of Society*. Englewood Cliffs, N.J.: Prentice-Hall.

Nisbet, R. (1976). *Sociology as an Art Form*. New York: Oxford University Press.

Olsen, M. (1968). *The Process of Social Organization*. New York: Holt, Rinehart and Winston.

Parsons, T. (1951). *The Social System*. New York: The Free Press.

Parsons, T. (1959). "General theory in sociology." In R. Merton et al. (eds.), *Sociology Today*, pp. 3–38. New York: Basic Books.

Parsons, T. (1966). *Societies: Evolutionary and Comparative Perspectives*. Englewood Cliffs. N.J.: Prentice-Hall.

Parsons, T. (1971). *The System of Modern Societies*. Englewood Cliffs, N.J.: Prentice-Hall.

Phillips, B. (1969). *Sociology: Social Structure and Change*. New York: Macmillan.

Popper, K. (1959). *The Logic of Scientific Discovery*. New York: Harper and Row.

Price, J. (1968). *Organizational Effectiveness—An Inventory of Propositions*. Homewood, Ill.: Richard D. Irwin.

Ravetz, J. (1971). *Scientific Knowledge and Its Social Problems*. New York: Oxford University Press. Used with permission.

Reynolds, P. (1971). *A Primer in Theory Construction*. Indianapolis: Bobbs-Merrill.

Riley, M. W. (1964). "Sources and types of sociological data." In R. E. Faris (ed.), *Handbook of Modern Sociology*, pp. 978–1026. Chicago: Rand McNally.

Ritzer, G. (1975a). "Sociology: A multiple paradigm science." *The American Sociologist* 10 (August): 156–167.

Ritzer, G. (1975b). *Sociology: A Multiple Paradigm Science*. Boston: Allyn and Bacon. Used with permission.

Rogers, E. (1962). *Diffusion of Innovations*. New York: The Free Press.

Rose, A. M. (ed.) (1962). *Human Behavior and Social Processes: An Interactionist Approach*. Boston: Houghton Mifflin.

Rosenberg, M. (1968). *The Logic of Survey Analysis*. New York: Basic Books.

Rudner, R. (1966). *Philosophy of Social Science*. Englewood Cliffs, N.J.: Prentice-Hall.

Schachter, S. (1959). *The Psychology of Affiliation*. Stanford, Calif.: Stanford University Press.

Schrodinger, E. (1957). *Science, Theory and Man*. New York: Dover. Used with permission.

Schutz, A. (1964). *Collected Papers*, Vol. 2. The Hague: Martinus Nijhoff.

Selltiz, C., et al. (1963). *Research Methods in Social Relations*. New York: Holt, Rinehart and Winston.

Shibutani, T. (1961). *Society and Personality*. Englewood Cliffs, N.J.: Prentice-Hall.

Shibutani, T. (ed.) (1970). *Human Nature and Collective Behavior*. Englewood Cliffs, N.J.: Prentice-Hall.

Skinner, B. F. (1971). *Beyond Freedom and Dignity*. New York: Knopf.

Smelser, N. J. (1969). "The optimum scope of sociology." In R. Bierstedt (ed.), *A Design for Sociology: Scope, Objectives and Methods*, pp. 1–21. Philadelphia: The American Academy of Political and Social Science.

Stinchcombe, A. D. (1968). *Constructing Social Theories*. New York: Harcourt, Brace and World.

Stone, G., and H. Farberman (1970). *Social Psychology Through Symbolic Interaction*. Waltham, Mass. Ginn-Blaisdell.

Sudman, S. (1976). "Sample surveys." In A. Inkeles (ed.), *Annual Review of Sociology*, Vol. 2, pp. 107–120. Palo Alto, Calif.: Annual Reviews.

Sullivan, M., et al. (1958). "Participant observation as employed in the study of a military training program." *American Sociological Review* **23**: 660–667.

Sztompka, P. (1974). *System and Function: Toward a Theory of Society*. New York: Academic Press.

Thibault, J., and H. Kelly (1959). *The Social Psychology of Groups*. New York: Wiley.

Tumin, M. (1973). *Patterns of Society*. Boston: Little, Brown.

Turner, J. (1974). *The Structure of Sociological Theory*. Homewood, Ill.: Dorsey Press.

Wallace, W. (ed.) (1969). *Sociological Theory*. Chicago: Aldine.

Warriner, C. (1956). "Groups are real: A reaffirmation." *American Sociological Review* **21**: 549–554.

Warshay, L. (1975). *The Current State of Sociological Theory*. New York: D. McKay.

Webb, E., et al. (1966). *Unobtrusive Measures: Nonreactive Research in the Social Sciences*. Chicago: Rand McNally.

Weber, M. (1947). *The Theory of Social and Economic Organization*. New York: The Free Press.

Weiss, G. (1973). "A scientific concept of culture." *American Anthropologist* **75**: 1376–1413.

Wiseman, H. (1966). *Political Systems*. New York: F. A. Praeger.

Wolfenstein, M. (1951). "The emergence of fun morality." *Journal of Social Issues* **7**: 3–16.

Zeitlin, I. (1973). *Rethinking Sociology: A Critique of Contemporary Theory*. New York: Appleton-Century-Crofts.

Zetterberg, H. I. (1965). *On Theory and Verification in Sociology*, 3rd. ed. Totowa, N.J.: The Bedminster Press. Used with permission.

PART 2
SPORT AND
MICROSOCIAL
SYSTEMS
Social Systems of Sport

Chapter 3
SPORT GROUPS

3.1 INTRODUCTION

3.1.1 Psychosociological Analysis of Small Groups

Why Study Small Groups?

According to Mills (1967), there are four cogent reasons why the study of small groups is an important and worthy endeavor for social scientists. The first is pragmatic in nature, namely: "We need to understand what happens within such groups, both because their decisions have a critical effect upon the history of communities, and because their dynamics affect the way individuals lead their daily lives." The second reason is social-psychological in nature, namely: "Because social pressures and pressures from the individual meet in the small group, it is a convenient context in which to observe and to experiment on the interplay among these pressures." The third reason is sociological in nature in that "The direct task is to understand small groups in their own right and to create empirically based theories about the dynamics of these many billions of transitory systems, much as the task of physiology is to formulate working theories of the dynamics of transitory living organisms" (Mills, 1967).

The fourth reason is also sociological but more ambitious and comparative in nature:

> Small groups are a special case of the more general type of system, the social system. Not only are they micro-systems, they are essentially microcosms of larger societies. They present in miniature, societal features, such as a division of labor, a code of ethics, a government, media of exchange, prestige rankings, ideologies, myths, and religious practices . . . Small-group research is thus a means of developing effective ways of thinking about social systems in general. (Mills, 1967, pp. 2–3)

Approaches to the Study of Small Groups

In Section 2.1.2 a group was defined as a social system organized around a set of interacting personalities. This chapter focuses on this approach by studying individuals in a social context and emphasizing the process of social interaction. This social interaction can be treated as a function of human biological nature and personality on the one hand, and as a function of social structure, culture, and environment, on the other hand (see Hare, 1964). Moreover, it is noted that the behavior of individuals in interaction may be analyzed from a number of different perspectives. As Hare (1964) points out in the context of small group research, "some observers focus on interpersonal behavior, . . . some focus on intrapersonal behavior, . . . and still others focus on aspects of *individual performance* which may characterize an individual whether he is alone or in a group."

The study of small groups, social interaction, and interpersonal behavior falls primarily in the domain of social psychology. Although social psychology is sometimes considered as an academic discipline in its own right, it is most often considered as a subfield or speciality within both the discipline of psychology and the discipline of sociology. As we defined in Chapter 2, sociology is the study of the structure and composition, functioning and change, of social systems and their relation to human behavior. On the other hand, psychology may be defined as " . . . the study of the structure and functioning of the personal system, the system of action which characterizes a particular biological organism, notably a human being" (Inkeles, 1959). As can be surmised from these definitions, psychologically oriented social psychologists tend to study small groups from a different perspective than sociologically oriented social psychologists do.

Following Inkeles (1959) we shall refer to the perspective of the former group of social scientists as social psychology, and to the perspective of the latter group of social scientists as psychosociology. Specifically, we " . . . designate as social psychology the study of personality, which seeks to explain individual action not only by considering the psychological properties of the person but also by giving systematic attention to socio-cultural forces in the individual's action situation" (Inkeles, 1959). Further, we " . . . designate as psychosociology efforts to explain the functioning and change of social systems which not only consider properties of social systems but give systematic consideration to general personality theory or to the modal personalities of the system's participants and their psychological adjustment to the social forces impinging upon them" (Inkeles, 1959).

3.1.2 Psychosociological Analysis of Sport Teams as Task Groups

Why Study Sport Groups?

Since sport groups are a type of small group, Mills's four-fold rationale for the importance of small-group research provides adequate reasons for the study of sport groups. In addition, sport groups possess unique structural features that offer special advantages with respect to small-group research. Schafer (1966) has stated four such special advantages: "First, the sports group is a 'natural' rather than an artificial or laboratory group." Thus, sport groups provide research settings for studying (1) the life cycle of groups from their initial emergence to final extinction, (2) the internal and external systems of groups, that is, the relationships between groups and their organizational context and the larger external social environment in general, and (3) whether findings about small groups obtained in laboratory research reflect generalizable patterns of behavior or only experimental artifacts.

Second, research focused on a particular sport controls a number of confounding variables by automatically holding them constant. Examples of such variables include group size, role structure, and rules of conduct (Schafer, 1966). Third, because sport groups are typically in pursuit of zero-sum goals, they often provide an ideal context for the study of cooperation and competition and intergroup and intragroup conflict. Finally, sport groups with an emphasis on winning typically offer objective measures of group effectiveness in terms of the number of errors made, points scored for or against, and percentage of games won. That is, they offer ideal settings " . . . for the study of the effects of such variables as membership composition, cohesion, informal norms, leadership, and social environment on the attainment of group goals" (Schafer, 1966).

Conceptual Approaches to the Study of Sport Groups

A dominant characteristic of small-group research in sport settings is its atheoretical nature. Few studies of sport groups are based on a well-formulated theoretical perspective. In fact, many, if not most, studies of sport groups are highly descriptive in terms of both theoretical framework and empirical findings. For example, numerous investigations of group composition have simply measured the personality characteristics of individuals in different sport groups, with no a priori hypotheses predicting what specific traits are associated with the modal personality type of a particular sport group.

Two factors may account for the largely atheoretical nature of sport-group research. First, although there are a number of active researchers in sport psychology interested in the study of personality and the study of motor performance, there are few individuals actively engaged in the study of sport groups. Second, notwithstanding the several thousand small-group studies in psychology and sociology conducted since the 1930s, there is a general absence of theoretical formulations that might be utilized in the study of sport groups (see Shaw, 1971, p. 360).

However, several general paradigms of group dynamics have been developed that might be used as conceptual frameworks in the analysis of sport groups (see, for example, Hackman and Morris, 1975; Landers, 1974; Luschen, 1969; McGrath, 1964; Mills, 1967; Olmsted, 1959; and Steiner, 1972). In order to illustrate the present state of research regarding the psychosociological analysis of sport groups, this chapter focuses on certain components of group dynamics depicted in McGrath's (1964) frame of reference (Fig. 3.1) and in Hackman and Morris's (1975) modification of McGrath's model (Fig. 3.2). Specifically, Section 3.2 discusses group leadership, which is considered a special aspect of group composition; Section 3.3 is devoted to a second aspect of group composition, namely, the personal characteristics of group members; while Section 3.4 deals with the relationships between and among group structure, group process, and group performance.

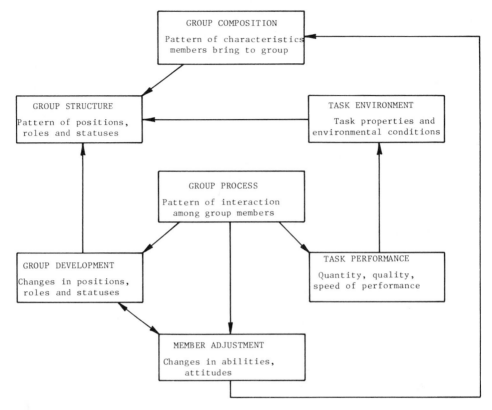

Fig. 3.1 *A frame of reference for the analysis of groups. (From* Social Psychology: A Brief Introduction *by Joseph E. McGrath. Copyright © 1964 by Holt, Rinehart and Winston. Reprinted by permission of Holt, Rinehart and Winston.)*

3.2 GROUP LEADERSHIP

3.2.1 Introduction

Functions of Leaders

Leadership is a much discussed but seldom studied topic in the context of sport. Notwithstanding the limited research about leadership in sport groups, it is evident that the leadership role is a complex one since group leaders fulfill many different functions. For example, Krech et al. (1962) note that a leader, to some degree, must serve as (1) executive, (2) planner, (3) policymaker, (4) expert, (5) external group representative, (6) controller of internal relations, (7) purveyor of rewards and punishments, (8) exemplar, (9) symbol of the group, (10) substitute for individual responsibility, (11) ideologist, (12) father figure, and (13) scapegoat.

The importance of any given leadership function depends on the type of group in which it is carried out. In general, however, the first seven functions

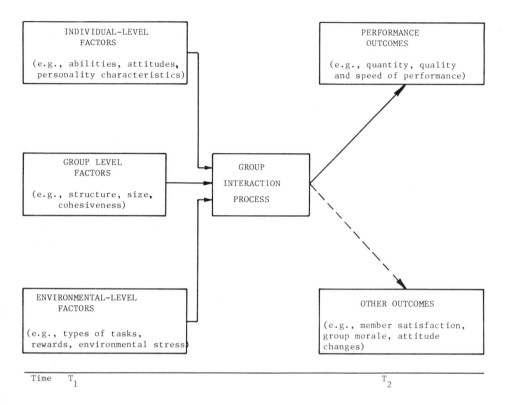

| | INPUT | PROCESS | OUTPUT |

INPUT   **PROCESS**   **OUTPUT**

INDIVIDUAL–LEVEL
FACTORS

(e.g., abilities, attitudes,
personality characteristics)

GROUP LEVEL
FACTORS

(e.g., structure, size,
cohesiveness)

ENVIRONMENTAL–LEVEL
FACTORS

(e.g., types of tasks,
rewards, environmental stress)

GROUP
INTERACTION
PROCESS

PERFORMANCE
OUTCOMES

(e.g., quantity, quality
and speed of performance)

OTHER OUTCOMES

(e.g., member satisfaction,
group morale, attitude
changes)

Time T_1 T_2

Fig. 3.2 *A paradigm for the analysis of group interaction. (From Hackman and Morris, 1975, p. 50)*

listed above are *primary* functions "essential to the exercise of leadership," whereas the latter six functions are *accessory* functions which " . . . a leader may assume or may be assigned by the group by virtue of his leadership position . . . " (Krech et al., 1962).

Definition of Leadership

In view of the many functions fulfilled by leaders, it is difficult to state both a precise and a comprehensive definition of leadership. Given the multifaceted nature of the concept, Hemphill's definition seems a reasonable and useful one. He states that: "To lead is to engage in an act which initiates a structure in the interaction of others as part of the process of solving a mutual problem" (cited in Gibb, 1969).

Hemphill's definition holds a number of implications for the study of leadership behavior. First, it suggests that leaders can be identified "by the relative frequency with which they engage in such acts" (Gibb, 1969). Second, it suggests that groups may have many leaders and several individuals in a group may engage in such acts simultaneously or at different times. Third, it suggests that "leadership is probably best conceived as a group quality, as a set of functions which must be carried out by the group" (Gibb, 1969). Finally, "if there are leadership functions which must be performed in any group, and if these functions may be 'focused' or 'distributed', then leaders will be identifiable both in terms of the frequency and in terms of the multiplicity or pattern of functions performed" (Gibb, 1969).

The Study of Leadership

In general, leadership behavior has been studied in terms of traits, styles, and situations (see, for example, Gibb, 1969; Shaw, 1971). The first approach stresses the search for dominant characteristics of leaders, including physical and constitutional factors, personality variables, and specific skills and abilities. The second approach emphasizes what leaders actually do and how they do it—for example, making decisions in a democratic manner. The third approach assumes that leadership is always relative to a specific situation. Moreover, as Gibb has written:

> The situation includes: (1) the structure of interpersonal relations within a group, (2) group or syntality characteristics . . . , (3) characteristics of the total culture in which the group exists and from which group members have been drawn, and (4) the physical conditions and the task with which the group is confronted. (Gibb, 1969, p. 246)

Each of these perspectives is examined below with respect to leadership in sport groups.

3.2.2 Leadership Traits

General Leadership Characteristics

Since the turn of the century many empirical studies have sought to determine the outstanding personal attributes of leaders in a variety of group settings. In an early review of research regarding leadership traits, Stogdill (1948) found that the factors having the highest overall correlation with leadership were " . . . originality, popularity, sociability, judgment, aggressiveness, desire to excel, humor, cooperativeness, liveliness, and athletic ability, in approximate order of magnitude of average correlation coefficient."

In a similar review based on reported research from 1900 to 1957, Mann (1959) concluded that there were highly significant and positive relationships between leadership and the factors of intelligence, adjustment, and extraversion. In addition, he found that dominance, masculinity, and interpersonal sensitivity were positively related to leadership, while conservatism was negatively related to leadership.

With the development of a number of standardized personality inventories (see Cattell, 1965), many studies since the early 1950s have examined the relationship between personality traits and leadership characteristics and success. These studies have usually compared those fulfilling leadership and nonleadership roles in a variety of social organizations. For example, Cattell, and Stice (1954) administered the Cattell Sixteen Personality Factor Inventory (16PF) to newly recruited military personnel and found that leaders could be characterized by four dominant personality factors: superego strength and conscientiousness, venturesomeness, worrying anxiousness, and will power.

Although many generalizations can be made on the basis of similar studies, most correlations between personality traits and leadership measures are not large and vary in magnitude from one study to another. Moreover, as Krech et al. (1962) have stated: "It is of interest to speculate that the personality traits which have been found to characterize leaders may, in part, *develop* in individuals as they act as leaders." For example, a moderately submissive individual when placed in a leadership position may become more assertive and dominant as a result of the newly gained power and responsibility.

Personality Characteristics of Coaches

Within sport groups the primary responsibility for leadership rests with the coach. Although laypeople appear to hold a relatively common stereotype of the coach as a conservative, dogmatic, and manipulative individual, relatively few studies have investigated the personality structure of coaches (Hendry, 1974; Sage, 1975a). One of the earliest investigations of the personality structure of coaches examined the personality profiles of 64 coaches in four major sports: baseball, basketball, football, and track (Ogilvie and Tutko, 1966). They reported that as a group coaches represent highly success-driven, dominant, organized, conscientious, emotionally stable, and persevering individuals. In addition, the coaches were found to be sociable, trusting, willing to accept blame and responsibility, and " . . . very high in leadership qualities when compared with norms based on men who were selected or elected leaders" (Ogilvie and Tutko, 1966). Similar traits have been reported by Andrud (1970), Gagen (1971), and Hendry (1968).

On the other hand, Ogilvie and Tutko found that coaches were characterized by two traits that might detrimentally influence their exertion of leadership in sport situations. First, they expressed a low interest in the dependency needs of others, and thus might not provide much emotional support to others. Second, they expressed a marked degree of psychological inflexibility and extreme conservatism, and thus might be expected " . . . to limit their use of new information or different thinking in terms of dealing with new problems" (Ogilvie and Tutko, 1966).

In contrast, four relatively comprehensive investigations of the personality structure of coaches indicate that the stereotype of the athletic coach as a conservative, dogmatic, and manipulative individual is not supported. First, Longmuir (1972) administered Rokeach's (1960) *Dogmatism Scale* to samples of high school basketball and football coaches, and discovered that coaches do not differ significantly in their degree of dogmatism from members of a wide variety of occupational groups that were assessed by Rokeach et al. (Rokeach, 1960).

Second, Sage (1972a) obtained measures of Machiavellianism for randomly selected national samples of collegiate basketball, football, and track coaches, as well as randomly selected high school basketball and football coaches in the state of Colorado. He used the *Mach scale* (see Christie and Geis, 1970), which is purported to be a reliable and valid measure of the degree to which individuals endorse duplicity, guile, manipulation, and opportunism in interpersonal relations. However, Sage discovered no significant differences between high school and college coaches and male undergraduate students in terms of mean scores on the Mach scale.

Third, Walsh and Carron (1977) compared the degree of Machiavellianism among three groups of Canadian coaches—high school physical education coaches, non-physical education high school coaches, community volunteer coaches—and a control group of noncoaching teachers. On the basis of Mach scale scores, they reported that community volunteer coaches were significantly lower in Machiavellianism than either the non-physical education coaches or the noncoaching teachers. Other intergroup comparisons revealed no significant differences.

Finally, Sage (1972b), in a second study, assessed the value orientations (liberalism vs. conservatism) of randomly selected national samples of collegiate basketball, football, and track coaches using the *Polyphasic Values Inventory* (PVI) developed by Roscoe (1965). In comparing his findings for the coaches with those earlier reported for male college students (see Teglovic, 1968), Sage concluded that coaches express a greater degree of conservatism than male undergraduates. However, he goes on to point out that: " . . . an item-by-item analysis of the response choices certainly does not support the assertions which have been made recently that coaches are extremely conservative—even reactionary—in value orientation" (Sage, 1972b). Further, in comparing his findings for the coaches with those reported for businessmen (see Elliott, 1969), Sage (1972b) states that all coaches considered as a group demonstrated more liberal tendencies in such domains as the treatment of communists, international relations, educational methodology, academic freedom, and racial and sexual relations. However, they were more conservative than the businessmen on such issues as labor unions and the use of alcoholic beverages.

In summary, despite the paucity of research, there is some evidence that coaches have a relatively consistent set of personality characteristics.[1] However, the issue as to how these characteristics were acquired initially is unresolved. To date, the only theoretical interpretation of the matter is Sage's (1975b) discussion that the beliefs and behaviors of coaches may result from selected child-rearing practices, parental values, sport participation patterns, and the process of occupational socialization. Limited evidence suggests that the personality orientations of coaches, however acquired, influence both coach-player relationships (see Albaugh, 1972: Hendry, 1968; Pease, 1970; Snyder, 1975) and group performance.

Personality Orientations and Performance Measures

Although a limited number of investigations have assessed the personality structure of coaches, few studies have examined the relationships between the personality traits of coaches and the performance of these coaches in sport situations. Four studies that have examined these relationships are briefly reviewed below.

Penman et al. (1974), using the Rokeach Dogmatism Scale to measure degree of authoritarianism, examined the relationship between team success and authoritarianism of selected samples of head high school basketball and football coaches. They noted that: "It has been traditionally assumed that the development of successful athletic teams is based on a strict adherence to discipline, organization, and conformance on behalf of players." They tested and found support for the related hypothesis " . . . that the more successful coaches were more authoritarian than the less successful coaches" (Penman et al., 1974).

Sage (1972a), however, on the basis of scores on the Mach scale, found no significant differences in Machiavellianism between coaches with won-loss records over 60 percent and those with won-loss records under 60 percent. His samples consisted of college football coaches and high school basketball and football coaches. Moreover, he found that college basketball coaches with won-loss records over 60 percent had significantly lower Machiavellian scores than those with won-loss records under 60 percent. Similarly, Walsh and Carron (1977), in their study of three groups of Canadian coaches, discovered no significant differences between degree of Machiavellianism and won-loss records.

Cooper and Payne (1972) examined the relationship between personality and performance by administering the Bass Orientation Inventory (see Bass, 1960, 1962) to the staff and players of 17 soccer teams in the senior division of the English Football League. This inventory provides scores on three general types of personality characteristics: self-orientation, interaction orientation, and task orientation. Cooper and Payne obtained a significant correlation ($r = .72$) between the task orientations of coaches and trainers and team success, but found no significant correlations between the task orientations of managers and captains and team success. With respect to managers they suggest that, since managers are concerned mainly with administration and have little contact with the players, task orientations are not as relevant for them as for coaches and trainers. With respect to team captains they suggest that since " . . . captains are not appreciably more task oriented than players, their task behavior is presumably not sufficiently different to have much influence on the players' performances" (Cooper and Payne, 1972).

In concluding this discussion of the relationship between personality and performance, we must recognize that team success is not the only performance measure that should be examined. For example, the extent to which a coach is willing to experiment with innovations in equipment, skill techniques, and training methods is also a reflection of the influence of leadership. Thus, one might ask what personality factors characterize innovative coaches. One study that addresses this question is Loy's (1968) analysis of the psychosociological characteristics of early and late adopters of the "controlled internal training method" (CIM) among a sample of English swimming coaches. On the basis of data obtained through a background questionnaire and the 16PF questionnaire, he found a significant multiple correlation of 0.80 between the time of adoption of the new training technique and ten social-psychological attributes of swimming coaches. The ten factors and their partial correlation with time of adoption of the technique were professional status (0.54), cosmopoliteness (0.48), venturesomeness (0.44), sociability (−0.43), occupational status (0.41), dominance (−0.39), sensitivity (−0.33), imaginativeness (0.33), shrewdness (−0.33), and experimentiveness (0.33). Loy's findings directly indicate that sociological factors, in addition to psychological factors, should be considered in leadership studies, and indirectly suggest that leadership behaviors should be considered in addition to leadership traits.

3.2.3   Leadership Behaviors

Dimensions of Leadership Behavior

As Shaw (1971) has stated: "Since characteristics of individuals presumably reflect behavioral tendencies, it has seemed to many students of leadership that investigations should deal with behavior directly." As a result, many studies have been directed toward determining dimensions of leadership behavior (see Gibb, 1969). One of the more notable investigations is Halpin and Winer's (1952) factor-analytic study of leader behavior among aircrew commanders. Their analysis suggests that there are four dimensions of leadership behavior, two of which are of primary importance. These four dimensions and the percentage of the total variance accounted by each are summarized below in order of importance (Gibb, 1969):

1. *Consideration* (49.6%): This dimension is probably best defined as the extent to which the leader, while carrying out his leader functions, is considerate of the men who are his followers.

2. *Initiating structure* (33.6%): This dimension represents the extent to which the leader organizes and defines the relation between himself and his subordinates or fellow group members.

3. *Production emphasis* (9.8%): This represents a cluster of behaviors by which the leader stresses getting the job done.

4. *Sensitivity (social awareness)* (7.0%): The leader characterized by this factor stresses being a socially acceptable individual in his interactions with other group members.

It is significant that these four dimensions of leadership behavior parallel the three kinds of personality orientations measured by the Bass Orientation Inventory: self-orientation, interaction orientation, and task orientation. Moreover, they are similar to the three dimensions of individual behavior observable in small groups, which were identified by Carter as follows:

Factor I: Individual Prominence. The dimension of behavior which is interpreted as indicating the prominence of that individual as he stands out from the group. The behavior associated with the traits of aggressiveness, leadership, confidence, and striving for individual recognition seems to have a common element which is interpreted as the member's attempting to achieve individual recognition from the group.

Factor II: Group Goal Facilitation. The dimension of behavior which is interpreted as being effective in achieving the goal toward which the group is oriented. Efficiency, adaptability, cooperation, etc., all seem to have a common element which facilitates group action in solving the group's task.

Factor III: Group Sociability. The dimension of behavior which is interpreted as indicating the positive social interaction of an individual in the group. The traits heavily loaded in this factor—sociability, striving for group acceptance and adaptability—all have a common element which represents a friendly interpersonal behavior pattern of the individual toward the other group members. (Carter, 1954, pp. 479–481)

The dimensions of leader and group behavior just outlined suggest that the differences between leaders and followers are one of degree and not kind. That is, leaders display the same behaviors as other group members but their patterns of behavior are typically more frequent and dominant. Moreover, the preceding account of the dimensions of leadership behavior " . . . suggests that if a leader is to successfully exert influence and move a group toward its goals, he must motivate the members and maintain harmony and satisfaction, while at the same time directing and coordinating the efforts of the group" (Krech et al., 1962).

Types of Leaders

Instrumental vs. expressive leadership types.   In many groups a leader fulfills both of these functions. But if an official leader is incapable of fulfilling both functions, then an unofficial or informal leader may assume responsibility for ensuring that the neglected function is fulfilled. Moreover, in some complex task groups two or more official leaders will be respectively assigned responsibilities related to one of the two functions. For example, it is currently common practice within intercollegiate basketball teams in the United States for the head coach to be responsible for directing and coordinating the tasks efforts of the team, and for the assistant coach to be responsible for maintaining harmony and morale among team members.

Finally, " . . . where there is no official leader, the two functions are often assumed by two *different* emergent leaders . . .": an expert leader or "task specialist" and a socioemotional leader or "maintenance specialist" (Krech et al., 1962). A primary reason for the emergence of the two types is that there are conflicting expectations associated with a leader in his or her leadership role. For example, it is difficult for leaders to be friendly with their followers (that is, to be "one of the gang") and simultaneously make impersonal and difficult decisions that may often be contrary to the wants and wishes of the majority of group members.

In summary, group leadership involves both internal and external problems and must deal with both the instrumental and expressive aspects of group activity. Because these matters are complex and demanding, "the differentiation of the leadership role into task and maintenance specialists appears to be a primitive and widespread phenomenon" (Krech et al., 1962).

Although a number of studies provide evidence of the phenomenon of dual leadership in small groups (see, for example, Bales, 1953; Burke, 1967, 1968; Etzioni, 1965; Mann, 1961; Slater, 1955; Verba, 1961; Zelditch, 1955), the study of the phenomenon of dual leadership in sport groups is largely nonexistent. However, it is hypothesized that on both the coaching and player levels there is differentiation of the leadership role. On the one hand, certain individuals act as task specialists and deal with the instrumental problem of group effectiveness (i.e., achievement of group goals). On the other hand, certain individuals act as maintenance specialists and deal with the expressive problem of group efficiency (i.e., satisfaction of group members). Figure 3.3 presents a functional framework or paradigm that may prove useful for the consideration of leadership role differentiation in sport groups.

Authoritarian vs. democratic leadership types.   A major typology of leadership types is based on the distinction between authoritarian and democratic styles of leadership. This typology is largely based on the pioneering investigations of small-group behavior by Lewin and his associates nearly 40 years ago (Lewin, Lippett, and White, 1939; Lippett and White, 1943). The behavioral styles of the authoritarian and democratic types of leaders have been well characterized by Krech et al. as follows:

> The authoritarian leader wields more absolute power than the democratic leader; he alone determines policies of the group . . . he alone serves as the ultimate agent and judge and as the purveyor of rewards and punishments. Hence, the fate of each individual within the group is in his hands.

> The democratic leader does not necessarily differ from the authoritarian leader in amount of power but he does differ in the way he seeks to evoke the maximum involvement and participation of every member in the group activities and in the determination of group objectives. He seeks to spread responsibility . . . encourage and reinforce interpersonal relations . . . to reduce intragroup tension and conflict . . . (and) . . . to prevent the development of a hierarchical group structure in which special privilege and status differentials predominate.*

Numerous accounts have strongly stated that the leadership styles of coaches are basically authoritarian and autocratic in nature, if not outright dictatorial (Meggyesy, 1971; Ogilvie and Tutko, 1971; Scott, 1971; Tutko and Richards, 1971). However, within a more analytical framework, Sage (1973) has pointed out that the general leadership style of coaches is very similar to that represented by the scientific management perspective, which evolved from the work of Frederick W. Taylor. Specifically, Sage states that:

---

*From *Individual in Society* by D. Krech et al. Copyright 1962 by McGraw-Hill Book Company. Used with permission of McGraw-Hill.

	External dimension	Internal dimension	
Instrumental dimension	*Adaptation*: Problem of ensuring group survival and adapting to external social system (e.g., winning games in order to ensure monetary support and membership in a given league or conference). *Leader role*: Coach as "task specialist" with emphasis on coach as technical expert, policymaker, and executive leader.	*Goal attainment*: Problem of relating team members to each other in order to carry out group decisions and in order to reach group goals. *Leader role*: Team captain or member as "instrumental leader" with emphasis on calling plays and coordinating task activities.	Concern with members as means and group effectiveness
Expressive dimension	*Pattern maintenance*: Problem of ensuring continuity of beliefs and standards and obtaining consensus about collective values, norms, and sanctions. *Leader role*: Coach as "maintenance specialist" with emphasis on coach as teacher, morale leader, father-figure, and group symbol.	*Integration*: Problem of relating team members to each other in order to achieve group harmony and member satisfaction. *Leader role*: Team captain or member as "expressive leader" with emphasis on maintaining group morale and "team spirit."	Concern with members as ends and group efficiency
	Concern with cultural problems	Concern with social structure problems	

Fig. 3.3 *A paradigm of leadership role differentiation in sport groups. (Adapted from Loy, 1969, p. 69, and Olmsted, 1959, p. 139)*

. . . many coaches have tended to view team members as objects in a machine-like environment where emphasis is on instrumental rather than consummatory behaviors . . . Accordingly, coaches have structured coach-player relations along authoritarian lines; they have analyzed and structured sports team positions for precise specialization of the performers, and they have endeavored to control player behavior not only throughout practice and contest periods but also on a round-the-clock basis . . . an observer at many athletic team practice sessions might believe that he was viewing a factory assembly-line work shift. (Sage, 1973, pp. 36–37)

Notwithstanding the several polemic perspectives about the autocratic leadership of coaches, only a few empirical investigations have examined the leadership behaviors of coaches.

Leadership Behavior of Coaches

In order to assess the relationship between type of coaching leadership (i.e., laissez-faire, democratic-cooperative, autocratic-submissive, autocratic-aggressive) and success, Swartz (1973) compared 72 college coaches classified as successful (won-loss record over 50 percent) or unsuccessful (won-loss record under 50 percent). He did not find any differences between the leadership behavior patterns of successful and unsuccessful coaches.

In the only other reported comparison of "authoritarian" and "democratic" styles of coaching, Lenk (1977) points out that rowing crews coached in both styles have won international championships and thus neither style has been proven to be the more effective one. He further notes that each style of coaching possesses particular advantages and disadvantages. More specifically, Lenk states that:

Whereas the "authoritarian" style seems to be simpler and easy to procure and to have a larger range of applicability, the "democratic" method certainly involves or engenders a greater degree of internal identification and commitment on the side of intellectual athletes . . . Because of this higher-grade identification it is hypothesized that, under a "democratic" style of coaching athletes, teams, and crews may be able to mobilize psychic reserves not accessible otherwise, in particular not "on command." (Lenk, 1977a, p. 88)

An interesting case study of leadership behavior in a sport situation is Tharp and Gallimore's (1976) observation of John Wooden's behavioral acts during practices in his last season as head basketball coach at UCLA. They recorded 2326 acts of teaching by Wooden, which they classified in terms of ten categories of leadership behavior. They found that 50.3 percent of Wooden's behavioral acts during practice sessions constituted instructions (that is, "verbal statements about what to do or how to do it"). In short, the case study of Tharp and Gallimore suggests that while coaches may be the "take-charge" type of individual, they are far from autocratic in nature, and in fact invest most of their time in communicating information.

This latter observation is empirically supported by the analysis by Danielson et al. (1975) of coaching behavior as perceived by high school hockey players. On the basis of multidimensional scaling and factor analysis of 57 frequently reported coaching behaviors, they concluded that "commonly perceived behaviors in hockey coaching are mainly of a communicative nature with surprisingly little emphasis on domination" (Danielson et al., 1975).

Finally, mention is made of Mudra's (1965) study of the leadership behaviors of intercollegiate football coaches. He found that coaches at small colleges tend to endorse a gestalt-field approach to coaching, which stresses insight and problem-solving behavior, whereas major-college coaches tend to utilize stimulus-response principles of learning, which emphasize acquisition of habits and involve greater authority and control. Mudra speculated that the difference in leadership behavior of college coaches is closely associated with contrasting philosophies regarding the role and objectives of athletic programs at small and large institutions. In sum, Mudra's findings and interpretation suggest that leadership behaviors are likely to be situation-specific.

3.2.4 Leadership Interactions: Styles and Situations

In the conclusion of his extensive review of research on leadership, Gibb stated that:

> Leadership is an interactional phenomenon, and an interaction theory is required to provide a framework for studies of leadership . . . In general, it may be said that leadership is a function of personality and of the social situation, and of these two in interaction. (Gibb, 1969, p. 273)

The Contingency Model of Leadership Effectiveness

To date, the most explicit theoretical interpretation of the reciprocal effects of personality and situational variables is the contingency model of leadership developed by Fiedler (1967, 1971a, 1971b). His model is outlined below in terms of types of task groups, leadership styles, leadership situations, and the interactions between leadership styles and situations.

Types of task groups.   Fiedler (1967) identified three types of task groups: interacting, coacting, and counteracting. *Interacting* task groups " . . . require the close coordination of several team members in the performance of the primary task." Examples of interacting task groups are baseball, basketball, and football teams. In *coacting* task groups " . . . each of the group members does his job relatively independently of other team members." Examples of coacting task groups are bowling, gymnastic, and rifle teams. Finally, *counteracting* task groups " . . . consist of individuals who are working together for the purpose of negotiating and reconciling conflicting opinions and purposes" (Fiedler, 1967). An example of a counteracting task group would be a group of player representatives and management in a professional sport attempting to negotiate a new pension plan.

Leadership styles. For Fiedler (1971a), leadership style signifies ". . . a motivational system expressed in various goal-seeking behaviors that the individual perceives as rewarding or necessary for his emotional well-being." Fiedler and his co-workers have identified two general motivational patterns of group leaders, namely, "task motivated" and "relationship motivated." Both task-oriented and relationship-oriented leaders are empirically identified by the calculation of a least preferred co-worker (LPC) score. This score is obtained by means of a simple eight-point bipolar[2] scale " . . . that asks the individual (a) to think of everyone with whom he has ever worked and (b) to describe the one person with whom he could work *least well*" (Fiedler, 1971a). A *high* LPC score indicates that an individual perceives his or her least preferred co-worker in a relatively *favorable* manner, while a *low* LPC score denotes that an individual perceives his or her least preferred co-worker in very *unfavorable* terms.

Fiedler summarized the general behavioral characteristics of high and low LPC leaders as follows:

> . . . high LPC leaders are concerned with having good interpersonal relations and with gaining prominence and self-esteem through these interpersonal relations. Low LPC leaders are concerned with achieving success on assigned tasks, even at the risk of having poor interpersonal relations with fellow workers. The behaviors of high and low LPC leaders will thus be quite different if the situation is such that the satisfaction of their respective needs is threatened. Under these conditions the high LPC leader will increase his interpersonal interaction in order to cement his relations with other group members while the low LPC leader will interact in order to complete the task successfully.*

It must be noted, however, that LPC scores cannot always be simply interpreted in the above manner. As Fiedler (1971b) takes care to point out, ". . . only in situations which are unfavorable (that is, stressful, anxiety arousing, giving the leader little control) do we find leader behaviors which correspond to these terms."

Leadership situations. Fiedler suggests that leadership situations can be usefully categorized according to three dimensions, which he labels "leader position power," "task structure," and "leader-member relations." Further, these dimensions can be readily conceptualized in dichotomous terms. Thus, a leader can be seen as having a strong or a weak position of power, the task activities of a group may be highly structured or relatively unstructured, and leader-member relations may be viewed as good or poor. Fiedler's classification of group task situations based on these three dimensions is shown in Table 3.1. This table indicates the favorableness of a given situation for a leader in the left-hand column, with category I representing the most favorable and category VIII representing the least favorable set of conditions.

---

*From *A Theory of Leadership Effectiveness* by F. E. Fiedler. Copyright 1967 by McGraw-Hill Book Company. Used with permission of McGraw-Hill.

Table 3.1

Classification of group task situations on the basis of three factors

	Leader-member relations	Type of task structure	Leader position power
I	Good	High	Strong
II	Good	High	Weak
III	Good	Weak	Strong
IV	Good	Weak	Weak
V	Moderately poor	High	Strong
VI	Moderately poor	High	Strong
VII	Moderately poor	Weak	Strong
VIII	Moderately poor	Weak	Weak
VIII-A	Very poor	High	Strong

From *A Theory of Leadership Effectiveness* by F.E. Fiedler. Copyright 1967 by McGraw-Hill Book Company. Used with permission of McGraw-Hill.

Interactions of leadership styles and situations. The key theoretical question addressed by Fiedler's contingency model is "What kind of leadership is required for what kind of situation?" (Fiedler, 1971a). The major prediction of Fiedler's theory of leadership effectiveness, which he develops in his contingency model, is that ". . . a task-oriented style will be maximally effective in favorable leadership situations, a relationship-oriented style will be effective in intermediate situations, and a task-oriented style will again be most effective in unfavorable group situations" (Fiedler, 1967).

Although Fiedler's contingency model and theory of leadership have been criticized on methodological, statistical, and theoretical grounds (Ashour, 1973; Butterfield, 1968; Graen et al., 1970; Korman, 1971; Shiflett, 1973), they have been strongly supported in whole or part by numerous empirical investigations (Fiedler, 1967, 1971b, 1973; Graham, 1973; Larson and Rowland, 1973). In view of such strong empirical support and self-evident theoretical implications for the study of leadership in sport groups, it is somewhat surprising that Fiedler's model and theory have received only limited application in the analysis of sport groups.

Leadership Effectiveness in Sport Groups

The findings of four studies of interacting sport groups and three studies of co-acting sport groups, based in part on Fiedler's contingency model of leadership effectiveness, are reviewed below.

Interacting sport groups. Some 20 years ago, when setting forth the initial formulations of his model, Fiedler (1954) made two exploratory investigations of leadership and team effectiveness using high school basketball teams. Interestingly, the findings of these two studies were directly opposite to the predicted results. First, Fiedler hypothesized that the assumed similarity scores of the teams' "most preferred co-worker" would be positively related to team success. Instead, he found that ". . . the teams in which squad members chose their friends as co-workers performed more poorly than did those in which the team members' best friend and best co-worker were not necessarily the same person" (Fiedler, 1967). Second, Fiedler hypothesized that teams ". . . in which the leaders perceived the most and their least preferred co-workers in an accepting, positive manner would be the most effective" (Fiedler, 1967). Once again, however, results ran counter to the prediction, thus indicating that effective basketball teams are primarily concerned with performance and task objectives, whereas ineffective teams are overly concerned with interpersonal relations and member satisfaction.

In sum, the studies of basketball teams led to the formulation of another hypothesis: "Members of effective teams will prefer co-workers who assume relatively little similarity between the persons whom they choose and those whom they reject as their own co-workers" (Fiedler, 1954). Fiedler (1954) obtained support for this hypothesis in a study of surveying teams. These early studies by Fiedler resulted in less stress being placed in future research on assumed similarity measures and measures of most preferred co-worker, and more emphasis being given to least preferred co-worker (LPC) scores as predictors of leadership and team effectiveness.

Vander Velden (1971) used LPC scores as a measure of task attitude in a study to account for the success of high school basketball teams. One explicit hypothesis concerning leadership style tested in his investigation was the proposition that: "Group effectiveness is a function of the leader's task relevant attitude; more specifically, (a) the more positive the formal leader's task attitude, the more effective the group, and (b) the more positive the informal leader's task attitude, the more effective the group" (Vander Velden, 1971). A positive task relevant attitude was operationally defined as a *low* LPC score, the coach was defined as the formal group leader, and the informal leader was a team member sociometrically selected by his teammates. Finally, two separate but related operational measures of team effectiveness were obtained: (a) team winning percentage in conference play, and (b) the difference between the number of points scored and allowed during conference competition (Vander Velden, 1971).

Vander Velden found no empirical support for the stated hypotheses. However, when controlling for selected situational factors he did discover significant relationships between the task attitude of leaders and team success. First, with respect to the three dimensions of group situations described by Fiedler, Vander Velden assumed that task structure remained constant for all teams and that formal leaders had relatively equal position power, and thus only leader-member relations might vary significantly among teams. When controlling for the tone of leader-member relations, Vander Velden (1971) found that ". . . while the task attitudes of coaches were not related to team performance in either friendly or less friendly groupings, the informal leader's task attitude was significantly related to winning percentage in the more congenial groups."

Second, when holding task ability constant Vander Velden discovered that task attitudes of leaders were significantly related to team performance. Specifically, results revealed that within high ability groups a combination of a task-oriented coach and a relationship-oriented team leader contributed to success, whereas within low ability groups a combination of a relationship-oriented coach and a task-oriented team leader was most effective (Vander Velden, 1971).

Third, in an effort to replicate Fiedler's model Vander Velden determined the degree of situational favorableness by combining team task ability, group satisfaction, and leadership experience in a single measure. He reports that:

> The classification of teams into three categories similar to Fiedler's model showed task oriented informal leaders to be most effective under unfavorable conditions with formal leaders performing maintenance functions in the group. In favorable situations, the roles were reversed. Groups intermediate on the favorableness continuum performed best when both leaders were less directive. (Vander Velden, 1971, p. 137)

Finally, in discussing the limitations of his investigation, Vander Velden (1971) points out that: "according to Fiedler's definition of high and low LPC persons, there were few coaches or team members with low LPC scores, i.e., few task oriented leaders."

In yet another investigation of interacting sport groups in which LPC scores were used to measure leadership styles, Bird (1977) studied the relationships among leadership, cohesion, skill, and success of women's intercollegiate volleyball teams in two different divisions. She found in the case of the more highly skilled and competitive division (Division I) that players on winning teams perceived their coaches to be relationship-oriented, whereas players on losing teams perceived their coaches to be task-oriented. But in the case of the less skilled and competitive division (Division II) the results were reversed: Members of successful teams perceived their coaches as task-oriented, whereas members of unsuccessful teams perceived their coaches as relationship oriented. Bird suggests that:

> Some explanation for these results might be within structural changes which may occur owing to the skill level of players. Perhaps on less highly skilled teams, effective coaching strategy demands greater use of designated positions such as hitters or setters, whereas on more highly skilled teams, such as Division I, positions are more flexible because of the type of playing strategy employed. If this is so, then the prediction which was generated from Fiedler's contingency model for highly structured groups would indeed be applicable to less highly skilled teams such as those in Division II. An alternative explanation may be that players on more highly skilled teams may be sufficiently motivated and, therefore, respond more to a supportive, socio-emotional coach. In either case, the results strongly suggest that effective leadership or coaching style is somewhat related to situational factors such as player skill. (Bird, 1977, p. 31)

Coacting sport groups.   Fiedler (1967) states that: "Whether the Contingency Model can be generalized to all coacting task groups is questionable. Where the position power of the leader is very weak his influence over individual members of the group and hence over their work performance is likely to be minimal." In support of these observations Fiedler refers to De Zonia's (1958) study of recreational bowling teams in which little relationship was found between leadership style and team performance.

However, there are some coacting sport groups in which the leader's power position is a fairly strong one, as, for example, on gymnastic teams. In an investigation of the leadership process among 30 high school gymnastic teams, Kjeldsen (1976) examined Fiedler's theory from several points of view and found general support for the contingency model. For example, he found that coaches of successful teams were more task-oriented, while coaches of less successful teams were highly relationship-oriented.

More specifically, with respect to the degree of favorableness of the situation, Kjeldsen's findings indicated that task-oriented coaches tended to be associated with successful teams in situations of low favorability, while relationship-oriented coaches tended to be associated with successful teams in situations of moderate favorability. Kjeldsen reports a number of other findings concerning relationships between LPC scores, leadership behavior, and team performance, which are beyond review here. However, it must be noted that his work represents the most comprehensive study of leadership in sport groups to date.

In summary, although studies of leadership in sport groups are few in number, and while reported findings are often inconsistent, research to date supports Gibb's observation that leadership is an interactional phenomenon and highlights the importance of studying situational variables as well as personal variables. Combined consideration is given to these two sets of factors in the following section on group composition.

3.3 GROUP COMPOSITION AND STRUCTURE

3.3.1 Introduction

As McGrath (1964) has defined the concepts: "Group *composition* refers to the properties represented by the aggregate of persons who are members of a given group at a given time," whereas "group *structure* refers to the relatively stable patterns of relationships that exist among members of groups." In brief, the concept of group composition is usually used in reference to individualistic characteristics of group members, while the concept of group structure usually refers to the relationships among group members.

Structure of the Group

Group structure is a form of social structure. Although not entirely consistent among themselves, social scientists use the term *social* structure in reference to macrosocial systems such as social classes, institutions, and societies, the term *formal* structure in reference to the social structure of complex organizations, and the term *group* structure in reference to the social structure of small groups. In effect, group structure is a special form of social structure that is based on the patterned interaction among the occupants of a specific set of social positions having particular ranks, roles, and statuses (see Section 2.1.1).

Moreover, just as social structure in general is comprised of specific substructures, group structure in particular can be differentiated in terms of four underlying substructures (see McGrath, 1964), which include:

1. A *task* structure based on the pattern of task activities among group members.
2. A *power* structure based on the patterns of authority and influence among group members.
3. A *communication* structure based on the pattern of communication among group members.
4. A *friendship* structure based on the patterns of affective and emotional relations among group members.

Composition of the Group

Properties of group composition include abilities, aptitudes, personality characteristics, physical or constitutional factors, and social identities. These properties or elements of group composition can be examined from three perspectives. First, the modal value of a property in terms of group frequency or average level may be considered. For example, the achievement motivation (n Ach) of each group member can be assessed and a group mean of n Ach can be determined.

Second, the variation or distribution of a particular property or set of properties among group members may be considered. This perspective focuses on the similarity or homogeneity–heterogeneity of group membership. Moreover, a given analysis of group composition can consider either *trait* or *profile* homogeneity. Shaw (1971) defines trait homogeneity as "the degree to which the members of a group are similar with respect to a single individual characteristic," whereas profile homogeneity refers to "the degree to which the members of a group are similar on a variety of individual characteristics, considered collectively."

Third, the compatibility among group members may be considered. Various kinds of compatibility can be analyzed but two general categories of compatibility are *need* compatibility and *response* compatibility. The former category refers to the extent to which the needs of group members are mutually satisfying, whereas the latter category refers to the extent to which the behaviors of group members are mutually agreeable (see Shaw, 1971, pp. 396, 398).

The three perspectives of group composition just described are treated in turn below. In general, the concept of group composition is given primary attention in this chapter, while the concept of group structure receives major consideration in the following chapter. However, as indicated by the definitions above and illustrated by the descriptions below, it is difficult to talk about any one of the concepts without speaking about the other.

3.3.2 Modal Characteristics of Group Membership

Groups were previously defined as systems organized around interacting sets of personalities. Accordingly, the personal characteristics that individuals bring into a group situation greatly influence both individual and group behavior (Davis, 1969; Haythorn, 1968; Heslin, 1964; Shaw, 1971). More specifically, ". . . the personal characteristics of each group member serve as stimuli for all other members, and those of other members serve as stimuli for each individual member" (Shaw, 1971).

Since personal characteristics of group members are infinite in number, they are arbitrarily classified into three categories: physical characteristics, social characteristics, and personality characteristics.

Physical Characteristics of Group Members

It is obvious that personal physical characteristics play a major role in sport situations since sport competition is based on physical performance. While it is beyond the scope of a text on the sociology of sport to present a detailed analysis of the biological basis of sport (see Asmussen, 1965), it is relevant to emphasize that any complete explanation of sport group performance must take into account quantitative and qualitative biological differences due to age, race, sex, size, and a variety of anatomical and physiological parameters.[3] Moreover, such biological differences have social implications, as evidenced by current concerns about the effects of athletic competition on children (see Albinson and Andrew, 1976; Magill, 1978), racial variations in sport, and coeducational sport participation.

Perhaps the clearest example of modal physical characteristics in sport groups is the predominant physiques or body types found within specific sports (see, for example, Carter, 1970; Cureton, 1941, 1951; De Garay, 1974; Tanner, 1964). This research shows that athletes, both male and female, tend to be of marked mesomorphic build in comparison to nonathletes. However, the degree of mesomorphy varies greatly among members of different sport groups (see Table 3.2). In general, a high degree of mesomorphy is characteristic of the somatotypes of male championship athletes and athletes in contact sports; it is also the major component of the somatotypes of combat pilots (Damon, 1955) and juvenile delinquents (Sheldon, 1949; Glueck and Glueck, 1956; Cortes, 1961), two groups that have often been compared with athletes.

The significance of body build for the analysis of the composition of sport groups is that it has been shown to be related to athletic performance, to a variety of behavioral and temperament patterns (see Cortes, 1961; Cortes and Gatti, 1965; Domey et al., 1964; Parnell, 1958; Sheldon, 1942; Walker, 1962, 1963), and to social image (Kiker and Miller, 1967; Miller et al., 1968; Miller and Stewart, 1968; Staffieri, 1967; Sugerman and Haronian, 1964; Wells and Siegel, 1961). For example, notwithstanding the limitations of constitutional psychology, especially the much maligned work of William H. Sheldon, the relationship between components of physique and temperament may predispose certain individuals to seek stimulation to a greater degree than others.

In his early work, Sheldon (1942) found a very high correlation ($r = .82$) between his scale of somatotonia and his measure of mesomorphy. The traits underlying his scale of somatotonia clearly indicate a personality type predisposed to a high need for stimulation as, for example, (1) love of physical adventure,

Table 3.2
Mean mesomorphy values for 1968 male olympic athletes

Selected sport sample	n	Mesomorphy
1. Weightlifters (all classes)	59	7.1
2. Weightthrowers (discus, shotput, hammer)	14	7.1
3. Wrestlers, Greco-Roman (all classes)	40	6.4
4. Wrestlers, free-style (all classes)	49	6.3
5. Gymnasts	28	5.9
6. Decathlonists	8	5.6
7. Javelin throwers	8	5.6
8. Canoeists (all events)	49	5.5
9. Divers	16	5.4
10. Boxers (all classes)	142	5.3
11. Rowers (all events)	85	5.3
12. Water polo players	71	5.3
13. Modern pentathlonists	24	5.3
14. Cyclists (all events)	100	5.0
15. Swimmers (all events)	65	5.0
16. Sprinters (100 m, 200 m, 4×100 m, 220 m hurdles)	78	5.0
17. Pole vaulters	8	4.8
18. Walkers (20 km, 50 km)	21	4.7
19. Reference group	265	4.6
20. 400m Runners (400 m, 4×400 m, 400 m hurdles)	49	4.5
21. Jumpers (high, long, and triple jumps)	31	4.4
22. Marathon runners	20	4.3
23. Basketball players	63	4.3
24. Middle-distance runners (800 m, 1500 m)	41	4.2
25. Long-distance runners (3000 m, 5000 m, 10,000 m, steeple chase)	34	4.1

From De Garay et al. (1974).

(2) need and enjoyment of exercise, (3) love of risk and chance, (4) physical courage for combat, (5) competitive aggressiveness, (6) Spartan indifference to pain, (7) general noisiness, (8) need of action when troubled, (9) freedom from squeamishness, and (10) orientation toward goals and activities of youth (Sheldon, 1942).

Social Characteristics of Group Members

Members of sport groups are also characterized by a variety of social identities, including age, race, sex, and social status. These social characteristics, in relation to sport involvement, are treated at length elsewhere in the text (see Chapters 6, 9, and 10). Therefore, the focus here is on the frequency of individuals of given birth order found in different sports.

Birth order has been shown to be related to a large number of psychological and sociological factors (see, for example, Adams, 1972; Althus, 1966; Kammeyer, 1967; Sampson, 1965; Sutton-Smith and Rosenberg, 1970; Warren,

1966). For example, research findings indicate that first-borns are more fearful, display greater avoidance behavior toward dangerous situations, and tolerate less pain than later-borns. Thus, with respect to group composition, later-borns when compared with first-borns are more likely to be found in physically demanding and sensory-stimulating activities as shown by the studies cited below.

Birth order, like mesomorphic body build, seems to be related to delinquency (Sletto, 1932) and combat pilot effectiveness (Torrance, 1954). Studies of other high-stress situations also show that later-borns are overrepresented as group members. For example, Lester (1969), in his study of stress among 17 members of a 1963 expedition to Mount Everest, found that the majority of climbers were later-born children. Similarly, in their account of stress studies associated with the Sealab II project, Radloff and Helmreich report that:

> . . . first born and only children did not perform as well under stress as did later-borns. More than half of the divers were first-born or only children, and these men spent significantly less time in the water than divers who were later-borns. They also reported themselves more frightened than later-borns. . . . (Radloff and Helmreich, 1969, p. 59)*

Experimental results closely match the field findings given above. For example, it has been shown that first-borns display greater avoidance of dangerous situations (Longstreth, 1970); that first-born females score higher on extreme fear (Mealiea and Farley, 1971); that they express more fear when faced with the prospect of physical harm (Helmreich and Collins, 1967); that they are more fearful and sensitive to pain in dental situations (Defee and Himelstein, 1969); and that they have a lower degree of tolerance to electrical shock than later-borns (Schachter, 1959).

The reported relationships between birth order and sport participation are largely consistent with the field and experimental findings just reviewed. For example, three studies of general patterns of sport participation and sport preferences show that second-born individuals are overrepresented. Landers (1972) examined the effects of ordinal position and the sex of siblings on males' sport participation among 394 junior high school athletes and nonathletes and 115 high school varsity baseball players. He found that second-born males with an older sister were over-represented among high school baseball players and competed in more varsity and junior varsity sports than individuals who fall elsewhere in the birth order. De Garay et al. (1974), in their study of 1200 athletes who competed in the 1968 Olympic Games, found that second-born individuals were markedly overrepresented in their sample of athletes. Finally, in a survey of sibling interest preference, Sutton-Smith and Rosenberg (1970) administered a recreational inventory to 83 male and 90 female college students. They discovered that second-born males with an older brother had the highest mean scores for games of physical skill and strategy, including the high-risk sports of boxing, football, hockey, and wrestling.

---

*Reprinted by permission of *Psychology Today Magazine.* Copyright © 1969 Ziff-Davis Publishing Company.

Three other investigations report more direct relationships between birth order and participation in dangerous sports. Nisbett (1968) examined the ordinal position of high school, college, and professional athletes competing in what he considered three high-risk or dangerous sports: football, rugby, and soccer. He found that first-borns are less likely to participate in these sports than later-borns and that the probability of an individual participating in these sports increases with family size.

Yiannakis (1976) analyzed the relationship between birth order and degree of sport preference for a sample of 166 male university students. Sport preferences were assessed for three types of sports representing varying degrees (low, intermediate, high) of severity of injury: (1) individual contact sports: boxing, judo, and wrestling; (2) team contact sports: football, ice hockey, lacrosse, rugby, and soccer; and (3) individual noncontact (dangerous) sports: flying, gymnastics, motorcycle racing, rock climbing, scuba diving, ski jumping, and sky diving. On the basis of discriminant function analysis, Yiannakis (1976) concluded that: "First borns are more likely to avoid sports in which the severity of physical injury is perceived to be high and the opportunity to affiliate, under stress, tends to be low."

More recently, Casher (1977) studied the relationship between birth order and participation in dangerous sports for a sample of 127 varsity athletes attending Ivy League universities. Considering only individual high-harm sports (diving, hurdling, skiing, tumbling, and wrestling) and low-harm sports (golf, swimming, tennis, and throwing), Casher found that ". . . the proportion of athletes in dangerous sports increased as birth order increased from first born (41%) to second born (45%) to third born (76%)."

In summary, research suggests that birth order is an important variable to consider when analyzing the composition of sport groups. Specifically, findings suggest that later-born individuals possess a greater need for stimulation than first-born individuals, and thus tend to be overrepresented in high-risk sport groups.

Personality Characteristics of Group Members

Many, if not most, individuals subscribe to the notion that personality and sport participation are highly interrelated. Either explicitly or implicitly assumed are a number of beliefs, including the following:

1. Certain personality characteristics motivate or predispose selected individuals to participate in sport; thus athletes are held to possess particular personal attributes that clearly distinguish them from nonathletes.

2. Specific personality factors are a prerequisite for sport success; thus championship athletes possess particular psychological attributes that distinguish them from less successful athletes.

3. The specific personality traits prerequisite for sport success vary from sport to sport; thus athletes competing in different sports have different psychological profiles.

Several extensive reviews of the research literature concerning personality and athletics (see, for example, Cofer and Johnson, 1960; Husman, 1969; Kane, 1964; Layman, 1960; Ruffer, 1975–1976) indicate that evidence at best is inconclusive concerning the validity of the preceding beliefs. Moreover, research investigations conducted since many of these reviews were made also fail to substantiate the beliefs stated above (see Kroll, 1967; Kroll and Carlson, 1967; Kroll et al., 1973; Rushall, 1970, 1972; Sage, 1972a).[4] Kroll has aptly summarized the state of the art:

> Any honest appraisal of the work in athletic personality must conclude that the picture is unsettled. Only clinical interpretations have been able to come up with anything approaching a definite conclusion while studies with objective measurements of personality continue to offer conflicting results. (Kroll, 1970, p. 362)

Perhaps the only exceptions to Kroll's observations are the relatively recent studies of the relationship between need for stimulation (n Stim) and sport participation. It is evident that some individuals clearly enjoy engaging in sports involving intense sensory stimulation through physical contact, interpersonal competition, pain, risk-taking, increased social interaction, high speeds, etc., whereas other individuals prefer to participate in less stimulating sports, or prefer to participate only vicariously by means of direct or indirect forms of spectatorship. Still others are "asportual," preferring total noninvolvement with sport situations.

A great deal of empirical evidence has been generated which bears upon n Stim, many methods have been developed to measure n Stim, and several theoretical explanations for individual differences in n Stim have been set forth (Donnelly, 1976; Loy and Donnelly, 1976). The most noted work on the topic has been completed by Sales and co-workers (Sales, 1971, 1972; Sales and Throop, 1972; Sales et al., 1974), who proposed a theory to explain individual differences in n Stim, which is founded on three assumptions:

1. Exposure to a stimulus does not affect all individuals the same way. Some subjects' nervous systems "damp down" (reduce) objective stimulus inputs, while other subjects' nervous systems "augment" these inputs.

2. Individuals have an "optimum" level of internal, received stimulation. If current stimulation evokes an internal response which is either "too small" or "too large," subjects attempt to change their input and react negatively to the current input. If current stimulation evokes an internal response which is "just right," subjects attempt to maintain this input and react positively to it.

3. The optimum level of internal, evoked stimulation tends to be similar for all individuals. (Sales et al., 1974, p. 16)

Sales and colleagues have derived a number of testable propositions from the theory that have been generally confirmed. In their initial investigations, the kinesthetic aftereffects task (KAE) (Petrie, 1967) was used to assess need for stimulation in terms of degree of perceptual augmentation or reduction. In terms of KAE task scores, perceptual augmenters represent individuals with low n Stim, while perceptual reducers represent individuals with high n Stim. Later investigations by Sales and associates used measures of "strength of the nervous system" to assess n Stim. Individuals with "strong" nervous systems have high n Stim, whereas individuals with "weak" nervous systems have low n Stim. Although not employed by Sales, other investigations have used Vando's (1969) Reducing-Augmenting (R-A) Scale to assess n Stim. A number of studies of individuals in sport situations have used one or more of these measures.

In a study of male delinquents, Petrie et al. (1962) assessed perceptual styles by means of the KAE task and found that reducers participated in sports and other activities more frequently than augmenters. Ryan and Foster (1967) investigated the relationship between perceptual style and athletic participation using the KAE task and found that athletes in contact sports tended to be reducers, nonathletes tended to be augmenters, and athletes in noncontact sports tended to fall between the two extremes.

Other investigators of the relationship between n Stim and sport participation have used the Vando R-A scale to measure n Stim. The findings of their studies are summarized in Table 3.3. For comparative purposes it is noted that scores on the Vando R-A scale range from 0 to 54 and that Vando (1969), in his initial investigation, obtained a mean score of 29.13 for a sample of 80 female nurses at Columbia University.

In summary, limited research to date in sport settings suggests that n Stim is a worthy variable to consider in the analysis of sport group composition. Future investigations of n Stim among members of sport groups should consider the distribution of n Stim among members in addition to measuring the mean value of n Stim for a given sport group.

3.3.3 Homogeneity–Heterogeneity of Group Membership

Similarity of group membership is an important consideration in the analysis of group composition, especially concerning the relationship between group membership and group performance. On the one hand, there is some empirical support for the argument that homogeneous groups are the most effective. This argument is based on the rationale that when members of groups are very similar in personal characteristics there is less clique formation and internal interpersonal conflict, greater group cohesiveness and member satisfaction, and thus better group performance.

On the other hand, there is some empirical support for the argument that heterogeneous groups are the most effective. This argument is based on the rationale that the attainment of group goals requires a division of labor among group members, resulting in role differentiation that necessitates diverse abilities, aptitudes, and personality characteristics among group members.

There is probably some degree of validity in both arguments. The conflicting evidence suggests that homogeneity on some characteristics and heterogeneity on others are related to effective group performance. Moreover, it remains likely that homogeneity or heterogeneity on still other individual characteristics is not at all related to group effectiveness. The relative support for each of these posi-

Table 3.3
Need for stimulation and sport participation

Samples: Subjects and Sports	Mean Vando Scale Score
Cornell, Harvard, and Yale Universities (Berger, 1970)	
Male varsity athletes (*n* = 132)	*33.48*
Tennis	29.60
Swimming	33.52
Wrestling	34.75
Skiing	35.15
University of Massachusetts (Donnelly, 1976)	
Female undergraduates in general P.E. skill classes (*n* = 174)	*29.88*
Orienteering	27.40
Bowling	28.66
Archery	29.17
Figure control	29.48
Tennis and badminton	29.89
Swimming	31.00
Fencing	32.00
Mountaineering	33.42
Scuba diving	33.83
Male undergraduates in general P.E. skill classes (*n* = 135)	*32.12*
Bowling	28.37
Tennis and badminton	31.09
Orienteering	31.25
Karate	32.78
Mountaineering	32.94
Scuba diving	35.44

tions in reference to the composition of sport groups is indicated by the research reviewed below.

Task Ability Homogeneity–Heterogeneity

With respect to sport groups, the pros and cons of homogeneous versus heterogeneous membership is most often discussed in reference to playing ability. A perennial debate is whether teams comprised of highly skilled players are always more successful against teams comprised of less skilled players. Surprisingly, few investigations have directly assessed the relationship between group effectiveness and individual or subgroup effectiveness.

An example of the type of research that needs to be pursued is Jones's (1974) study of group effectiveness as a function of individual or subgroup effectiveness among baseball, basketball, football, and tennis teams. Based on regression analysis, taking into account a wide variety of individual and group performance measures, Jones found significant relationships between individual effectiveness and group effectiveness for each type of sport. The results, however, revealed

Table 3.3 *continued*
Need for stimulation and sport participation

Samples: Subjects and Sports	Mean Vando Scale Score
Northfield Academy (Walsh, 1976)	
Male secondary school students ($n=141$)	*32.34*
Interscholastic athletic competition	33.07
Intramural sport participation	31.64
Track: fall (cross-country)	27.62
Track: winter (indoors)	29.67
Track: spring (outdoors)	28.40
Water polo	30.10
Basketball	30.18
Tennis	34.26
Swimming	31.50
Baseball	32.00
Football	33.04
Skiing	33.21
Soccer: fall	33.60
Soccer: spring	33.14
Crew	34.50
Hockey	35.31
Wrestling	35.78
Lacrosse	37.71
Female secondary school students ($n=149$)	*29.68*
Interscholastic athletic competition	30.33
Intramural sport participation	29.48

that the relationship between individual and group performance was less significant in the case of basketball teams. Rather, basketball teams were found to be strongly balanced with respect to the relative playing ability of their members, and tended not to have more than one "super star" or highly superior player. These findings about basketball teams support a general conclusion of research regarding task groups, namely that:

> . . . a group does not necessarily need the *highest possible* levels of ability in all members. What it needs is a *distribution* of levels and types of abilities which best fits the requirements of its task. (McGrath, 1964, p. 73)

In contrast to Jones's findings for professional basketball teams, Vander Velden (1971), in his investigation of high school basketball teams, found that homogeneity rather than heterogeneity of ability was most strongly related to team effectiveness. However, Vander Velden's findings were only significant for 15 teams from large schools. Moreover, Vander Velden's measures of task ability were based on subjective ratings of players by coaches, whereas Jones's measures of task ability were based on objective performance measures of players. Thus, the limited evidence to date suggests equivocal findings concerning the homo-geneity–heterogeneity of task ability. We now consider this same issue on a psy-chological, rather than a physical, level.

Psychological Homogeneity–Heterogeneity

Personality traits. As we observed previously (see Section 3.3.2), current find-ings about athletic personality types are ambiguous. Moreover, most investi-gations of the personality characteristics of individuals in selected sports have focused on ascertaining the modal characteristics of a group and thus have not examined the distribution of personality types within a group. Three exceptions to this trend are investigations by Kroll and Petersen (1965), Kroll et al. (1973), and Loy (1969).

By means of multiple discriminant function analysis, Kroll and Petersen (1965) assessed the personality factor profiles of five collegiate football teams and found significant discrimination between teams on four factors of the 16PF test: factor B (intelligence), factor H (shy vs. bold), factor O (confident vs. worrying), and factor Q3 (casual vs. controlled). Moreover, in a comparative analysis of the actual versus predicted group membership of the teams, they found that the per-centage of correct classifications was 55. Further, when the teams were classified into winning and losing categories, the percentage of correct classifications was 82. Their study suggests the merit of multiple discriminant function analysis and use of the 16PF in studying the homogeneity–heterogeneity of the psychological composition of sport groups.

In perhaps the most comprehensive study to date of athletic personality types, Kroll et al. (1973), on the basis of data obtained by means of the 16PF questionnaire, analyzed the personality profiles of 358 nationally ranked male and female Czechoslovakian athletes participating in 20 different sports. They found by means of discriminant function analysis that all 16 personality factors constituted significant discriminatory variables for both male and female subjects. However, their findings, summarized in Tables 3.4 and 3.5, ". . . which compare the assignment of subjects on the basis of sport participation with their assignment on the basis of personality do not offer substantial support for the supposition that there are distinctive personality types associated with selected sport groups" (Kroll et al., 1973). Moreover, they suggest that: "Part of the cause for such weakness in discrimination between participants in various sport groups may be due to a deficiency in the classification scheme utilized.

As Vanek and Cratty (1970) have suggested, some sports may actually belong in similar classification categories" (Kroll et al., 1973). To illustrate this point the reader should examine the data given in Table 3.4, which shows that one trackman had the personality profile of a gymnast and two trackmen had the personality characteristics of weightlifters. Interestingly, the trackman with the profile of a gymnast was found to be a pole vaulter, while the trackmen with the weightlifter profile were shotput and discus throwers.

In order to confront the problem of the arbitrary classification of sport groups, Kroll et al. (1973) analyzed their data by means of numerical taxonomy analysis which offers ". . . the alternative *of first* forming mutually exclusive and

Table 3.4
Classification of male athletes

Sport group	1	2	3	4	5	6	7	8	9	10	11	12	13	14	15	16	17	18	19	20	Percent correctly classified
														Number of correct classifications by sport group							
Basketball	2	0	0	1	0	0	0	0	1	0	1	1	0	0	5	1	1	0	0	0	15
Boxing	0	4	0	0	0	0	0	0	0	1	0	0	0	0	1	0	0	1	0	0	57
Canoeing (channel)	0	1	10	0	0	0	0	1	2	0	0	0	0	3	1	1	0	0	0	1	50
Canoeing (rapids)	0	0	1	5	0	0	1	1	0	0	0	3	2	0	2	1	0	1	1	1	26
Cycling	0	1	1	1	3	0	1	1	2	2	0	0	1	1	0	1	2	1	1	0	16
Gymnastics	0	1	0	0	0	6	0	0	0	2	0	0	0	0	0	0	0	1	0	0	75
Ice-hockey	0	2	3	1	2	2	6	1	1	3	0	1	6	1	1	0	1	1	3	2	16
Motorcycling (cross-country)	0	0	2	0	0	0	1	2	1	0	0	0	2	0	1	0	0	1	3	0	15
Motorcycling (track)	0	1	3	1	0	0	1	2	3	1	1	0	0	2	0	0	1	0	0	0	19
Mountaineering	1	0	0	0	0	0	0	0	1	6	0	0	0	0	0	1	1	0	1	0	46
Orienteering	0	0	0	0	1	0	0	1	1	0	5	0	0	0	0	3	0	0	0	0	83
Rowing	1	0	2	1	0	0	1	0	0	1	1	7	0	1	0	1	1	1	1	0	33
Shooting	0	0	1	0	1	4	1	2	0	0	0	0	3	0	1	0	0	0	0	1	21
Skiing (downhill)	1	0	0	1	1	0	0	2	0	2	0	0	1	4	1	0	0	1	3	0	24
Ski jumping	1	0	0	0	0	0	0	0	1	0	0	0	1	0	4	0	0	0	1	0	50
Skiing (Nordic)	0	0	0	0	0	0	0	0	1	0	0	0	0	0	0	4	0	0	0	0	80
Track & Field	0	0	1	0	0	1	0	0	0	0	0	0	0	1	0	0	6	0	2	1	50
Volleyball	0	2	0	0	0	1	1	0	0	0	1	0	0	0	0	0	1	7	2	1	44
Weight lifting	0	1	0	0	0	0	0	0	0	0	1	0	0	0	0	0	0	0	2	0	40
Wrestling	2	0	0	0	0	0	0	0	1	0	0	0	1	0	0	0	0	0	0	5	55

From Kroll et al. (1973), "Multivariate analysis of the personality profiles of championship Czechoslovakian athletes," *International Journal of Sport Psychology* 4: 135. Used with permission.

Table 3.5
Classification of female athletes

Sport group	Number of correct classifications								Number of Ss	Percent correctly classified
	1	2	3	4	5	6	7	8		
Basketball	7	1	0	1	2	1	1	1	14	50
Canoeing (C)	0	5	0	0	1	0	0	0	6	83
Canoeing (R)	1	0	7	2	0	0	0	1	11	64
Gymnastics	3	1	2	3	1	1	1	1	13	23
Orienteering	0	1	0	0	4	0	1	1	7	57
Skiing (D)	1	0	0	0	0	6	0	0	7	86
Track & field	0	0	0	0	0	0	5	0	5	100
Volleyball	2	2	0	4	0	1	0	8	17	46

From Kroll et al. (1973), "Multivariate analysis of the personality profiles of championship Czechoslovakian athletes," *International Journal of Sport Psychology* 4: 136. Used with permission.

optimally homogeneous groups *and then* considering the criteria capable of explaining the resultant classifications." This technique is based on a simple distant function that can range from 0.0 (shortest distance or greatest similarity) to 1.0 (longest distance or least similarity). Figure 3.4 shows the similarity-dissimilarity of male Czechoslovakian sport groups. As Kroll et al. states:

> Perhaps the most interesting cluster of sport groups is the matching of male motor cyclists, mountaineers, downhill skiers, ski-jumpers and cyclists. Although these sport groups appear to be quite diverse at first glance, they may be analytically viewed as agonetic activities involving physical experiences which provide ". . . at some risk to the participant, an element of thrill through the medium of speed, acceleration, sudden change of direction, or exposure to dangerous situations, with the participant usually remaining in control" (Kenyon, 1968, p. 100). Thus, the clustering of these specific sport groups offers empirical evidence for the "category of vertigo" in Callois's (1955) classification of games, and for the subdomain entitled "pursuit of vertigo" in Kenyon's (1968) conceptual model for characterizing physical activity.*

Whereas the first two studies reviewed analyzed the psychological profiles of athletes, the third study analyzes the psychological profiles of coaches. Specifically, Loy (1969) compared the social psychological characteristics of British swimming coaches who were relatively early or late in adopting a technological innovation, namely, a new training method for swimmers. In terms of their date of adoption of the innovation, coaches were classified in four categories: innova-

*From Kroll et al. (1973), "Multivariate analysis of the personality profiles of championship Czechoslovakian athletes," *International Journal of Sport Psychology* 4: 140, 144. Used with permission.

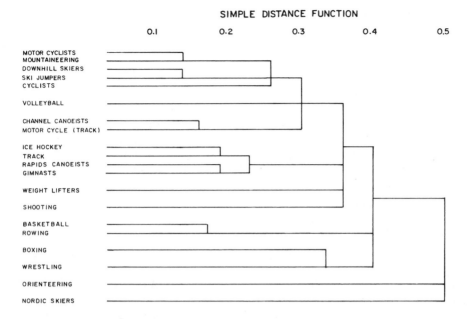

Fig. 3.4 *A dendogram of male sport groups. (From Kroll et al. (1973), "Multivariate analysis of the personality profiles of championship Czechoslovakian athletes," International Journal of Sport Psychology 4: 142. Used with permission.)*

tors, early majority adopters, late majority adopters, and laggards. By means of multiple discriminant function analysis Loy discovered significant differences for the four adopter categories with respect to factors on the 16PF test and selected social characteristics. The most discriminating variables in order of significance were venturesomeness, professional status, imaginativeness, educational status, dominance, sociability, cosmopoliteness, and self-sufficiency.

In terms of these factors, the members of the four adopter categories were found to have very homogeneous sociopsychological profiles. In fact, only one coach was misclassified in that a late majority adopter was found to have a psychological profile similar to an early majority adopter. In summary, the findings of Loy's study have implications for the explanation of social change in sport situations and indicate the importance of analyzing the sociopsychological composition of sport groups.

Motivational characteristics. Another crucial aspect of the psychological composition of sport groups has to do with the level and distribution of motivational characteristics among group members. Extensive research on motives and goals in groups has been conducted by Alvin Zander and his associates at the University of Michigan (Zander, 1971, 1974). Zander (1975) described the significance of his work for the study of group-oriented motivation in sport situations and has indicated ways in which the desire for group success can be ensured among team members.

Unfortunately, as is true with so many important problems, group achievement orientation has seldom been studied by social psychologists interested in sport. There has been, however, a limited number of investigations of the relationship between the task motivation of team members and team effectiveness. To illustrate, Vander Velden (1971), in his study of high school basketball teams, found no significant relationship between task-relevant attitudes of team members as measured by LPC scores and team success.

Similarly, Cooper and Payne (1972), in their investigation of English professional soccer teams, found no significant relationship between team success and highly task-motivated players as measured by Bass Orientation Inventory scores. Likewise, Widmeyer (1977), in a study of experimentally contrived basketball teams, found no direct relationship between performance outcome and three types of participation motivation: affiliation motivation, self-motivation, and task motivation. However, in an investigation of 144 college intramural teams, Martens (1970) reported that high task-motivated teams were more successful than low task-motivated teams.

In one of the few field studies of individual motivation and group goals, Emerson (1966) observed the members of the 1963 Mount Everest expedition. On the basis of this longitudinal case study in a natural field setting, Emerson formulated a theory of group achievement orientation which ". . . suggests that individual motivation and effort in goal-striving is a function of uncertainty about goal outcomes." However, his theory has not been tested in a group situation, although it appears generalizable to all task-oriented teams.

To date, only one study has examined the homogeneity–heterogeneity of achievement motivation among members of sport groups. Klein and Christiansen (1969) studied achievement motivation as a group composition variable among experimentally contrived three-man basketball teams. They reported three significant findings. First, teams with high-average achievement motivation were more successful than teams with low-average achievement motivation. Second, among teams with high-average achievement motivation, heterogeneous teams were more successful than homogeneous teams. Third, high-average achievement-motivated heterogeneous teams had greater status consensus than high-average achievement-motivated homogeneous teams.

In summary, few investigations have examined the psychological homogeneity–heterogeneity of sport groups. But limited research to date indicates that this dimension of group composition is worthy of further study.

Sociological Homogeneity–Heterogeneity

Social status homogeneity. A review of the literature indicates that few studies have directly attempted to determine the relationship between the social characteristics of individuals in sport groups and measures of overall group performance. For example, only three studies (see Loy, 1968, 1969; Eitzen, 1973; Tamashe, 1976) have analyzed group composition in terms of more than one social characteristic (i.e., profile homogeneity). To illustrate, in his analysis of member composition in terms of father's occupation, place of residence, religion, and family prestige in the community, Eitzen (1973) found moderate but significant support for the following hypotheses: (1) "the greater the homogeneity of a group on selected social characteristics, the smaller the probability of cliques being present," and (2) "the greater the homogeneity of a group on selected social characteristics, the greater the probability of goal attainment by the group."

In addition to the three studies of the social profile homogeneity of sport groups, three investigations of social trait homogeneity have analyzed the relationship between group performance and member's status consensus (i.e., agreement among members about their relative position in the status hierarchy within the group). Klein and Christiansen (1969) studied experimentally contrived basketball teams and found that high status consensus teams were more successful than low status consensus teams. They concluded that: "It can be assumed that status consensus about the role distribution facilitates interactions within the group and thus is a prerequisite to the success of the group" (Klein and Christiansen, 1969).

Contrary to Klein and Christiansen, Melnick and Chemers (1974) discovered no significant relationship between member status consensus and team success in their investigation of 21 college intramural basketball teams. By way of explanation, the relationship may be conditional in that it is related to status consensus between both coach and players. For example, Vander Velden (1971), in his investigation of high school basketball teams, reported that:

> . . . high status consensus was evident within all teams prior to the start of competition, a stable condition which endured throughout the basketball season. Consequently, there was no direct relationship between members' consensus and team success. (But) importance of members' consensus to team success was demonstrated with the level of task ability held constant; specifically, groups with both high task ability and high consensus were most effective . . . Also, a unique measure of consensus, i.e., agreement between the leader and members on the status hierarchy of the group was related to team effectiveness. (Vander Velden, 1971, pp. 130–131)

Racial heterogeneity. A crucial variable in the analysis of sport group composition is ethnicity, especially degree of ethnicity based on racial identification. Somewhat surprisingly in view of all that has been said about the role of sport in aiding racial integration and reducing racial prejudice, only two studies have addressed the matter of interracial contact and the reduction of prejudice within sport groups. In one investigation, McIntyre (1970a) conducted a field experimental study of attitude change in four biracial sport groups. In brief, he observed the behavior of four experimentally contrived flag football teams composed of nearly equal numbers of black boys from an urban school and white boys from a suburban school who competed in 20 contests over a five-week period. Using the Own Categories technique to measure attitudes toward ethnicity, McIntyre analyzed attitude change among team members during the course of competition and compared their attitudes with random control groups from each of the two schools from which players were drawn.

Although significant behavioral changes were observed, findings of the study revealed no significant changes in racial attitudes between biracial groups of players and their respective control groups. Moreover, members of high cohesive interracial playing groups were found not to differ significantly in ethnic attitudes from members of less cohesive interracial playing groups. McIntyre did find, however, that black subjects expressed a higher commitment and stronger involvement than whites on issues of ethnicity.

In a second investigation dealing with racial heterogeneity, McClendon and Eitzen (1975) tested Sherif's theory of subordinate goals (see McClendon, 1974) in an analysis of interracial contact on collegiate basketball teams. In short, findings of their investigation indicate that for whites, but not for blacks, superordinate goal achievement is related to more favorable racial attitudes.

3.3.4 Compatibility of Group Membership

As we noted earlier, group composition can be viewed from three perspectives: (1) the modal or average values of individual characteristics of members of a group, (2) the distribution of characteristics among members of a group, and (3) the compatibility of group members. Having discussed the first two perspectives, we now turn to the third.

Compatibility of group membership is reflected in positive perceptions of interpersonal relationships in general, and in membership satisfaction in particular. Concepts related to membership satisfaction include esteem of teammates, perceived acceptance, and social adjustment. Studies examining these variables in sport situations are reviewed below.

Positive Interpersonal Relations

Social scientists who study social groups are basically concerned with the relationship between personality and social structure. Investigations of these relationships tend to center on two critical issues. First, how does the structure and composition of groups affect the behavior of individuals within them? Second, how do the many particular personal attributes and actions of group members affect the functioning and change of groups? These two issues are well illustrated in the context of sport groups by the complementary studies of Myers (1962) and McGrath (1962). Specifically, Myers shows how group performance influences individual behavior, while McGrath shows how individual behavior influences group performance. Both investigations emphasize personal adjustment and positive interpersonal relations which relate to the compatibility of group members.

Myers's study. Myers investigated the effects of competition and success on the personal adjustment of rifle team members by testing three hypotheses: (1) "Individuals in successful teams will tend to have more favorable interpersonal perceptions of their teammates than individuals on unsuccessful teams"; (2) "success in a competitive situation will generate more favorable perceptions of teammates than success in noncompetitive situations"; and (3) "failure in a competitive situation will tend to generate more unfavorable perceptions of team-mates than failure in noncompetitive situations" (Myers, 1962).

Myers organized 180 ROTC students into 60 three-man rifle teams, which participated in a recreational rifle tournament extending over several weeks. The teams were evenly divided into competitive and noncompetitive leagues. Three types of measures were obtained from all subjects: (1) esteem for teammates, (2) perceived acceptance of self by teammates, and (3) perception of where blame should be placed when the team performed poorly.

Myers (1962) found that " . . . the competitive teams showed more improve-ment in team esteem than did the noncompetitive teams. In addition, the high success teams showed an improvement in average esteem during the course of the tournament while the low success teams deteriorated." Hence, the first hypothesis was supported. The second hypothesis was also substantiated in that Myers found that members of successful competitive teams perceived "a far more favorable relationship between their teammates and themselves" in comparison to members of other teams.

Results, however, did not support the third hypothesis, since Myers discovered that low-success competitive teams obtained better adjustment scores than low-success noncompetitive teams. A final finding of interest is that members of competitive teams did not hold their teammates responsible for poor performance, as was the case for noncompetitive teams. In summary, the findings of Myers's study indicate that in a competitive situation greater team effective-ness results in better adjustment of individual team members.

McGrath's study. In the investigation discussed above, Myers treated team effectiveness as an independent variable and assessed its effect on group adjust-ment, the dependent variable. In a related study McGrath (1962) treated team effectiveness as the dependent variable and sought to determine how it is in-fluenced by positive interpersonal relations, the independent variable. In short, he tested the assumption that positive interpersonal relations among teammates result in greater team effectiveness.

McGrath used the same subjects that Myers used in his study. On the basis of previously measured interpersonal perception scores, he assembled two types of teams: (1) teams composed of individuals who had given favorable ratings to former teammates, and (2) teams composed of individuals who had not given favorable ratings to former teammates. McGrath labeled the first set of teams the Positive Interpersonal Relations (PR) group and called the second set of teams the Nonpositive Interpersonal Relations (NR) group. These two sets of teams partici-pated in a one-hour, six-trial, handicap marksmanship contest for a monetary prize.

McGrath (1962) found that "the NR group had significantly better marks-manship scores and showed significant improvements in marksmanship while the PR group did not improve." In attempting to account for these findings, McGrath hypothesized a posteriori " . . . that members of the PR group focused their at-tention and energies primarily on the social or inter-personal aspects of the team interaction, while members of the NR group concentrated on their own task performance to the neglect of interpersonal relations." In summary, results of McGrath's investigation suggest that two contrasting types of personal orientation may be found among members of sport teams, namely, those who are oriented to task success and those who are oriented to interpersonal success. Thus, it may be hypothesized that task-oriented individuals would achieve greater member satisfaction in a task group, whereas relationship-oriented individuals would experience greater member satisfaction in a social group (see Mikalachi, 1969).

Membership Satisfaction

Only three published studies have directly compared the relationship between member satisfaction and the success of sport groups. In the first investigation Martens (1970) examined the effect of affiliation and task motivation on the satisfaction and success of 144 college intramural basketball teams composed of 1200 male students. Team success was defined in terms of the number of games won, while affiliation and task-motivation and member-satisfaction measures were assessed by means of players' responses to pre- and post-season questionnaires. Teams were classified into low, moderate, and high levels for both measures of motivation. In brief, Martens (1970) found that: (1) high affiliation-motivated teams were less successful but more satisfied than moderate and low affiliation-motivated teams, and (2) high task-motivated teams were more satisfied and more successful than moderate or low task-motivated teams.

In the second study, Martens and Peterson (1971) analyzed group cohesiveness as a determinant of success and member satisfaction for a sample of 144 male college intramural basketball teams. Their findings show that higher levels of cohesiveness are associated with greater member satisfaction and team success. They note that:

> These results suggest a circular relationship between satisfaction, cohesiveness, and success. Those teams which are more cohesive are more successful, and teams which are successful have greater satisfaction from participation than unsuccessful teams. Greater satisfaction, in turn, leads to higher levels of cohesiveness, thus maintaining a circular relationship. In actuality though, this cause-effect triangulation is bombarded with a number of other important factors that may influence this sequence of events. (Martens and Peterson, 1971, p. 58)

In the third investigation Kjeldsen (1976) took into account measures of member satisfaction in an analysis of leadership among 30 high school gymnastics teams. He discovered several conditional relationships between team success and member satisfaction. For example, he found support for the hypothesis that high individual performance leads to winning, which in turn leads to both higher member satisfaction and to higher member perceptions of the influence of the coach. Kjeldsen (1976) notes, however, that there appears to be no causal connection between member satisfaction and perceptions of the influence of the coach, but both seemed to be based on winning.

Another interesting finding of Kjeldsen's investigation was that there is a positive correlation between the coach's age and member satisfaction. This finding is counter to conventional wisdom that athletes tend to prefer younger coaches. Kjeldsen tested a number of models in an effort to account for this unexpected relationship between the coach's age and member satisfaction. Although he was able to account for 49 percent of the variation in member satisfaction by a number of behavioral measures, he reached no conclusive interpretation for the relationship between coach's age and member satisfaction.

In summary, this review of research regarding the composition of sport groups has shown that team success is related to three sets of factors: attributes of group members, attributes of groups, and situational conditions. In the concluding section of this chapter, the dynamic interaction among these three sets of factors is illustrated as they relate to group performance.

3.4 GROUP PROCESS AND PERFORMANCE

3.4.1 Group Cohesion and Team Success

Cohesion has been variously considered as a "compositional" variable (Shaw, 1971), as a "structural" variable (McGrath, 1964), and as a "process" variable (Widmeyer, 1977). These different perspectives are associated with the fact that cohesion (or cohesiveness) has a number of different meanings, represents many different behaviors of group members, and has been measured in several different ways. Thus, not surprisingly, definitional, methodological, and theoretical problems have plagued investigations of cohesion in small groups in general, and in sport groups in particular.

Cohesion has been discussed in the literature under a variety of titles, including cooperation (Deutsch, 1949), integration (Landecker, 1955), interpersonal attraction (Lott and Lott, 1965), and morale (Zeleny, 1939). Shaw (1971) summarizes the situation by noting that " . . . at least three different meanings have been attached to the term 'cohesiveness': (1) attraction to the group, including resistance to leaving it, (2) morale, or the level of motivation evidenced by group members, and (3) coordination of efforts of group members." Because of its manifold meanings researchers have most often followed Festinger (1950) by defining cohesiveness " . . . as the resultant of all the forces acting on the members to remain in the group." However, this definition has received much criticism, especially concerning the difficulty of operationalizing the concept (Gross and Martin, 1952).

Cartwright (1968) has discussed five major approaches to measuring group cohesiveness, namely: (1) interpersonal attraction among members, (2) evaluation of a group as a whole, (3) closeness or identification with a group, (4) expressed desire to remain in a group, and (5) composite indexes. Unfortunately, several studies show that there is little relationship among these different operational measures of cohesion (see Eisman, 1959; Ramuz-Nienhuis and Van Bergen, 1960; Van Bergen and Koekebakker, 1959). However, there is some support in the literature for the notion that cohesion is a bidimensional property of small groups and that operational measures of both instrumental and intrinsic (or inter-personal) attraction are required (see Enoch and McLemore, 1967; Feldman, 1968: Hagstrom and Selvin, 1965; Loy, 1972). Interestingly, in a recent comprehensive investigation of cohesiveness within sport groups, Widmeyer (1977) also discovered two major cohesion factors when he factor-analyzed eight cohesion variables. He labeled the two cohesion factors as "descriptive cohesion" and "inferential cohesion."

The preceding observations, while highlighting the complex (and often confusing) nature of cohesion, may have unintentionally led the reader to assume that cohesion is largely a static concept. Therefore, it must also be emphasized that cohesion is a dynamic concept and may be best considered as a process variable in sport group research. To illustrate, Widmeyer notes that:

> Cohesion, then, is not something which is brought to the group but instead is something that develops and occurs within the group. Cohesion may thus be regarded as a process variable which mediates the relationship between group inputs and group outputs. Even though cohesion is often referred to as a "structural" variable such a view is not incompatible with the present view if one accepts Davis' (1969) point that structure is simply "frozen" process. As such, cohesion's relationship to group outputs can be altered by the demands of the task, by certain group inputs, and by other process variables. (Widmeyer, 1977, p. 15)

Having outlined this perspective of the concept, the following represents a review of research regarding cohesion as a mediating process variable in sport groups.

Cohesion and Performance

Studies conducted in a variety of sport situations have found a positive, a negative, or no relationship between measures of selected aspects of team cohesion and effectiveness. Specifically, a *positive* relationship between these two variables has been reported in studies of:

1. Baseball teams (Landers and Crum, 1971)
2. Basketball teams (Arnold and Straub, 1973; Chapman and Campbell, 1957; Klein and Christiansen, 1969; Martens and Peterson, 1971; Nixon, 1976, 1977; Smith, 1968; Vander Velden, 1971; Widmeyer, 1977)
3. Bowling teams (Walters, 1955)
4. Football teams (McIntyre, 1970b, Stogdill, 1963; Trapp, 1953)
5. Rifle teams (Chapman and Campbell, 1957)
6. Soccer teams (Essing, 1970; Veit, 1973)
7. Volleyball teams (Bird, 1977; Slepicka, 1975; Vos and Brinkman, 1967).

However, empirical evidence concerning the relationship between team cohesion and team effectiveness is equivocal. That is, a number of investigations have found a *negative* or no relationship between the two variables. These investigations include studies of:

1. Basketball teams (Fiedler et al., 1952; Grace, 1954; Melnick and Chemers, 1974)

2. Bowling teams (Landers and Luschen, 1974)

3. Rifle teams (McGrath, 1962)

4. Rowing teams (Lenk, 1969).[5]

Many ex post facto explanations have been offered to account for the apparent discrepancies in the findings regarding the relationship between group cohesion and group performance. The most often cited reason is that the inconsistent findings likely result from the extreme variability in the measurement of cohesiveness in the studies cited above. In addition, in a number of the earlier investigations cohesiveness was inferred from indirect measures of interpersonal perceptions and personal distance scales rather than from straightforward indexes of cohesion. A related difficulty is the fact that many investigations have measured only one form of cohesion, and thus do not adequately account for the multidimensional nature of the concept.

A second possible reason for discrepant results stems from the variety of methods used to measure performance or performance outcome. Although the percentage of events won and lost has been most commonly used as an index of team effectiveness, numerous other criteria have also been utilized. A related problem is that most investigators have not distinguished between the concepts of performance and performance outcome. That is, "Performance refers to overt goal-directed behavior, whereas performance outcome is the consequence of such behavior" (Widmeyer, 1977). Although there is usually a close association between the two concepts, the fit is far from perfect. That is to say, good performance doesn't always result in a favorable performance outcome (e.g., winning), and bad performance doesn't necessarily produce an unfavorable performance outcome (e.g., losing) (see Lowe, 1973).

A third possible reason for inconsistent findings relates to the diverse types of sport groups that have been studied. Landers and Luschen (1974), for example, have argued that cohesion is more likely to be related to team success within interacting sport groups that emphasize complementary tasks, than within coacting sport groups which emphasize additive tasks. In support of their argument they point out that positive findings regarding the relationship between cohesion and performance have most often been found for interacting sport groups such as baseball, basketball, football, and volleyball teams, which involve cooperative interaction and interdependent tasks. On the other hand, negative findings are often characteristic of studies of coacting sport groups such as bowling and rifle teams, which involve independent tasks whose performance outcomes are additive in nature. Landers and Luschen (1974) further suggest that cohesion, and its opposite concept "in-group conflict," are related to arousal levels. In short, Landers and Luschen provide a rationale for the hypothesis that cohesion is positively related to performance within interacting groups, but negatively related to performance in coacting groups.

A fourth possible reason for the inconclusive findings is closely related to the preceding reason. This explanation concerns group emotionality, a special aspect of cohesion. Nixon (1977), for example, states that: "The element of physical contact may make overt displays of group emotion or team spirit a positive factor in team competitive efforts, while in noncontact sports, group emotionality may impede group goal attainment." Thus Nixon, like Landers and Luschen, argues that the type of sport team must be taken into account when considering the matter of cohesiveness and team success.

A fifth possible explanation for the equivocal findings has to do with the different competitive levels underlying the several investigations of cohesion in sport groups. That is, the influence of cohesion on performance may vary in terms of whether team members are professional or amateur athletes, highly skilled or unskilled, very competitive or noncompetitive, etc.

A sixth possible reason for mixed results is that investigations of cohesion and performance have seldom taken into account the organizational and environmental contexts in which sport groups are embedded. For example, sport groups in cohesion studies have been considered largely as closed systems and the possible and likely social impact of the larger surroundings within which they interact has been ignored. Yet several studies indicate that environmental effects have a strong influence on the interactions between personality and performance (Kroll and Petersen, 1965; Rushall, 1972; Straub, 1971) and thus can be expected to influence the relations between cohesion and performance (Martens, 1971).

A seventh possible explanation for the inconclusive findings is that the sport groups that have been studied have varied markedly with respect to the tenure and stability of their memberships. For example, several groups were experimentally contrived and thus their ongoing social interaction was of limited duration, whereas other groups represented "natural groups" whose members had interacted over long periods of time. In short, investigators have not adequately assessed the primary or secondary nature of the task groups that they sampled (Stone, 1966). To illustrate, in their investigation of the relative efficiency of primary versus secondary group interactions on improvement in performance, Cratty and Sage noted that:

> A *primary* group . . . (is) characterized by a common feeling of unity, exhibiting a fusion of individuals into a common whole . . . (and) involves long-lasting friendship; . . . a *secondary* group involves no such cohesion, and within the present context included individuals who, when asked, did not know each other's names. They had been brought together specifically to perform the experimental task. (Cratty and Sage, 1964, p. 266)

An eighth possible, and very probable, reason for discrepant findings is that researchers have typically examined only the direct relationship between cohesion and performance and have ignored the complex interaction of variables that underly the relationship.[6]

In summary, several reasons have been suggested that may account in whole or part for the apparent discrepancies reported in the literature regarding the relationship between team cohesion and team effectiveness. These ex post facto explanations have implicitly, if not explicitly, leveled a number of criticisms at investigations of cohesion in sport groups. Many, if not most, of these implied criticisms can be extended to small sport group research in general. This is aptly illustrated by Martens's concluding comments in his report on the field of sport psychology:

> At this time sport psychology is obviously deficient in group dynamics research. A few isolated studies exist in certain areas, but all too often these studies are replete with methodological and conceptual problems. Cohesiveness has received considerable attention but the majority of the research is unsystematic and lacks a sound theoretical base. Investigators have typically failed to consider the dynamic nature of group structure and group process has been universally ignored. (Martens, 1976c, p. 192)

3.4.2 Group Competition, Conflict, and Performance

Martens' comments about the state of group dynamics research in sport psychology also hold true for the state of group dynamics research in sport sociology, especially concerning the study of group process within sport situations. Theoretical and/or empirical treatments of the major social processes underlying sport group performance are the exception rather than the rule. For example, the social processes of competition and conflict are inherent elements of all sport situations, but ironically represent the least studied aspects of sport groups. In fact, notable discussions of these processes are largely confined to the work of less than a half dozen individuals (see Elias and Dunning, 1966; Heinila, 1966; Kiviaho and Mustikkamaa, 1976; Lenk, 1969, 1977; Luschen, 1970; Martens, 1975; Oglesby, 1974; Sherif, 1973).

Notwithstanding the paucity of literature on the subject, it is evident that conflict and tension are essential components of the dynamics of sport groups. As Elias and Dunning have observed in reference to forms of football (i.e., soccer and rugby):

> . . . a complex of interdependent polarities built into the game pattern provides the main motive force for the group dynamics of a football game. In one way or another they all contribute towards maintaining the "tone," the tension-balance of the game. Here is a list of some of them:
>
> 1. The overall polarity between two opposing teams.
> 2. The polarity between attack and defense.
> 3. The polarity between co-operation and tension of the two teams.
> 4. The polarity between co-operation and competition within each team. . . .
>
> Other polarities are of a slightly different type. These are a few examples:

5. The polarity between the external controls of players on a variety of levels (by managers, captains, team-mates, referees, linesmen, spectators, etc.) and the flexible control which the individual player exercises upon himself.

6. The polarity between affectionate identification and hostile rivalry with the opponents.

7. The polarity between the enjoyment of aggression by the individual and the curb imposed upon such enjoyment by the game pattern.

8. The polarity between elasticity and fixity of rules. (Elias and Dunning, 1966, pp. 398–400)

The basic thrust of the observations of Elias and Dunning can be extended to group dynamics in general. For example, Coser has written:

> Groups require disharmony as well as harmony, dissociation as well as association, and conflicts within them are by no means altogether disruptive factors. Group formation is the result of both types of processes. The belief that one process tears down what the other builds up, so that what finally remains is the result of subtracting the one from the other is based on a misconception. On the contrary, both "positive" and "negative" factors build group relations. Conflict as well as co-operation has social functions. Far from being necessarily dysfunctional, a certain degree of conflict is an essential element in group formation and the persistence of group life. (Coser, 1956, p. 31)

Coser illustrates this perspective of the importance of conflict in social life by means of a detailed theoretical examination of 16 propositions derived largely from Simmel's (1955) classic analysis of conflict. His derived propositions represent hypotheses that are worthy of being tested in sport situations.

The Functions of Social Conflict

To illustrate the function of conflict in sport situations, four of Coser's (1956) propositions are cited and given a sport interpretation.

The function of group binding.   Conflict between groups tends to establish clear boundaries, heighten group consciousness, and lead to greater group recognition and identity (Coser, 1956). This process is a common occurrence and is readily seen in sport, beginning with the distinction between those who "make" the team and those who do not (the "in group" vs. the "out group"). It is further illustrated by the "reciprocal antagonism" that develops between teams and forces the members of each team into more cohesive social units. By maintaining the resulting clear boundaries the larger system remains intact. Moreover, the concept of "we-they" is highly functional in sport and has less ambiguity than in most other group settings, especially as it applies to a team or the fans.

Conflict as a safety valve for releasing hostility.   Conflict between groups allows for the expression of hostilities (Coser, 1956) which, in turn, functions to increase group cohesion. While the concept of catharsis, or the releasing of pent-up emotions of individuals through aggressive behavior, has found little support in the psychological literature (see Berkowitz, 1962), perhaps the case is more compelling in group settings. In sport, a number of avenues toward the expression of socially approved revenge are available, such as boxing, wrestling, and, in earlier historical periods, dueling. For example, Coser notes that:

> Dueling brings potentially disruptive aggressive self-help under social control and constitutes a direct outlet for hostilities between members of the society. The socially controlled conflict "clears the air" between the participants and allows a resumption of their relationships. (Coser, 1956, p. 42)

Coser goes on to discuss the phenomenon of displaced hostility. Again, sport provides ample opportunity to express antagonism, even "unwittingly" or through a "war without weapons" (Goodhart and Chataway, 1968). However, the reader should not overlook the fact that displaced hostility, whether through sport or any other means, can also be *dysfunctional*. For example, joking about players who belong to a minority group may be useful to reduce tension and enhance team cohesion, but it does little to alleviate fundamental forms of discrimination that, in the long run, could lead to team disruption.

Searching for enemies. In the absence of other mechanisms, group cohesion and attention to the task at hand are often enhanced by focusing attention on the "enemy"; for example, the denigration of the opponent in war is common. Coser (1956) suggests that if real or imagined threats to the group can be highlighted, group integration increases. In sport, examples abound, from the symbolic burning of the opponent in effigy to pep rallies before college football games. By characterizing the opponent as stronger than fact, a greater sacrifice for the "common cause" is achieved. Often the media reinforce this function by discussing the exploits of the opposing team and its individual players. If empirical support for such a proposition is forthcoming, coaches may wish to reconsider the nature of their own public relations programs, lest they backfire.

Conflict creates associations and coalitions. In some situations conflict may bring together otherwise competing groups for both short- and long-term gain (Coser, 1956). For example, the rise of the trade union movement forced alliances between employers, who otherwise were competing for the same markets. Other examples include center and right-of-center political parties joining forces against the left, the agreement among manufacturers to fix prices on common products, and any number of international alliances and treaties.

In sport, where institutionalized conflict is central, a number of coalitions and alliances have appeared that collectively enhance one or more aspects of the game (for example, the creation of leagues). As sport becomes a multinational corporation, the occurrence of league agreements or mergers increases, such as the long-standing relationship between the National and American leagues in baseball, the mergers of the National Football League with the American Football League and the NBA with the ABA, and, more recently, the possibility of some organizations in the World Hockey Association merging with the National Hockey League. On the players' level, there have been a number of developments such as player associations which seek to protect the players' opportunity to compete. While the creation of such sport alliances often changes the nature of the game, in many instances the results have strengthened particular leagues and thus maintained the sport order.

In summary, using only a few of Coser's propositions as examples, the argument that social conflict has certain functions, not all negative, can be applied to the sport group in particular. Perhaps this is not so surprising, given the realization that in sport, the contest—and therefore the conflict—is essential (see Luschen, 1970).

The Process of Competition

Although among the most fundamental elements of sport, *competition* remains a most elusive phenomenon. As Martens (1975) points out, competition has been defined in various ways, depending on whether it has been seen as a process, a

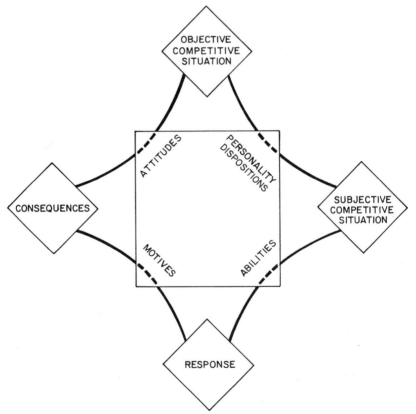

Fig. 3.5 *The competition process. (From* Social Psychology and Physical Activity *by Rainer Martens. Copyright © 1975 by Rainer Martens. By permission of Harper & Row, Publishers, Inc.)*

specific behavior, a behavioral tendency, or a specific situation. As a result, little consensus has emerged from the many research efforts related to this process.

In response to this conceptual state of affairs, Martens rejects the common "reward" definition and instead suggests the need to make careful distinctions between competition (or the competition process), competitiveness, and competitive behavior. The *competition process* consists of "a four category frame of reference with the individual as the focal organism . . . the objective competitive situation, the subjective competitive situation, the response, and the consequences of the response" (Martens, 1975). The four elements and their relationships are shown in Fig. 3.5. *Competitiveness* "is defined as a disposition to strive for satisfaction when making comparisons with some standard of excellence in the presence of evaluative others in sport" (Martens, 1976b). *Competitive behavior* is the overt action taken in both objective and subjective competitive situations.

Given the distinction among the three terms, research becomes more manageable. For example, one might seek a better understanding of competitiveness and its role in precipitating competitive behavior. Obviously, the development of such a behavioral disposition or motive will depend on a number of antecedent and situational factors, some of which would occur in early childhood. In an attempt to build on Martens's typology, Scanlan (1974) developed a "theoretical framework for the antecedents of competitiveness." Figure 3.6 will help the reader to appreciate the complexity of the hypothesized process.

In summary, the process of competition is far from being well understood. However, recent efforts to reconceptualize competition phenomena promise to set the stage for new investigations that could lead to more satisfying explanations in both sport and nonsport situations.

3.4.3 Toward a Theory of Team Success

The review of research concerning the performance of sport groups suggests that team success is due to many factors, including intrapersonal factors, interpersonal factors, and social structural factors. To date, only Nixon (1974) has attempted to integrate the many factors associated with team success. Based on a review of several of the studies in this area, Nixon (1974) identified 12 psychological and social factors associated with team success. These correlates are listed and defined below.

Correlates of Team Success

Intrapersonal factors (aggregated over group).

1. Group Achievement Orientation (GAO): The "degree of importance of team versus individual success."

2. Perceived Ability Discrepancy (PAD): The "amount of perceived discrepancy between the task ability level of one's own group and a competitive group."

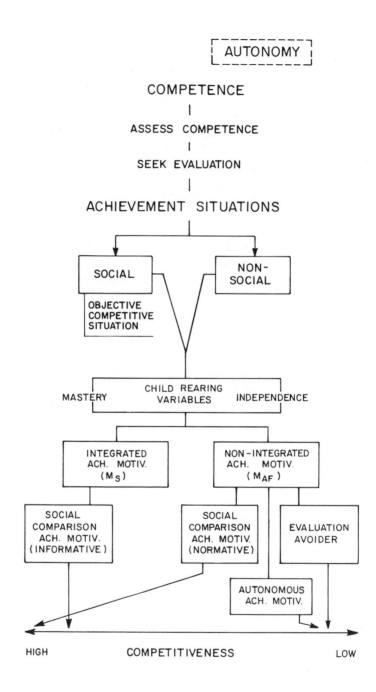

Fig. 3.6 *Theoretical framework for the antecedents of competitiveness. (From Scanlan, 1974, p. 179)*

3. Expected Competitive Outcome (ECO): The "degree of closeness in expected relative group competitive outcome."

4. Success Expectation Fulfillment (SEF): The "degree of fulfillment of expectation of group competitive success."

5. Member Satisfaction (MS): The "amount of individual member satisfaction with group involvement."

Interpersonal factors

6. Interpersonal Rivalry (IR): The "degree of interpersonal rivalry."

7. Affective-Task Discrepancy (A-TD): The "amount of discrepancy between positive affective and task orientations."

8. Perceived Teamwork (TW): The "amount of perceived integration of group activities."

Social structural factors

9. Status Consensus (SC): The "amount of status consensus."

10. Group Cohesion (GC): The "amount of attraction to the group as a whole."

11. Group Success (GS): The "amount of success in group goal attainment efforts."

12. Past Group Success (PGS): The "amount of immediate past group success." (Nixon, 1974, pp. 6–8)

Based on a review of research regarding team effectiveness, Nixon developed 25 propositions stating the expected relationships among given combinations of the 12 variables just defined. These hypothesized relationships are summarized in Table 3.6. However, for purposes of parsimony, perceived teamwork (TW) is considered (see Nixon, 1974) as an aspect of group cohesion (GC).

An Axiomatic Theory

Collectively considered, the 25 propositions set forth by Nixon represent an axiomatic theory of team success. The axiomatic nature of Nixon's theoretical formulation is illustrated by taking selected propositions as postulates from which the other propositions can be derived and taken as theorems. Propositions are defined as "primary" theorems if they can be derived from the postulates alone, "secondary" theorems are based on the consideration of both postulates and primary theorems, and "tertiary" theorems are based on the consideration of all preceding propositions, etc.

For example, using the following four propositions, two primary theorems can be deduced.

Postulate I: The greater the Group Achievement Orientation (GAO), the less the Interpersonal Rivalry (IR).

Postulate II: The less the Interpersonal Rivalry, the greater the Status Consensus (SC).

Table 3.6

A propositional inventory of Nixon's hypothesized determinants and results of team effectiveness

Variables	1 GAO	2 PAD	3 ECO	4 SEF	5 MS	6 IR	7 A-TD	8 SC	9 GC	10 GS	11 PGS
1. Group Achievement Orientation						$-^1$		$+^2$	+	+	
2. Perceived Ability Discrepancy			+				+			−	
3. Expected Competitive Outcome							+			−	
4. Success Expectation Fulfillment					+						
5. Member Satisfaction	+										
6. Interpersonal Rivalry								−	−	−	
7. Affective-Task Discrepancy											
8. Status Consensus									+		
9. Group Cohesion[3]								+	+	+	
10. Group Success											
11. Past Group Success	+			+	+	−		+	+	+	

1. A negative symbol (−) indicates an inverse relationship: "The greater the group achievement orientation, the less the interpersonal rivalry."
2. A positive symbol (+) indicates a direct relationship: "The greater the group achievement orientation, the greater the status consensus."
3. Includes "perceived teamwork."

From Nixon (1974).

Postulate III: The greater the Status Consensus, the greater the Group Cohesion (GC).

Postulate IV: The greater the Group Cohesion, the greater the Group Success (GS).

Primary Theorem I: The greater the GAO, the greater the SC (from P I and P II).

Primary Theorem II: The less the IR, the greater the GC (from P II and P IV).

From the postulates and primary theorems above, two secondary theorems can be derived:

Secondary Theorem I: The greater the GAO, the greater the GC (from PT I and P III).

Secondary Theorem II: The less the IR, the greater the GS (from PT II and P IV).

Finally, from the foregoing, a tertiary theorem can also be derived:

Tertiary Theorem I: The greater the GAO, the greater the GS (from ST I and P IV).

Using such a logical deductive procedure, at least 25 propositional statements can be derived from Nixon's theory of team success. The reader should appreciate, however, that such an exercise must meet some rather stringent requirements. For example, each of the above propositions expresses a *relationship* between two phenomena, or, if causality is assumed, between determinant and result. Further, as Zetterberg (1966) points out, such relationships may be (1) reversible or irreversible, (2) deterministic or stochastic, (3) sequential or coextensive, (4) sufficient or contingent, or (5) necessary or substitutable. Given these considerations and other requirements of theory construction and given the imprecision of the subject matter, the shortage of robust theories explaining social phenomena in general and sport phenomena in particular should not be surprising. However, since the ultimate goal of science is explanation (see Section 2.3), the serious sociologist interested in sport should not be daunted by having to meet such standards when developing and testing propositions explaining the small group in sport.

Future Directions

A complete analysis of the pros and cons of Nixon's theory is beyond the scope of this text. Rather, it has been presented to illustrate both the components and the complexity of explaining successful team performance. Obviously, considerably more work, theoretical and empirical, is needed if we are to achieve satisfying explanations and ultimately predictions. In closing, in the realm of explaining and predicting team success Martens (1976c) has specified some needed directions, including the following.

1. Greater consideration should be given to the influence of task characteristics on group process; and task classifications relevant to sports skills are needed.

2. Nonperformance as well as performance outcomes should be investigated, and the influence of outcomes at one point in time on subsequent group process should be considered.

3. Group development or changes in group structure over time should be investigated using alternative measures of group structure that consider the total pattern of relationships within the group.

4. Relevant group processes for sport teams must be identified and adequate coding systems must be developed so that greater attention may be given to group process as the critical mediating component between input factors and outcomes.

5. Undoubtedly, the greatest need of sport psychology in the group dynamics area is for the initiation of systematic programs of research, rather than isolated studies, operating from a sound theoretical base directed at specifying precisely the dynamic processes that occur in sport teams. (Martens, 1976c, pp. 192–193)

NOTES

1. There is a special dearth of research regarding female coaches (an exception being Clark, 1976), and few cross-cultural studies of coaches have been conducted (an exception being Hammer and Skubic, 1976).

2. Examples of bipolar adjectives used in the scale are friendly–unfriendly and cooperative–uncooperative.

3. For a detailed discussion of the interrelationships between biological and sociological processes, the reader is referred to Barchas (1976).

4. Although we place stress on "negative findings," several studies have found "positive findings" to support the stated beliefs; see, for example, Balazs (1975, 1976) for findings regarding the psychosocial profiles of outstanding female athletes, and Morgan (1974) for findings concerning significant psychological differences between high- and low-level performers.

5. Two recent investigations with conditional findings about cohesion and team performance are Lefebvre and Cunningham's (1977) study of a successful football team, and Ball and Carron's (1977) study of Canadian intercollegiate ice hockey teams.

6. For detailed discussions of the kind of variables that mediate the relationship between cohesion and performance, the reader is referred to recent work by Nixon (1977) and Widmeyer (1977).

REFERENCES

Adams, B. (1972). "Birth order: A critical review." *Sociometry* **35**: 411–439.

Albaugh, G. (1972). "The influence of ressentience as identified in college basketball coaches." In *The 75th Proceedings of the National College Physical Education Association for Men*, pp. 60–68.

Albinson, J., and G. Andrew (eds.) (1976). *Child in Sport and Physical Activity*. Baltimore, Md: University Park Press.

Althus, W. D. (1966). "Birth order and its sequelae." *Science* 151 (January): 44–49.

Andrud, W. E. (1970). "The personality of high school, college and professional football coaches as measured by the Guilford-Zimmerman temperament survey." Unpublished M.A. thesis, University of North Dakota.

Arnold, G., and W. Straub (1973). "Personality and group cohesiveness as determinants of success among interscholastic basketball teams." In I. Williams and L. Wankel (eds.), *Proceedings of the Fourth Canadian Psycho-Motor Learning and Sport Psychology Symposium*, pp. 346–353. Ottawa, Canada: Department of National Health and Welfare.

Ashour, A. (1973). "The contingency model of leadership effectiveness: An evaluation." *Organizational Behavior and Human Performance* 9: 339–355.

Asmussen, E. (1965). "The biological basis of sport." *Ergonomics* 8: 137–142.

Balazs, E. K. (1967). "Psycho-social study of outstanding female athletes." *Research Quarterly* 46: 267–273.

Balazs, E. K. (1976). *In Quest of Excellence.* Waldwick, N.J.: Hoctor Publications.

Bales, R. F. (1953). "The equilibrium problem in small groups." In T. Parsons, R. F. Bales, and E. A. Shils (eds.), *Working Papers in the Theory of Action*, pp. 111–161. Glencoe, Ill. Free Press.

Ball, J. R., and A. V. Carron (1977). "The influence of team cohesion and participation motivation upon performance success in intercollegiate ice hockey." *Recreation Research Review* 5: 53–58.

Barchas, P. R. (1976). "Physiological sociology: Interface of sociological and biological processes." In A. Inkeles (ed.), *Annual Review of Sociology*, Vol 2, pp. 299–333. Palo Alto, Calif.: Annual Reviews, Inc.

Bass, B. M. (1960). *Leadership, Psychology and Organizational Behavior.* New York: Harper and Row.

Bass, B. M. (1962). *Manual of the Orientation Inventory.* Palo Alto, Calif.: Consulting Psychologists Press.

Berger, B. G. (1970). "Relationships between the environmental factors of temporal-spatial uncertainty, probability of physical harm, and nature of competition, and selected personality factors." Unpublished Ph.D. dissertation, Columbia University.

Berkowitz, L. (1962). *Aggression: A Social Psychological Analysis.* New York: McGraw-Hill.

Bird, A. M. (1977). "Development of a model for predicting team performance." *Research Quarterly* 48 (March): 24–32. Used with permission.

Burke, P.J. (1967). "The development of task and social-emotional role differentiation." *Sociometry* 30: 379–392.

Burke, P. J. (1968). "Role differentiation and the legitimation of task activity." *Sociometry* 31: 404–411.

Butterfield, D. A. (1968). "An integrative approach to the study of leadership effectiveness in organization." Unpublished Ph.D. dissertation, University of Michigan.

Carter, J. E. L. (1970). "The somatotypes of athletes—a review." *Human Biology* 42: 535–569.

Carter, L. F. (1954). "Recording and evaluating the performance of individuals as members of small groups." *Personnel Psychology* 7: 477–484. Used with permission.

Cartwright, D. (1968). "The nature of group cohesiveness." In D. Cartwright and A. Zander (eds.), *Group Dynamics*, pp. 91–109. New York: Harper and Row.

Casher, B. B. (1977). "Relationship between birth order and participation in dangerous sports." *Research Quarterly* 48 (March): 33–40.

Cattell, R. B. (1965). *The Scientific Analysis of Personality.* Baltimore, Md.: Penguin Books.

Cattell, R. B., and G. F. Stice (1954). "Four formulae for selecting leaders on the basis of personality." *Human Relations* 7: 493–507.

Chapman, L. J., and D. T. Campbell (1957). "An attempt to predict the performance of three-men teams from attitude measurements." *Journal of Social Psychology* 46: 277–286.

Christie, R., and F. L. Geis (1970). *Studies in Machiavellianism*. New York: Academic Press.

Clark, M. I. (1976). "An assessment of characteristics of successful women intercollegiate athletic coaches." Paper pressented at the 91st National Convention of AAHPER, Milwaukee, Wisconsin (April).

Cofer, C. N., and R. Johnson (1960). "Personality dynamics in relation to exercise and sports." In W. R. Johnson (ed.), *Science and Medicine of Exercise and Sports*, pp. 525–559. New York: Harper and Row.

Cooper, R., and R. Payne (1972). "Personality orientations and performance in soccer teams." *British Journal of Social and Clinical Psychology* 11: 2–9.

Cortes, J. B. (1961). "Physique, need for achievement and delinquency." Unpublished Ph.D. dissertation, Harvard University.

Cortes, J. B., and F. M. Gatti (1965). "Physique and self-description of temperament." *Journal of Consulting Psychology* 29: 432–439.

Coser, L. A. (1956). *The Functions of Social Conflict*. New York: Free Press.

Cratty, B. J., and J. N. Sage (1964). "Effects of primary and secondary group interaction upon improvement in a complex movement task." *Research Quarterly* 35: 265–274. Used with permission.

Cureton, T. K. (1941). "Body build as a framework of reference for interpreting physical fitness and athletic performance." *Research Quarterly* 12 (May): 301–330.

Cureton, T. K. (1951). *Physical Fitness of Champion Athletes*. Urbana, Ill.: University of Illinois Press.

Damon, A. (1955). "Physique and success in military flying." *American Journal of Physical Anthropology* 13: 217–252.

Danielson, R. R., et al. (1975). "Multidimensional scaling and factor analysis of coaching behavior as perceived by high school hockey players." *Research Quarterly* 46 (October): 323–334.

Davis, J. H. (1969). *Group Performance*. Reading, Mass.: Addison-Wesley.

Defee, J., and P. Himelstein (1969). "Children's fear in a dental situation as a function of birth order." *Journal of Genetic Psychology* 115: 253–255.

De Garay, A., et al. (eds.) (1974). *Genetic and Anthropological Studies of Olympic Athletes*. New York: Academic Press. Used with permission.

Deutsch, M. (1949). "An experimental study of the effects of cooperation and competition upon group process." *Human Relations* 2 (August): 199–231.

De Zonia, R. H. (1958). "The relationship between psychological distance and effective task performance." Unpublished Ph.D. dissertation, College of Education, University of Illinois.

Domey, R. G., et al. (1964). "Taxonomies and correlates of physique." *Psychological Bulletin* 62: 411–426.

Donnelly, P. (1976). "A study of need for stimulation and its relationship to sport involvement and childhood environment variables." Unpublished M.A. thesis, University of Massachusetts.

Eisman, B. (1959). "Some operational measures of cohesiveness and their correlations." *Human Relations* 12 (April): 183–189.

Eitzen, D. S. (1973). "The effect of group structure on the success of athletic teams." *International Review of Sport Sociology* 8: 7–17.

Elias, N., and E. Dunning (1966). "Dynamics of group sports with special reference to football." *British Journal of Sociology* **7**: 388–402. Used with permission of Routledge & Kegan Paul Ltd.

Elliott, T. L. (1969). "A determination and comparison of the values of various student groups, secondary business teachers and businessmen." Unpublished Ed.D. dissertation, Colorado State College.

Emerson, R. M. (1966). "Mount Everest: A case study of communication feedback and sustained group goal-striving." *Sociometry* **29**: 213–227.

Enoch, J., and S. McLemore (1967). "On the meaning of group cohesion." *Southwestern Social Science Quarterly* **48** (September): 174–182.

Essing, W. (1970). "Team line-up and team achievement in European football." In G. S. Kenyon and T. M. Grogg (eds.), *Contemporary Psychology of Sport*, pp. 349–354. Chicago: Athletic Institute.

Etzioni, A. (1965). "Dual leadership in complex organizations." *American Sociological Review* **30**: 688–698.

Feldman, R. (1968). "Interrelationships among three bases of group integration." *Sociometry* **31** (March): 30–46.

Festinger, L. (1950). "Informal social communication." *Psychological Review* **57**: 271–282.

Fiedler, F. E. (1954). "Assumed similarity measures as predictors of team effectiveness." *Journal of Abnormal and Social Psychology* **49**: 381–388.

Fiedler, F. E. (1967). *A Theory of Leadership Effectiveness*. New York: McGraw-Hill.

Fiedler, F. E. (1971a). "Leadership." Morristown, N.J.: General Learning Press.

Fiedler, F. E. (1971b). "Validation and extension of the contingency model of leadership effectiveness: A review of empirical findings." *Psychological Bulletin* **76**: 128–148.

Fiedler, F. E. (1973). "The contingency model—a reply to Ashour." *Organizational Behavior and Human Performance* **9**: 356–368.

Fiedler, F., et al. (1952). *The Relationship of Interpersonal Perception to Effectiveness in Basketball Teams*. Urbana, Ill.: Bureau of Records and Service, University of Illinois.

Gagen, J. J. (1971). "Risk-taking within football situations of selected football coaches." Unpublished M.A. thesis, Kent State University.

Gibb, C. A. (1969). "Leadership." In G. Lindzey and E. Aronson (eds.), *The Handbook of Social Psychology*, 2nd ed., Vol. 4, pp. 205–282. Reading Mass.: Addison-Wesley.

Glueck, S., and E. Glueck (1956). *Physique and Delinquency*. New York: Harper.

Goodhart, P., and C. Chataway (1968). *War without Weapons*. London: W. H. Allen.

Grace, H. (1954). "Conformance and performance." *Journal of Social Psychology* **40**: 233–237.

Graen, G. B., et al. (1970). "Contingency model of leadership effectiveness: Antecedent and evidential results." *Psychological Bulletin* **74**: 285–296.

Graham, W. K. (1973). "Leader behavior, esteem for the least preferred co-worker and group performance." *Journal of Social Psychology* **90**: 59–66.

Gross, N., and W. E. Martin (1952). "On group cohesiveness." *American Journal of Sociology* **57**: 546–554.

Hackman, J. R., and C. G. Morris (1975). "Group tasks, group interaction process, and group performance effectiveness: A review and proposed integration." In L. Berkowitz (ed.), *Advances in Experimental Social Psychology*, Vol. 8, pp. 45–99. New York: Academic Press.

Hagstrom, W., and H. C. Selvin (1965). "The dimensions of cohesiveness in small groups." *Sociometry* **28** (March): 30–43.

Halpin, A. W., and B. J. Winer (1952). *The Leadership Behavior of the Airplane Commander*. Columbus: Ohio State University Research Foundation.

Hare, A. P. (1964). "Interpersonal relations in the small group." In R. E. L. Faris (ed.), *Handbook of Modern Sociology*, pp. 217–271. Chicago: Rand McNally.

Haythorn, W. W. (1968). "The composition of groups: A review of the literature." *Acta Psychologica* 28: 97–128.

Heinila, K. (1966). "Notes on the inter-group conflicts in international sport." *International Review of Sport Sociology* 1: 31–40.

Helmreich, R. L., and B. E. Collins (1967). "Situational determinants of affiliative preference under stress." *Journal of Personality and Social Psychology* 6: 79–85.

Hendry, L. B. (1968). "The assessment of personality traits in the coach-swimmer relationship, and a preliminary examination of the 'father-figure' stereotype." *Research Quarterly* 39 (October): 543–551.

Hendry, L. B. (1974). "Human factors in sport systems: Suggested models for analyzing athlete-coach interactions." *Human Factors* 16: 528–544.

Heslin, R. (1964). "Predicting group task effectiveness from member characteristics." *Psychological Bulletin* 62: 248–256.

Husman, B. F. (1969). "Sport and Personality dynamics." In *The 72nd Proceedings of the National College Physical Education Association for Men*, pp. 56–70.

Inkeles, A. (1959). "Personality and social structure." In R. K. Merton, et al. (eds.), *Sociology Today*, pp. 249–276. New York: Basic Books.

Jones, M. B. (1974). "Regressing group on individual effectiveness." *Organizational Behavior in Human Performance* 11: 426–451.

Kammeyer, K. (1967). "Birth order as a research variable." *Social Forces* 46 (September): 71–80.

Kane, J. E. (1964). "Personality and physical ability." *Proceedings of the International Congress of Sports Sciences*, Tokyo.

Kiker, V. L., and A. R. Miller (1967). "Perceptual judgement of physiques as a factor in social image." *Perceptual and Motor Skills* 24: 1013–1014.

Kiviaho, P., and U. Mustikkamaa (1976). "Intragroup conflict in sport audiences intergroup competition: A test of the conflict-integration hypothesis." Paper presented at a Disciplinary Seminar on Sociology of Sport, International Congress of Physical Activity Sciences, Quebec City (July).

Kjeldsen, E. K. (1976). "An investigation of the leadership process in organizationally embedded task groups." Unpublished Ph.D. dissertation, University of Massachusetts.

Klein, M., and G. Christiansen (1969). "Group composition, group structure and group effectiveness of basketball teams." In J. W. Loy and G. S. Kenyon (eds.), *Sport, Culture and Society*, pp. 397–408. New York: Macmillan.

Korman, A. (1971). "On the development of contingency theories of leadership: Some methodological considerations and a possible alternative." Presented at the University of Chicago Graduate School of Business, December.

Krech, D., et al. (eds.) (1962). *Individual in Society*. New York: McGraw-Hill.

Kroll, W. (1967). "Sixteen personality profiles of collegiate wrestlers." *Research Quarterly* 38: 49–57.

Kroll, W. (1970). "Current strategies and problems of personality assessment of athletes." In L. E. Smith (ed.), *Psychology of Motor Learning*, pp. 349–367. Chicago: Athletic Institute.

Kroll, W., and B. R. Carlson (1967). "Discriminant function and hierarchical grouping analysis of karate participants' personality profiles." *Research Quarterly* 38 (October): 405–411.

Kroll, W., and K. H. Petersen (1965). "Personality factor profiles of collegiate football teams." *Research Quarterly* 36 (December): 433–440.

Kroll, W., et al. (1973). "Multivariate analysis of the personality profiles of championship Czechoslovakian athletes." *International Journal of Sport Psychology* 4: 131–147. Used with permission.

Landecker, W. (1955). "Types of integration and their measurement." In P. Lazarsfeld and M. Rosenberg (eds.), *The Language of Social Research*. New York: Free Press.

Landers, D. M. (1972). "The effects of ordinal position and sibling's sex on males sport participation." In A. Taylor and M. Howell (eds.), *Training: Scientific Basis and Application*, pp. 235–241. Springfield, Ill.: Charles C. Thomas.

Landers, D. M. (1974). "Taxonomic considerations in measuring group performance and the analysis of selected group motor performance tasks." In M. G. Wade and R. Martens (eds.), pp. 204–221. *Psychology of Motor Behavior and Sport*. Urbana, Ill.: Human Kinetics.

Landers, D., and T. Crum (1971). "The effect of team success and formal structure on inter-personal relations and cohesiveness of baseball teams." *International Journal of Sport Psychology* 2: 88–95.

Landers, D., and G. Luschen (1974). "Team performance outcome and cohesiveness of competitive co-acting groups." *International Review of Sport Sociology* 9: 57–69.

Larson, L. L., and K. M. Rowland (1973). "Leadership style, stress, and behavior in task performance." *Organizational Behavior and Human Performance* 9: 407–420.

Layman, E. M. (1960). "Contributions of exercise and sports to mental health." In W. R. Johnson (ed.), *Science and Medicine of Exercise and Sports*, pp. 560–599. New York: Harper and Row.

Lefebvre, L. M., and J. D. Cunningham (1977). "The successful football team: Effects of coaching and team cohesiveness." *International Journal of Sport Psychology* 8: 29–41.

Lenk, H. (1969). "Top performance despite internal conflict: An antithesis to a functionalistic proposition." In J. W. Loy and G. S. Kenyon (eds.), *Sport, Culture and Society*, pp. 393–397. New York: Macmillan.

Lenk, H. (1977a). "Authoritarian or democratic style of coaching?" In H. Lenk (ed.), *Team Dynamics*, pp. 81–89. Champaign, Ill.: Stipes. Used with permission.

Lenk, H. (ed.) (1977b). *Team Dynamics*. Champaign, Ill.: Stipes.

Lester, J. T. (1969). "Stress on Mount Everest." *Psychology Today* 3 (September): 30–32, 62.

Lewin, K., R. Lippitt, and R. K. White (1939). "Patterns of aggressive behavior in experimentally created social climates." *Journal of Social Psychology* 10: 271–299.

Lippett, R., and R. K. White (1943). "The 'social climate' of children's groups." In R. G. Barker et al. (eds.), *Child Behavior and Development*, pp. 485–508. New York: McGraw-Hill.

Longmuir, C. E. (1972). "Perceived and actual dogmatism in high school athletes and coaches." Unpublished Ph.D. dissertation, University of New Mexico.

Longstreth, L. E. (1970). "Birth order and avoidance of dangerous activities." *Developmental Psychology* 2: 154.

Lott, A., and B. Lott (1965). "Group cohesiveness as interpersonal attraction: A review of relationships with antecedent and consequent variables." *Psychological Bulletin* 64 (October): 259–309.

Lowe, R. (1973). "A new look at the relationship between arousal and performance." Unpublished Ph.D. dissertation, University of Illinois.

Loy, J. W. (1968). "Sociopsychological attributes associated with the early adoption of a sport innovation." *Journal of Psychology* 70: 141–147

Loy, J. W. (1969). "Social psychological characteristics of innovators." *American Sociological Review* 34 (February): 73–82.

Loy, J. W., and P. Donnelly (1976). "Need for stimulation as a factor in sport involvement." In T. T. Craig (ed.), *The Humanistic and Mental Health Aspects of Sports, Exercise and Recreation*, pp. 80–89. Chicago: American Medical Association.

Loy, P. (1972). "Cohesiveness as interpersonal and instrumental attraction." Unpublished M.A. thesis, University of New Hampshire.

Luschen, G. (1969). "Small group research and the group in sport." In G. S. Kenyon (ed.), *Aspects of Contemporary Sport Psychology*, pp. 57–75. Chicago: Athletic Institute.

Luschen, G. (1970). "Cooperation, association, and contest." *Journal of Conflict Resolution* 4: 21–34.

Magill, R. (ed.) (1978). *Children and Youth in Sport: A Contemporary Anthology*. Champaign, Ill.: Human Kinetics Publishers.

Mann, R. D. (1959). "A review of the relationships between personality and performance in small groups." *Psychological Bulletin* 56: 241–270.

Mann, R. D. (1961). "Dimensions of individual performance in small groups under task and social-emotional conditions." *Journal of Abnormal and Social Psychology* 62: 674–682.

Martens, R. (1970). "Influence of participation motivation on success and satisfaction in team performance." *Research Quarterly* 41: 510–518.

Martens, R. (1971). "The influence of success and residential affiliation on participation motivation." *Journal of Leisure Research* 3 (Winter): 53–58.

Martens, R. (1975). *Social Psychology and Physical Activity*. New York: Harper and Row.

Martens, R. (1976a). "Competition: In need of a theory." In D. M. Landers (ed.), *Social Problems in Athletics*, pp. 9–17. Urbana, Ill.: University of Illinois Press.

Martens, R. (1976b). "Competitiveness in sport." Presented at the International Congress of Physical Activity Sciences, Quebec City (July 13).

Martens, R. (1976c). "State of the field of sport psychology." Final report prepared for Fitness and Amateur Sport Branch, Department of Health and Welfare, Government of Canada. Used with permission.

Martens, R., and J. A. Peterson (1971). "Group cohesiveness as a determinant of success and member satisfaction in team performance." *International Review of Sport Sociology* 6: 49–61. Used with permission.

McClendon, M. J. (1974). "Interracial contact and the reduction of prejudice." *Sociological Focus* 7 (Fall): 47–65.

McClendon, M. J., and D. S. Eitzen (1975). "Interracial contact on collegiate basketball teams: A test of Sherif's theory of subordinate goals." *Social Science Quarterly* 55: 926–938.

McGrath, J. E. (1962). "The influence of positive interpersonal relations on adjustment and effectiveness in rifle teams." *Journal of Abnormal and Social Psychology* 65: 365–375.

McGrath, J. E. (1964). *Social Psychology: A Brief Introduction*. New York: Holt, Rinehart and Winston. Used with permission.

McIntyre, T. D. (1970a). "A field experimental study of attitude change in four bi-racial small groups." Unpublished Ph.D. dissertation, Pennsylvania State University.

McIntyre, T. D. (1970b). "A field experimental study of attitude change in four bi-racial small sport groups." Presented at the annual meeting of the Canadian Association of Sport Sciences, Quebec City, Canada (October 29).

Mealiea, W., Jr., and F. H. Farley (1971). "Birth order and expressed fear." In *Proceedings of the 79th Annual Convention of the American Psychological Association*. pp. 239–240.

Meggysey, D. (1971). *Out of Their League*. New York: Ramparts Press.

Melnick, M. J., and M. M. Chemers (1974). "Effects of group social structure on the success of basketball teams." *Research Quarterly* 45 (March): 1–8.

Mikalachi, A. (1969). *Group Cohesion Reconsidered*. London, Ontario: School of Business Administration, University of Western Ontario.

Miller, A. R., and R. A. Stewart (1968). "Perception of female physiques." *Perceptual and Motor Skills* 27: 721–722.

Miller, A. R., et al. (1968). "Experimental analysis of physiques as social stimuli: Part II." *Perceptual and Motor Skills* 27: 355–359.

Mills, T. M. (1967). *The Sociology of Small Groups*. Englewood Cliffs, N.J.: Prentice-Hall.

Morgan, W. P. (1974). "Selected psychological considerations in sports." *Research Quarterly* 45: 374.

Mudra, D. E. (1965). "A critical analysis of football coaching practices in light of a selected group of learning principles." Unpublished Ph.D. dissertation, University of Northern Colorado.

Myers, A. E. (1962). "Team competition, success, and the adjustment of group members." *Journal of Abnormal and Social Psychology* 65: 325–332.

Nisbett, R. E. (1968). "Birth order and participation in dangerous sports." *Journal of Personality and Social Psychology* 8: 351–353.

Nixon, H. L. (1974). "An axiomatic theory of team success." *Sport Sociology Bulletin* 3 (Spring): 1–12. Used with permission.

Nixon, H. L. (1976). "Team orientations, interpersonal relations, and team success." *Research Quarterly* 47 (October): 429–435.

Nixon, H. L. (1977). "Cohesiveness and team success: A theoretical reformulation." *Review of Sport and Leisure* 2 (June): 36–57.

Ogilvie, B. C., and T. A. Tutko (1966). *Problem Athletes and How to Handle Them*. London: Pelham Books.

Ogilvie, B. C., and T. A. Tutko (1971). "Sport: If you want to build character, try something else." *Psychology Today* 5 (October): 61–63.

Oglesby, C. (1974). "Social conflict theory and sport organization systems." *Quest* 22: 63–73.

Olmsted, S. (1959). *The Small Group*. New York: Random House.

Parnell, R. W. (1958). *Behavior and Physique*. London: Arnold.

Pease, D. A. (1970). "Player-coach compatibility: A study of the relationship of interpersonal relations orientations to athletic exclusion in junior high school baseball programs." Unpublished Ph.D. dissertation, University of New Mexico.

Penman, K. A., et al. (1974). "Success of the authoritarian coach." *Journal of Social Psychology* 92: 155–156.

Petrie, A. (1967). *Individuality in Pain and Suffering*. Chicago: University of Chicago Press.

Petrie, A., et al. (1962). "The perceptual characteristics of juvenile delinquents." *Journal of Nervous and Mental Disorders* 134: 415–421.

Radloff, R., and R. Helmreich (1969). "Stress: Under the sea." *Psychology Today* 3 (September): 28–29, 59–60.

Ramuz-Nienhuis, W., and A. Van Bergen (1960). "Relations between some components of attraction-to-group: A replication." *Human Relations* 13 (August): 271–277.

Rokeach, M. (1960). *The Open and Closed Mind*. New York: Basic Books.

Roscoe, J. T. (1965). "The construction and application of the polyphasic values inventory." Unpublished Ph.D. dissertation, Colorado State University.

Ruffer, W. A. (1975-1976). "Updated biographies—personality traits of athletes." *Physical Educator*, Part I, 32 (2): 105–109; Part II, 32 (3): 161–165; Part III, 32 (4): 213–217; Part IV, 33 (1): 50–55; Part V, 33 (2): 105–108.

Rushall, B. S. (1970). "An investigation of the relationship between personality variables and performance categories in swimmers." *International Journal of Sport Psychology* 1: 93–104.

Rushall, B. S. (1972). "Three studies relating personality variables to football performance." *International Journal of Sport Psychology* 3: 12–24.

Ryan, E. D., and R. Foster (1967). "Athletic participation and perceptual reduction and augmentation." *Journal of Personality and Social Psychology* 6: 472–476.

Sage, G. H. (1972a). "An assessment of personality profiles between and within intercollegiate athletes from eight different sports." *Sportwissenschaft* 2: 408–415.

Sage, G. H. (1972b). "Machiavellianism among college and high school coaches." In *75th Proceedings of the National College Physical Education Association for Men.* pp. 45–60.

Sage, G. H. (1972c). "Value orientations of American college coaches compared to male college students and businessmen." In *75th Annual Proceedings of the National College Physical Education Association for Men.* pp. 174–186.

Sage, G. H. (1973). "The coach as management: Organizational leadership in American sport." *Quest* 19 (January): 35–40.

Sage, G. H. (1975a). "An occupational analysis of the college coach." In D. W. Ball and J. W. Loy (eds.), *Sport and Social Order: Contributions to the Sociology of Sport*, pp. 391–455. Reading, Mass.: Addison-Wesley.

Sage, G. H. (1975b). "Socialization of coaches: Antecedents to coaches' beliefs and behaviors." In *Proceedings of the 78th Annual Meeting of the National College Physical Education Association for Men*, pp. 124–132.

Sales, S. M. (1971). "Need for stimulation as a factor in social behavior." *Journal of Personality and Social Psychology* 19: 124–134.

Sales, S. M. (1972). "Need for stimulation as a factor in preferences for different stimuli." *Journal of Personality Assessment* 36: 55–61.

Sales, S. M., and W. F. Throop (1972). "Relationship between kinesthetic after-effects and strength of the nervous system." *Psychophysiology* 9: 492–497.

Sales, S. M. et al. (1974). "Relationship between strength of the nervous system and need for stimulation." *Journal of Personality and Social Psychology* 29: 16–22. (Copyright 1974 by the American Psychological Association. Reprinted by permission.)

Sampson, E. E. (1965). "The study of ordinal position: Antecedents and outcomes." In B. Mahzer (ed.), *Progress in Experimental Personality Research*, Vol. 2, pp. 175–228. New York: Academic Press.

Scanlan, T. K. (1974). "Antecedents of competitiveness." In M. G. Wade and R. Martens (eds.), *Psychology of Motor Behavior and Sport*, pp. 171–194. Champaign, Ill.: Human Kinetics Publishers. Used with permission.

Schachter, S. (1959). *The Psychology of Affiliation*. Stanford, Calif.: Stanford University Press.

Schafer, W. E. (1966). "The social structure of sport groups." Presented at the First International Symposium on the Sociology of Sport, Koln, West Germany, April 15–16.

Scott, J. (1971). *The Athletic Revolution*. New York: The Free Press.

Shaw, M. E. (1971). *Group Dynamics*. New York: McGraw-Hill.

Sheldon, W. H. (1942). *The Varieties of Temperament*. New York: Harper.

Sheldon, W. H. (1949). *Varieties of Delinquent Youth*. New York: Harper.

Sherif, C. W. (1973). "Intergroup conflict and competition: Social psychological analysis." *Sportwissenschaft* 3: 138–153.

Shiflett, S. C. (1973). "The contingency model of leadership effectiveness: Some implications of its statistical and methodological properties." *Behavioral Science* **18** (November): 429–440.

Simmel, G. (1955). *Conflict*. Translated by K. H. Wolff. Glencoe, Ill.: The Free Press.

Slater, P. E. (1955). "Role differentiation in small groups." *American Sociological Review* **20**: 300–310.

Slepicka, P. (1975). "Interpersonal behavior and sports group effectiveness." *International Journal of Sport Psychology* **6**: 14–27.

Sletto, R. F. (1932). "Sibling position and juvenile delinquency." *American Journal of Sociology* **39**: 657–669.

Smith, G. (1968). "An analysis of the concept of group cohesion in a simulated athletic setting." Unpublished M.A. thesis, University of Western Ontario, London, Canada.

Snyder, E. E. (1975). "Athletic team involvement, educational plans, and the coach-player relationship." *Adolescence* **10** (Summer): 191–200.

Staffieri, J. R. (1967). "A study of social stereotype of body image in children." *Journal of Personality and Social Psychology* **7**: 101–104.

Steiner, I. D. (1972). *Group Process and Productivity*. New York: Academic Press.

Stogdill, R. M. (1948). "Personal factors associated with leadership: A survey of the literature." *Journal of Psychology* **25**: 35–71.

Stogdill, R. M. (1963). *Team Achievement Under High Motivation*. Columbus: Bureau of Business Research, College of Commerce and Administration, Ohio State University.

Stone, G. P. (1966). "Begriffliche Probleme in der Kleingruppenforschung" (Conceptual Problems in Small Group Research). In G. Luschen (ed.), *Kleingruppenforschung und Gruppe im Sport*. Koln: Westdeutscher Verlag.

Straub, W. F. (1971). "Personality traits of college football players who participated at different levels of competition." *International Journal of Sport Psychology* **2**: 33–41.

Sugerman, A. A., and F. Haronian (1964). "Body type and sophistication of body concept." *Journal of Personality* **32**: 380–394.

Sutton-Smith, B., and B. G. Rosenberg (1970). *The Sibling*. New York: Holt, Rinehart and Winston.

Swartz, J. L. (1973). "Analysis of leadership styles of college level head football coaches from five midwestern states." Unpublished Ph.D. dissertation, University of Northern Colorado.

Tamasne, F. (1976). "Study on favored sociological and sociopsychological factors influencing performance of athletic teams in rowing." *International Review of Sport Sociology* **4**: 17–32.

Tanner, J. M. (1964). *The Physique of the Olympic Athlete*. London: Allen and Unwin.

Taylor, F. W. (1911). *The Principles of Scientific Management*. New York: Harper.

Teglovic, S. (1968). "American college student values: A normative study." Unpublished Ph.D. dissertation, Colorado State University.

Tharp, R. G., and R. Gallimore (1976). "What a coach can teach a teacher." *Psychology Today* **9** (January): 75–78.

Torrance, E. P. (1954). "A psychological study of American jet aces." Presented at the Annual Meeting of the Western Psychological Association, Long Beach, California.

Trapp, W. G. (1953). "A study of social integration in a college football squad." In *Proceedings of the 56th Annual Meeting of the College Physical Education Association*, pp. 139–141. Washington, D.C.

Tutko, T. A., and J. W. Richards (1971). *Psychology of Coaching*. Boston: Allyn and Bacon.

Van Bergen, A., and J. Koekebakker (1959). "Group cohesiveness in laboratory experiments." *Acta Psychologica* 16: 81–98.

Vander Velden, L. (1971). "Relationships among member, team, and situational variables and basketball team success: A social-psychological inquiry." Unpublished Ph.D. dissertation, University of Wisconsin. Used with permission.

Vando, A. (1969). "A personality dimension related to pain tolerance." Unpublished Ph.D. dissertation, Columbia University.

Vanek, M., and B. J. Cratty (1970). *Psychology of the Superior Athlete.* New York: Macmillan.

Veit, H. (1973). "Interpersonal relations and the effectiveness of ball game tennis." In *Proceedings of the Third International Congress of Sport Psychology.* Madrid: Instituto Nacional de Educacion Fisicay Deportes.

Verba, S. (1961). *Small Groups and Political Behavior.* Princeton, N.J.: Princeton University Press.

Vos, K., and W. Brinkman (1967). "Success en Cohesie in Sportgroepen." *Sociologiesche Gids* 14: 30–40.

Walker, R. N. (1962). "Body build and behavior in young children." *Child Development Monograph* 33: 75–79.

Walker, R. N. (1963). "Body build and behavior in young children." *Child Development Monograph* 34: 1–23.

Walsh, J. M., and A. V. Carron (1977). "Attributes of volunteer coaches." Presented at the Annual Meeting of the Canadian Association of Sport Sciences, Winnipeg, Spetember 28–October 1.

Walsh, M. (1976). "Need for stimulation among private secondary school sport groups." Unpublished paper, Department of Sport Studies, University of Massachusetts.

Walters, C. E. (1955). "A sociometric study of motivated and nonmotivated bowling groups." *Research Quarterly* 26: 107–112.

Warren, J. R. (1966). "Birth order and social behavior." *Psychological Bulletin* 65: 38–49.

Wells, W. D., and B. Siegel (1961). "Stereotyped somatotypes." *Psychological Reports* 8: 77–78.

Widmeyer, W. N. (1977). "When cohesiveness predicts performance outcome in sport." Unpublished Ph.D. dissertation, University of Illinois. Used with permission.

Yiannakis, A. (1976). "Birth order and preference for dangerous sports among males." *Research Quarterly* 47 (March): 62–67.

Zander, A. (1971). *Motives and Goals in Groups.* New York: Academic Press.

Zander, A. (1974). "Team spirit vs. the individual achiever." *Psychology Today* 8 (November): 65, 67, 68.

Zander, A. (1975). "Motivation and performance of sport groups." In D. M. Landers et al. (eds.), *Psychology of Sport and Motor Behavior II,* pp. 25–39. Penn State HPER Series, No. 10. Pennsylvania State University.

Zelditch, M. (1955). "Role differentiation in the nuclear family: a comparative study." In T. Parsons et al. (eds.), *Family, Socialization and Interaction Process,* pp. 307–351. Glencoe, Ill.: The Free Press.

Zeleny, L. (1939). "Sociometry of morale." *American Sociological Review* 4 (December): 799–808.

Zetterberg, H. L. (1966). *On Theory Verification in Sociology,* 3rd ed. Totowa, N.J.: Bedminster Press.

Chapter 4
SPORT
ORGANIZATIONS

4.1 INTRODUCTION

The study of formal and complex social organizations has long attracted the interest of sociologists. Moreover, "with each passing year the likelihood becomes greater that this area of social inquiry can be described by linked propositions, analytical models, and statements carrying high probabilities" (Caplow, 1964). Sociological analysis of formal organizations can be readily justified on the grounds that such social systems are a fundamental part of modern life, affecting the social behavior of every member of society at every stage of his or her life cycle. The very ubiquity of formal organizations, then, is reason enough to merit the attention of sociologists, whose research has contributed to an understanding of their basic structures and processes (see Blau, 1974; Blau and Scott, 1962; Caplow, 1964; Dornbusch and Scott, 1975; Etzioni, 1964; Gouldner, 1954; Hall, 1972; March, 1965; Mouzelis, 1968; Perrow, 1970; Scott, 1975; Silverman, 1970; and Tausky, 1970).

4.1.1 Sociological Analysis of Formal Organizations

The sociology of organizations has been specifically cited for its potential contribution to the advancement of the sociological enterprise. For example, Blau and Scott (1962) state that they ". . . consider the study of formal organizations to be capable of making the greatest contributions to the advancement of systematic sociology at this juncture." They offer a four-fold rationale for their somewhat presumptuous, but nevertheless forceful, contention.

First, Blau and Scott (1962) note that there is a growing refusal on the part of students of social organization to be impaled on the horns of the dilemma posed by abstract theorizing without recourse to scientific evidence on the one side, and sterile empiricism devoid of theoretical interpretation on the other.

Second, they argue that formal organizations represent an ideal level of social system analysis. On the one hand, with respect to microsocial systems, study of formal organizations provides opportunities for the examination of a variety of problems of organizational life that ". . . cannot be clarified on the basis of observations of small groups because they simply do not occur in these groups" (Blau and Scott, 1962). On the other hand, with respect to macrosocial systems such as communities or entire societies, formal organizations are smaller and less complex, and thus less complicated to study. More specifically, "in contrast to the communities or societies, formal organizations are characterized by explicit goals, an elaborate system of explicit rules and regulations, and a formal structure with clearly marked lines of communication and authority" (Blau and Scott, 1962).

Third, Blau and Scott point out that formal organizations are especially amenable to comparative analysis and thus relatively controlled social inquiry. "Since the most serious problem in the investigation of social life is to establish causal relations by disentangling the interplay among a large number of social forces, the fact that some of these are relatively fixed in a formal organization and others vary simplifies the analysis" (Blau and Scott, 1962).

Fourth, they argue that in addition to its theoretical significance the study of formal organizations has practical application. For example, Blau and Scott (1962) note that "acquiring knowledge about bureaucractic organizations is an important first step in meeting the threat they pose for democratic institutions."

4.1.2 Sociological Analysis of Sport Organizations

The contention that formal organizations merit the attention of sociologists in part because of their pervasiveness can be extended to the more specific study of sport organizations. Interest in sport is widespread and the intensely expressed concern about the fate of sport teams by participants and nonparticipants alike affords ample justification for studying these organizations.

A more significant rationale from a sociological perspective, however, is that the structural features of sport organizations make them especially suitable social systems for comparative organizational analyses (see, for example, Grusky, 1963a; Ball, 1975). With respect to any given sport and organizational level (e.g., interscholastic, intercollegiate, and professional teams), sport organizations typically possess similar authority structures, are of the same size, have equal technological resources, share common goals, conform to mutual norms, and not only have the roles of each organizational position explicitly prescribed, but replicate positional interrelationships across all teams within an organizational set.

Another characteristic of sport organizations that enhances their utilization in comparative investigation is their set of extensive records and statistics. As Ball observed:

> There are few activities which are as assiduously recorded and publicly recorded as sport. Additionally, much of this public information involves a highly precise and quantitative mode of measurement. Scores, team standings, batting averages, percentage of passes completed are just a few: some measuring league phenomena, some team performance, and others those of individual actors in the drama of sport. (Ball, 1975, p. 43)

The sociological import of the precise and public recordkeeping of sport organizations is two-fold. First, sport records often provide reliable and valid measures of significant sociological processes such as organizational effectiveness and social mobility that are not usually as easily operationalized in other types of organizations (Katz and Klein, 1966). Second, sport records provide comparable measures of critical variables for large numbers of similar organizations for extended periods of time, thus making comparative analyses of a historical nature more feasible (Grusky, 1963b; Eitzen and Yetman, 1972).

A final feature of sport organizations that makes them especially suitable social systems for purposes of comparative organizational analysis is their structural stability. It is often difficult to conduct meaningful longitudinal comparative studies in industrial or educational settings because organizations associated with such settings may rapidly change in size, degree of specialization, level of technology, and even goal orientation. However, sport organizations experience relatively few of these changes. Structural changes are obviously not absent in sport organizations, as evidenced by the recent creation of a new player role in professional baseball: the designated hitter. Still, when compared with other types of formal organizations, sport teams are exceptionally stable in their structural features. This stability tends to increase their analytic utility, since a greater body of standardized data is available for comparative purposes.

Sport organizations generally possess structural characteristics not commonly found among other types of formal organizations, and these special features make them especially amenable to comparative study. Equally important for purposes of analysis, however, is the fact that sport organizations do share some structural features in common with other types of formal organizations, and deal with a number of problems and processes also confronted by other kinds of formal organizations. Illustrations of these problems and processes are given in the following sections of the chapter, including the problems of organizational leadership, composition, and performance.

4.2 ORGANIZATIONAL LEADERSHIP

The following discussion illustrates the interrelationship between organizational structure and organizational process through an analysis of the effects of formal structure on leadership recruitment in sport organizations. This analysis is based largely on a review of studies that have drawn on Grusky's (1963a) theory of formal structure in examining patterns of behavior in sport organizations. Thus, by way of introduction, Grusky's theory is outlined below in terms of its underlying model, theoretical system, and operational system.

4.2.1 Grusky's Theory of Formal Structure

The *rationale* underlying Grusky's model suggests that:

1. "The formal structure of an organization consists of a set of norms which define the system's official objectives, its major offices or positions, and the primary responsibilities of the position's occupants;

2. "This formal structure . . . patterns the behavior of its constituent positions along three interdependent dimensions: (1) spatial location, (2) nature of the tasks, and (3) frequency of interaction; and

3. "This patterning tends to influence the chances of a position's occupant to assume a leadership role in a given organization." (Grusky, 1963a, p. 345)

More specifically, because of the three interdependent dimensions that pattern behavior, two specialized types of organizational positions are differentiated: high interaction positions and low interaction positions. Grusky argues that the occupancy of one or the other type of position influences the kind of role skills that are acquired, and thereby influences the chances for moving into a leadership position in an organization.

The formalized theoretical system that may be derived from Grusky's model consists of the following sets of nominal definitions, assumptions, and propositions.

Nominal definitions. The basic concepts associated with Grusky's model are nominally defined as follows:

1. *Central spatial locations:* Positions located close to other positions in a given organization.

2. *Peripheral spatial locations:* Positions located relatively distant from other positions in a given organization.

3. *Independent tasks:* Tasks performed without the necessity of coordination with the activities of other positions.

4. *Dependent tasks:* Tasks that must be coordinated with the activities of other positions.

5. *High interactors:* Occupants of positions in central spatial locations.

6. *Low interactors:* Occupants of positions in peripheral spatial locations.

Assumptions. The major assumptions of Grusky's (1963a) model are that "all else being equal, the more central one's spatial location":

1. "The greater the likelihood dependent or coordinative tasks will be performed; and,

2. "The greater the rate of interaction with the occupants of other positions; also,

3. "Performance of dependent tasks is positively related to frequency of interaction."

Propositions. Grusky's model includes four primary propositions:

1. "Since interaction is positively related to liking, high interactors should be selected more often than low interactors as the most popular and respected members of the organization.

2. "High interactors should be more likely to learn cooperative social skills and

develop a strong commitment to the welfare of the organization [than low interactors].

3. "Low interactors should be more likely to focus on individualistic rather than team values and tend to be psychologically distant or aloof.

4. "High interactors should be selected for executive positions more often than low interactors." (Grusky, 1963a, p. 347)

4.2.2 Effects of Formal Structure on Leadership Recruitment

Baseball

Professional baseball managers. Grusky (1963a) attempted to empirically validate part of his theoretical system by testing the fourth proposition, namely, that "high interactors should be selected for executive positions more often than low interactors." He operationally defined high interactors as catchers and infielders and low interactors as pitchers and outfielders, and formulated the empirical hypothesis that "catchers and infielders are more likely to be recruited as managers than pitchers and outfielders." To test his empirical hypothesis, data were collected from a sample consisting of " . . . the total population of field managers of the sixteen professional baseball teams during the period 1921–1941 and 1951–1958" (Grusky, 1963a). Analysis of this data supported the hypothesis and provided some support for the validity of Grusky's theoretical system. Specifically, he found that for all managers during the two time periods, 76.9 percent were recruited from high interaction positions while only 23.1 percent were recruited from low interaction positions. More particularly, managers most often represented former catchers (26.2 percent), shortstops (14.0 percent), and third basemen (13.1 percent).

Professional baseball umpires. Based on a similar theoretical framework, Breglio (1976) suggested that an opposite pattern may exist for the recruitment of baseball umpires because of the nature of the task. That is, he hypothesized that low interactors would more likely become umpires because of the need to be independent and aloof. He found that of a total population of umpires ($n = 1257$) up to 1970, 656 had been players in the major leagues. More specifically, 67.7 percent of these umpires previously occupied peripheral positions (i.e., outfielders) as players.

High school and college captains and coaches. Loy and Sage (1970) and Loy, Sage, and Ingham (1970) replicated and extended Grusky's study on the basis of data obtained from high school and college baseball teams. Drawing on Grusky's theory of formal structure, they hypothesized that high interactors (i.e., catchers and infielders) are more likely (1) to be selected for official leadership positions (i.e., coaches or team captains), and (2) to be better liked by teammates. Furthermore, those who occupy central positions that involve both dependent and independent tasks (i.e., catchers and pitchers) would be more likely to be perceived as more valuable to an organization than those who occupy central positions requiring only dependent tasks (i.e., infielders) or those who occupy peripheral positions (i.e., outfielders).

In the study of high school players Loy and Sage (1970) found that of the 15 captains and co-captains among the 12 teams, 14 were high interactors (including 6 shortstops, 4 catchers, 3 second basemen, and 1 third baseman). Moreover, catchers and infielders were more likely to be perceived as better liked than pitchers and outfielders, and the pitchers and catchers were perceived to be more valuable than occupants of other positions.

Because of the small sample associated with the replication of Grusky's study at the interscholastic level, Loy, Sage, and Ingham (1970) sent two postcard questionnaires to the head baseball coach of every other college listed in the *Blue Book of College Athletics* (1968–1969) whose enrollment of male students was over 1000. Findings of the investigation indicated that 72 percent of all college baseball coaches were recruited from high interaction positions and that 69 percent of all team captains and co-captains were selected from high interaction positions. Moreover, 39 percent of the most valuable players on intercollegiate baseball teams were pitchers or catchers.

Similar to Grusky's findings in professional baseball that the greatest number of managers were former catchers (that is, 26 percent), within the ranks of intercollegiate baseball the greatest number of team leaders were recruited from the position of catcher (i.e., 27 percent of the coaches and 15 percent of the captains and co-captains). However, in contrast to Grusky's findings that only 6.5 percent of all managers were former pitchers, 23 percent of the college coaches and 12 percent of the college team captains and co-captains were selected from the pitching position.

Football

Although playing positions cannot be as readily classified as central or peripheral in football as they can in baseball, Grusky's theory of formal structure has nevertheless been used with some success in the study of leadership recruitment in both intercollegiate and professional football organizations. With respect to spatial location and positions of high and low interaction, the investigations of leadership recruitment in football have considered centers, guards, quarterbacks, and linebackers as central, and all other positions as peripheral for purposes of analysis.

College captains and coaches. Sage (1974) analyzed the association between playing position and team captaincy within intercollegiate football over a three-year period. He reported that college football teams over the 1970–1972 seasons selected a total of 1212 team captains (594 offensive and 618 defense captains). By the laws of probability, 36 percent of the offensive captains and 27 percent of the defensive captains should have been recruited from central playing positions. However, Sage discovered that 51 percent of the offensive captains (i.e., center, guards, and quarterbacks) and 51 percent of the defensive captains came from central positions (i.e., left, right, and middle linebackers).

On the basis of data contained in the 1975 "press guides" obtained from member institutions of Division I of the NCAA ($n = 136$), Massengale and Farrington (1977) examined the influence of playing position on the recruitment of major college football coaches. They found that 65 percent of all head coaches, 63 percent of assistant head coaches (including offensive and defensive coordinators), but only 49 percent of assistant coaches were recruited from central playing positions. In short, experience as a player at a central position increases the chances of moving into a head coaching position.

Professional coaches. Drawing on the biographical profiles contained in the *Media Information Books* annually prepared by the National Football League, Roland (1977) determined the college and professional playing experience by position of the entire coaching staff of all teams in the NFL from 1970 to 1976. He found that 366 individuals had served in some coaching capacity in professional football during this seven-year period. Of these, 196 had both professional and college playing experience, 170 had only college playing experience, and 9 had no college or professional playing experience. In particular, with respect to college playing experience, Roland reported that nearly 50 percent of his sample of professional coaches were recruited from central playing positions.

Hockey

In what is perhaps the most extensive study to date of the effects of formal structure on leadership recruitment, Roy (1974) examined the relationship between centrality of playing position and occupational mobility in the context of professional hockey. For purposes of analysis, central positions were operationally defined as center and defense, while the positions of goaltender and wings were considered peripheral positions. On the basis of a review of related research, Roy proposed nine theoretical hypotheses and, using both primary and secondary data sources, tested nine related empirical hypotheses in his investigation, including the following two sets of predictions.

First, Roy tested the empirical hypothesis that: "Players occupying the positions of defense and center are more likely than wings and goaltenders to have access to the positions of general manager and coach." In general, findings of the investigation supported the empirical hypothesis in that 66.7 percent of the managers and 74.4 percent of the coaches were recruited from central playing positions.

Second, Roy proposed the theoretical hypothesis that: "Players occupying central positions are more likely than players occupying peripheral positions to be selected for leadership positions at levels of organization other than that of management." He tested the related empirical hypothesis that: "Players occupying the positions of defense and center are more likely than wings and goaltenders to be selected as captain and co-captain." Results of the study indicated that 76.0 percent of the captains and 77.9 percent of the co-captains were selected from central playing positions.

Basketball

Using as a data base the coaching records of 67 coaches who had been professional players in the National Basketball Association between 1946 and 1975, Klonsky (1975) investigated the effects of formal structure on leadership recruitment in basketball. With respect to centrality of playing position, Klonsky contended that forwards occupy the most peripheral playing positions. He further argued that although the position of center in basketball denotes by definition the most central playing position, guards in fact represent the position of greatest centrality because of their high rate of interaction and the performance of dependent and coordinative tasks. The record of previous playing experience for his sample of coaches indicated that 63.5 percent were guards, 28.6 percent were forwards, and 7.9 percent were centers, thereby offering further support for the centrality hypothesis.

4.2.3 A Consideration of "Centrality" in Sport Organizations

In order to assess the usefulness of centrality as a theoretical concept for understanding sport organizations, this section raises some theoretical and methodological issues that must be considered and resolved.

The Problem of Definition

Spatial centrality. Grusky (1963a) explicitly described three interdependent dimensions of formal organizational structure: spatial location, nature of the task, and frequency of interaction. Moreover, he stressed the combination of these three dimensions in order to differentiate between high interactors and low interactors in organizational settings. However, notwithstanding his multidimensional perspective, Grusky primarily focused on the dimension of spatial location. Similarly, other investigators whose work was reviewed above also emphasized the dimension of spatial location by stressing the distinction between central and peripheral playing positions within sport organizations. This emphasis on spatial location denotes what might best be termed *spatial centrality*, which has been defined by Mulder as follows:

> Centrality reflects the extent to which one position is strategically located in relation to other positions in the pattern. The *most central position* in a network is the *position closest to all other positions.* (Mulder, 1963, p. 9)

At first glance this definition seems ideal for the analysis of centrality in sport situations. For example, the pitcher in baseball, the center in basketball, and the quarterback or middle linebacker in football represent the most central position in a network and the position closest to all other positions. However, this definition places too much emphasis on the positional aspect and tends to neglect the dynamic aspect of organizational structure.

Functional centrality. The preceding review of the effects of formal structure on leadership recruitment revealed at least two instances in which the static aspect of centrality (that is, spatial location) did not correlate closely with the dynamic aspect of centrality (that is, nature of the task and frequency of interaction). First, in the case of professional baseball, although the pitcher is the most centrally located field position, Grusky (1963a) defined it as a low interaction position because the pitcher performs largely independent tasks and typically pitches one out of every four games if a regular pitcher or a few innings per game if a relief pitcher. Second, in the case of professional basketball, although the center is the most centrally located playing position, Klonsky (1975) defined it as a low inter-action position because the center does not assist and coordinate plays to the same degree as the guards do.

These anomalies between the dimension of spatial location and the dimensions of type of task and frequency of interaction indicate a need for an emphasis on *functional centrality* rather than spatial centrality. A focus on functional centrality, while not mitigating the importance of spatial location, nevertheless highlights the importance of coordinative tasks and both quantity and quality of interaction. To paraphrase Hopkins (1964), this type of centrality designates how close an individual is to the "center" of the interaction network of a social organization. Thus, it refers simultaneously to the frequency with which an individual participates with other individuals and the number or range of other individuals with whom he or she interacts, as well as the degree to which he or she must coordinate tasks and activities with other individuals. This definition, while incorporating the three interdependent dimensions of Grusky's theory of formal structure, emphasizes the dynamic aspects of centrality and indicates new directions for future research in terms of models, methods, and theories.

The Problem of Model Building

A focus on the dynamic aspects rather than the static aspects of centrality in sport organizations leads to a consideration of other models of formal structure. For example, in the case of baseball, a "line-of-power" model might be as useful in explaining the process of leadership recruitment as Grusky's model is. Specifically, the line-of-power model represents a type of functional centrality for the coach or manager wherein the most critical (i.e., "skilled") positions are sequentially aligned down the center of the field (i.e., catcher, pitcher, second baseman, shortstop, and center fielder). Some support for this model is given by a reanalysis of the Loy, Sage, and Ingham (1970) data in which it was shown that, in terms of Grusky's model, 73.63 percent of college baseball coaches were recruited from positions of high interaction and 28.37 percent from positions of low interaction. Placing the data into a line-of-power model indicates that 81 percent of the coaches were recruited from positions of functional centrality.

As a second example of an alternative model that might be applied to leadership recruitment we note Ball's (1973) "primary-supporting" model of the formal structure of football teams. In brief, within the offensive and defensive units of football teams:

> . . . positions can be differentiated on the basis of task-orientation into primary and supporting positions. The former, the *primary positions*, are those within the organization charged with the basic achievement and realization

Table 4.1
Ball's model of formal structure:
The case of professional football

Primary and supporting positions on offense and defense

	Offense	Defense
Primary	Quarterback* Running backs* Flankers, wide receivers+ Ends+	Tackles Ends Linebackers
Supporting	Center Guards Tackles	Backs Safeties

*Proactive
+Reactive
Adapted from Ball (1973, p. 106).

of the organization's goals. *Supporting positions,* on the other hand, are defined as those responsible for assisting the primary positions in their efforts toward goal-achievement, but not ordinarily directly involved in such accomplishment. (Ball, 1973, p. 105)

A further refinement within the primary offensive positions is the distinction between those that are *proactive* and initiate goal-directed activity and/or carry it out independently, and those that are *reactive* or dependent upon the activities of other primary positions for participation. (Ball, 1973, p. 106)

Ball's operational definitions of primary and supporting positions in football are schematically illustrated in Table 4.1. The import of Ball's model for the investigation of leadership recruitment is indicated by a reanalysis of Roland's (1977) data regarding the college playing positions of professional football coaches. When his data are placed in the context of Ball's model, findings show that 70.6 percent of professional football coaches played at primary positions at the intercollegiate level (50.7 percent at offensive and 19.9 percent at defensive positions), while only 29.3 percent played at supporting positions (25.1 percent at offensive and 4.2 percent at defensive positions). Moreover, Roland's data reveal that among primary offensive positions, 34.4 percent of professional football coaches played at "proactive" positions and only 16.3 percent played at "reactive" positions.

A third model includes the dimensions of *propinquity* and *task dependence* (Chelladurai and Carron, 1977). The propinquity dimension includes the

attributes of (1) *observability,* the extent to which the position affords the knowledge of ongoing action (including locations and movements of other positions) relevant to the accomplishment of the task; and (2) *visibility,* the degree to which a position is seen and watched by other positions on the playing field including the opponents. (Chelladurai and Carron, 1977, p. 14)

Thus, a more propinquitous position would have greater observability and visibility and would enable the occupant to obtain greater knowledge, authority, and prestige. The task dimension refers to the level of performance interaction with others in the required tasks.

The authors hypothesized that the two dimensions interacted to create four categories of positions that have greater or lesser amounts of actual and ascribed status, prestige, and importance. Thus, in order of decreasing rank, the following types of positions were denoted: (1) high propinquity and high dependence, (2) low propinquity and high dependence, (3) high propinquity and low dependence, and (4) low propinquity and low dependence. The authors noted as a caveat that "the relative level of task dependence and/or propinquity in a specific situation will vary as a result of external factors such as coaching decisions relating to strategy" (Chelladurai and Carron, 1977, p. 12). As an example, they cite the difference between a zone and a man-to-man defense in football: In the former a defensive back would be high in task dependence, while in the latter the position would be low in dependence (that is, independent).

In order to illustrate this model, Chelladurai and Carron (1977) combined the two intermediate categories into one and reanalyzed the data on baseball and football that were reported in the earlier studies by Grusky (1963a), Loy, Sage, and Ingham (1970), and Ball (1973). In both baseball (see Fig. 4.1) and football, they found support for the propinquity-task dependence model.

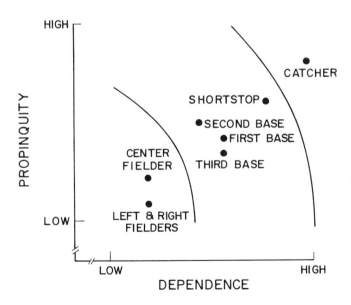

Fig. 4.1 *Categorization of baseball positions on the basis of the interaction of propinquity and task dependence. (From Chelladurai and Carron, 1977, p. 12)*

The Problem of Methodology

An emphasis on the dynamic rather than the static aspect of formal structure demands a different approach to research design in future studies of the effects of formal structure on leadership recruitment in sport organizations. As indicated by the above review of research, most studies of the relationship between playing position and occupational mobility have utilized secondary data sources for their analyses. These sources are adequate for determining the spatial location of playing positions but seldom permit adequate assessment of the types of tasks and rates of interaction associated with particular playing positions.

Accordingly, future investigators who direct their attention to the dynamic aspects of formal structure will have to conduct their studies in field settings in order to obtain objective measures of task coordination, rates and range of interaction, acquisition of specific role skills, degree of interpersonal attraction, etc. Such studies will require more precise methods of instrumentation, as, for example, using a battery-operated interaction process recorder to record the range and rate of interaction among players in a field situation. These kinds of studies will also require more complex and dynamic forms of theory construction.

The Problem of Theory Construction

With respect to what we have termed spatial centrality, Mulder (1963) has written that "the *topological* structure, characterized by invariability, determines which behavior is *possible*; *dynamic* variables, however, determine which behavior will *actually* happen." The first step toward the development of a theory of functional centrality, which emphasizes dynamic rather than static variables, is to order psychosociological propositions by means of inventories of determinants (independent variables) and results (dependent variables) (see Zetterberg, 1965, pp. 87–100). The second step in theory construction is to incorporate sets of psychosociological propositions into theories of centrality. These theories may take one or more of the forms of theory construction described in Chapter 2 (see Section 2.3.1). In order to illustrate the types of dynamic variables and problems of theory construction associated with centrality, examples of the three forms of theory are given below.

Set-of-laws form of theory. Explicit examples of lawlike statements about centrality are given in Hopkins's (1964) analysis of the exercise of influence in small groups in which he develops a systematic model of centrality focused on five variables interrelated in a set of fifteen propositions. For example, Hopkins (1964) states that: "For any member of a small group, the greater his centrality, then the greater his (a) observability, (b) conformity, (c) influence, and the higher his (d) rank."

Axiomatic form of theory. Various combinations of the theoretical propositions proposed by Hopkins can be set forth in a form that suggests an axiomatic theory. For example:

> *Axiom I:*   If centrality, then influence.

Axiom II: If influence, then rank.

Theorem A: Therefore, the greater the degree of centrality, the higher the rank.

It must be noted, however, that such a systematic set of propositions does not constitute a true axiomatic theory since any one of the three propositions can be derived from the other two. "The order in which the propositions are written does not, so to speak, make any difference. But in a real explanation at least one of the propositions cannot be derived from the others" (Homans, 1969).

Causal process form of theory.   Although Hopkins's set of theoretical propositions does not permit the formulation of true hypothetical-deductive theories, it does nevertheless allow the formulation of sets of sequential propositions that can be incorporated into a causal process form of theory, which was schematically illustrated in Fig. 2.1.

The most complete transformation of Hopkins's set of propositions into a causal process form of theory has been made by Blalock (1969) and is diagrammatically described in Fig. 4.2. The causal models displayed in Figs. 2.1 and 4.2 reveal the complexity of relations associated with the analysis of centrality in sport situations. In short, it may be exceedingly difficult to sort out the several reciprocal relations and to assess the relative influence of the many "feedback processes" underlying the sets of dynamic variables related to centrality. For example, if one were to examine the relationship between centrality and influence while taking into account only the factors of conformity and observability, one would have to entertain four possible "causal paths" (see Fig. 4.2).

In summary, while the illustration presented here may dishearten some individuals interested in constructing significant and testable theories of centrality, the development of dynamic models of behavior in sport organizations is within the realm of possibility (see Blalock, 1969; Stinchcombe, 1968).

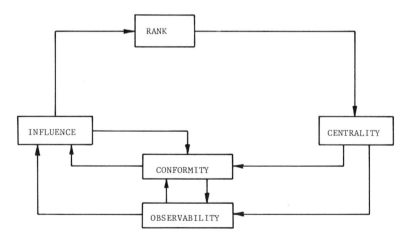

Fig. 4.2 *A causal model for Hopkins's axioms. (From Blalock, 1969, p. 22, as adapted from Hopkins, 1964, p. 52)*

4.3 ORGANIZATIONAL STRUCTURE AND COMPOSITION

4.3.1 Introduction

It is evident from the preceding discussion of the effects of formal structure on leadership recruitment that social systems of sport are characterized by a high degree of social differentiation. This social differentiation is indicated clearly by the specific roles and responsibilities that occupants of particular positions within given sport organizations fulfill. Moreover, this social differentiation often represents a type of social stratification.

Social Stratification in Sport Organizations

A detailed analysis of the nature of social stratification and its relation to sport involvement is presented in Chapter 9. However, the underlying processes of social stratification in sport organizations may be summarized as follows:

1. All social systems require a division of labor which results in role differentiation.

2. Differential roles characteristic of the occupants of particular positions within given social systems are typically ranked according to one or more criteria.

3. The rank order of positional roles in a social system are generally evaluated in terms of social worth on the basis of their perceived prestige, preferability, and popularity, and assigned an overall social status.

4. Statuses are differentially rewarded in terms of property, power, and psychic gratification, and the inequalities associated with this rewarding influence an individual's life chances and life style.

The processes of stratification just described are associated with all forms of social stratification, including those based on age, class, ethnic, racial, and sex (gender) statuses, which are found in sport organizations.

Social Discrimination in Sport Organizations

A major consequence of social stratification in sport organizations is the resulting social inequalities between and among selected social statuses. For example, in the context of professional sport, "rookies" normally receive a lower annual average salary than "veterans," female golfers compete for smaller amounts of prize money than male golfers, and blacks do not have the same opportunities as whites for leadership positions in sport. Sometimes such inequalities are relatively justified, as in the case of a salary differential based on objective criteria of playing ability and experience. At other times, however, such inequalities are unjust—for example, the exclusion of individuals from participation on the basis of characteristics such as age, race, or sex. This exclusion, of course, constitutes discrimination.

Broadly conceived, *discrimination* ". . . denotes the unfavorable treatment of categories of persons on arbitrary grounds" (Moore, 1964). A major mode of discrimination involves *segregation*, when certain categories of persons are excluded "from specific social organizations or particular positions within organizations on arbitrary grounds, that is, grounds which have no objective relation to individual skill and talent" (Loy and McElvogue, 1970).

Throughout history sport has been characterized by segregation. Moreover, segregation remains a feature of modern sport: the exclusion of blacks from participation in sport with whites in South Africa, the exclusion of females from participation in contact sports with males in North America, and the exclusion of professionals from participation in numerous contests with amateurs in all parts of the world.

A special form of segregation in sport, especially evident in professional sports in North America, is what has been termed "stacking" (see McPherson, 1974, 1976a). Generally defined, ". . . *stacking* in sport involves assignment to a playing position, an achieved status, on the basis of an ascribed status" (Ball, 1973). The term was first used in reference to black athletes who were allegedly assigned to particular playing positions in sport organizations on the basis of particularistic rather than universalistic criteria (see Edwards, 1969; Meggesey, 1970; Olsen, 1968). However, the phenomenon of stacking is not restricted to the case of the black athlete (Ball, 1973), since members of a number of social categories have been shown to be differentially allocated to particular playing positions.

Ethnic Stratification in Sport Organizations

As indicated in the studies reviewed below, it is often difficult to determine whether the marked presence of members of specific ethnic groups at particular playing positions results from discriminatory practices per se. Thus, we use the more neutral term *ethnic stratification*, and analyze "structural segregation" in somewhat broader terms than those of stacking. Specifically, the percentage of particular ethnic groups represented at playing positions, ability levels, and leadership roles is examined within professional baseball, basketball, football, and hockey organizations.[1]

4.3.2 Patterns of Organizational Integration in Sport

Playing Personnel

Baseball. Although major league professional baseball made the initial attempt at integration over 30 years ago with the recruitment of Jackie Robinson (see Dodson, 1954), substantial organizational integration of both black and Latin American players has been a slow process. For example, 10 years after the "color line" was broken by Robinson, there were only 12 black and 2 Latin American players in the National League, while 15 years after the significant but nevertheless token integration of Robinson, there were only 6 black and 7 Latin American players in the American League (Loy and McElvogue, 1970).

As indicated in Table 4.2, the overall organizational integration of black and Latin American players into major league baseball has followed a very orderly

Table 4.2

Distribution of white, black, and Latin American players in major league
professional baseball, 1960–1975

Year	Total number of players	White players		Black players		Latin players	
		n	%	n	%	n	%
1975	295	176	59.66	81	27.46	38	12.88
1974	283	162	57.24	82	28.98	39	13.78
1973	282	163	57.80	76	26.95	43	15.25
1972	270	155	57.41	72	26.67	43	15.93
1971	281	168	59.79	69	24.56	44	15.66
1970	290	169	58.28	72	24.83	49	16.90
1969	301	185	61.46	68	22.59	48	15.95
1968	243	144	59.26	59	24.28	40	16.46
1967	225	132	58.67	55	24.44	38	16.89
1966	—	—	—	—	—	34	—
1965	230	150	65.22	47	20.43	33	14.35
1964	234	151	64.53	49	20.94	34	14.53
1963	232	163	70.26	42	18.10	27	11.64
1962	—	—	—	—	—	25	—
1961	203	145	71.43	34	16.75	24	11.82
1960	181	138	76.24	25	13.81	18*	9.94

*The number of Latin American players increased from 4 in 1950, to 11 in 1955, to 15 in 1959.
Adapted from McElvogue (1969) and Henderson (1975).

stepwise progression from 1960 to 1975. The greatest degree of integration of
Latin American players occurred in 1970 when 49 Latin American athletes held
starting positions and represented 17 percent of active playing personnel. The
greatest degree of integration of black players occurred in 1974 when 82 black
athletes held starting positions, representing 29 percent of the active playing
personnel.

Football. Like baseball organizations, football teams have been and remain
stratified along ethnic lines. Also similar to baseball teams, football organizations
did not achieve substantial organizational integration until after the mid-1960s
and did so in a very orderly progression. For example, in the case of intercollegiate football, although black athletes were playing on predominantly white
college teams before the turn of the century, the Southeastern Conference did not
become integrated until 1967 when two black athletes played for Kentucky and
one black athlete played for Tennessee (Schrag, 1970). However, ten years later
33 percent ($n = 81$) of the starting football players at the ten Southeastern Conference schools were black athletes (Caruso, 1976).

In American major league professional football, the figures for black athletes
were 12 percent in 1960, 19 percent in 1964, 28 percent in 1968, and 40 percent in
1971 (Eitzen and Sanford, 1975), and by 1976 42 percent of the players in the
National Football League were black (see "The black dominance," *Time*, 9 May

Table 4.3
Distribution of blacks in the Canadian Football League, 1954–1969

Year	Number of blacks	Year	Number of blacks
1954	14	1962	36
1955	12	1963	43
1956	15	1964	49
1957	24	1965	44
1958	25	1966	47
1959	32	1967	45
1960	32	1968	42
1961	37	1969	50

From G. Smith and C. Grindstaff, "Race and sport in Canada." In A. Taylor and M. Howell (eds.), *Training: Scientific Basis and Applications*, 1972. Courtesy of Charles C Thomas, Publisher, Springfield, Illinois.

1977, p. 57). As shown in Table 4.3, a similar pattern of increasing integration occurred in the Canadian Football League.

Basketball. Among professional sports, basketball has achieved the highest degree of organizational integration. For example, in 1977 nearly two-thirds of the players in the National Basketball Association (NBA) were black. However, notwithstanding the fact that organizational integration of the NBA is now substantial, the data given in Table 4.4 indicate that the pattern of integration during the past 25 years is similar to that previously shown for other professional sports.

Historically considered, the changing racial composition of intercollegiate basketball teams has paralleled that of professional basketball teams. To illustrate, by 1970 nearly 80 percent of the NCAA teams were integrated and more than a quarter of the college players were black athletes. "The percentage composition of black players on college teams is even more striking when, according to the *Chronicle of Education* (October 4, 1971), blacks comprised only 6.9 percent of undergraduate students in 1970 and that nearly half (44 percent) attended predominantly black institutions" (Yetman and Eitzen, 1972).

Hockey. In professional hockey, patterns of ethnic stratification are largely based on forms of social differentiation between Anglophone (English-speaking) and Francophone (French-speaking) players. The former category represents high ethnic status, while the latter category represents lower ethnic status in Canadian society.

Table 4.5 reveals that the organizational integration of Francophones in the National Hockey League closely parallels that in other professional sports. An important difference, however, is revealed when comparisons are made between the percentage of given ethnic groups in professional sport relative to their percentage in the national population. Specifically, in American professional baseball, basketball, and football, black athletes are overrepresented when compared with their proportional membership in the general population of the United

Table 4.4

Racial composition of professional basketball teams, 1954–1973*

	Year	No. of teams	No. of black players	Black players as percentage of total	Percentage of teams with blacks	Average no. of blacks per team
NBA	1954	9	4	4.6	44 (4)	0.4
	1958	8	11	11.8	87 (7)	1.3
	1962	9	34	30.4	100 (9)	3.8
	1966	9	57	50.9	100 (9)	6.3
	1970	14	94	54.3	100 (14)	6.7
	1973	17	140	64.5	100 (17)	8.2
ABA	1970	11	80	57.3	100 (11)	7.3
	1973	10	80	62.0	100 (10)	8.0

*Data for the years 1954, 1958, 1962, 1966, and 1970 were compiled by N.R. Yetman and D.S. Eitzen and reported in their article "Black Americans in sports: Unequal opportunity for equal ability," *Civil Rights Digest* (August 1972): 21–34. Leonard and Schmidt (1975, p. 30).

Table 4.5
Distribution of Francophones and Anglophones in the
National Hockey League, 1949–1950 to 1972–1973

Years	Francophones		Anglophones		All players	
	n	%	n	%	n	%
1949–1954	60	9.4	578	90.6	638	100.0
1955–1960	115	17.6	539	82.4	654	100.0
1961–1966	127	18.9	544	81.1	671	100.0
1967–1972	293	19.1	1240	80.9	1533	100.0

From Roy (1974, p. 76).

States. However, in the case of professional hockey in the context of Canadian society, French Canadians are underrepresented in relation to their proportional membership in the general population (that is, 32.2 percent for the 1951 and 30.0 percent for the 1971 Canadian census).

Leadership Personnel

Baseball. Ethnic stratification also has consequences for the process of leadership recruitment within sport organizations. It was shown in Section 4.2.2 that managers in professional baseball are most often recruited from central playing positions (especially those of catcher and shortstop). It will also be demonstrated in Section 4.3.2 that black athletes most often occupy peripheral playing positions and least often occupy the positions of catcher and shortstop. Thus, it is perhaps not surprising that there are so few blacks and Latin Americans in leadership roles in major league baseball. To illustrate, during the 1977 baseball season there were no minority members on the executive staff of the league offices, no black managers, and only eight black and five Latin American coaches in the two major leagues.

Football. Similarly, in football there is only one black on the executive staff of the National Football League and although there are a few officials and a number of assistant coaches, not a single head coach is black.

Basketball. In view of the substantial degree of organizational integration at the player level, it is perhaps not surprising that when compared with other professional sports, basketball has the greatest number of blacks in decision-making positions at the coaching and management levels. For example, in 1975–1976 the NBA had a black serving as deputy commissioner of the league, two blacks in the position of general manager, and five blacks among its eighteen head coaches. However, a black has not as yet obtained the position of club president within the NBA.

A similar degree of integration of blacks into decision-making roles has been achieved at the collegiate level. For example, Yetman and Eitzen (1972) reported that in 1971 there were only two major colleges that had head basketball coaches who were black, whereas Leonard and Schmidt (1975) found that in 1973 there were approximately 21 black head coaches and 44 black assistant coaches within the NCAA.

Hockey. Since Francophones in hockey are well represented at central positions, they should have access to management positions. However, there were only nine coaches and one general manager with French Canadian backgrounds in the National Hockey League from 1949 to 1973 (Roy, 1974).

An Interpretation of Organizational Integration Patterns

The slow and incomplete stepwise progression for racial groups gaining entry to professional sport may be explained by the presence of three distinct factors. First, it has been suggested that there is unequal opportunity for equal ability. That is, a black athlete must demonstrate greater skill than a white player in order to have an equal chance of being recruited or drafted to a team. For example, based on a sample of 784 major league baseball players, Pascal and Rapping (1972) found that on the average a black player must be better than a white player if he is to have an equal chance of moving into the major leagues. Similarly, Scully (1974) concluded that blacks must outperform whites throughout their careers in order to remain in the major leagues. Finally, Pascal and Rapping (1972) suggest that there are significant "between league" differences in the number of blacks admitted to major league baseball. In short, entrance into professional sport may be more difficult for the black athlete if higher performance expectations are established, especially for sport roles in which a subjective rating on the part of a manager or coach is involved in the decision-making process.

A second factor that has limited the entry of blacks is an alleged quota system whereby each team would have only a predetermined number of blacks on the team or in the starting lineup. Interviews with black athletes (Charnofsky, 1968, p. 45; Olsen, 1968; Smith and Grindstaff, 1972) have in fact suggested that such a system operates in college and professional sport. Because of the lack of empirical data it is difficult to substantiate this charge, other than to note incidences in which stacking occurs. However, there seems to be more recent agreement that a quota system no longer exists, or at least has been relaxed, as evidenced by the appearance of starting lineups comprised entirely of black players.

A third factor accounting for the slow rate of organizational integration results from educational discrimination. Until recently, relatively few blacks were offered athletic scholarships, and hence were denied access to the necessary preprofessional occupational socialization. Thus they were underrepresented at both the college and professional level for many years, especially in basketball and football.

In summary, the slow stepwise progression for organizational integration in sport has been the result of higher entrance and performance requirements, the presence of a quota system, and discrimination in gaining access to college sport teams. However, with increased civil rights legislation, a rapid expansion of sport leagues creating more positions, and an increasing recognition of the superior skills of blacks, management has increasingly created greater opportunities for members of ethnic and racial minority groups in college and professional sport. Unfortunately, despite this social change, there is still great variation within teams, leagues, and sports.

4.3.3 Patterns of Positional Segregation in Sport Organizations

Patterns of Segregation

Baseball. As well as being stratified according to the percentage of ethnic players participating per year in a given league, sport is stratified by the percentage of players from racial or ethnic groups occupying particular field positions. For example, in baseball during the past 20 years white players have been overrepresented at central (i.e., infield) positions, black players have been overrepresented at peripheral (i.e., outfield) positions, and Latin American players have been relatively evenly distributed between central and peripheral playing positions (Dougherty, 1976; Henderson, 1975; Leonard, 1977; Loy and McElvogue, 1970).

More particularly, with respect to central playing positions, white players most predominantly occupy the position of catcher, black players the position of first base, and Latin American players the position of shortstop. Table 4.6 indicates this data pattern for 1974.

It should be noted that pitchers have been excluded from the preceding analyses since researchers have found it difficult to obtain adequate data about them when using secondary source materials for their investigations. However, the relative percentage of white, black, and Latin American pitchers appearing at least once during a season has remained relatively constant over time. For example, in 1969, 88 percent ($n = 351$) of all pitchers were white, 5 percent ($n = 21$) were black, and 7 percent ($n = 26$) were Latin American; similarly, in 1975, 87 percent ($n = 306$) of all pitchers were white, 7 percent ($n = 25$) were black, and 6 percent ($n = 22$) were Latin American (Winfield, 1977). In summary, Leonard (1977) has recently demonstrated that, with or without pitchers included in the analysis, whites are more centrally located than either blacks or Latins, but Latins are more often found in central positions than blacks are.

Football. A striking example of ethnic stratification in football organizations was the relative distribution of black and white athletes by playing position within the American and National Football Leagues in 1968. Specifically, black athletes within offensive teams comprised only 4 percent of the playing personnel at central positions and 34 percent at peripheral positions, and within defensive teams black athletes comprised 8 percent of the playing personnel at central positions and 42 percent at peripheral positions. Moreover, the majority of black athletes occupied defensive (59 percent) rather than offensive (41 percent) playing positions (Loy and McElvogue, 1970).

These patterns of ethnic stratification in professional football in 1968 also held in 1974 as shown in Dougherty's (1976) replication of the Loy and McElvogue study. It is evident that five years later black athletes remained markedly underrepresented at central playing positions, but some degree of rela-

Table 4.6
Distribution of white, black, and Latin American players by position in major league baseball, 1974*

Position	Total number of players	Whites		Blacks		Latins		Percentage blacks vs. whites	Percentage Latins vs. whites	Percentage blacks vs. Latins
		n	%	n	%	n	%			
Catcher	26	22	85	1	4	3	11	4	12	25
Shortstop	25	18	72	0	0	7	28	0	28	0
Second base	29	11	38	7	24	11	38	39	50	38
Third base	24	19	79	4	17	1	4	17	5	80
First base	26	11	42	11	42	4	15	50	27	73
Outfield	78	31	40	34	44	13	17	52	30	72
n and %	208 (100%)	112	54%	57	27%	39	19%	34%	26%	59%

Distribution according to centrality

Position	All players		White players		Black players		Latin players	
	n	%	n	%	n	%	n	%
Central positions	130	62 (100)	81	62	23	18	26	20
Peripheral positions	78	38 (100)	31	39.7	34	43.6	13	16.6
n and %	208	100%	112	54%	57	27%	39	19%

*Based on all starting players, excluding pitchers.
Adapted from Dougherty (1976) and Henderson (1975).

tive change had taken place. Specifically, Dougherty's data show that in 1974, black athletes within offensive teams represented 19 percent of the playing personnel at central positions and 42 percent at peripheral positions, and within defensive teams black athletes represented 10 percent of the playing personnel at central positions and 56 percent at peripheral positions. Interestingly, the percentage of black athletes on offense and defense remained the same over the five-year period (i.e., 41 percent and 59 percent, respectively).

The Loy and McElvogue study of centrality, stacking, and race was also replicated in the context of the Canadian Football League by Ball (1973). Based on data for the 1971 season, Ball found that the distribution in the Canadian league was nearly identical to that obtained by Loy and McElvogue, and later by Dougherty, for the American leagues. Ball (1973) extended earlier investigations of positional occupancy and ethnicity in two ways. First, he examined centrality of position according to national origin (nativity) as well as race. That is, he compared the relative percentage of Canadians and non-Canadians occupying particular positions. Second, he examined positional occupancy with respect to both race and nativity in terms of his alternative primary-supporting positions model of formal structure (see Section 4.2.3). In brief, Ball (1973) found that the centrality model had greater explanatory power in accounting for positional occupancy in the case of race, but the primary-supporting model had greater explanatory power in accounting for positional occupancy in the case of national origin.

Hockey.   In hockey, a basic difference is the fact that "contrary to other professional sports like baseball and football, where the relationship between race or national origin and centrality is strong, the relationship between ethnicity and centrality in professional hockey does not exist" (Roy, 1974).

Alternative Explanations of Positional Segregation and Racial Variations in Sport Organizations

The preceding review of research regarding positional segregation within sport organizations illustrates clearly that black athletes are markedly overrepresented at particular playing positions and often on a comparative basis display a greater degree of athletic ability than white athletes. To date, no thoroughly valid theoretical explanation of the reported structural and behavioral differences between white and black athletes has been set forth. However, several diverse explanations with varying degrees of empirical support have been made. In concluding this account of positional segregation, these explanations are briefly reviewed below.

Biological explanations.   Numerous biologically oriented investigations have found statistically significant differences between selected samples of black and white subjects concerning certain anatomical and physiological parameters. For example, reviews of many of these investigations by Jordan (1969), Malina (1972), and Norman (1968) suggest that blacks in comparison to whites have longer arms, greater hand and forearm length, longer lower legs, shorter trunks, narrower hips, greater muscle mass, greater skeletal weight, wider bones in the upper arm, thigh, and calf, more muscle tissue in the upper arms and thighs, less muscle mass in the calves, a higher degree of mesomorphy, a lower vital lung capacity, and a higher specific gravity.

These racial variations have been cited by some authorities (see Kane, 1971; *Time*, 1977) as the major underlying reasons why blacks are overrepresented or underrepresented in specific sports and at particular playing positions. For example, the anatomical differences in arm and leg length between blacks and whites are held to account for the superiority of blacks over whites in running and jumping events. To illustrate, blacks are predominant in basketball and track and field, and are overrepresented at outfield, defensive back, running back, and wide receiver positions in baseball and football. Similarly, the greater meso-morphy, lower vital lung capacity, and higher specific gravity of blacks over whites is held to account for the underrepresentation of blacks in swimming and endurance events.

A number of criticisms, however, may be made of these biological explana-tions for racial variations in sport situations. First, there is little evidence that a number of the discovered racial differences affect athletic performance. For example, there is little evidence that buoyancy is related to swimming ability.

Second, the reported physical advantages of blacks over whites may offset one another. For example, ". . . the greater weight and density of the Negro skeleton, might possibly offset the advantage suggested by mechanical principles relative to body proportions; further, since strength of muscle is physiologically related to its cross-sectional area, it is difficult to assume that the Negro calf musculature produces more power, enabling him to excell in the sprints and jumps" (Malina, 1972).

Third, most of the reported differences between blacks and whites are *mean* differences and thus do not adequately reflect the wide overlap of characteristics shared between blacks and whites or the wide variation of physical characteristics among blacks or whites.

Fourth, studies of racial variations have seldom been based on adequate samples, especially of top-level athletic performance. Phillips (1976) points out that "any effort to discover whether a given group is better endowed for superior performance must focus on the top one percent or so of the population. . . ." He also outlines the methodological steps that must be taken to establish a "physical endowment theory" of racial superiority and concludes that while "this appears to be a prodigious task, . . . until it is done physical endowment explanations cannot be uncritically accepted" (Phillips, 1976).

Psychological explanations. Numerous psychological explanations have been given to account for racial differences in athletic performance. One that is currently receiving a fair amount of attention is Worthy and Markle's (1970) thesis that whites tend to excell at self-paced activities. "A self-paced activity is one in which the individual responds, when he chooses, to a relatively static or unchanging stimulus," whereas "a reactive activity . . . is one in which the individual must respond appropriately and at the right time to changes in the stimulus situation" (Worthy and Markle, 1970).

To test their thesis, Worthy and Markle examined racial variations in professional baseball and basketball. First, they hypothesized that since pitching is a self-paced activity and hitting is a reactive activity, whites would excel as pitchers and blacks would excel at other positions. In support of this hypothesis, Worthy and Markle show that in major league baseball only 7 percent of the pitchers are black, whereas 24 percent of the nonpitchers are black. Second, they hypothesized that since free-throw shooting is a self-paced activity and field-goal shooting is a reactive activity, difference scores derived by subtracting the percentage of successful field-goal attempts from the percentage of successful free-throw attempts would be higher for whites than blacks. In short, they did find that whites had significantly higher free-throw minus field-goal scores than did blacks.

Jones and Hochner (1973) criticized Worthy and Markle's investigation on the grounds that their baseball data were based on frequencies rather than performance data, and that their method of treating basketball data did not demonstrate white superiority at free throws and black superiority at field goals. In their replication of Worthy and Markle's investigation, Jones and Hochner obtained data in support of superior performance of blacks at hitting and superior performance of whites at free-throw shooting. However, contrary to Worthy and Markle, they found that black pitchers, although fewer in number, were superior to white pitchers, and they found no racial differences in field-goal shooting accuracy.

In a third study of racial differences in self-paced and reactive sports activities, Dunn and Lupfer (1974) assessed the performance of 55 white and 122 black fourth-grade boys playing a modified game of soccer. Specifically, they determined the number of points won by each boy when playing in the offensive (self-paced) and defensive (reactive) positions. Their analysis provides strong support for the Worthy–Markle hypothesis, since black boys averaged 4.98 points when playing in reactive positions and 4.00 points when playing in self-paced positions, whereas white boys averaged 5.45 points in self-paced positions and 4.25 points in reactive positions.

In summary, data in support of the Worthy–Markle hypothesis is inconclusive. On the one hand, the hypothesis may account for why blacks are (1) overrepresented in reactive playing positions such as the outfield, running back, wide receiver, and cornerback, and (2) underrepresented in self-paced sports such as bowling, golf, and swimming. On the other hand, the hypothesis does not account for why blacks are underrepresented in such reactive sports as autoracing, fencing, skiing, squash, and tennis.

Sociopsychological explanations. A third category of explanations of racial variation in athletic performance is sociopsychological in nature and emphasizes the importance of socialization. For example, Jones and Hochner:

. . . argue that the manner in which an individual is socialized into sports activities will have a significant effect on his sports personality. And further, this sports personality will have a significant effect on sports preference and performance. (Jones and Hochner, 1973, p. 92)

They offer a general sociopsychological model based on three personality orientations measured as bipolar dimensions (team–individual, success–style, competition–play) and reflecting three dominant motives (approval or affiliation, achievement, and power). With respect to racial variations in athletic performance, Jones and Hochner suggest that, in contrast to white athletes, black athletes (1) emphasize an individualistic rather than a team orientation, (2) stress style or expressive performance rather than success or technical performance, and (3) reflect a personalized power orientation associated with individual winning rather than a socialized power orientation associated with team winning. Although Jones and Hochner cite examples from basketball to illustrate the basic personality orientations of black athletes, their observations could be readily extended to the performance of black athletes in outfield positions in baseball, and in running back, wide receiver, and defensive back positions in football.

Another sociopsychological model emphasizing socialization has been developed by McPherson (1975), who hypothesized that since success increases visibility, there is a greater likelihood that those occupying a given role would be imitated by novices. Based on this rationale, the minority-group socialization hypothesis was proposed in which it was argued that black youth would seek to play the specific sport roles occupied by blacks in professional sport who have attained a high level of achievement and therefore visibility. While there is little direct empirical support for this differential socialization hypothesis, there do appear to be some differences in the early socialization experiences of black and white track and field athletes (Kenyon and McPherson, 1973). Moreover, based on interviews with 23 white and 20 black high school athletes, Brower (1972) found that 90 percent of the black athletes reported having one or more black role models and that a majority of the black football players in the sample aspired to play traditionally black positions.

In the only direct empirical test of this minority-group socialization hypothesis, Castine and Roberts (1974) concluded that there was some support for the modeling hypothesis based on their finding that 57 percent of the black college athletes in their sample who had a black idol played the same position as the idol when they were in high school. Further, 48 percent of these played the same position as their idol while in college. Thus, rather than racial discrimination being the cause of positional segregation, blacks may learn and subsequently occupy specific roles held by those who have attained success. However, Eitzen and Tessendorf (1975) note that "although the role model hypothesis does not explain the initial discrimination that caused early entry blacks to take non-central positions, it helps explain why . . . the pattern of discrimination by player position tends to be maintained."

Economic explanations. The sociopsychological frameworks just outlined imply that positional segregation in sport organizations is self-initiated. That is, they suggest that, because of particular personality orientations and unique socialization experiences, blacks selectively seek out specific sports and particular playing positions and thus their marked overrepresentation in given sports and playing positions is not held to result from discriminatory practices.

One type of economic explanation also endorses the self-selection thesis. In brief, this explanation holds that black athletes are predisposed to selecting playing positions that offer the greatest opportunity for individual achievement, prestige, popularity, and monetary rewards. For example, outfield positions in baseball, and runningback, wide receiver, and cornerback positions in football typically involve independent task activities, receive a great deal of visibility and publicity, and generally are associated with high average salaries in relation to other playing positions. It must be noted, however, that this economic explanation does not explain the underrepresentation of blacks among catchers, pitchers, and quarterbacks,[2] nor does it explain the absence of blacks in the lucrative and individualistic sport of professional golf. Moreover, as noted in Section 7.1.3, the salaries of black athletes in professional sports may not be commensurate with their playing ability.

Sociocultural explanations.   Contrary to biological, sociopsychological, and economic explanations of ethnic stratification in sport organizations, sociocultural explanations of organizational integration and positional placement indicate that discriminatory processes are at work. First, there are sociocultural explanations based on social stereotyping. For example, in a series of studies Williams and Youssef (1972, 1975) have shown in the context of college football that: "(a) players' race was correlated with position assignments, e.g., blacks were proportionately over-represented in certain positions and under-represented in others; (b) coaches stereotyped football positions, that is, they judged some personal characteristics to be more important for success in some football positions than in others; and coaches stereotyped according to race, that is they rated black players as different from white players on most . . . personal characteristics."

Findings similar to those of Williams and Youssef have been reported by Brower (1972) in the context of professional football. A summary of Brower's analysis is given in Table 4.7, which shows the relative percentage of blacks and whites at different playing positions and indicates the perceived personal characteristics associated with different types of playing positions. It is evident from the table that black athletes are overrepresented at playing positions perceived to require strength, quickness, emotion, instinct, and speed, and are underrepresented at those positions believed to require intellect, leadership, poise under pressure, finesse, technique, and control.

A second category of sociocultural explanations focuses on the concepts of social interaction and social distance (Loy and McElvogue, 1970). This form of explanation can be summarized in terms of three positions: (1) "There is a range within discriminatory practice such that there is most discrimination and most prejudice as the practice comes closer to intimate personal contact" (Berelson and Steiner, 1964); (2) intimate personal contact varies directly with degree of social interaction; and (3) degree of social interaction varies directly with degree of

Table 4.7

Comparison of 1970 black and white National Football League players by position requirement

Positions	White	Black	Position requirements
Quarterback Center Linebacker	34.6% (245)	6.8% (25)	Intellect and leadership
Kicker Punter	2.5% (18)	0% (0)	Brief stress and pressure
Guard Tackle Tight end	23.1% (164)	12.8% (47)	Finesse, technique, and control
Defensive end Defensive tackle	14.4% (102)	17.9% (66)	Strength, quickness, and emotion
Running back Wide receiver Defensive back Kick returner Punt returner	25.4% (180)	62.5% (230)	Instinct and speed
Column total	65.8% (709)	34.2% (368)	100% (1077)

From Brower (1972, Table 9).

centrality. For heuristic purposes these three propositions can be taken as axioms from which a fourth theoretical proposition accounting for lack of black athletes at central positions in sport organizations can be derived, as follows:

Axiom I: Discrimination leads to personal contact.

Axiom II: Personal contact leads to social interaction.

Axiom III: Social interaction leads to centrality.

Theorem A: Discrimination leads to centrality.

In short, this axiomatic theory predicts that black athletes when compared with white athletes will be overrepresented in playing positions characterized by distant (i.e., peripheral) spatial location, low rates of interaction, and the performance of independent tasks.

The most thorough theoretical analysis to date of occupational discrimination is given in the work of Blalock (1962, 1967). His analysis is summarized in terms of 13 theoretical propositions, which are listed in Table 4.8. On the one hand, this set of propositions offers explanations for the overrepresentation of blacks in professional sport over other occupations. On the other hand, it offers explanations for the overrepresentation of blacks in specific sports and at

Table 4.8
Occupational discrimination: Blalock's theoretical propositions

A low degree of minority discrimination is a function of:

1. The greater the importance of high individual performance to the productivity of the work group.

2. The greater the competition among employers for persons with high performance levels.

3. The easier it is to accurately evaluate an individual's performance level.

4. The degree to which high individual performance works to the advantage of other members of the work group who share rewards of high performance and status within the group.

5. The fewer the restrictions placed on performance by members of the work group.

6. The degree to which a work group consists of a number of specialists interacting as a team and where there is little or no serious competition among these members.

7. The degree to which a group member's position is threatened by anonymous outsiders rather than other members of his own group.

8. The extent to which an individual's success depends primarily on his own performance, rather than on limiting or restricting the performance of specific other individuals.

9. The degree to which high performance does not lead to power over other members of the work group.

10. The degree to which group members find it difficult or disadvantageous to change jobs in order to avoid minority members.

11. The extent to which it is difficult to prevent the minority from acquiring the necessary skills for high performance. This is especially likely when:
    a) Skill depends primarily on innate abilities,
    b) Skill can be developed without prolonged or expensive training, or
    c) It is difficult to maintain a monopoly of skills through secrecy or the control of facilities.

12. The extent to which performance level is relatively independent of skill in interpersonal relations.

13. The lower the degree of purely social interaction on the job (especially interaction involving both sexes).

Adapted from H. M. Blalock, Jr., "Occupational discrimination: some theoretical propositions." *Social Problems* 9: 3 (Winter 1962), pp. 245–246. Used with permission.

particular playing positions and their underrepresentation in others. For example, if one were to rate every professional sport on a scale from 1 to 10 with respect to each of Blalock's 13 propositions (range = 0 to 130), then one could obtain an index of potential discrimination for any given professional sport and could correlate the scale with the relative percentage of black athletes in given sports. That is, lower scores on the potential discrimination scale are hypothesized to correlate with high degrees of racial integration.

In summary, while many alternative explanations have been proposed, a definitive account of why blacks are overrepresented or underrepresented at specific playing positions is lacking.

4.3.4 Performance Differentials in Sport Organizations

Baseball. A third way in which major league baseball is ethnically stratified is with respect to relative playing ability. Specifically, although black and Latin American athletes represent minority groups in professional baseball, they nevertheless reflect higher levels of athletic skill on a percentage basis than whites. For example, since 1969, roughly one-third of the members of the major league all-star teams have been black athletes. Another example is the fact that black athletes have won the National League's Most Valuable Player Award 16 times in the past 28 seasons ("The black dominance," *Time*, 9 May 1977, p. 57).

A major reason for the disproportionate representation of members of minority groups on all-star teams and in MVP selections is the fact that on the average they display greater batting superiority. As is evident from the data presented in Table 4.9, black and Latin American players had higher batting averages than white players for every season from 1953 to 1965 and again in 1973. It is also interesting to note that Latin American players had higher batting averages than black players during eight of the fourteen seasons examined. Most recently, Leonard (1977) reported finding significant differences in favor of blacks in batting average, slugging percentage, home run production, and runs batted in. However, for pitching and fielding performance there were only slight but insignificant differences between ethnic groups.

Table 4.9
Major league batting averages* by ethnic group: 1953–1965, 1973

Year	(1) Blacks	(2) Latins	(3) Whites	% diff (1)−(3)	% diff (2)−(3)	% diff (1)−(2)
1953	.288	.274	.257	.031	.017	.014
1954	.262	.282	.244	.018	.038	−.020
1955	.271	.266	.251	.020	.015	.005
1956	.270	.268	.248	.022	.020	.002
1957	.264	.265	.252	.012	.013	−.001
1958	.274	.264	.249	.025	.015	.010
1959	.265	.269	.246	.019	.023	−.004
1960	.264	.271	.248	.016	.023	−.007
1961	.264	.272	.247	.017	.025	−.008
1962	.276	.270	.250	.026	.020	.006
1963	.262	.265	.238	.024	.027	−.003
1964	.255	.273	.238	.017	.035	−.018
1965	.252	.271	.234	.018	.037	−.019
1973	.274	.267	.257	.017	.010	.007

*At least 30 at bats per season, pitchers excluded.
Adapted from Rosenblatt (1967), Henderson (1975), and Leonard (1977).

The higher batting average of minority group members is no doubt related to the fact that a greater percentage of the populations of black and Latin American players are "starters" in comparison to the population of white players. For example, between 1968 and 1975, 68 to 83 percent of all black athletes in major league baseball were starting players (Winfield, 1977).

Basketball. It was previously shown in the case of professional baseball that blacks have a higher degree of relative playing ability than whites.[3] Two studies indicate that this same situation obtains in both college and professional basket-

Table 4.10
Percentage of NBA players by race in each scoring quartile

1957–1958

	Black		White		Difference	
Upper quartile	25.0 ⎱ 66.7		27.7 ⎱ 49.4		− 2.7 ⎱ +17.3	
Upper middle	41.7 ⎰		21.7 ⎰		+20.0 ⎰	
Lower middle	8.3 ⎱ 33.3		26.5 ⎱ 50.6		−18.2 ⎱ −17.3	
Lower quartile	25.0 ⎰		24.1 ⎰		+ 0.9 ⎰	
	100.0		100.0			

1961–1962

	Black		White		Difference	
Upper quartile	32.4 ⎱ 70.6		21.8 ⎱ 41.0		+10.6 ⎱ +28.4	
Upper middle	38.2 ⎰		19.2 ⎰		+19.0 ⎰	
Lower middle	23.5 ⎱ 29.4		25.6 ⎱ 58.9		− 2.1 ⎱ −28.5	
Lower quartile	5.9 ⎰		33.3 ⎰		−27.4 ⎰	
	100.0		100.0			

1965–1966

	Black		White		Difference	
Upper quartile	29.8 ⎱ 57.9		20.0 ⎱ 41.8		+ 9.8 ⎱ +16.1	
Upper middle	28.1 ⎰		21.8 ⎰		+ 6.3 ⎰	
Lower middle	24.6 ⎱ 42.1		25.5 ⎱ 58.2		− 0.9 ⎱ −16.1	
Lower quartile	17.5 ⎰		32.7 ⎰		−15.2 ⎰	
	100.0		100.0			

1969–1970

	Black		White		Difference	
Upper quartile	30.5 ⎱ 55.8		17.9 ⎱ 42.3		+12.6 ⎱ +13.5	
Upper middle	25.3 ⎰		24.4 ⎰		+ 0.9 ⎰	
Lower middle	25.3 ⎱ 44.2		24.4 ⎱ 57.7		+ 0.9 ⎱ −13.5	
Lower quartile	18.9 ⎰		33.3 ⎰		−14.4 ⎰	
	100.0		100.0			

From Yetman and Eitzen (1972, p. 30).

ball. First, Yetman and Eitzen (1972) found that for the period from 1954 to 1970 blacks in both college and professional basketball were systematically over-represented in starting positions and among the leaders in scoring. Their findings for professional basketball are summarized in Table 4.10.

Johnson and Marple (1973) replicated the investigation of Yetman and Eitzen (1972) and also discovered that within college teams, blacks are disproportionately represented at starting positions. However, Johnson and Marple found no clear evidence that blacks are systematically overrepresented at starting positions within professional teams. But they did find evidence that " . . . blacks who are only marginal players are dropped from the league earlier than are marginal whites" (Johnson and Marple, 1973). They also found support for their hypothesis that "the performance of blacks in their last year in the professional league will be greater than the performance of whites in their last year in the league."

Contrary to Yetman and Eitzen (1972) and Johnson and Marple (1973), Leonard and Schmidt (1975), on the basis of an analysis of the top 25 NBA and ABA scorers for the 1972–1973 season, found no statistically significant differences between the relative performances of blacks and whites with respect to average point production, games played, minutes played, field goals made, free throws made, rebounds, assists, and total number of points. It may be that, as Yetman and Eitzen (1972) noted, "the magnitude of these differences has declined as the percentage of black players in the league has increased."[4] That is, although blacks may have had to "be better" before they were recruited to a college team or before they gained a position in professional basketball during the early years of integration, with greater ease of access in recent years, black athletes of average ability may now be included in the comparative statistics. Further, with less emphasis on a quota system in recent years, more journeymen black athletes are being included in these statistical patterns, thereby lowering the mean scores for blacks.

4.4 ORGANIZATIONAL PROCESS AND PERFORMANCE

4.4.1 Sociological Analysis of Replacement Processes

All formal organizations seek to maintain relatively stable populations and thus must continually fill positional vacancies resulting from a variety of forms of attrition, including death, demotion, firing, promotion, resignation, retirement, and transfer. As Ball has observed, organizational replacement is typically viewed from one of two sociological perspectives:

> (1) internally, it is characterized by the study of *organizational succession* [italics added]; (2) externally, it is subsumed under the rubric of *labor-force turnover*. Both of these perspectives, in turn, may be seen as aspects of the more general process of *replacement;* what Sorokin (1931) long ago conceptualized as the metabolism of organizations—specifically, the metabolic process of personnel circulation. When the focus is upon the position in and out of which people move, the perspective is on succession, when it is upon

the aggregate of people who move in and out of these positions, it is turnover. When the two are combined—e.g., varied rates of positional succession and varied rates of labor-force turnover—the problematic of *organizational replacement* is described.*

In general, the study of organizational succession has been within the purview of sociologists (see Carlson, 1961; Gamson and Scotch, 1964; Glasser, 1968; Gordon and Becker, 1964; Grusky, 1960, 1961, 1963, 1964, 1969; Grusky and Miller, 1970; Guest, 1962; Kriesburg, 1962; Perrucci and Mannweiler, 1968; and Trow, 1960, 1961), whereas investigations of personnel turnover have largely been within the province of economists (see, for example, the work of Bowen and Finegan, 1969). Exceptions to the latter observation include the studies of Argyle et al. (1958), Evan (1963), Price (1975, 1976, 1977), and Trice (1961).

In view of the fact that there is an extensive body of literature concerning organizational replacement, and in light of the fact that sport organizations must annually deal with the problem of organizational replacement, it is somewhat surprising that so few studies in the area of the sociology of sport have focused on the phenomenon of organizational replacement. However, notwithstanding the limited literature on the subject, a review of the research regarding succession and turnover in sport organizations is given in this section. Specifically, seven hypothesized correlates of organizational replacement are presented and discussed.

4.4.2 Replacement Processes in Sport Organizations

Member Replacement Rates Vary by Organizational (Player) Position.

Football. As with most organizations, there are varying degrees of role specialization and skill required for different positions in sport. For example, a team's success is often related to the ability of the personnel occupying such highly skilled positions as the pitcher, quarterback, center, or goaltender. Moreover, this recognition of varying degree of skill is reflected in the differential salary paid to occupants of particular positions (Ball, 1973). Because of the premium placed on physical skill and prowess in sport, which is subject to fluctuation, player positions can be expected to experience a high degree of succession (turnover) (see McNeil and Thompson, 1971, p. 626). Thus, in the context of sport organizations, it may be hypothesized that member replacement rates vary by organizational (player) position.

In order to test this hypothesis, Ball (1974) analyzed replacement rates in the National Football League from 1966 to 1970. He found empirical support for the hypothesis in that the percentage of occupants (that is, "stayers" vs. "movers") filling the same offensive position on the same team for five years was as follows:

*From Donald W. Ball, "Replacement Processes in Work Organizations: Task Evaluation and the Case of Professional Football." Reprinted from *Sociology of Work and Occupations* Vol. 1, No. 2 (May 1974), pp. 197–217 by permission of the Publisher, Sage Publications, Inc.

tackles (76 percent), guards (75 percent), centers (74 percent), running backs (67 percent), flankers and wide receivers (56 percent), tight ends (55 percent), and quarterbacks (38 percent). The percentage of "stayers" among occupants of defensive positions ranged from 67 percent to 57 percent, while the overall percentage of "stayers" for all positions was 62 percent.

In an effort to discover a potential explanation for varying replacement rates by playing position, Ball tested a related but more powerful hypothesis predicting that "positional replacement rates are directly related to the precision and availability of evaluative opportunities and techniques." In terms of the degree of quantitative evaluation, player positions were categorized as *high* (quarterbacks, running backs, flankers, wide receivers, tight ends, and kickers), *high-intermediate* (defensive backs), *low-intermediate* (linebackers), and *low* (center, guards, tackles, and defensive ends). Ball found support for this second hypothesis, with the only notable finding that ran counter to his hypothesis being the fact that running backs (whose performance can be easily evaluated) were relatively stable occupants of that position.

Ball also found support for the more general hypothesis that "the higher the rate of positional replacement, the higher the salaries at that position" (Ball, 1974). Interestingly, his hypothesis and findings are in direct contrast to the correlate of turnover cited by Price (1977) that "lower income members have higher rates of turnover than higher income members."

Finally, Ball attempted to assess positional replacement rates in terms of race and, although his findings were somewhat inconclusive, there is a tendency for blacks to occupy positions characterized by a high degree of visibility and ease in evaluating performance. Ball's tentative conclusions concerning positional occupancy by race are related to Blalock's (1962) prediction that: "The easier it is to accurately evaluate an individual's performance level, the lower the degree of minority discrimination by employers."

Hockey. Turning to professional hockey, McPherson (1976b) tested the hypothesis that "role positions in professional hockey have varying turnover rates." Looking at both managerial and member turnover rates in the National Hockey League from 1950 to 1966, McPherson (1976b) found the following turnover rates by position: managers (0.50), coaches (1.75), goalies (2.50), defensemen (4.72), wings (7.53), and centers (8.25). Thus, the lowest turnover rate was for managers and the highest for centers. Although these findings support those of Ball, McPherson suggests that the explanation for varying turnover rates by position may be sport specific:

> . . . whereas Ball attributed some of the variation in turnover rates in professional football to the degree of visibility of the position, this argument may not apply to hockey where all positions are equally visible to coach and spectator alike. In fact, the role of goaltender may be so visible to the spectator that the incumbent may receive undue criticism if his goals against average is high. This explanation also counters the "ease of quantification and evaluation" argument (Rose, 1969; Ball, 1974). That is, despite the presence

of a quantifiable evaluative measure (goals against average), the turnover rate for goaltenders is the lowest for any player category. (McPherson, 1976b, p. 10)

On the other hand, McPherson (1976b) points out that although accurate salary data is not available, the high turnover rates for centers and wings may support Ball's conclusion that positions having the greatest replacement rates also receive the highest remuneration.

Baseball. A third study testing this hypothesis analyzed personnel succession in professional baseball (Theberge and Loy, 1976). This study gives a two-fold analysis of succession rates by player position. First, Theberge and Loy compared the percentage of new starters at each position (excluding pitchers) for the eight teams in the National Baseball League from 1951 through 1960. The following variation in replacement rates was found: leftfielders (58 percent), second and third basemen (48 percent), centerfielders (46 percent), first basemen (45 percent), rightfielders (43 percent), catchers (41 percent), and shortstops (35 percent). Interestingly, these findings show that the most "demanding" positions (i.e., catcher and shortstop) have the highest replacement rates (excluding the unanalyzed position of pitcher). Second, they computed the annual percentage of replacement for infielders (excluding pitchers, but including catchers) and outfielders for teams in both the American and National Baseball Leagues from 1951 to 1960. They found that the replacement rate for infielders was 58 percent, while that for outfielders was 55 percent.

Theberge and Loy point out that Ball's ease of quantification explanation of turnover rates, which McPherson (1976b) has suggested, may not be applicable to hockey, and also does not seem to hold for baseball, where all members' contributions can easily be quantified through a variety of offensive and defensive statistics. They also note that one possible explanation for the fact that succession rates do not vary markedly among organizational positions in baseball may be that there is very little difference in the role requirements of baseball positions in relation to other sports. Baseball players, for example, at all positions must be capable of batting, catching, fielding, and throwing.

In summary, studies of professional baseball, football, and hockey suggest that member replacement rates vary by organizational (player) position. However, the nature of replacement rates by position appears to be sport specific and adequate theoretical explanations of varying replacement rates by position are largely lacking.

Replacement Rates Vary with Managerial Replacement Rates.

A folk adage holds that "change at the top brings about change at the bottom." This bit of folk wisdom is supported by some evidence indicating that administrative succession in formal organizations leads to member succession. For example, Grusky (1969) discusses a procedure which he calls "strategic replacement" whereby "the successor, particularly if he is new to the firm, often finds it necessary to bring new persons into the organization to support his policies and buttress his position." The concept of strategic replacement has obvious implications for sport organizations, wherein owners, managers, and coaches possess particular philosophies of management and coaching and seek to attract personnel who will act in accordance with their personal philosophies. Thus, it seems reasonable to suggest that member replacement rates may vary with managerial replacement rates. Moreover, a leader appointed from outside an organization may have a different style of leadership from the previous occupant than a person appointed from within the organization. Therefore, a second hypothesis is proposed that "external managerial succession has a greater impact upon member succession than internal managerial succession."

In order to test the first hypothesis, Peckham (1970) and Theberge and Loy (1976) used data from the American and National Baseball Leagues. Peckham (1970) calculated the mean player succession rate for each team from 1948 to 1968. He obtained a total mean value of player succession, which was then compared to the number of new players obtained by a team every time a managerial change occurred. His results clearly indicated that player succession was positively related to managerial succession. Similar results were obtained by Theberge and Loy (1976) for the period from 1951 to 1960.

In testing the second hypothesis concerning external versus internal managerial replacement, Peckham (1970) found that there was a higher rate of player turnover under conditions of external managerial succession than internal managerial succession. Theberge and Loy (1976), on the other hand, found no significant differences between external and internal managerial succession and player turnover rates.

In summary, for professional baseball, there is strong evidence that "member replacement rates vary with managerial replacement rates," but inconclusive support for the hypothesis that "member replacement rates are more strongly influenced by external managerial replacement rates than by internal managerial replacement rates."

Personnel Replacement Rates Vary by Type of Sport Organization.

Sport organizations vary in terms of a variety of characteristics such as size, number of organizational positions, level of competition, and length of playing season. Thus, different types of sport organizations may also be characterized by differential rates of personnel replacement. Unfortunately, however, for purposes of comparative analysis, few of the several studies of replacement processes in sport organizations report overall succession rates. Moreover, the few studies that cite rates seldom have used comparable measures of replacement processes. Three examples suffice to illustrate this point.

Theberge and Loy (1976) report an annual average player succession rate of 57 percent for major league professional baseball based on the average percentage of new players per team per year for the period 1951–1960. Kjeldsen (1976) reports an annual average withdrawal rate of 21.2 percent for interscholastic gymnastics. His index of withdrawal rate is based on the total number of athletes trying out for a team on the first day of the season, minus the number of athletes on a team on the last day of the season, divided by the total number of athletes trying out for the team at the start of the season. McPherson (1976c) reports that for the 16-year period of the National Hockey League ". . . there were an average of 35.25 player changes per year, 5.88 player changes per team per year, and 94 new players per organization." In short, overall replacement rates have been reported in selected studies of sport organizations but their different bases of operational measurement virtually preclude comparative analysis.

It appears that Schwartz's (1973) unpublished pilot study provides the only direct comparative test to date of the proposition that personnel replacement rates vary by type of sport organization. On the basis of secondary data analysis, Schwartz determined the average succession rate for playing personnel of the National Basketball, Baseball, and Football Leagues over the 1960–1969 seasons. He operationally defined succession rate as the ratio of players used by a team in a particular season who were not used the previous season, compared to the total number of players used by a team.

Schwartz found that average player succession rates varied among the three professional sports as follows: football (0.334), basketball (0.367), and baseball (0.403). These relative succession rates are somewhat striking in view of the fact that they are inversely related to the injury rates characteristic of the three sports. That is, unlike many formal organizations, the turnover rates of sport teams are hypothesized to be in part a function of physical injury suffered by playing personnel, yet football, which annually loses many players because of injury, has been shown to have a lower player succession rate than basketball or baseball.

Schwartz observes that since the annual average team size was 12.7 players for basketball, 31.1 for baseball, and 43.4 for football, the differential succession rates by sport can not be accounted for by organizational size per se. Although several studies of formal organizations report strong relationships between the variables of size and succession, Schwartz offers a series of speculations as to why the relationship does not obtain for professional sport teams. First, he notes that succession in professional sport is generally of an involuntary nature (McPherson, 1976b), whereas in most formal organizations there is a good deal of voluntary turnover. Second, Schwartz points out that the expansion of teams in the three National sport leagues during the period studied and the formation of new competing leagues (e.g., the American Basketball and Football Leagues) during the same period may have influenced the succession rates reported above. For instance, in four of the seven years between 1960 and 1966, an era in which the NBA expanded by only one team, basketball experienced lower succession rates than did football.

Third, he contends that basketball rates could conceivably have been higher than expected because of the growing domination of the playing rosters by black athletes. He also mentions the possibility that black players experienced higher turnover rates than white players during this period. Fourth, Schwartz suggests that succession rates in baseball were possibly highest among the three professional sports because player trades seem to be more inherent to those sports than to others. Moreover, all major league baseball teams operate multitiered "farm systems" of minor league teams from which players can be brought up to the major leagues or sent down to the minor leagues during the course of a season. In any event, for whatever reasons, in no year did baseball achieve the lowest succession rate among the three sports, and in only three years during the period studied did it experience any rate but the highest.

Fifth, and finally, Schwartz speculates that the internal dynamics of the three professional sports compared might possibly account for differential personnel succession rates. For example, teamwork, interaction, and performance of mutually interdependent tasks seem more characteristic of football than basketball, and in turn, more characteristic of basketball than baseball. And since effective teamwork requires that players on a given team interact as a cohesive unit over a significant period of time, turnover rates should vary as a function of the number of dependent and coordinate tasks required of positional occupants in a specific sport.

In summary, there is some empirical support for the proposition that personnel replacement rates vary by type of sport organization. But the precise nature of personnel succession rates of various sports is unknown, and explanations are notably absent.

Organizational Effectiveness Varies with Managerial Replacement Rates.

The initial stimulus for the study of replacement processes in sport organizations was Grusky's (1963a) analysis of managerial succession and organizational effectiveness based on the examination of records for 16 professional baseball teams over two time periods, 1921–1941 and 1951–1958. Grusky assumed that the variables of succession and success have reciprocal effects and thus hypothesized that: "High rates of succession should produce declining organizational effectiveness, and low effectiveness should encourage high rates of administrative succession" (Grusky, 1963a). Grusky found that his hypothesis was empirically supported by negative correlations between number of successions and average team standings for the two time periods considered, both separately (e.g., $r = -0.40$ and -0.60) and in combination (e.g., $r = -0.43$). In an effort to theoretically account for these negative relationships Grusky set forth a hypothetical causal model based on the interrelationship among ten organizational factors.

In a critique of Grusky's analysis, Gamson and Scotch (1964) take issue with his "two-way causality theory" and posit two alternative explanations, which they label "the common-sense one-way causality theory" and "the ritual scapegoating no-way causality theory." The first explanation assumes, like Grusky's explanation, that a field manager has an important influence on team performance; thus when a team performs poorly the manager is held responsible, accordingly fired, and replaced by a new manager who can improve team performance by avoiding the mistakes of his predecessor. The second explanation offered by Gamson and Scotch assumes that field managers exert relatively little effect on team performance, but since blame has to be placed somewhere when a team is doing poorly, managers serve as effective scapegoats. Gamson and Scotch tentatively tested the three theories using data concerning 22 midseason managerial changes from 1954 to 1961. They found that no firm conclusion regarding the respective merit of the three alternative explanations could be drawn, but state that until all data is in they personally "prefer the scapegoating explanation of the correlation between effectiveness and rate of managerial succession" (Gamson and Scotch, 1964).

In a reply to Gamson and Scotch, Grusky (1964) stresses the importance of considering whether managerial change is a result of internal or external succession. He contends that "inside successors tend to be less disruptive than outside successors, and mid-season successions in baseball frequently tend to involve inside replacements" (Grusky, 1964). In support of his thesis Grusky presents an analysis of managerial change and team performance for the years 1954 to 1961 that shows that "five of six managers who showed improvement were inside successors and ten of eleven of those whose teams deteriorated were outsiders" (Grusky, 1964).

The pilot studies of Peckham (1970) and Theberge and Loy (1976) also test the general hypothesis that "organizational effectiveness is negatively related to managerial succession" and the more specific hypothesis that "organizational effectiveness is more adversely influenced by external managerial succession than by internal managerial succession." Peckham examined managerial changes in professional baseball for the years 1948 to 1968, considering only those individuals who served in managerial roles for at least 20 games. Theberge and Loy also examined managerial changes in professional baseball but only for the years 1951 to 1960 and included all individuals who had managed a team for at least 10 games.

In brief, Peckham found, contrary to Grusky, that team performance usually improved following a managerial change and that there was no significant difference between team effectiveness following external or internal managerial succession. Theberge and Loy (1976), on the other hand, found support for the general hypothesis that managerial change was correlated in the predicted direction with three measures of organizational effectiveness: percent of games won, league standing, and games behind the first-place team. However, they found no statistically significant differences between the type of managerial change (internal vs. external) and the three performance measures: percent of games won, league standing, and games behind.

Eitzen and Yetman (1972) also replicated Grusky's initial investigation by analyzing college basketball records for four decades (1930–1970). They found a small but statistically significant negative correlation between measures of coaching changes and winning percentages for the forty-year period. However, "as a forty-year period might be too lengthy and therefore insensitive to shorter periods of team success or failure, as well as to coaching stability or instability, a ten-year period, 1960–1969, was also selected to test the relationship between turnover rate and winning percentage" (Eitzen and Yetman, 1972). Although a slightly higher correlation was obtained in the predicted direction, the results indicate that losing teams are more likely to be characterized by high turnover rates.

Contrary to Eitzen and Yetman, McPherson (1976c) found no relationship between managerial change and organizational effectiveness for his sample of National Hockey League teams. He observes that "the results . . . are not surprising in view of the almost equal probability of a team experiencing an improvement or decrement in performance in a given year" (McPherson, 1976c).

In summary, a review of current research regarding replacement processes in sport organizations warrants no firm conclusions concerning the hypothesis that organizational effectiveness varies with managerial replacement rates. However, the nature of the hypothesized relationship is examined in more detail below, wherein the important conditional factors of managerial tenure and long-term team performance are taken into account.

Organizational Effectiveness Varies with Member Replacement Rates.

Much of the literature on formal organizations points to the dysfunctional effects of member turnover on organizational effectiveness. Turnover is seen as costly for a number of reasons, including a consequential reduction in effective communication (McNeil and Thompson, 1971; Shelley, 1964), an upsetting of established routines (Shelley, 1964), the additional costs of finding new personnel, and the reduced effectiveness of new employees while they become adjusted to an initially strange work situation. Caplow (1964) indicates that the successful socialization of recruits into a formal organization results in new self-images, involvements, values, and accomplishments on the part of incumbents. Achieving adequate socialization of recruits may also impose a strain on the organization. Clearly, then, turnover and the resulting positional succession are seen as potentially disruptive to an organization. Thus, it may be readily hypothesized that organizational effectiveness is negatively related to member replacement rates. Several studies of sport organizations provide tests of this hypothesis.

The only direct comparative test of the stated hypothesis is Schwartz's (1973) study of 91 basketball teams, 94 baseball teams, and 142 football teams in the national professional leagues from 1960 to 1969. He found significant negative correlations between winning percentages and personnel succession rates for each of the professional sports: basketball ($r = -0.47$), baseball ($r = -0.51$), and football ($r = -0.54$). Peckham (1970) and Theberge and Loy (1976) report similar correlations for professional baseball. In contrast to the findings of Peckham, Schwartz, and Theberge and Loy, McPherson (1976c) found no association in his analysis of replacement processes in professional hockey between ". . . the total number of new players; the number of new goaltenders, defensemen, wings or centers; the number of new stars or the number of new marginals; and, any of the following four dependent variables: direction of difference (improvement, decrement, or no change) in team performance from the previous year's league standing, total goals scored, total goals against or total team points."

Notwithstanding the nonsignificant results reported by McPherson, it can be logically hypothesized that organizational effectiveness is more adversely influenced by central member succession than by peripheral member succession. The role requirements of central positions in organizations typically require greater interaction and task coordination than those of peripheral positions (Grusky,

1963b). Therefore, high rates of turnover among occupants of central positions may be more likely to disrupt patterns of social and task interaction, and thus detrimentally affect group performance than high rates of turnover among incumbents of peripheral positions. This argument is supported by Blau and Scott (1962) who cite research revealing the importance of centralized communication and organization to an organization's effectiveness. The studies of Peckham (1970) and Theberge and Loy (1976) provide tests of the predicted relationship between organizational effectiveness and rates of succession among occupants of central and peripheral positions. In their examination of replacement rates in professional baseball, these investigators operationally defined central and peripheral positions as infield and outfield positions, respectively.

Theberge and Loy compared the correlations between three measures of organizational effectiveness (i.e., winning percentage, league standing, and games behind) and succession rates for occupants of central and peripheral positions (percentage of new players). Their data clearly indicate that organizational effectiveness is influenced more by central personnel succession than peripheral personnel succession.

Similarly, Peckham (1970) found that the number of new starters at infield positions correlated -0.47 with percentage of games won, whereas the number of new starters at outfield positions correlated -0.37 with percentage of games won. Some insight into the difference in correlations between organizational effectiveness and central and peripheral succession rates is gained by considering the factor of team errors. The correlation between the number of new starting infielders and team errors is 0.37, while the correlation between the number of new starting outfielders and team errors is only 0.17. The importance of this difference is clear when the significance of total team errors for overall team performance is taken into account. The correlation between total team errors and team won/lost percentage (-0.49) is as high as that between team batting average and winning percentage (0.47). Thus, an increase in errors is an important factor to consider when examining the relationship between player turnover and team performance.

A fourth study that supports the hypothesis that organizational effectiveness is negatively related to member replacement rates is Kjeldsen's (1976) investigation of interscholastic gymnastic teams. He found an association of -0.27 between winning percentage and withdrawal rate, and an association of -0.38 between a measure of member satisfaction with performance and withdrawal rate.

In summary, studies of professional baseball, basketball, football, and high school gymnastics strongly support the hypothesis that organizational effectiveness varies with member replacement rates. However, an analysis of data in a study of professional hockey does not support the hypothesis.

The Relationship Between Organizational Effectiveness and Personnel Replacement Rates Varies with the Tenure of Managers and Members.

This hypothesis focuses on the relationships stated in the previous two hypotheses, but takes into account the important additional factor of the tenure of playing and managerial personnel. The initial examination of the conditional nature of the relationship between organizational effectiveness and personnel replacement rates was Grusky's (1963a) early investigation. He tested the hypothesis ". . . that a change in the rate of administrative succession is negatively correlated with a change in organizational effectiveness" (Grusky, 1963a) by determining the relationship between change in average length of managerial tenure and average team standing from period I (1921–1941) to period II (1951–1958) for 15 professional baseball teams. "That is, (he) wanted to see if teams that kept their managers for shorter periods (experienced more succession) in period II than they had in period I were less effective in the later period and vice versa" (Grusky, 1963a). Grusky obtained strong support for his hypothesis, since "all eight teams that increased considerably their rate of managerial succession over that of the earlier period experienced a decline in average team standing" (Grusky, 1963a).

Eitzen and Yetman (1972), in their replication of Grusky's investigation, made a number of comparisons of coaching turnover and team performance by controlling for longevity of tenure and relative performance. They draw two major conclusions from their several analyses. On the one hand, they conclude ". . . that turnover rate and team performance are inversely related, but that this relationship depends upon the team's performance prior to the change." Specifically, they observe ". . . that when the preceding coach's winning percentage is taken into account, a change in coaches makes no difference. . . . poor teams tend to improve the following year and successful teams tend to deteriorate strictly as a matter of probability" (Eitzen and Yetman, 1972). On the other hand, they conclude that "although a coaching change appears to have little effect upon initial team performance, the introduction of a new coach provides a possibility for long-term change and improvement. . . ." Specifically, they observe that:

> Coaches who left after eight or nine years tended to leave as winners in comparison with their early years. Coaches whose tenure lasted ten, eleven, or twelve years were split evenly into those whose records were improving and those whose records were deteriorating. For those coaches whose longevity at one post exceeded twelve years (the longest tenure was twenty-eight years), every year but one showed a disproportionate number of coaches ending their career at a school with last-half records poorer than their first (comparing five year segments in each case). (Eitzen and Yetman, 1972, p. 115).

In summary, Eitzen and Yetman's study represents one of the few systematic examinations of the effects of managerial longevity on organizational effectiveness.

A review of the literature reveals no published studies of the relationship between the tenure of athletes and team performance. However, two unpublished papers provide a preliminary examination of this relationship. Marin (1969) compared the performance records and the average annual playing experience of the members of the 12 teams of the National Football League for each year from 1955 to 1959. His findings indicate that although experienced teams are not always winning teams, losing teams are usually inexperienced teams. In a second study analyzing the relationship between player longevity and team performance, Donnelly (1975) obtained a negative correlation ($r = -0.46$) between mea-

Table 4.11
A comparison of organizational half-life
and organizational effectiveness

Half-life	n	Mean games behind
2 years	175	28.38
3 years	126	19.33
4 years	60	13.79
5 years	20	*11.33*
6 years	9	13.58
7 years	4	13.70

From Donnelly (1975).

sures of the half-life[5] of teams and mean games behind the leader for six major league professional baseball teams at various points in time from 1901 to the mid-1960s. An analysis of team performance in terms of varying degrees of half-life (see Table 4.11) indicates that baseball teams having a half-life of five years are more effective than teams with shorter or longer half-lifes. It is also noted that, performance aside, the years to half-life shown in Table 4.11 strikingly illustrate the high player succession rates in professional baseball discussed earlier.

In summary, evidence from recent empirical investigations indicates that the relationship between organizational effectiveness and personnel replacement rates in sport organizations is markedly influenced by the longevity of tenure of managers and by the length of service and experience of members. Moreover, although findings are far from firm, recent research suggests that longevity of service by managers and members of sport organizations is related to performance in an inverted-U manner. This inverted-U hypothesis implies that neither very new nor very old coaches are as effective as coaches with tenure of median duration; the hypothesis also suggests that teams with few experienced players and teams with large numbers of very old players are not as effective as teams having players with moderate levels of playing experience.

The Relationship Between Organizational Effectiveness and Personnel Replacement Rates Varies with the Relative Level of Performance of Teams and Players.

This hypothesis focuses on the relationships stated on pp. 163–169 above, but takes into account the important conditional factor of relative level of performance of both teams and players. Rose (1969) examined the major league baseball careers of managers and players between 1902 and 1960 in order to test two hypotheses concerning organizational failure. "Organizational failure was operationally defined as the situation in which a team finished lower in the league standings than it had finished the preceding season" (Rose, 1969). The first hypothesis tested:

. . . was that managers would show the greatest tendency for career termination in a declining season, pitchers the least such tendency and all other players an intermediate degree of such tendency. The hypothesis was based on the assumption that to managers are attributed the widest scope of responsibility for organizational failure while pitchers, being the most specialized performers, are least likely to be assigned responsibility for organizational failure. (Rose, 1969, p. 327).

Rose obtained strong support for this hypothesis in a comparison of the percentage of pitchers, other players, and managers terminating major league careers with teams of differing performance levels (i.e., improving, remaining the same, declining).

The second hypothesis tested by Rose was ". . . that a manager's rated effectiveness is related to the extent to which the performance of his team exceeds or falls short of the performance of the team under the managership of his immediate predecessors" (Rose, 1969). He found that length of tenure is associated with improvement at high, medium, and low levels of team performance. Moreover, he points out that ". . . the manager of a medium-performance team who improves on the performance of his predecessors is more likely to attain high tenure than one whose team finishes more strongly, but whose record is poorer than that of his predecessors" (Rose, 1969).

In their examination of coaching turnover and team performance among college basketball teams, Eitzen and Yetman (1972) controlled for the relative level of team performance by dividing teams into three categories on the basis of winning percentages (i.e., less than 45 percent, 45–54 percent, and more than 55 percent. They found that unsuccessful teams had the highest rate of turnover (60.9 percent), average teams had a moderate rate of turnover (51.1 percent), and successful teams had the lowest rate of turnover (43.3 percent).

Turning from the managerial level to the member level of sport organizations, only two studies have tested the hypothesis that the greater the differential improvement on performance measures between new and replaced players, the greater the organizational effectiveness. McPherson (1976c) tested the hypothesis on the basis of a secondary analysis of National Hockey League records for the period from 1950 to 1966. On the one hand, he reported that "a comparison of the new and replaced players on goals scored, assists, total points, penalty minutes, and goaltender's goals against average indicated that in most cases the new players slightly outperformed the replaced players and therefore one would expect that team effectiveness would increase" (McPherson, 1976c). On the other hand, he found ". . . with two exceptions, the direction of performance differential between new and replaced players had little influence on organizational effectiveness" (McPherson, 1976c). He found a statistically significant but weak relationship between the direction of differential performance between new and replaced players in goals scored and the direction of difference in league standing from the previous year. He also found a statistically significant but weak relationship between direction of differential performance between the new and replaced goaltender's goals against average and the direction of difference in league standing from the previous year.

Theberge and Loy (1976) replicated McPherson's study in the context of professional baseball using data for eight major league teams for the period from 1951 to 1960. They specifically compared the league standing and winning percentage of each team with the comparative batting and fielding averages of new and replaced players. Unlike McPherson, Theberge and Loy found little directional difference in the comparative performance measures of new and replaced players. For example, 46 percent of the new players had batting averages in the same range as the team batting average for the previous season and 49 percent of all new players showed no directional differences in the fielding averages between themselves and those they replaced. Not surprisingly, in view of these findings, Theberge and Loy discovered that league standing was not significantly related to the batting average or the fielding average of new players, and that a team's percentage of games won was not related to the fielding performance of its new players. However, they did find a weak but statistically significant relationship between winning percentage and comparative batting average of new players.

In summary, empirical findings indicate that organizational effectiveness and personnel replacement rates are related to the relative level of performance of teams and players. But the nature of the interrelationships among these factors appears rather idiosyncratic when the present state of knowledge is considered.

4.4.3 Summary and Conclusions

A review of recent research, both published and unpublished, reveals several studies of sport organizations that have examined the phenomenon of organizational replacement, often with special reference to organizational effectiveness. Although many of these studies represent preliminary investigations and while most analyses are entirely dependent on secondary data sources, the several studies in combination provide empirical tests of explicit hypotheses regarding replacement rates. Tests of these hypotheses need to be further replicated in sport organizations and in other formal organizations, especially those defined as work organizations (see Tausky, 1970).

Notwithstanding the special characteristics of sport organizations that make them most amenable to comparative analysis (see the introduction to this chapter), it must be recognized that the uniqueness of sport organizations may in fact preclude the generalization of findings from them to other formal organizations. For example, the degree of involuntary turnover, the standardized size of sport teams, and the monopolistic nature of organizational sets in professional sport are not commonly found in combination in other work organizations. Moreover, some studies of work organizations indicate important differences in replacement rates for blue- and white-collar workers, but in professional sports it is difficult to determine whether playing personnel should be classified as blue- or white-collar workers. The fact that their job performance is based on physical skill suggests that they are semiskilled craftsmen, but their education, relations with management (notwithstanding recent attempts at unionization), and employment during the off-season suggest that they should be classified as minor professionals.

Perhaps work organizations in the entertainment industry would afford the most appropriate units of analysis for the comparative examination of hypotheses of replacement processes generated in sport situations. This comparison might be useful since the performance of actors, artists, dancers, and musicians also depends on well-developed motor skills.

The primary purpose of the final section of this chapter was to determine through a review of literature the degree of empirical support for seven hypothesized correlates of replacement rates in sport organizations. Although a degree of empirical support was found for each hypothesis, the evidence was usually of a correlational nature, which precludes all but the most dubious inferences about the causal nature of the relationships. On the basis of available data it is difficult to determine whether the seven relationships examined are reversible or irreversible, deterministic or stochastic, sequential or coextensive, sufficient or contingent, necessary or substitutable (see Zetterberg, 1965, pp. 69–74). The specific nature of the relationships hypothesized above must be ascertained before adequate theories of replacement rates can be developed. As Zetterberg has warned:

> The types of causal linkage should be kept in mind in all manipulations of propositions. So long as all propositions used in our theorizing are of the same type, there are few dangers involved. However, when they are of different varieties, pitfalls appear, and one must proceed with caution. (Zetterberg, 1965, p. 74)

In short, and quite obviously, future studies of replacement processes in sport organizations should give greater attention to both theoretical and methodological issues. McPherson (1976c) has suggested that future studies should examine:

1. The effect of trading for future draft choices;
2. The impact of the mechanism of player turnover (i.e., draft, trade, promotion, or retirement);
3. The impact of personnel turnover on team effectiveness over a longer period of time; and
4. The influence of adding inexperienced (i.e., rookies) or experienced (i.e., veterans) personnel to the organization.

In all of these studies, a comparative analysis with a variety of sport organizations should be initiated to control for sport-specific phenomena. Cross-cultural studies might also prove fruitful in the sport domain. For example, in Japan baseball managers are sent off on retreats but are never fired when their team is losing. This procedure is related, of course, to the cultural norm of "saving face" (see Whiting, 1976, pp. 46–54).

From a theoretical and methodological perspective Theberge and Loy (1976) suggest that future studies should examine:

1. The utility of a variety of measures of replacement rates and organizational effectiveness;

2. The utility of multivariate methods of analysis and such statistical models as "Markov models" (Guppy and Fraser, 1973) and "vacancy chain models" (White, 1970); and

3. The utility of a variety of methods of data collection other than secondary data analysis, including the possibility of experimental investigation (Trow, 1960).

Finally, future studies should pay greater attention to the theoretical assumptions underlying the models that they use. To illustrate, Corwin (1971), in reaction to the work of Eitzen and Yetman (1973), states:

> We can only infer the model on which these interpretations rest, but there seems to be an unhealthy rationality about it all. . . . Why assume that team performance has anything to do with turnover any more than we should assume that the profit motive explains why big corporations grow or that the goals of learning can explain the affairs of universities? (Corwin, 1971, p. 2)

The preceding quotation does not do justice to the several critical and cogent observations made by Corwin concerning the analysis of the relationship between turnover and performance, but hopefully underscores the importance of critically examining the theoretical assumptions underlying studies of replacement processes in work organizations. In short, research regarding replacement processes in sport organizations has hardly begun.

NOTES

1. Income differentials by ethnicity may also be present. This topic is discussed in Section 7.1.3.
2. Another type of economic explanation may explain why blacks are underrepresented at these central positions. Specifically, Medoff (1977) proposes: "The economic hypothesis is (that) the result is due to differential costs. Relatively few blacks will choose these positions since the costs of acquiring skills are expensive."
3. Marple (1975) has found that there is also a performance differential in the scoring (goals and assists) in hockey. Specifically, Francophone players outperform Anglophone players.
4. This observation receives additional support in a more recent examination of discrimination in sport by Eitzen and Yetman (1977).
5. "Half-life" refers to the length of time required for a group or organization to experience a fifty-percent change in its original membership.

REFERENCES

Argyle, M., et al. (1958). "Supervisory methods related to productivity absenteeism, and labour turnover." *Human Relations* 11: 23–40.

Ball, D. W. (1973). "Ascription and position: A comparative analysis of 'stacking' in professional football." *Canadian Review of Sociology and Anthropology* 10 (May): 97–113. Used with permission.

Ball, D. W. (1974). "Replacement processes in work organizations: Task evaluation and the case of professional football." *Sociology of Work and Occupations* 1 (May): 197–217.

Ball, D. W. (1975). "A note on method in the sociological study of sport." In D. Ball and J. Loy (eds.), *Sport and Social Order: Contributions to the Sociology of Sport,* pp. 35–47. Reading, Mass.: Addison-Wesley.

Berelson, B., and G. A. Steiner (1964). *Human Behavior: An Inventory of Scientific Findings.* New York: Harcourt, Brace and World.

Blalock, H. M., Jr. (1962). "Occupational discrimination: Some theoretical propositions." *Social Problems* 9 (Spring): 240–247.

Blalock, H. M. (1967). *Toward a Theory of Minority Group Relations.* New York: John Wiley.

Blalock, H. (1969). *Theory Construction.* Englewood Cliffs, N.J.: Prentice-Hall.

Blau, P. (1974). *On the Nature of Organizations.* New York: John Wiley.

Blau, P. M., and W. R. Scott (1962). *Formal Organizations: A Comparative Approach.* San Francisco: Chandler.

Bowen, W. G., and T. A. Finegan (1969). *The Economics of Labor Force Participation.* Princeton, N.J.: Princeton University Press.

Breglio, J. (1976). "Formal structure and the recruitment of umpires in baseball organizations." Presented at the American Sociological Association Annual Meeting, New York (August).

Brower, J. (1972). "The racial basis of the division of labor among players in the National Football League as a function of racial stereotypes." Presented at the Pacific Sociological Association Meeting, Portland, Oregon. Used with permission.

Caplow, T. (1964). *Principles of Organization.* New York: Harcourt, Brace and World.

Carlson, R. (1961). "Succession and performance among school superintendents." *Administrative Science Quarterly* 6: 211–228.

Caruso, G. (1976). "Black is beautiful." *Atlanta Journal* (October 25): 1D, 7D.

Castine, S., and G. Roberts (1974). "Modeling in the socialization process of the black athlete." *International Review of Sport Sociology* 9: 59–73.

Charnofsky, H. (1968). "The major league baseball player: Self-conception versus the popular image." *International Review of Sport Sociology* 3: 39–55.

Charnofsky, H. (1975). "Social class, the black athlete, and success in sports." Presented at the Pacific Sociological Association Meetings, Victoria, British Columbia (April).

Chelladurai, P., and A. Carron (1977). "A reanalysis of formal structure in sport." *Canadian Journal of Applied Sport Sciences* 2 (April): 9–14. Used with permission.

Corwin, R. (1971). "Reaction to Eitzen and Yetman's paper on managerial change, longevity and organizational effectiveness." Paper presented at the Ohio Valley Sociological Society Meetings, Cleveland, Ohio (April 22–24). Used with permission.

Dodson, D. (1954). "The integration of Negroes in baseball." *Journal of Educational Sociology* 28 (October): 73–82.

Donnelly, P. (1975). "An analysis of the relationship between organizational half-life and organizational effectiveness." Unpublished paper, Department of Sport Studies, University of Massachusetts.

Dornbusch, S. M., and W. R. Scott (1975). *Evaluation and the Exercise of Authority.* San Francisco: Jossey-Bass.

Dougherty, J. (1976). "Race and sport: A followup study." *Sport Sociology Bulletin* 5 (Spring): 1–12.

Dunn, J., and M. Lupfer (1974). "A comparison of black and white boys' performance in self-paced and reactive sports activities." *Journal of Applied Social Psychology* 4: 24–35.

Edwards, H. (1969). *The Revolt of the Black Athlete.* New York: The Free Press.

Edwards, H. (1971). "The sources of the black athlete's superiority." *The Black Scholar* (November): 32–41.

Edwards, H. (1972). "The myth of the racially superior athlete." *Intellectual Digest* **2** (March): 58–60.

Eitzen, D. S., and D. C. Sanford (1975). "The segregation of blacks by playing position in football: Accident or design?" *Social Science Quarterly* **55** (March): 948–959.

Eitzen, D. S., and I. Tessendorf (1975). "Racial segregation by position in sports: The special case of basketball." In D. Landers et al. (eds.), *Proceedings of the 2nd Conference for the North American Society for the Psychology of Sport and Physical Activity*, pp. 321–332. University Park, Pennsylvania State University.

Eitzen, D. S., and N. R. Yetman (1972). "Managerial change, longevity and organizational effectiveness." *Administrative Science Quarterly* **17** (March): 110–116. Used with permission.

Eitzen, D. S., and N. R. Yetman (1977). "Immune from racism." *Civil Rights Digest* **9**: 3–13.

Etzioni, A. (1964). *Modern Organizations*. Englewood Cliffs, N.J.: Prentice-Hall.

Evan, W. M. (1963). "Peer-group interaction and organizational socialization: A study of employee turnover." *American Sociological Review* **28**: 436–440.

Gamson, W. A., and N. A. Scotch (1964). "Scapegoating in baseball." *American Journal of Sociology* **70**: 69–72.

Glasser, B. G. (1968). *Organizational Careers*. Chicago: Aldine.

Gordon, G., and S. Becker (1964). "Organizational size and managerial succession: A reexamination." *American Journal of Sociology* **70**: 215–222.

Gouldner, A. W. (1954). *Patterns of Industrial Bureaucracy*. Glencoe, Ill.: The Free Press.

Grusky, O. (1960). "Administrative succession in formal organizations." *Social Forces* **39** (December): 105–115.

Grusky, O. (1961). "Corporate size, bureaucratization, and managerial succession." *American Journal of Sociology* **67**: 261–269.

Grusky, O. (1963a). "The effect of formal structure on managerial recruitment: A study of baseball organization." *Sociometry* **26**: 345–353.

Grusky, O. (1963b). "Managerial succession and organizational effectiveness." *American Journal of Sociology* **69** (July): 21–31.

Grusky, O. (1964). "Reply to Gamson and Scotch." *American Journal of Sociology* **69**: 72–76.

Grusky, O. (1969). "Succession with an ally." *Administrative Science Quarterly* **14**: 155–170.

Grusky, O., and G. A. Miller (eds.) (1970). *The Sociology of Organizations: Basic Studies*. New York: The Free Press.

Guest, R. (1962). "Managerial succession in complex organizations." *American Journal of Sociology* **68**: 47–56.

Guppy, L. N., and E. D. Fraser (1973). "Occupational mobility in professional baseball: A Markov model as a tool for measurement." Paper presented at the First Canadian Congress for the Multi-Disciplinary Study of Sport and Physical Activity, Montreal, Quebec (October 12).

Hall, R. H. (1972). *Organizations—Structure and Process*. Englewood Cliffs, N.J.: Prentice-Hall.

Henderson, F. (1975). "Latin Americans in baseball: The absence of stacking." Unpublished paper, Department of Sport Studies, University of Massachusetts.

Homans, G. (1969). "Prologue: The sociological relevance of behaviorism." In R. L. Burgess and D. Bushell (eds.), *Behavioral Sociology*, pp. 1–26. New York: Columbia University Press.

Hopkins, T. (1964). *The Exercise of Influence in Small Groups*. Totowa, N.J.: The Bedminster Press.

Johnson, N., and D. Marple (1973). "Racial discrimination in professional basketball: An empirical test." *Sociological Focus* 6 (Fall): 6–18.

Jones, J., and A. Hochner (1973). "Racial differences in sports activities: A look at the self-paced versus reactive hypothesis." *Journal of Personality and Social Psychology* 27: 86–95.

Jordan, J. (1969). "Physiological and anthropometrical comparisons of Negroes and whites." *Journal of Health, Physical Education and Recreation* 40 (November/December): 93–99.

Kane, M. (1971). "An assessment of black is best." *Sports Illustrated* (January 18): 72–83.

Katz, D., and R. Klein (1966). *The Social Psychology of Organizations*. New York: John Wiley.

Kenyon, G. S., and B. D. McPherson (1973). "Becoming involved in physical activity and sport: A process of socialization." In G. L. Rarick (ed.), *Physical Activity: Human Growth and Development*, pp. 303–332. New York: Academic Press.

Kjeldsen, E. (1976). "An investigation of the determinants of effectiveness in small, task-oriented groups." Unpublished Ph.D. dissertation, Department of Sociology, University of Massachusetts.

Klonsky, B. (1975). "The effects of formal structure and role skills on coaching recruitment and longevity: A study of professional basketball teams." Unpublished paper, Department of Psychology, Fordham University.

Kriesburg, L. (1962). "Careers, organizational size, and succession." *American Journal of Sociology* 68: 355–359.

Leonard, W. M. (1977). "Stacking and performance differentials of whites, blacks and Latins in professional baseball." *Review of Sport and Leisure* 2: 77–106.

Leonard, W., and S. Schmidt (1975). "Observations on the changing social organization of collegiate and professional basketball." *Sport Sociology Bulletin* 4 (Fall): 13–35. Used with permission.

Loy, J. W., and J. F. McElvogue (1970). "Racial segregation in American sport." *International Review of Sport Sociology* 5: 5–24.

Loy, J. W., and J. Sage (1970). "The effects of formal structure on organizational leadership: An investigation of interscholastic baseball teams," pp. 363–373. In G. S. Kenyon and T. Grogg (eds.), *Contemporary Psychology of Sport*, pp. 363–373. Chicago: The Athletic Institute.

Loy, J. W., J. Sage, and A. Ingham (1970). "The effects of formal structure on organizational leadership: An investigation of varsity baseball teams." Unpublished paper, Department of Sport Studies, University of Massachusetts.

Malina, R. M. (1972). "Anthropology, growth and physical education." In R. Singer et al. (eds.), *Physical Education: An Interdisciplinary Approach*, pp. 237–309. New York: Macmillan.

March, J. (ed.) (1965). *Handbook of Organizations*. Chicago: Rand McNally.

Marin, V. (1969). "Experience—a factor in pro-football success." Unpublished paper, Department of Physical Education, UCLA (March).

Marple, D. (1975). "Analyse de la discrimination que subissent les Canadiens Français au hockey professionel." *Mouvement* 10: 7–13.

Massengale, J., and S. Farrington (1977). "The influence of playing position centrality on the careers of college football coaches." *Review of Sport and Leisure* 2 (June): 107–115.

McElvogue, J. (1969). "Discrimination in sport." Unpublished paper, Department of Physical Education, University of California at Los Angeles.

McNeil, K., and J. D. Thompson (1971). "The regeneration of social organizations." *American Sociological Review* 36: 624–637.

McPherson, B. D. (1974). "Minority group involvement in sport." In J. Wilmore (ed.)., *Exercise and Sport Sciences Reviews*, Vol. 2, pp. 71–101. New York: Academic Press.

McPherson, B. D. (1975). "The segregation by playing position hypothesis in sport: An alternative explanation." *Social Science Quarterly* 55 (March): 960–966.

McPherson, B. (1976a). "The black athlete: An overview and analysis." In D. Landers (ed.), *Social Problems in Athletics*, pp. 122–150. Urbana, Ill.: University of Illinois Press.

McPherson, B. (1976b). "Involuntary turnover: A characteristic process of sport organizations." *International Review of Sport Sociology* 11: 5–15. Used with permission.

McPherson, B. (1976c). "Involuntary turnover and organization effectiveness in the National Hockey League." In R. Gruneau and J. Albinson (eds.), *Canadian Sport: Sociological Perspectives*, pp. 259–275. Don Mills, Ontario: Addison-Wesley (Canada).

Medoff, M. H. (1977). "Positional segregation and professional baseball." *International Review of Sport Sociology* 12: 49–54.

Meggesey, D. (1970). *Out of Their League*. Berkeley, Calif.: Ramparts Press.

Moore, H. E. (1964). "Discrimination." In J. Gould and L. Kolb (eds.), *A Dictionary of the Social Sciences*, pp. 203–204. New York: Free Press.

Mouzelis, N. P. (1968). *Organization and Bureaucracy*. Chicago: Aldine.

Mulder, M. (1963). *Group Structure, Motivation and Group Performance*. The Hague: Mouton. Used with permission.

Norman, S. L. (1968). "Collation of anthropometric research comparing American males: Negro and Caucasian." M.S. thesis, University of Oregon, Eugene, Oregon.

Olsen, J. (1968). *The Black Athlete: A Shameful Story*. New York: Time Publications.

Pascal, A., and L. Rapping (1972). "The economics of racial discrimination in organized baseball." In A. Pascal (ed.), *Racial Discrimination in Economic Life*, pp. 119–156. Lexington, Mass.: Heath.

Peckham, V. (1970). "A study of the relationship between personnel succession and organizational effectiveness." Unpublished paper, Department of Sport Studies, University of Massachusetts.

Perrow, C. (1970). *Organizational Analysis: A Sociological View*. Belmont, Calif.: Wadsworth.

Perrucci, R., and R. A. Mannweiler (1968). "Organization size, complexity and administrative succession in higher education." *The Sociological Quarterly* 9: 343–355.

Phillips, J. (1976). "Toward an explanation of racial variations in top-level sports participation." *International Review of Sport Sociology* 11: 39–53.

Price, J. L. (1975). "A theory of turnover." In B. O. Bettman (ed.), *Labor Turnover and Retention*, pp. 51–75. Epping, Essex: Gower Press.

Price, J. L. (1975–1976). "A Theory of Turnover." *Industrial Relations* 6 (Winter): 33–46.

Price, J. L. (1976). "The effects of turnover on the organization." *Organization and Administrative Science* 7: 61–88.

Price, J. L. (1977). *The Study of Turnover*. Ames, Iowa: Iowa State University Press.

Roland, P. (1977). "Ascription and position: A comparative analysis of the influence of playing position on the careers of professional football coaches." Unpublished paper, Department of Sport Studies, University of Massachusetts.

Rose, J. D. (1969). "The attribution of responsibility for organizational failure." *Sociology and Social Research* 53 (April): 323–332. Used with permission.

Rosenblatt, A. (1967). "Negroes in baseball: The failure of success." *Transaction* 5 (September): 51–53.

Roy, G. (1974). "The relationship between centrality and mobility: The case of the

National Hockey League." M.S. thesis, Department of Kinesiology, University of Waterloo.

Sage, J. (1974). "The effects of formal structure on organizational leadership: An investigation of collegiate football teams." Presented at the National AAHPER Convention, Anaheim, California (March).

Schrag, P. (1970). "Tennessee lonesome end." *Harper's Magazine* **240** (March): 59–67.

Schwartz, G. (1973). "A comparative analysis of succession, size and success among professional sport organizations." Unpublished paper, Department of Sport Studies, University of Massachusetts.

Scott, W. R. (1975). "Organizational structure." In A. Inkeles (ed.), *Annual Review of Sociology*, Vol. 1, pp 1–20. Palo Alto, Calif.: Annual Reviews, Inc.

Scully, G. (1974). "Discrimination: The case of baseball." In R. Noll (ed.), *Government and the Sports Business*, pp. 221–273. Washington, D.C.: The Brookings Institution.

Shelley, M. W. (1964). "The mathematical representation of the individual in models of organization problems." In W. W. Cooper et al. (eds.), *New Perspectives in Organizational Research*. New York: Wiley.

Silverman, D. (1970). *The Theory of Organizations*. London: Heinemann.

Smith, G., and C. Grindstaff (1972). "Race and sport in Canada." In A. Taylor and M. Howell (eds.), *Training: Scientific Basis and Application*, pp. 197–206. Springfield, Ill.: Charles C. Thomas.

Stinchcombe, A. (1968). *Constructing Social Theories*. New York: Harcourt, Brace and World.

Tausky, C. (1970). *Work Organizations*. Itasca, Ill.: B. E. Peacock.

Theberge, N., and J. W. Loy (1976). "Replacement processes in sport organizations: The case of professional baseball." *International Review of Sport Sociology* **11**: 73–93.

Time (1970). "Sport." (April 6): 79.

Time (1977). "The black dominance." (May 9): 57–60.

Trice, H. M. (1961). "Rural-reared workers and labor turnover." *Rural Sociology* **26**: 299–304.

Trow, D. B. (1960). "Membership succession and team performance." *Human Relations* **13**: 259–268.

Trow, D. B. (1961). "Executive succession in small companies." *Administrative Science Quarterly* **6**: 229–239.

White, H. C. (1970). *Chains of Opportunity: System Models of Mobility in Organizations*. Cambridge, Mass.: Harvard University Press.

Whiting, B. (1976). "Bowed but never bloodied." *Sports Illustrated* **44** (June 17): 46–54.

Williams, L., and Y. Youssef (1972). "Consistency of football coaches in stereotyping the personality of each position's player." *International Journal of Sport Psychology* **3**: 3–11.

Williams, R., and Y. Youssef (1975). "Division of labor in college football along racial lines." *International Journal of Sport Psychology* **6**: 3–13.

Winfield, A. L. (1977). "Racial variations in starting positions: The case of professional baseball." Unpublished paper, Department of Sport Studies, University of Massachusetts.

Worthy, M., and A. Markle (1970). "Black Americans in reactive versus self-paced sports activities." *Journal of Personality and Social Psychology* **16**: 439–443.

Yetman, N., and D. S. Eitzen (1972). "Black Americans in sports: Unequal opportunity for equal ability." *Civil Rights Digest* **5** (August): 20–34. Used with permission.

Zetterberg, H. L. (1965). *On Theory and Verification in Sociology*, 3rd ed. Totowa, N.J.: Bedminster Press. Used with permission.

Chapter 5
SPORT
SUBCULTURES

5.1 INTRODUCTION

5.1.1 Definitions of Subcultures

Despite the presence of many descriptive analyses of unique normative systems in a society (e.g., class, racial, ethnic, regional, avocational, occupational, or deviant groups), there is a paucity of theoretical and empirical work concerning the concept "subculture" (Arnold, 1970). It was not until 1947 that Gordon first defined the concept as "a subdivision of a national culture . . . a functioning unity which has an integrated impact on the participating individual." More recently it has been defined as "a culture theme, a sub-ethos, or a cluster of values that is differentiated from those in the total culture" (Wolfgang and Ferracuti, 1967), and as "a set of modal beliefs, values, norms and customs associated with a relatively distinct social subsystem . . . existing within a larger social system and culture" (Fischer, 1975).

Central, then, to the idea of subculture are values and norms that arise within a unique social situation. Once these values and norms become accepted by a number of individuals, who may or may not interact with each other, they begin to influence both avocational and occupational life styles. Wolfgang and Ferracuti (1967) suggest that a given system of values and norms may lead to the formation of a subculture when a number of these values and norms are different from the mainstream culture in content and importance, when they are unacceptable to some degree in the larger culture, when they become stable over time (i.e., they are not a fad), and when they begin to regulate behavior.

In short, an individual's life style is influenced by his or her degree of identity and involvement with a particular subculture, which is characterized by values, norms, beliefs, attitudes, and language that differ from, but are related to, the mainstream society. The degree of interaction with the dominant culture or with other subcultures may range from little or none (e.g., a subsistence commune in the mountains) to a great deal (e.g., revolutionaries who employ violent tactics while in conflict with the dominant group). As a general principle, the more the subculture has special meanings, symbols, dress, values, norms, beliefs, attitudes, language, rituals, etc., for those involved, the greater the spiritual or physical distance from outsiders. This holds even if individuals seldom or never interact with "others" within the subculture.

5.1.2 Models of Subcultures

In recent years social scientists have attempted to analyze how subcultures are created, why they persist, how individuals come to be members, and what impact they have on the individual and on society. In order to assist in this process of explanation, a number of theories have been formulated. Although most were developed to explain deviant subcultures, some have been concerned with occupational or leisure social worlds.

Generally, the theories (see Arnold, 1970) have argued that subcultures arise (1) in response to some problem, deprivation, or opportunity that is common to a group of people or to a specific natural environment (e.g., poverty); (2) as a result of interaction which creates social distance, social conflict, or the awareness of life-style differences (e.g., ethnic group insulation and isolation); and (3) when a shared frame of reference and group action emerges (e.g., violence to induce change). Accordingly, a subculture emerges in response to a situation which is accompanied by interaction and remains viable and recruits new members when interaction occurs over an extended period of time. This view has been identified in a process model of subcultures, which suggests that "individuals sharing similar status interact more with each other than would be expected by chance, and that out of this interaction comes a system of beliefs, values, and norms—i.e., a subculture" (Arnold, 1970).

Whereas the work of Arnold (1970) and others (Cohen, 1955) stresses the necessity of face-to-face interaction, Shibutani (1955), employing a symbolic interactionist perspective, argues that the essential component for the development and continuation of a social world is a formal communication network such as that found in occupational subcultures. This network serves as a reference group in the individual's social world because of its special meanings and symbols. Furthermore, it may accentuate differences and increase the social distance from outsiders. For example, the worlds of horse racing, professional wrestling, and poolrooms all have their own unique language and communication networks for acquiring and disseminating information among "insiders."

In order to synthesize the process of subcultural emergence and development, Pearson (1976) derived a model that operates on three levels and accounts for both the antecedent conditions and the actual process (Fig. 5.1). Using this model, the emergence of sporting subculture X can be explained. First, a group of individuals with an interest in X (e.g., X = surfing, skiing, hang gliding, etc.) find themselves in a common social situation or structural position that facilitates differential interaction whereby those not involved in X are excluded (e.g., these individuals may have joined a club or be engaging in the sport in the same milieu). As a result, shared attitudes, beliefs, and behaviors unique to individuals and to the group become salient, while facets of the dominant culture are

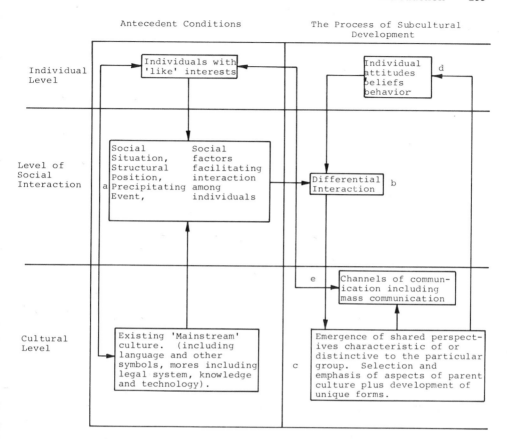

Antecedent Conditions   The Process of Subcultural
                                          Development

Fig. 5.1   *The process of subcultural emergence and development. (From Pearson, 1976)*

selectively (consciously or unconsciously) eliminated. Thus, individual and group beliefs, attitudes, and behavior are solidified and a new reference group or subculture emerges. The more this cycle (b to c to d in Fig. 5.1) is repeated, the greater the likelihood that channels of communication will be expanded beyond the original group, thereby attracting new recruits to the subculture, although perhaps not to the original group because of geographical or ideological differences. That is, even if individuals do not formally join the original group, they become part of the subculture if they adhere to some of the attitudes, beliefs, norms, and values as communicated to them. For example, the surfing subculture has diffused throughout the world and different social worlds, such as those of the surfboard riders and surf lifesavers in New Zealand, have evolved.

5.1.3 Problems in the Study of Subcultures

To date, many of the analyses of subcultures have been descriptive, qualitative ethnographies based on a participant observation study of one specific social milieu. Hence, typologies and structural characteristics are described that may not be general across all situations within that subculture. That is, to observe and describe the scene at one beach, ski resort, or health club may be insightful, but it may be atypical of the surfing, skiing, or pumping-iron subcultures in general. Much of this problem has been created due to the lack of a general theoretical framework that would facilitate systematic comparisons and theory development. More specifically, there are some conceptual and methodological problems in this area of sociological inquiry that must be considered.

First, it has been suggested that social interaction is not required in order for values to be shared and therefore a subculture in which members do not interact face-to-face may arise. For example, Pearson (1976) notes that surfboard riders in Australia comprise a subculture because they share a common meaning and way of life (e.g., norms, values, symbols), yet members seldom, if ever, interact with each other. In short, subculture is a concept that is independent of individuals and collectivities and represents a pattern whereby people share a universe of meanings.

A second problem is how to delineate subcultural boundaries from each other and from the dominant culture itself. This definitional and measurement problem has led some investigators to conclude that a subculture can only be identified and understood when components of both the dominant culture and the subculture are measured and compared to note differences, similarities, and possibilities for conflict. For example, Wolfgang and Ferracuti (1967) suggest that there are two types of subcultural values: concordant values, which are tolerated, and discordant values, which are not. The number and importance of each type identify the degree of agreement or conflict between a given subculture and both the dominant culture and other subcultures. Schematically, Pearson (1976) has illustrated how a subcultural norm that is discrepant with a cultural norm may lie within a tolerable range of behavior of those sharing the cultural norm (Fig. 5.2).

A final problem, this from the perspective of the individual, is how to determine the degree of involvement in one or more subcultures among the many that may interact (in either a cooperative or conflict relationship) in a pluralistic society. That is, an individual may participate in one or more subcultures with varying degrees of commitment, identity (Clarke, 1974), and intensity, ranging from marginal or peripheral status (i.e., almost an outsider) to a central or leadership position (i.e., a committed insider). For example, an individual may visit a ski area for one week a year or may migrate to the area, establish roots, and become an informal or formal task or social leader in the community. Similarly, individuals may enter related subcultures sequentially (e.g., from skier to hang-glider to glider pilot to balloonist) or, because of similar physical or structural components, there may be multiple involvement in a variety of avocational or occupational social worlds (e.g., surfing, diving, and skiing, or dune-buggy riding, motocross racing, and snowmobiling). Notwithstanding these problems, this chapter describes and analyzes the types of sport subcultures, their functional problems, and the opportunity they provide for developing and testing character traits of those who are involved.

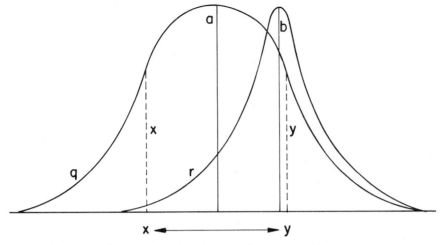

Fig. 5.2 *Illustrating how a subcultural norm discrepant with a cultural norm may lie within a tolerable range of behavior of those sharing the cultural norm. The q curve represents the distribution of behavior around the cultural norm; the r curve represents the distribution of behavior around the subcultural norm; a is the culturally prescribed norm; b is the subculturally prescribed norm; and the area of the q curve between x and y represents the range of tolerable behavior within the parent culture. (From Pearson, 1976)*

5.1.4 Types of Sport Subcultures

Subcultures might be expected to develop within the social system of sport in that by virtue of interaction patterns and specialized role expectancies, unique symbols, meanings, argot (i.e., language), beliefs, norms, and values arise and are shared among members. This operates on either a microsystem level within one sport where there is frequent and intense interaction (e.g., one team in professional football), or on a macrosystem level in a sport where there may be little or no face-to-face interaction (e.g., surfing).

Phillips and Schafer (1970, 1971) have suggested that there is one athletic subculture that is comprised of all athletes, regardless of their sport. They argue that this subculture exists on the basis of studies indicating that athletes are different from nonathletes in character traits, degree of social adjustment, educational aspirations and achievement, and life style. Since the findings of many of these studies are equivocal, the evidence for a general athletic subculture is not sufficiently strong. Rather, it may be more meaningful to talk about specific sport subcultures and how they relate to each other and to nonsport subcultures.

There appear to be three major types of subcultures: occupational, avocational, and deviant, although elements of the latter can interact with the other two types. Each type is faced with a number of functional problems, which will be discussed throughout the chapter. These include (1) *pattern maintenance,* such as the recruitment and socialization of new members, the retention of members through rewards and inducements, retirement and desocialization from the scene, and the maintenance of cultural elements (e.g., norms, values, beliefs, symbols, language, dress, legends, traditions, technology); (2) *integration*, such as the learning of job-related skills and moral attributes, the functional specialization of tasks, the social status and mobility paths (career benchmarks) within the structure, the rites of passage, and the establishment of reciprocal collegial relationships; (3) *goal attainment*, such as information control and the acquisition and demonstration of cognitive and motor skills unique to the subculture; and (4) *adaptation*, such as differential relations with the dominant culture and with "outsiders."

Occupational Subcultures

Occupational subcultures appeared within the world of professional sport when the degree of professionalization, commercialization, and bureaucratization increased (see Ingham, 1975). As a result, participation in sport became a work role rather than a leisure role and necessitated a process of socialization, formalization, and role differentiation. To illustrate, each professional sport is characterized by a variety of interacting, yet unique subcultures including the athlete and coach, the owner and management personnel, the sport consumers, the media, and the league officials. Since there are different life styles within and between sports, the career contingencies and the way of life characteristic of sport occupations has served as the focus of analysis for a number of subcultures within professional sport, including the world of *boxing* (Weinberg and Arond, 1952; Hare, 1971), *professional wrestling* (Stone, 1972; Rosenberg and Turowetz, 1975), *baseball* (Andreano, 1965; Bouton, 1970; Charnofsky, 1968; Haerle, 1975), *horse racing* (Scott, 1968), *football* (Kramer, 1969; Meggesey, 1970; Shaw, 1973), *hockey* (Faulkner, 1975; Smith and Diamond, 1976; Vaz, 1972), and *college coaching* (Massengale, 1974; Sage, 1975).

More specifically, using the participant observation or survey research technique, these studies have described and to varying degrees attempted to explain anticipatory socialization; the prerequisite technical and social skills; recruitment patterns; the informal and formal occupational socialization process; the behavioral norms, value components, and expectations concerning interaction with those inside (e.g., the team) and outside (e.g., owners, media, fans, officials) the subcultural system; the argot (language) of the sport system; the social structure, social organization, social status, and social mobility within the sport; and the process of coping with failure, demotion, dismissal, and retirement, and the subsequent adjustment to the dominant culture.

Avocational Subcultures

Avocational subcultures are created when a leisure activity provides a social milieu in which individuals can pursue a central life interest and interact with others who have similar life styles. That is, an avocational leisure pursuit may represent an "ephemeral role," which Steele and Zurcher (1973) define as "a temporary or ancillary position-related behavior pattern chosen by the enactor to satisfy social-psychological needs incompletely satisfied by the more dominant and lasting roles he regularly must enact in everyday life positions." Furthermore, these activities, pursued under the guise of leisure and fun, may constitute identity-seeking activities not attainable within the normal organizational or institutional channels that usually provide status (Klapp, 1969). For example, Jacobs (1976) describes the karate dojo as a "place where some aspect of their many-sided selves can become rooted, a place where a uniform and a colored belt become the criteria of who they are and what they do, in this time, in that place." From a functional perspective Fritschner (1977) argues that karate appeals primarily to working-class males, many of whom occupy deadend jobs, because it permits a class of potential malcontents to experience vertical mobility in their leisure world, which is denied them in the larger economic and political system. Moreover, she stresses that the dojo reinforces the idealized values of diligence, hard work, suffering, and honesty among the working class.

Within any given leisure world, the pattern and degree of involvement is patternlike, but differential (see Section 2.2.3). For example, McPhee (1963) suggested that patterns of consumption may be "explosive," "chronic," "divergent," "normal," "abortive," or "aversive" in that not everyone is involved to the same degree or at the same time interval. For some, involvement is cyclical; for others it is regular and well-integrated into their life style; for still others it is a pattern of being ". . . carried away toward consumption ever rising beyond any bounds and without return . . ." (McPhee, 1963). Ultimately, the degree of involvement in the subculture may result in a fulltime commitment whereby the individual moves into an occupational subculture. For example, the recreational skier may become a ski instructor or the surfer may open a surf shop at a favorite beach.

Similarly, what is ostensibly an avocational subculture can become a preoccupational subculture (Vaz, 1972) when a leisure activity emulates the work world and seeks to socialize individuals into work roles. Youth sport programs have increasingly become training environments for high school, college, and professional sport in which appropriate norms, values, attitudes, and skills are acquired. To illustrate, within youth sport there have evolved occupationally oriented patterns of behavior (only the highly skilled play and are rewarded; recruiting for the best talent), values (winning is all that counts; be aggressive; deviate from the rules when and if necessary), beliefs (an elite career is initiated early in life and includes extensive competition), and symbols (trophies, uniforms, jackets, bonuses for playing for a specific team). Some of these practices and views are reported by Ralbovsky (1974) and Voigt (1974) in their perceptive analyses of Little League baseball. For example, Voigt wrote the following based on his experience as a Little League baseball manager.

1. . . . thanks to a new league ruling that changed to our advantage the month of a boy's age eligibility. It was a ruling Fred and I helped to push through. . . . Given this diplomatic coup, I planned to . . . lure one of the star players from the Updyke Boy's League into our camp. If this new strategy worked we had a darned good shot at the championship. . . . (Voigt, 1974, p. 13)

2. . . . make the most of a recruiting campaign. (Voigt, 1974, p. 15)

3. With only eleven good players on hand we had no problem identifying the six "plumbers" whose fate would be to ride the bench and work to develop their skills for shots at starting posts in 1974 (Voigt, 1974, p. 13). Being a plumber meant spending hours standing in the field waiting to get in somewhat fewer licks. It was a clear caste system. . . . (Voigt, 1974, p. 23)

4. Vic's best asset was a father who worked him daily and saw to it that he moonlighted in another league with kids his own age. (Voigt, 1974, p. 19)

In a similar vein, Vaz and Thomas illustrate the ideology of the minor hockey league occupational milieu in the following pregame speech and statement by a coach:

1. . . . Let's be ready tonight . . . you're going to get mad at them right now, and we are going to hit them . . . (Vaz and Thomas, 1973, p. 4); and

2. As long as they are playing competitive hockey, there's nothing wrong with playing it tough, and that's the way kids should be taught . . . otherwise they should go to the park with a puck and stick and go for a skate. That's the game . . . you take Gordie Howe . . . you try to out-muscle him in the corner with the puck and you'll get 17 elbows in the face . . . if you want to play the game, play it tough, don't play it like a sissy. (Vaz and Thomas, 1974, p. 9)

While having many of the same characteristics and processes as an occupational subculture, an avocational subculture is unique in a variety of ways. For example, the meaning of the activity is normally more expressive than instrumental; there is normally less time commitment, at least in the initial stages; the recruitment and socialization process is less formalized; the social organization is less bureaucratic; withdrawal from the world is normally voluntary and less traumatic; there is less status differentiation and mobility within the system, although prestige rankings based on skill evolve; and the activity is more likely to occur without an audience in a nonurban environment. Furthermore, as Toffler (1970) notes, many avocational subcultures are organized around a technological device such as a parachute, hot rod, dune buggy, or glider. Thus, as society becomes increasingly technocratic, we can expect to see the emergence of new avocational subcultures that will reflect the new technology.

Deviant Subcultures

Most occupational and avocational subcultures represent normative patterns of social participation. However, some leisure or work domains have been considered sufficiently different from the normative system in society to be labeled by the dominant culture as a deviant subculture. Some examples include those sport environments in which hustling, cheating, gambling, institutionalized violence, or deviant social acts take place.

Deviant behavior, which is often a dysfunctional product of the socialization process, involves a violation of formal (public) or informal (private) norms, either within the dominant society or within any given subsystem. Whether an act is labeled as deviant or not often depends on the normative reference group or individual evaluating the behavior and enforcing the norms. Because of social differentiation and pluralistic socialization patterns, deviance varies across class, ethnic, racial, cultural, and occupational lines and is considered to be a process and product of a particular subculture.

Thus what is viewed as deviance by outsiders is often more likely to be considered "sanctioned deviance" by insiders within the specific subculture. For example, tripping or pushing an opponent who is about to score in a game violates the norm of fair play and the formal norms of the game, yet may be sanctioned by coaches, players, and spectators. In fact, it may be institutionalized as an informal norm within the particular sport subculture. Similarly, fighting in hockey (Faulkner, 1974a), hustling in pool (Polsky, 1969, 1972), or drinking at sport events[1] is viewed by outsiders as deviant behavior unique to a specific subculture. In short, whether a subculture is labeled as deviant depends on the norms and values of the salient reference group within mainstream society.

From the perspective of the individual, deviant behavior is learned in unique subcultures that value and reinforce certain behavioral skills or patterns. For example, Wolfgang and Ferracuti (1967) have demonstrated that violent behavior results from values supportive of violence being learned in certain subcultures. Similarly, hustling is an art acquired by "hanging out" in poolrooms where one can hustle and be hustled.

Notwithstanding the fact that some sporting subcultures are labeled as deviant, deviant behavior is present to some extent in most sport subcultures. In addition to perceived deviant acts in the playing milieu, athletes sometimes engage in behavior that is considered legally or morally unacceptable by society. Although the acts themselves may or may not have serious consequences, they are viewed with concern because they are committed by a member of a sporting subculture. Although numerous incidents of deviant acts by athletes could be cited, we present the social life of the rugby subculture as an example of deviant interactions within the sport system. The unique feature of this world is that the behavioral patterns are highly institutionalized in a similar form in many cultures (that is, the game, as well as its subcultural characteristics, has been diffused to other nations) and they are considered normative within the subculture of rugby players.

The most interesting sociological fact of this world is that historically it has been a "male preserve" (Sheard and Dunning, 1973) wherein deviant behavior has become a ritualized and integral facet (McElroy, 1971; Sheard and Dunning, 1973; Thomson, 1977) of the life style away from the field. More specifically, rugby players consider it normative to violate societal norms regarding fighting, obscene language and songs, nakedness (e.g., a male strip tease), drunkenness, and vandalism against property. Sheard and Dunning (1973) argue that historically this behavior resulted because of the threat to the masculinity of middle- and upper-class males by the suffragette movement. This threat necessitated the creation of a private refuge from women. Vestiges of this attitude of exclusionism are found in other sporting subcultures such as surfing (Pearson, 1974), skydiving (Arnold, 1972), boxing (Weinberg and Arond, 1952) and pool-rooms (Polsky, 1972). Even recent excursions of women into these worlds have not posed a perceived threat, since the women are relegated to obscure positions and continue to be abused verbally (in songs) or physically (for example, the "butt bite" is a traditional initiation rite for a woman entering the rugby social world for the first time). Deviation from everyday norms is therefore characteristic of the rugby social world in many countries since players are allowed:

> to behave with impunity in a manner which would bring immediate condemnation and punishment were it to occur among other social strata or even among members of the upper and middle classes in a different social setting. (Sheard and Dunning, 1973, p. 7)

Thomson (1977) suggests that this antisocial behavior is underreported or ignored because the values of sport are not in conflict with the values of the dominant ideology, whereas similar behavior by a motorcycle gang might be negatively sanctioned because most of the gang's values appear to conflict with those of society. A second explanation (Thomson, 1977) is that "traditions of deviance" in sport have led to the behavior being viewed as "legitimate" deviance, which is condoned and perhaps even encouraged as a socially sanctioned safety valve for releasing tension (Listiak, 1974). In short, the emphasis in the literature has been on identifying the degree to which deviant acts are present within sport subcultures and on determining to what extent involvement in sport serves as a deterrent to deviant behavior outside the sporting subculture.

5.2 SPORT SUBCULTURES: WHERE THE ACTION IS

Goffman (1967) argues ". . . that action is to be found whenever the individual knowingly takes consequential chances that are perceived as avoidable. Ordinarily, action will not be found during the week-day work routine at home or on the job." There are, of course, certain occupations involving high personal risk and, thus, action. For example, there are the physical risks associated with construction work, the military service, and police work; the financial risks associated with salesmen, speculators, and stockbrokers; the social risks associated with live entertainers, politicians, and social commentators; and the combined risks associated with racketeers and other criminal figures (Goffman, 1967). But these occupations tend to be the exception rather than the rule. Moreover, although they permit the display of moral attributes such as courage and coolness, the social situations in which they are displayed are often viewed as deviant and immoral (for example, the daring courage of a bank robber or the coolness of a pool hustler). Further, such display of moral character is not typically witnessed by the general public.

In North American culture, *action* in the clearest and most legitimate sense is generally seen in subcultural sport situations. Goffman (1967), for example, describes four social settings in which action is routinely found, and each situation by coincidence is sport related. He specifically suggests that contestants typically find action in (1) commercialized competitive sports, (2) nonspectator high-risk sports, (3) commercialized places in which sporting equipment and playing facilities can be rented, and (4) social settings such as casinos, race tracks, and jai alai frontons where individuals can engage in a special type of action that Goffman calls "fancy milling."

Of course, most members of society do not routinely engage in direct sport participation and thus only indirectly expose themselves to action situations. Perhaps one of the basic appeals of indirect sport involvement through the mass media is the fact that individuals do not have to put their own character to test. Rather, they vicariously appropriate the moral identities of those public figures whom they most admire. In any event, television and the popular press provide idealized moral role models. These function as comparative standards of preferred moral attributes to which individuals may lay claim and discern as defining their own character.

5.2.1 Commercialized Spectator Sport

Within the context of professional sport a number of unique subcultures develop, many of which have common patterns and characteristics. For example, all professional sport teams must recruit and socialize new members, develop and maintain stability in the organization, and require or permit members to leave when their interest or utility declines.

Recruitment and Socialization

The process of recruiting and socializing potential members into a professional sport role actually begins in early childhood and continues, for some sports, during the high school and college years. The process begins indirectly when youth identify early in life with role models in professional sport. For some, this may involve a face-to-face interaction, as in the case of boxers who "hang out" in a neighborhood gym or club; or it may involve vicarious participation through consumption of the traditional team sports that appear in the mass media. Whether an individual becomes socialized into a specific type of sport subculture (e.g., boxing rather than tennis) is often related to the social class and ethnic and/or racial background of the family.

Once an interest in sport is aroused, an individual becomes involved in organized youth sport programs, which are almost identical to the appropriate professional sport model, including its rules, rankings, uniforms, practices, norms, attitudes, values, language, rituals, and symbols. To illustrate, Vaz (1972) reports that the values and institutionalized aggressive behavior characteristic of professional hockey are learned early in life in minor hockey programs. Here the aspiring professional acquires definitions, meanings, and skills concerning the means to an end in that sport.

Having demonstrated some potential in a youth sport subculture, athletes are then recruited to the more formal preprofessional stages, which may or may not be conducted within an educational environment. For example, professional football and basketball depend on colleges and universities for training new members, while baseball, hockey, and tennis depend on the private sector and minor league affiliates. In other sports such as wrestling, promoters recruit former football players or college wrestlers because of their potential skill, or they recruit an individual because of some unique physical characteristic (e.g., the obese heavyweight, the midget, the aggressive female, or the ethnic stereotype). In wrestling athletes are trained first to acquire the physical skills and then to "work up" a social identity that will appeal to the wrestling audience who demand a "display" (Stone, 1972; Rosenberg and Turowetz, 1975).

Although much of the general socialization in terms of skill is complete by the time an athlete enters a professional sport subculture, further socialization into the subculture of a specific team is necessary. For example, McElroy (1971) suggests that a sport subculture can be seasonal and thereby may require re-socialization at the beginning of each season for both veterans and new recruits. That is, there is a need to develop a "functioning and integrated unit" with clearly established and understood values, norms, and skills deemed essential for the success of that specific team.

The Maintenance of a Professional Sport Subculture

The continued existence of any professional or occupational subculture depends on the presence of a clearly identified social structure. Generally this consists of "insiders," such as athletes, coaches, owners, scouts, managers, or trainers, and "outsiders," such as league officials, media personnel, and fans. Since both systems place varying demands on the individual, role conflicts often arise that can only be resolved by quitting or by being consistent and successful at impression management or identity makeup. For example, although the fan values baseball as a game, the owner values it as a business (Haerle, 1975). From the athletes' perspective, different role performances can be utilized for insiders and outsiders. Furthermore, the external criteria can be changed, however slowly, to permit unique innovative role players to enter the subculture and survive. However, this range of tolerance varies greatly from sport to sport and from organization to organization within a given sport.

Within given subcultures there are varying degrees of prestige or status attached to roles depending on skill, the level of competition, or the ability to work up a marketable identity. Thus, in most team sports and in some individual sports, there are major and minor leagues, each with unique values, norms, and life styles. Furthermore, within most sports there is a system of rankings or ratings that place individuals somewhere on a vertical ladder, either within a given organization (for example, baseball players are assigned to a team that is designated as major league, Triple A, Double A, etc.) or across the sport (for example, tennis players and boxers are ranked from 1 to n both within their own countries and throughout the world). This has the effect of encouraging mobility (that is, an incentive plan), as well as inducing age grading, whereby individuals recognize that they must be at a certain level of competition by a specific age if they are to be successful in their chosen sport. Often this opportunity is related to chance as much as ability, especially if a player is drafted by a successful organization in which the competition for positions at the highest level is more demanding.

Once an athlete enters the subculture at the highest professional level, socialization continues, but it is more informal and is more concerned with developing a social identity and learning to interact with the internal and external social systems. In order for the subculture to continue, certain values and coping styles must be internalized by individuals. This involves learning occupational norms and the art of impression management in order to establish respect, avoid conflict, and become a marketable performer. Each actor-athlete, then, must learn the tolerable range of behavior in order to gain and keep the approval of his or her teammates, opponents, management, and fans. Thus Faulkner (1974b) stresses the importance of hockey players "making respect" or establishing a reputation in a new league and team by demonstrating physical toughness and a willingness to fight when challenged. Similarly, boxers learn to put up a tough fight and to demonstrate "heart," even when faced with defeat by a superior opponent (Weinberg and Arond, 1952), while wrestlers are expected to play their agreed-upon roles and not attempt to "shoot" a match (that is, not go against the prescribed outcome and try to win on skill alone) (Stone, 1972). Further, novices in wrestling must work at developing and maintaining an identity for outsiders, whether it be hero or villain. This involves learning cues, learning how to display and dramatize identity characteristics, and learning how to generate a response from the audience. In short, they must engage in convincing performances of the roles assigned to them by the promoter during both the entrance and performance phases of their career (Rosenberg and Turowetz, 1975). Yet this process involves risks since the wrestler may come to believe that he is truly invincible or evil. That is, he goes beyond the dramatized identity and adopts these characteristics in everyday life. Stone (1972) cites examples of former wrestlers whose careers ended abruptly when their ring identity was considered real by themselves or others, resulting in personal attacks by fans or bizarre personal behavior, which proved fatal in at least one case.

It is necessary, then, to recognize that professional athletes become adept at impression management or identity work in the "front" (Goffman, 1959) or public region of their social world. These images are rigorously and systematically maintained in order to create a certain image acceptable to the fan. As Charnofsky (1968) has noted, baseball players have traditionally accepted public criticism, signed autographs by the thousands, avoided fraternization off the field with opponents who are friends, and presented images as "All-American" males in order to sell tickets and thereby earn their salary. Yet these beliefs, attitudes, and behaviors may be violated in the "back"[2] or private region of the locker or hotel room, where players often comment that the adult fan is naive, uninformed, and fickle (Charnofsky, 1968).

The role of the audience in maintaining the subculture varies from having no influence (in jai alai) to some (in some professional team sports) to a great deal (in professional wrestling where the audience is part of the scene). While the professional wrestling fan accepts the fact that the match is staged, he or she demands that it be done well and that "good" win out over "evil," regardless of whether the contest represents a conflict between social classes, ethnic groups, racial groups, normative and deviant actors, or beauty and beast. As Stone (1972) suggests, the lower-class status of the audience, with its rather unquestioning attitude, makes it more susceptible to staging, so long as it is done well and represents a conflict with which the audience can identify.

Finally, a sporting subculture is dependent for its continuation on a link with its history, a continuing development of an argot, and the presence of rituals, superstitions, and taboos unique to the social world. For example, most subcultures search for and draw comparisons of new recruits with past heroes to promote continuity as well as interest among the fans. Similarly, the development of a new argot reflects innovation and increasing sophistication, and can serve to isolate athletes from fans or provide a stimulus to greater cognitive involvement by the fan. This can best be illustrated by the evolution of such football terminology as the "pass rush," the "red dog," the "blitz," and the "safety blitz."

Withdrawal from the Sporting Subculture

For those players who become well established in an occupational subculture within sport, retirement comes early in life (usually before 35 years of age) and may be voluntary or involuntary (McPherson, 1977). In boxing, the fighter may be left with physical impairments, yet he may have few skills to fall back on and may not even have much money. Thus, the general pattern for boxers, as described by Weinberg and Arond (1952), is a rapid economic and status descent, often accompanied by severe emotional problems in adjusting to the social world outside the boxing subculture. The result is that many return to the boxing world and attempt to fight past their prime, or occupy a secondary position within a local boxing club.

The pattern may be somewhat similar in other sports and is partially related to the process through which they entered the social world initially. For example, there are basically two methods of entering professional baseball (Haerle, 1975). First, there is the noncollegiate player who appears to be more involved in the occupation and who signs his professional contract much earlier. He spends a long period of time in professional baseball (17 or more years), postpones planning for the retirement years, and plays into his 40s before finally retiring as a player. It is this player who tends to resist retirement and who spends years at the end of his career in the low minor leagues before leaving the baseball subculture. Not surprisingly, this individual has limited options available once his playing career has ended. In short, withdrawal is traumatic because he has lived within the subculture for his entire adult life. Many, in fact, never leave as they search for and occupy insecure lesser status roles as scouts, coaches, or trainers. That is, faced with an identity crisis that often leads to maladjustment in the nonsport dominant culture of mainstream society, they retreat to safety within the sport subculture.

The other career profile is represented by college-educated players who begin their professional playing career later and usually end their career much earlier. For these individuals baseball may serve as a mobility device through which they are looking for prestigious positions in the outside world and will accept an offer should it come prior to their being forced from the world of professional sport. That is, they have an option and may retire from sport at an early age. Moreover, these individuals are usually less committed to the subcultural life surrounding professional sport. It is quite likely that similar career profiles for getting in and getting out are present in other professional sports, although they have yet to be studied.

Marginal, or less successful players, faced with the fact that they are unlikely to be promoted to the major leagues or to get a chance at the "big money," may engage in "face-saving" mechanisms to maintain a front of success. For example, Faulkner (1974b) indicated that structural and personal mechanisms are utilized to sustain the commitment and motivation of minor league hockey players. These include a redefinition of the self to account for a lack of mobility or for a demotion, through which they stress the personal benefits of their present position (e.g., "the kids are in a good school; it is a nice community; the money is good here"); the price to be paid in moving up the career ladder (e.g., more pressure, instability for the family, loss of good friends); the acceptance of average recognition or esteem (e.g., "I am well known here"); and the development of other interests in addition to the career (e.g., family, leisure pursuits in a smaller community, off-season career possibilities). Similarly, Scott (1968) indicates that unsuccessful jockeys "cop out" by becoming exercise boys in order to save face.

One additional pattern of withdrawal is unique to professional wrestling. Because the wrestler may have another occupational commitment (such as being a professional football player), retirement may be temporary as he moves into another subcultural environment. Alternatively, where identity work fails, a wrestler may be forced to retire from one specific subculture, rework a new identity, and enter a new subculture (that is, another wrestling alliance) in another part of the country. If successful, he may be recruited back to the original subculture.

5.2.2 Nonspectator Risky Sport Subcultures

In contrast to the commercialized form of action described above, nonspectator risky sports are characterized by a lack of remuneration and little or no public identity resulting from the involvement. Furthermore, participation is voluntary, challenging, and vigorous, and does not constitute work. As Goffman (1967) notes, those "who can afford the time, travel and equipment . . . seem to get the best of both worlds, enjoying the honor of chance-taking without greatly threatening their routinized week-day involvements." Some examples of nonspectator sports that contain varying degrees of risk include skiing (Boroff, 1969), surfing, parachuting (skydiving), rock climbing (Csikszentmihalyi, 1969), mountain climbing,[3] the martial arts, and the technologically based sports such as gliding (soaring), bobsledding, scuba diving, drag racing, hot rodding, dune-buggy riding, snowmobiling, and motocross riding.

Each of these stress-seeking or action-seeking activities comprises a unique subculture that enables a participant to escape the dominant culture and engage in social interaction with others who have similar interests, knowledges, norms, and experiences. For some, involvement in the subculture may be sporadic and limited only to weekends and holidays, whereas for others it may comprise their central life interest and activity. Regardless of the degree of commitment to a specific subculture, there appear to be some common meanings of the activity for an individual. These include a desire to escape or to search for and experience freedom, a desire to challenge the self, and a desire to escape the urban scene and interact with a more natural environment. To illustrate, Pearson (1974, 1976) describes the surfboard riding and surf lifesaving subcultures. Each group has a different meaning of surfing and contrasting value orientations. The surfboard riders are hedonistic, mobile, and expressively oriented in their pursuit of surfing, whereas the surf lifesavers are achievement-oriented, stable, and instrumentally oriented (to compete as a member of their club and to save lives) in their involvement. Table 5.1 lists a number of differences between the two surfing subcultures.[4]

Occasionally conflict between members of the subculture and "outsiders" arises because of different values, life styles, or interpretations as to how individuals should interact with the environment. To illustrate, conflict has occurred between rock climbers and park administrators and between the public and members of the climbing subculture. Conflict can also occur within a subculture as contrasting meanings of the activity evolve, accompanied by different values, norms, beliefs, attitudes, symbols, and life styles. For example, for some rock climbers (Donnelly, 1976) the activity is a mystical or expressive experience, while for others it is a competitive or instrumental experience. Similarly, some skiers identify with racing while others identify with the aesthetic element and are labeled freestylers.

Conflict in meaning or style seldom occurs, however, in the martial arts (for example, judo and karate). This subculture tends to have a highly organized social structure with strict adherence to norms, attitudes, and beliefs being demanded of the participants. For example, the Master of the club is the peer group leader, a father figure, and a folk hero who functions as a benevolent dictator. While many individuals become interested in the martial arts for the instrumental goal of self-defense, those who become fully socialized do so because the appeal lies in the ritual, mystique, discipline, and challenge of progressing through clearly defined statuses, which range from the novice white belt to several stages in the black belt level. This subculture is also unique in the physical and social interaction that is dictated by status (that is, the color of one's belt). This status distance is maintained by the practice of "making poker faces" (Jacobs, 1976). As a result of this status hierarchy, cliques within a given subculture change as individuals improve their skills and earn the right to wear a different belt, thereby interacting with those at a higher level.

Table 5.1
Areas of difference between surf lifesavers and surfboard riders

Surf lifesavers	Surfboard riders
Surf weekends and on holidays in the summer.	Surf all year at every opportunity, not just weekends and holidays. More likely to surf full time in the summer or winter.
Surf after work.	Surf before, after, or during the work week.
Can't drop work to surf (typically).	Can drop work to surf.
More likely to live in one place most of the year.	Less likely to live in one place for most of the year (though a majority do).
Surf close to home at a few spots.	Travel further to more spots.
Prefer to surf well-known beaches or surf spots.	Prefer to surf lesser known spots.
Definitely in favor of surf lifesaving competition.	Neutral or uncertain about surf lifesaving competition.
In favor of competitive boardriding.	Less in favor of competitive boardriding.
Belong to clubs and associations.	Typically do not belong to clubs or associations.
Highly likely to own a regular (sedan type) car.	More likely to own a panel van, or similar vehicle, which may be used for sleeping.
Only sleep in a vehicle on occasional weekends or holidays.	Likely to sleep in a vehicle frequently or even to live in it for weeks or months at a time.
Authorities' attitude perceived in a most unthreatening manner.	Authorities' attitude perceived as threatening or hostile.
Most likely to consider that drugs play no part or a small part in surfing.	Likely to consider drugs a definite part of surfing.
Work should be more important than leisure.	Leisure should be more important than work.
Work activities were more important in life compared with leisure.	Work activities were less important in life compared with leisure.

Adapted from Pearson (1976).

Regardless of the specific sport, all nonspectator subcultures evolve in a similar pattern. Based on an analysis of surfing, Irwin (1973) suggests that a "scene" begins to emerge when a number of individuals with common beliefs, values, norms, and interests engage in face-to-face verbal and behavioral inter-action. During this process they fit certain components (e.g., the wave, rider, and beach; or the mountain, skis, and lodge) together into a subcultural configuration and unique life style. This is facilitated by being free of other commitments, by developing new patterns of behavior and language,[5] and by focusing their interest on one activity (surfing, skiing, skydiving, etc.). Once this life style comes to the attention of outsiders, they in turn may become insiders in a different locale. However, sooner or later, a mass of outsiders discover the scene and "want in." (This process is often stimulated by the media—for example, the movie *The Endless Summer* and the Beach Boys' music helped the growth of the surfing sub-culture.) This results in an influx of new or "pseudo" members who change the scene in a variety of ways, which may include the introduction of competition, the creation of social organization(s), an influx of conspicuous display (e.g., clothing and equipment), the introduction of bizarre or deviant behavior, and a redefinition of the central meaning of the activity or life style. The result is that the original members move on or out and a redefined subculture emerges. In effect, then, a subculture is a dynamic social entity that is constantly undergoing change in personnel, structure, and meaning.

5.2.3 Commercialized Sport Scenes

Commercialized places of action enable an individual to participate in a sub-culture that requires facilities, equipment, and a structure that cannot normally be provided by the participant. Examples include racetracks, poolrooms, and bowling alleys, where chances can be taken and some element of competence demonstrated, either legally or illegally (see Section 7.1.5). Within these sub-cultures, perhaps more than in any other, an individual may resort to cheating or hustling in order to attain success.

In an analysis of cheating in sport, Luschen (1976) suggested that it occurs because there is a high uncertainty of outcome,[6] especially if the opponents are relatively equal in ability; because there are high rewards at stake; and because it is often a zero-sum event in which one opponent gets the entire reward and the other receives nothing. Furthermore, in accordance with both the differential association and conflict perspective, cheating may be class-based. That is, values learned in a deviant subculture may be transferred to the sport milieu, or members of one class may not agree with the established means of attaining specific goals and therefore may cheat. As Luschen (1976) suggested, members of both the lower and upper classes may cheat; however, the method may differ be-tween classes and the upper class may be less seriously reprimanded if caught.

Cheating involves changing the conditions in a contest in favor of one side. In games in which rules are subject to a range of interpretation, both opponents will often test the officials to determine what they consider acceptable and un-acceptable behavior. Occasionally cheating may even become part of a planned strategy to upset an opponent (e.g., hitting after the whistle, calling a tennis shot out that lands on the line). Although this type of cheating is overt, most is un-observable and remains undetected, a fact that makes it difficult to determine and study the degree of cheating,[7] including competing below (e.g., point shaving) or above (e.g., using drugs) one's level of ability or changing the playing conditions (e.g., watering the infield, raising or lowering the pitching mound, stealing or selling playbooks in football).

Hustling is another form of cheating in which an individual manipulates the game interaction, by misrepresenting his or her true ability, with naive others in order to succeed. It is crucial that the hustler enter the contest on even or favorable terms and that the contest be sustained as long as possible in order for the hustler to realize maximal success or profit. For the interested reader, Prus and Sharper (1977) suggest that the five basic skills of hustling involve (1) locating a target or mark, (2) consolidating oneself with the target by making the target think that he or she is better than the hustler, (3) promoting the target's investment in one's enterprise, (4) obtaining the target's investment, and (5) cooling out the target. These latter two principles involve winning by a small margin in the hope that the target will continue to play or will come back for more. In recent years participant observation analyses have been completed of hustlers in bowling (Steele, 1976), cards (Martinez and La Franchi, 1972; Mahigel and Stone, 1976; Prus and Sharper, 1977), and pool (Polsky, 1972).

In order to be successful, hustlers must spend most of their free time in the social milieu of their activity (at the bowling alley, poolroom, card parlor, golf course) in order to perfect their game. This is especially important in games other than cards in which the opponent cannot be deceived by cheating. Rather, hustlers must deceive on the basis of their performance (for example, they must miss shots, leave themselves in a bad position, deliberately lose a game) in order to con their "mark" into entering or continuing a game. As Polsky (1972) notes, hustlers must never show their "real speed" (unless they find themselves being hustled) since they will exhaust the potential of that scene and be forced to move on to another milieu.

From the perspective of the dominant society, a hustler violates norms concerning what is morally correct behavior and what is a legitimate occupation. As a result the hustler is often stigmatized and branded as a criminal who victimizes people. Yet, in common with many facets of social life, double standards exist, in that many people engage in various forms of hustling in their own leisure or occupational worlds.

5.2.4 "Fancy Milling": The Consumption of Valued Sport Products

The action of consumption provides adults with an opportunity to be entertained and to be seen in sport settings, some of which are luxurious and exclusive in nature. These include casinos, private sport clubs, and the clubhouse at racetracks where the use of sporting symbols, dress, argot, and gestures is used for impression management concerning the skill level of an individual. For example, the "peacock" dressed in the latest fashions and using sport argot may masquerade to the masses as a highly skilled participant. However, to insiders the true "speed" or identity is known, although the individual is seldom, if ever, tested. In this way vicarious action continues, thereby allowing adults to "obtain a taste of social mobility by consuming valued products, by enjoying costly and modish entertainment, by spending time in luxurious settings, and by mingling with prestigeful persons" (Goffman, 1967). There is little doubt that part of the explanation for the increasing membership in health, tennis, golf, and squash clubs is closely linked with the opportunity to "mill" in a fancy or lavish environment with successful people. In fact, some individuals spend more time "hanging out" and being seen than actually participating in the activity.

Although Goffman (1967) characterized the milling process as "fancy," this criterion may not be present in all situations in which individuals assemble for the purpose of consuming a sport product. Rather, individuals may enter or gather at any sport scene to seek "action" that "a tightly packed gathering of reveling persons can bring" (Goffman, 1967). The action that results represents a form of collective behavior that is normally unstructured and unpredictable in that it lacks clearly defined institutionalized norms. This type of behavior is more likely to result when individuals who already belong to an existing subculture (e.g., social class, ethnic group, students at one college) come together to form a crowd.

To date, many instances of collective behavior in sport have involved violence, such as soccer "hooliganism" among working class youth in Great Britain (Taylor, 1972) and riots at major sporting events throughout the world. While this phenomenon was once limited almost exclusively to soccer, it is increasingly appearing in other sports (Fimrite, 1974; Lang, 1970; Lang and Lang, 1961; Smith, 1975b, 1976a). As Beisser, cited in Fimrite (1974), noted: "the old fan yelled 'Kill the Umpire'—the new fan tries to do it." Each year, then, a regular consumer of sport news can expect to read about or see collective violence in sport (Smith, 1976b).

Although it appears that most instances of "unfancy" milling reflect a subculture of violence, pregame and postgame celebrations are also examples of collective milling in a sport milieu. For example, McPhail and Miller (1973) analyzed the "assembling" process, whereby college students and fans came together to welcome home a winning college basketball team after an upset victory. Among the most powerful factors influencing the gathering of a crowd were suggestions and requests from others, including a radio broadcaster, to go to the airport, the availability of transportation to the airport, the number of prior home games attended, and the absence of competing alternatives. A second example is Ponting's (1974) descriptive analysis of a milling crowd in a hotel lobby the night prior to Canada's national football final, the Grey Cup. Using the unobtrusive method of film and tape recording he found that although the turnover rate in the mostly male audience was high, common patterns of behavior emerged, which he interpreted in terms of Goffman's (1959) dramaturgical model of impression management or the "staging" of social behavior. A final example is the Listiak (1974) study of bar behavior prior to a Grey Cup game in Canada. He compared the pregame celebrations in lower- and middle-class bars and found that only in the middle-class bars were the patrons engaged in excessive or aggressive festival-related behavior. He attributed this to the fact that this "time-out" festival with its accompanying legitimate deviance is more functional for relieving the frustrations and tensions of daily living for the middle class.

5.3 SPORT SUBCULTURES
AND THE DISPLAY OF "MORAL" CHARACTER

While engaging in action, a person can ask "What am I?" and thereby attempt to ascertain what set of qualities distinguish him or her as a unique human being. A given set of qualities characteristic of a particular person is composed of both extrinsic (or objective) and intrinsic (or subjective) attributes. Examples of objective attributes include physical qualities (height, weight, attractiveness, etc.), psychological characteristics (intelligence, need to achieve, spatial ability, etc.), and social statuses (education, income, occupation, etc.).

There are many types of intrinsic qualities that define a social self, but the most highly valued subjective characteristics are those associated with moral character. The morai traits are not necessarily those held to be of significance by a priest or philosopher, but rather those traits representing exemplary conduct in everyday life.

Among the many heroes of the Western world portrayed in the mass media, the athlete has received special attention as a moral leader. In his insightful book *The Racing Game*, Scott states the case as follows:

> Worship, as Durkheim has taught us, involves the collective reaffirmation of moral values. Now if we ask where the virtues of moral character—courage, integrity, dignity, and so forth—are reaffirmed in action, we arrive at the curious irony that the race track and not the church is a place of worship.

> At the race track, we find a sphere of life where men are out to establish character, demonstrate virtue, and achieve honor. These men are the jockeys; and while on stage they are putting on the line their money, their reputations, and their lives. (Scott, 1968, p. 25)

Scott stresses, then, that the test of moral character is "coolness in risky situations," such as during a race. In this situation jockeys can best demonstrate their character to themselves, the owner, the trainer, and the fans. Character in racing is essential to a jockey since the social organization of the track dictates that he or she exhibit the traits of integrity, gameness, and coolness in order to be in demand. The greater the demand, the greater the choice in selecting mounts for a given race. Once it is perceived that a jockey has lost his or her moral character, such as after a fall, the jockey encounters difficulty in getting mounts. In light of this norm, jockeys fear not only the physical trauma of a spill but also the social consequences and subsequent labeling. In short, as clearly stated by Scott (1968), "the traits of moral character are generated by social organization." For example, the benchmark of winning the first handicap or stakes race provides confirmation that the jockey possesses moral character. Scott's analogy can be readily extended to other sports since the moral traits he ascribes to the jockey have been attributed to athletes in a variety of sports.

There are many valued moral traits believed to be characteristic of the athletic hero, but the most highly valued moral attributes are those related to the control of fateful events in action situations. Goffman (1967) has defined five major forms of character related to the management of fateful events. These seem especially germane to the consideration of sport as a context of action and the athlete as a moral leader. These include courage, gameness, integrity, gallantry, and composure.

In addition to developing moral traits, sporting subcultures provide opportunities in which an individual can "lay himself on the line and place himself in jeopardy during a passing moment" and thereby draw "self-respect" (Goffman, 1967). More explicitly, Scott states:

> Attributes of moral character are established only in risk-taking situations: before we are ready to impute to a person the quality of strong character, he must be seen as voluntarily putting something on the line. (Scott, 1968, p. 25)

To illustrate, character contests for the hustler are related to deceiving the opponent and playing consistently. Among the job-related skills and traits that must be developed and tested are argumentative skill for "making a game"; knowing when to resist the temptation to play when the action does not provide him or her with an advantage; "heart" (courage) to play well when the action is heavy (that is, when a lot of money is riding on the game); coolness so as not to let a bad break, audience distractions, or falling behind in the score disrupt his or her game; having imaginative "con" techniques in reserve when needed; and having the flexibility and sense to break rules when necessary.

Since individuals seldom put themselves to test in the home or job milieu, sport can serve as a symbolic, yet relatively safe, mechanism for testing moral character. This section outlines the development of moral traits, including examples of character testing that may occur in sport subcultures.

5.3.1 Courage

"There are various forms of *courage*, namely, the capacity to envisage immediate danger and yet proceed with the course of action that brings danger on" (Goffman, 1967). Perhaps the best examples of courage in sport are provided by extraordinary performances in aggressive contact sports, such as professional hockey. To illustrate, in the article "Courage and fear in a vortex of violence" *Time*, 24 February 1975), the requisite attributes of a hockey goalie were described as follows:

> He needs the glove of an all-star shortstop, the agility of a gold medal gymnast, the reflexes of a championship racing-car driver, the eye of a .400 hitter and the mind of a geometrician. Even then he is nothing if he has not conquered fear, for he lives in a vortex of violence in the world's fastest team sport.*

---

*Reprinted by permission from TIME, The Weekly Newsmagazine; copyright Time Inc. 1975.

The article further states with respect to Bernie Parent, the goalie of the Phila-delphia Flyers, that he " . . . is ridden by repressed fear on ice. Like a soldier under fire, he finds fear real and physical, and he has to fight it off."

Similarly, for hockey players other than the goalie, violent acts such as fighting become institutionalized as part of the role expectation. This normative character trait is legitimized and reinforced for some players early in life by signi-ficant others such as parents, coaches, fans, peers, and the media (Smith, 1975a; Vaz, 1972). At the professional level, Faulkner (1974b) notes that players learn to "make respect," which "involves acting in terms of standardized expectancies so that others will impute to the actor the kind of identity he would desire them to see him as possessing." Hockey players test others early in their career by en-gaging in character contests in the corners and around the net:

> You line up the opposition and you nail 'em . . . you give 'em a warning about what's going to happen the rest of the season, you find out how different guys react. (Faulkner, 1974b, p. 296)

> If you have to drop your gloves to establish yourself with these guys then that's what you do. (Faulkner, 1974a, p. 798)

As a result of these character contests, players determine who can be intim-idated and thereby dominated, as well as assert their own character. For some players, constant testing is needed to reaffirm their courage and utility to the team. Similarly, from the perspective of the individual being tested, a cardinal rule is that it is "better to have fought and lost, then never to have fought at all." In short, refusal to fight when challenged is considered cowardly and generates disrespect from teammates as well as opponents. In fact, it is viewed as a failure in the character contest within this occupational world.

Other clear examples of the display of courage are found in accounts of soli-tary competition against the natural elements and against self-doubt. These accounts are given in both books and films; examples are Lord Chichester's story (Chichester, 1967) of his solitary trip around the world in a small sailboat christened the "Gypsy Moth," the descent on skis of the highest mountain in the world, which was portrayed in the film *The Man Who Skied Down Everest*, and in the ten accounts of individual courage described in *Gifford on Courage*. Still other striking examples of courage are revealed in combative sports such as boxing and bullfighting, which feature classic life-and-death duels (for example, the movie *Rocky*). Finally, it is noted that in all sport contests courage is often displayed by the *underdog* who manages to achieve victory (if only "moral" victory) in the face of overwhelming odds. For example, the biggest upset in Super Bowl history occurred when Joe Namath led the New York Jets, considered a 17½ point underdog, to a 16–7 victory over the Baltimore Colts in 1969.

5.3.2 Gameness

Gameness is "the capacity to stick to a line of activity and to continue to pour all effort into it regardless of set backs, pain or fatigue. This occurs not because of some brute insensitivity but because of inner will and determination" (Goffman,

1967). Gameness is often reflected in endurance events such as long-distance running, swimming, and Nordic skiing, or by athletes who overcome severe physical handicaps to achieve success in sport. A ready example is the cross-country skier in the 1976 Winter Olympic Games who completed the last several kilometers on only one ski.

Gameness is closely related to the concept of *heart* in sport situations. Weinberg and Arond, in their analysis of the occupational culture of the boxer, state that:

> There is . . . a cult of a kind of persevering courage, called a "fighting heart," which means "never admitting defeat." The fighter learns early that his exhibited courage—his ability, if necessary, to go down fighting—characterizes the respected, audience-pleasing boxer . . . This common attitude among boxers is reinforced by the demands of the spectators who generally cheer a "game fighter." (Weinberg and Arond, 1952, pp. 462–463)

Similarly, in his description of the poolroom hustler, Polsky notes that:

> Without exception, hustlers contend that "heart" (courage or toughness) is as essential to hustling as playing ability is . . . hustlers, in their preoccupation with it, often use judgments about "heart" to confer or withhold prestige. (Polsky, 1969, p. 63)

In his account of the racetrack, Scott (1968) shows that the concept of heart applies to "animal athletes" as well as human athletes, observing that "the ultimate display of heart is to die in the cause of victory." To illustrate the latter point, Scott (1968) reports ". . . an eyewitness account of a crowd's reaction to a horse that won by a nose and then dropped dead after passing the finish line."

Another moral trait related to gameness is the concept of *comeback*. For example, in horseracing the first fall experienced by a jockey provides a baseline against which to measure gameness, and enables horsemen to evaluate whether the jockey has the character to make a successful comeback. There are also many tales of both major and minor sport figures who have gone from tragedy to triumph after suffering severe physical injury. A dramatic account of a comeback resulting in a moral victory is the film and book *The Other Side of the Mountain* (Valens, 1975). This story describes how Jill Kinmont was paralyzed from the shoulders down after a fall in the last qualifying race before the Olympic trials and, after years of suffering and struggle, managed to achieve a full and useful life. Another recent and poignant example of a successful comeback in the world of sport is given in the autobiography of Rocky Bleier, *Fighting Back* (Bleier, 1975), which describes Bleier's struggle to overcome the handicap of severe shrapnel wounds suffered in combat in Viet Nam and his success in establishing himself as a running back for the Pittsburgh Steelers.

5.3.3 Integrity

"A fundamental trait of character from the view of social organization is *integrity,* meaning here the propensity to resist temptation in situations where there would be much profit and some impugnity in departing momentarily from moral standards" (Goffman, 1967). The best examples of integrity in sport situations are probably covert acts not witnessed by others, in which athletes act as their own umpire and referee, as, for example, when a professional golfer marks the ball or assesses a penalty for an illegal shot. As Gavit has expressed the matter:

> I heard character defined as "the sum total of things a man will do when nobody is looking." Pretty good, as far as it goes; but history justifies by adding: ". . . when he thinks he can get away with it." (Gavit, 1941, p. 37)

More overt examples of the display of integrity in sport situations are efforts by athletes to equalize what they perceive to be a "bad call" on their opponent. For example, when a tennis player thinks that his or her opponent has lost a point because of a bad call by the linesman, he or she will at the first opportunity intentionally "double fault" or stroke the ball into the net in order to offset the opponent's bad luck. Interestingly, displays of integrity are often more characteristic of individual sports than team sports.

5.3.4 Gallantry

Gallantry ". . . refers to the capacity to maintain the forms of courtesy when the forms are full of substance" (Goffman, 1967). Acts of gallantry are most clearly illustrated in sport situations when athletes give assistance to their opponents when it jeopardizes their own chances of winning. Illustrations of gallantry in action include the runner who stops to pick up a fallen opponent, and the jockey who, in mid-race, hands his whip to another jockey who has lost his own in the heat of action. More detailed examples of gallant acts that jeopardized an athlete's own chance for victory are given by the following accounts of Eugenio Monti and Willye White:

> This incident occurred in Innsbruck (Austria) at the Winter Olympic Games in 1964. In the two-man bobsled trials, the Italian champion, Eugenio Monti, had just made his final run at remarkable speed. Only the English team with Tony Nash could still beat his time. But it was then learnt that Nash could not take off because a part of his sled was broken. Monti then detached the part in question from his own sled and sent it up to Nash, who made his repair, finished in record time and won the gold medal. . . .
>
> The case of the American athlete, Willye White, has similarities with Monti's. During the long-jump trials in the international indoor athletics championship in the United States of America in 1965, Mary Rand, the English Olympic champion in this event, misled by various marks on the ground, missed her third try and was eliminated from the finals. Feeling that her English rival had been unfairly treated, Willye White of her own accord requested the Jury to give Mary Rand (who was her most dangerous opponent) another try. The jury acceded to her arguments and Mary Rand then made another jump which enabled her to qualify and ultimately to win. (*Fair Play*, 1974, pp. 4–5)

Although of less consequence because victory has been achieved, another class of gallant acts in sport situations constitutes what might be best termed *gracious gestures.* These gestures reflect modern forms of chivalry in which athletes perform actions that show their high moral qualities and demonstrate that athletes fully appreciate their opponents' qualities or regret their having suffered an irremediable stroke of bad luck. At the same time they reflect, in general, a spirit of fellowship with opponents.

> For example, at the end of the 200 meter race in the French athletics championships of 1967, Sylvie Telliez spontaneously handed over her gold medal to Gabrielle Mayer, who had fallen, when clearly in the lead, just before she reached the tape. . . .

> In the same way, Annie Famose who, in the Winter University Games at Sestriere in 1966, finished 0.01 seconds ahead of Therese Obrecht in the special slalom, feeling that her Swiss companion had equally deserved to win, pulled her up beside her on the topmost step of the podium to share in her victory. (*Fair Play*, 1974, pp. 7–8)

A similar, but more dramatic example of a gracious gesture is the case of Lanny Bassham and Margaret Murdock who tied for first place in the small-bore rifle competition at the 1976 Summer Olympic Games in Montreal. Due to the ruling of the international shooting union, the International Olympic Committee could not award each of the American shooters a gold medal. As a result of a tie-breaking procedure based on a comparative analysis of the shooters' last ten shots, Bassham was given the gold medal. However, on the victory stand Bassham invited Ms. Murdock to stand with him while the national anthem was played, in order to demonstrate that he considered her performance to be the equal of his (Moore, 1976).

5.3.5 Composure

Finally, there are those character traits related to ". . . *composure,* that is, self-control, self-possession, or poise" (Goffman, 1967). Three dimensions of composure are physical control, emotional control, and dignity. Physical control is best exemplified in athletics by the controlled display of physical skill shown by divers, gymnasts, and figure skaters. Their performances present in a realistic manner what heroic figures of the mass media present in a fictitious manner. As Lyman and Scott state:

> The moral worth of many heroes of the Western world is displayed in their willingness and ability to undergo trials of pain and potential death with stylized equanimity and expert control of relevant motor skills. Modern fictional heroes, such as James Bond and Matt Dillon, for example, face death constantly in the form of armed and desperate thugs and killers; yet they seem never to lose their nerve or skill. It is not merely their altruistic service in the cause of law and country that makes them attractive, but also, and perhaps more importantly, their smooth skill—verbal and physical—that never deserts them in time of risk. (Lyman and Scott, 1968, p. 93)

The counterpart of the modern fictional hero who exhibits "stylized equanimity and expert control of relevant motor skills" is the bullfighter who enacts a ritualized duel with his animate opponent with indifferent despatch and graceful finesse.

Adroit athletic movement by sport performers typically represents emotional as well as physical control. In current parlance the defining attribute of emotional control is *coolness*. As Lyman and Scott have succinctly characterized the concept:

> Coolness is exhibited (and defined) as poise under pressure. By pressure we mean simply situations of considerable emotion or risk, or both. Coolness, then refers to the capacity to execute physical acts, including conversations, in a concerted, smooth, self-controlled fashion in risky situations, or to maintain affective detachments during the course of encounters involving considerable emotion. (Lyman and Scott, 1968, p. 93)

In the argot of various sporting subcultures the term "ice" is often used in reference to an athlete who displays extraordinary emotional control. For example, within the ranks of professional tennis Arthur Ashe has often been referred to as the "Ice Man" and Chris Evert has been given the appellation of "Ice Maiden" for her consistent display of emotional control in the course of action. Similarly, Scott has observed in the case of the jockey:

> Above all, the jockey with strong character possesses the perceived virtue of coolness. A jockey who possesses this attribute is said to always "keep his cool," "to ride like an ice man," or to "have ice in his veins." The ideal horse-jockey combination is a fiery animal and an icy rider. . . . Coolness is sparing the whip on a front-running horse when another animal has passed into the lead. . . . All these activities are taken by observers as instances of a jockey's character. In short, moral character is coolness in risky situations. (Scott, 1968, p. 26)

Although not always coterminous with physical and emotional control, a third important dimension of the moral trait of composure is *dignity*. This term typically denotes decorum, as, for example, being gracious to an obnoxious or superior opponent, or calmly accepting all the referee's decisions. But the concept decorum when applied to sport also indicates moral courage—personal effort to refrain from meeting violence with violence, or using devious play when faced with unfair tactics. In short, an athlete displaying dignity or decorum is viewed as a gentleman or a lady and not as a gamesman or gameswoman.

In sport situations, dignity is perhaps most often illustrated by the degree of consideration that athletes give to spectators, officials, and their opponents. As Herbert Warren Wind has written about the long-standing rivalry between tennis players Evonne Goolagong and Chris Evert:

> They are considerate of all their opponents but Evert is especially careful not to rob Goolagong of the play of a deserved victory, and Goolagong has the same concern in regard to Evert . . . (Wind, 1976, p. 104)

Wind further states of Chris Evert that:

> She is an unfailingly courteous and gracious competitor, but because she devotes her attention exclusively to playing tennis and remains so cool and unsweaty (hence her appellation Ice Maiden) galleries have a tendency to overlook these attributes. (Wind, 1976, p. 105)

A final aspect of composure is what Goffman (1967) calls ". . . *stage confidence*, the capacity to withstand the dangers and opportunities of appearing before large audiences without becoming abashed, embarrassed, self-conscious, or panicky." To illustrate, Birrell and Turowetz (1977) stress that gymnasts and wrestlers must develop "poise" and "color," respectively, which they must learn to display and maintain during performance. As one gymnast noted when asked about the audience:

> I'm not paying very much attention to them . . . I don't even pay attention to people because I figure I'm the one that's going to get the personal satisfaction out of it. They're going to enjoy watching me no matter if I hit or miss because I'm exciting to watch. (Birrell and Turowetz, 1977, p. 21)

On the other hand, there are numerous accounts of athletes in a variety of sports who, while possessing excellent physical abilities and skills, nevertheless fail to excel in certain situations because they "lose their cool," "tighten up," and "clutch" when performing before large groups of spectators.

In summary, the problem of self-construction implied by the question "What am I?" is closely related to the problem of moral character. Greater moral character indicates greater social worth and thus a more highly valued social identity. As previously noted, moral character is displayed and moral attributes are defined in a context of action. Dramaturgically viewed, from the perspective of the active participant, sport situations provide idealized contexts of action wherein character can be tested and moral attributes objectively evaluated. From the perspective of the passive participant (i.e., spectator), sport situations provide idealized moral role models that function as comparative standards of moral character to which individuals may vicariously lay claim and discern as defining themselves.

Two concluding points are necessary with reference to action situations and moral attributes. First, all of the action situations described above have, until recent years, characteristically represented male behavior or male bonding (Tiger, 1969) rather than female activity. Indeed, as Goffman (1967) has stated: ". . . action in our Western Culture seems to belong to the cult of masculinity. . . . " Second, all of the character traits described above represent the aristocratic ethic associated with the renaissance man and the noble English norms of sportsmanship and character building. When considered in combination, these factors suggest that such moral qualities as talent and intelligence are in short supply, and that only select social categories (e.g., young, white males of noble birth) possess these scarce social resources. In sum, such considerations suggest that in every age and in every culture, social categories and identities are stratified in terms of valued moral characteristics (see Section 10.3).

NOTES

1. Listiak (1974) suggests that a certain amount of socially sanctioned deviant behavior serves as a safety valve or "time-out" from social control to reduce the strains and tensions in a social system.

2. Although it was considered a norm to maintain the secrecy of the back region and not expose it to the public, the back region is becoming increasingly public as athletes gain more freedom and the media become more open and critical in their reporting of the sport milieu (e.g., Bouton, 1970; Meggesey, 1970; Shaw, 1973; Voigt, 1974).

3. *Rock climbing* involves climbing the sheerest faces of a mountain, whereas *mountain climbing* involves attaining the summit using the easiest route.

4. In North America a similar contrast and conflict exist between the "purists" who do not view it as a competitive sport but rather as an individual experience, and the "innovators" who seek to shape the activity into institutionalized competition (fixed or free style) and to create occupational options (e.g., teacher, professional competitor, surf shopowner or employee).

5. The argot may reflect the ethnic history of a sport (Jarka, 1963) and may change yearly in some subcultures. The following is an example of that found in one avocational subculture in the 1970s:

   She was wedeling a headwall loaded with bathtubs, but caught an edge, helicoptered down the fall line and wound up with a spiral in the tibia.

   Translated this passage recounts how the individual was making a series of tight parallel turns (wedeling) on a steep incline (headwall) full of depressions (bathtubs) made by fallen skiers, when she caught an edge of the ski and fell head over heels straight down the hill, suffering a spiral fracture of the tibia.

6. Other responses to a high uncertainty of outcome include the use of magic, rituals, and violence.

7. For example, does it occur more frequently in amateur or professional sport? This may be related to the values held concerning the rewards for success (that is, a cup, ribbon, or money may be differentially valued). Also, there are often fewer agents of control at the amateur level and therefore the possibility exists for a higher incidence of cheating.

REFERENCES

Andreano, R. (1965) "The affluent baseball player." *Transaction* (May/June): 2, 4, 10–13.

Arnold, D. (ed.) (1970). *The Sociology of Subcultures.* Berkeley: The Glendessary Press.

Arnold, D. (1972). "The social organization of sky diving: A study in vertical mobility." Presented at the Pacific Sociological Association Annual Meeting, Portland, Oregon (April).

Birrell, S., and A. Turowetz (1977). "Character work-up and display in collegiate gymnastics and professional wrestling." Presented at the annual meeting of the Canadian Sociological and Anthropological Association, Fredricton, New Brunswick (June).

Bleier, R. (1975). *Fighting Back.* New York: Warner Books.

Boroff, D. (1969). "A view of skiers as a sub-culture." In J. W. Loy and G. S. Kenyon (eds.), *Sport, Culture and Society: A Reader on the Sociology of Sport,* pp. 453–456. New York: MacMillan.

Bouton, J. (1970). *Ball Four.* New York: Dell.

Charnofsky, H. (1968). "The major league professional player: Self conception versus the popular image." *International Review of Sport Sociology* 3: 39–56.

Charnofsky, H. (1970). "The occupational culture of the ball player and the boxer: A comparison." Presented at the Pacific Sociological Association Meetings, Anaheim, California (April).

Chichester, F. (1967). *"Gypsy Moth" Circles the World.* London: Hodder.

Clarke, M. (1974). "On the concept of subculture." *British Journal of Sociology* 25: 428–441.

Cohen, A. (1955). *Delinquent Boys.* New York: The Free Press.

Csikszentmihalyi, M. (1969). "The Americanization of rock climbing." *The University of Chicago Magazine* LXI (May/June): 21–26.

Donnelly, P. (1976). "Outsiders"—The climber as a deviant: A reply to Grietbauer and Kingsley." *Climbing* (January–February): 31–33.

Fair Play. (1972). Paris: French Committee For Fair Play.

Faulkner, R. (1974a) "Coming of age in organizations: A comparative study of career contingencies and adult socialization." *Sociology of Work and Occupations* 1 (May): 131–173.

Faulkner, R. (1974b). "Making violence by doing work: Selves, situations, and the world of professional hockey." *Sociology of Work and Occupations* 1 (August): 288–312.

Faulkner, R. (1975). "Coming of age in organizations: A comparative study of career contingencies of musicians and hockey players." In D. W. Ball and J. W. Loy (eds.), *Sport and Social Order,* pp. 525–558. Reading, Mass.: Addison-Wesley.

Fimrite, R. (1974). "Take me out to the brawl game." *Sports Illustrated* 40 (June 17): 10–13.

Fischer, C. (1975). "Toward a subcultural theory of urbanism." *American Journal of Sociology* 80 (May): 1319–1341.

Fritschner, L. (1977). "Karate: The making and the maintenance of an underdog class." Presented at the annual meeting of the American Sociological Association, Chicago (September).

Gavit, J. (1941). "Through neighbor's doorways—blossoms of democracy." *Survey Graphic* 30 (January): 37–38.

Gifford, F. (1976). *Gifford on Courage.* New York: Bantam Books.

Goffman, E. (1959). *The Presentation of Self in Everyday Life.* Garden City, N.Y.: Anchor Doubleday.

Goffman, E. (1967). *Interaction Ritual.* Chicago: Aldine.

Gordon, M. (1974). "The concept of subculture and its application." *Social Forces* 26: 40–42.

Haerle, R. (1975). "Career patterns and career contingencies of professional baseball players: An occupational analysis." In D. W. Ball and J. W. Loy (eds.), *Sport and Social Order,* pp. 461–519. Reading, Mass.: Addison-Wesley.

Hare, N. (1971). "A study of the black fighter." *The Black Scholar* 3 (November): 2–9.

Ingham, A. (1975). "Occupational subcultures in the work world of sport." In D. W. Ball and J. W. Loy (eds.), *Sport and Social Order,* pp. 337–389. Reading, Mass.: Addison-Wesley.

Irwin, J. (1973). "Surfing: The natural history of an urban scene." *Urban Life and Culture* 2 (July): 131–161.

Jacobs, G. (1976). "Urban samurai: The karate dojo." In A. Yiannakis et al. (eds.), *Sport Sociology: Contemporary Themes,* pp. 134–142. Dubuque, Iowa: Kendall/Hunt.

Jarka, H. (1963) "The language of skiers." *American Speech* 38 (October): 202–208.

Klapp, O. (1969). *Collective Search for Identity.* New York: Holt, Rinehart and Winston.

Kramer, J. (1969). *Farewell to Football.* New York: Bantam Books.

Lang, G. E. (1970). "Riotous outbursts in sports events." Presented at the Seventh World Congress of the International Sociological Association, Varna, Bulgaria.

Lang, K., and G. E. Lang (1961). *Collective Dynamics*. New York: Crowell.

Listiak, A. (1974). "Legitimate deviance and social class: Bar behavior during Grey Cup week." *Sociological Focus* 7 (Summer): 13-44.

Luschen, G. (1976). "Cheating in sport." In D. Landers (ed.), *Social Problems in Athletics*, pp. 67-77. Urbana: University of Illinois Press.

Lyman, S., and M. Scott (1968). "Coolness in everyday life." In M. Truzzi (ed.), *Sociology and Everyday Life*, pp. 92-101. Englewood Cliffs, N.J.: Prentice-Hall.

Mahigel, E. L., and G. P. Stone (1976). "Hustling as a career." In D. Landers (ed.), *Social Problems in Athletics*, pp. 78-85. Urbana: University of Illinois Press.

Martinez, T. M., and R. La Franchi (1972). "Why people play poker." In G. P. Stone (ed.), *Games, Sport and Power*, pp. 55-73. New Brunswick, N.J.: Transaction Books.

Massengale, J. (1974). "Coaching as an occupational subculture." *Phi Delta Kappan* (October): 140-142.

McElroy, D. (1971). "Socialization and the seasonal subculture." Presented at the Third International Symposium on the Sociology of Sport, Waterloo, Ontario (August).

McPhail, C., and D. Miller (1973). "The assembling process: A theoretical and empirical examination." *American Sociological Review* 38 (December): 721-735.

McPhee, W. (1963). *Formal Theories of Mass Behavior*. New York: The Free Press.

McPherson, B. (1977). "The occupational and psychological adjustment of former professional athletes." Presented at the annual meeting of the American College of Sports Medicine, Chicago (May).

Meggesey, D. (1970). *Out of Their League*. Berkeley, Calif.: Ramparts Press.

Moore, K. (1976). "Enough to take his breath away." *Sports Illustrated* (August 2): 31-35.

Pearson, K. (1974). "The symbol of the revolution: A surfboard." Presented at the Sociological Association of Australia and New Zealand Conference, University of New England, Armidale, NSW, Australia.

Pearson, K. (1975). "Subcultures and leisure." Presented at the Sociology section of the ANZAAS Conference, Canberra, Australia (January).

Pearson, K. (1976). "Subcultures, drug use and physical activity." Presented at the International Congress of Physical Activity Sciences, Quebec City (July). Used with permission.

Phillips, J., and W. Schafer (1970). "The athletic subculture—a preliminary study." Presented at the American Sociological Association Annual Meeting (August).

Phillips, J., and W. Schafer (1971). "Subcultures in sport: A conceptual and methodological approach." In R. Albonico and K. Pfister-Binz (eds.), *Sociology of Sport: Theoretical and Methodological Foundations*, pp. 66-74. Magglingen, Switzerland: Birkhauser, Verlag Basel.

Polsky, N. (1969). *Hustlers, Beats and Others*. New York: Anchor Books.

Polsky, N. (1972). "Of pool playing and poolrooms." In G. P. Stone (eds.), *Games, Sport and Power*, pp. 19-54. New Brunswick, N.J.: Transaction Books.

Ponting, J. R. (1974). "Grey Cup revelry: A collective behavior analysis." Presented at the Annual Meeting of the Canadian Sociology and Anthropology Association, Toronto (August).

Prus, R., and C. R. D. Sharper (1977). *Road Hustler*. Toronto: D. C. Heath.

Ralbovsky, M. (1974). *Destiny's Darlings*. New York: Hawthorn Books.

Rosenberg, M., and A. Turowetz (1975). "The wrestler and the physician: Identity work-up and organizational arrangements." In D. Ball and J. Loy (eds.), *Sport and Social Order*, pp. 563-574. Reading, Mass.: Addison-Wesley.

Sage, G. (1975). "An occupational analysis of the college coach." In D. W. Ball and J. W. Loy (eds.), *Sport and Social Order*, pp. 395–455. Reading, Mass. Addison-Wesley.

Scott, M. (1968). *The Racing Game*. Chicago: Aldine.

Shaw, G. (1973). *Meat on the Hoof*. New York: Dell.

Sheard, K. G., and E. Dunning (1973). "The rugby football club as a type of male preserve: Some sociological notes." *International Review of Sport Sociology* 8: 5–21.

Shibutani, T. (1955). "Reference groups as perspectives." *American Journal of Sociology* 60 (May): 562–569.

Smith, M. D. (1975a). "The legitimation of violence: Hockey players' perceptions of their reference groups' sanctions for assault." *Canadian Review of Sociology and Anthropology* 12: 72–80.

Smith, M. (1975b). "Sport and collective violence." In D. W. Ball and J. W. Loy (eds.), *Sport and Social Order*, pp. 281–330. Reading, Mass.: Addison-Wesley.

Smith, M. D. (1976a). "Hostile outbursts in sport." In A. Yiannakis et al. (ed.), *Sport Sociology: Contemporary Themes*, pp. 205–207. Dubuque, Iowa: Kendall Hunt.

Smith, M. D. (1976b). "Precipitants of crowd violence in sport." Unpublished paper, York University.

Smith, M., and F. Diamond (1976). "Career mobility in professional hockey." In R. Gruneau and J. Albinson (eds.), *Canadian Sport: Sociological Perspectives*, pp. 275–293. Don Mills, Ontario: Addison-Wesley (Canada).

Steele, P. D. (1976). "The bowling hustler: A study of deviance in sport." In D. Landers (ed.), *Social Problems in Athletics*, pp. 86–92. Urbana: University of Illinois Press.

Steele, P., and L. Zurcher (1973). "Leisure sports as ephemeral roles." *Pacific Sociological Review* 16 (July): 345–356.

Stone, G. (1972). "Wrestling: The great American passion play." In E. Dunning (ed.), *Sport: Readings from a Sociological Perspective*, pp. 301–335. Toronto: University of Toronto Press.

Taylor, I. R. (1972). "Football mad: A speculative sociology of football hooliganism." In E. Dunning (ed.), *The Sociology of Sport*, pp. 353–377. Toronto: University of Toronto Press.

Thomson, R. (1977). "Sport and deviance: A subcultural analysis." Ph.D. dissertation, University of Alberta, Edmonton.

Tiger, L. (1969). *Men in Groups*. London: Thomas Nelson and Sons.

Time (1975). "Courage and fear in a vortex of violence." 105 (February 24): 48–54.

Toffler, A. (1970). *Future Shock*. New York: Bantam Books.

Valens, E. G. (1975). *The Other Side of the Mountain*. New York: Warner Books.

Vaz, E. (1972). "The culture of young hockey players: Some initial observations." In E. Taylor (ed.), *Training: A Scientific Basis*, pp. 222–234. Springfield, Ill.: Charles C. Thomas.

Vaz, E., and D. Thomas (1974). "What price victory: An analysis of minor hockey players' attitudes towards winning." *International Review of Sport Sociology* 9: 33–53.

Voigt, D. (1974). *A Little League Journal*. Bowling Green, Ohio: Bowling Green University Popular Press. Used with permission.

Weinberg, S., and H. Arond (1952). "The occupational culture of the boxer." *American Journal of Sociology* 57 (March): 460–469.

Wind, H. W. "The sporting scene—the ever more complex world of tournament tennis." *The New Yorker* (October 11): 93–125.

Wolfgang, M., and F. Ferracuti (1967). *The Subculture of Violence*. London: Tavistock.

PART 3
SPORT AND MACROSOCIAL SYSTEMS
Sport and Societal Subsystems

Chapter 6
SPORT
AND SOCIALIZING
INSTITUTIONS

6.1 INTRODUCTION

6.1.1 Perspectives on Social Learning

Every institutionalized system needs to recruit and train new members for the social roles that must be performed. The process by which this recruitment and learning occurs is known as socialization. It is a complex process designed to produce an individual who is socialized for the requirements of participating as a functioning member of society in general, and for the performance of specific social roles in a variety of social systems within society. More specifically, socialization into particular social roles involves the acquisition of skills (physical and social), traits, values, knowledges, attitudes, norms, and dispositions that can be learned in one or more social institutions.

Specific sport roles can be learned in more than one institutional setting; thus in this chapter the influences of the family, the school, peer groups, and voluntary sport associations are considered from two perspectives. First, individuals, formally and informally, are socialized *into* sport roles and the interest here concerns who gets involved in sport, how they learn sport roles, at what stages in life these roles are learned, and whether individuals receive the opportunity to realize their inherent potential to become involved in specific sport roles or to ultimately perform at an elite level.

Whereas the physical sciences may be able to account for physical and structural differences between those who are involved in sport and those who are not, between athletes who are successful and those who are unsuccessful, between males and females, and between those of varying racial origins, they are unable to explain all of the variations accounting for socialization into specific sport roles or the attainment of elite performance in a specific sport. Furthermore, the physical sciences cannot totally explain why individuals from one country are more involved or successful in a particular sport role than those in other countries with similar population, size, and geographical characteristics, or why one region of a country produces more elite athletes than another region (see Rooney, 1974).

It is the process of socialization in different cultural environments that influences who has the opportunity to participate and achieve in a specific sport role and that explains why individuals who are structurally and physiologically similar do, or do not, become involved in sport roles. For example, few Indians, blacks, or Francophones in North America have been given the opportunity to achieve elite status in national or international sport competitions (Boileau, Landry, and Trempe, 1976; Gruneau, 1972; McPherson, 1974b).

A second perspective on social learning is related to socialization *via* sport. This concerns the degree to which skills, traits, values, attitudes, knowledges, and dispositions learned in one social system can be generalized to other social situations. For example, for many years sport and physical education have been legitimated by those within the system on the basis that what is learned in these social environments is transferred to other domains. More specifically, claims have been made that character and moral traits such as "sportsmanship," "honesty," "courage," "citizenship," "cooperation," and "achievement orientation" are learned when a child is participating in such sport roles as that of Little League athlete or intramural participant. As a later section of this chapter suggests, the "socialization-via-sport" theme is an assumption that has little theoretical or empirical support (Loy and Ingham, 1973; Kenyon, 1968; Stevenson, 1975).

In view of the fact that socialization may occur in a variety of social institutions, in a variety of social environments, and throughout the life cycle, the process may vary by gender, social class, ethnic background, and nationality. Throughout this chapter the reader should recognize that the values, attitudes, opportunity set, and past experiences of the socializing agents may greatly influence the process for given individuals. For example, differing values and beliefs concerning gender role identification held by significant others in different nations or within a nation greatly influence the socialization process and opportunity set for females to learn and enact sport roles.

6.1.2 One Approach to Social Learning: A Social Role–Social Systems Model

A concern with the process of socialization is present in many of the social sciences, including social anthropology, psychology, political science, and sociology. As a result, a number of theoretical and conceptual approaches[1] have been developed to explain how a novice learns the goals, values, norms, and preferred behavioral patterns of a society or of a specific social system.

One of the more fruitful approaches has been the social imitation process proposed by Bandura and Walters (1963) and Bandura (1969). They argue that most social behavior is learned by observing and internalizing the behavior of others, without the observer actually reproducing the observed behavior and receiving direct reinforcement, as in the traditional stimulus-response pattern of learning. The models for this imitation process are both exemplary (e.g., parents, siblings, peers, teachers, coaches, etc.) and symbolic (e.g., television personalities or fictional characters with whom the individual does not have face-to-face

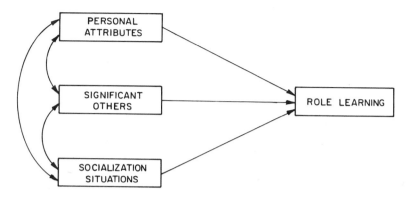

Fig. 6.1   *The three elements of the socialization process. (From Kenyon and McPherson, 1973, p. 305)*

contact). Moreover, the process operates over the entire life cycle and may lead to the learning of deviant as well as normative behavioral patterns, depending on the models that are available.

In addition to social imitation theory, role theory (Sarbin and Allen, 1968) also helps to explain the process whereby an individual acquires the pattern of expected behavior, or role, for social positions within a social structure. In fact, if a social system is to survive, individuals must be found to fill the institutionalized roles. Based on this theory, the learning process involves interaction and imitation between the role of socializer, occupied by established members of the system (i.e., significant others, reference groups, role models), and the role of novice.

In order to provide a synthesis of the social learning process, Sewell (1963) combined psychological and sociological parameters in a "social role–social system" model (see Fig. 6.1). This approach states that a *role aspirant*, characterized by a set of ascribed and achieved physical, sociological, and psychological characteristics, is exposed to *significant others* (Woelfel and Haller, 1971) found within a variety of *social systems*. More specifically, role learners (with unique personality traits, attitudes, motivations, values, motor skills, and gender, racial, and ethnic differences) are exposed directly and indirectly to significant others in a variety of social systems (e.g., the home, school, church, playground, the mass media, sport teams) at various stages in the life cycle (Fig. 6.2).

Each social system is viewed, then, as an institution that can potentially facilitate or inhibit the learning of a specific role. The degree to which each system operates in the learning process depends on the role being learned, the sex of the socializee, and the stage in the life cycle. For example, whereas the family and school are the most important systems during childhood, the place of employment and the peer group are most important during the adult years. Furthermore, within a given social system the values, norms, and situational facilities may lead that system to be supportive of, indifferent to, or in direct opposition to the learning of a specific role. To illustrate, if sport is not ranked

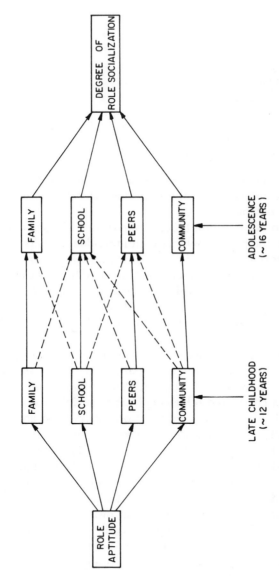

Fig. 6.2 *Postulated social role-social system two-stage block-recursive model for sport socialization. (From Kenyon and McPherson, 1973, p. 309)*

highly in the leisure or career hierarchy of values held by parents, peers, or teachers, if positive reinforcement for participating and competing in sport is not received from significant others, and if opportunity sets are not created so that equipment, coaching, and competition are available, then it is unlikely that an individual exposed to this type of socialization setting would ever become involved in sport, regardless of how great an innate ability he or she may have.

The process of role acquisition involves four stages: anticipatory, formal, informal, and personal (Thornton and Nardi, 1975). Thornton and Nardi (1975) suggest that role acquisition is not fully accomplished until the individual has "anticipated it (the role), learned anticipatory, formal, and informal expectations comprised in it, formulated his own expectations, . . . and accepted the final outcome." Regardless of the role, the process is influenced by a number of macrosystem and microsystem factors as well as by achieved and ascribed social categories. For example, at the macro level, within a given society, the dominant ideologies reflecting social values and norms can greatly influence the behavioral patterns that are learned and perpetuated in that nation or community. At the micro level, ascribed or achieved categories such as social class, ethnicity, religion, gender, place and type of residence, ordinal position, and age are often influential in allocating rights, expectations, and opportunities in a variety of domains. It is these factors that influence an individual's life chances to learn and acquire specific social roles.

6.1.3 Socialization into Primary and Secondary Sport Roles

Major questions of interest to both coaches and researchers include why some individuals become involved in sport and why others do not, why individuals are attracted to specific sport roles but not to others, and why some who are involved become elite athletes, while others with apparently similar physical attributes do not. Although definitive answers to these questions are not yet available, research efforts in recent years have been directed toward the study of socialization into both primary and secondary sport roles.[2] One general finding is that the socialization that takes place within a given social system varies according to the sport role and the component of the role being learned (i.e., the behavioral, affective, or cognitive component) and according to the stage in the life cycle and the sex of the role aspirant.

The process whereby elite athletes (i.e., college, Olympic, or professional athletes) become interested and involved in sport indicates that interest and participation is aroused early in life, often before the age of six or seven. This initial interest is stimulated in the home, neighborhood, and school and normally involves exposure to one of the traditional team sports such as baseball, basketball, or football. Later, either through the school or voluntary associations, interest and participation in other sports such as track and field, gymnastics, wrestling, and tennis may occur. Many of those who eventually become elite athletes participate in a number of sports before they begin to specialize, and often their early experiences result in a high level of success. Moreover, combined with a favorable opportunity set (such as living close to a sport facility), at specific stages in the life cycle they receive positive sanctions from a variety of significant others, of whom the family, peer group, and coaches appear to be the most influential. Many of these role models did compete or still do compete in one or more of the sports being learned by the role aspirant. Thus, they serve as direct role models in addition to providing verbal, emotional, or financial support. Finally, although the general sport-role socialization process has a number of common elements, there are patterned differences in the processes between sports, for each sex, and at different stages in the life cycle.

For the general population (that is, those who do not compete at a high level of competition), studies suggest that early socialization is also a major factor in involving young adults in sport during the college years or during the early years of adulthood. Further, those who are socialized early and receive reinforcement from significant others are more likely to continue to be involved in later adulthood. Interestingly, there appear to be unique differences in the socialization process for the learning of sport roles by the general population. For example, it appears that for the members of some ethnic groups, two, three, or four institutions must provide an opportunity set, reinforcement, and role models, in order for those individuals to become involved in sport.

Similar to the learning of primary sport roles, socialization into secondary roles is a complex process that appears to vary depending on the sport role and the social class, sex, and ethnicity of the role aspirant. Moreover, unlike primary sport role socialization, which tends to occur during childhood, adolescence, or early adulthood, the process of learning secondary roles can occur at any stage of the life cycle. More so than for the learning of primary sport roles, however, socialization into secondary sport involvement at one stage in the life cycle appears to be highly dependent on the degree of socialization that has occurred at earlier stages (McPherson, 1976c). That is, there appears to be greater continuity or stability in the consumption of sport than in the degree of involvement in active sport roles. Once learned, the role tends to be enacted much later in life than the role of athlete. In short, being socialized and involved at one stage in the life cycle appears to account for much of the involvement at the next stage, more so than current situational correlates that may be operating at that point in time.

6.2 SPORT, FAMILY, AND KINSHIP SYSTEMS

6.2.1 The Family as a Socializing Institution

Throughout history the family has been a basic and dominant social institution, to the extent that the nuclear family in most societies is one of the more universal institutions (along with play, games, and sport). The nuclear family and the extended family (e.g., grandparents) are most responsible for the socialization process in the early years. However, other relatives (e.g., aunts, uncles, cousins, in-laws) comprise a kinship network and may also serve as socializing agents.

The structure of the nuclear family permits two-way interaction between parents and children and among siblings. It is within the interaction framework of this primary group that social participation begins for the infant. Although this is usually an exchange process in which resulting behavior is influenced by the rewards and costs (as determined by a comparison of expectations and the competing alternatives), conflict may occur. This is more likely to happen during the preadolescent and adolescent years when the individual encounters new reference groups (e.g., school personnel, the peer group) with possible conflicting interests, values, and goals. Nevertheless, during the childhood years the nuclear family serves as the major socializing institution by confirming ascribed social status, providing economic and emotional (i.e., reinforcement) support, providing role models for the internalization of values, knowledge, and behavioral patterns, and providing the opportunity set for voluntary association involvement (e.g., youth groups). Furthermore, by serving as a gatekeeper for mass media consumption, the family controls access to public opinion and the learning and internalization of societal norms. In short, the family provides a basic frame of reference from which to view social reality. Thus it continues to be a critical social institution, although other institutions such as education, religion, voluntary associations, the mass media, the polity, and the economy have usurped some of the family's traditional functions.

6.2.2 Factors Influencing Family Leisure Role Socialization

Many of the earliest parent-infant interactions are playlike in nature and are closely related to the social class milieu of the parents. From these early play experiences the child is gradually exposed to more formal play and game experiences within the family unit. This exposure is closely related to the sex-role socialization process in which from an early age boys and girls receive toys and games (Lewis, 1972) "appropriate" to their biological gender. In its most extreme form, early sex-role socialization is exemplified by the parent who places a football in a son's crib and a doll in a daughter's crib.

Most studies of socialization into primary and secondary sport roles indicate that the family of origin is an influential social system, especially for females (Theberge, 1977). In general, this influence results from a climate that values sport and from the presence of role models who engage in the specific behavior and/or provide reinforcement and an opportunity set. For young children, the values of sport are transferred from generation to generation along with those in other cultural domains. Thus, a positive evaluation of sport by parents is likely to give rise to sport interests among the offspring. Moreover, children are more likely to consume and participate if the parents presently participate in sport or if they did so in the past, if the parents attend sport events or watch them on television, if the parents have expectations or aspirations for their children in sport, if the parents actively encourage participation, and if sport is a salient topic of conversation in the home.

Although it represents a "chicken-egg" phenomenon, the question as to why and how parents come to value sport in varying degrees must be considered. That is, why are some children raised in an environment in which sport is valued, while others are not, thereby increasing the sporting life chances of the former considerably? First, as the continuity theory (see Atchley, 1977) of social behavior has suggested, life style at one stage in life influences subsequent life chances and life style. Therefore, if the individual was socialized into one or more sport roles as a child within the family unit and if the activities were pleasurable, the activity is more likely to be introduced to subsequent generations (Sofranko and Nolan, 1972). Second, if members of valued reference groups are involved in an activity, a role model is provided and similar patterns of behavior are encouraged. Therefore, even parents who had never been socialized themselves might begin to socialize their child if other parents in the child's immediate reference group introduce their children to sport activities. Third, a deprivation hypothesis would suggest that individuals may attempt to compensate for activities or experiences they missed during childhood by consciously and actively socializing their offspring into these activities. This may partially account for the adult domination of children's sport programs at the present time.

A final phenomenon that may influence the specific sport roles to which children are exposed is the father's occupation. While the evidence is contradictory at this time, there has been support for both a "compensatory" hypothesis, which suggests that adults seek leisure activities that are different in form and structure from their daily occupation (i.e., a safety valve effect), as well as for a "similarity" hypothesis, which suggests that people seek consistency in their life style and engage in leisure activities similar in form to their daily occupation.

In summary, whatever pattern is exhibited by parents within a family of procreation serves as the model for their children. Thus, within the family unit, the form of leisure role socialization is influenced by factors in the parents' family of orientation (e.g., their social class, their opportunity set as a child, their pleasurable experiences in sport as a child), by factors within the family of procreation (e.g., family size, social status, opportunity set, age of the children), and by the influence of extended family and nonfamily reference groups for the parents, both in the past and at present.

In addition to the influence of the parents, sibling interaction also facilitates or inhibits socialization into sport roles. Although considerable significance has been attached to sibling relations by social scientists, little empirical research has been completed on the interaction patterns within the youngest generation in an extended family (Irish, 1964). Thus, if a more adequate understanding of the socialization process during childhood is to be gained, research on sibling interaction must be initiated (Sutton-Smith and Rosenberg, 1970).

Among some of the factors that influence patterns of sibling interaction are the effects of density in the physical environment in the home, ordinal position or birth order, family size, sex and age differences, and systematic differences in parental interaction with different siblings. To date, the effects of birth order or ordinal position have received the most attention from social scientists (Adams, 1972; Kammeyer, 1967; Miley, 1969; Rosenberg and Sutton-Smith, 1964; Sampson, 1965), partly because the concept is easy to quantify or operationalize, and partly because being the only child, the oldest child, or the youngest child has intuitively suggested differences in life chances and behavioral patterns, including involvement in sport. Most of this research has been concerned with the question "Does ordinal position make a difference in the learning of social behavior, and if so, what are the differences?" Unfortunately, less effort has been spent asking *why* we would expect differences or *why* there are differences. One important premise to remember, however, is that birth order creates a particular kind of social structure within the family that may influence psychological (e.g., personality, attitudes) and social development patterns.

Many theories or tentative explanations have been postulated to explain why birth order should make a difference. The physiological theories argue that early-borns are healthier and have greater intelligence because they developed in a more nutritious uterine environment. Yet another view holds that since later deliveries are easier, forceps are less likely to be used and there is less likelihood of cerebral damage during birth. Another theoretical view holds that the only child is unique because of the social environment in which he or she is socialized. That is, lacking siblings with whom to interact, he or she becomes adult-oriented or self-centered earlier in life and to a greater degree. However, most research has found that the only child is not very different from first-borns in families in which there are siblings.

A third perspective suggests that parents are more overprotective, anxious, and indulgent with their first child and thus the child is more dependent. However, this may apply solely to only children since once a sibling arrives to compete for attention, the first-born receives less attention (dethronement). A fourth view (Sutton-Smith and Rosenberg, 1970) suggests that first-born siblings interact and serve as role models and competitors for younger siblings. This implies a one-way socialization process in which the behavior of later-borns is primarily accounted for by the presence of older siblings. Birth order, in this context, is usually considered in conjunction with the sex of the older sibling. Thus, a male with an older brother will have a different learning environment than a male with an older sister because a different modeling and interaction process may operate. It is this latter theoretical framework that has been utilized most by those interested in explaining involvement in sport according to birth order and sibling sex.

The relationships among ordinal position, sex of siblings, and involvement in sport has normally been studied in two-children families, with no attempt to control for age differences between the siblings. Further, the research has been mainly descriptive, with some attempt to explain the findings on the basis of either the "sibling-similarity" hypothesis (later siblings assimilate the behavioral patterns of the older sibling, regardless of sex) or the "sibling-opposite" hypothesis (the older sibling functions as a negative model of how *not* to behave; this usually occurs when the model is a member of the opposite sex). Ordinal position, then, may influence the socialization process in that first-borns serve as positive or negative role models who are to be imitated. However, they do not experience this advantage themselves and therefore may have different life chances than later-borns. For example, it has been found that first-borns are less likely than later-borns to participate in "dangerous" sports such as hockey, football, and wrestling (Casher, 1977; Gould and Landers, 1972; Nisbett, 1968; Yiannakis, 1976), supposedly because they have less freedom in selecting activities, are more vulnerable to stress and pain, and are more psychologically dependent on adults.

First-borns, especially females, are also hypothesized to be the "conservators of tradition" within the family (Kammeyer, 1966; Edwards and Klemmack, 1973) in that they are more likely to assume traditionally defined occupational roles. For example, Schachter (1959) noted that later-borns are overrepresented among professional baseball players. This hypothesis, which has equivocal support at best, argues that there is a differential socialization process between first-borns and later-borns in that the first-borns are more likely to adopt a traditional orientation and to internalize parental aspirations concerning educational and occupational expectations.

It has been hypothesized that the sex of the older sibling in relation to that of the younger sibling influences the type and frequency of sport involvement by the latter. To date, the research evidence is conflicting in that the "sibling-similarity" and "sibling-opposite" hypotheses have both been supported or rejected (see, for example, Landers, 1970, 1971, 1972; Landers and Luschen, 1970; and Portz, 1973). That is, it can *not* be predicted that a second-born male with an older brother will more likely be involved in sport, or that a later-born female with an older brother will be more involved than her age-peers. The equivocal state of knowledge in this area suggests that although siblings may serve as role models, consistent birth order by sex interaction patterns are not present and therefore caution should be exercised in predicting involvement in sport based on these variables. In sum, more theoretically based research is needed to increase our knowledge about the dynamics of the relationship between birth order, sibling sex, family socialization, intragenerational interactions, and involvement in sport.

6.2.3 Outcomes of Family Sport Role Socialization

Based on the available evidence, the family of orientation seems to provide the main social context in which initial sport and leisure role socialization takes place. Furthermore, interest generated in childhood within the family is likely to persist or be adopted at later stages in the life cycle (Kelly, 1974). If a child is socialized into sport so that participation and/or consumption become an integral facet of his or her life style, this influence will likely remain throughout the adult years (e.g., continuity theory). There may be a shift, however, from participation in the traditional team sports to individual sports, or a shift from enactment of primary roles to involvement in secondary roles.

Another outcome of family involvement in sport role socialization is the presence of sex differences in both the process and the result. Although little empirical work has been completed concerning the socialization of females into primary sport roles, the process does appear to be differentiated by gender, just as it is for most aspects of socialization. This may result in discrimination, which often occurs because there are different expectations (because of socially induced sex-appropriate values, norms, and sanctions) for the female and the male roles in most facets of life. This is especially true with respect to involvement in sport, where socialization into status equality or inequality can occur within the family. For example, within a given community a female may see her mother and older female siblings participating and competing in sport within the family environment and thus she may become involved because of modeling and direct reinforcement. On the other hand, she may interact with a peer group that does not receive similar support from the family or she may attend a school where negative sanctions for sport participation are dispersed. In general, the evidence suggests that it is almost essential that young girls have female role models (especially the mother) or female reference groups (same-sex peers) available in their social world if they are to be socialized into primary sport roles (Smith, 1976; Snyder and Spreitzer, 1976). Furthermore, it is likely that girls need support from more than just the family (for example, peers or teachers); otherwise role conflict may occur. To illustrate, in an analysis of factors associated with socialization into the role of professional woman golfer, Theberge (1977) found that few players ever perceived contradictions between the roles of woman and athlete. One explanation for this lack of conflict may be that the golfers reported receiving support for sport involvement first from their parents and later from male and female friends and teaching professionals. That is, they were socialized into this sport role in a supportive environment.

While little research has been concerned with understanding the relationship between sport and family life or the function of sport within the family environment, it has been stated that "the family that plays together stays together"—that is, sport facilitates familial consensus, integration, or solidarity. To date, there is no evidence to support this view and, in fact, there may be just as much anecdotal evidence to suggest that sport is a disruptive element. For example, (1) there is a high divorce rate and incidence of absentee parent when one of the marital partners is a professional athlete; (2) when family members develop different sport interests and join different associations, the opportunity for sport-related family interaction decreases (e.g., the "golf widow"); (3) the excessive amount of sport consumption by adult males often creates marital strain or conflict (e.g., the "football widow"); and (4) a conflict often results when a father-child-mother triad has differing views concerning the relative values of education and sport.

In a series of studies that analyzed the function of children's sport in family life, Watson (1973, 1974, 1975, 1977) suggests that there is a decline in the socialization function and power of the family in general and that although parents have lost power over their children, they are still responsible for their socialization. At the same time, the peer group and community agencies have increased their influence over the child. Therefore, parents attempt to institutionalize their children's free-time activities, especially in sport, in order to test their effectiveness as parents and to compare their child's development with age-peers. Specifically, Watson indicates that Little League baseball (and, by inference, other youth sports) provides a testing environment for both the child and parent. Watson also reported that there are differences in how parents from different social classes view Little League baseball. For example, middle-class parents consider the game to be a form of training through which the child learns cooperative interaction in a group—a basic value in the middle-class status system. On the other hand, working-class parents evaluate the game as a form of training for social integration through exposure to highly organized authority figures and authority structures. Hence, the function of sport as viewed by the family is perceived differently according to social-class background.

The Little League game is highly attractive to members of the family since it enables parents and children to mirror interactions that occur in society under expressive conditions (Ralbovsky, 1974a; Voigt, 1974). In order to accomplish this goal the youth sport milieu includes the following features: adult control, social disorganization, social conflict, unpredictability, ritual, fun, a Gemeinschaft[3] environment in which the seating arrangements and degree of involvement during the game by parents vary according to social class background, and status passage during the course of the game (Watson, 1974). Because of these features the world of children's sport exposes the family to the processes and problems operating in adult society. Finally, a comparison of parents who were involved in youth sport with those who were not suggests that the involved parents have a greater concern for the successful development of their children through highly institutionalized community organizations, rather than depending exclusively on the family environment to realize these goals.

In summary, the family as an institution is intimately related to sport in a variety of ways. The family serves as a socializing agent for the learning of sport roles (especially mothers for their daughters); it provides a structure from which ascribed and achieved attributes impinge on an individual in a sport system, and it uses sport as an expressive microcosm of the larger society in its attempt to socialize children. Moreover, there is little evidence to support the myth that participation in sport contributes significantly to family integration or solidarity.

6.3 SPORT, SCHOOL, AND EDUCATIONAL SYSTEMS

6.3.1 Introduction

Prior to, and especially after, the Industrial Revolution, there was an increasing recognition that the family could not socialize the individual for all the potential roles he or she might play throughout the life cycle. Accordingly, the formal educational system was greatly expanded to provide the basic and more specialized skills needed by a more complex division of labor. Later, because of increasing specialization, higher education was developed to provide both a general "liberal" education and highly specialized training for specific occupations (for example, engineering, physical education, law, biology, sociology, etc.). This functionalistic view is based on the premise that occupations require specific skills that can best be acquired through a formal curriculum in the elementary, secondary, or higher educational institutions.

In contrast, a conflict perspective, more concerned with equality of educational opportunity (see Coleman et al., 1966), argues that the growth of the educational system has resulted from an attempt by status groups to solidify their elite position in the occupational hierarchy by imposing restrictions on the entry into specific occupations. Moreover, in addition to the imposition of achievement criteria, the educational system inculcates values and patterns of behavior related to the more advantaged groups in societies. In short, this view argues that the educational system was created to maintain the status quo, whereas the functionalist view would argue that the system serves as a mechanism facilitating upward social mobility. Although the debate continues (see Collins, 1971), it is likely that both perspectives have some explanatory value in accounting for the role of education in the socialization process in general and as it pertains to sport in particular.

First in the form of physical education classes and later in intramural and extramural competition, sport was introduced into the educational system to promote health through fitness, to socialize youth into sport skills, and to inculcate values and character traits deemed essential by society. In fact, much of the early rationale for the inclusion of physical education in the curriculum was the belief that socialization via play, games, and sport was possible and necessary. (More will be said about this assumption in Section 6.5.)

The role of sport within the educational milieu appears to adhere to both a functionalist and a conflict perspective. On the one hand, it has been suggested that sport is functional for raising educational aspirations, for encouraging academic achievement, for fostering social integration, and for serving as a catalyst or mechanism for upward social mobility. Similarly, the system itself is functional in socializing individuals into sport roles. On the other hand, it has been argued that sport interferes with the attainment of the basic educational goals.

Closely related to the functional and conflict perspectives is the more basic question of the purpose of education. One polar view is that education should be designed for enculturation through which children are fitted into the religious, cultural, and economic values and behavioral patterns exhibited by their parents. Thus, the main function of the educational system, according to this view, is to provide individuals with skills and knowledges that will guarantee that the individual has sufficient vocational skills to fit into the existing social structure. In this type of program, the learning tends to be more authoritarian—the student is provided with information that he or she passively accepts. An alternative view is that the primary goal of the educational system is to develop maturity within the individual so that he or she becomes an autonomous person who is ultimately responsible for his or her own life chances. This approach emphasizes questioning, both of self and of others.

To date enculturation, or the functional approach, has been the model that has been used most within the educational system. As a result, as Schafer (1971) noted, interscholastic athletics have come to serve an enculturation function whereby students are molded into mainstream society by acquiring the normative attitudes, values, and behavioral patterns considered acceptable by the majority.

Through the influence of coaches within the school system, values, norms, beliefs, and attitudes thought to be desirable for success in later life are internalized. In short, Schafer suggests that a high school sport program promotes dominant community values and life styles rather than providing individuals with the opportunity to question the existing form or to try alternative models. The result is a structure whereby only the elite participate, while the subelites become spectators and support those who are on the representative team. Schafer further argues that school athletic programs should contribute more to the maturity and development of each student. In this way all will have an opportunity to engage in a variety of sports purely for the enjoyment of participation, rather than for the sole purpose of elite competition. The result would be adults who are in a better position to make an individual choice as to the type of physical recreation that best meets their interests and needs in adulthood. That is, they will have a much wider range of choice if they have experienced a number of sport opportunities during their school years.

6.3.2 The Role of the School in Sport Role Socialization

To date, there is little evidence to suggest that the elementary school plays a key role in the process of sport-role socialization. Rather, most of the socialization at this stage occurs in the family, neighborhood, peer group, and voluntary sport associations. This is not surprising considering the state of development of physical education and interschool athletic programs in most elementary schools.

At the secondary school level, sport becomes an integral part of the youth subculture and tends to be highly valued in most secondary schools. As a result, the individual is exposed to an opportunity set and to significant others who value sport highly. More specifically, interest in consuming a variety of sports is often stimulated and reinforced within the school, especially if consumption is encouraged to promote school solidarity or identification. In terms of socialization into primary roles, the secondary school provides role models and reinforcement from significant others for the learning of specific sport roles, especially those sports that an individual is unlikely to have experienced during the elementary school years. For example, a high percentage of Olympic calibre gymnasts (Roethlisberger, 1970) and track and field athletes (Kenyon and McPherson, 1973) have reported that although they were involved in a variety of team sports during childhood, the initial interest in their present sport was aroused during the high school years. In fact, over 80 percent of the track and field athletes reported that they attended a high school where the students and teachers considered track and field to be an important extracurricular activity.

At the college or university level, a professional socialization process operates to prepare elite athletes for professional or amateur careers in sport. It is during this stage in the life cycle that an athlete, already socialized to some degree, becomes almost fully socialized into the values, skills, and knowledges essential for subsequent involvement in sport at the highest level (e.g., professional or Olympic sport). This period of socialization involves learning and testing oneself against other elites before making a final decision concerning a career in sport. Again, similar to the high school period, the university environment further socializes students into the role of sport consumer, especially of football and basketball. In fact, those who are most likely to consume professional football on a regular basis are those who have attended college. Moreover, they have likely graduated from a college at which attendance at football games was an integral component of the social scene during the first semester each year. That is, they become socialized into the role of football spectator and this type of social participation becomes integrated into their leisure life style as adults.

In summary, the school, along with the family and peer group, is an influential institution in the process of sport-role socialization. However, like other social systems, the role of the educational system in the process varies by sport, by roles within sports, by sex, and by stage in the life cycle. For example, professional female golfers are largely socialized into their sport role by agents (that is, parents and friends) outside of school settings (Theberge, 1977).

6.3.3 Sport and Educational Attainment

Unlike many subtopics in the sociology of sport, an interest in the relationship between involvement in sport and academic performance has generated not only a great deal of research in a number of countries, but also some cumulative research findings. Interest in this relationship led to a number of empirical studies in the early 1900s. For example, Davis and Cooper (1934) reviewed 41 studies, which appeared between 1903 and 1932. On the basis of this review they concluded, in contrast to more recent findings, that the nonathlete performs slightly better in schoolwork than the athlete does. Moreover, they noted that athletes tend to get better grades after the end of the sport season. More recently, the descriptive work of Eidsmore (1961, 1963) has stimulated renewed empirical interest in this topic. He found that high school male and female basketball players and male football players were "brighter" students than their classmates, based on a comparison of grade point averages (GPA). Although not explicitly stated, the results implied that participation in sport "caused" better academic performance. Other studies have found similar results in the United States (Bend, 1968; Schafer and Armer, 1968) and Great Britain (McIntosh, 1966; Start, 1967), although Jerome (1971) did not find support for the relationship in Canada.[4]

Although the finding that athletes have a higher level of academic performance than nonathletes appears to be almost universal, a definitive explanation for the relationship is lacking. It has been suggested that there is a link between mental and physical ability, that the better student is differentially selected by coaches for sport teams, or that the better students are involved in a variety of extracurricular activities, of which sport is just one of many pursuits (Spady, 1970).

In order to account for this relationship Schafer and Armer (1968) suggested eight possible explanations: (1) athletes are graded more leniently; (2) values acquired in sport are applied in the academic domain; (3) superior physical condition improves mental performance; (4) athletes work harder to obtain grades in order to remain eligible; (5) athletes make more efficient and effective use of their limited study time; (6) athletes are motivated to achieve in order to be eligible for an athletic scholarship at college; (7) they obtain additional tutoring and advice from peers, coaches, and teachers because they are athletes; and (8) the prestige earned in athletics gives them a better self-concept and promotes higher aspirations in other domains (Schurr and Brookover, 1970). A more analytical account by Rehberg (1969) hypothesizes that there are five intervening constructs between athletic participation and academic achievement: (1) association with highly achievement-oriented peers; (2) transfer of achievement values from sport to the classroom environment; (3) an increasing self-esteem, which creates higher levels of aspiration in other domains; (4) pressure applied internally and externally to present a consistent image in all domains as a successful individual; and (5) more scholastic and career guidance from adult significant others, especially those within the school environment (Snyder, 1972).

One of the major limitations of studies in this area is that they have been cross-sectional. That is, the athletes are studied at only one point in time, normally during one year at high school. One exception is the study by King and Angi (1968), which compared the academic performances in grade 9 and again in grade 12 of boys playing on hockey teams outside the school system. They found that as freshmen the hockey players had grades similar to those students who did not play hockey. However, by the time they were seniors they had significantly lower grades. That is, as their degree of involvement in higher levels of hockey increased, their academic performance declined. Thus, it may be the degree of involvement rather than the fact of their involvement in sport that leads to differential academic performance. Some support for this explanation is offered by Schutz et al. (1977), who concluded that boys who participate in organized hockey at the level of juvenile or lower do not differ in academic achievement from boys who do not participate in hockey. Academic achievement was measured by either average grade or percent who graduate from high school.

The influence of ceasing to participate in organized sport on academic performance also needs to be examined to determine whether grades change after disengagement from sport. In the only attempt to answer this question to date, Sage (1967) considered the academic performance at college of 85 former high school athletes, 43 of whom participated in college sport and 42 of whom did not. He found that the nonparticipating students achieved better grades and were more occupationally oriented at college.

In summary, athletes do appear to receive grades at least as high, and perhaps higher, than nonathletes (Clarke, 1975), but it is not known how many potential athletes have been eliminated from studies because they were academically ineligible to be a member of the school team that was sampled. Further, the relationship may change over a period of time, especially if the athlete becomes involved in higher levels of competition, and there may be cross-national differences. Finally, all that may really be known at this stage is that participation in institutionalized scholastic or collegiate sport does not have a serious detrimental effect on academic performance.

6.3.4 Sport and Educational Aspirations and Expectations

At some point during the high school years an individual begins to consider and decide how much education he or she would like to attain and whether there is a chance to realize this goal. In recent years it has been found that athletes have higher expectations than nonathletes, even when the studies have been controlled for class background, mental ability, academic performance in high school, and parental encouragement. For example, Bend (1968), Rehberg and Schafer (1968), Spreitzer and Pugh (1973), and Otto and Alwin (1977) found that a greater proportion of high school male athletes than nonathletes expected to enroll in a four-year college program. Moreover, the recent Otto and Alwin (1977) study extended previous research and found that participation in athletics also has a positive effect on occupational aspirations and attainment and on income. Finally, in one of the few studies concerned with women in sport, Snyder and Spreitzer (1977) found a similar positive relationship between athletic involvement and educational expectations for high school girls.

A number of explanations for this relationship between sport participation and academic expectations have been proposed. Rehberg and Schafer (1968) suggested that it occurs because (1) there is a link between participation in sport and high academic performance; (2) athletes are members of the "leading" crowd in the high school subculture and therefore are influenced to achieve in the academic domain by their peers, who have similar aspirations; (3) a high level of self-esteem gained through positive feedback from others influences the level of aspiration; (4) they receive a quantity and quality of career counseling and encouragement from teachers and coaches beyond that received by the nonathlete; (5) they desire to attend college in order to continue their athletic career; and (6) some might have been approached about accepting an athletic scholarship, which would arouse their interest and aspirations. In their replication of the Rehberg and Schafer (1968) study, Spreitzer and Pugh (1973) obtained similar results and concluded that involvement in sport leads to high peer status, which in turn fosters a desire for further recognition through college attendance. However, this process seemed to operate only in those high schools in which sport achievement was valued higher than scholastic achievement.

Most recently, in a more sophisticated study, Otto and Alwin (1977) refuted the findings of Spady (1970) and Spreitzer and Pugh (1973) in that they found no support for the psychological hypothesis that perceived peer status serves as an intervening mechanism between sport participation and educational or occupational aspirations. Rather, they found empirical support for a sociopsychological explanation that the influence of sport participation is mediated by the influence of significant others. In their discussion Otto and Alwin (1977) suggest three additional explanations for the process: (1) By participating in sport athletes may acquire "interpersonal skills" that can be utilized outside athletics, (2) involvement in sport may serve an "allocation function" that increases the visibility of athletes and labels them as successful individuals, and (3) because of their participation in sport they may experience "interpersonal networks, contacts, and information channels that are beneficial in establishing careers."

On a more psychological level, it has been suggested that the need for achievement acts as an intervening mechanism to account for the positive relationship between high school athletic participation and educational aspirations and achievement (Rehberg, 1969). However, in an empirical test of 558 high school males, Birrell (1978) found no support for the hypothesis that achievement motivation is a significant factor in the relationship between athletic participation and educational aspirations. Rather, support was obtained for a model wherein athletic participation and achievement motivation exert separate effects on educational aspirations.

In an empirical study of the role of coaches in providing advice to their players concerning where and when to attend college, Snyder (1972) found a positive relationship between the advice given by a coach and the decision to attend college. Moreover, many players reported that the coaches' advice was instrumental in their decision to attend college. Also, it was found that the higher skilled players perceived their coach to be more influential to them in terms of educational advice than did the average or substitute players.

While sport participation may stimulate aspirations to attend college, it may not be sufficient to provide the skills and resources necessary for subsequent success as a student in college. Spady (1970) found that general extracurricular involvement in high-status activities within the school is an important influence on college attainment. Moreover, he suggests that students who are active in both athletics and other student groups have the highest aspirations. This indicates that the high educational expectations reported by athletes may be a consequence of their popularity within the school milieu, which further stimulates a desire for recognition at higher levels. As Spady (1970) noted, this process may have the resultant consequence of inflated educational aspirations in the absence of prerequisite skills for academic success. More recent evidence by Otto (1976) and Otto and Alwin (1977) confirms Spady's finding that extracurricular activities serve a mediating function on subsequent educational and occupational attainment.

In summary, there appears to be a relationship between participation in sport and both educational and occupational aspirations. This relationship seems to hold for those from a lower socioeconomic background, for those who attend a high school at which the athlete role is highly valued (perhaps more than the scholar role), for those who receive advice to pursue their sport or academic career from significant others, and perhaps for those who have attained high status within the peer subculture because of their involvement in school athletics and their involvement in other activities common to the "leading" crowd. Furthermore, some of these factors may operate in combination to create a greater likelihood of attending college, especially among those who would not normally be inclined toward attending college. For example, athletes from low socioeconomic backgrounds whose parents do not encourage them to continue their education beyond high school, who have below average grades in high school, and who come from a rural environment may have higher educational aspirations than nonathletes from a similar background (Picou and Curry, 1974). However, these inflated aspirations may not "fit" with their ability or previous life style and may result in academic or sport problems in the college or university environment. This may partially account for the academic difficulties experienced by minority group athletes at college. In summary, longitudinal data are needed before many of these interpretations can be clarified or supported.

6.3.5 Sport and Interference with Educational Goals

Another area of interest within the educational domain has been the extent to which interscholastic sport programs enhance or detract from the educational goals of a school. In a classic study completed in the 1950s, Coleman (1961) hypothesized that the emphasis on athletics in high school diverts the energies of athletes and nonathletes away from academic pursuits. He found that achievement in athletics was more valued than academic achievement or social background within the status system of high school males. For example, when asked how they would most like to be remembered by their peers, the boys responded as follows: 44 percent said they would like to be remembered as an athletic star, 31 percent said they would like to be remembered as a brilliant student, and 25 percent reported that they would like to be remembered as the most popular student.

Since values may change over time, Eitzen (1976) used items similar to those used in the Coleman study and found that athletics is still an important part of the status system of teenage males. However, based on a number of controls (e.g., social class background, grade in school, type of academic program, place of the respondent in the school status hierarchy, size of the school, tradition of winning or losing teams in the school, and size of the community), the study showed that the strongest support for sport was among those with less-educated fathers, among those in the smaller schools, among those in less affluent communities, among those at the center of the status hierarchy in the school, and among those attending schools with a strict authority structure. Eitzen also asked the girls in the schools to rank their dating preferences. He found that 52 percent favored the best-looking male, 19 percent the lead guitar player in a local band, 18 percent the star athlete, and 11 percent the best student. Thus, it appears that in the subculture of some high schools, the role of athlete carries less prestige now than it did in the past. In addition to changes over time, there may also be cultural differences in the values students place on school athletics. For example, in a study of Canadian high school students, Friesen (1968) found that the order of preference among males was to be remembered as an outstanding student, as an athletic star, and then as the most popular student.

Whereas most of the studies have ignored girls, work by Buhrmann and Jarvis (1971), Buhrmann and Bratton (1977), and Birrell (1977) suggests that the role of the female athlete has been reevaluated in the past 15 years. Specifically, they found that the criteria for status in the high school system are similar for boys and girls, and that being a female athlete is now a viable role for gaining access to the leading crowd for both girls and boys. Moreover, Buhrmann and

Bratton (1977) found that the quality of athletic performance is a more important determinant of status for girls than the amount of athletic involvement.

In that it has been demonstrated that sport is highly valued in the youth subculture, it has been suggested that sport programs may interfere with academic achievement. Schafer and Armer (1968) suggested that there are at least five ways in which this interference might operate; however, no empirical evidence was presented. First, they suggested that sport diverts resources (both personnel and facilities) from more fruitful activities. Second, parents provide more support and demonstrate greater interest in the athletic events of the school than in the academic pursuits. Third, the psychic energy of the students is diverted from intellectual pursuits to the support of school teams. Fourth, students of high academic ability may be discouraged by the lack of awards and perhaps even scorn and ridicule of their peers, and may never realize their true potential because of the value climate in the school that favors athletics. Finally, athletes may not have the opportunity to realize their full academic potential because of their intensive involvement in sport. This appears to be a very plausible reason why many college athletes fail to graduate, either during the normal four-year period or even after their class has graduated.

In summary, while some investigators have suggested that interscholastic sport is diversionary and detrimental to the ultimate and real goals of the school, there is insufficient evidence at this time to support this position. Furthermore, since only high school settings have been examined, studies at the elementary school and college level should be initiated in any attempt to understand the extent to which sport either aids or detracts from the educational system. For example, Roper and Snow (1976) studied academic excellence in institutions engaged in "big-time" athletics. They found that good students and programs of academic excellence do not necessarily occur in institutions engaged in "big-time" athletics, as is commonly claimed in order to justify the large expenditure on intercollegiate athletics.

6.4 SPORT, PEER GROUPS, AND VOLUNTARY ASSOCIATIONS

6.4.1 Introduction

As soon as the child is given the freedom to venture from the home and its immediate environment (i.e., a Gemeinschaft[3] world), he or she begins to participate first in peer groups and later in voluntary associations (i.e., a Gesellschaft world), which are characterized by an informal structure rather than the more formal structure of the family and school systems. Moreover, unlike ascribed membership in the family and school, membership in these groups is voluntary and an individual may belong to one or more groups at the same time. Membership in a given group, however, does not imply complete and continuing involvement, since individuals may vary in their degree of interest and participation.

Since social organization is pluralistic, a theory of differential association (Sutherland and Cressey, 1970) suggests that at different stages in the life cycle individuals are involved in primary and secondary groups in many social worlds in addition to the family. In these groups they are likely to be exposed to either competing or complimentary values, norms, expectations, sanctions, goals, and ideologies. As the child moves away from the home and school environment, socialization increasingly occurs in the context of social systems that are more impersonal and less intense.

The peer group frequently becomes a socializing agent before the child enters the school system and either reinforces or opposes the ideas, values, attitudes, behavioral patterns, and skills learned in the home and in the school. During childhood the peer group provides experience in egalitarian relationships, teaches "taboo" subjects, helps the child become more independent of parents and other authority figures, and exposes him or her to ideas, values, and experiences that may not be encountered in the nuclear family. Later in the individual's life, and especially during the adolescent years, the peer group provides opportunities to engage in a decision-making process, to test leadership capabilities, to usurp the role of the family in the socialization process, especially if the peer group is cohesive and highly integrated, and to become integrated into an age-graded subculture (i.e., youth culture) with its own unique values, norms, sanctions, etc. For example, Coleman concluded that:

> The adolescent lives more and more in a society of his own; he finds the family a less and less satisfying psychological home. As a consequence, the home has less and less ability to mold him. (Coleman, 1961, p. 312)

During the childhood, adolescent, and adult years, individuals gravitate toward and join voluntary associations that exist or are created to achieve some common instrumental[5] or expressive goal. An examination of the theoretical approaches to the phenomenon of participation in voluntary associations indicates the consequences of such networks for the stability of society and for the integration of individuals into society (Amis and Stern, 1974; Cutler, 1973; Smith, 1975; Tomeh, 1973).

To date there have been two major theoretical approaches. The functionalist orientation operates on two levels: (1) the social-psychological level, with an interest in the function of voluntary associations for the social participation and goal attainment of the individual; and (2) the macro level, which is interested in the function of the formal group for attaining goals, socialization, supporting established institutions, allocating power and influence, fostering social integration, and initiating social change (Amis and Stern, 1974).

The second conceptual approach is organizational theory, which considers the association as the unit of analysis. In this micro orientation the emphasis is on the structure and processes within an association and the association's relationship to other social organizations within the society. Hoyle (1971) and Schlagenhauf and Timm (1976) have suggested procedures and frameworks to be used when analyzing sport organizations and sport clubs, respectively. For example, future analyses of the organization of sport clubs might include the following dimensions:

1. The degree of demand for instrumental objective services.
2. The degree of homogeneity of demands of the membership.
3. The degree of internal or external orientation.
4. The degree of orientation toward individuals on the part of the club's management.
5. The degree of professionalization in the management.
6. The degree of the purposeful and rational aspect in the decision-making process. (Schlagenhauf and Timm, 1976, p. 21)

They argue that these dimensions are useful in explaining variations between the structure and the purpose of different sport clubs and are of use in analyzing changes in the social organization of sport clubs over time. For example, Schlagenhauf and Timm (1976) found that sport clubs in Germany are in a transitory stage at the present time wherein there is less emphasis on ideological values and a trend toward greater professionalization and purposeful rationality in the organizations.

Voluntary associations, then, have been and are an integral facet of contemporary life styles[6] and serve several specific functions, including stimulating and inducing social change by majority or minority groups, facilitating expressive involvement in specific interests, promoting the interests of special groups, providing affectual support for individuals, providing the play element in society, supporting and maintaining the normative order, distributing power at the grassroots level, reinforcing societal or subcultural values, integrating the individual and assimilating subgroups into society, and socializing individuals into existing roles, organized skills, and social values (Amis and Stern, 1974; Babchuk and Booth, 1969; Hausknecht, 1962; Smith and Freedman, 1972; Tomeh, 1973). In short, formal voluntary organizations are a conspicuous and integral facet of contemporary social structures, although the purpose and degree of involvement appear to vary cross-nationally depending on the degree of modernization in the society (Tomeh, 1973).

The degree of participation in at least one formal voluntary association by the general adult population is difficult to measure but appears to range from 53 to 84 percent (Tomeh, 1973), although the degree of commitment or actual involvement is quite likely considerably less than the percentage who report they are members. What are some of the factors, then, that induce a propensity to become involved in voluntary associations? Generally, these can be classified into social-structural and demographic characteristics and attitudinal and personal orientation variables.[7]

Based on empirical studies to date, it appears that participation is related to (1) a higher socioeconomic status in terms of types of organizations joined, degree of involvement, and the holding of leadership positions; (2) age, with increasing involvement to about 50 or 60 years, followed by a decline (i.e., disengagement); (3) sex, with males being more affiliative in general and being more likely to join instrumental groups, whereas females are more likely to join expressive groups; (4) race, with blacks being more involved that whites at comparable social class levels; (5) religion, with higher Protestant involvement; and (6) availability of role models, with higher participation rates by those whose parents and peers are involved (Smith and Freedman, 1972; Tomeh, 1973). Variables such as size of community and length and place of residence do not appear to be consistently related to affiliative behavior.

In terms of attitudes, there is much less research evidence, although initial and continued involvement does appear to be related to "satisfaction, a feeling of control, optimism, confidence in a society, a sense of predictability, and feelings of happiness and adjustment" (Tomeh, 1973). It is quite likely that, whereas the demographic factors play a more important role in influencing an individual to join an association, the attitudinal factors may be more influential in determining the intensity and duration of involvement. Moreover, many of the above factors interact to influence the socialization process whereby one becomes and remains a member of an association and to provide variation in the process, so that some individuals join while others do not.

To summarize, in addition to the family and school, peer groups and voluntary associations are influential socializing institutions throughout the life cycle. In fact, unlike the family and school, which decrease in importance, these institutions become increasingly important in the socialization process and must be considered in any attempt to account for social participation patterns in the discretionary or nonwork segment of adult life. The following subsections examine the role of peer groups and voluntary associations in the process of socialization into and the enactment of sport roles.

6.4.2 Peer Groups and Sport Role Socialization

Although an initial interest in sport is often stimulated in the home, peer groups have the potential to reinforce or inhabit subsequent development. The research evidence overwhelmingly supports the importance of peer group support for involvement and success in sport. In most instances the degree of support or influence increases with age or until the individual ceases to be involved. In fact, the lack of a sport-oriented peer group often leads individuals to reduce their involvement in sport, especially at the participation level. Similarly, entrance into a new peer group at work can suddenly revive an earlier interest or stimulate a new interest in primary or secondary involvement, especially if breaks from work are dominated by sport-oriented conversation, if an office "pool" on weekly or special sport events is available, or if the work peers enter a team in a recreational sport league.

During childhood and early adolescence, most of the peer influence is sex-linked, especially for males. However, many female athletes report having been a member of a male-dominated peer group during their childhood years. During the high school years, female athletes report receiving more support from female friends than from male friends (Snyder and Spreitzer, 1976). Later in life, and especially after dating begins or after marriage, opposite-sex peers become more influential in encouraging or discouraging various forms of sport involvement for females.

In summary, there is little question but that peer pressure operates to influence sport-related facets of our life style. During childhood, peer groups are found in the immediate neighborhood and tend to be somewhat similar in values to the individual; during the adolescent years, peer groups (youth subculture) are located within the high school and therefore may include individuals with different values and interests; and during adulthood, influential peer groups are normally comprised of peers at the place of employment, providing an even greater likelihood of there being diversity in interests and values concerning sport. However, despite this influence throughout the life cycle, it is still not possible to determine whether an individual selects a peer group to "fit" with their previously established life style or whether an individual can experience dramatic changes in life style because of the influence of a peer group.

6.4.3 Voluntary Associations and Sport Role Socialization

Historically, institutionalized sport in North America was first promoted and provided for adults by voluntary associations that tended to be class-related. For example, Metcalfe (1972, 1976a, 1976b), Wettan and Willis (1976), and Willis and Wettan (1976) describe the class background of voluntary sport clubs in Canada and the United States, respectively, during the late 1800s and early 1900s. For the most part the membership was of the middle or upper class, although there were a few working-class sport clubs formed in the working-class districts of some communities. However, few working-class males had either the time or the money to join sport clubs. When they did participate, much of their sporting activity took place in taverns that either sponsored sport teams or served as the meeting place for the working-class teams that existed.

In view of this early involvement, it is not surprising that most sporting opportunities for adults are provided through voluntary associations. Most of these associations provide male and female members of all social classes who can afford to join a given club with an opportunity to participate (e.g., golf, tennis) or to be secondarily involved (e.g., booster or quarterback clubs). However, social differentiation is still prevalent in that there are clubs that adhere to membership criteria based on gender, wealth, occupation, religion, race, or ethnicity.

On the other hand, there are clubs that exist for a variety of purposes, with sport being just one domain of interest. One example is the ethnic clubs that sponsor sport programs such as soccer. Pooley (1976) found that involvement in ethnic soccer clubs in Milwaukee did not promote assimilation into the dominant group because the policies of the club promoted ethnic homogeneity. For example, members were recruited exclusively from the same ethnic group and the native language was used on the playing field, during business meetings, and at all social events. Thus, interactional processes within the voluntary association discouraged assimilation into the larger community and strengthened integration into the ethnic community. In a similar study in Toronto, McKay (1975) found that the clubs were more heterogeneous in that players were recruited on the basis of ability rather than ethnicity. Thus, the members of these ethnic clubs experienced greater interethnic contact and were more likely to be acculturated into the majority group, especially if they had lived in Canada for many years. These studies illustrate how voluntary associations that sponsor sport for adults can have quite different assimilation outcomes depending on their sport-related policies.

In Europe the sport club has been the central social institution promoting sport for many years. European children attend these clubs with other members of their family and are normally exposed to a wide variety of sports early in life. For example, in the Federal Republic of Germany there are over 43,000 sport clubs with a total membership of over 14,000,000 (Schlagenhauf and Timm, 1976). These clubs serve both social and sport functions and provide opportunities for both mass and elite sport.

In North America, the organization of sport was originally the domain of professional educators within the schools. However, as Berryman (1975) notes, the philosophy of highly organized sport competition for preadolescents was questioned in the 1930s and led to a refusal by the educational sector to provide sport competition for this age group. At about this same time, there was a growing awareness of the need to provide varied opportunities for children if they were to develop and realize their full potential. As a result many boys' clubs were formed, which ultimately took over responsibility for organizing sport competition for children and adolescents. Thus, when the educational system renounced competition for boys, the voluntary sector, comprised mostly of parents, took control. The result has been the establishment of highly organized and bureaucratized structures (for example, Little League baseball, formed in 1939, has become an incorporated business organization), which exist to provide competition for children under the age of twelve. Many of these organizations are no longer truly "voluntary" associations in that they employ professional, full-time employees.

As a result of the present opportunity set, over 20 million children in North America are involved in competitive sport programs, many beginning as early as six years of age. These voluntary sport organizations are a significant socializing institution for children. First, because of their presence they create an opportunity set by which sport roles can be learned. Second, they provide coaches as role models. These coaches also serve as recruiters of potential talent and directly encourage children to become involved in sport. Third, many parents strongly encourage their children to become involved in one of the many local sport programs, but, in the end, may become as involved themselves as coaches, executives, or spectators. Some, in fact, may become more intrinsically involved than their children.

Finally, sport in voluntary associations has been promoted as a mechanism by which children can be socialized into the values and characteristics deemed desirable by the community. This untested assumption has been indirectly responsible to a great extent for the expansion and growth of this phenomenon with each succeeding generation. However, the milieu that has been created has the capacity to enhance or inhibit the personal growth of a child, and in recent years, as the following section notes, some conditions in the child's sport milieu have become intolerable to the extent that the phenomenon is presently considered an emerging social problem.

6.4.4 Problems with Voluntary Sport Associations for Children

In recent years there has been increasing concern expressed about the dysfunctional outcomes of a child's involvement in competitive sport programs. Most of this attention has resulted from anecdotal accounts by journalists (Ralbovsky, 1974a, 1974b), field observations by social scientists (Orlick and Botterill, 1975; Voigt, 1974), literature reviews (Albinson and Andrews, 1976; Magill, et al., 1978; McPherson, 1978; Rarick, 1973), or conceptual analyses of a particular sport (McPherson, 1974c). Thus, there is little empirical evidence to help explain how or why some of the following problems develop or how they can be controlled or eliminated.

In recent years unrealistic career aspirations in the world of sport have been stimulated by well-meaning parents who provide excessive encouragement for their child to aspire to a career in professional or elite amateur sport. Unfortunately, the chances of pursuing a career in sport are somewhat limited, in that the success ratio for this career is relatively low considering the numbers who participate at the youth level. For example, only about 1 in 20,000 Little League baseball players ever make it to the major leagues for even a tryout. In addition, there are only about 3100 positions in professional sport and the annual turnover is relatively small. Parents, then, must encourage their children to achieve in both the educational and sport domains so that they will have a resource to fall back on once their career in sport is terminated, either voluntarily or involuntarily. This is especially important for minority groups such as blacks who, as Arthur Ashe suggested (Ashe, 1977), must send their children to the libraries to instill a desire for learning. In this way they will reduce the school dropout rate and provide themselves with insurance when their athletic career ends, whether it is at 13 or 35 years of age.

A second major problem in the child's sport milieu is the increasing tendency for adults to enter and dominate that world. Today children's sport is highly organized and controlled by adults who become involved in order to vicariously experience success, to invest emotion in their children, to seek prestige or status that is lacking in their own world, or in some cases to protect their child from the practices and values of other parents. One consequence of this interference is that adult expectations are imposed and the levels of aspiration held by the child become externally induced and often lead to unrealistic norms, goals, and practices within the sport system, regardless of the age of the child. For example, adults scream at the kids, criticize them harshly, demand skills that their level of maturation will not permit, and, in short, take much of the fun out of playing sport. Moreover, the emphasis on winning and excessive competition introduces such practices as all-star competition, children sitting on the bench for the duration of games or seasons, recruitment beyond the immediate community for better players, an increase in the number of games played, and the professionalization of coaching, which has occurred in swimming. As Devereux (1976) noted, there must be an increasing concern for "what the ball is doing to the boy rather than what the boy is doing to the ball." Included in this concern should be a reduction in adult involvement and perhaps a modification in the rules, size of the playing area, and organizational structure of children's sport.

Closely related to the influx of adult domination has been a declining involvement in sport on the part of children. Not only are children increasingly dropping out of organized sport programs, but an increasing number are deciding not to become involved in the first place because of the experiences of their older siblings. In addition, many who do wish to remain involved are eliminated by coaches because they do not exhibit the level of ability that is needed at that particular time or place. Many of these children never return to competitive sport or to any other form of sport because of this early rejection. It is especially important that children be given the opportunity to remain involved, at a variety of levels, in order to account for varying maturational levels. For example, a child who is eleven or twelve years of age and is "cut" from a team could potentially, with a later growth spurt than those who make the team, be a better athlete by 15 or 16 years of age than his or her chronological-age peers.

In summary, there are many apparent problems in voluntary sport associations that are ostensibly organized for children. Most of these are possible to solve because they result from the overemphasis on competition and the over-organization imposed by adults. If children are given the opportunity to participate spontaneously and at their own level of ability and interest, it is quite likely that more individuals would be socialized into a variety of sport roles that would continue to be enacted throughout the life cycle. At the present time, many children are forced out of sport at an early age and never return. These individuals likely remain sedentary throughout life and may never be interested in socializing their own children to participate in sport. Thus, noninvolvement becomes a self-perpetuating cycle in which future generations become less likely to be socialized into sport roles.

6.5 SPORT AS A SOCIALIZING SYSTEM: SOCIALIZATION VIA PLAY, GAMES, AND SPORT

6.5.1 Socialization via Play and Games

Throughout history anthropologists, psychologists, and sociologists have noted the saliency of play and games during infancy and childhood, and have suggested that they are structurally isomorphic to experiences in the larger society. For example, imitative play in some societies provides the mechanism by which children are acculturated to the ways of life and serves as a form of anticipatory socialization for interpersonal skills that will be needed later in life. In Meadian (1934) terms, the child learns to take the perspective of others through the symbolic processes of interaction, or, as Denzin (1975) noted, "all forms of play teach or socialize young children into the illusory worlds of social reality." Similarly, Erikson (1963) stressed the role of play in personality development and socialization in general, based on the finding that children go through three recognized stages of play (autocosmic, microcosmic, macrocosmic) during infancy and early childhood.

As the child develops, play becomes more structured and complex, and he or she begins to participate in games, many of which are a reflection of the cultural values of a given society. Moreover, games are universal, although the type of game found in a specific society is related to the cultural demands of that social group. To illustrate, Roberts and Sutton-Smith (1962) found that games of strategy are more likely to be found in structurally complex societies and are linked directly with obedience training, and that games of chance are found where a culture's religious beliefs emphasize the benevolence or coerciveness of supernatural beings and are linked with training for responsibility, while games of physical skill are prominent whenever the culture places a high value on the mastery of the environment and on personal achievement.

As a result of their extensive work in the area of games in culture, Roberts and Sutton-Smith developed a conflict-enculturation hypothesis, which relates the game form to the socialization demands of the society. This hypothesis argues that conflicts induced by the child-training processes and subsequent learning lead to involvement in game forms, which in turn provide buffered learning experiences or the enculturation deemed important both to the child and to the society. In short, they argue that there is a relationship between the type of games played, variations in child-training practices, and general cultural demands.

A summary of the literature suggests that the social learning derived from play and game experiences can be classified into three types. First, there is the development of individual traits and skills such as sex-role identity, personality traits, need-achievement, independence, emotional dispositions, and mental reactions. Second, play and games facilitate learning about the environment, including norms and the roles of others. Finally, play and, in particular, games provide valuable skills for effective interaction with the environment, such as how to interact with others in cooperative or competitive situations.

The process by which this socialization takes place through play and game forms has usually been explained by either an interactionist or a conflict model. The interactionist model suggests that children develop the self through interaction in play and games (Mead, 1934) and acquire a cognitive understanding of norms that require responsible forms of behavior. For example, Mead (1934) suggests that the game of baseball is an illustration of the situation from which an organized personality can develop. However, as Watson (1977) notes, games in the past were played in a social environment that was normally devoid of adult involvement. Today, however, the interaction model may be less useful because many game activities such as youth sport are dominated by adults (Watson, 1977; Watson and Kando, 1974), hence children do not gain the same experiences they once did. As a result, less socialization may be occurring.

The conflict model (Roberts and Sutton-Smith, 1962) suggests that forms of expressive behavior such as games foster an "enculturative outcome so that after many years of gaming, players ultimately become persons with wide repertoires of adaptive skills . . . relevant to the matters of crisis that concern the larger culture" (Sutton-Smith, 1973). Although some cross-cultural correlational evidence is available to support this model (Roberts and Sutton-Smith, 1962), a causal relationship has yet to be supported. Moreover, field studies in Jersualem with "advantaged" and "disadvantaged" children (Eiferman, 1971) fail to support the "specific conception of the relations between style of games and their enculturative functions." Eiferman argues that the challenge of a game to a player is an important determinant of the extent of game involvement. She also added a fourth dimension of game type, memory and attention, which was found to be preferred by girls and by disadvantaged (i.e., low-ability) children. In summary, a definitive or complete explanatory model for the hypothesized function of play and games in socialization is lacking.

Most of the evidence above suggests that play and game experiences are functional. However, some critics, such as Spencer (1896), Soule (1955), and Aries (1962), have argued that they are dysfunctional and essentially a waste of time. Bend (1971) similarly argues that sport can lead to personality problems (e.g., unrealistic self-perceptions, overaggressive achievers, narrow range of interests) or the learning of deviant norms (e.g., cheating, violence, "win at all costs"). Most of these critics, however, lack empirical evidence and therefore the dysfunctional element of play and games must be considered tentative until tested.

In summary, play and games are an important element of childhood socialization (Bruner et al., 1976; Caplan and Caplan, 1973; Denzin, 1975; Erikson, 1977; Herron and Sutton-Smith, 1971; Ellis, 1973; and Millar, 1968) in that they provide a social milieu in which children develop cognitive abilities (Lieberman, 1977; Piaget, 1962), learn to interact with others in both a cooperative and a competitive context (Bruner et al., 1976, pp. 300–366), learn sex roles (Bruner et al., 1976, pp. 368–391; Lever, 1976) and become indoctrinated into their culture (Bruner et al., 1976, pp. 466–489). The exact process by which this socialization occurs is still not well understood and merits further investigation.

6.5.2 Socialization via Sport

Because of the apparent relationship between participation in play and games during infancy and childhood and certain socialization outcomes, this evidence has often been extrapolated to account for social learning that may result from participation in institutionalized sport, both within and outside the school. The initiation and rationalization of new sport programs and the continuation of those already in existence, have often been based on the common belief or untested assumption that participation in sport is an element of the socialization process that contributes to mental and social development. More specifically, it has been argued that there are psychological, behavioral, and attitudinal outcomes derived from involvement in competitive sport programs (Stevenson, 1975).

However, because of a variety of theoretical and methodological problems (e.g., sampling, instrumentation) the research evidence is weak. That is, in addition to many value-laden statements, the studies have been correlational in nature and have been unable to establish a cause-effect relationship. For example, although some studies have found personality differences between athletes and nonathletes, among athletes of different abilities, and among athletes in different sports, other studies have been unable to demonstrate differences between the various groups. Similarly, while some studies have shown that athletes compared to nonathletes have higher grade point averages, are less delinquent, or demonstrate highly valued traits (e.g., sportsmanship), others have failed to find differences. One reason for these findings may be that there is a selection process operating by which the weaker students and the nonconformers are eliminated before the researcher enters the scene.

The empirical evidence to date provides little support for the socialization-via-sport hypothesis, at least for institutionalized sport. For example, research reviews by Ingham, Loy, and Berryman (1972), Kenyon (1968), Loy and Ingham (1973), McPherson (1978), and Stevenson (1975) have all concluded that there is little, if any, valid evidence that participation in sport is an important or essential element of the socialization process, or that involvement in sport teaches or results in the learning of specific outcomes that might not be learned in other social milieu. These outcomes have been hypothesized to include character building, moral development, a competitive and/or a cooperative orientation, good citizenship, or certain valued personality traits. In fact, there is little evidence that what is learned in any social environment (e.g., sport) will be transferred to another (e.g., work). Further, the child is not exposed to merely a single sport system but rather to many systems that could have an influence on his or her social learning. Thus, it is difficult to isolate the learning that takes place in any given social system. More specifically, Loy and Ingham conclude that:

> Socialization via play, games and sport is a complex process having both manifest and latent functions, and involving functional and dysfunctional, intended and unintended consequences. Since research on the topic is limited, one must regard with caution many present empirical findings and most tentative theoretical interpretations of these findings. (Loy and Ingham, 1973, p. 298)

Until empirical evidence is available, parents, children, physical educators, coaches, and administrators must seriously question attempts to justify a program because of its inherent socializing value or hypothesized socialization outcomes. Although many years have passed since the Battle of Waterloo, there is still no concrete evidence that the war was won on the playing fields of Eton.

6.6 DESOCIALIZATION FROM SPORT ROLES

Inevitably, at some stage in the life cycle, individuals cease to be involved in institutionalized sport as competitors. For some this occurs voluntarily early in life when they decide to pursue other forms of social participation; for others it occurs later in life when they decide to retire from a full- or part-time career as an elite amateur or professional athlete; and for others it can occur quite suddenly and unvoluntarily when they are seriously injured or are "fired" from a team. Thus, voluntary or involuntary retirement from a sport can occur at any age. The reaction or adjustment to this state can range from satisfaction, if the process is voluntary or planned for in advance, to traumatic psychological or life-style adjustment problems, if the process is involuntary. In many cases the reaction depends on age, the options or alternative life styles available, the degree of sport involvement, the amount of preplanning or socialization for alternative roles, and the available mechanisms for desocialization from the role (McPherson, 1977).

Most withdrawal occurs during childhood and adolescence since a large proportion of youth in all countries are initially socialized into one or more sport roles. More specifically, the number of participants is quite large by the age of nine or ten years, yet by late adolescence relatively few are involved in organized sport programs. For example, in 1975–1976 the Canadian Amateur Hockey Association registered 60,356 Bantams (13–14 years), 50,489 Midgets (15–16 years), 16,987 Juveniles (17 years and older), 9011 Junior B, C, and D (16 years and older) players, and 2450 Junior A players, who are the elite preprofessional players. Moreover, there are fewer than 400 professional hockey players. Thus, there is a decrease in participation from 60,356 at the lower levels to approximately 400 at the professional level. This drop-off rate occurs either when a child is cut from a team by a coach or when an individual decides for a variety of reasons to no longer continue his or her involvement in either a particular sport or in sport in general (Orlick and Botterill, 1975). If the withdrawal is involuntary, it is perceived as failure by the individual and the reaction can be traumatic, especially for a child whose peers continue to be involved and whose parents expect him or her to participate in sport. Unfortunately, there is little empirical research on the process of failure and the reaction to failure in sport at very young ages. Rather, most researchers have been primarily interested in the reaction of elite performers to failure.

At the professional level, attention has been devoted to the analysis of failure, downward mobility (demotion), and adjustment to retirement after the playing career. This is an interesting sociological question since athletes are a unique cohort in the work force in that they retire early in life (usually in their late twenties or thirties) and are constantly faced with the possibility of failure at any time during their career.[8]

A theoretical framework for the analysis of failure in sport (Ball, 1976) indicates that the process includes the reaction of the members of the former group toward the failed individual, as well as the individual's reaction to his or her own failure. The reaction of the group involves either degradation, when the player is ignored, or cooling out, when sympathy and rationalizations are extended, expected, and accepted. The failed individual experiences embarrassment in that expectations are left unfulfilled and he or she must face significant others to whom he or she expressed career plans. The individual also utilizes new frames of reference by joining cliques on the new team (if he or she is sent down to a lower level of classification), which may be comprised of other organizational failures.

Ball (1976) suggests that the reaction processes vary according to the structure of the sport. In baseball, which is a two-tiered caste system (comprised of major and minor leagues), players who fail at the major league level are usually "sent down" to a minor league affiliate (that is, they experience downward mobility). However, they are still in the system and can be seen by the public and by their playing peers. Thus, they have second-class status and are constantly reminded of their marginality within the organizational set. However, because they are sent down to the minor league, there is always the hope that they will be promoted and resocialized into a team at the highest ability level. Because the individual remains somewhere in the "system," degradation and embarrassment may operate more frequently. To illustrate the feeling experienced by an individual, Ball cites from Bouton (1971):

> As I started throwing stuff into my bag, I could feel the wall, invisible but real, forming around me. I was suddenly an outsider, a different person, someone to be shunned, a leper. (Ball, 1976, p. 731)

This process would seem to operate in sports such as hockey (Smith and Diamond, 1976), professional baseball, and perhaps tennis and golf, where there are satellite tours.

On the other hand, there are sports such as football and basketball in which there is no formal minor league structure so that players who fail either are released outright or remain on a "taxi squad." In this situation they are removed from public visibility and do not experience the public embarrassment of being seen in a marginal role. Moreover, many of the failures in these systems are "rookies," who may have a college education to fall back on and therefore may have greater alternatives outside the specific sport. Ball (1976) suggests that a cooling-out mechanism operates in this type of sport structure because there are alternatives. Furthermore, because there is no lower subsystem, there is a higher expected rate of failure; therefore failure is not as traumatic as it may be in those sports in which an option to perform at a lower level is available.

Another mechanism for handling failures was described by Goldner (1968) as "zigzag" mobility, when a demotion is masked as a horizontal move. In this case an individual may be given the implied hope that there will be a promotion in the future. Another version of this strategy occurs when a "fading" star is encouraged to retire by the promise of a relatively powerless, but prestigious, title within the organization for which he or she formerly played.

The process of retirement and the subsequent adjustment to it by former athletes has been described in journalistic accounts of former Olympic athletes (Johnson, 1972), professional athletes (Jordan, 1975; Kahn, 1973; Kramer, 1969), and little League baseball players (Ralbovsky, 1974a). Whether the process is voluntary or involuntary, the professional and dedicated amateur athlete must change careers at a time in life when their age peers are attaining stability, recognition, and perhaps mobility in their chosen occupation. However, these athletes are often handicapped by a failure to preplan for their retirement, by not having an education or training for a second career, and by a desire to remain within the game in some capacity in order to satisfy an ego that has been fed by adulation from the masses for many years (Kramer, 1969).

One of the first empirical attempts to analyze this phenomenon was a study of 44 former soccer players in Yugoslavia (Mihovilovic, 1968). He found that 95.4 percent of the athletes in his sample reported the process of retirement was imposed on them, thereby suggesting that there is a conscious attempt to extend the playing career as long as possible. For those who had no profession to move into, retirement was a traumatic experience characterized by personal conflict, frustration, increased smoking and drinking, and loss of friends in the work (team) group. One of the reasons for these side effects is that retirement has a negative connotation in that it represents a devaluation in status and a reduction in income or travel and necessitates the acquisition of new skills and resocialization into new roles in a new social world.

In an extensive analysis of the retired athlete, Haerle (1975) examined the adjustment to retirement among former professional baseball players on both a sociopsychological and an occupational dimension. He found that 75 percent of the 312 respondents in his study did not begin to consider the post-career life until they were in their early or mid-thirties, that approximately 50 percent reported that they were oriented more toward the past than to the future at the time of retirement, that the forced decision led to feelings of regret, sadness, and shock at the reality of the aging process, and that only 25 percent were future-oriented in that they were confident and accepted the inevitable fact of retirement. For example, compare the responses of a past-oriented with a future-oriented retiree from professional baseball: "It scared hell out me. I wanted to stay in baseball in some capacity for the rest of my life" (Haerle, 1975) and "I knew I was out of baseball so didn't worry too much. I had my mind made up that I could do about anything I selected by hard work" (Haerle, 1975).

Athletes represent a unique group of individuals in the labor force in that they are required to change careers in midlife. The transition from one career to another, however, seems to be more problematic for those who begin a "skidding" process late in their career by continuing to play until they are involuntarily removed. That is, those who end their career after a period of downward mobility (Smith and Diamond, 1976) may find that they continue sliding in their post-playing life. Haerle found that those who remained inside baseball as coaches, managers, or scouts had a less stable career pattern in the post-playing years than did those who moved into a career outside baseball immediately upon the conclusion of their playing career. Similar results have been found for former professional hockey players (Roy, 1974). Moreover, there were other distinct differences between those who remained in baseball and those who moved into other careers. For example, Haerle (1975) found that those who remained in baseball retired as players at a later age, often ending their career in a lower minor league, and they spent more time during their playing career in the minor leagues. Thus, for those employed outside baseball the playing career may have been a stepping-stone to a more secure occupation. In fact, in Haerle's (1975) causal model, baseball fame acquired during the playing career was a most important predictor of immediate occupational attainment, with the respondents' educational attainment second in importance. However, over the long run, ability to perform at a high level and high educational attainment were equally important.

Since many athletes now recognize that their playing career will inevitably be terminated, many are initiating skill training or off-season permanent careers during the playing years. Moreover, an increasing number are recognizing the importance of an education and the need to invest earnings wisely in order to build equity for later life. Similarly, almost all professional sports now have players' associations that generate pension and disability programs to protect the retiree in later life. It is quite likely that from an economic point of view, future former athletes will be less likely to experience economic problems. However, they may still experience psychological trauma as they adjust their life style to a more autonomous social world in which they are less likely to be a central actor with high prestige. In this respect, desocialization or withdrawal from one social role may be more of a psychologcial problem than a sociological problem.

NOTES

1. For a more detailed discussion than that which follows, see Zigler and Child (1969) and Loy and Ingham (1973).

2. For a detailed review see Kenyon and McPherson (1973), Greendorfer (1977), and McPherson (1978).

3. The "Gemeinschaft" world implies a kinshiplike community into which people are born or grow, whereas a "Gesellschaft" world consists of a voluntary, special-purpose association in which the bond between people is voluntary and serves as a means of attaining some objective.

4. This relationship may only hold for individuals who participate in a sport that is within the jurisdiction of the school. For example, studies comparing Canadian students who play high school hockey with those who play Junior A or B hockey for organizations outside the school have shown that the latter group not only have lower grades than the school athletes, but also progress at a slower rate through the school system and are more likely to drop out of high school.

5. An instrumental association is goal-oriented and is organized to maintain or change the existing social order by performing some service (e.g., the Peace Corps), whereas expressive associations are ends in themselves and are formed to provide activities in order to bring gratification to the membership (e.g., Little League baseball). In reality, elements of both can often be found in any given association.

6. For example, as early as 1835 de Tocqueville (1961), in his classic study of America, noted the penchant for forming a variety of associations, while more recently Americans have been classified as a "nation of joiners" by Hausknecht (1962).

7. For the most part studies in this area have been correlational, with few attempts to account for multivariate additive or interactive effects, especially in terms of including both sociocultural and attitudinal components.

8. Blitz (1973) states that the average career length of professional athletes ranges from five years (in football and basketball) to about ten years (in racecar driving).

REFERENCES

Adams, B. (1972). "Birth order: A critical review." *Sociometry* 35 (September): 411–439.

Albinson, J., and G. Andrews (eds.) (1976). *Child in Sport and Physical Activity.* Baltimore: University Park Press.

Amis, W., and S. Stern (1974). "A critical examination of theory and functions of voluntary association." *Journal of Voluntary Action Research* 3 (July, October): 91–99.

Aries, P. (1962). *Centuries of Childhood.* New York: Vintage Books.

Ashe, A. (1977). "Send your children to the libraries: An open letter to black parents." *New York Times* (February 6): S2.

Atchley, R. (1977). *The Social Forces in Later Life,* 2nd ed. Belmont, Calif.: Wadsworth.

Babchuck, N., and A. Booth (1969). "Voluntary association membership: A longitudinal analysis." *American Sociological Review* 34 (February): 31–45.

Ball, D. W. (1976). "Failure in sport." *American Sociological Review* 41 (August): 726–739.

Bandura, A. (1969). "Social learning theory of identificatory process." In D. Goslin (ed.), *Handbook of Socialization Theory and Research,* pp. 213–262. Chicago: Rand McNally.

Bandura, A., and R. H. Walters (1963). *Social Learning and Personality Development.* New York: Holt, Rinehart and Winston.

Bend, E. (1968). *The Impact of Athletic Participation on Academic and Career Aspiration and Achievement.* New Brunswick, N.J.: National Football Foundation and Hall of Fame.

Bend, E. (1971). "Some potential dysfunctional effects of sport upon socialization." Paper presented at the Third International Symposium on the Sociology of Sport, Waterloo (August).

Berryman, J. (1975) "From the cradle to the playing field: America's emphasis on highly organized competitive sports for preadolescent boys." *Journal of Sport History* 21: 112–131.

Birrell, S. (1977). "The neglected half of the adolescent society: Status and educational consequences of high school athletic participation for girls." Unpublished paper, McMaster University.

Birrell, S. (1978). "An analysis of the inter-relationships among achievement motivation, athletic participation, academic achievement, and educational aspirations." *International Journal of Sport Psychology* 8.

Blitz, H. (1973). "The drive to win: Careers in professional sports." *Occupational Outlook Quarterly* 17: 2–16.

Boileau, R., F. Landry, and Y. Trempe (1976). "Les Canadiens Français et Les Grands Jeux Internationaux (1908–1974)." In R. Gruneau and J. Albinson (eds.), *Canadian Sport: Sociological Perspectives,* pp. 141–169. Don Mills, Ontario: Addison-Wesley (Canada), Ltd.

Bouton, J. (1970) *Ball Four.* New York: Dell.

Bruner J., et al. (1976). *Play: Its Role in Development and Evolution.* New York: Penguin Books.

Buhrmann, H., and R. Bratton (1977). "Athletic participation and status of Alberta High School girls." *International Review of Sport Sociology* 12: 57–67.

Buhrmann, H., and M. S. Jarvis (1971). "Athletics and status." *Journal of the Canadian Association for Health, Physical Education and Recreation* 37 (January–February): 14–17.

Caplan, F., and T. Caplan (1973). *The Power of Play.* Garden City, N.Y.: Anchor Press.

Casher, B. (1977). "Relationship between birth order and participation in dangerous sports." *Research Quarterly* 48 (March): 33–40.

Clarke, H. H. (ed.) (1975). "Athletes: Their academic achievements and personal social status." *Physical Fitness Research Digest* 5 (July): 1–23.

Coleman, J. S. (1961). *The Adolescent Society*. New York: The Free Press.

Coleman, J. S., et al. (1966). *Equality of Educational Opportunity*. Washington, D.C.: Government Printing Office.

Collins, R. (1971). "Functional and conflict theories of educational stratification." *American Sociological Review* 36 (December): 1002–1019.

Cutler, S. (1973). "Voluntary association membership and the theory of mass society." In E. Laumann (ed.), *Bonds of Pluralism: The Form and Substance of Urban Social Networks*, pp. 133–159. New York: John Wiley.

Davis, E., and J. Cooper (1934). "Athletic ability and scholarship." *Research Quarterly* 5 (December): 68–78.

Denzin, N. (1975). "Play, games and interaction: The contexts of childhood socialization." *The Sociological Quarterly* 16 (Autumn): 458–478.

de Tocqueville, A. (1961). *Democracy in America*. New York: Schocken Books.

Devereux, E. (1976). "Backyard versus Little League baseball: Impoverishment of children's games." In D. Landers (ed.), *Social Problems in Athletics*, pp. 37–56. Urbana: University of Illinois Press.

Edwards, J., and D. Klemmack (1973). "Birth order and the conservators of tradition hypothesis." *Journal of Marriage and the Family* 35 (November): 619–626.

Eidsmore, R. M. (1961). "The academic performance of athletes." *School Activities* 32 (December): 105–107.

Eidsmore, R. M. (1963). "Highschool athletes are brighter." *School Activities* 35 (November): 75–77.

Eiferman, R. (1971). *Determinants of Children's Game Styles—On Free Play in a "Disadvantaged" and in an "Advantaged" School*. Jerusalem: Israel Academy of Science and Humanities.

Eitzen, D. S. (1976) "Sport and social status in American public secondary education." *Review of Sport and Leisure* 1 (Fall): 139–155.

Ellis, M. J. (1973). *Why People Play*. Englewood Cliffs, N.J.: Prentice-Hall.

Erikson, E. (1963). *Childhood in Society*. New York: Norton.

Erikson, E. (1977). *Toys and Reason*. New York: Norton.

Friesen, D. (1968). "Academic-athletic-popularity syndrome in a Canadian high school society." *Adolescence* 3 (Spring): 39–51.

Goldner, F. (1968). "Demotion in industrial management." In B. Glaser (ed.), *Organized Careers: A Source Book for Theory*, pp. 267–279. Chicago: Aldine.

Gould, D., and D. Landers (1972). "Dangerous sport participation: A replication of Nisbett's birth order findings." Presented at the North American Society for the Psychology of Sport and Physical Activity Conference. Houston (March).

Greendorfer, S. (1977). "Socialization into sport." In C. Oglesby (ed.), *Woman Sport: From Myth to Reality*. Philadelphia: Lea and Febiger.

Gruneau, R. S. (1972). "A socioeconomic analysis of the competitors of the 1971 Canada Winter Games." M. A. thesis, University of Calgary.

Haerle, R. (1975). "Career patterns and career contingencies of professional baseball players: An occupational analysis." In D. Ball and J. Loy (eds.), *Sport and Social Order*, pp. 461–519. Reading, Mass.: Addison-Wesley.

Hausknecht, M. (1962). *The Joiner: A Sociological Description of Voluntary Association Membership in the United States*. New York: Bedminster Press.

Herron, R., and B. Sutton-Smith (1971). *Child's Play*. New York: John Wiley.

Hoyle, E. (1971). "Organization theory and the sociology of sport." In R. Albonico and K. Pfister-Binz (eds.), *Sociology of Sport*. Switzerland: Birkhauser Verlag Basel.

Ingham, A., J. Loy, and J. Berryman (1972). "Socialization, dialectics and sport." In D. Harris (ed.), *Women and Sport: A National Research Conference*, pp. 235–276. University Park: Pennsylvania State University.

Irish, D. P. (1964). "Sibling interaction: A neglected aspect in family life research." *Social Forces* 42 (March): 279–288.

Jerome, W. C. (1971). "A study of the academic achievement of highschool students when sport participation and selected sociological variables are considered." Unpublished Ph.D. dissertation, University of Oregon.

Johnson, W. (1972). "After the golden moment." *Sports Illustrated* 37 (July): 28, 30–34, 39–41.

Jordan, P. (1975). *A False Spring*. New York: Bantam Books.

Kahn, R. (1973). *The Boys of Summer*. New York: Signet.

Kammeyer, K. (1966). "Birth order and the feminine college women." *American Sociological Review* 31 (August): 508–515.

Kammeyer, K. (1967). "Birth order as a research variable." *Social Forces* 46 (September): 71–80.

Kelly, J. (1974). "Socialization toward leisure: A developmental approach." *Journal of Leisure Research* 6: 181–193.

Kenyon, G. S. (1968). "Sociological considerations." *Journal of the American Association of Health, Physical Education and Recreation* 39 (November–December): 31–33.

Kenyon, G. S., and B. D. McPherson (1973). "Becoming involved in physical activity and sport: A process of socialization." In G. L. Rarick (ed.), *Physical Activity: Human Growth and Development*, pp. 303–332. New York: Academic Press.

King, A. J., and C. E. Angi (1968). "The hockey playing student." *Journal of the Canadian Association for Health, Physical Education and Recreation* 35 (October–November): 25–28.

Kramer, J. (1969). *Farewell to Football*. New York: Bantam Books.

Landers, D. (1970). "Sibling-sex-status and ordinal position effects on females sport participation and interest." *Journal of Social Psychology* 80: 247–248.

Landers, D. (1971). "Sibling-sex and ordinal position as factors in sport participation." Paper presented at the Third International Symposium on the Sociology of Sport, Waterloo.

Landers, D. (1972). "The effects of ordinal position and siblings' sex on male sport participation." In A. Taylor and M. Howell (eds.), *Training: Scientific Basis and Application*, pp. 235–241. Springfield, Ill.: Charles C. Thomas.

Landers, D., and G. Luschen (1970). "Sibling-sex status and ordinal position effects on the sport participation of females." In G. S. Kenyon (ed.), *Contemporary Psychology of Sport*, pp. 411–419. Chicago: The Athletic Institute.

Lever, J. (1976). "Sex differences in the games children play." *Social Problems* 23: 479–487.

Lewis, M. (1972). "Culture and gender roles: There is no unisex in the nursery." *Psychology Today* 5 (May): 54–57.

Lieberman, J. N. (1977). *Playfulness*. New York: Academic Press.

Loy, J. W., and A. Ingham (1973). "Play, games, and sport in the psychosocial development of children and youth." In G. L. Rarick (ed.), *Physical Activity: Human Growth and Development*, pp. 257–302. New York: Academic Press.

Magill, R., et al. (1978). *Children and Youth in Sport: A Contemporary Anthology*. Champaign-Urbana, Ill.: Human Kinetics.

McIntosh, P. C. (1966). "Mental ability and success in school sport." *Research and Physical Education* 1: 1.

McKay, J. P. (1975). "Sport and ethnicity: Acculturation, structural assimilation, and voluntary association involvement among Italian Immigrants in Metropolitan Toronto." Unpublished M.Sc. thesis, Department of Kinesiology, University of Waterloo.

McPherson, B. D. (1974a). "Career patterns of a voluntary role: The minor hockey coach." Presented at the Annual Meetings of the Canadian Sociology and Anthropology Association, Toronto (August).

McPherson, B. D. (1974b). "Minority group involvement in sport: The black athlete." In J. H. Wilmore (ed.), *Exercise and Sport Sciences Reviews*, Vol. 2, pp. 71–101. New York: Academic Press.

McPherson, B. D. (1974c). "The social milieu of minor hockey in Canada." Paper prepared for the Technical Advisory Committee, Canadian Amateur Hockey Association (May).

McPherson, B. D. (1976a). "Consumer role socialization: A within-system model." *Sportwissenschaft* **6** (February): 144–154.

McPherson, B. D. (1976b). "Socialization into the role of sport consumer: A theory in causal model." *Canadian review of Sociology and Anthropology* **13** (May): 165–177.

McPherson, B. D. (1976c). "The sport role socialization process for Anglophone and Francophone adults in Canada: Accounting for present patterns of involvement." Paper presented at the Disciplinary Seminar on the ICSS Cross-National Project on Leisure Role Socialization at the International Congress of Physical Activities Sciences, Quebec, Canada (July).

McPherson, B. D. (1977). "The occupational and psychological adjustment of former professional athletes." Presented at the American College of Sports Medicine Annual Meeting, Chicago (May).

McPherson, B. D. (1978a). "The child in competitive sport: Influence of the social milieu." In R. Magill et al. (eds.), *Children and Youth in Sport: A Contemporary Anthology*. Champaign-Urbana: Human Kinetics.

McPherson, B. D. (1978b). "Socialization and sport involvement." In G. Sage and G. Luschen (eds.), *Encyclopedia of Physical Education*, Vol. 5. Reading, Mass.: Addison-Wesley.

Mead, G. H. (1934). *Mind, Self and Society*. Chicago: University of Chicago Press.

Metcalfe, A. (1972). "Sport and social stratification in Toronto, Canada: 1860–1920." Paper presented at the American Sociological Association Annual Meeting, New Orleans (August).

Metcalfe, A. (1976a). "Organized sport and social stratification in Montreal: 1840–1901." In R. Gruneau and J. Albinson (eds.), *Canadian Sport: Sociological Perspectives*, pp. 77–101. Don Mills, Ontario: Addison-Wesley (Canada), Ltd.

Metcalfe, A. (1976b). "Working class physical recreation in Montreal: 1860–1895." Paper presented at the North American Association for the Study of Sport History, Eugene, Oregon.

Mihovilovic, M. (1968). "The status of former sportsmen." *International Review of Sport Sociology* **3**: 73–93.

Miley, C. (1969). "Birth order research, 1963–1967: Bibliography and index." *Journal of Individual Psychology* **25**: 64–70.

Millar, S. (1968). *The Psychology of Play*. New York: Penguin Books.

Nisbett, R. (1968). "Birth order and participation in dangerous sports." *Journal of Personality and Social Psychology* **8**: 351–353.

Orlick, T., and C. Botterill (1975). *Every Kid Can Win*. Chicago: Nelson-Hall.

Otto, L. B. (1976). "Social integration and the status-attainment process." *American Journal of Sociology* **81** (May): 1360–1383.

Otto, L. B., and D. Alwin (1977). "Athletics, aspirations, and attainments." *Sociology of Education* 42 (April): 102–113.

Piaget, J. (1962). *Play, Dreams and Imitation in Childhood.* New York: W. W. Norton.

Picou, J., and E. Curry (1974). "Residence and the athletic participation-educational aspiration hypothesis." *Social Science Quarterly* 55: 768–776.

Pooley, J. D. (1976). "Ethnic soccer clubs in Milwaukee: A study in assimilation." In M. Hart (ed.), *Sport in the Socio-Cultural Process,* 2nd ed., pp. 328–359. Dubuque, Iowa: W. C. Brown.

Portz, E. (1973). "Influence of birth order, sibling-sex on sports participation." In D. Harris (ed.), *Women and Sport: A National Research Conference,* pp. 225–234. University Park: Pennsylvania State University.

Ralbovsky, M. (1974a). *Destiny's Darlings.* New York: Hawthorn Books.

Ralbovsky, M. (1974b). *Lords of the Locker Room.* New York: Peter H. Wyden.

Rarick, G. L. (1973). "Competitive sports in childhood and early adolescence." In G. L. Rarick (ed.), *Physical Activity: Human Growth and Development,* pp. 364–386. New York: Academic Press.

Rehberg, R. (1969). "Behavioral and attitudinal consequences of high school inter-scholastic sports: A speculative consideration." *Adolescence* 4 (April): 59–68.

Rehberg, R. A., and W. E. Schafer (1968). "Participation in interscholastic athletics and college expectations." *American Journal of Sociology* 73 (May): 732–740.

Roberts, J. M., and B. Sutton-Smith (1962). "Child training and game involvement." *Ethnology* 1: 166–185.

Roethlisberger, G. A. (1970). "Socialization into the role of gymnast." Unpublished M.Sc. thesis, University of Wisconsin.

Rooney, J. (1974). *A Geography of American Sport.* Reading, Mass.: Addison-Wesley.

Roper, L. D., and K. Snow (1976). "Correlation studies of academic excellence and big-time athletics." *International Review of Sport Sociology* 11: 57–68.

Rosenberg, B., and B. Sutton-Smith (1964). "Ordinal position and sex-role identification." *Genetic Psychology Monographs* 70: 297–328.

Roy, G. (1974). "The relationship between centrality and mobility: The case of the National Hockey League." M.Sc. thesis, Department of Kinesiology, University of Waterloo.

Sage G. (1967). "The academic performance of former highschool athletes at college." Unpublished paper, University of Northern Colorado.

Sampson, E. (1965). "The study of ordinal position: Antecedents and outcomes." In B. Maher (ed.), *Progress in Experimental Personality Research, Vol. 11,* pp. 175–228. New York: Academic Press.

Sarbin, T., and V. Allen (1968). "Role theory." In G. Lindzey and E. Aronson (eds.), *Handbook of Social Psychology, Vol. 1,* pp. 488–567. Reading, Mass.: Addison-Wesley.

Schachter, S. (1959). *The Psychology of Affiliation.* Stanford, Calif.: Stanford University Press.

Schafer, W. (1971). "Sport, socialization and the school." Paper presented at the Third International Symposium on the Sociology of Sport, Waterloo (August).

Schafer, W. E., and J. M. Armer (1968). "Athletes are not inferior students." *Trans-Action* (November): 21–26, 61–62.

Schlagenhauf, K., and W. Timm (1976). "The sport club as a social organization." *International Review of Sport Sociology* 11: 9–27.

Schurr, T., and W. Brookover (1970). "Athletes, academic selfconcept and achievement." *Medicine and Science in Sports* 2: 96–99.

Schutz, R., et al. (1977). "Relationships among academic achievement and active competition in amateur hockey." Project completed for the Canadian Amateur Hockey Association (May).

Sewell, W. H. (1963). "Some recent developments in socialization theory and research." *The Annals of the American Academy of Political Science* 349 (September): 163–181.

Smith, C., and A. Freedman (1972). *Voluntary Associations: Perspectives on the Literature.* Cambridge, Mass.: Harvard University Press.

Smith, D. H. (1975). "Voluntary action and voluntary groups." In A. Inkeles (ed.), *Annual Review of Sociology,* Vol 1, pp. 247–270. Palo Alto, Calif.: Annual Reviews.

Smith, M. (1976). "Getting involved in sport: Sex differences." Presented at the International Congress of Physical Activity Sciences, Quebec City (July).

Smith, M., and F. Diamond (1976). "Career mobility in professional hockey." In R. Gruneau and J. Albinson (eds.), *Canadian Sport: Sociological Perspectives,* p. 175–293. Don Mills, Ontario: Addison-Wesley (Canada), Ltd.

Snyder, E. (1972). "High school athletes and their coaches: Educational plans and advice." *Sociology of Education* 45 (Summer): 313–325.

Snyder, E., and E. Spreitzer (1973). "Family influence and involvement in sports." *Research Quarterly* 44 (October): 249–255.

Snyder, E., and E. Spreitzer (1976). "Correlates of sport participation among adolescent girls." *Research Quarterly* 47 (December): 804–809.

Snyder, E., and E. Spreitzer (1977). "Participation in sport as related to educational expectations among high school girls. *Sociology of Education* 50 (January): 47–55.

Sofranko, A., and M. Nolan (1972). "Early life experiences and adult sports participation." *Journal of Leisure Research* 4: 6–18.

Soule, G. (1955). *Time for Living.* New York: Viking Press.

Spady, W. G. (1970). "Lament for the letterman: Effects of peer status and extra curricular activities on goals and achievement." *American Journal of Sociology* 75 (January): 5–31.

Spencer, H. (1896). *The Principles of Psychology.* New York: Appleton.

Spreitzer, E., and M. Pugh (1973). "Interscholastic athletics and educational expectations." *Sociology of Education* 46 (Spring): 171–182.

Start, K. B. (1967). "Sporting and intellectual success among English secondary school children." *International Review of Sport Sociology* 2: 47–53.

Stevenson, C. L. (1975). "Socialization effects of participation in sport: A critical review of the research." *Research Quarterly* 46 (October): 287–301.

Sutherland, E., and D. Cressey (1970). *Criminology.* Philadelphia: Lippincott.

Sutton-Smith, B. (1973). "Games: The socialization of conflict." *Canadian Journal of History of Sport and Physical Education* 4 (May): 1–7.

Sutton-Smith, B., and B. G. Rosenberg (1970). *The Sibling.* New York: Holt, Rinehart and Winston.

Theberge, N. (1977). "An occupational analysis of women's professional golf." Ph.D. dissertation, University of Massachusetts.

Thornton, R., and P. M. Nardi (1975). "The dynamics of role acquisition." *American Journal of Sociology* 80 (January): 870–885.

Tomeh, A. (1973). "Formal voluntary organizations: Participation, correlates, and interrelationships." *Sociological Inquiry* 43: 89–122.

Voigt, D. (1974). *A Little League Journal.* Bowling Green, Ohio: Bowling Green University Popular Press.

Watson, G. (1973). "Game interaction in Little League baseball and family organization." Unpublished doctoral dissertation, University of Illinois.

Watson, G. G. (1974). "Family organization and Little League baseball." *International Review of Sport Sociology* 2: 5–31.

Watson, G. G. (1975). "The meaning of parental influence and intrinsic reward in children's sport: The case of little athletics." Paper presented at the Conference on Sport, Society and Personality, Bundoora, Victoria, Australia (May).

Watson, G. (1977). "Games, socialization and parental values: Social class differences in parental evaluation of Little League baseball." *International Review of Sport Sociology* **12**: 17–47.

Watson, G., and T. Kando (1974). 'The meaning of rules and rituals in Little League baseball." Presented at the International Sociological Association Meetings, Toronto (August).

Weinberg, S., and W. Arond (1952). 'The occupational culture of the boxer." *American Journal of Sociology* **57**: 460–469.

Wettan, R., and J. Willis (1976). "Social stratification in the New York Athletic Club: A preliminary analysis of the impact of the club on amateur sport in late 19th century America." *Canadian Journal of History of Sport and Physical Education* **7**: 41–53.

Willis, J., and R. Wettan (1976). "Social stratification in New York City athletic clubs, 1865–1915." *Journal of Sport History* **3**: 45–63.

Woelfel, J., and A. Haller (1971). "Significant others, the self-reflexive act, and the attitude formation process." *American Sociological Review* **36** (February): 74–87.

Yiannakis, A. (1976). "Birth order and preference for dangerous sports among males." *Research Quarterly* **47**: 62–67.

Zigler, E., and I. L. Child (1969). "Socialization." In G. Lindzey and E. Aronson (eds.), *A Handbook of Social Psychology*, Vol 3, pp. 450–589. Reading, Mass.: Addison-Wesley.

Chapter 7
SPORT
AND REGULATIVE
INSTITUTIONS

In the previous chapter we analyzed institutions that help the individual to become involved in sport. There are other social institutions, however, that regulate the structure and function of institutionalized sport. These include the economic, legal, political, and military[1,2,3] systems. Although political and military systems have influenced the form and function of sport at varying times throughout history, the economic, legal, and political systems have increasingly gained control over institutionalized sport in the twentieth century because of the rationalization and professionalization of sport. This chapter analyzes the relationship between sport and three social institutions that regulate its structure and function: the economic, legal, and political systems.

7.1 SPORT AND ECONOMIC SYSTEMS

7.1.1 Introduction

Institutionalized sport at the university, professional, and international levels has become heavily embedded in the bureaucratic dimensions of a mass-consuming society and is therefore an integral part of the marketplace. In fact, as Shecter (1970) noted: "winning, losing, playing the game, all count far less than counting the money." Not only has sport itself become an economic enterprise, it has also stimulated economic growth in a variety of ways, so that sport and related enterprises represent an estimated 100-billion-dollar business in the United States alone (Kowet, 1977; Meyers, 1975). This industry includes (1) large corporations that manufacture sporting goods in an estimated 10.5-billion-dollar industry; (2) clothing manufacturers who produce practical, attractive athletic attire to be worn while playing or consuming sport (e.g., swimsuits, tennis clothes, footwear); (3) architects, building contractors, and consulting engineers who design, construct, or remodel stadiums, games sites, ski resorts, etc., at a large profit (see Auf der Maur, 1976); (4) concession owners and operators who engage in a million-dollar industry selling food and beverages at sporting events; (5) part-time entrepreneurs such as those who recover golf balls from ponds and lakes for resale in a million-dollar business, much of which is illegal; (6) bookies and betting syndicates who handle over one billion dollars a year in wagers on professional and college sport events; (7) agents and lawyers who represent the contractual and commercial interests of athletes; and (8) various forms of the mass media, especially television, which sell commercial time to business corporations which can then advertise their products to a relatively homogeneous set of potential consumers. Within the sport world itself, a large number of personnel directly receive incomes in exchange for services in the production of sport; these include athletes, coaches, field and business managers, scouts, trainers, officials, maintenance personnel, publicity officers, sportwriters and sportcasters, etc.

As sport has become increasingly "worklike" and professionalized, the concepts and methods used to analyze sport have become similar to those in any other industry. Thus, such concepts as productivity, exchange of goods and services, division of labor, competition for and allocation of resources, intrinsic versus extrinsic rewards, job dissatisfaction, strikes, unions, franchises, monopolies, depreciation, tax concessions and subsidies, operating revenues, direct and indirect costs, maximization of profits and minimization of losses, and bonuses, etc., have been used in recent years to examine the relationship between sport and economics. Although a text could be written on this subject alone (see Auf der Maur, 1976; Dauriac, 1977; Demmert, 1973; Durso, 1971; Hellerman, 1975; Miller, 1966; Noll, 1974b), the following sections limit the analysis to university sport, professional sport, elite international amateur sport, and gambling.

7.1.2 The Economics of University Sport

In many countries university or college sport programs began as clubs in which the players organized their schedule, appointed a coach, and payed all or most of their expenses. However, in North America, as sport became more professionalized, departments of athletics were formalized and charged with the administrative and financial responsibility for intercollegiate athletics. Today, cross-national differences in the social structure and economic basis of college athletics are based on value differences and economic necessity. For example, intercollegiate athletics in the United States, and to a lesser extent in Canada, are considered to be an essential part of the social life of the student body and important for the prestige of the institution. As a result departments of athletics are normally separate economic entities within the institution, run by an athletic director who may administer a budget of over five million dollars.

In brief, the structure of college sport in North America has resulted from an emphasis on excellence, specialization, high-level elite competition, the desire to consume sport by the student body and alumni, and the belief that a successful college athletic program will enhance the prestige of the institution and thereby assist in recruiting students and generating revenue in the form of alumni contributions and television rights. As a result, college sport has become an ancillary business enterprise dependent on gate receipts, television and radio rights, alumni assistance, and, in the case of football, guarantees for playing in bowl games.

Concomitant with this structure is the principle that the economic base of a given department influences policies concerning scheduling, recruiting,[4] educational standards for eligibility, and the variety of sports available at the intercollegiate level. For the major sports, and especially football, winning on the field is essential if athletic programs are to remain economically viable, especially in the United States.

Contrasted with this structure is the Council of University Sport Clubs found in Great Britain, Australia, the German Federal Republic, Japan, and many other countries. Under this structure each club sends one representative to the governing council, which assists in arranging competitions with other universities or community sport clubs. There is no athletic department or full-time athletic administrator. Other differences in sport at the extramural level between North America and other areas of the world include the following: (1) the coaches are normally volunteers if the club structure predominates; (2) there are no paid admissions; (3) the athletes do not view their participation as preprofessional occupational socialization; (4) competition is available at up to four or five levels of ability; (5) the players do not receive athletic scholarships; and (6) the games are not televised (Bennett, Howell, and Simri, 1975).

American Intercollegiate Athletics

In order to illustrate the economics of intercollegiate athletics in the United States, a brief descriptive account follows. In 1969, according to an NCAA study, football revenues totaled about $145 million of the total $205 million revenue for all sports (Raiborn, 1970). No doubt this has increased since then, assisted by the $18 million received annually by the NCAA from one television network for the right to televise 41 regular-season games. Each team involved in a nationally televised regular-season game receives more than $475,000, while a trip to the Rose Bowl could result in revenue of $1.5 million, which is shared by the participating school and the conference.

This income is required because of the increasing costs of producing intercollegiate sport. For example, at one university, athletic scholarships cost over $700,000 per year, administrative costs were approximately $270,000, and team and game expenses cost over $800,000. Thus, the total operating expenditures for the 1975–1976 year at this university were approximately $4.5 million, against a total revenue[5] of approximately $4.8 million. However, because of a previous deficit, the net profit for a two-year period was only $59,000 (Raiborn, 1970).

In short, college sport has attained the magnitude of big business; thus, like other enterprises, it is faced with inflation and a need to cut costs and increase revenues. Yet costs can only be reduced through a reduction in salaries or in the number of scholarships offered, both of which may reduce the quality of the program and thereby influence revenues. At the same time, most stadia have a fixed seating capacity, which would be extremely expensive to expand; therefore revenues can normally be increased only by raising ticket prices. If this is done, the administrators run the risk of pricing themselves out of the entertainment market. Thus, athletic departments today find themselves in a "Catch-22" situation. This has been further compounded by the Title IX Educational Amendment of 1972, which states that women's athletic programs at institutions that receive federal funds must receive equality in budgeting and facilities. Quite obviously this means that either men's athletic programs must be reduced or budgets must be expanded considerably. The result, then, of the present and future economic state is that more schools will either operate their athletic budgets in the red or drop out of "big-time" competition as a trend toward a diminished margin of profit increases.

On a more analytical level, "big-time" college athletics in the United States is structured within a cartel, the NCAA, which functions (1) to establish input prices for student-athletes in the form of maximum grants-in-aid; (2) to regulate the years of eligibility and the practice of redshirting; (3) to establish the rules of the game and limit the number of games; (4) to pool and divide profits accruing to the cartel from television rights, royalties, and tournament receipts; (5) to inform members of the cartel of transactions, market conditions, and business procedures; and (6) to monitor rules and impose sanctions (e.g., probations, no television exposure and the accompanying revenue) on members who deviate from the rules (Koch, 1971). In addition to the national cartel (e.g., the NCAA), there are regional conferences (e.g., the Big Ten), which may impose further rules and regulations.

The structure also operates at the local level through universities that produce one or more products (i.e., sports) in competition with other universities. The output, then, is not very different from that of professional or amateur sport in which prosperity depends on producing successful teams that will enhance gate receipts, television rights, and, theoretically, alumni donations. However, as Davenport (1968), Jones (1969), Koch (1971), and Neale (1964) state, not every firm can win and therefore the cartel attempts to promote equalization of competition and/or revenue.

To illustrate, Koch (1971) noted that the NCAA emphasizes the former approach by establishing rules governing the maximum amount of money to be expended on recruiting and subsidizing athletes, the minimum grade point average to be eligible, and the maximum number of years of participation. Of course, similar rules do not exist in professional sport, where bonuses and inflated salaries are limitless and where one organization may raid another to hire away "star" athletes who have completed their contract. However, college athletes do have a contract in the form of a "letter of intent," which binds them to one university for at least one year. In effect this makes them ineligible to play for another university for two years, since if they transfer they cannot compete for one year. Thus, mobility from one firm to another is subtly discouraged, partly to prevent the wealthier firms from raiding the less successful teams.

In short, at the present time the cartel arrangement at the intercollegiate level facilitates the equalization of competition mainly through regulations dealing with recruitment and playing rules. However, increasingly in the future the cartel must do more to equalize costs and revenues through direct and indirect regulations pertaining to the sharing of gate receipts and television rights and to the number of grants-in-aid that may be offered in both major and minor sports (Koch, 1971).

"Big-Time" versus "Middle-Time" Athletics

Notwithstanding the cartel-like framework of the NCAA, there are unique and commonly accepted economic, philosophical, and structural differences among certain categories of institutions affiliated with the NCAA. For example, Raiborn (1970) classified NCAA membership ". . . into five homogeneous groups based upon the criteria of dominance of particular sports within the program and apparent strength of programs as determined by the nature of the scheduled opposition." His five-fold classification is as follows:

Class A.   This category includes the 118 institutions which the NCAA in 1969 designated as constituting its University Division. These institutions sponsor football teams that the NCAA Football Statistics and Classification Committee defines as "major" on the basis of the relative strength of their football schedules. Somewhat tautologically, a major football team is defined as one that plays a majority of its regularly scheduled games against teams in its own division.

Class B.   This category includes the 157 institutions which the NCAA in 1969 designated as comprising College Division I. In terms of relative strength in football, these institutions may occasionally compete against institutions in the University Division, but generally schedule the majority of their games against institutions in their own division.

Class C.   This category includes 170 institutions designated as comprising College Division II. In terms of relative strength in football, these institutions rarely ever play a Class A institution, and only periodically compete against a Class B institution.

Class D.   This category includes the 40 member institutions which do not sponsor an intercollegiate football team but do sponsor an intercollegiate basketball team which the NCAA Basketball and Classification Committee defines as "major."

Class E.   This category includes the 170 member institutions of the NCAA which do not sponsor an intercollegiate football team or a "major" intercollegiate basketball team.

Philosophically considered, class-A institutions represent big-time athletics and stress the concept of "athletics for entertainment"; classes C and E and, to some extent, class-D institutions represent small-time athletics emphasizing the concept of "athletics for education," while class-B institutions represent middle-time athletics ambivalently trying to blend the concepts of "athletics for pay" and "athletics for play." In brief, small-time athletic institutions have elected not to enter the economic rat race of intercollegiate athletics, big-time athletic institutions are running the race with varying degrees of success, and middle-time athletic institutions are attempting to compete in the race with limited resources. The result is that many middle-time institutions are being financially squeezed.

The basic economic difficulty confronting middle-time (i.e., class B) athletic institutions is that in order to field "quality" football teams they must spend nearly as much money on their football programs as big-time (i.e., class A) ath-letic institutions do, but they have little chance of generating similar revenues. For example, with respect to expenses, Jackson points out:

> Such a school must begin by competing with the Big Time for a share of the best high-school talent. Tuition, room and board, books and fees cost about the same at a Middle Time as at a comparable Big Time school, so grants-in-aid must be roughly the same. In some cases the upper Middle Time school must spend more on player recruitment than Big Time schools spend . . . Many basic expenses—coaches, promotion, entertainment, football uni-forms, training room facilities, laundry, etc.—are roughly comparable to Big Time expenses . . . (Jackson, 1969, p. 239)

With respect to income, Raiborn (1970) estimated that NCAA members generated $205 million for the 1969 fiscal year, with $162.3 million or 79.1 percent of this aggregate figure being produced by class-A institutions and $31.1 million or 15.2 percent being generated by class-B institutions. Table 7.1 illus-trates the approximate annual income and expenses for one class-A institution.

In addition to marked contrasts between class-A and class-B institutions with respect to total revenue generated, there are striking differences in terms of how revenue is generated. One example is the fact that in 1969 class-A institutions generated 51 percent of their revenue from ticket sales compared to 20 percent for class-B institutions, whereas class-B schools generated 33 percent of their revenue from student fees for athletic admissions compared to 7 percent for class-A schools (Raiborn, 1970). A second example is the fact that in 1969 football revenues accounted for 68 percent of all revenues generated by class-A insti-tutions, but only 34 percent of all revenues produced by class-B institutions (Raiborn, 1970).

The principal expenses for intercollegiate athletic programs among Class A, B, C, D, and E institutions are shown in Table 7.2. It is evident from this table that class-B schools, compared to class-A schools, spend *as a percentage of total expenses* identical amounts of monies for salaries and wages, slightly more monies for travel, equipment, and uniforms, and 11 percent more monies for grants-in-aid. In sum, the preceding financial analysis of intercollegiate athletics suggests that *upper-level* middle-time schools have expenses that often approxi-mate those of big-time schools, but receive only about 20 percent of the revenue obtained by big-time institutions.

A major consequence of the income differentials between class-A and class-B institutions is that the latter are caught in a financial squeeze and are often faced with the difficult decision of attempting, on the one hand, to upgrade the quality of their football and basketball programs and go for the big-time money, or attempting, on the other hand, to reduce costs and expenses by dropping to the small-time level of competition. The former alternative involves a great deal of financial risk and economic "ifs." The latter alternative means a loss of insti-tutional prestige and the glamour associated with big-time athletics. However, as Jackson has summarized the situation:

If all these "ifs" add up to a negative decision, the future need not be so bleak as alumni might think. Colleges playing below the $40,000 level will find themselves in the pleasurable company of other institutions of higher learning that are moving back to amateur football—Small Time, no grants, no worry, no guilt, little profit, little loss, and after all is said and done still a fairly rousing game. (Jackson, 1969, p. 243)

Table 7.1
Athletic program income and expenses, 1971–1972

Income

Incidental fee	$142,000
Athletic privilege cards (faculty and staff)	60,000
Football games	1,025,000
Basketball games	
Regular season	424,238
Postseason	66,319
Football TV (national and regional)	222,747
Football delayed telecast	65,000
Football radio	31,875
Basketball TV (live and delayed)	87,300
Basketball radio	10,625
Football postseason (Rose Bowl)	155,000
Concessions and programs	17,500
Donations	80,000
Track meets	15,000
Gymnastic meets	3,000
Varsity Club	2,000
All other sports including television	15,000
	$2,386,547

Expenses

Director's office	$701,860
General expense	222,159
News bureau	57,746
Ticket office	58,965
Football—general	315,778
Football games	510,000
Basketball—general	85,500
Basketball games	233,500
Track & field	69,406
Other sports	244,277
Fellowships	4,000
Varsity Club	600
	$2,503,791

Balance   ($117,244)*

*This deficit is funded from accumulated reserves. From *UCLA Bruin,* 9 May 1972.

7.1.3 The Economics of Professional Sport Organizations

For many years the owners of professional sport franchises have perpetuated a number of myths designed to disguise or rationalize their profit-maximization motives and practices. This section illustrates that the following myths appear to have little empirical validity: (1) that the reserve system is essential to equalizing the distribution of playing strength; (2) that the owners of professional teams are sportsmen who are not interested in profit maximization; (3) that higher ticket prices are necessary because of higher player salaries; (4) that sport franchises are financially weak; and (5) that local broadcasting of games reduces gate receipts.

Essentially, professional sport consists of franchises within a cartel that is designed to provide monopoly rights and restrictions against competition. A cartel is a group of firms (e.g., teams in a league) that are structurally linked to produce a product through agreement on rules, the end product, prices, advertising, hiring policies, revenue sharing, etc. In effect, the result is that owners have a monopoly on access to players, the protection of their geographical territory from competition in the same sport, control over local broadcast rights, and control over concession rights. Furthermore, at least until the last few years, sport teams have been an example of monopsonistic power wherein the buyer has control in any bargaining relationship. Although the balance of power is shifting to the athlete in some sports (for example, where free-agent status can be attained), the economic structure of professional sport continues to be complex. Therefore, the following subsections describe and analyze the revenue and expenses, the salaries and profits accruing to athletes, owners, and associated personnel, the restrictions on economic freedom, and some theories and models of the economic processes within professional sport.

Revenue and Expenses for Professional Sport Teams

There are three main sources of income for professional sport teams: gate receipts, radio and television rights, and ancillary enterprises such as concessions, parking, and the sale of programs and souvenirs. The sale of tickets results in over $300 million annually for teams in the major sports. These tickets range in price from a low in baseball of approximately $3.00 to a high in football of approximately $18.00. Moreover, the prices increase for postseason games. In some sports such as hockey (in some cities) and football (in most cities), the annual revenue from tickets is predictable, because a high percentage of sales are season tickets and thus the revenue is "banked" before the season begins. However, in other sports ticket sales fluctuate on a daily basis, often depending on the success of the team to date, the opposition for a specific game, or the weather. In short, ticket sales are an essential component of the revenue, but tend to be unpredictable.[6]

Improvement in the standing in the league, winning a championship, or having a "star" on the team will influence attendance patterns. For example, Noll (1974a) found that a baseball team that improves its position by ten games over the previous year will draw an additional 18,000 fans for each million residents in the area, while winning a pennant will increase attendance more than 850,000 for

Table 7.2

Principal expenses classified by object and percentage of total expenses, fiscal years 1965–1969 (in thousands of dollars)

Expense classification	1965 Mean	1965 Per-cent	1966 Mean	1966 Per-cent	1967 Mean	1967 Per-cent	1968 Mean	1968 Per-cent	1969 Mean	1969 Per-cent
Grants-in-aid										
Class A	$219	19%	$239	20%	$257	20%	$279	20%	$308	20%
Class B	63	29	71	28	78	27	96	30	115	31
Class C	35	13	37	12	39	12	47	13	55	13
Class D	61	31	67	32	73	32	74	33	76	32
Class E	26	23	29	24	32	24	40	26	40	24
Guarantees and options										
Class A	$181	15%	$210	16%	$217	15%	$227	15%	$247	14%
Class B	9	4	10	4	10	3	11	3	12	3
Class C	2	1	2	1	2	1	2	1	2	1
Class D	14	7	13	6	13	6	10	4	10	4
Class E	3	1	3	1	3	1	3	1	4	1

Salaries and wages										
Class A	$280	26%	$304	28%	$341	28%	$378	29%	$421	29%
Class B	48	24	53	24	66	25	83	29	94	29
Class C	29	36	32	36	36	37	40	36	46	37
Class D	59	30	64	31	69	31	71	31	77	32
Class E	26	38	28	37	30	36	34	36	36	36
All travel expenses										
Class A	$106	10%	$118	11%	$131	11%	$144	11%	$155	11%
Class B	28	14	32	14	39	15	44	15	47	14
Class C	14	18	15	17	16	16	18	16	20	16
Class D	25	14	25	13	28	14	28	14	31	14
Class E	11	16	12	16	14	17	17	18	19	19
Equipment and uniforms										
Class A	$ 45	4%	$ 49	4%	$ 55	4%	$ 58	4%	$ 64	4%
Class B	17	8	18	7	22	7	25	8	24	6
Class C	12	15	14	16	15	15	17	15	17	14
Class D	12	7	12	7	12	6	16	8	16	7
Class E	9	10	11	11	13	12	13	11	12	9

From Raiborn (1970).

each million in the area. He also noted that the presence of a star on the team will increase attendance at home games by an additional 22,000 per season for each one million residents in the metropolitan area. In dollars, the presence of a star may add approximately $175,000 to the gate receipts at home games alone, with another $25,000 being added to revenues at away games. As a result, owners are increasingly willing to pay high salaries to the superstars for both economic and performance reasons. Noll (1974a) also suggested that a metropolitan area population of only 900,000 is necessary to provide adequate financial support for a professional football team. Many additional cities could therefore theoretically support a professional football team.

A far more stable source of revenue, and an increasingly essential source, is radio and television rights for local and national broadcasts. In recent years the local and national rights to televise regular-season baseball and football games have been over $50 million annually in each sport. For example, in 1977 the television rights for baseball totaled $52.1 million, with the amount a given team received ranging from $2 million for the Red Sox to $350,000 for the Royals (Kahan, 1977). In football, each team divided $57.2 million in television rights for a net share of $2.2 million. In some sports (for example, football), the revenue for national rights is divided equally among the firms in the cartel while in others (for example, hockey) it is divided so that the teams in larger cities, or the more successful teams that appear more frequently, receive larger shares. This latter arrangement is a version of the "rich get richer" theme. The importance of this source of revenue is so critical that franchises are shifted to enter more lucrative television markets (for example, the Milwaukee Braves were moved to Atlanta) and new leagues or teams fail or remain economically depressed if a national television contract is not present (e.g., the World Football Association or the World Hockey Association). Further, Horowitz (1974) noted that not a single major league baseball team would have earned a profit in 1952 or in 1970 if television rights were not available.

In order to pay these rights, television networks in turn sell advertising time to sponsors at a high cost per minute. The income derived from the sale of commercial time provides the network with a profit, even after paying the radio

Table 7.3
Estimated cost per minute for television advertising time

Event	Estimated cost per minute
Stanley Cup playoff game	$25,000
Saturday afternoon baseball game	$30,000
Monday evening baseball game	$52,000
NFL—Sunday game	$85,000
NFL—Monday night game	$120,000
All-Star baseball game	$140,000
World Series	$150,000
Super Bowl	$250,000

or television rights. In the end, these costs are, of course, passed on to the consumer. Table 7.3 illustrates the approximate cost per minute paid by manufacturers for advertising time on specific sport events. It should be noted that these costs vary by sport and by viewing time.

Because of this dependency, professional sport owners strive to sign a multi-year contract with the media in order to provide some stability to their revenue. Yet, once locked into a long-term contract, they have little flexibility to meet inflationary costs and increased salary demands by free agents. According to Horowitz (1974), the size of the rights negotiated for local television depends on such factors as the profit orientation of the owner, the size of the potential viewing audience, the past interest demonstrated in the team, the past performance and future prospects of the team, the number of competitive sport broadcasts, the length of the contract, and the bargaining skill and position of those involved (for example, the viability of a threat to move a franchise to another city may increase the revenue). For national rights, Horowitz (1974) suggests that the influential factors are mainly the interest of one or more sponsors in gaining monopoly rights to advertise through a given sport and the degree of interest (as expressed via the television ratings of viewer interest) of fans in consuming that sport. For example, hockey is no longer televised nationally, tennis is reducing the amount of its coverage, and soccer has yet to attain a national contract primarily because of anticipated low ratings.

In summary, local and national television and radio rights enable teams that are less financially stable to survive. They also provide some long-term financial stability to the teams and, more important, to a league. Furthermore, in recent years, the acquisition of a national television contract has been essential to the creation and ultimate survival of new leagues.

The third source of revenue, and the least understood, is the income derived from concessions, parking lots, and the sale of programs and souvenirs. By far the largest proportion of this source is that obtained from the sales of food and beverages at athletic contests. Although it has been estimated that this is a billion-dollar industry, little factual information is available other than estimates that the average fan attending a game spends between fifty cents and a dollar on food or drinks. The revenue derived from these sales accrues directly to the owner who operates the parking lot and concessions. Alternatively, the owner of the team receives a fixed income, or an income plus percentage, from the sale of concession rights to another entrepreneur. For example, many of the concession rights at stadia and arenas in North America have been purchased by one large corporation, and the owner of the sport team is guaranteed a fixed source of revenue.

Another increasing source of revenue is the emergence of rights fees for the use of league or team logos on a multitude of products ranging from T-shirts and caps to drinking and eating utensils. Again, these rights are often sold in advance to a marketing firm to ensure a certain amount of income for the league or team. In short, the source of revenue for a sport organization is three-fold, although the sale of players or the addition of new franchises may add additional revenue on an ad hoc basis.

On the other side of the ledger, teams are faced with increasing expenses[7] in the form of salaries, operating costs (recruiting, food, travel), equipment, taxes, and, in some situations, stadium or arena rentals. Again, these expenses are difficult to estimate because most teams are not public corporations and therefore are not required to publish their annual audit.

Until the late 1960s the salaries paid to professional athletes were relatively low,[8] especially in view of the actual profits made by the owners. This situation existed because legislative rules imposed by the cartel (e.g., the reserve system) gave a team monopoly rights to a player for life, because there were no competing cartels for the player's services, and because player associations (i.e., unions) were nonexistent. Since the 1960s, the emergence of competing cartels, changes initiated through collective bargaining (e.g., free-agent status), increased revenues from television, expanded leagues, and an awareness of the actual profits made by owners have all operated to inflate salaries considerably. As a result minimum salaries have increased, the number of athletes on a payroll has increased, some athletes now earn more than $200,000 per annum, pension and other fringe benefits have increased, and multiyear contracts are being encouraged by the owners.

There is great variation, however, in salaries between sports, between leagues in a given sport, and within clubs depending on the position played, the level of ability, and the degree of "charisma" generated. To illustrate, some teams spend over $2 million per annum on player salaries, which can range from 20 percent (in football) to 45 percent (in basketball and hockey) of their revenue. Table 7.4 shows the estimated average and maximum salaries of professional athletes in 1977. In sports in which there are two competing cartels (hockey), average salaries are higher, but they decline with a merger of the leagues or the failure of one league. However, salaries for the superstars or "quality" performers may continue to escalate or remain high because of the ability of these athletes to improve both the team's performance and the attendance figures at home and away games. This is especially true if free-agent status enables lawyers to bargain in a

Table 7.4
Estimated average and maximum annual salaries for professional sport, 1977

Sport	Approximate number of players	Estimated average salary	Estimated maximum salary
Baseball	600	$ 95,000	$500,000
Football	1200	50,000	450,000
Basketball	200	120,000	600,000
Hockey*	600	75,000	250,000
Golf	300	30,000	300,000
Tennis	200	50,000	600,000
Horse racing (jockeys)	2500	10,000	450,000

*This is the only sport in which there are two leagues competing for playing personnel. However, there is the possibility of a merger between the NHL and WHA in 1978–1979.

relatively free market. For example, one quality player in professional basketball earns an estimated $600,000 per annum, while a free agent in baseball negotiated a contractual agreement that includes a salary of $100,000 per year for five years, a bonus[9] of $125,000 payable within one month of signing, an investment account of $250,000, an off-season job worth $50,000 for the duration of the contract, deferred payments of $450,000 plus 5 percent interest compounded quarterly, payable over 15 years after he retires, a new car each year, a guarantee on the contract in case of disability or death, and $200,000 in fees and service commission for his agent (The *Globe and Mail*, 6 December 1976, p. S2).

Faced with inflated salaries and increased operating expenses because of expanded schedules and travel costs, owners complain that it is virtually impossible to break even or realize a profit. Yet new stadia are constructed and more entrepreneurs are attempting to purchase new or existing franchises. The following section suggests why sport franchises are in demand.

Professional Sport as an Investment

Although professional sport owners are increasingly publicizing their losses, little has been revealed about profits realized either directly from the sport franchise or indirectly from tax concessions applied to other investments. Profits in sport can result from a salary paid to the owner, from dividends on stock in the franchise, from expansion rights, from tax benefits that can be applied to other enterprises, and from the sale of a franchise. One reason for the difficulty in obtaining accurate information about the economic stability of teams is that there are many different accounting procedures used. For example, one team may report real losses, while another can show a loss on paper, but in reality this loss is used as a tax deduction against another corporation or against the owner's personal income tax. The latter procedure enables the owner to accrue an indirect profit (Okner, 1974). A closer analysis suggests that contrary to the popular myth, most owners are entrepreneurs who strive to maximize profits either directly or indirectly.

One way to realize a profit in professional sport is to acquire a franchise and then sell it later at a profit. This is possible because there are many wealthy individuals or corporations who would like to acquire a franchise for intrinsic reasons or for the special tax advantages or advertising value it can bring to other business interests. For example, whenever a new owner acquires a franchise, he or she negotiates an agreement with federal tax personnel as to what percentage of the purchase price can be allocated to player contracts. These contracts can be depreciated over a five-year period so that they offset the tax payable on income. As Quirk (1974) noted, this tax advantage approximately doubles the value of the franchise. Quirk (1974) reports that the average price per sale of a franchise between 1970 and 1974 was $4.6 million in basketball, $10.4 million in baseball, and $15.2 million in football. More specifically, he cites the following resale history of the Philadelphia Eagles: In 1933 the franchise was sold for $2500, in 1949 for $250,000, in 1963 for $5.5 million, in 1967 for $14.5 million, and in 1969 for $16.2 million. This represents a rate of return on the franchise of 15 percent per year over the past 35 years, and this was over and above the profits earned annually.

These annual profits can be quite high but the franchise may still appear to be in financial difficulty after dividends are paid to shareholders. For example, one professional hockey team reported a pretax profit of $2.3 million in August 1975. Then, in October 1975, a $1.00 dividend was voted to all shareholders. However, 547,000 of the 735,580 shares were held by the owner. Three years earlier a $3.00 dividend had been paid to stockholders, resulting in an approximate $1.5 million bonus for the owner. Thus, an estimated $2 million was transferred to the owner's pocket over a three-year period.

Another source of income and profit results for original owners when a league expands and admits new teams. For example, a franchise in the NFL costs approximately $15 million, while an NHL fanchise costs $6 million. The money derived from this admission fee is divided equally among the existing teams.

Many owners in recent years have reported losses ranging from $200,000 to over $1 million. No doubt there are some new teams or financially weak franchises for which these figures are accurate. However, based on an extensive economic analysis of professional sport, Noll (1974c) reported that many basketball and baseball teams realized an annual profit of $200,000 and $500,000, respectively, while some established professional hockey and football teams may accumulate one million dollars per team per year, depending on the success of the team. Similarly, Burman (1974) estimated that the average pretax profit in the NFL was $2 million per team in 1973.

In order to identify the factors that may influence the size of team profits, Noll (1974a) utilized regression analyses for baseball attendance between 1969 and 1971. The most important factors appeared to be winning a league championship, a superstar on the team, tickets being in demand, a high standing in the league, and being situated in a large city. Moreover, he suggested that league attendance, along with profits, would be higher if several teams alternated winning championships.

Although the costs and revenues cited earlier might suggest that sport is a risky financial investment, individuals continue to invest their money in sport, and many realize a profit either directly or indirectly. One major reason for many franchises remaining in the black is the presence of local and federal subsidies in the form of tax concessions or low rental payments for facilities. Okner (1974) found that at the local level more than 70 percent of the stadia or arenas were owned by municipalities that rented the facility to the owner at a rate lower than that which a comparable facility would demand. These low rentals are tolerated by other businessmen and citizens because it is believed that a professional sport team enhances the prestige of the community, stimulates the economy in general,[10] generates employment at the sport facility, and improves the morale of the citizens (Okner, 1974).

Similarly, there are indirect subsidies in the form of property taxes below the market value, which may amount to between $9 and $12 million annually in foregone taxes. At the federal level, Okner (1974) found that professional sport teams receive tax exemptions on bonds sold to finance the construction of new facilities, are permitted to depreciate player contracts on income tax returns, and are exempt from capital gains tax on the sale of players, franchises, or equipment. To illustrate, Davis and Quirk (1975) present a formal model of the valuation of a sport franchise for an owner who owns a team forever, and for the case in which an owner sells the franchise and is subject to a capital gains tax. In effect these models indicate that if an owner can assign 90 percent of the purchase price to player contracts, a team is worth twice as much to an owner in the former case and 3⅔ times as much to an owner in the latter case, if all tax advantages are utilized. However, they conclude that even though the average sale price for franchises between 1970 and 1974 was between $4 and $15 million, the rate of return is "less than could be earned in less risky tax shelters" (Davis and Quirk, 1975). As a final example, one professional sport team recently attempted to sell its star player for $700,000 to cover the expected annual deficit. If the deal had been concluded, a capital gains tax would not have been imposed, thereby enabling the sport owner to acquire $700,000 in tax-free revenue. Yet, if a manufacturer in some other industry opted to sell a piece of machinery for $700,000, he would be required to pay a capital gains tax.

In total, it has been estimated (Okner, 1974) that over $40 million per year accrues to professional sport owners through either rentals below the market value, low property taxes, or federal tax provisions. Through these subsidies (and certain cartel monopolistic restrictions to be discussed in the next section), profits can be realized by those who have the capital to invest in professional sport franchises. However, it is becoming more risky to purchase a sport club; there are many professional baseball clubs that would be sold if the right buyer made an offer. Part of this risk is related to the rising costs combined with tax reforms that make sport clubs a less attractive tax shelter than they were in the past (Block, 1977). For example, the maximum amount of the purchase price owners are able to write off as depreciation attributable to player contracts has been reduced from 90 percent to 50 percent of the purchase price. As a result, owners may lose up to $150 million in tax savings over a six-year period (Horvitz and Hoffman, 1976), because they will be forced to tie up capital that previously was used for other investments. In addition, this reform also reduces the value of a franchise.

Sport can also be profitable for those athletes who invest a significant part of their life, often at the expense of an education, in preparing for the career. Those who attain positions at the highest level of competition, can earn not only high salaries, but significant incomes through endorsements of products, fringe benefits, and wise investment of their income during the playing career. For example, some star professional athletes annually earn the equivalent of their salary through commercial endorsements. Through sound investments by business managers, many will have guaranteed annual incomes sufficient to maintain a high standard of living long after their playing career, without ever being employed full-time.

On the other hand, sport may not be a profitable career for those who ultimately don't make it, or who only remain in the system from one to five years. These individuals may have few alternatives open to them outside sport; thus they experience not only the loss of potential income but the loss of a feeling of self-worth. Many of these "failures" experience downward social mobility and a life of marginal existence. In short, their investment in professional socialization for the athlete role has not materialized.

Restrictions on Individual and Team Economic Freedom

Within professional sport there are individual and team restrictions on profit maximization. From the individual's point of view, a player is bound to a contract and can only increase his salary by negotiation with the owner, by becoming a "free agent" after a specified number of years in the league (six years in major league baseball, four years in football), or by playing out the option year of a contract. In the latter arrangement the player continues to play for the year during which the contract dispute occurs, but his salary can be cut by a certain percentage (usually 10 to 20 percent). At the end of this option year the player is then free to continue negotiation with the original owner or to attempt to sell his services in the open market. Among the problems that may result from this trend are: (1) owners may begin to experience "real" losses, especially if the team doesn't win and attract spectators; (2) some players may price themselves out of the market and find themselves unemployable at what they believe to be their market value; or (3) marginal players will be forced to settle for minimum or relatively low salaries in order to have one or two stars on the team.

Another limiting factor on the freedom to maximize income is hypothesized to have its basis in the racial origin of the player. A commonly held assumption for many years was that blacks are discriminated against in terms of salary. However, Pascal and Rapping (1972), using a linear regression model, concluded that, regardless of position, black baseball players with major league status experienced no salary discrimination. Moreover, they found that the salaries of black players were, on the average, higher than those for white players. Similar results for professional football have been reported (Mogull, 1973). However, based on a reanalysis of the Pascal and Rapping data, Scully (1974a) found that blacks actually earn more, position by position, than whites do. He suggested that the salary differentials favoring blacks are due to equal pay for superior performance. For example, he noted that to earn $30,000 black outfielders must outperform white players by approximately 65 points on the "slugging" average. Thus, in effect, there is salary discrimination against blacks, since they must be better athletes, or, to state it another way, they earn less than whites for equivalent performance.

Other economic areas in which blacks may experience discrimination are the bonus received for signing the initial contract and the opportunity for remuneration from commercial endorsements. Pascal and Rapping (1972) reported that, whereas blacks did receive smaller bonuses when they were first permitted to play major league baseball (from 1947 on), by the mid-1960s the differential between the races was minimal or nonexistent. However, Pascal and Rapping (1972) did find that black athletes were underrepresented in television commercials during 1966. Similarly, Yetman and Eitzen (1972) reported that only 2 of 13 blacks compared to 8 of 11 whites in the starting lineup of one professional football team were endorsing an advertised product.

Until recently there have been racial differences in the economic opportunity within professional sport. Scully (1974a) developed a theory of racial discrimination for major league baseball in which it was suggested that racial differentiation in salary could be accounted for by fan, owner, or white player discrimination, combined with the lower bargaining strength of blacks because of inexperience and fewer alternative avenues of employment outside sport. While inequities may still exist, they are less pronounced, and are probably nonexistent for the black "stars." Similarly, while opportunities to demand a salary commensurate with perceived market value were nonexistent in the past, contemporary professional athletes, black and white, are in a stronger bargaining position and are able to place themselves in open competition in a free market under certain legislative procedures that have been instituted.

In order to strive for equity of competition and a high level of spectator interest, most professional sport leagues have instituted legislative rules within the league. They argue that a universal draft and a reserve clause are necessary to prevent the wealthier teams, usually in the large cities, from buying up the contracts of the stars and thereby disturbing the balance of playing strength. Similarly, a draft of amateur players based on the less successful teams getting priority in the selection process is believed to lead to more equitable competition and therefore, by inference, greater profit. In the absence of these two systems, it is argued that the wealthy teams would be able to offer the highest salaries to players. Under this system, while the league may benefit, players are discriminated against in their attempt to maximize their opportunities in a free market system.

Recent legislation whereby a player can become a free agent has resulted in some economic chaos for the owners. For example, in 1976 one baseball owner negotiated the sale (for an estimated $3.5 million) of three players who were in the "option" year of their contract, but the sales were declared illegal by the commissioner of baseball. The owner subsequently lost, without compensation, six players who became free agents and signed contracts with other teams for an estimated total of over $8 million. Thus, he lost not only a large number of playing personnel, but also the $3.5 million he had originally thought was his because of the sale. As a result of such practices, the high salaries and bonuses offered by other teams for free agents are establishing a trend that may result in the rich getting richer, at least until fans stop attending games. This has happened in professional hockey in recent years—inflated salaries (an estimated 48 percent of gross income) have been accompanied by a 10-percent decline in attendance and many franchises filing for bankruptcy.

For many years it has been assumed that the reserve system and universal draft were essential to monopolize the labor market and thereby promote uncertainty of competition and maintain spectator interest. However, these mechanisms have recently been demonstrated to be ineffective in ensuring equity of competition. First, player contracts can be purchased or traded among teams within a league and, since a star may have more market potential in a large city, small-city teams can sell or trade a star to a big-city team in return for a number of players, cash, or "future considerations" such as draft choices. For example,

Quirk and El Hodiri (1974) suggest that the universal draft has little effect on equality of competition, since the weaker teams function as "conveyor belts": They obtain talent at low prices and then trade or sell these athletes to those willing to pay a high price, normally the more affluent and successful teams. Second, based on a number of analytical arguments (Canes, 1974; Okner, 1974; Rottenberg, 1974), it has been concluded that there is little, if any, relationship between equality of competition and the presence of a reserve system.

A third source of evidence concerning the ineffectiveness of the reserve system and universal draft is the empirical studies that show that contractual arrangements do not alter the distribution of playing talent from that in a market without such arrangements. For example, Canes (1974) compared teams that won championships in the four major professional sports before and after each of the contractual arrangements (the reserve clause, the free-agent draft, and the intra-league draft) were instituted. He found that restrictive league rules have no significant effect on the distribution of playing talent. Similarly, Daymont (1975) found that equality of competition is independent of each of the three legislative procedures, both independently and when they were combined to determine the net interactive effect. Like others, he suggested that the procedures are ineffective because organizations can sell or trade players or draft choices at will, and it is these practices that really influence equality of competition.

Neither the draft nor the reverse system can guarantee economic balance among the teams in a league. Rather, it would appear that additional legislation is necessary to restrict the practice of trading or selling players in order to maximize success and/or income. Rules prohibiting the sale of player contracts might guarantee convergence over time to equal playing strength, if it can be demonstrated that this goal truly equalizes opportunties for profit maximization. Another alternative is to subsidize the weak clubs with players or to establish more than one franchise in large cities. In this way teams in strong market areas are reduced in revenue potential equivalent to that of a team in a small city (Demmert, 1974). Perhaps the simplest mechanism to equalize profit maximization would be to pool the revenue from tickets and television rights, have the league pay all player salaries, and divide the profits equally. But then this practice goes against the principle of free enterprise on both an individual and a collective level.

Theories and Models Explaining the Economics of Professional Sport

Having presented some descriptive and analytical information in the previous sections, we now introduce theoretical analyses of cartel behavior (Davis, 1974), the economic structure of professional sport (Canes, 1974; El Hodiri and Quirk, 1971; Jones, 1969; Quirk and El Hodiri, 1974; Rottenberg, 1956; Sloane, 1971), the wage determination process (Dabscheck, 1975; Scully, 1974b), estimating attendance and determining the location of new clubs (Rivett, 1975), and factors influencing team movements (Quirk, 1973).

In order for professional team sports to generate a product, a cartel, which is an organized structure adopted by firms in an oligopolistic industry, is created. In this economic structure the optimum goal of the cartel (that is, the league) is to maximize joint profits of all members, whereas the optimum goal of each firm (that is, the team) is to gain more profit than others in the cartel. In an oligopoly situation, neither optimum is ever attained because the two goals are really in opposition; thus a "qualified joint maximizing position" (Jones, 1969) is normally realized, whereby the clubs earn sufficient profits to keep them and the league economically viable. However, there is great disparity in the profits realized by teams within the cartel because some may not follow the rules of the cartel (Davis, 1974), especially if the rules are difficult to enforce or if the sanctions are minimal if caught (e.g., negotiating with a player under contract to another firm). Furthermore, the voting rules of cartels usually make it difficult to initiate such changes as a reorganization or distribution of income, profits, or players to financially weaker franchises. For example, since 75 percent of the major league baseball teams must ratify any rule change, the four or five wealthier teams (usually those in the largest cities) can oppose any rule change. Hence they maintain their advantaged position of greater profits because of larger gate receipts and broadcast rights.

In short, professional sport does not represent a true oligopolistic structure, since collusion among members for equal benefit is incomplete in that each firm has a greater incentive to win than to maintain uncertainty of outcome (which is hypothesized to maximize profits). Furthermore, despite cartel regulations to offset disequilibrium, playing talent is distributed unequally among members, since each team attempts to maximize its pool of talent in order to win a championship (Jones, 1969). The result is conflict between league and team goals that must be resolved if the cartel is to survive as a stable organization based on mutual interdependence[11].

In order to apply economic theory to an analysis of the business operations of professional sport, Quirk and El Hodiri (1974) developed a theoretical model[12] based on the assumptions of profit maximization as a goal of each owner and the existence of an equilibrium within the system at each point in time (that is, the stock of playing skills for each team remains fixed with new players replacing those whose skills depreciate). The elements of the model include a basic unit of playing skill that can be assigned to each player, so that the playing skills of the team represent a sum of these skills. Each owner then must decide on the number of units of playing skill he or she must buy or sell in the market in order to realize success on the field and to maximize profits. In effect, the owner must establish a wage rate per unit of playing skill and balance this against revenues from gate receipts, broadcast rights, and the sale of player contracts. One additional unique feature of the model is that each firm operates in conjunction with others. Therefore, revenues and access to units of playing skill are dependent on the product (i.e., the equity of competition) and the success of one team compared to the others (for example, the least successful gets first choice for the contract of players desiring to enter the professional leagues).

Based on their model, Quirk and El Hodiri conclude that the distribution of playing strength within a league moves toward a position where:

1. Franchises located in areas with high drawing potential have stronger teams than franchises in low drawing potential areas.

2. On balance, franchises in low drawing potential areas sell players to franchises in high drawing potential areas.

3. If local television revenues are ignored, the distribution of playing strengths among teams is independent of the gate-sharing arrangements, which, instead, determine the level of player salaries and bonuses and the purchase price of player contracts.

4. The home team's gate share must exceed 50 percent in order for a steady-state situation to exist, and the higher the home team's gate share, the higher the costs of players and the smaller the chance of survival for franchises in low drawing potential areas.

5. The higher the share of television and radio revenues accruing to the home team, the higher the costs of players and the smaller the chance of survival for low drawing potential franchises.

6. The distribution of playing strengths is the same as it would be if the league were operated as a syndicate with central control over the allocation of players among teams.

7. The speed of convergence to an equilibrium, given an arbitrary initial allocation of players among teams, is greater the fewer the teams in the league and the shorter the average playing lifetime of players.

8. Equalization of playing strengths among teams can be achieved only by eliminating the sale of player contracts among teams or by assigning franchise rights so as to equalize drawing potential rather than on the basis of geographic area.*

The implication of such a model is that an owner will strive to produce a team with a total number of units of playing skill that is higher than the league average, but not so high that uncertainty of outcome will approach zero, since fan interest declines and revenues from gate receipts are lost.[13] Further, being interested in profit maximization, an owner will "add additional units of playing skills only to the point where the last unit acquired adds as much to revenue as it does to cost" (Quirk and El Hodiri, 1974). The authors also qualify their model by noting that the rule structure of each league differs in such areas as the reserve clause, the option clause, gate and broadcast-rights sharing arrangements, degree of autonomous decision making, the extent to which cartel rules are enforced, the degree to which owners are motivated by profits, the degree of expansion, contraction, and franchise mobility, which does not imply steady-state conditions, and the degree of structural or marketing innovations (Quirk and El Hodiri, 1974).

---

*Reprinted with permission from J. Quirk and M. E. Hodiri, "The economic theory of a professional sports league." In R. Noll (ed.), *Government and the Sports Business*, pp. 36–37. Copyright © 1974, The Brookings Institution, Washington, D.C.

Based on an empirical test of their model, Quirk and El Hodiri conclude that (1) big-city teams tend to win more league championships than do teams situated in small cities; (2) franchises in smaller cities tend to be mobile or to disappear more frequently than those situated in large cities; and (3) generally there is little evidence to support the commonly held assumption that the present structural rules balance playing strengths among teams, but rather that the imbalance is due to differential attraction potentials of franchises. For example, in the early 1920s the St. Louis Cardinals were successful in baseball, in the 1960s the Green Bay Packers were successful in professional football, and currently the Winnipeg Jets are successful in professional hockey.

Although most of the analytical studies have focused on explaining the profit-maximization process of professional sport, an analysis of the process of wage determination has been relatively neglected. Rottenberg's (1956) analysis assumed that baseball clubs will only pay players according to the income expected to be derived from gate receipts. Thus extra sources of income are ignored, unlike in the Victorian Football League in Australia, in which extra income is directed to ensuring that a club fields the best possible team (Dabscheck, 1975). Another unique feature of this Australian league is that players' wages are a function of seniority (i.e., number of games played) rather than skill differences. All players are theoretically treated equally no matter what club they play for; therefore, the wealthier clubs cannot buy up all the best talent. However, in reality this rule is not enforced and special payments and allowances are made at the discretion of the club so that star players can earn between $15,000 and $20,000 per year (Dabscheck, 1975). This practice of rewarding players has resulted from the clubs' desire to recruit players to win as many games as possible (utility-maximization) rather than maintaining equitable competition (profit-maximization) for the benefit of joint profits by members of the cartel.

In order to understand the wage determination process, there is a need to consider the factors that affect the supply and demand for athletes. First, there is the tendency for firms to operate as utility maximizers rather than as profit maximizers; thus, they are willing to pay higher salaries to better players to retain the better players and to use income as an incentive to win.

Second, the players use an "orbit of coercive comparison"—they demand higher salaries when they see other players' demands being met. As Ross (1956) noted, "comparisons are important to the worker . . . it is an affront to his dignity and a threat to his prestige when he receives less than another worker with whom he can legitimately be compared."

Third, Dabscheck (1975) suggests that owners will use the wages fund (i.e., the total payments that an owner can pay to the labor force) of the firm to pay each player his supply price (i.e., the minimum wage necessary to induce a player to play to the best of his ability) so as to maximize the efficiency of the team's playing personnel for a given wage fund. Further, the internal wage structure of the firm is established to maximize winning and minimize dissatisfaction among the players because of the orbit of coercive comparison. Because of this practice, a skilled player on a financially weak team may earn less than a less skilled player on a wealthier team.

A fourth factor in the wage determination process, at least in the past, was the bargaining skill demonstrated by a player. Today, however, agents trained in contract law do much of the negotiation for athletes in North America; hence the athlete has a more knowledgeable and equal representation in the negotiation process with the owner or his representative.

A final factor influencing the process is the method of payment, which can be based either on results demonstrated during the previous year or on a guaranteed income for an established number of years. While owners would prefer the former system, most players prefer a guaranteed income, especially late in their career when skills may depreciate. In short, based on his analysis of professional football in Australia, Dabscheck (1975) concluded that the utility-maximization model reflects the domination by a few teams in most sports and is most relevant for analyzing the wage determination process in sport.

Another approach to examining the wage determination process is based on a labor relations model of the sport market. This model is based on the demand for players, as determined by the number of teams and roster size permitted; the number of players that can be supplied from the labor pool in three categories of workers (stars, journeymen, marginals); and the player's own reservation price of minimum acceptable salary. This reservation price is influenced by the player's potential earning in another occupation, by the presence of a reserve system, which reduces competition for his or her services, and by the degree to which the player will sacrifice a higher income for the psychic gratification or prestige acquired throughout the sport career. Scoville (1974) states that in a competitive player market the salaries of journeymen and marginals equals the reservation price of the most recent player in that category to enter the specific sport. However, since the supply of stars is inelastic, peer salary in all likelihood will exceed a star's reservation price but would still equal the value of the last star added to a team.

In order to determine the economic loss to players due to the restrictions of the reserve clause, Scully (1974b) developed and tested a model of marginal revenue product for professional baseball. Although he found that salaries are related to performance, he concluded that the economic loss to professional ballplayers because of the reserve clause was considerable. More specifically, he indicated that an average player would receive a salary equal to about 20 percent of their net marginal revenue product while a star would receive only about 15 percent if the reserve clause were present.

In an attempt to provide another mathematical model of salary determination, Scoville (1974) notes that league rules assist the team in placing the salary of each player close to his or her reservation price. However, the extent to which a team succeeds in this plan depends on the bargaining experience of the players and the team representative and differs significantly among the three classes of players.

A final area of theoretical interest has been the impact of franchise movements from one city to another. Quirk (1973) suggests that although many franchises have been shifted within professional sport, this practice has only a temporary effect on compensating for imbalanced competition and economic losses, and in the long run may actually increase the imbalance. Rather, he argues that the basic problem is the tendency for the largest cities to dominate the sport. If a franchise moves to a market with a greater revenue potential, the result may be more evenly balanced playing strengths, hence an increase in spectator interest and ultimately total league revenues, but only in the short term. Based on an analysis of franchise moves in professional baseball between 1946 and 1972, Quirk (1973) concluded that franchise moves have not led to more evenly balanced revenue potential in the league, that the assignment of local television revenues to the home team has been an important element in approximately one half of the moves, and that, in the long run, the franchises have not been highly viable in the new location.

7.1.4 The Economics of International Sport

Although amateur sport at the international level is ostensibly organized for the competitor, the evidence increasingly suggests that it is an integral part of the marketplace and is not much different in economic structure than professional sport. This section briefly outlines the economic basis of the Olympic Games and one major international "professional" event—the Canada Cup hockey series of 1976.

The Canada Cup was an invitational hockey tournament comprised of the six teams with the best players in the world. Each team was guaranteed a minimum of $45,000, while the winning team would receive $150,000. The gross revenue from the round-robin series was between $7 and $10 million, with a minimum profit after expenses of $2 million. The gate receipts accounted for about $100,000 of the revenue, with the majority coming from the sale of television rights ($5 million), advertising, and commercial products that featured the Canada Cup symbol (T-shirts, etc.). Companies wishing to advertise their products during the television coverage paid $23,000 per commercial minute. In light of this evidence, we can certainly say that international sport events are economically equivalent to professional sport.

Turning to a description of what Auf der Maur (1976) called "the billion-dollar game," it can be seen that the Olympic Games have ceased to be a religious festival and have truly become big business (Table 7.5). One justification for this investment is that the host city will gain an excellent sport facility, will benefit from urban and regional development, and will gain additional housing (the Olympic Village). Unfortunately, in Mexico City, Munich, and most recently Montreal, the Olympic Village apartments have never been fully occupied and the sport facilities are so expensive to operate on a daily basis that only a few events can be held there. In short, as Cicarelli and Kowarsky (1973) conclude, in economic terms, the benefit/cost ratio is less than one.

To illustrate further, in 1970, despite a debt of $12.3 million to the Canadian federal government for assistance with Expo 67 (the World Fair), the city of Montreal won the right to host the 1976 Summer Olympic Games. Although it

Table 7.5
Estimated costs for hosting the Summer[1] Olympic Games

Games	Estimated cost, in millions of dollars
1932: Los Angeles	6
1936: Berlin	6
1948: London [2,3]	2
1952: Helsinki	7
1956: Melbourne	15
1960: Rome	32
1964: Tokyo	70
1968: Mexico City	160
1972: Munich	200
1976: Montreal	750–1000 (i.e., nearly one billion)

[1] The Winter Olympic Games have also been characterized by rising costs, although to a lesser magnitude (e.g., 1960, $14 million; 1964, $25 million; 1968, $85 million).

[2] The cost was low because priorities in Great Britain were directed toward reconstruction following the destruction caused by World War II.

[3] This is the only series of Summer Olympic Games to realize a profit.

had been predicted in 1968 that the cost would range from $10 to $15 million, in 1973 a revised but balanced budget of $310 million was struck, accompanied by a statement from the mayor of Montreal that "the 1976 Olympics can no more have a deficit than a man can have a baby." This budget was based on expenses that included $250 million for the facilities, not including the Olympic Village, which was to be constructed by a private developer, and $32.5 million in operating expenses. The balanced revenue was to be derived from the sale of Olympic coins, stamps, rights to the Olympic symbol, television rights, gate receipts, and a national lottery. By May 1976 the revenue included $5 million from the sale of stamps, $100 million from the sale of coins, $170 million from the sale of lottery tickets, $20.4 million from the sale of tickets, $34.4 million from the sale of television rights, and $30 million from endorsement rights, for a total of $359.8 million in revenue two months before the Games opened.

On the other side of the ledger, however, estimated[14] expenses through inflation, labor problems, corruption, and mismanagement had risen to $1.4 billion, with the best final estimate of revenue being approximately $400 million, leaving a deficit of somewhere between $0.5 to $1 million, depending on which financial statement is believed. In more dramatic terms, it has been estimated that the Games cost each Montreal taxpayer $726. By comparison, Auf der Maur (1976) reports that the St. Lawrence Seaway was completed in 1959 at a cost of $470 million, or $1.23 billion in 1975 dollars, and that the 2200-mile Trans-

Canada gas pipeline would cost $970 million in 1975. Moreover, he noted that a billion-dollar investment in the city of Montreal in 1976 would have provided either low-rental housing for 120,000 citizens, free public transportation for ten years, or 400 community arenas.

Although these figures are only estimates, they do reflect the inflationary and escalating cost of producing international sport events. Among the reasons cited for this financial investment are the facts that it enhances the prestige of the city and country, it promotes personal prestige or political gain by the organizers, and it brings revenue into the city and country.

In addition to the operating costs for the host city and country, the cost of winning an Olympic medal has escalated since the athlete must train year-round in order to be competitive. To illustrate, national coaches and executives are paid annual salaries, while athletes are compensated through bursaries, scholarships, jobs, or per diems for salary lost, living expenses, training costs, and travel. However, depending on the athlete, the sport, and the country, the percentage of expenses recovered by the athlete or his or her family varies widely. For example, one speed skater in North America (who didn't win a medal in 1976) estimated that training expenses for his family were $20,000 over a 20-year period. In some cases athletes cannot afford the time to work full- or part-time during an Olympic year and must be subsidized by the family or by some outside organization. In summary, like professional sport, international competition has become a big business that may have to adhere to the economics and business practices of any other enterprise if it is to remain viable.

7.1.5 Sport and Gambling

Gambling on sport events is a universal, democratized form of leisure behavior pursued by both sexes and by members of all social classes, ethnic groups, nationalities, and ages. While some of this action is legal, such as betting at race-tracks or off-track shops in North America or at betting offices for football (i.e., soccer) pools in Great Britain, much of it is illegal and is on the fringe of a highly secretive subculture. A number of social scientists (Bloch, 1951; Herman, 1967b, 1976; Morin, 1976; Scott, 1968; Suits and Kallick, 1976) and journalists (Cady, 1975; Merchant, 1973; Underwood, 1963) have sought to describe and analyze the system by which this phenomenon operates, to identify motives or explanations for this behavior, and to discuss some of the concomitant problems such as gambling by athletes, the "fixing" of games, and the role of organized crime in the sport system. To date, most of this work has been concerned with the legal world of horse racing, and thus the extent to which it can be generalized to specific sports remains tenuous.

In short, it is not really known what percentage or segment of the population is involved, how much money is wagered legally or illegally, how many people are compulsive or casual gamblers, where the profits end up, or what effect legalization would have on the individual (would it increase or decrease his or her involvement?) or on the economic basis of the sport system.

Some tentative trends, which may answer some of these questions, have been identified from a recent national probability study of gambling in the United States (Suits and Kallick, 1976). They found that 61 percent of the sample, or 88 million adults over 18 years of age, gambled during 1974. While much of this gambling was between friends, 48 percent, or about 70 million adults, engaged in commercialized gambling. It was estimated that $22.4 billion was wagered in 1974, with $17.3 billion being legal (e.g., at racetracks, legal off-track betting parlors, casino games, bingo games, lotteries) and $5.1 being illegal (e.g., sports books, horse books, numbers, sports cards). This total represents about 2 percent of the 1974 United States personal income. The study found that gambling was more prevalent among males, whites, the young, the better educated, the higher income groups, those who live in the suburbs, Catholics, those who live in the Northeast (off-track betting is legal in New York), and among people of Eastern European and Italian descent.

With the increase in direct and indirect sport consumption, gambling has also increased since the placing of a wager heightens personal involvement and interest by providing additional vicarious excitement. That gambling is a major leisure activity for a significant percentage of the population in Great Britain is clearly demonstrated by the estimated $100 million annual turnover by just *one* of the largest bookmaking firms in England (see Herman, 1967a). Similarly, in the United States, Cady (1975) reported that an estimated $50 billion per year is bet with illegal bookmakers on team sports. More specifically, Merchant (1973) estimated that $15 million is bet on professional football games each week, and indicates that at least one bookmaker reported handling $7.3 million in sport bets during one year, realizing a tax-free profit of $55,000 after expenses and bad debts.

Although several sociological interpretations of gambling as a form of leisure behavior have been suggested, generally they can be subsumed under four inter-related motives: a reaction to deprivation, a need to manage tension, a need to make decisions (Knox and Inkster, 1968), and a technique for demonstrating a culturally induced interest and knowledge in sport. Faced with a perceived restrictive and deprived social environment, individuals gamble to escape from the boredom of a routine life, to relieve societally induced tensions, to strive for social mobility by winning money, and to indicate to themselves and others that they can regulate and control their destiny (Bloch, 1951; Devereux, 1949; Herman, 1967b, 1976; Scott, 1968). The latter explanation suggests that skill and control can be attained by engaging in a decision-making process in which money only verifies the involvement of the individual in the action. In fact, if winning money were the only objective, there are other more certain and efficient ways of acquiring wealth.

Herman (1967b) further suggests that involvement in gambling is a substitute for a decision-making void in the life style of lower- and middle-class men. For lower-class women, who tend to make "show" bets, gambling is hypothesized to be related to their need to experience frequent symbolic rewards in an otherwise deprived and unrewarding life style. For the upper classes who suffer few deprivations, large amounts of money are gambled, perhaps to display "conspicuous consumption" in order to establish signs of esteem and power. Moreover, because they are more concerned with social interaction, they play the "favorites" since they don't have time to study and engage in a rational decision-making process.

In summary, not much is really known about sport gambling, other than that it is engaged in by a large number of people. Moreover, while illegal, there is less likely to be a criminal link than is commonly assumed. For example, Cady (1975) concluded that bookies are not hoods who assault clients if they don't "pay up," that bookies don't have to fix games since they realize a profit by making a commission (i.e., vigorish in the argot) on each bet, that few police officers are bribed even though many of the federal gambling laws are not enforced, that there are many amateur bookies in offices, bars, schools, and colleges who organize pools to realize a profit, and that, because of gambling, attendance at sport events increases since the fans want to be "where the action is" in order to try to influence their bets.

7.2 SPORT AND LEGAL SYSTEMS

7.2.1 Introduction

With increasing rationalization and professionalization, sport has become more dependent on the basic institutions of law and economics, both for its continued existence and for social control. This section considers the legal process as an increasingly salient facet of contemporary sport (Appenzeller, 1975; Joyal-Poupart, 1975; Sobel, 1977), especially at the professional and international levels.

First, it is not surprising that those trained in law are being selected for positions in sport as commissioners or presidents, player representatives, arbitrators, executive directors or negotiators for player associations, and organizers of international sport events. Furthermore, to meet this need for a stronger relationship between law and sport, a number of law schools in North America either offer a course on law and sport, or include cases involving sport in specific components of the curriculum such as contract, civil, tax, corporate, or criminal law. To illustrate, in recent years litigation has been initiated to promote equitable competition, maximize tax gains, eliminate discrimination against minority groups, negotiate player contracts, arbitrate and resolve labor disputes, gain individual rights guaranteed by civil law, control the amount and level of violence in professional sport, and adjudicate slander suits (for example, *G. Atkinson* vs. *the NFL and C. Noll*).

7.2.2 Sport and Litigation

Most litigation in professional sport has occurred as a result of an interaction between the desire of the owners to maintain equitable levels of competition by means of the reserve clause, the option clause, and the player draft, and the desire of the athletes to maximize their individual earnings by placing themselves in a free market in which they can rent services to the highest bidder. The reserve clause in a player's contract binds the player to that club for life and prevents other firms, usually those that are the wealthiest, from negotiating for their services.

In recent years the reserve clause has become less restrictive because an "option" clause was introduced into the contract in some sports. This arrangement meant that a team had the exclusive right to retain a player's services, without his consent, for one year after the original contract expired. During this one-year period, the player's salary could be reduced to 90 percent of what it was under the contract, and the club could attempt to negotiate a new contract, trade the player, or ignore him. If a new contract was not signed by the end of the option year, the player was considered a free agent who could negotiate with other teams. However, this was not always successful because of the indemnity rule (i.e., the Rozelle rule in football) whereby the firm that signed the free agent had to compensate the former team for their loss. For example, a recent agreement in football requires the team signing a free agent to compensate the player's former team with draft choices based on the player's salary.

The drafting system gave the league the right to decide which team would hire specific players. That is, players were not free to test their true market value at the beginning of their professional career. Furthermore, however dissatisfied a player might be with the club that originally drafted him, until recently he could not offer his services to another team. Now, however, depending on the sport, a player has considerably more freedom, both initially and later in his career.

In order to gain freedom from this serflike contractual arrangement, a number of players challenged the Sherman Antitrust Act of 1890 and the Clayton Act of 1910 in the United States and the Combines Investigation Act of 1966 in Canada. Basically these acts are aimed at preserving free competition in business so that monopolies, and the resultant high prices and low quality of goods, are declared illegal. Recently, players have taken civil action[15] in all four major sports, arguing that the universal draft and the reserve clause violate antitrust laws. In defense, the owners argue that sport is a unique business or a service that needs monopolistic practices in order to provide the best product. This product can only be realized within a system of equitable competition, and thus these contractual arrangements are essential to prevent the wealthy teams from acquiring all the best talent.

While basketball, football, and hockey have been found to have violated the antitrust laws, baseball has repeatedly been declared exempt in a number of cases that went to court. In 1975, however, the courts ruled that a baseball player could become a free agent after the option year. In short, through civil litigation and the process of collective bargaining (Fraser, 1975), players now have considerably more freedom, both initially and later in their career.[16] In addition, professional sport is now regarded as a major profit-maximizing industry and is no longer considered a unique, struggling enterprise that needs the assistance of specific laws or interpretations in order to survive. The result will likely mean higher salaries for the superstars, slight increases for some journeymen, and decreases for the marginal players.

Other areas of dispute in sport have been concerned with civil rights. For example, many young girls and women have had to resort to civil suits in order to participate in male sport organizations or sport contests. The incidence of these cases will decrease in the future, however, because of the initiation in 1972 of Title IX of the Education Amendments in the United States.

Other cases have involved parents in amateur sport seeking the right for their child to play for the team of their choice rather than a team to which they have been arbitrarily assigned. At the other extreme, some parents in Canada have created legal guardians in another community for their young sons or daughters in order to allow them to play or swim for a more prestigious or successful minor hockey team or swim club. To counteract this practice, minor-sport organizations have instituted civil action.

Perhaps the most serious form of litigation has been the increasing need to resort to the criminal code to charge spectators and athletes who engage in violent acts within the sport milieu. For many years, sport leagues argued that they should be responsible for policing and enforcing their own business since professional sport was beyond the legal and moral jurisdiction of the criminal code. However, legal authorities have found it increasingly necessary to lay formal charges against spectators because of assaults on players, officials, or other spectators. This has occurred in many countries prior to, during, and after soccer matches, and in North America it has most frequently occurred at baseball, football, and hockey games at both the professional and youth sport level. In fact, some of the most bizarre cases have involved parents, coaches, players, or referees at highly organized children's sport events.[17]

In order to introduce some element of social control to sport, crown attorneys or public prosecutors are also increasingly intervening to indict professional or amateur athletes on charges of aggravated assault with a dangerous weapon. While none of the professional athletes has yet been convicted, similar cases involving amateur athletes have resulted in fines or modest jail sentences.

The social significance of this legal intervention has not been studied, although the long-range impact of this action may result in significant social change, both in the attitudes and behavior of the players and in the expectations concerning the role of violence in sport by the media, the public, and the owners. In hockey, the first court case was the Maki–Green trial in Ottawa in 1970. The defendent (Maki) was cleared of a charge of assault causing bodily harm on the grounds of self-defense against a player (Green) who had struck him and who was known by reputation (Faulkner, 1974) to be very aggressive. In his closing remarks the judge implied that a defense of consenting adults would have failed and that, in the future, no sport league should render the players in that league immune from criminal prosecution.

Similarly, in the United States, criminal proceedings were initiated in July 1975 in the *State* (Minnesota) vs. *Forbes*[18] trial. This case raised the issue of whether participation in professional sport exempts players from criminal sanctions (Binder, 1975; Kuhlman, 1975). Since the trial resulted in a hung jury and dismissal of the charge, the question remains unanswered. Other major sports viewed the proceedings with interest, however, because of such practices as spearing in football and the beanball and spike-high slide in baseball.

While there are four possible defenses that might be used in these cases (implied consent, self-defense, provocation, and mutual combat), the judge in the Forbes case instructed the jury that "no one could consent to an assault either explicitly or implicitly" (*Minneapolis Tribune,* 19 July 1975). That is, there seems to be a limit on the degree of danger to which one is expected to consent. Nevertheless, as Binder (1975) indicates, the consent defense is not sufficiently clear concerning sport cases and as a result will not assist in protecting participants or in eliminating violent practices. Rather, there must be more severe internal sanctions (e.g., suspensions) within the league rules, or the law will not pursue the laissez-faire policy that professional sport desires. To date, the cases brought to trial have not clearly established guidelines as to when the law should or will intervene (Binder, 1975).

Another approach, yet to occur, is that legal action may be taken against coaches, owners, or the league for encouraging and rewarding violent behavior. That is, conspiracy statutes might be utilized to establish criminal responsibility (Kuhlman, 1975). While the above cases have been initiated by representatives of the law, future suits may be originated by a player who is attacked by another player in a manner beyond the spirit or letter of the rules. For example, the Marichal–Roseboro bat-swinging incident in 1965 was settled out of court, but more recently a former NFL player has brought suit against an opposing player who ended his career because of a spinal fracture caused by the excessive use of forearm and fist.

Since criminal law in sport is such a new area, precedents are few and prosecutors are still somewhat reluctant to prosecute. As a result, athletes have remained relatively immune from criminal prosecution for acts committed during their work (for example, Marichal's attack on Roseboro). Kuhlman (1975) suggests that there are four possible explanations for this immunity. First, there may be differential enforcement because of the normative structure of the subgroup. For example, fighting is a common occurrence or norm among professional hockey players (Faulkner, 1974). Thus, the defense of consent may be seen as a deterrent to legal action. A second explanation is that the victim and the offender will compete against each other in the future and a trial may only increase the hostility of the parties involved and their teammates, especially if they view the action as superceding in-house prosecution (i.e., fines and/or suspensions, which are quickly forgotten). A third explanation for failing to prosecute is that a conviction may not really serve as a deterrent. A fourth reason is that there has been a tacit agreement that informally delegates legal authority to the league.

Kulhman (1975) further suggests (1) that league officials know the risks assumed by the players and can discern what conduct is deemed unreasonable; (2) that because of the diversity of geographical location, there may be differential treatment in each jurisdiction, thereby undermining the economic and moral solidarity of the league[19]; (3) that outside interference would hurt the league financially; and (4) that only the league can adequately police its own employees. The latter point is the key to the degree of future intervention by the legal system. If sport leagues will not impose severe sanctions and alter the normative requirements of their employees concerning violence or utilize commonly accepted contractual procedures, then criminal and civil action is likely to increase in an effort to bring order to the sport world.

7.3 SPORT AND POLITICAL SYSTEMS

The relationship between sport and politics is one of the oldest and most pervading examples of institutional interaction. From a historical perspective, the governments of the city-states in ancient Greece used sport to enhance the fitness of their citizens for war and to demonstrate the superiority of one state over another through athletic competition. In fact, large incentives were provided for athletes to be successful and thereby bring prestige to their city. During the Roman era, sport was used for military fitness and, in the later years, sportlike events were part of the circuses used to control the masses. Although sport was less important in subsequent societies, by the late eighteenth and early nineteenth centuries the growth of nationalism again revived the importance of sport and games for national fitness and national integration. Although the Olympic Games were ostensibly revived in 1896 to provide a stimulus to improve the fitness level of French children, they soon became a vicarious mechanism of cold-war combat, culminating in the present situation in which sport and politics are inexorably intertwined, often to demonstrate political gains over another nation.

While little empirical or theoretical work has been completed pertaining to sport and politics, there have been a number of descriptive historical, philosophical, sociological, or journalistic analyses that have sought to refute the belief that sport is an apolitical institution. For example, analyses have been completed in England (McIntosh, 1963; Goodhart and Chataway, 1968; Natan, 1969), France (Meynaud, 1966; Bouet, 1968), the Soviet Union (Morton, 1963; Riordan, 1974, 1977), Germany (Mandell, 1971), Canada (McKelvey, 1972; Pooley and Webster, 1972), New Zealand (Thompson, 1969, 1975), South Africa (Draper, 1963), and Rhodesia (Cheffers, 1972). More detailed reviews concerning the international scene have been presented by Goodhart and Chataway (1968), Petrie (1975), and Douglas (1975).

Although the examples cited by these authors vary, the themes tend to be similar and include the increasing nationalism in sport, the use of sport as political propaganda for national or foreign policy, the use of sport to encourage national integration or unity, the use of sport to foster or sustain existing social conflict, and the increasing politicization of the decision-making process in sport at all levels.

These themes are most prevalent at the international level because (1) there are competing political ideologies on both the societal level and in the sport milieu; (2) there is involvement by national governments in the organization and control of sport; (3) athletes are used by the state to symbolically represent national strength; (4) sport is thought to be a visible medium for communicating national policies and ideological beliefs to the masses; and (5) sport is a visible and effective means of expressing opposition (through defections or boycotts) to the political or racial policies of one's own or other national governments. Thus, the descriptive accounts suggest that sport is definitely not apolitical, nor is politics free of sport. As a result, it is naive to place much credence in the following statement by Avery Brundage, former president of the International Olympic Committee, after six nations withdrew from the 1956 Olympic Games:

> By their decision these countries show that they are unaware of one of our most important principles, namely, that sport is completely free of politics. (Natan, 1969, p. 204)

Most of the analyses adhere to either a functionalist or a conflict perspective. From the functionalist view, sport is used to promote common values believed to be essential to the integration of a society. Furthermore, it is argued that all groups strive to maintain the social order and that sport can facilitate this process. On the other hand, the conflict perspective is based on the premise that the domination of particular groups, either within a country or between countries, rests on control of economic and political resources. Conflict, then, is generated among groups in order to gain control of these resources so that they will have power in the decision-making process. In the absence of declaring outright war, sport is vicariously used to demonstrate superiority over opposing groups. Denial of opportunities for sport competition can also be used to impose sanctions on groups (for example, in South Africa) with which a particular nation is in conflict.

Although it is beyond the scope of this section to document or describe the many incidents within sport that have had political overtones (see Goodhart and Chataway, 1968; Petrie, 1975), the following suggests that the relationship between sport and politics involves a two-way interaction process that includes two dimensions: sport in politics and the politics of sport. Since no definitive explanations have been advanced to account for the increasing political intervention in organized sport, the following is a list of hypothesized reasons: (1) to enhance international prestige through athletes who win medals or championships and thereby symbolically represent national strength, (2) to use sport successes as propaganda for both the masses within the country and for external visibility via the mass media, (3) to improve the growth and structure of sport in a community or nation, (4) to provide social control for certain sports (e.g., boxing, violence in hockey), (5) to impose sanctions on other nations because of national policies (for example, apartheid in South Africa), (6) to facilitate military training, (7) to provide exposure and an image of the "common man" for incumbents or those seeking office (politicians in North America always appear at major sport events where they either are spectators or have some formal function in the opening or closing ceremonies), (8) to mold national unity or a political consciousness, (9) to express the views of minority groups (for example, the Black Power salute at the 1968 Olympic Games in Mexico City), (10) to attempt to democratize sport at the grass-roots level by eliminating ethnic, economic, and racial barriers to involvement in sport, or (11) to facilitate social differentiation in sport (e.g., apartheid in South Africa).

For many political factions there is a two-way interaction at the municipal, state, national, or international level. The higher the level of government, the more likely the interaction is one-way, with politics having more influence on sport. For example, international disputes between governments or political ideologies carried into the sport milieu have included the 1936 Nazi Olympics, which were hosted by Hitler to demonstrate the superiority of the German race; the opposition of the United States to the entry of a USSR team into the 1952 Summer Olympic Games; the Suez invasion and the Hungarian Revolution in 1956, which led many nations to withdraw their teams in protest; the occurrence of the blood bath between the USSR and Hungary in a water-polo match; the student riots in Tokyo in 1964; the black athlete protest in Mexico City in 1968; the assassination of the Israeli athletes by the Arabs in the Olympic Village at Munich in 1972; and the boycott by black African nations and the banning of Taiwan from the 1976 Olympic Games at Montreal. It is not surprising that the Summer Olympics have been used for political purposes to a much greater extent than the Winter Olympics since they have generally been accorded much greater prestige and include many more participating nations.

In addition to political differences expressed through international sport, there are also political actions within the social structure of sport organizations. That is, sport organizations are no different than any other organization in which internal politics plays a role in policy making, recruitment of new members, succession to executive roles, and evaluation of performances. Again, much of the discussion concerning the politics within sport is based on anecdotal information. However, studies by Ball (1973) and Kiviaho (1975) have provided some empirical evidence. For example, a perennial complaint in such sports as diving, figure skating, and gymnastics is that there is a politically based bias on the part of judges in international events in which the outcome is dependent on subjective, evaluative decisions. Ball (1973) examined the results of four events at the World Figure Skating Championships between 1967 and 1971 to determine whether there was a relationship between the judges' nationality and their scoring practices. He found a high degree of agreement between judges, but no relationship between nationality and the score given by each judge. The only consistent bias was a tendency for judges to rank contestants from their own nation somewhat higher than the average awarded by other judges. Yet, despite these findings, claims and counterclaims have been made by gymnastic officials and figure skaters at recent Olympic Games. It would appear that more work is needed in this area to resolve whether sports with subjective evaluations are susceptible to political biases.

In an analysis of sport organizations in Finland, Kiviaho (1975) found that support of the various sport federations varies regionally. A closer examination, however, based on the assumption that political factors are essential in sport organization policy, found that political cleavages in a region are essential factors in accounting for the distribution of support for the region's sport organizations. That is, the membership in the major sporting organizations in Finland appears to be based more on political party preference than on sport interests.

A common conception in the sport milieu has been that athletes and coaches are basically conservative and apolitical. As a result, studies of the political attitudes and behavior of athletes and coaches have been initiated. Much of this work originated in the United States during the period of student unrest in the late 1960s (Norton, 1971; Petrie, 1973, 1975; Rehberg and Cohen, 1976; Sage, 1974). Generally these studies suggest that although there was a concomitant rise in political and social awareness among some athletes during this period of unrest, it was generally hypothesized and subsequently confirmed (Norton, 1971; Rehberg and Cohen, 1976; Sage, 1974) that those involved in sport are more conservative than nonathletes in a variety of domains. At the present time, this is not a major area of interest within the sociology of sport, since there is little theoretical basis to suggest why athletes should be different from nonathletes in their political attitudes or behavior.

To summarize, there appears to be a reciprocal relationship between politics and sport, which, although not well understood at this point in time, has been illustrated in numerous descriptive articles. This is one area within the sociology of sport where comparative, empirical, and theoretical efforts might better assist in explaining the relationship between specific patterns and processes in the two social institutions. Moreover, there is a need to examine further the pattern by which federal governments have sought power within sport in order to achieve their goals. Specifically, many governments have moved from the role of sport supporter to that of sport controller. For example, in most nations of the world there are now central government agencies responsible for funding, organizing, and controlling sport at both the mass and elite levels.

NOTES

1. Historically the military has been linked with sport from earliest times when physical education, games, and sport were utilized for a variety of purposes: to prepare citizens or military personnel for war, to develop esprit de corps (e.g., the Army–Navy football game), to develop character and skills (e.g., strategy) necessary for military service, and to promote the goals of the state through sport. For example, in the Eastern European nations the military often serves as a place of employment for elite athletes, who are given release time while competing for the state. This illustrates the increasing mix of political and military strategy (Goodhart and Chataway, 1968), wherein victories in sport symbolize the functional equivalence of a victory by one country over another (e.g., the "unofficial" point standings at the Olympic Games).

2. The military has been instrumental in the diffusion of sport throughout the world since off-duty military personnel have participated in sports native to their own country, and thereby directly or indirectly introduced them in the host society (Lindsay, 1970). Further, whereas the Greeks stopped wars to participate in athletic competitions, more recent history reveals that sport has continued uninterrupted during periods of war and has, in some periods, gained greater popularity because of

the war effort (Betts, 1971; Lewis, 1973; Schleppi, 1972). For example, Lewis (1973) attributes the emergence of interest in sport by the masses in North America in the early twentieth century to the inclusion of sport in the military life for thousands of young men, and by the required sport programs that were initiated in educational institutions because of the need to be physically fit for involvement in World Wars I and II.

3. This relationship between sport and war has been examined by Sipes (1973). He studied 20 societies classified as "warlike" or "not warlike" and found a significant correlation between warlike tendencies and the presence of combative sports.

4. See Durso et al. (1975) for a description of the "business" of recruiting college athletes, including the pressures on high school athletes and abuses of the NCAA rules. He concludes that college athletics are commercial enterprises that are only vaguely related to the educational process in institutions of higher learning.

5. In addition to the revenue derived by the university, local retail businesses, such as clothing and souvenir stores, restaurants, bars, hotels, and gasoline stations, reap expanded business profits during football weekends, especially in those communities in which "big-time" football is played. Moreover, these private enterprises place subtle pressure on the university to increase its success on the playing field, often through alumni donations and special courtesies to visiting recruits, parents of players, and distinguished alumni.

6. For example, the New York Mets were relatively unsuccessful on the field when they entered the league, yet were successful in drawing spectators to the games. On the other hand, while successful on the ice, the Boston Bruins had difficulty in 1976–1977 attracting spectators who were protesting against the failure of the team owners to re-sign Bobby Orr to a contract.

7. Boe (1975), owner of the New York Nets, reported that in five years the expenses to operate the Nets increased from $650,000 to $2.5 million per annum. Over this same period player salaries increased from $200,000 to $1.1 million.

8. There were exceptions, however. Scully (1974c) has noted that Babe Ruth's salary at the peak of his career would be valued at $316,699 per annum in the equivalent value of 1973 dollars.

9. A bonus is offered to a player in relation to the perceived net return that player will generate for the club. A player expects a bonus in order to cover the risk he is taking in trying a career in professional sport and the amount is related to the expected earnings foregone. Thus, the opportunity to gain exclusive right to a player, along with the right to drop a player if he is unsuccessful, enables the bonus system to operate. Moreover, owners often offer a large bonus instead of a large salary in the first year, since league rules regulate the percentage by which a player's salary may be cut in succeeding years (Ross, 1975).

10. For example, a report prior to the Montreal Olympics estimated that because of the multiplier effect, the Games would result in $2.2 billion being added to the Canadian economy. This would result from rising employment and the subsequent income and sales tax revenue and from increased tourism, through which foreign money is exchanged into Canadian funds and spent on accommodation, transportation, food, entertainment, clothing, souvenirs, etc. Similarly, a report cited by Block (1977) indicated that the Pittsburgh Pirates were directly or indirectly responsible for $21 million being added to the city economy in 1976. To illustrate, 16 percent of the attendees spent an average of $4 each at some establishment en route to the game, while 28 percent spent an average of $5.77 each after the game.

11. One unique feature of the economic structure of football (i.e., soccer) in Great Britain is that there is a system of promotion and demotion between divisions

depending on the playing success of a team. This mobility has obvious economic correlates that encourage member clubs of the Football Association to strive to maintain or improve performance. Another unique feature is that it is an open system: Non-member clubs can apply and, if admitted, an existing member of the fourth division is dropped.

12. A mathematical version is derived in an appendix to the paper by Quirk and El Hodiri (1974).

13. An interesting paradox is that sometimes a loser generates greater fan interest (e.g., the New York Mets during their first years in the league). For example, Sloane (1971) noted that occasionally there is greater attendance when two lower-level teams meet to decide who will be demoted to a lower division in the English Football League.

14. It must be emphasized that these statistics are estimates since it is unlikely that the real costs and revenues will ever be known or publicly stated. For a journalistic critique of the 1976 Montreal Games and the gross overexpenditure of public funds, see Auf der Maur (1976).

15. Basically, there are two issues in the controversy. First there is a value issue as to whether procedures should exist in sport and not in other domains, and second, there is the question as to whether they really serve the function they are purported to serve, namely, ensuring equity of competition. In fact, equality of competition may be independent of each of the three procedures (draft, reserve system, free agent) acting alone, probably because the practice of selling or trading draft choices or players is permitted.

16. In baseball a player has some initial freedom in that if he has not signed a contract within one year of being drafted he is placed back in the pool and can be drafted by the same team or another team, depending on who selects first. However, the player cannot negotiate with more than one team at a given point in time. Similarly, a recent agreement (March 1977) in professional football introduced a modified draft whereby a player is eligible to be drafted the following year if he doesn't sign with the team that originally drafted him. Moreover, if he refuses to sign after two years, he becomes a free agent. There is also an intraleague draft in hockey and baseball at the end of each season whereby each team "protects" (i.e., retains the rights to) a certain number of players on their payroll. The unprotected players may then be drafted by other teams in the league.

17. For example, two mothers supporting opposing teams trade punches, fathers attack hockey or football referees during or after the game, a fifteen-year-old hockey player is charged with manslaughter in the death of an opponent outside the arena after the game.

18. Dave Forbes was indicted for aggravated assault with a dangerous weapon on Henry Boucha who needed 25 sutures to close a stick-inflicted cut next to his eye. Boucha subsequently underwent surgery because of continuing double vision thought to be caused by a small fracture of the right eye socket.

19. This was the reaction in 1976 when four NHL players were charged in Toronto with assault. Teammates claimed their action was no worse than similar acts performed in other cities in the league.

REFERENCES

Appenzeller, H. (1975). *Athletics and the Law*. Charlottesville, Virginia: Michie.

Auf der Maur, M. (1976). *The Billion-Dollar Game: Jean Drapeau and the 1976 Olympics*. Toronto: James Lorimer.

Ball, D. W. (1973). "A politicized social psychology of sport: Some assumptions and evidence from international figure skating competition." *International Review of Sport Sociology* **8**: 63–71.

Bennett, B., M. Howell, and U. Simri (1975). *Comparative Physical Education and Sport*. Philadelphia: Lea and Febiger.

Betts, J. (1971). "Home front, battle field and sport during the Civil War." *Research Quarterly* **42** (May): 113–132.

Binder, R. (1975). "The consent defence: Sports, violence and the criminal law." *The American Criminal Law Review* **13**: 235–248.

Bloch, H. (1951). "The sociology of gambling." *American Journal of Sociology* **57**: 215–222.

Block, A. (1977). "So, you want to own a ball club." *Forbes* (April): 37–40.

Boe, R. (1975). "Basketball and hockey." In D. Hellerman and Company (eds.), *Sports Business and Finance*, pp. 14–23. New York: D. Hellerman.

Bouet, M. (1968). *Signification du Sport*. Paris: Editions Universitaires.

Burman, G. (ed.) (1974). *Proceedings of the Conference on the Economics of Professional Sport*. Washington, D.C.: The National Football League Players' Association.

Cady, S. (1975). "Gambling and sport." *The New York Times* (January 20–24).

Canes, N. (1974). "The social benefits of restrictions on team quality." In R. Noll (ed.), *Government and the Sports Business*, pp. 81–114. Washington, D.C.: The Brookings Institution.

Cheffers, J. (1972). *A Wilderness of Spite or Rhodesia Denied*. New York: Vintage Press.

Cicarelli, J., and D. Kowarsky (1973). "The economics of the Olympic Games." *Business and Economic Dimensions* **9**: 1–5.

Dabscheck, B. (1975). "The wage determination process for sportmen." *The Economic Record* **51** (March): 52–64.

Davenport, D. S. (1968). "Collusive competition in major league baseball: Its theory and institutional development." *American Economist* **13**: 6–30.

Dauriac, C. (1977). *L'économie du sport en France*. Paris: Centre d'Etude des Techniques Economiques Modernes.

Davis, L. (1974). "Self-regulation in baseball, 1909–1971." In R. Noll (ed.), *Government and the Sports Business*, pp. 349–386. Washington, D.C.: The Brookings Institution.

Davis, L., and J. Quirk (1975). "Tax writeoffs and the value of sports teams." In P. Ladany (ed.), *Management Science Applications to Leisure-Time Operations*, pp. 263–275. Amsterdam: North-Holland.

Daymont, T. (1975). "The effects of monopsonistic procedures on equality of competition in professional sport leagues." *International Review of Sport Sociology* **10**: 83–97.

Demmert, H. (1973). *The Economics of Professional Team Sports*. Lexington, Mass.: Lexington Books.

Demmert, H. (1974). "The relationship between labor market restrictions and product market restrictions in professional sport." In G. Burman (ed.), *Proceedings of the Conference on the Economics of Professional Sport*, pp. 5–8. Washington, D.C.: National Football League Players' Association.

Devereux, E. (1949). "Gambling and the social structure—a sociological study of lotteries and horse racing in contemporary America." Unpublished Ph.D. dissertation, Harvard University.

Douglas, S. (1975). "Uses of sport in domestic politics." Presented at the Fifth Popular Culture Association Meeting, St. Louis (March).

Draper, M. (1963). *Sport and Race in South Africa*. Johannesburg, South Africa: Johannesburg Institute of Race Relations.

Durso, J. (1971). *The All-American Dollar: The Big Business of Sports*. Boston: Houghton Mifflin.

Durso, J., et al. (1975). *The Sports Factory: An Investigation into College Sports*. New York: Quadrangle-New York Times Book Co.

El Hodiri, M., and J. Quirk (1971). "An economic model of a professional sports league." *Journal of Political Economy* 79 (November–December): 1302–1319.

Faulkner, R. R. (1974). "Making violence by doing work: Selves, situations, and the world of professional hockey." *Sociology of Work and Occupations* 1 (August): 288–304.

Fraser, E. (1975). "Labour relations in professional sport: Special reference to the National Hockey League." M.A. thesis, Department of Sociology, University of Waterloo, Waterloo, Ontario.

Goodhart, P., and C. Chataway (1968). *War Without Weapons*. London: W. H. Allen.

Hellerman, D., and Company (eds.) (1975). *Sports Business and Finance*. New York: D. E. Hellerman and Co.

Herman, R. (ed.) (1967a). *Gambling*. New York: Harper and Row.

Herman, R. (1967b). "Gambling as work: A sociological study of the race track." In R. Herman (ed.), *Gambling*, pp. 87–104. New York: Harper and Row.

Herman, R. (1976). *Gamblers and Gambling: Motives, Institutions, and Controls*. Lexington, Mass.: Lexington Books.

Horowitz, I. (1974). "Sports broadcasting." In R. Noll (ed.), *Government and the Sports Business*, pp. 275–323. Washington, D.C.: The Brookings Institution.

Horvitz, J., and T. Hoffman (1976). "New tax developments in the syndication of sports franchises." *Taxes—The Tax Magazine* (March): 175–184.

Jackson, M. (1969). "College football has become a losing business." In J. W. Loy and G. S. Kenyon (eds.), *Sport, Culture and Society*, pp. 232–243. New York: MacMillan.

Jones, J. (1969). "The economics of the National Hockey League." *Canadian Journal of Economics* 2 (February): 1–20.

Joyal-Poupart, R. (1975). *La Responsabilité civile en matière de sports au Québec et en France*. Montreal: Presses de l'Université de Montreal.

Kahan, O. (1977). "TV–radio revenue important to major leagues." *The Sporting News* (April 9): 13–38.

Kiviaho, P. (1975). "The regional distribution of sport organizations as a function of political cleavages." *International Review of Sport Sociology* 10: 5–14.

Knox, R., and J. Inkster (1968). "Postdecision dissonance at post time." *Journal of Personality and Social Psychology* 8: 319–323.

Koch, J. (1971). "The economics of 'big-time' intercollegiate athletics." *Social Science Quarterly* 52 (September): 248–260.

Kowet, D. (1977). *The Rich Who Own Sports*. New York: Random House.

Kuhlman, W. (1975). "Violence in professional sports." *Wisconsin Law Review*: 771–790.

Lewis, G. (1973). "World War I and the emergence of sport for the masses." *The Maryland Historian* IV (Fall): 109–122.

Lindsay, P. (1970). "The impact of the military garrisons on the development of sport in British North America." *Canadian Journal of History of Sport and Physical Education* 1 (May): 33–44.

Mandell, R. (1971). *The Nazi Olympics*. New York: MacMillan.

McIntosh, P. (1963). *Sport in Society*. London: C. A. Watt.

McKelvey, G. (1972). "Sport and politics in Canada." Presented at the Symposium on Sport, Man and Contemporary Society, Queens College of the City University of New York (March).

McPherson, B. (1975). "Sport consumption and the economics of consumerism." In D. Ball and J. Loy (eds.), *Sport and Social Order: Contributions to the Sociology of Sport*, pp. 243–275. Reading, Mass.: Addison-Wesley.

Merchant, L. (1973). *The National Football League Lottery*. New York: Holt, Rinehart and Winston.

Meyers, J. A. (1975). "Background and history of sports." In D. E. Hellerman and Company (eds.), *Sports Business and Finance*, pp. 1–12. New York: D. E. Hellerman and Co.

Meynaud, J. (1966). *Sport et Politique*. Paris: Payot.

Miller, G. (1966). "A study of the economics of professional spectator sports." Unpublished Ph.D. dissertation, The Claremont Graduate School.

Mogull, R. (1973). "Football salaries and race: Some empirical evidence." *Industrial Relations* 12 (February): 109–112.

Morin, C. H. (1976). *Second Interim Report of the Commission on the Review of the National Policy toward Gambling*. Washington, D.C.: Government Printing Office.

Morton, H. (1963). *Soviet Sport*. New York: Cromwell-Collier.

Natan, A. (1969). "Sport and politics." In J. W. Loy and G. S. Kenyon (eds.), *Sport, Culture and Society*, pp. 203–210. Toronto: Collier-MacMillan Canada Ltd.

Neale, W. C. (1964). "The peculiar economics of professional sports." *Quarterly Journal of Economics* 76: 1–14.

Noll, R. (1974a). "Attendance and price setting." In R. Noll (ed.), *Government and the Sports Business*, pp. 115–157. Washington, D.C.: The Brookings Institution.

Noll, R. (ed.) (1974b). *Government and the Sports Business*. Washington, D.C.: The Brookings Institution.

Noll, R. (1974c). "The United States team sports industry: An introduction." In R. Noll (ed.), *Government and the Sports Business*, pp. 1–32. Washington, D.C.: The Brookings Institution.

Norton, D. (1971). "A comparison of political attitudes and political participation of athletes and nonathletes." Masters thesis, University of Oregon.

Okner, B. (1974). "Taxation and sports enterprises." In R. Noll (ed.), *Government and the Sports Business*, pp. 159–184. Washington, D.C.: The Brookings Institution.

Pascal, A., and L. Rapping (1972). "The economics of racial discrimination in organized baseball." In A. Pascal (ed.), *Racial Discrimination and Economic Life*, pp. 119–156. Lexington, Mass.: D. C. Heath.

Petrie, B. (1973). "The political attitudes of Canadian university students: A comparison between athletes and nonathletes." Presented at the National A.A.H.P.E.R. Convention, Minneapolis (April).

Petrie, B. (1975). "Sport and politics." In D. W. Ball and J. W. Loy (eds.), *Sport and Social Order*, pp. 189–237. Reading, Mass.: Addison-Wesley.

Pooley J., and A. Webster (1972). "Sport and politics: Power play." Presented at a symposium on Sport, Man and Contemporary Society, Queens College of the City University of New York (March).

Quirk, J. (1973). "An economic analysis of team movements in professional sports." *Law and Contemporary Problems* 38: 42–66.

Quirk, J. (1974). "Professional sport franchise values." In G. Burman (ed.), *Proceedings of the Conference on the Economics of Professional Sport*, pp. 25–32. Washington, D.C.: National Football League Players' Association.

Quirk, J., and M. El Hodiri (1974). "The economic theory of a professional sports league." In R. Noll (ed.), *Government and the Sports Business*, pp. 33–80. Washington, D.C.: The Brookings Institution.

Raiborn, M. (1970). *Financial Analysis of Intercollegiate Athletics*. Shawnee Mission, Kansas: The National Collegiate Athletic Association. Used with permission.

Rehberg, R., and M. Cohen (1976). "Political attitudes and participation in extracurricular activities." In D. Landers (ed.), *Social Problems in Athletics*, pp. 201–216. Urbana: University of Illinois Press.

Riordan, J. (1974). "Soviet sport and Soviet foreign policy." *Soviet Studies* **26** (July): 322–343.

Riordan, J. (1977). *Sport in Soviet Society*. London: Cambridge University Press.

Rivett, P. (1975). "The structure of league football." *Operational Research Quarterly* **26**: 801–812.

Rose, D. (1974). "University of Massachusetts athletic expansion, 1957–1972: A case study of 'middle time' athletics." Unpublished paper, Department of Sport Studies, University of Massachusetts.

Ross, G. (1975). "The determination of bonuses in professional sport." *The American Economist* **19** (Fall): 43–46.

Ross, R. (1956). *Trade Union Wage Policy*. Berkeley: University of California Press.

Rottenberg, S. (1956). "The baseball player's labour market." *The Journal of Political Economy* **64** (June): 242–258.

Sage, G. (1974). "Value orientations of American college coaches compared to those of male college students and business men." In G. Sage (ed.), *Sport and American Society*, 2nd ed., pp. 207–228. Reading, Mass.: Addison-Wesley.

Schleppi, J. (1972). "A history of sport in England during World War II, with an emphasis on the professional sports." In *Proceedings of the Second Canadian Symposium on the History of Sport and Physical Education*, pp. 147–159. Ottawa: Department of National Health and Welfare Canada, Sport Canada Directorate.

Scott, M. (1968). *The Racing Game*. Chicago: Aldine.

Scoville, J. (1974). "Labour relations in sports." In R. Noll (ed.), *Government and the Sports Business*, pp. 185–219. Washington, D.C.: The Brookings Institution.

Scully, G. (1974a). "Discrimination: The case of baseball." In R. Noll (ed.), *Government and the Sports Business*, pp. 221–273. Washington, D.C.: The Brookings Institution.

Scully, G. (1974b). "Pay and performance in major league baseball." *American Economic Review* **64** (December): 915–930.

Scully, G. (1974c). "Player salaries." In G. Burman (ed.), *Conference on the Economics of Professional Sport*, pp. 33–37. Washington, D.C.: National Football League Players' Association.

Shecter, L. (1970). *The Jocks*. New York: Warner Books.

Sipes, R. (1973). "War, sports and aggression: An empirical test of two rival theories." *American Anthropologist* **75** (February): 64–87.

Sloane, P. (1971). "The economics of professional football: The football club as a utility maximizer." *Scottish Journal of Political Economy* **18** (June): 121–146.

Sobel, L. S. (1977). *Professional Sports and the Law*. New York: Law-Arts Publishers.

Suits, D., and M. Kallick (1976). *Gambling in the United States. A Summary Report*. Ann Arbor: Survey Research Center, Institute for Social Research, University of Michigan.

Thompson, R. (1969). *Race in Sport*. New York: Oxford University Press.

Thompson, R. (1975). *Retreat from Apartheid: New Zealand's Sporting Contacts with South Africa*. London: Oxford University Press.

Underwood, J. (1963). "The true crisis." *Sports Illustrated* **18** (May 20): 16–19, 83.

Yetman, N., and D. Eitzen (1972). "Black Americans in sports: Unequal opportunity for equal ability." *Civil Rights Digest* **5** (August): 20–34.

Chapter 8
SPORT
AND CULTURAL
INSTITUTIONS

8.1 INTRODUCTION

In Chapter 2, *culture* in its broadest sense was said to be a normative subsystem composed of beliefs, folkways, ideologies, laws, mores, norms, and values. These elements come together as subcultures (Chapter 5) and as analytic social institutions, which can be classified into three spheres: *socializing* institutions (Chapter 6), *regulative* institutions (Chapter 7), and *cultural* institutions. The latter, recognizable as the arts, mass media, and religious and scientific networks, are recreational (Panunzio, 1949), expressive, or higher institutions, as opposed to the service (i.e., socializing and regulative) institutions, which are functionally more instrumental (Feibleman, 1968). The purpose of this chapter, then, is to describe and attempt to account for the linkage between such expressive institutions and sport. In doing so, it should be realized that culture is not behavior itself, but rather a *social product* that originates and develops through human interaction to provide a symbolic order to social life in a group. Traditionally, *culture* (e.g., ideas, values, beliefs) has been sustained symbolically through material culture such as works of art, technological innovations, and other objective artifacts produced by expressive institutional networks.

Obviously, the term culture[1] is less definitive than many other concepts used in the social sciences; however, it becomes more explicit when placed in a particular social context or orientation. That is, its meaning becomes clearer when such concepts as "high culture," "mass culture," "popular culture," and "taste culture" are introduced. Although values (that is, good and bad) are often associated with most of these terms, some common understandings have evolved. For example, *high culture* (or "Kultur" in German) refers to classical music, ballet, theater, poetry, and the fine arts. As such, it has traditionally been considered the domain of the upper class or well-educated social elite, particularly in Western countries, and consequently involves a relatively small segment of a given population. At the opposite end of the spectrum, *mass culture* is the collection of cultural elements that are transmitted via the printed press, the electronic media, or other forms of mass communication—in other words, "the culture of the numerical majority" (Kando, 1975). Finally, *popular culture* refers to "the typical cultural and recreational activities of typical segments of a society" (Kando, 1975). Sport, then, is one element of popular culture, especially since it appeals to all strata in society in one or more of its divergent forms. But, at the same time, it is very much an element of mass culture since it is transmitted via mass communication networks.

For some, the distinction between high and popular culture rests on aesthetic standards. Gans (1974), however, rejects the implied dichotomy: ". . . instead of assuming a single popular culture, I propose that the number of cultures is an empirical and a conceptual problem, to be determined in part by studies of who chooses what content, and what relationships exist among content choices." He goes on to suggest the concept of "taste cultures"[2] wherein membership is determined by ". . .class, age, religion, ethnic and racial background, regional origin and place of residence, as well as personality factors which translate themselves into wants for specific types of cultural content . . ., although age and class seem to be the major factors in American society" (Gans, 1974). Following this approach, Gans identifies five taste cultures: *high culture, upper-middle culture, lower-middle culture, low culture,* and *quasi-folk low culture.*

Although the consumption of a particular cultural product such as music may be common to several taste publics, the form and complexity of a given product could vary greatly. In the case of sport, preference for particular games and activities would depend on the taste culture with which one is identified. However, in some form, sport appeals to persons of all taste cultures.

The meaning and function of sport in a particular society is reflected in the cultural institutions of that society. In this way sport becomes a cultural product. By examining the interaction between sport and the cultural institutions (Maheu, 1962), understanding of the values, needs, beliefs, and patterns of life in various societies can be gained. That is, institutionalized sport is symbolic of the way of life in a society and can have various meanings in different cultures. For example, in one group it may be viewed as work, in another as leisure. Similarly, in one it may stress competition, aggressiveness, and violence (e.g., in North America), while in another it may stress friendly cooperative social interaction as a means of promoting physical fitness, friendship, and a respite from the normal requirements of daily life (e.g., in The Peoples Republic of China). Furthermore, by reflecting the values of a culture, the symbolic elements from sport can be transferred to other domains of life. To illustrate, many terms that originated in sport slang have been incorporated into the language of everyday life: "I'll take a raincheck," "that's not cricket," "behind the eightball," "I struck out," etc.

As a cultural product, sport is influenced by the economic, political, religious, and ideological forces in a society and a given sport may change its form, structure, and meaning as it is diffused into a new cultural milieu. This is illustrated by Riesman and Denney (1951) in their analysis of how rugby became a game (i.e., American football) that reflected unique and different life-styles and values in the host society after it was introduced to the United States from England. As such, the game in its new form acculturates immigrants.

Although a sport such as baseball may not undergo a change in form or structure[3] as it is diffused throughout the world, it may reflect a variety of meanings in different societies. For example, in Libya, in the 1930s, baseball served ritualistic functions (Gini, 1939); in America it represents individualism and teamwork, pastoral simplicity in the cycle of the seasons, and quantification (Guttman, 1975); and in primitive Pueblo society it represents a competitive intrusion into an essentially noncompetitive social system and provides for the acting out of aggressive and competitive tendencies both within and among the villages (Fox, 1961). In Japan (Andreano, 1965), baseball reflects a traditional pattern of group loyalty (players are not traded, for example), a strong social organization, and a compatibility with the slow-paced tempo of life in the country; more recently, with continued modernization, it represents an avenue for upward mobility.

Within a given society, then, different sports can represent a variety of values and needs. To illustrate, Ross (1971) suggests that baseball is a pastoral sport that stresses harmony, the individual, a slower pace, and ritualized actions, whereas football is a heroic sport that is more complex, violent, sudden, and warlike, and reflects a collective pattern of life. In short, Ross suggests that football has become the more popular sport in North America because it is more representative of contemporary culture, yet baseball survives because it reflects a way of life that people would still like to see exist.

Based on a comparison with other forms of football (e.g., soccer, rugby), another interpretation is supplied by Finlay (1971). He argues that football is now the dominant game in North America because it represents a corporate sport that is more attuned than baseball to the present stage of mature capitalism. Finlay (1971) further notes that baseball is a game of the early stages of capitalism, and that this is illustrated by the current Japanese penchant for baseball rather than football. Similarly, the increasing popularity of squash in North America has been attributed to its being an intense, competitive game that is in tune with an achievement-oriented, urbanized society in which aggressiveness, self-discipline, and domination of the opponent are essential for success (Wool, 1975).

Thus sport becomes a valued life interest and, in turn, mirrors society in both subtle and overt ways: Canadians value hockey, the Chinese swimming and Ping-Pong, the Basques jai alai, the Japanese baseball and sumo wrestling, the Nordic countries alpine skiing, the Americans baseball, football, and basketball, the British soccer, and the Latin Americans soccer and baseball. It is interesting to note that Eastern European countries do not appear to value one specific sport[4] that is endemic to their culture. Instead, most sports that involve international competition have been incorporated into the life-style for instrumental rather than expressive purposes.

In addition to national differences in values held for sport, there are also regional differences in that certain regions of a country may adopt a sport to a greater degree than other regions. This adaptation may be reflected in more people playing, talking about, or watching the sport or in the production of high-quality performers. To illustrate, on the basis of an analysis of the birthplace of elite athletes, Rooney (1974) indicated that in the United States baseball is associated with California and the south, football with Texas, Ohio, and Pennsylvania, basketball with Illinois, Indiana, and Kentucky, stock-car racing with the Carolinas, and soccer with the Northwestern states.

To summarize, sport is inextricably linked with culture in that (1) it is functional (e.g., provides entertainment, promotes social integration, enhances physical development and prestige, develops achievement orientation, competitiveness, and aggressiveness), (2) it is highly valued, (3) it is institutionalized, and (4) it has a set of enduring rules and traditions. Furthermore, there is an interdependent relationship between the meaning, structure, and the rules of sports and the ideological characteristics of the culture in which they originate or in which they are diffused (see Clignet and Stark, 1974; Dunlap, 1951; Geertz, 1972; Zurcher and Meadow, 1967). Thus, sport is one of a variety of institutions that reinforce the most sacred values of a given society. For example, Haerle (1974) stated that sport is one institution in which the basic cultural values of "success and failure, the individual versus the group, the ultimate nature of man, the need for social order and social control" can be tested and reinforced. At the same time sport does not operate in a vacuum, but rather as a social institution it interacts with and is reflected in other cultural institutions such as religion, the mass media, and the arts. The following three sections examine this cultural interplay while the final section notes that sport is also a cultural product influenced by a variety of social institutions.

8.2 SPORT AND RELIGION

8.2.1 Introduction

Until the twentieth century, when the private sector and educational institutions took control, sport was traditionally under the jurisdiction of the church or state. For example, the religious festivals in Greek antiquity were among the first known sporting competitions. For many centuries thereafter, leisure activities and therefore sport and games were under church control because of their concern for the body and the soul. As a result, sport competition was permitted only on holidays (holy days) or was associated with the celebration of religious rites or festivals (e.g., births, baptisms, confirmations, weddings, funerals). For example, Huizinga (1976) states that "the great competitions in archaic cultures had always formed part of the sacred festivals and were indispensable as health and happiness-bringing activities."

During the medieval period sporting activities tended to remain part of the religious feasts and festivals, but in the Middle Ages sporting competition began to be pursued on a regular basis outside the control of religious leaders. Later, competition between communities and clubs became a regular phenomenon in nineteenth-century England. However, it did not thrive without opposition since leaders of some religious groups (for example, the Puritans) discouraged sport by branding it as sinful (Metcalfe, 1968). Furthermore, they exerted sufficient influence on the government to force the banning of sport on Sunday. However, with the rise of industrialization and urbanization in England and North

America, sport became even more popular (Betts, 1953, 1974). In an effort to regain some control, church leaders legitimized sport, even going so far as to sponsor social or sport clubs and to include sport facilities within the church environs such as gymnasiums and tennis courts (Andrus, 1962; Betts, 1974).

Since the early 1900s, the rise of sport has been related to, but independent of, religious control[5] (Geldbach, 1975; Grupe et al., 1972; Meyer, 1973; Schloz et al., 1973). For example, religious organizations have been responsible for organizing and promoting sport (e.g., YMCA, CYO), religious groups such as the Fellowship of Christian Athletes have gained increasing membership among high school, college, and professional athletes (Deford, 1976; Koppett, 1977; Simonson, 1962), and new religions have evolved such as the Church of Perfect Liberty in Japan, which promotes golf as a means of searching for self-expression.

By the 1920s there were few religious restrictions on sport, although abstinence on Sunday was still required in many communities (Huskel, 1926). This reflects the general weakening of power and control that religion had traditionally held over most social institutions in Western societies. In fact, this shift suggests that the relationship between the Protestant ethic and the spirit of capitalism was extended to sport (Luschen, 1967) with its increasing emphasis on competition, success, and a "win-at-all-costs" ethic. The result has been the development of sport as work, as a business, and as a form of entertainment. Yet, despite the decreasing influence of religion on sport as a result of social change, the two institutions remain functionally related.

8.2.2 The Function of Sport as a Religion

From a Marxist perspective in the nineteenth century, religion was the "opiate of the masses." It has been suggested that sport has now replaced religion in this sense. As such, it functions as a civil religion or quasi-religious institution, which replaces sectarian religion for the purpose of fostering social integration (Duncan, 1968; Durkheim, 1947; Radcliffe-Brown, 1964; Warner, 1953). Although this is a difficult hypothesis to test empirically, there are a number of interesting parallels between sport and religion, including the "worship" of athletes as gods and heroes, the "idolization" of former athletes in Sport Halls of Fame (Lewis and Redmond, 1974), the dependence of "followers" (fans) for economic stability, the daily "reading" of the sport pages by the "devout" fan, the collection of "symbols of faith" (Edwards, 1973) such as trophies, baseballs, game balls, and sport-related souvenirs, and the charisma that is attached to the elites and leaders in the sport milieu. More specifically, religious language has been extensively used in the literature and rhetoric on the Olympic movement. For example, MacAloon (1976) concluded that the writings of Pierre de Coubertin indicate that an important source of the Olympic movement was the search for a "humanistic" or "civil" religion. Furthermore, he reports that the sentiments, themes, conceptions, and actions pervading Olympism and the Olympic Games have religious connotations.

From another perspective, Milton (1972) hypothesized that sport is a functional equivalent of religion. Employing a functionalist analysis, he found several studies of sectarian religion in which various functional structures of integration were present. An examination of selected studies of sport revealed a similar set of functional structures. Based on the similarity between the two sets of studies, he concluded that sport is a functional equivalent of religion, particularly with respect to its contribution to integration. As such, sport integrates individuals into their society by inculcating and reinforcing dominant social values and providing regulatory norms as controlling mechanisms. In a similar vein, the bullfight in Spain is regarded as a modern-day religious ritual in which the bull is sacrificed (Desmonde, 1952).

There is also some evidence of a mutual interdependence between religion and sport. First, as we note in Section 8.5, there appears to be a relationship between religion and success in sport, both individually (personal level) and collectively (national level). In addition, there are many religious values or practices present in sport, including ceremony, ritual, magic, and superstition. These have remained a part of sport because it is commonly believed that they are necessary for the continued institutionalization of a sport, or are somehow related to the outcome of a specific sport event. Moreover, ritual and ceremony, whether in religion or sport, reinforce values and beliefs. In terms of ceremony, examples include the spectacle of the modern Olympic Games with the ritualistic and lavish opening and closing ceremonies complete with torch, oath, flags, and symbolism, and the half-time spectaculars at football games in North America, including the annual Superbowl extravaganza (*Time*, "The Super Show," 1977).

8.2.3 Magic in Sport

The use of magic as a form of religion involves the application of techniques for manipulating supernatural or natural forces believed to ensure desired results. In sport, because of the lack of outcome control and the uncertainty of outcome, chance plays a role and rituals, taboos, fetishes, and superstitions abound. Many of these practices have very definite functions. This is illustrated clearly in a study by Scotch (1961) in which the focus of attention was not so much on the religiosity of groups but on the magic and sorcery of football among the urban Zulu. For these people, witchcraft functions to explain why certain things occur, such as why one team always wins or why one team manages to attract all the good players. Scotch goes on to say that it is very difficult to destroy such beliefs in witchcraft because they form a system that helps to explain failures. Furthermore, each soccer team carries a Zulu doctor who uses his supernatural powers in every possible way to produce a successful team. As well, rituals and ceremonies are performed that sanction and support team efforts. Thus, the practices unite the team members in much the same way that religion provides an opportunity for identification with a particular social group.

Although it is difficult to assess the extent to which magic is used in sport, reference to it appears frequently in the popular sport literature (Bouton, 1970; Kramer, 1969). In recent years, there have been some descriptive and conceptual analyses and at least one empirical study of the phenomenon. Wrigley (1970) provided a number of examples of magic in sport that were used to promote good fortune, to reduce tension, anxiety, and fear of failure, to contribute to team morale (Sheard and Dunning, 1973), and to justify or rationalize a defeat when a ritual was forgotten. Wrigley also noted the difference between "sorcery," which is done so that some event will happen, and "taboo," which is not done so that some event will not occur. Although rituals are usually individualistic and are associated with playing equipment or with the act of preparing for a contest (such as a favorite bat, a specific order of getting dressed), they can be collective as well (for example, team prayer or cheer, or no mention of a "no-hitter" on the bench). Based on a participant-observation study, Gmelch (1972) analyzed the use or function of magic in professional baseball, including the role of rituals, taboos, and fetishes (that is, ordinary objects that are regarded as having extraordinary powers). In almost all cases, he found that these acts were associated with hitting or pitching and were directed toward improving the performance of the actor himself. That is, unlike many forms of magic, there is no attempt to put a "hex" on the opponent. This supports Malinowski's (1948) hypothesis that magic is most likely to appear in situations of chance and uncertainty.

Increasingly mysticism is appearing in sport, primarily because those individuals who are exposed to risks (which in turn creates anxiety) often resort to practices that assist them in their quest for success or safety. For example, it has been suggested that with the number of Latin-Americans participating in baseball, the emphasis on voodoo and religious incantations has increased. While there have been many descriptive articles written in newspapers and journals listing the superstitions of well-known athletes, two empirical studies by Gregory and Petrie (1973, 1975) attempted to compare the superstitions of male and female nonathletes and intercollegiate athletes in six sports. They found that male athletes listed fewer general superstitions than did nonathletes, that male and female athletes listed twice the number of superstitions associated with sport as did nonathletes, that females in both the nonathlete and the athlete groups listed more general superstitions than did males, that there were more superstitions associated with athletes on team sports than on individual sports, and that many superstitions were sport-specific.

In summary, the relationship between sport and religion has been present throughout history, with the dependence of sport on religion being almost total in earlier times, although today the two institutions are related but independent. However, as society shifted from the sacred to the secular, the direct influence of religion on sport decreased. Nevertheless, there are similar characteristics in both institutions such as worship, ritual, and ceremony (Smith, 1976a). Although it has been frequently hypothesized that sport is a functional equivalent of religion or that sport conflicts with religion, empirical evidence is lacking at the present time. Thus, statements such as the following continue to be made:

Sports are our nations' strongest forms of natural religion, inculcating discipline, a taste for perfection, and the experience of beautiful and perfect acts. Writers on the sports page need to know that they are guardians of important treasures of the human spirit. (Novak, 1976, p. 38)

In a word, at the present time, the two institutions appear to have eliminated the conflict characteristic of earlier historical periods.

8.3 SPORT AND MASS MEDIA

8.3.1 Introduction

The mass media are a technical system by which a relatively few number of people can communicate rapidly and simultaneously with a large percentage of the population, thereby narrowing physical, temporal, and social distances. Generally, the media consist of printed communication such as newspapers, magazines, and books, and electronic communication such as radio, television, and the movies. Because the media reach a large, yet diverse population, as a social institution they can serve a variety of needs, including providing information, promoting status or social integration, presenting an aesthetic experience, and serving as an escape mechanism from the realities of everyday life. Sport has been hypothesized to serve these needs as well and therefore the use of the media to present sport is somewhat understandable.

The advance of modern technology has led to the creation of a mass culture, often referred to as "popular culture," which is oriented toward the entertainment of large audiences, usually through one or more forms of the mass media. Sport has become one of the major forms of this popular culture (along with popular music, movies, and television shows), primarily through its association with the dominant form of the media in each era. As a result, a symbiotic relationship between sport and the media has evolved in order to satiate the demands of the masses who seek to indirectly consume sport for a variety of real or imagined reasons. Whereas the following subsections discuss some theories of mass communication, the degree to which, and why, the masses consume sport, and the relationship between sport and various forms of the media, this introductory section provides a brief historical overview of the relationship between sport and the mass media.

The first sport story in an American newspaper appeared on 5 May 1733 in the *Boston Gazette* as a reprint from a report of a boxing match held in England (Greendorfer, in press). In the 1700s and 1800s newspapers occasionally published news about prize fights, horse races, and boat races. However, it was not until 1819 that the first American periodical on sport, *The American Farmer*, began to publish the results of hunting, fishing, shooting, and bicycling matches, plus articles on the philosophy of sport. By the 1850s items on sport began to appear regularly, but it was not until the 1890s that a sport department and a sport section were created. In Europe, daily newspapers devoted exclusively to sport were established at about the same time. By the 1850s the electronic media were beginning to be used for sport communication, as illustrated by the use of the telegraph to report results of horse and yachting races and boxing matches. By the late 1800s, the Atlantic Cable carried sport news from England (Betts, 1953); by the 1920s, live radio broadcasts of sport events were being carried, at first locally and then nationally; and by the 1930s, experimental telecasts of sport events were made. For example, a baseball game was telecast between New York and Philadelphia in the 1920s and the 1936 Olympic Games were televised and shown on the Games site. However, it wasn't until the 1950s that sport events became part of the regular program format of the television networks. A more detailed time-line of when and how sport was presented in the media appears in Table 8.1.

It is television, however, that has become so involved with both national and international sport. In North America the major television networks produce 1200 to 1500 hours of sport annually, which is approximately 15 percent of all scheduled programs. This represents approximately 25 hours per week, although in some large cities there may be over 30 hours per week of televised sport. At the same time, radio stations in North America broadcast over 400,000 hours of sport annually, with a large percentage of this time devoted to professional baseball and college sport events. Internationally, there are now regular transmissions of sport events throughout the world, especially during an Olympic year.

As a result of television's commitment to sport, a number of innovations in sport have occurred, including a change in the form and structure of sport (for example, early starting times on the west coast to accommodate the television market in the east, a new scoring system in tennis to enable matches to be completed within predetermined maximum time periods, time-outs in most sports for the purpose of presenting commercials); the expansion of existing leagues and the creation of new leagues to take advantage of new "market" areas; and, the construction of new stadia with excellent lighting for color television. In addition, athletes have received sufficient public exposure to enable them to become corporate executives (Arnold Palmer is an example); many college and professional sport programs have remained financially solvent because of television rights; athletes have received high salaries because of television rights; some sports have gained exposure and therefore popularity both for viewing and participating (e.g., golf and tennis); satellites have been launched to improve international telecasting; and sportlike spectacles have been created because of the general interest in sport (e.g., the "super-stars competition").

A further example is the impact that television has had on professional baseball, including divisional play-offs to increase the ratings late in the season; the increased number of night games; the opening of the World Series on a Saturday instead of the traditional Wednesday; and scheduling of midweek World Series games at night rather than the afternoon to take advantage of "prime-time" television. Thus, whereas newspapers have been used to promote a team or sport and radio has assisted in popularizing a sport while providing some economic returns, television virtually controls the destiny of professional sport, in both its form and its economic basis.

Table 8.1   *Time line—mass media and sport*

Year	Event
1733	(May 5) First sports story in an American newspaper. *The Boston Gazette* carries the prizefight between John Faulconer and Bob Russel on the "Bowling Green at Harrow on the Hill." It was copied directly from a London daily.
1796	The *Charleston City Gazette* carries notices for Charleston Golf Club.
1801	The first sports publication in England: "The Sports and Pastimes of People in England."
1819	Colonel John Stuart Skinner, postmaster of Baltimore, publishes the first American periodical on sports, *The American Farmer*. Published the results of hunting, fishing, shooting, and bicycling matches as well as essays on the philosophy of sports.
1823	The *New York Evening Post* carries the first full-scale account of a boxing match.
1831	*The Spirit of the Times*, the first weekly on sport, is started. Most successful of all early sporting periodicals.
1850s	The only member of newspaper staff who in any way resembled the modern sports editor was the turf man. Horse racing and cricket were the most popular sports of the day, and only the *New York Anglo-American* and the *Albion* covered cricket. Henry Chadwick began to cover cricket matches between the United States and Canadian teams for the *New York Times*. (He received no pay.) The visit of a British cricket team in 1859 caused so much interest that the *Herald* finally hired Chadwick. He later reported baseball.
1862	Chadwick becomes the first sport reporter, baseball.
1866	Opening of the Atlantic cable.
1870	Middie Morgan becomes the first female sportswriter. She covered races and cattle shows for the *New York Times*.

8.3.2   Theories of Mass Communication

Although there are many approaches to the description and explanation of mass communication (see Emery et al., 1965; McQuail, 1969; Schramm, 1960; Steinberg, 1966; Stephenson, 1967), this discussion is delimited to four theories outlined by De Fleur (1970).

The *individual-differences theory* argues that the media present images that appeal to individual differences in the personality characteristics of the viewers. This approach suggests that individuals have specific needs that predispose them to use the media in order to satisfy these needs. Katz, Gurevitch, and Haas (1973) identified four categories of needs that the media could fulfill: cognitive (strengthening information, knowledge, understanding); affective (providing an aesthetic, pleasurable, emotional experience); integrative (providing credibility, confidence, status, contact with family and friends); and escapist (providing release of tension and separation of the self from one's required social roles).

In a sport context, Birrell and Loy (1977) recently proposed the following four functions of media sport. The *information* function provides knowledge of

Table 8.1   *continued*

Year	Event
1883	Joseph Pulitzer bought the *World* and set up the first sport department. (By 1892, all great papers had them.) Reports of baseball, horse racing, pedestrian tournaments, and other events were combined into a single article. They were less concerned with personalities than with final scores.
1886	The *Sporting News*, a St. Louis weekly, began. It was and is devoted to baseball. It has become the bible of the diamond.
1889	Joe Villa, sports editor of the *New York Sun*, uses the play-by-play technique for the first time in covering the Harvard–Princeton football game. The *Sun* devoted three columns to the game.
1895	Hearst begins the first sport section in a newspaper.
1899	The wireless was used for news reporting in connection with the international yacht races.
1921	Baseball games and fights are on KDKA. Florent Gibson becomes the first sport broadcaster. The Dempsey-Carpentier fight becomes the first million-dollar gate.
1923	The first televised broadcast between New York and Philadelphia.
1925	The first play-by-play broadcast of major league baseball and football.
1940	Emergence of sport cartoons.
1945	The AP sports wire is established for the opening day of major league baseball.
1963	The first instant replay on television.
1973	Congress enacts Public Law 93-107, which amends Communication Act of 1934. (This is the Anti-blackout ruling: If home game is sold out 72 hours prior to the game, the game cannot be blacked out in home area.)

Adapted from Greendorfer (in press).

the game itself, game results, and statistics concerning players or teams, while the *integration* function provides affiliation with a social group and a social experience with other spectators. Similarly, the *arousal* and *escape* functions serve affective needs by providing excitement and by facilitating the release of pent-up emotions, respectively. The authors further suggest that different forms of secondary sport involvement are selected on the basis of the individual's perceived need. Thus, a predisposition toward information will lead to "hot media" involvement (McLuhan, 1964) in books, newspapers, and films where there is low participation by the audience. On the other hand, integrative and arousal predispositions will incline the individual toward "cool media" consumption (e.g., direct attendance at events, television, and radio) where there is higher sensory involvement. More specifically, cognitive needs in sport can best be met by newspapers and magazines, followed in order by television and radio; integrative needs can best be met by attending an event, followed in order by television, radio, and newspapers; affective needs can best be met by direct attendance or television; and escapist needs can probably be gratified by every form of the media.

The *social-categories theory* argues that "there are broad collectivities, aggregates or social categories in urban industrial societies whose behavior in the face of a given set of stimuli is more or less uniform" (De Fleur, 1970). This theory has some support since there are age, sex, social class, educational, and marital status differences in sport consumption patterns. One limitation of this approach is that the social categories tend to be considered apart from each other so that the pattern of a lower-class, poorly educated, fifty-year-old black is not usually identified; that is, the life-styles of specific subgroups and cohorts are often overlooked.

The *social-relationships theory* suggests that "informal social relationships play a significant role in modifying the manner in which a given individual will act upon a message which comes to his attention via the mass media" (De Fleur, 1970). This theory suggests that the concept of life-style may influence media behavior. Life-style, according to Feldman and Thielbar (1972), is a group phenomenon influenced by participation in social groups and interaction with significant others. It pervades many aspects of life, it implies a central life interest, and it varies according to relevant sociological variables (Zablocki and Kanter, 1976).

Some support for this theory is found in a study of the process through which adolescents are socialized into the role of sport consumer (McPherson, 1976a, 1976b). The results indicated that the degree of consumer role socialization is related to the number of significant others who consume sport, the frequency of sport consumption by significant others, the amount of interaction with significant others who consume sport, the number of sanctions received from significant others in the family who are ego-involved in sport, the intensity with which they are ego-involved, the importance of sport in the hierarchy of parents' leisure-time pursuits, the amount of primary sport involvement engaged in by the adolescent, the opportunity set to participate in sport in the adolescent's social milieu, and the general degree of system-induced propensity provided by the family, school, peer group, and community. In short, an individual's pattern of media sport consumption is influenced by significant others in their social world (see Chapter 6).

The final model presented by De Fleur (1970), the *cultural-norms theory*, argues that the mass media selectively present and emphasize certain themes that are perceived by viewers as cultural norms and that subsequently guide future behavior and use of the media. De Fleur notes that normative perceptions of individuals can be influenced by the media in three ways: (1) existing norms and patterns are reinforced; (2) new ideas, norms, or expectations are created; and (3) existing norms can be changed, thereby leading to new forms of behavior.

Although empirical evidence is lacking, the way in which the mass media present sport may be somewhat instrumental in changing social stereotypes of blacks and females, in changing beliefs and attitudes concerning amateurism, professionalism, and Olympic ideals, and in influencing patterns of both primary and secondary sport involvement. However, as Breed (1958) noted, the media are more likely to support and maintain the status quo than to initiate social change. The one exception in recent years, however, has been the appearance in the printed media of critical columnists and "athletes-turned-author." While "telling it like it is," they invariably call for a change within institutionalized sport.

Nevertheless, what appears in the media serves for the most part as a symbolic representation of established norms, values, and sanctions, including those within institutionalized sport.

To summarize, while no definitive explanation of mass communications is yet available, the four theories outlined by De Fleur provide a framework for studying the hypothesized functions of sport consumption, much of which occurs via the mass media. The following two subsections outline the degree of primary and secondary sport involvement and the hypothesized functions of sport consumption. These sections are included here to highlight the pervasiveness of sport as a cultural product, and to emphasize that most sport involvement occurs via the mass media.

8.3.3 The Degree of Sport Involvement

Primary Involvement

Because sport events appear so frequently in the media and are therefore consumed by a significant proportion[6] of the population, casual observers of the social scene have assumed that a large percentage of the population must participate in sport as well. Although this observation might be confirmed by noting the crowds at public golf courses or tennis courts on any summer weekend, a closer examination of several empirical studies suggests that this assumption may have little validity. In fact, in comparison to the number who consume sport indirectly via the media, relatively few adults actively participate in sport (i.e., primary involvement) or attend sport events (i.e., direct secondary involvement).

In most countries, the evidence suggests that while young children and early adolescents are highly involved as participants, declining involvement with age is the general pattern, especially after an individual enters the labor force. However, at all age levels, participation rates are higher for males, for those with higher levels of educational attainment, and for those in occupations with higher prestige rankings (see Table 9.3). The following are some examples of this trend.

As noted earlier in the text, over 20 million people are involved in organized youth sport in North America alone. However, even in youth activities, declining participation rates by age appear. For example, a 1973 report by the United States Department of Labor indicated that only 400,000 of 2,000,000 Little League baseball players play high school ball, with 25,000 of these playing at the college level and perhaps only 100 making a major league team (see *Sports Illustrated*, "Few and Far Between," 1973). Similar rates could be cited for other organized youth sports. The net effect is a shift from active participation to vicarious consumption, which begins during the high school years and continues throughout adulthood (see Section 9.5). Moreover, there are regional variations in participation rates for specific sports (Table 8.2) that reflect differences in culture, climate, or opportunity set.

Secondary Involvement

In contrast, an analysis of the degree of secondary sport involvement suggests that when compared to the minority who actually participate, a moderate proportion of the population attend sport events, while a significant majority con-

Table 8.2
Participation rates in specific sports by region (province in Canada)*

| Sport | Percentage of population involved | | | |
	Newfoundland	Ontario	British Columbia	All Canada
Golf	1.6	9.1	8.8	7.5
Tennis	2.6	5.6	7.2	5.0
Bowling	5.4	13.5	11.8	11.8
Skiing	1.8	6.2	7.5	6.8
Jogging	5.2	6.7	8.3	7.1
Hockey	9.7	8.3	4.6	8.1
Swimming	22.9	35.7	28.5	28.5

*These percentages represent responses to a national survey of 49,750 Canadians in March and April, 1972. More detailed information is available in Kirsch et al. (1973).

sume sport through the mass media. Notwithstanding the fact that much of the evidence in this domain is provided by sport organizations, television networks, popularity polls, or independent media rating systems and therefore may be biased, there is little doubt that sport consumption via the media is a significant leisure activity for both adolescents and adults.

Direct sport consumption by adolescents is high because of the importance of sport in the high school subculture. For example, Kenyon (1968) found that two thirds of the adolescents consumed sport directly once a month or more. Similar trends were found by McPherson (1972) in a study of urban-dwelling Canadian adolescents. In fact, only 4.8 percent of the males and 4.3 percent of the females reported that they never attended a sport event. However, the pattern of declining involvement by age appears to hold for direct sport consumption as well as for active sport participation. To illustrate, Kenyon (1966) found that only 29 percent of adult males and 21 percent of adult females attended sport events once a month or more during the summer months. An even smaller percentage attended at other times of the year. More recent evidence in Canada suggests that sport events are less popular than movies, but more appealing than live theater and art galleries at all age levels (Table 8.3). While these participation patterns may partly be explained by opportunity set, it is more likely that they reflect the current "tastes" of the masses.

Despite these low percentages, the number who attend in absolute terms is relatively high in that the estimated annual attendance at professional and college sport events is over 300 million. Included in this total, however, are many who attend one sport regularly (e.g., season-ticket holders) or who are multisport attendees. The more popular sports, with 1977 estimated annual paid admissions, are horse racing (82 million), automobile racing (49 million), college and professional football (44 million), baseball (44 million), basketball (34 million), hockey (23 million), greyhound racing (19 million), soccer (6 million), professional wrestling (5 million), tennis (4 million), boxing (3 million), and golf (3 million).

Table 8.3
Attendance (percentage of population) at paid events*

Age	Sports events	Movies	Live theater	Art galleries
14	41.6	51.5	14.1	3.9
15–16	44.1	57.5	19.3	5.6
17–19	40.7	65.4	20.5	5.4
20–24	31.0	62.5	14.7	4.4
25–34	25.0	45.9	11.6	3.4
35–44	22.6	33.0	9.1	2.8
45–54	17.2	26.2	10.2	3.2
55–64	10.4	17.1	7.0	2.9
65–69	6.2	12.3	5.1	1.8
70+	3.1	6.1	3.2	1.0
Total population	23.4	38.1	11.3	3.4

*These percentages represent responses to a national survey of 49,750 Canadians in March and April, 1972. More detailed information is available in Kirsch et al. (1973).

Moreover, special events such as the Super Bowl, the World Series, and the Olympic Games attract even those who are only marginally interested in the contest.

By far the greatest involvement in sport occurs indirectly through television, radio, books, and magazines. Robinson (1970) reported that 30 percent of American adults follow sport on television each day, while Kenyon (1966) found that over 50 percent of those in his sample listened to sport on the radio or watched it on television at least once a week. Even greater indirect secondary involvement was reported by adolescents in a similar study (Kenyon, 1968). Table 8.4 illustrates the fact that the type of indirect consumption by adolescents varies by sex.

Although more detailed information can be found in Birrell and Loy (1974, 1977), McPherson (1975), and the media trade journals and reports (e.g., *Advertising Age* and A. G. Neilsen's *Let's Look At Sports*), the following examples are illustrative of the extent to which the age of high mass consumption (Rostow, 1971) has arrived. First, during any given month of the year, a viewer has a choice of consuming at least three different sports, while during some months eight sports are regularly televised. For example, in May a viewer can watch basketball, baseball, hockey, bowling, golf, tennis, horse racing, and auto racing. Moreover, since 1975 the three major networks in the United States have offered more than 1200 hours of sport telecasts annually, many of which receive the highest ratings for both number of viewers and degree of enjoyment. For example, in recent years it has been estimated that over 100 million view the entire World Series, that Monday night football has an audience of 11.5 million, that 5 million view a regular season National Basketball Association game, that 80 million view the Super Bowl, that over 1 billion viewed the 1976 Summer Olympic Games, that over 800 million throughout the world consume the World

Table 8.4
Type of indirect consumption by adolescents

Type of consumption	At least once per week		Never	
	Males (%)	Females (%)	Males (%)	Females (%)
Television	64.3	40.4	1.3	1.4
Radio	21.7	19.1	29.9	36.9
Reading	57.4	34.0	12.1	12.1
Talking	69.3	47.6	1.9	0.7

From McPherson (1972).

Cup football (soccer) championship, and that 35 million (or over 40 percent of the potential viewing audience) saw Hank Aaron break Babe Ruth's home run record. In addition, sport can be consumed anywhere by radio, especially baseball in the summer and college football in the fall. The estimates generally range from 100,000 to 500,000 listeners per event depending on the importance of the game and the number of radio stations presenting a given event.

Finally, an increasing source of indirect consumption is the appearance of many general and specific sport magazines that are published on a daily, weekly, monthly, or annual basis. For example, *Sports Illustrated* has a weekly circulation of over 2.4 million copies, many of which are read by more than one individual. In fact, the increasing publication of specialty magazines for sports such as skiing, tennis, roller derby, auto racing, and skydiving provides further evidence that certain sports have become institutionalized.

In summary, the rate of sport consumption is high, especially in North America. Whether individuals consume sport initially and to what degree and whether they are direct or indirect consumers can partially be accounted for by personal attributes such as age, sex, socioeconomic status, nationality, place of residence, occupation, and education. While a more detailed examination of the influence of these factors on sport consumption is available in Birrell and Loy (1974) and McPherson (1975), we can state generally that males, those under 30, the middle class, the higher educated, and the urban dweller are those who consume sport the most, although democratization in secondary sport involvement has occurred more rapidly than in primary sport involvement.

8.3.4 The Function of Sport Consumption

A number of scholars have attempted to account for the function served by consuming spectator sports. Brill (1929) stated that vicarious spectator sport meets an important need in providing for the release of our aggressive combative instincts. Similarly, Gerth and Mills (1954) reported that many mass audience situations, with their "vicarious components," serve psychologically the unintended function of channeling and releasing emotions. Thus, great amounts of aggression are, theoretically, released by crowds of spectators cheering for their favorite stars and jeering the umpire.

Some studies, however, have found that observers may be more aggressive after viewing violence than before (Bandura and Walters, 1963; Berkowitz, 1969; Dollard et al., 1939; Goldstein and Arms, 1971). Thus, the findings in this area are equivocal and the reaction to a sport contest may be sport- or person-specific. In addition, studies in this area have not examined similar phenomena with small groups who may view a sport event on television.

Closely related to the functions of spectator sports are the factors causing vast numbers of people to consume sport. Again, only impressionistic information is generally available. Elias and Dunning (1970) suggest that a quest by people for pleasurable excitement and a need to "lose themselves" were factors causing the rise of sport consumption. They suggested that one of the motives for consuming soccer in Britain may be a desire to compensate for the fact that one's own work offers few opportunities for the expression of physical skill, hence one vicariously experiences the high level of skill displayed by the athletes. Furthermore, they argue that everyone needs to release tensions, and as a consequence some time must be devoted to the affective component of one's life.

Real (1975) argues that the Super Bowl functions to represent a symbolic form of myth in that one is permitted to become a vicarious participant and personally identify with one team. Furthermore, the spectators or viewers can identify and worship heroic archetypes, experience a feeling of collective participation, and break the monotony of secular time and space in an industrial society. Real (1975) also reiterates that this special televised event sustains the economic order through the presentation of commercials.

Beisser (1967) states that sport consumption is a socially sanctioned mode of behavior in which an individual can share something in common on an equal basis with others in the community. This may not be possible in other spheres of what is normally an anonymous society. Stone (1969) argues that the consumption of sport provides mutual accessibility to members of the mass society. However, there is some doubt concerning Stone's argument that a knowledge of sport can help penetrate the barriers of anonymity in a society by leading an individual into interaction with others. For example, Smith (1976c) found that people do talk about sport with strangers, but only rarely, and that sport conversations tend to be more instrumental in reinforcing primary group relationships. Among those who talk with strangers about sport, the majority are middle- and upper-class males who, in their work role, find themselves interacting with strangers to a much greater extent.

Hoch (1972) suggests that sport in capitalist countries is an opiate that distracts the underprivileged and keeps them from confronting the source of their alienation. Of course, this is not a new idea since the initiation of the "bread and circuses" in Roman times supposedly performed a similar function. Edwards (1973) argues that those who are involved in instrumental pursuits are more likely to be interested in sport. Furthermore, he states that since most instrumental pursuits involve security, leadership, and control, these functions are most often performed by males, and particularly by males from the middle and upper classes. Thus, he notes that it is not surprising that males from these social strata comprise the greatest percentage of sport consumers.

Finally, in a comprehensive impressionistic analysis, Spinrad (1970) suggests that there are six functions of spectator sport: (1) it serves as a mechanism of vicarious combat; (2) it provides psychic gratifications through identification with sport heroes in the local community; (3) it enables the individual to participate in a subcultural folklore through the accumulation of knowledge about the history and strategy of a particular sport; (4) it enables the individual to accumulate a set of statistics and thereby retain and express an interest in a subject; (5) it stimulates rational dialogue about players and teams; and (6) it enables an individual to play the role of owner, manager, or coach by making appropriate strategy decisions ("the armchair quarterback").

In addition to conceptual or theoretical analyses, many market research studies have sought to determine why the masses consume sport. The following survey by Harris (1972) illustrates the types of responses that are given by the masses. Using a probability sample of all households in the United States, the motivating factors behind the appeal of professional football were investigated. Based on interviews with 1614 sport fans, 18 years of age and over, it was found that football is a favorite sport in cities and towns in every region of the country. When asked what it is about football that appeals to them, 43 percent indicated that it is entertaining and enjoyable; 7 percent indicated that it draws the family together; 6 percent stated that they watch it because it gives them something to talk about with friends; and 6 percent felt that it gives them an outlet for tensions and pressures. When asked whether they watch football on television alone or with others, 25 percent reported that they watch it alone, 34 percent watch it with one other person, and 18 percent watch it with two or more friends or relatives. In short, studies such as the foregoing provide little or no explanation for the phenomenon. Thus, no definitive conclusions should be drawn as yet concerning why people consume sport.

8.3.5 The Influence of Sport on the Media

The regulative effect of sport on the media suggests that the two social institutions are interrelated at the present time and will likely continue this relationship in the future (see Parente, 1977).

Newspapers have been involved in the presentation of sport longer than any other medium, perhaps because individuals want to read about sport for knowledge and information. As a social institution, the newspaper reflects the culture of a society. To illustrate, Cozens and Stumpf (1953) cite an unpublished study that indicates that general social problems in the United States from 1929 to 1935 were given indirect discussion on the sport pages; these included the depression, race relations, public morality, technological change, and a propensity to favor and help the underdog.

This relationship is further illustrated every time that a cartoon appears on the editorial page. These typically use a sport metaphor or scene to comment on some nonsport phenomenon, or to depict a sport-related event that is considered sufficiently important to merit comment on the editorial page. Van Dalen (1976), for example, examined how political cartoons employing sport themes were used as communication media during the nineteenth century. He found that "sport imagery was used to promote the candidacy of a favored politician, to enlighten voters about the strengths or shortcomings of politicians, to express public fears or dissatisfactions, to attack evils, to inform or inflame the public about issues, to test or crystalize dissent or consensus, and to bolster morale in the North during the civil war." A recent example is the number of editorial cartoons that appeared in Canadian newspapers in 1975 and 1976 concerning the scandals, the escalation of costs, the construction schedule, and the political differences associated with the hosting of the Montreal Olympic Games.

Sport has also increasingly appeared in the comics, either in the form of characters who appear as athletes or in the use of themes to comment on sport issues in a given society. These issues include aggression in sport, an overemphasis on sport, adult domination of children's sport, and sport for national prestige. In one of the few analyses of sport in the comics, Schroeter (1975) suggests that comic strips and comic books enable children to learn about their culture through a visual-verbal medium created for their level of comprehension. Many of the comic heroes symbolically represent "good" as opposed to "evil," and are depicted with athletic-looking physiques (Superman). In sum, comic strips using sport themes, while drawn in a lighter vein, often provide serious social commentary (for example, the Doonesbury and Tank McNamara cartoon series). However, scholars still wait for a "sociology of sport according to 'Peanuts'."

At the local level, newspapers, radio, and television have become indirectly responsible for the promotion of sport in that the product often represents the work of a master of ceremonies (Shecter, 1970; Smith, 1976b; Surface, 1973), rather than a news commentator, news reporter, or journalist. This results in only favorable news for the sport or team being presented. Hence, little incisive reporting about the business side of sport or about any news that might be considered unfavorable advertising by the owners appears. This is reflected in the presentation of sport news, in which mainly scores and strategies are reported. Seldom, if ever, are criticisms leveled, and seldom are stories with a negative theme followed up as nonsport news items would be.

This favorable, advertising approach to sport reporting results from a club-like milieu within the sport system in which obligations bind the media personnel to adhere to a cohesive, consistent presentation of the news or event. For example, many local radio and television play-by-play announcers are hired directly by the club, or the club has the right to approve who broadcasts its games. Furthermore, the club executives may monitor the broadcasts to ensure that a favorable image of the team is being presented. Those who adhere to this policy may receive complimentary drinks or meals, or they may be given a stipend to serve as official scorers or statisticians. An additional bonus is complimentary tickets which they can sell or give away in return for favors they wish to receive from friends or acquaintances (Surface, 1973).

Newspaper reporters have even greater obligations since they are more likely to travel with a team and to report exclusively about one team. In this situation, they often experience a role conflict as to whether they should function as a reporter and objectively report the news (that the team played poorly) or function as a publicity man and try to sell the sport, and their newspaper, to the public (report that the team had bad luck). In this respect they are similar to reporters following a particular candidate during an election campaign.

Most sportwriters are dependent on the publicity personnel of the team for reasons of both information and economics. First, they receive team statistics and news about trades, promotions, and demotions on a regular basis and in sufficient time to meet the press deadlines. A reporter who falls out of favor may receive a news release too late to be included in that day's newspaper. Additionally, they may not be notified of a press conference, or they may be banned from the press box or locker room. On the other hand, if they "fit" in, they may receive direct gratuities such as expenses while traveling with the team or an honorarium for writing press releases or feature stories for the program that is sold at the game. Thus, as McFarlane (1955) has noted, there is an economic interdependence between writers and broadcasters and club executives that ensures an element of social control over media personnel at the local level.

As a result of the power held by sport owners, expected behavioral patterns and norms have evolved within the sport promotion milieu. These enable the individual to appease any element of conflict by economic gains. In this way the sport promoters (i.e., the owners) have a monopoly on the media to shape news and public opinion to meet their needs. Thus, at least until the recent emergence of independent critical columnists, the masses often received a biased view of the world of sport in the absence of any critical writing or counterpropaganda. In effect, there is some censorship of sport stories and sport broadcasts. To date, these practices continue because of tradition, because of their acceptance by the masses, and because of the lack of challenge of these practices on a legal or moral basis.

8.3.6   The Influence of the Media on Sport

Since the 1960s television programs, and especially sport events, have become an increasingly important source of low-cost entertainment for the masses, as well as the major source of fixed revenue for sport organizations. In effect, the media serve as a middleman by collecting revenues from commercial sponsors (see Table 7.3), deducting their expenses and retaining a profit, and then diverting a large proportion of this revenue to sport leagues or individual teams so that they in turn can survive economically. However, in reality the process works in reverse since the league or owners have options in the sale of local and national broadcast rights. At the local level they can package and present the games themselves, they can sell the rights directly to a sponsor who then negotiates a radio or television package, or they can sell the rights to a station or network which packages the games and sells commercial time to sponsors. The latter arrangement is most prevalent at both the local (i.e., team) and the national (i.e., league) level. In fact, because of the insatiable demand for sport on television, owners have been in a position to annually raise the value of the rights. As a result, however, they have become almost totally dependent on this source of revenue to break even or to realize a profit. For example, Horowitz (1974) reported that only one major league baseball team would have realized a book profit in either 1952 or 1970 if broadcast revenues had not been present, and only four would have made a profit in 1965. This situation appears to hold for other sports as well. Furthermore, in all sports there are wide between-team differences in the amount of local or national rights received. This depends on the arrangement with the league for national rights (that is, either each team receives an equal share or the share is based on frequency of appearance) and for local rights (that is, on the size of the local population, the local fan interest, and indirectly the interest by sponsors in becoming affiliated with that team). To illustrate, the broadcast rights accruing to a team can range from approximately $800,000 to $2.5 million, depending on the sport, the team, and the year. For special events such as the Super Bowl or the Olympic Games, television rights have in recent years been approximately $3 million and $25 million, respectively (see Horowitz, 1977).

While some network executives have claimed that sport broadcasts are a bad investment and that they are produced as a public service rather than to make profits (Durso, 1971), certain events are profitable. For example, in the case of the 1974 Super Bowl, the rights were purchased for $2.75 million, the commercial time was sold for over $200,000 per minute, and the net profit for the network after expenses was an estimated $1.2 million (Lalli, 1974).

Thus, the sponsor, and ultimately the consumer, is paying for the sport events that appear on television. Sponsors, in effect, gain a monopoly on the consumer's attention and can direct their advertising to people who are known purchasers of a given product. It is no accident that sponsors of sport events sell products of special appeal to adult males below 50 years of age—namely, beer, automobiles, tires, petroleum products, shaving products, and insurance. Although the cost of sponsoring sport events is increasing, the cost per household is considerably lower than that for other television shows because of the size of the audiences and because of the predictability of the composition of the sport audience (that is, males 20–50 years of age). Nevertheless, because of the escalating cost of television advertising,[7] only the largest industries and firms within each industry can afford to get involved. Hence they gain a monopoly on the advertising market. Furthermore, through long-term contracts they erect a barrier that prevents their competitors from becoming involved.

In summary, the mass media are a social institution, which, although influenced itself to some extent by sport, has had a profound impact on the growth and stability of institutionalized sport. This has occurred largely because of the increasing economic dependence of sport on television, thereby giving the media the opportunity to be innovative and to utilize their power to change the structure and form of sport.

8.4 SPORT AND THE ARTS

8.4.1 Introduction

In Chapter 1 the reader was exposed to the question, "What is sport?" Given the complexity of the answer, it should come as no surprise that the question "What is art?" has no simple answer either. In fact, many more writers have addressed this topic over a much longer period of time with equally diverse results. Thus, a discussion of the relationship between sport and art is less than straightforward. The most common aspect of the resulting collection of issues is the query, "Is sport art?" Most thoughtful answers begin with, "It all depends . . . ."

There is little dispute about whether sport, in both expressive and instrumental modes, has been a subject of artistic creation—that is, an artistic cultural product depicting one or more facets of sport. Moreover, sport historians have depended on artifacts and art objects for knowledge of primitive and pre-industrial game forms and sport pursuits. For example, the poet Pindar's description of the triumph and struggle in early Greek contests reveals the greater importance placed on participation than on success; early Greek vases and sculptures indicate the events, age, sex, and physical structure of participants in the early Olympic Games; (see Boardman, 1964); wall paintings on the tomb of Beni-Hassan in Egypt demonstrate the presence of hopping, jumping, and ball games in the ancient East (see Gardiner, 1967); and the games and pastimes of peasant children in the 1560s are portrayed in Peter Bruegel's classic painting *Children's Games.*

More recently, artists such as LeRoy Nieman have portrayed the events of the modern Olympic Games through canvas and lithographs, poets have described the beauty of sport or criticized the role of sport in contemporary society, and novelists have been obsessed with sport because it is an integral facet of contemporary life-styles. Sport is part of culture and, although normally excluded from a discussion of the art forms of self-expression, it does appear in literature and in the visual and performing arts (Bell, 1976; Betts, 1974; Gerber, 1972; Miller and Russell, 1971).

Since the sociology of the arts is not well developed as a subfield,[8] it is not surprising that sport as an art form has been ignored from an analytical perspective. Rather, much of the analysis has been in the form of social or art criticism, often by those who represent powerful positions in the arts (critics or patrons). They frequently label sport as "popular" or "folk" art that is associated with the masses rather than elite culture and therefore not worthy of critical comment or serious evaluation. Thus, there is a need for a critical, but objective analysis of sport as a part of the aesthetic belief system (i.e., the arts) in a culture (Lowe, 1977). Such an analysis might begin by utilizing a historical perspective to identify and account for changes over time in four elements of the art structure: the medium selected by the producers, the end product, the composition and taste of the audience, and the role, techniques, and values of the distributors (e.g., dealers) and gate-keepers (e.g., critics). In this respect the macroscopic and middle-range models proposed by Huaco (1965) may be applicable for an historical analysis of changes in art forms. Further, a sociological explanation of the arts, and therefore sport art, may operate on three levels: (1) The causal explanation, in which art forms are believed to be the result of social conditions at the time they are created; (2) the expressive level, in which art forms express or reflect the social conditions in which they were created; and (3) the anecdotal level, in which each piece of art is considered a separate entity that may or may not have been influenced by some social or economic fact (Wollheim, 1976).

The art system, then, is just another social system which is comprised of normative, structural, and behavioral subsystems (see Section 2.1.1). These serve the function of depicting, idealizing, or compensating for society. As such, it is similar to and interacts with the sport system. The following two sections offer brief illustrative examples of how sport has been depicted in literature, music, and the visual arts.

8.4.2 Sport and Visual Art Forms

An examination of art books or a visit to most art galleries, museums,[9] or the art exhibit at each Olympiad clearly indicates that sport has been a theme for paintings, prints, drawings, and sculptures[10] throughout history (Masterson, 1974). In these art forms, the value or role of sport in society at a particular period is depicted, sport heroes are idolized, or a sport theme serves as a metaphor for a comment on some other facet of social life. For example, a cursory examination of much of this work clearly reveals social differentiation in sport as in other facets of life. This is evidenced by the emphasis on elites in the art forms (e.g., males, Caucasians, the young, and the highly successful). Seldom portrayed are females, minority groups, children, older athletes (or former athletes when they are past their athletic prime), or the unsuccessful.

Other visual art forms using sport as a theme include documentary and commercial movies, photography, and stamps. In recent years, the artistic expression of athletes competing in specific events has been filmed (*Olympia I and II, Walk, Don't Run, The Man Who Skied Everest*, and *The Endless Summer*), often to the accompaniment of music (*An Olympic Symphony*, in which athletes perform to the music of Beethoven and Verdi). However, most sport films have been produced as mass entertainment in response to anticipated interests or needs. In this respect, movies produced at a specific period in history often reflect the values of that society. For example, Mosher (1976) argues that the need for or interest in violence by North Americans has been vicariously provided by the movies. As evidence, he cites the increased violence appearing in films following the cessation of both World War II and the American involvement in Vietnam—that is, during nonviolent periods in history.

Generally the movies have depicted or used sport as an autobiography of a particular hero or antihero (*Brian's Song, The Other Side of the Mountain, Fear Strikes Out, The Babe Ruth Story*); as an analysis of a subculture with its structure, rules, roles, and function (*Muscle Beach Party, The Endless Summer, Paper Lion, Downhill Racer, The Hustler, Rocky, North Dallas Forty, Semi-Tough, Pumping Iron*); as a comment on the ethics of sport that attempts to raise social consciousness (*The Loneliness of the Long Distance Runner, Roller Ball, Bad News Bears, Slap Shot*); or as a background or subtheme in advancing the main theme or plot of a movie (*Love Story, The Longest Yard, One Flew Over the Cuckoo's Nest, MASH, Black Sunday, Kansas City Bombers*).[11]

While mainly North American examples have been cited here, the reader should recognize that most countries of the world have produced commercial or documentary films with similar themes and for similar purposes. In fact, many foreign film festivals, regardless of the host country, increasingly include sport-related films as part of the program. Sport photography has also become an institutionalized art form through a system of competition and awards.

The appearance of sport stamps (e.g., the 1896 issue by Greece to commemorate the revival of the Olympic Games) has also led to a proliferation of sport art in most countries of the world. A stamp is often initially created as an art form to honor famous athletes or significant sport events in the culture and history of a nation. Today, the collection of sport stamps (there are over 6000 available) represents an avid hobby for sport philatelists[12] who may specialize in the collection of specific sports, specific events (e.g., the Olympic Games[13]), or the sports of a specific nation. Interestingly, several countries (Poland and Canada, for example) have capitalized on the popularity of sport and sport stamps by levying a surcharge for such issues.

8.4.3 Sport, Music, and Literature

The relationship between music and sport has a long history (see Betts, 1974). Although recorded artifacts are not available, music was part of the early training sessions and Olympic competitions in ancient Greece. Since that time, a number of compositions have had sport-related titles (e.g., "The Olympiade" by Pergolesi and "Les Jeux Olympiques" by Mouret written in the 1700s), have been part of the Olympic Games (a piece of music is commissioned for the opening and closing ceremonies of each Olympiad), have commented on contemporary lifestyles (for example, "Raised On Robbery" by Joni Mitchell or "Roller Derby Queen" by Jim Croce), or have been used to augment the visual image in sport competitions that serve as a medium for artistic expression (e.g., gymnastics, figure skating). Thus music plays both instrumental and expressive roles in sport contexts.

Throughout literary history, sport themes have appeared in poetry for a variety of purposes including (1) social criticism, (2) a satirical comment on the participants ("Rugby League Game" by J. Kirkup, which illustrates the absurdity of sport as men try to prove their virility and retain their youth), (3) to illustrate the human pathos of former heroes ("To An Athlete Dying Young" by A. E. Houseman and "Ex-Basketball Player" by John Updike), (4) to depict the beauty and precision of sport ("Tennis" by M. Avison and "Skiers" by R. Warren), (5) to illustrate the physical attributes and skill of athletes ("Two Wrestlers" by R. Francis), (6) to record the triumph and the struggle of sport, as in life ("Casey at Bat" by E. Thayer); and (7) to illustrate the cultural uniqueness of sport ("Matador" by R. Eberhart, "Monsieur Joliat" by W. MacDonald, which depicts ice hockey in Canada, and "At The Ball Game" by W. Williams). Thus, poets have demonstrated their view of sport as a cultural institution in a variety of ways. Detailed analyses of the themes of modern poetry can provide an insightful view of contemporary sport.

Increasingly, the novel or play has become an influential art form that fictionally or autobiographically treats sport in either a serious or frivolous manner. Authors have used sport as the setting for their novel or play to develop a major character or to include an element of realism in their plot. For example, sport material has been used for social criticism, satire, and fantasy.[14]

Recent examples of sport in novels or plays include *Bang the Drum Slowly* (M. Harris), *The Great American Novel* (P. Roth), *Rabbit Run* (J. Updike), *A Fan's Notes* (F. Exley), *End Zone* (D. Delillo), *North Dallas Forty* (P. Gent), *Sports in America* (J. Michener), and *The Universal Baseball Association, J. Henry Waugh, Prop.* (R. Coover). Furthermore, over 30 novels since 1960 have either referred to football or used it as a central theme. The dominant themes in these novels have included idealism, egocentric pragmatism, isolationism, sexuality, racism, commercialism, gambling, and drugs (Burt, 1975). According to Burt (1975), this increasing interest in football serves as a metaphor to depict modern life-styles and the accompanying social problems. In a similar vein, Haerle (1974) completed a content analysis of baseball autobiographies which demonstrated that players' values with respect to the game change over time.

Finally, content analyses of children's literature over time suggests that until recently a masculine world has been presented. Moreover, because childhood socialization may occur through novels with sport themes, the central characters reflect the dominant values of a particular society. Surprisingly, there have been few differences over time in the character traits that have been presented in children's books about sport, although the values and traits presented vary with the specific sport being described. Among the traits most commonly portrayed are obedience, unselfishness, consideration for others, hard work, determination, honesty, impulse control, intelligence, high achievement orientation, success, physical prowess, and emotional control.

In summary, sport has appeared as a topic or theme in a number of art forms throughout history. Notwithstanding the debate as to whether sport is art, its appearance in music, literature, and visual art forms has provided a valuable understanding of sport, both historically and as a social comment on life at the period of time in which the work was created. It appears likely that sport will continue to appear in the arts and may be perceived to be a more integral or legitimate form of art by those both within and outside artistic institutions.

8.5   SPORT AS A CULTURAL PRODUCT:
THE INFLUENCE OF SOCIAL INSTITUTIONS
ON INVOLVEMENT AND SUCCESS IN SPORT

The process of becoming involved in sport varies cross-culturally, partly due to factors operating at the macro level such as a dominant ideology, the type of political system, the degree of government stability, the state of the economy, and unique societal values and norms concerning play and sport. At the macro level within a given society there is often a dominant ideology that reflects a social value and norm concerning the behavioral patterns in that country, region, or community, including those related to sport. For example, if there is a dominant ideology that considers sport participation and the attainment of elite performance to be important, human and economic resources are usually allocated to enhance the opportunity for athletic involvement and success.[15] Thus, there tend to be both intrasocietal and intraregional differences as well as cross-national differences in the degree and type of involvement in sport.

Although the Olympic Games are supposedly held to facilitate competition among individuals, they have become a source of national pride and prestige. As a result, cross-national differences in success in the last 20 years have appeared because some nations have utilized more of their resources to increase their performance level in the "unofficial" team standings. Thus, within some countries many human and economic resources have been allocated to enhance the opportunity for athletic success; values have changed so that the pursuit of elitism in sport is more highly valued than other social issues; a tradition of success has come to be expected and required; and government agencies have promoted mass participation in sport so that those who have the potential will have every opportunity to attain success. In summary, a number of macro-level factors found within the economic, political, and religious institutions of a society influence the degree of involvement and success in international sport competitions.

In an attempt to account for cross-national differences in involvement and success, the number of participants and the number of medals won by each country at the Olympic Games have been correlated with social, political, economic, and religious variables.[16] Luschen (1975), controlling for population size, reported that there is a high level of involvement by smaller countries such as Iceland, Mongolia, Luxembourg, Norway, Switzerland, and Denmark. That is, countries send a significant number of representatives regardless of their relative size or degree of political strength. However, not all countries are successful and recent studies have attempted to account for this differential success rate by considering religious, political, economic, and social differences among nations.

The role of religion in success has been considered by Luschen (1967) and Seppanen (1970). Luschen (1967) examined the probable (based on the percentage of different religious groups in each country) religious preferences of Olympic medal winners of the 1960s. He found that more than 50 percent of the medal winners were from countries in which Protestantism dominated. Similarly, he cites a 1958 survey of young athletes in West Germany which indicated that there was an overrepresentation of Protestants, especially in the individual sports and among the elite athletes. Luschen also noted that since collectivity is highly valued by Catholics, it is not surprising to see them well represented in team sports in Germany, the United States, and South America.

A similar study by Seppanen (1970) hypothesized that Olympic success from 1896 to 1968 was a function of religious ideologies throughout the world. Using a success coefficient constructed for the study, he compared countries with a major religion that could be classified as having an "other-worldly" orientation (e.g., Hindu, Buddhist) with those with an "inner-worldly" orientation (e.g., Confucian, Islam, Hebrew, Christian). He found that the latter were more successful in Olympic competition. When he further examined the success coefficients for countries in which various Christian religions dominated, the Protestant nations were found to be three to four times more successful than the Catholic nations. As an additional analysis he compared the Protestant, Catholic, and Socialist nations and noted that up to 1956 the Protestant countries were more successful. However, beginning in 1960 the Socialist countries became more successful in both male and female events. Thus, it appears that the competitive and achievement ethos characteristic of both Protestantism and Socialism is reflected in Olympic success, especially for the Socialist countries in which the values of hard work and accomplishment are promoted in all facets of life, including sport.

Success in Olympic competition has also been hypothesized to be related to the type of political system and the presence of certain human and economic resources within a given social system. In the first analysis of athletic success from a social science perspective, Jokl et al. (1956) studied 4925 athletes at the 1952 Helsinki Olympic Games. This information was later combined with similar 1960 Olympic data and it was found that Olympic success was related to low national death rates, low infant mortality rates, and high per capita incomes (Jokl, 1964).

Seppanen (1970) noted the success of Germany, Russia, and Japan during and following high periods of nationalism in each country. More specifically, he noted the success of these countries in the 1930s at a time when they were intensifying their war preparations. Ball (1972) found that Olympic success was related to the possession of human and economic resources, along with a centralized form of political decision-making and authority that maximizes the allocation of these resources. More specifically, he concluded that a high level of Olympic success was related to modernized and westernized qualities, a centralized government, a high degree of political mobilization of the human and economic resources within the country, a high degree of social integration, and a Communist-dominated political system.

Similarly, on the basis of an analysis of the 1972 Summer Olympics, Grimes, Kelly, and Rubin (1974) concluded that the Communist countries were more successful because they seemed to be more effective in channelling their available population and economic resources into sport, rather than into other social domains. Novikov and Maximenko (1972) found correlations ranging from 0.41 to 0.74 between Olympic success at the 1964 Summer Olympic Games and such socioeconomic indices as per capita national income, calories of food consumed by the population, average life expectancy of the inhabitants, percentage of illiterates in the country, percentage of the population living in an urban area, and the total number of inhabitants. More recently, an analysis of the 1972 Summer Olympic Games by Pooley et al. (1975) found that military strength, military expenditure per capita, the gross national product, and the number of Olympic sports practiced in the schools were the factors that correlated most highly with Olympic success. The relationship between military strength and Olympic success was also found to hold when the two most powerful nations (the USSR and the USA) were eliminated from the analysis.

To illustrate the uncertainty of the "real" explanation of Olympic success, a study by Levine (1974), also utilizing the 1972 Summer Olympic Games, reported that the following four factors correlated highly with the number of Olympic medals won: the gross domestic product, the size of the area of each country, the presence of a socialist economy, and the presence of a wide newspaper circulation throughout the country. Thus the fact that two studies of the same Olympic games report different results suggests that there is a need to define more precisely and consistently what the dependent variables should be, and to arrive at a theoretical rationale for including specific independent variables. Moreover, there would seem to be a need to account for interaction among variables.

The one study that has attempted to account for some of these weaknesses (Shaw and Pooley, 1976) grouped the countries according to their international power or their ability to exert control over other states (Speigel, 1972). The results indicated that Olympic success varies depending on the political and economic conditions within certain types of countries.[17] To illustrate, population size and gross national product accounted for 63 percent of the variance in success for Western developed countries; military expenditure and the number of Olympic sports taught in the schools accounted for 32 percent of the variance in the socialist countries; and gross national product, military expenditure, and number of Olympic sports taught explained 94 percent of the variance in the developing countries of the Third World.

In summary, although definitive explanations are not yet available, it appears that Olympic success is influenced to varying degrees by the religious, economic, social, political, and military institutions found within a given society. More specifically, these institutions reflect and influence the cultural values and norms concerning the place of mass and elite sport in the value hierarchy of the country. In this way, sport becomes a cultural product. However, it still falls short of being equally accessible to all. This theme is expanded in the next chapter.

NOTES

1. A good conceptual account of the meaning of the term "culture" is given in Kessing (1974).

2. Gans defines taste culture as:

   . . . values, the cultural forms which express these values: music, art, design, literature, drama, comedy, poetry, criticism, news, and the media in which these are expressed—books, magazines, newspapers, records, films, television programs, paintings and sculpture, architecture, and insofar as ordinary consumer goods also express aesthetic values or functions, furnishings, clothes, appliances and automobiles as well. (Gans, 1974, pp. 10–11)

He goes on to indicate that "taste culture is the culture which results from choice; it has to do with those values and products about which people have some choice" (Gans, 1974). In pluralistic societies, so many taste cultures may appear that, in fact, they represent subcultures. Sport, then, comprises one element of taste culture that may be valued differently within societies with a stratified social structure.

3. Finnish baseball does, however, represent a cultural transformation into a unique game.

4. Some exceptions might be bandy in the Soviet Union and water polo in Hungary.

5. For a detailed summary of the place of sport in Catholicism, Protestantism, Judaism, Islam, Hinduism, and Zen Buddhism, see Grupe et al. (1972, pp. 59–115) and Schloz et al. (1973, pp. 595–606).

6. Over 96 percent of the households in North America have a television set.

7. For example, cost per commercial minute during baseball broadcasts is $30,000 for a Saturday afternoon season game, $52,000 for a Monday evening league game, $110,000 for an evening league championship game, $140,000 for the All-Star Game, and $150,000 for the World Series.

8. See the following for some general attempts to analyze this social phenomenon: Albrecht et al. (1970), Duvignaud (1972), Gans (1967), Kavolis (1968, 1973), and Rosenberg and White (1957).

9. A National Art Museum of Sport has been permanently located since 1968 in the new Madison Square Garden in New York City. This institution is funded by donations from artists, industries, patrons of the arts, and other private citizens. The museum annually sponsors a traveling exhibit of art prints depicting sport.

10. One of the most famous sculptors is R. Tait McKenzie, a Canadian surgeon. Among his creations are "The Joy of Effort" and the four facial reactions: "Effort," "Breathlessness," "Fatigue," and "Exhaustion."

11. Mosher (1976) provides a list of films by sport (boxing, college football, and professional baseball have been most popular) and a chronological list of sport films from 1894 to 1975.

12. An organization called the Sports Philatelists International publishes a monthly *Journal of Sports Philately* (H. Long, 148 S. Hemlock, Apt. 6, Ventura, Calif., 93001).

13. A catalog listing only Olympic stamps is over 300 pages in length.

14. A number of universities now offer courses on sport literature. Readers interested in this topic might want to examine W. L. Umphlett's *The Sporting Myth and the American Experience* (1975), which provides a critical analysis of twentieth-century sport literature, Higgs and Isaacs (eds.), *The Sporting Spirit—Athletes In Literature and Life* (1977), and A. Guttmann's "Sport in der Amerikanischen Literatur . . ." (1974).

15. For an application of quantitative methods and systems analysis to account for success in specific sport events, see Machol and Ladany (1976) and Ladany and Machol (1977).

16. It must be stressed that most of the results of these studies have been based on bivariate correlational analysis, with few attempts to control for spuriousness through the use of partial correlations or to utilize multiple regression analyses.

17. The USA, the USSR, and Kenya were eliminated from the analyses because they skewed the distributions on a number of variables. Moreover, this is one of the few studies to use partial correlation and multiple regression techniques.

REFERENCES

Albrecht, M., et al. (eds.) (1970). *The Sociology of Art and Literature: A Reader.* New York: Praeger.

Andreano, R. (1965). "Japanese baseball." In R. Andreano (ed.), *No Joy In Mudville: The Dilemma of Major League Baseball,* pp. 61–76. Cambridge, Mass.: Schenkman.

Andrus, R. (1962). "A history of the recreation program of the Church of Jesus Christ of Latter-Day Saints." Ph.D. dissertation, State University of Iowa.

Ball, D. W. (1972). "Olympic Games competition: Structural correlates of national success." *International Journal of Comparative Sociology* 15: 186–200.

Bandura, A., and R. Walters (1963). *Social Learning and Personality Development.* New York: Holt, Rinehart and Winston.

Beisser, A. (1967). *The Madness in Sports.* New York: Appleton-Century-Crofts.

Bell, J. (1976). "An investigation of the concept, sport as art." *The Physical Educator* 33 (May): 81–84.

Berkowitz, L. (1969). "The frustration-aggression hypothesis revisited." In L. Berkowitz (ed.), *Roots of Aggression,* pp. 1–29. New York: Atherton Press.

Betts, J. R. (1953). "The technological revolution and the rise of sport: 1850–1900." *Mississippi Valley Historical Review* XL: 231–256.

Betts, J. R. (1974). *America's Sporting Heritage: 1850–1950.* Reading, Mass.: Addison-Wesley.

Birrell, S., and J. Loy (1974). "Sport consumption via the mass media: Patterns, perspectives and paradigms." Presented at the Fourth National Convention of the Popular Culture Association, Milwaukee, Wisconsin (May).

Birrell, S., and J. W. Loy (1977). "Media sport: Hot and cool." Unpublished paper.

Boardman, J. (1964). *Greek Art.* New York: F. A. Praeger.

Bouton, J. (1970). *Ball Four.* New York: Dell.

Breed, W. (1958). "Mass communication and social-cultural integration." *Social Forces* 37 (December): 109–116.

Brill, A. (1929). "The why of the fan." *North American Review* 228 (October): 429–434.

Burt, D. (1975). "A helmeted hero: The football player in recent American fiction." Presented at the Popular Culture Association Meetings.

Clignet, R., and M. Stark (1974). "Modernization and the game of soccer in Cameroon." *International Review of Sport Sociology* 9: 81–98.

Cozens, F., and F. Stumpf (1953). *Sports in American Life.* Chicago: University of Chicago Press.

De Fleur, M. (1970). *Theories of Mass Communication,* 2nd ed. New York: David McKay.

Deford, F. (1976). "Religion in sport." *Sports Illustrated* 44 (April 19, April 26, May 3).

Desmonde, W. (1952). "The bullfight as a religious festival." *American Imago* 9: 173–195.

Dollard, J., et al. (1939). "Culture, society, impulse and socialization." *American Journal of Sociology* 45 (July): 50–63.

Duncan, H. (1968). *Symbols in Society.* London: Oxford University Press.

Dunlap, H. (1951). "Games, sports, dancing and other vigorous recreational activities and their function in Samoan culture." *Research Quarterly* 22: 298–311.

Durkheim, E. (1947). *The Elementary Forms of Religious Life.* Translated by J. Swain. London: George Allen and Unwin.

Durso, J. (1971). *The All-American Dollar: The Big Business of Sports.* Boston: Houghton Mifflin.

Duvignaud, J. (1972). *The Sociology of Art*. London: Paladin.

Edwards, H. (1973). *Sociology of Sport*. Homewood, Ill.: Dorsey Press.

Elias, M., and E. Dunning (1970). "The quest for excitement in unexciting societies." In G. Luschen (ed.), *The Cross-Cultural Analysis of Sport and Games*, pp. 31–51. Champaign, Ill.: Stipes.

Emery, E., et al. (1965). *Introduction to Mass Communication*, 2nd ed. New York: Dodd, Mead.

Feibleman, J. (1968). *The Institutions of Society*. New York: Humanities Press.

Feldman, S., and G. Thielbar (eds.) (1972). *Lifestyles: Diversity in American Society*. Boston: Little, Brown.

Finlay, J. (1971). "Homo Ludens (Americanus)." *Queen's Quarterly* **78**: 353–364.

Fox, J. (1961). "Pueblo baseball: A new use for old witchcraft." *Journal of American Folklore* **74**: 9–16.

Gans, H. (1967). "Popular culture in America: Social problems in a mass society or a social asset in a pluralistic society?" In H. Becker (ed.), *Social Problems: A Modern Approach*, pp. 549–620. New York: John Wiley.

Gans, H. (1974). *Popular Culture and High Culture: An Analysis and Evaluation of Taste*. New York: Basic Books. Used with permission.

Gardiner, E. N. (1967). *Athletics of the Ancient World*. London: Oxford University Press.

Geertz, C. (1972). "Deep play: Notes on the Balinese cockfights." *Daedalus* **101**: 1–37.

Geldbach, E. (1975). *Sport and Protestantismus*. Wuppertal, West Germany: R. Brockhaus Verlag.

Gerber, E. (ed.) (1972). *Sport and the Body*. Philadelphia: Lea and Febiger.

Gerth, H., and C. W. Mills (1954). *Character and Social Structure*. London: Routledge and Kegan Paul.

Gini, C. (1939). "Rural ritual games in Lybia." *Rural Sociology* **4**: 283–299.

Gmelch, G. (1972). "Magic in professional baseball." In G. P. Stone (ed.), *Games, Sport and Power*, pp. 128–137. New Brunswick, N.J.: Transaction.

Goldstein, J., and R. Arms (1971). "Effects of observing athletic contests on hostility." *Sociometry* **34**: 83–90.

Greendorfer, S. (In press). "Sport and the mass media." In G. Sage and G. Luschen (eds.), *Encyclopedia of Physical Education and Sport*, Vol. 5. Reading, Mass.: Addison-Wesley.

Gregory, C. J., and B. Petrie (1973). "Superstition in sport." In I. D. Williams and L. M. Wankel (eds.), *Proceedings of the Fourth Canadian Psycho-motor Learning and Sports Psychology Symposium*, pp. 384–402. Ottawa: Fitness and Amateur Sport Directorate.

Gregory, C. J., and B. Petrie (1975). "Superstitions of Canadian intercollegiate athletes: An inter-sport comparison." *International Review of Sport Sociology* **10**: 59–66.

Grimes, A., W. Kelly, and P. Rubin (1974). "A socio-economic model of national Olympic performance." *Social Science Quarterly* **55** (December): 777–783.

Grupe, O., et al. (eds.) (1972). *The Scientific View of Sport*. New York: Springer-Verlag.

Guttmann, A. (1974). "Sport in der Amerikanischen Literatur: Bestatingug der Neuen Sozialkritik?" *Sportwisseschaft* **4**: 384–394.

Guttmann, A. (1975). "Literature, sociology, and 'our national game.' " *Prospects* **1**: 119–136.

Haerle, R. (1974). "The athlete as single 'moral' leader: Heroes, success themes and basic cultural values in selected baseball autobiographies, 1900–1970." *Journal of Popular Culture* **8**: 392–401.

Harris, L. (1972). *A Survey of the Reactions and Opinions of Professional Football Fans*. Study Number 2153 (January). New York: Lou Harris and Associates.

Higgs, R. J., and D. N. Isaacs (eds.) (1971). *The Sporting Spirit—Athletes in Literature and Life*. New York: Harcourt Brace Jovanovich.

Hoch, P. (1972). *Rip Off the Big Game*. Garden City, N.Y.: Anchor Books.

Horowitz, I. (1974). "Sports broadcasting." In R. Noll (ed.), *Government and the Sports Business*, pp. 275–323. Washington, D.C.: The Brookings Institute.

Horowitz, I. (1977). "Sports telecasts: Rights and regulations." *Journal of Communication* 27 (Summer): 160–168.

Huaco, G. (1965). "The sociological model." In G. Huaco (ed.), *The Sociology of Film Art*, pp. 18–22. New York: Basic Books.

Huizinga, J. (1976) "The play element in contemporary civilization." In M. Hart (ed.), *Sport and the Sociocultural Process*, 2nd ed., pp. 18–34. Dubuque, Iowa: William C. Brown.

Huskel, E. (1926). "Should Christians play on Sunday?" *Literary Digest* 88: 27–28.

Jokl, E. (1964). "Health, wealth and athletics." In E. Jokl and E. Simon (eds.), *International Research in Sport and Physical Education*, pp. 218–222. Springfield, Ill.: C. C. Thomas.

Jokl, E. et al. (1956). *Sports in the Cultural Pattern of the World*. Helsinki, Finland: Institute of Occupational Health.

Kando, T. (1975). *Leisure and Popular Culture in Transition*. St. Louis: C. V. Mosby.

Katz, E., M. Gurevitch, and H. Hass (1973). "On the use of the mass media for important things." *American Sociological Review* 38 (April): 164–181.

Kavolis, V. (1968). *Artistic Expression: A Sociological Analysis*. Ithaca, N.Y.: Cornell University Press.

Kavolis, V. (1973). "The institutional structure of cultural services." *The Journal of Aesthetic Education* 7 (October): 63–80.

Kenyon, G. S. (1966). "The significance of physical activity as a function of age, sex, education, and socio-economic status of northern United States adults." *International Review of Sport Sociology* 1: 41–54.

Kenyon, G. S. (1968). "Values held for physical activity by selected urban secondary school students in Canada, Australia, England and the United States." Report of the U.S. Office of Education, Contract S-276. Washington: Educational Resources Information Center.

Kessing, M. (1974). "Theories of culture." *Review of Anthropology* 3: 73–97.

Kirsh, C., et al. (1973). *A Leisure Study—Canada, 1972*. Ottawa: Department of the Secretary of State, Arts and Culture Branch.

Koppett, L. (1977). "Athletes in action spread gospel efficiently." *New York Times* (March 15): 50.

Kramer, J. (1969). *Farewell to Football*. New York: Bantam Books.

Ladany, S., and R. Machol (eds.) (1977). *Optimal Strategies in Sport*. New York: North-Holland.

Lalli, R. (1974). "The $12 million businessman's special: And now for the pre-game scores." *Rolling Stone* 155 (February 28): 40–41.

Levine, N. (1974). "Why do countries win Olympic medals? Some structural correlates of Olympic Games success: 1972." *Sociology and Social Research* 28: 353–360.

Lewis, G., and G. Redmond (1974). *Sport Heritage: A Guide to Halls of Fame, Special Collections and Museums in the United States and Canada*. New York: Barnes.

Lowe, B. (1977). *The Beauty of Sport: A Cross-Disciplinary Inquiry*. Englewood Cliffs, N.J.: Prentice-Hall.

Luschen, G. (1967). "The interdependence of sport and culture." *International Review of Sport Sociology* 2: 127–139.

Luschen, G. (1975). "The institution of sport in sociological perspectives." Presented to UNESCO on Behalf of the International Committee for the Sociology of Sport.

MacAloon, J. (1976). "Religious themes and structures in the Olympic movement and the Olympic Games." Presented at the International Congress of the Physical Activity Sciences, Quebec City (July).

Machol, R., and S. Ladany (1976). *Management Science in Sports.* New York: North-Holland.

Maheu, R. (1962). "Sport and culture." *International Journal of Adult and Youth Education* 14: 169–178.

Malinowski, B. (1948). *Magic, Science and Religion.* New York: Doubleday.

Masterson, D. (1974). "Sport in modern painting." In H. T. Whiting and D. W. Masterson (eds.), *Readings in the Aesthetics of Sport,* pp. 69–88. London: Lepus.

McFarlane, B. (1955). "The sociology of sports promotion." Unpublished M.A. thesis, McGill University.

McLuhan, M. (1964). *Understanding Media.* New York: New American Library.

McPherson, B. D. (1972). "Socialization into the role of sport consumer: A theory and causal model." Ph.D. dissertation, University of Wisconsin, Madison.

McPherson, B. (1975). "Sport consumption and the economics of consumerism." In D. W. Ball and J. W. Loy (eds.), *Sport and Social Order,* pp. 243–275. Reading, Mass.: Addison-Wesley.

McPherson, B. (1976a). "Consumer role socialization: A within system model." *Sportwissenschaft* 6: 144–154.

McPherson, B. (1976b). "Socialization into the role of sport consumer: A theory and causal model." *Canadian Review of Sociology and Anthropology* 13 (November): 165–177.

McQuail, D. (1969). *Towards a Sociology of Mass Communications.* London: Collier-MacMillan.

Metcalfe, A. (1968). "Working class free time activities in Newcastle-upon-Tyne and South Northumberland, England 1780–1880." Ph.D. dissertation, University of Wisconsin, Madison.

Meyer, H. (1973). "Puritanism and physical training: Ideological and political accents in the Christian interpretation of sport." *International Review of Sport Sociology* 8: 37–51.

Miller, D., and K. Russell (1971). *Sport: A Contemporary View.* Philadelphia: Lea and Febiger.

Milton, B. (1972). "Sports as a functional equivalent of religion." Masters thesis, University of Wisconsin, Madison.

Mosher, S. (1976). "Everybody's a hero: A study of sport in the American cinema." M.A. thesis, Department of Sport Studies, University of Massachusetts.

Novak, M. (1976). *The Joy of Sports: End Zones, Bases, Baskets, Balls, and the Consecration of the American Spirit.* New York: Basic Books. Used with permission.

Novikov, A., and A. Maximenko (1972). "The influence of selected socio-economic factors on the level of sports achievements in the various countries." *International Review of Sport Sociology* 7: 27–44.

Panunzio, C. (1949). *Major Social Institutions.* New York: Macmillan.

Parente, D. E. (1977). "The interdependence of sports and television." *Journal of Communication* 27 (Summer): 128–132.

Pooley, J., et al. (1975). "Winning at the Olympics: A quantitative analysis of the impact of a range of socio-economic, politico-military, growth rate and educational variables." Presented at the Annual Conference of the APHERA, Charlottetown, Prince Edward Island (November).

Radcliffe-Brown, A. (1964). "Religion and society." In L. Schneider (ed.), *Religion, Culture, and Society*. New York: John Wiley.

Real, M. (1975). "Superbowl: Mythic spectacle." *Journal of Communication* 25 (Winter): 31–43.

Riesman, D., and R. Denney (1951). "Football in America: A study in culture diffusion." *American Quarterly* 3: 309–319.

Robinson, J. P. (1970). "Daily participation in sport across twelve countries." In G. Luschen (ed.), *The Cross-Cultural Analysis of Sport and Games*, pp. 156–173. Champaign, Ill.: Stipes.

Rooney, J. (1974). *A Geography of American Sport: From Cabin Creek to Anaheim*. Reading, Mass.: Addison-Wesley.

Rosenberg, B., and A. White (eds.) (1957). *Mass Culture: The Popular Arts in America*. Glencoe, Ill.: The Free Press.

Ross, M. (1971). "Football red and baseball green." *Chicago Review* (January–February): 30–40.

Rostow, W. (1971). *The Stages of Economic Growth*. London: Cambridge University Press.

Schloz, R., et al. (1973). "Sport and religions of the world." In O. Grupe et al. (eds.), *Sport and the Modern World*, pp. 595–606. New York: Springer-Verlag.

Schramm, W. (ed.) (1960). *Mass Communications*, 2nd ed. Urbana, Ill.: University of Illinois Press.

Schroeter, H. (1975). "Betrachtungen zu Asterix bei den Olympischen Spielen." *Kolner Beitrage zur Sportwissenschaft* 3: 171–183.

Scotch, N. (1961). "Magic, sorcery and football among urban Zulu: A case of reinterpretation under acculturation." *Journal of Conflict Resolution* 5: 70–74.

Seppanen, P. (1970). "The role of competitive sports in different societies." Presented at the Seventh World Congress of the International Sociological Association, Varna, Bulgaria (September).

Shaw, S., and J. Pooley (1976). "National success at the Olympics: An explanation." Presented at the Sixth International Seminar on the History of Physical Education and Sport, Trois Rivieres, Quebec (July).

Sheard, K., and E. Dunning (1973). "The rugby football club as a type of male preserve: Some sociological notes." *International Review of Sport Sociology* 8: 5–21.

Shecter, L. (1970). *The Jocks*. New York: Paperback Library.

Simonson, T. (ed.) (1962). *The Goal and the Glory—America's Athletes Speak Their Faith*. Westwood, N.J.: Revell.

Smith, G. (1976a). "Ritual, ceremony, and sport." *Katimavik* 3 (Winter): 3–4.

Smith, G. (1976b). "A study of a sports journalist." *International Review of Sport Sociology* 11: 5–25.

Smith, G. (1976c). "The use of the mass media for sports information as a function of age, sex and socio-economic status." Presented at the International Congress of the Physical Activity Sciences, Quebec City (July).

Spiegel, S. (1972). *Dominance and Diversity: The International Hierarchy*. Boston: Little Brown.

Spinrad, W. (1970). "Functions of spectator sports." Presented at the Seventh World Congress of the International Sociological Association, Varna, Bulgaria (September).

Sports Illustrated (1973). "Few and far between." (September 24): 22.

Steinberg, C. (ed.) (1966). *Mass Media and Communication*. New York: Hastings House.

Stephenson, W. (1967). *The Play Theory of Mass Communications*. Chicago: University of Chicago Press.

Stone, G. (1969). "Some meanings of American sport: An extended view." In G. Kenyon (ed.), *Aspects of Contemporary Sport Sociology*, pp. 5–27. Chicago: The Athletic Institute.

Surface, V. (1973). "The shame of the sports beat." In R. Glessing and W. White (eds.), *Mass Media: The Invisible Environment*, pp. 152–160. Toronto: Science Research Associates.

Time (1977). "The super show." (January 10): 28–34.

Umphlett, W. L. (1975). *The Sporting Myth and the American Experience*. Lewisburg, Penn.: Bucknell University Press.

Van Dalen, D. B. (1976). "Political cartoons employing sports as a communication medium." *Canadian Journal of History of Sport and Physical Education* **VII** (December): 39–57.

Warner, W. L. (1953). *American Life: Dream and Reality*. Chicago: University of Chicago Press.

Wollheim, R. (1976). "Sociological explanation of the arts: Some distinctions." In M. C. Albrecht et al. (eds.), *The Sociology of Art and Literature*. New York: Praeger.

Wool, R. (1975). "Capitalist squash." *New York Times Magazine* (April 13): 42–49.

Wrigley, J. R. (1970). "Magic in sport." Presented at the Seventh World Congress of the International Sociological Association, Varna, Bulgaria (September).

Zablocki, B., and R. M. Kanter (1976). "The differentiation of life styles." In A. Inkeles (ed.), *Annual Review of Sociology*, Vol. 2, pp. 269–298. Palo Alto, Calif.: Annual Reviews Inc.

Zurcher, L., and A. Meadow (1967). "On bull fights and baseball: An example of interaction of social institutions." *International Journal of Comparative Sociology* **8**: 99–117.

Chapter 9
INSTITUTIONALIZED STRUCTURES OF SOCIAL STRATIFICATION

9.1 THE NATURE OF SOCIAL STRATIFICATION

This chapter accounts for the differential role opportunities available to individuals in sport. This process of differential allocation derives from the fact that throughout history social systems have been characterized by the presence of individuals who can be identified on the basis of biological or social characteristics such as race, ethnic background, age, sex (gender), prestige, power, wealth, education, income, or occupation. These distinguishing attributes, which may be either ascribed (inherited) or achieved (acquired), often serve as the basis whereby individuals aspire to or are allocated to different but interrelated roles within a given social system. In effect, then, not everyone has an equal opportunity to play certain social roles because of this system of differential ranking known as *social stratification*.[1]

In his analysis of social stratification, Tumin (1967) states that this phenomenon has five characteristic features: It is (1) social, (2) ancient, (3) ubiquitous, (4) diverse in its forms, and (5) consequential. As well as having these five attributes, various forms of social stratification become institutionalized as a result of similar underlying social processes. Tumin (1967) identifies these processes as (1) differentiation, (2) ranking, (3) evaluation, and (4) rewarding. These processes are briefly described in the next section.[2]

9.1.1 Processes of Social Stratification

Role Differentiation

All social systems, be they micro or macro in nature, require a division of labor among their members in order to function effectively. The occupants of particular positions within a social system are assigned specific sets of rights and responsibilities (in other words, they are allotted distinctive social roles to perform). For example, among work organizations such as professional athletic teams, distinctions are made between the rights and responsibilities of owners, managers, coaches, and players. Moreover, among task groups (i.e., athletic teams) within such work organizations, there is further role differentiation in terms of functional specialization (for example, offensive roles vs. defensive roles, linemen vs. backs, etc.). Once positions in a social system have been differentiated on the basis of the roles performed by their occupants, it becomes possible to rank the positions and their related roles.

Ranking of Roles

Tumin (1967) points out that roles can be compared or ranked in terms of three criteria. First, they can be ranked according to *personal characteristics* of the role performer; for example, to be a first-rate quarterback requires intelligence, speed, strength, and good peripheral vision. Second, roles can be ranked according to the *trained skills and abilities* of the role performer; for example, to play the role effectively, a quarterback must possess the ability to read defensive alignments quickly and accurately and must have perfected the passing skills. Third, roles can be ranked according to the *consequences or effects* of role performance on others; for example, quarterbacks are judged on their leadership ability and the effects their actions have on team success. They may also be evaluated in terms of the degree to which they provide exciting entertainment for fans and spectators.

Role Evaluation

Major social roles selected for comparative ranking are characteristically evaluated on the basis of a subjective scale of social worth. "The graduations of this scale may . . . be described in terms such as superior to inferior, better to worse, more to less distinguished, or as evoking more to less favorable public opinion" (Tumin, 1967). In short, evaluation involves "moral judgments" of social worth and often leads to invidious distinctions between social categories representing age, sex, ethnic groups, and social classes.

Three basic dimensions of evaluation are *prestige, preferability*, and *popularity*. Conceptually, prestige refers to honor, preferability refers to an "idealized" choice of role or role model, and popularity refers to notoriety. The combination of the prestige, preferability, and popularity dimensions of role evaluation denotes the status of the role associated with a particular position. However, there is not always a high degree of correlation among the different dimensions of evaluation. For example, the role of professional athlete is not accorded high prestige as an occupational category in North America, and generally only receives high evaluation in terms of preferability on the part of young males; yet, as concerns popularity, it receives considerable public attention.

Finally, "it is important to distinguish between two major objects or foci of evaluation: one, a particular status or role, and two, a generalized social standing" (Tumin, 1967). The examples thus far have highlighted the first type of evaluative focus, whereas the examples that follow emphasize the second type of evaluative focus.

Rewarding of Roles and Statuses

The process of rewarding refers to the fact that the greater an individual's status in any given social system, the greater the rewards that person will receive in terms of property (including income), power, and psychic gratification (see Tumin, 1967, pp. 39–42). The consequences of inequalities associated with the process of rewarding are two-fold. First, inequalities determine in large measure the *life-chances* of an individual, including his or her physical and mental health, marital status, educational and occupational status, and social and geographical mobility. The second consequence is that such inequalities importantly influence *life-styles*, including manner of speech and dress, type of residence, type of leisure activities, and number and type of friends and social relations.

To summarize the nature of the underlying processes of social stratification, it is noted that (1) all social systems require a division of labor that results in role differentiation; (2) differential roles characteristic of the occupants of particular positions within given social systems are typically ranked according to one or more criteria; (3) the rank order of positional roles in a social system is generally evaluated in terms of social worth on the basis of perceived prestige, preferability, and popularity, and assigned an overall social status; and finally, (4) statuses are differentially rewarded in terms of property, power, and psychic gratification, and the inequalities associated with this rewarding affect an individual's life-chances and life-style.

The processes of stratification described above are associated with all forms of social stratification. The major institutionalized systems of stratification in North American society are those based on age, class, ethnic, racial, and sex (gender) statuses. The nature of these systems of stratification is outlined below.

9.1.2 Types of Social Stratification

Racial and Ethnic Stratification

In any pluralistic, multicultural, or multinational society, the social order may be stratified along racial or ethnic lines within the society or even within specific social strata. This division is more likely to occur in societies in which particularistic rather than universalistic criteria are used to evaluate individuals, resulting in minority groups who are differentiated on the basis of either inherited physical characteristics (e.g., skin color) or socially acquired cultural differences in language, national origin, or culture (ethnicity).

Although ethnic communities vary greatly in their degree of organization, it is possible for an individual to remain insulated within the environment of his or her own ethnic group for all social relationships throughout the life cycle. For example, Greeley points out that:

> Ethnic groups—even if they are not subcultures (and I suspect they are)—are at least substructures of the larger society, and in some cities, comprehensive substructures. The Polish community in Chicago, for example; the Jewish community in New York; the Irish community in Boston; the black community of Harlem all represent a pool of preferred associates so vast and so

variegated that it is possible, if one chooses, to live almost entirely within the bounds of the community. One can work with, play with, marry, attend church with, vote with and join fraternal organizations with people who are of exactly the same ethnic background. One can choose fellow ethnics to perform all the professional functions one requires, from decorator to psychiatrist to undertaker. One can belong to ethnic organizations, read ethnic newspapers, seek counsel from ethnic clergymen, play on ethnic baseball teams and vote for ethnic candidates in elections. While some of us may lament the exclusiveness in such ethnic communities, it is nonetheless true that the pattern of ethnic relationships constitutes an important part of the fabric of the larger community, organizing the amorphous population of the city into a number of clearly identifiable and elaborately structured subgroups. (Greeley, 1971, p. 47)

Because of prejudice, stereotyping, and ethnocentrism, institutionalized discrimination against members of minority groups often occurs, thereby imposing unequal opportunity for equal ability on individuals because of their race or ethnic background. For example, the apartheid policy in South Africa inhibits members of the indigenous black majority[3] from participating in a variety of social domains, including sport and leisure. Similarly, in the United States prior to 1947, blacks were excluded from major league baseball and were forced to establish their own leagues (see Peterson, 1970).

Although a variety of concepts, typologies, and models have been proposed or utilized to study ethnic stratification (see Kinlock, 1974; Shibutani and Kwan, 1965), there is no definitive theory at the present time. Rather, there are a number of different perspectives that may be of some explanatory use. The cyclical model (Park, 1950) suggests that ethnic mobility follows the irreversible cyclical pattern of contact, competition, accommodation, and assimilation. The latter stage was further delineated by Gordon (1964), who distinguished between cultural and structural assimilation, both of which must occur before the ethnic group disappears from the stratification system. Structural assimilation, which involves the minority groups gaining access to associations and institutions of the dominant group, has not occurred for many of the major ethnic groups in North America.

A second approach to ethnic stratification is derived from consensus theorists. They argue that ethnic groups are assimilated because there is a trend toward universalistic as opposed to particularistic norms, the result being integration and the removal of cultural pluralism, which may be dysfunctional for the system.

On the other side, conflict theorists argue that social change can occur only when the dominant and minority groups clash over the existing cultural norms and power structure. To illustrate, Mains and Williams (1975) developed a model to define the way in which different types of conflict facilitate or inhibit minority group members gaining access to power and authority in society. More specifically, they discussed the impact of four types of conflict on the process of acculturation and on minority/dominant group relations: intragroup nonrealistic, intragroup realistic, intergroup nonrealistic, and intergroup realistic. Mains and Williams conclude that:

> The solution to "our minority problem" would seem to lie not so much in the acculturational processes of these groups as in the conflict involved in re-defining the social situation of race and the racial stereotypes, which have historically stigmatized minority racial groups in this country. (Mains and Williams, 1975, p. 71)

A final approach is concerned with the interrelationship of social class and ethnic stratification, and the relative importance of each for influencing social behavior. Notwithstanding the fact that ethnicity could interact with religion, sex, age, and education, Gordon (1964) derived the concept of "ethclass," which refers to a group formed by the presence of a specific ethnic background and social class position. For example, within professional baseball lower-class blacks may have greater or lesser status than middle-class Puerto Ricans.

Regardless of the approach used to explain it, there is little doubt that ethnic stratification exists in North America and that it influences human behavior in a variety of social institutions, including sport. For example, during some periods of history, members of specific racial or ethnic groups have dominated certain sports, while at other times members of some ethnic groups experienced discrimination within the sport system.

Age and Gender Stratification

The social categories of age (Elder, 1975) and gender (Lipman-Blumen and Tickamyer, 1975) are universal and inevitable, both categories represent biological and social facts, and both types of social status reflect forms of ascriptive inequality. The importance of these social categories for sociological analysis is that each denotes an ascribed attribute or social identity that accounts for a considerable amount of the attitudes and behaviors in a variety of social situations (Riley, Johnson, and Foner, 1972). Furthermore, they are social categories that define role behavior at specific points in the life cycle and that facilitate or impede a number of social processes, including the processes of socialization into and desocialization out of sport roles.

One outcome of the systems of age and gender stratification is that normative criteria evolve for entering a given social system and relinquishing roles within it. For example, most youth sport organizations provide competition according to chronological age, without regard for the individual's unique physical or emotional readiness for that level of competition. As a result, children often encounter early failure and drop out of sport or, because they cannot compete with others of their chronological age, they often stop participating in that particular sport. Many of these children never return to involvement in sport or physical activity, and physical activity never becomes an integral facet of their life-style. Similarly, many professional sport organizations consider age to be a criterion in establishing benchmarks for career progress. To illustrate, Faulkner

(1975) reported in his study of hockey that "the players interviewed feel that unless they have been promoted into the NHL parent organization to play a continuous set of games before the age of 25, the occupancy of minor league status for the duration of their careers is heavily ruled in by existing social arrangements . . . As a result the probability of access to the major leagues declines in the late twenties."

A second outcome of stratification is the emergence of age- and sex-related norms concerning appropriate and inappropriate behavior in a variety of social situations, including the use of leisure time. For example, with regard to gender, it is appropriate for young girls to take up ballet and to compete in field hockey, but it is normally inappropriate for young boys to engage in such physical activities.

A third outcome of age and gender stratification is the appearance of *agism* and/or *sexism*, by which individuals of a particular chronological age and/or sex are discriminated against in terms of life-styles and life-chances. For example, after individuals leave school there is little opportunity to use physical activity facilities unless they join a private club. This is more characteristic in North America than in Europe where the sport club provides facilities for people of all ages in the family. That is, in Europe it is socially acceptable (i.e., normative) to continue involvement throughout the life-cycle.

This phenomenon of agism is more likely to be prevalent in age-heterogeneous than in age-homogeneous environments since there may be more conflict or competition between age strata for facilities. Furthermore, in an age-segregated environment the reference groups are from a similar generation; hence there may be less pressure to "act your age." To illustrate, in St. Petersburg, Florida, the Kids-and-Kubs, the Three-Quarter Century Softball Club, Inc., has become a social institution for the residents in that senior citizens compete in socially sanctioned institutionalized sport, often before spectators of all ages.

Although a definitive explanation for the existence and continuance of gender stratification is lacking, some insight can be gained by examining three models of gender stratification and by considering the process of sex-role identification and sex-role socialization. Eichler (1973) has presented and critiqued three analytical models of gender stratification. The first model suggests that females comprise a caste that is denied mobility because of an ascriptive attribute. A basic assumption is that they are less valued in the labor market. However, Eichler argues that there are many exceptions to the caste rules in that females do not socially avoid outsiders (i.e., males), they can be socially mobile through marriage when they marry outside their class, and there are differences in rank among women that are as great as those between the sexes. Furthermore, some women have higher status and higher skill levels than some men. In sum, although a few castelike qualities exist, there are too many exceptions to seriously compare the woman's position in the gender stratification system to that of a caste.

The second model views women as being members of a minority group that experiences economic and psychological disadvantages emanating from a power struggle between the two sexes. Eichler (1973) notes that this model also fails to fit reality completely, since these conditions should lead to the formation of a gender consciousness, which has not happened as yet to any great extent.

A third model argues that women form a unique class based on their ability to compete in the labor market (this includes housework). In fact, early in the twentieth century sex status was the basis for a classlike struggle for equal rights. Eichler criticizes this view because it does not distinguish between employed and nonemployed women. She further develops this model by stressing that there is a double standard by which women can be differentiated among those who are economically independent and those who are not.

The continuation of gender stratification and subsequent inequality is perpetuated through the sex-role socialization process through which sex-role identification occurs. This gender identification begins as soon as the child is born, in that significant others compulsively attempt to "make" a girl a girl and a boy a boy. That is, each society has definite conceptions as to what constitutes femininity and masculinity. In fact, research by Lewis (1972a, 1972b) suggests that social influences affect a child's type of play activity before he or she is even one year old. Moreover, once initiated, these influences may be irreversible (Mason and Bumpass, 1975) and thereby contribute to the perpetuation of gender stratification through generations.

Perhaps the most influential agents in maintaining these cultural expectations with respect to how and what roles children of each gender should play are the parents. For example, when a young girl expresses an interest in organized sport she is often discouraged by her parents from participating, so that she might maintain the socially sanctioned "image" of the female. Despite the fact that recent research has failed to support most of the psychological and physiological myths surrounding sport participation for females, institutional and legal barriers must still be overcome in order to achieve egalitarianism in sport. Therefore, if the opportunity for females is to improve, changes must be initiated at the system level by redefining the values, norms, and goals of significant others who are responsible for the socialization process. More specifically, the most appropriate target for change would be mothers, fathers, and elementary school teachers who are responsible for most of the socializing in the critical early years when lifestyles are being established.

Social and Economic Stratification

The term social stratification has been used most often to denote differences or social distances between social categories on the basis of their relative economic and/or generalized social status. Viewed from this perspective, the process of social stratification consists of the overall social structure of society being hierarchically divided into a number of distinct social classes or social strata. Much debate, however, centers on the nature of the dimensionality and composition of these social classes and strata. The following section introduces some theoretical perspectives on social and economic stratification.

9.1.3 Theoretical Perspectives on Social Stratification

Dimensions of Stratification

Some social theorists contend that social strata are unidimensional, while others contend that they are multidimensional. For example, Karl Marx argued that social strata are primarily based on economic considerations, while Max Weber argued that they must be viewed in terms of three analytically distinct dimensions: class, power, and status.

At present, there are three general categories of dimensions. *Objective status* represents the degree of power or control one has over the means of production, the amount of influence one has over the life-chances of others, or the amount of freedom one has in his or her place of employment. *Accorded status* is that given to an individual by others, depending on the position he or she occupies or the ascribed characteristics he or she brings to a position. Thus, the president of a professional sport team is accorded greater status by the media than the public relations officer. Finally, *subjective status* refers to the position at which individuals place themselves on some scale. This process is greatly influenced by the reference groups with which people identify and often results in identifying with a class, usually higher, to which an individual aspires.

Today most studies of social stratification utilize a self-rating (Cantril, 1944) or objective scale comprised of such factors as the level of educational attainment, the amount of annual income, or the prestige attached to a specific occupation. Some of the more frequently used objective measures include the NORC (North and Hatt, 1953) and the Blau–Duncan scale in the United States (Blau and Duncan, 1967), and the Blishen and McRoberts (1976) scale in Canada. The fact that there are so many different measures represents a major weakness in arriving at comparative information on which to base conclusions. That is, when different measures are used it is difficult to compare the results of two or more studies and to arrive at generalizations, both within a given society or cross-nationally.

Notwithstanding which of the above perspectives have the most empirical validity, the fact remains that the social stratum in which an individual is born may ultimately influence his or her life-chances and life-styles. In sum, social differentiation on the basis of social classes and/or social strata results in varying degrees of social inequality for some members of society.

The Conflict Model of Stratification

Historically, there have been two basic approaches to the study of social inequality: the conflict approach, which sees social inequality as unjust and perceives that it can be mitigated by changing the nature of the social structure; and the functionalist approach, which views social inequality as necessary and relatively just. The first perspective is adhered to by radicals, social critics, and reformers who take the presence of social class differences as a sign that social change is needed. That is, conflicts resulting from inequalities in power, privileges, and prestige cause pressure for change in the social order. This perspective is illustrated by the work of Marx (Bendix and Lipset, 1953), who argued that economic factors lead to the rise of class consciousness and therefore conflict between social classes. Similarly, Weber (1953) held that power and status were important elements by which hierarchies in a society are created and for which groups will come into conflict.

The relevance of the basic tenets of the conflict perspective (in the Marxist tradition) for the analysis of inequality in sport has been summarized by Gruneau, as follows:

1. Sport must be understood in the broader context of the material conditions of the capitalist societies.

2. Sport is intimately associated with classes that exist on the basis of widespread differences in wealth and power.

3. All competitive sport reflects bourgeois ideology; it is rationally utilitarian, meritocratic, and mobility-oriented and contains a belief in linear progress. Accordingly, it is control-oriented and helps to maintain a "false consciousness."

4. Sport is "alienating" to professional athletes caught up formally in the productive process.

5. A truly egalitarian, self-actualizing sport can be achieved only in a society having democratic control over societal economic life: a classless and egalitarian society where "competitive sport" in a rational sense is nonexistent. (Gruneau, 1975, pp. 136–137)

A contemporary case in sport that might well be explained by a Marxist analysis is the increasing conflict in recent years between professional athletes (i.e., the proletariat) and team owners (i.e., the bourgeoisie). This reflects an increasing "class consciousness" on the part of the athletes, leading to conflict in the form of labor strikes and possible resolution by legal arbitration.

The Consensus (Functional) Model of Stratification

The functionalist approach, characterized by the work of Davis and Moore (1945), argues that stratification (hence, social inequality) is necessary in order to motivate and place individuals in key social roles. That is, some positions are functionally more important than others for the survival of the social system, and there must be greater material rewards and prestige attached to these positions so that individuals will be motivated to make the necessary effort to train for these positions. The Davis–Moore theory can be concretely illustrated by looking at the role of the quarterback in football. The position of quarterback is the most "skilled" position in football, but few individuals have the innate ability to be good quarterbacks and, in turn, few of these naturally talented individuals are prepared to undergo the rigors and long years of training to become skilled quarterbacks. As a result (or so the theory suggests) quarterbacks are allotted greater power, higher prestige, and more privileges than other roles in football in order to ensure that scarce talent will be attracted, trained, and recruited.

The basic assumptions concerning inequality in sport from a functional perspective have been summarized by Gruneau, as follows:

1. Competitive sport reflects a set of values held to be important by the society. Therefore, recruitment into sport serves an integrative function.

2. Sport functions to make the stratification of a society more explicit. (Social systems stress a "need" for hierarchy of rewards that is related to a search for status under conditions of scarcity. Status is usually gained by a variety of means, including possessions and performance, both of which may be readily reflected in sport involvement. These reflections operate at two levels. Performance in sport may be a means of generating status at one level, but at another level, participation in sport, or in a specific sport, may function as a display of status. Thus, sport and specific sports may function as symbols of stratification in society and along the way provide arenas for the learning of important social roles.)

3. Sport functions as a mobility mechanism in the western industrial societies. ("Performance," as such, is a transitory and impermanent means of moving up the hierarchy of rewards, but high performance in sport may allow entrance into positions based on more durable criteria such as the possession of valuable material goods and the control of nonmaterial values.) (Gruneau, 1975, p. 142)

Table 9.1 presents a comparative summary of the dominant distributive and relational characteristics (with implications for sport) of the conflict and functional views of social class.

Although these two perspectives have predominated, a synthesis of the two views is represented in the work of Ossowski (1963) and Lenski (1966). They argue that individuals occupy more than one status position and thus inequality can be related to gender, race, ethnicity, class, income, education, property, age, power, or status. Moreover, there is likely both conflict and consensus within most social interaction.

9.2 SOCIAL STRATIFICATION IN SPORT

9.2.1 Historical Trends

Historically, the role of athlete has had varying degrees of status and the opportunity to play specific sport roles has been closely related to membership in a given social class. For example, in ancient Greece and Rome and in Eastern European countries today, the athlete was and is accorded high status and prestige, whereas in the post Greco-Roman period and in China during the early part of this century the athlete had low status. Similarly, the right to participate in sport, or in certain sports, has varied by social class. In the Middle Ages only the nobles and upper class were permitted to participate in sport and a sport was often abandoned by these elites when the lower classes began to participate. In fact, when a sport became dominated by the lower classes it very quickly became a professional sport. During the Victorian era sport became truly institutionalized in the elite "public schools" of England's dominant class and later, the establishment of sport governing bodies was initiated by the graduates of Oxford and Cambridge. Furthermore between-class or between-ethnic (e.g., in South Africa) competition in sport was traditionally discouraged or prohibited. It was not until

Table 9.1
A comparative summary of the dominant distributive and relational characteristics of divergent views of social class

Image of class structure	Dominant distributive characteristics		Dominant relational attributes	
	Class conflict	Functional-consensus	Class conflict	Functional-consensus
1. Classes as real groups	Market position and property ownership	Lineage and "estate"	Asymmetric dependence (exploitative)	Mutual dependence (functionally related)
2. Status continuum (nominalistic approach)	X* (compatible only in the sense of slight interstatus friction)	Interpersonal prestige and esteem	X* (possibly some element of nonegalitarian classlessness)	Mutual dependence
Implications for sport	Class conflict	Functional-consensus	Class conflict	Functional-consensus
1. Classes as real groups	Contours of sport shaped by productive process (highest market position guarantees access to participation, control, and administration)	Sport as a functionally important display of prestige related to lineage and "estate" (bars door to rationality)	Sport as ideologically hegemonic (leads to false consciousness on the part of the underclasses)	Sport as valuably integrative (aids in learning positionally associated social roles and beliefs)
2. Status continuum (nominalistic approach)	X*	Sport as a display of prestige and as a generator of prestige (fundamentally meritocratic)	X*	

*X signifies theoretical and empirical improbabilities.
From Gruneau (1975, p. 146).

the 1880s that working-class soccer clubs in England began to compete successfully against middle- and upper-class opponents, and until the late 1970s that
blacks, coloreds, and whites in South Africa competed with or against each
other.

In North America, elitism in sport was maintained through the formation of
private clubs, which restricted membership to those with specific ascribed or
achieved criteria. For example, Metcalfe (1972, 1976a) describes the hierarchical
structure (based on social class background) of the membership of sporting clubs
in Toronto between 1860 and 1920 and in Montreal between 1840 and 1901.
Similarly, Mallea (1975) reports that the first governing bodies of sport in Victorian England were composed of members of the aristocracy, while in Canada the
founding members of the Montreal Racket Club and the Toronto Cricket Club
were British army officers who restricted the membership to those of acceptable
social and financial standing. In the United States, the formation and early development of the influential New York Athletic Club was controlled by a social
elite comprised mainly of business owners, stock brokers, lawyers, corporation
officers, and bankers (Wettan and Willis, 1976). To illustrate further, Willis and
Wettan (1976) noted that the mean score on the NORC scale for the University
Athletic Club in New York City was 81.07. Although not strictly a valid comparison, the mean score for a 1975 national sample of adults over 18 years of age was
39.2, with the scores ranging from 12 to 82. At the other end of the social scale, a
small number of working-class (blue-collar) clubs were formed in the period after
1860, although they had little impact on the institutionalization of sport
(Metcalfe, 1976b). In short, the origin of modern institutionalized sport was characterized by ascription.

9.2.2 Social Stratification Among Elite Athletes

At the intercollegiate level, McIntyre (1959), Loy (1969, 1972), Webb (1969),
McPherson (1968), Petrie (1973), and Berryman and Loy (1976) have found sport
differences in the class background of athletes in a variety of intercollegiate
sports. While all investigators found a range of backgrounds, most athletes were
from a lower to upper middle-class background. However, this finding may be
influenced by the nature of the sample studied, which included athletes at
Harvard and Yale (Berryman and Loy, 1976), at UCLA (Loy, 1972), at Penn State
(McIntyre, 1959), at Michigan State (Webb, 1969), throughout the Big Ten Conference (Petrie, 1973), and in one province of Canada (McPherson, 1968). As a
result of these diverse samples, differences *within* sports, as well as *between*
sports, may result because of different recruiting policies or recruitment from different geographical regions of the country (see Rooney, 1974). In summary, those
involved in intercollegiate boxing and wrestling appear to be primarily from the
lower strata, while those involved in tennis, skiing, golf, and crew appear to be
from the upper strata. Most other sports, however, are characterized by a range
of backgrounds, although the middle classes tend to be overrepresented in all
sports.

In addition to studies of intercollegiate athletes, some evidence concerning the class basis of sport is found by studying elite amateur and professional athletes. Weinberg and Arond (1952) report that most boxers are recruited from the lower socioeconomic strata since most of the boxing clubs are located in this type of residential or commercial area. In a report of the background factors related to success in professional baseball, Haerle (1975) found that although there was a range of backgrounds, socioeconomic status had no discriminating power in predicting success. Gruneau (1972) found that male and female athletes competing in the 1971 Canada Winter Games came from a variety of class backgrounds, but that athletes from the upper-middle and upper strata were generally overrepresented. This pattern held even more so for the female athletes.[4] Similar to Webb (1969), Gruneau (1972) found that individual sports tend to outweigh team sports in terms of representation at the extreme ends of the socioeconomic scale. Furthermore, he noted that if any democratization is occurring at the elite levels of amateur sport, it is occurring in a downward trend. That is, those sports more closely identified with the lower strata have more middle- and upper-level participants than upper-strata sports have lower-strata participants.

9.2.3   Social Stratification and Mass Participation in Sport

In addition to the socioeconomic status of intercollegiate and elite amateur or professional athletes, there is also evidence of class differences in the primary and secondary sport involvement patterns by the masses or subelites. For example, in a classic study of the meaning of sport to adults, Stone (1957) found that the upper strata prefer hockey, golf, and tennis; the middle strata football, baseball, bowling, and hunting; and the lower strata combative sports such as boxing and wrestling. That preferences can change over time was illustrated in a replication of this study ten years later (Stone, 1969) in which it was noted that baseball was more salient for the lower strata, although it permeated all strata. However, based on a content analysis from 1900 to 1960 of four class-related magazines, Noe (1974) found both qualitative and quantitative differences in leisure life styles that were stable over time across social classes. Specifically, he noted that the lower-middle classes use sport as leisure to a greater extent than the upper and upper-middle classes do. In short, there is not mass equality in quantity, type, or style of leisure pursuits.

Further evidence for the lack of egalitarianism in sport at the level of mass participation can be found by analyzing differential expenditure patterns for sport equipment by social strata. For example, in spite of claims that democratization is occurring in tennis, those with incomes over $20,000 purchase the most tennis equipment, while those with incomes under $8000 purchase the least amount. Similar examples could be given for a variety of other sports ranging from boxing and bowling to polo and other equestrian events. Another factor closely related to income is the type of high school and college attended and their influence on life style. For example, a study by Berryman and Loy (1976) found that most athletes on the intercollegiate teams at Harvard and Yale were those who had attended a private school and who had therefore gained specific advantages in certain sports. This advantage results from differential social experiences in a private school, rather than from inherent sport aptitude (Eggleston, 1965).

Concomitant with class differences in primary sport involvement, there also appear to be class differences in secondary sport involvement. Kenyon (1966) suggested that for direct or indirect secondary involvement there may be variation by social class. In fact he found that while those in the lower strata did not attend sport events (i.e., direct consumption) as frequently as the higher strata, there were no significant differences across strata for various forms of indirect consumption. Rather, direct attendance at sport events is primarily a middle- to upper-class event, especially with rising admission prices and the sale of blocks of tickets to business organizations. The major exceptions appear to be horse racing, wrestling, and boxing. On the other hand, indirect secondary involvement, especially through television, is available to all. Unfortunately, accurate information is not available on the class background of viewers of specific sport events.

A final form of secondary involvement that is class-based pertains to the leadership roles within amateur sport held by adults. In a study of the sport executives in national swimming and volleyball associations in Canada, Bratton (1970) found that the executives of the swimming associations were from a higher class background. This may have been related to the fact that volleyball is more closely associated with ethnic groups who may be in a disadvantaged position. This point stresses the necessity of considering possible interaction between various stratification systems in any attempt to explain democratization in the sport system. McPherson (1974a) found that volunteer coaches in youth hockey programs had a range of class backgrounds, although the American coaches tended to be from a higher strata than the Canadian coaches. This may be partially explained by the fact that the diffusion of hockey throughout the United States has been initiated in the more affluent suburbs of the larger cities where the economic resources permit the building of expensive arenas. Similarly, a recent study by Beamish (1976) reported that 70 percent of all executives of the national sport governing bodies in Canada were engaged in professional occupations. Furthermore, most were originally from middle-class family backgrounds.

Unlike the above studies, which deal with officers at the middle administrative level, three recent studies have demonstrated that the "real" control of both professional and amateur sport is held by the social and economic elite. To illustrate, Kiviaho and Simola (1974) found that Finnish commercial leaders have increasingly gained representation in the executive positions of both bourgeoisie and working-class sport organizations. Similarly, in the United States, Clark (1977) has reported that there are direct relationships or connections between owning a professional football, baseball, or basketball team and decision making at the highest corporate, financial, political media or educational levels. Specifically, he found that for 56 of the 67 presidents of professional sport teams, there were 216 business links (e.g., automobile, oil, transportation, real estate, construction, insurance, banking), 72 government links (e.g., public officials, government committees or commissions, lawyers), 40 educational links, and 41 media links (e.g., television, radio, newspaper, book publishing, movies, theater). In the most detailed and analytical examination of control in sport, Gruneau (1976b) found that there is "an increased interlocking of professional team sports with the larger corporations." More specifically, he discovered through interviews and secondary analysis that the executive officers and directors of the Canadian Football League and the National Hockey League teams are linked with similar positions in the financial, trade, transportation, and communication sectors of the economy. As a result of this evidence there is little support for the hypothesis that mobility into the "elite" or "power" roles in sport have been opened up to any great extent.

9.2.4 Stratification in Sport in Comparative Perspective

In addition to studies completed in North America, the stratification process in sport has also been examined in societies that vary in culture, degree of industrialization, political structure, and ideology. Eggleston (1965) found that grammar school males in England, when compared to ex-public school males, are at a disadvantage in successfully competing in cricket and rugby at Oxford and Cambridge. This study was replicated in America by Berryman and Loy (1976) who similarly found that, with the exception of basketball, those who attended a private school are overrepresented on Harvard and Yale athletic teams. In the German Federal Republic, Luschen (1969) reported that 15–25-year-old youths with different social backgrounds had different favorite sports. Similarly, Ulrich concludes:

> The lower classes, which after all constitute half of the inhabitants of the FRG (Federal Republic of Germany), do not participate in high-level sport. The failure of many talented athletes to cope with the demands and to overcome the class barriers of today's competitive sport is *par excellence* a social inequality regarding chances. (Ulrich, 1976, p. 148)

At the mass level for adults, Renson (1976) found that sport involvement is related to the social class structure in Belgium, with skiing, golf, tennis, and fencing being at the top, and gymnastics, calisthenics, track and field, judo, boxing, soccer, and team handball at the bottom. As an indication that social events or social change may result in a different stratification system, Takenoshita (1967) noted that before World War II all national and international champion athletes in Japan were college students or college graduates. This is a reflection of the privileged status accorded students before the war. However, with the rise of industrialization after the war, the student's privileged position was lost and many industries began to sponsor sport activities. As a result, most male and female champion athletes since World War II have been industrial workers sponsored by their work organizations.

Although this cannot be considered in the purest sense a social class difference, both Starosta (1967) and Nowak (1969) indicated that Polish athletes have differential sport opportunities. For example, most of the students admitted to the Warsaw Figure Skating School were children of parents who belonged to the "intelligentsia with higher education" (Starosta, 1967). In a comparative analysis of figure skaters from other countries, it was similarly found that figure skaters of international calibre are children of well-to-do people who can afford to bear the expenses required to pursue elitism in sport. Similarly, although the recruitment process is reversed, Nowak (1969) found that over 70 percent of the elite boxers were from a working-class family environment, rather than a peasant or intelligentsia background.

Studies of elite athletes in Australia, Great Britain, and New Zealand also suggest that professional and high status families are overrepresented in athletics. For example, on the basis of a study of British male athletes at the Mexico Olympic Games, Collins (1972) derived the following four categories of sport: *egalitarian* (e.g., swimming, cycling, canoeing), *independent* (e.g., gymnastics and the modern pentathlon, which are not so firmly established in the British culture to have become class-based), *working class* (e.g., boxing, weight lifting, and wrestling), and *middle class* (e.g., track and field, rowing, fencing, field hockey, equestrian). In a similar study, Pavia (1973) analyzed the social class background of 174 male and female members of the 1972 Australian Olympic team and derived five sport categories, although 60 percent of these athletes belonged to the upper three social classes. Furthermore, in a more detailed study of Australian athletes in a variety of other sports, Pavia and Jaques (1976) noted that as a group they are overrepresented in the upper class and that a great number of females are of upper-class origin. This latter finding agrees with Luschen (1969) and Gruneau (1975) and suggests that there may be greater social obstacles for lower-class females than for lower-class males.

In a study of the New Zealand team at the Montreal Olympics, Crawford (1977) found that the athletes represented five categories of occupational prestige. Those involved in hockey, shooting, and rowing were drawn from a cross-section of prestige rankings and the sports were labeled as egalitarian (see Collins, 1972); those in track and field, boxing, and cycling were from a blue-collar/manual-labor category; those in canoeing, equestrian, weightlifting, wrestling, and yachting fit into a white-collar/nonmanual-labor category. He completed the five categories by noting that rowers fell into an intermediate category and that swimmers were an undetermined category, possibly because so many of them are students.

In summary, the evidence suggests that there is a stratification system operating cross-nationally that facilitates or inhibits access to specific sports and to the realization of elite status. However, the stratification system within any given country varies, often in relation to the inherent social structure in that society and perhaps in relation to the degree to which a sport is institutionalized in that society.

9.2.5 Sport, Class Conflict, and Social Integration

In addition to the question of class-based involvement in sport, the presence of a stratification system raises the possibility of class consensus or class conflict being manifested in the sport milieu. The appearance of consensus or conflict is related to the process of social integration by which a number of originally diverse individuals or groups are united into one common group, usually with the obliteration of former social and cultural group differences and previous group identities. Once this group has been formed, a new group identity and affiliation creates within-group consensus, which may or may not lead to conflict with other groups with different values or goals. This section examines the role of sport systems in facilitating social integration (Krawczyk, 1973), in transferring within-group consensus in sport groups to other social issues, in stimulating intergroup conflict, and in controlling the masses.

Since social integration occurs to a great extent through the process of acculturation and structural assimilation, sport organizations provide a medium whereby individuals might realize full participation in the social institutions of the host or dominant group (McKay, 1975; Pooley, 1976; Wohl, 1966). For example, Wohl (1966) describes how the introduction of volleyball into a Polish peasant community led to group identification and subsequently sport competitions with neighboring villages. The net effect was that sport competitions replaced the intervillage fights that had previously been taken seriously by those involved, but that had never attained the status of attracting spectators. Thus, the volleyball competitions served as an integrating mechanism. Similarly, Fox (1961) describes how baseball in Pueblo Indian society permits the acting out of aggressive and competitive tendencies in an essentially noncompetitive social system. This study further demonstrates how social conflicts are engendered when there are changes in the social structure without corresponding changes in the cultural structure of a social system.

Wohl (1966) also noted that within-group integration of social classes during national crises has been facilitated by sport groups. As an example he described the 1929–1934 period of class struggle for power in Poland in which the workers' sport organizations unified the working class and in fact drew most of the political party leaders from the leaders of the sport clubs. Through a sport club individuals interact with those of the same social class, and this facilitates the socialization of norms and values and the raising of class consciousness.

A similar phenomenon exists in other countries in which class background may explain a large part of the recruitment to membership in sport organizations. To illustrate, Kiviaho (1974a) indicated that in Finland the middle and upper strata are overrepresented in the leadership of the Central Sports Federation, whereas leaders of the Worker's Sports Federation are from the working class. Moreover, he noted that there appears to be an even closer link between the political ideology of the members and the club with which they affiliate. Naturally, in this type of structure there is the potential for intergroup conflict arising from institutionalized sport. Furthermore, Kiviaho (1974b) found that the selection of a favorite Finnish baseball team in a game in which the teams represent different sport organizations is based on class division and political opinion, rather than on the geographical regions that the two teams represent.

In contrast, Dunning and Sheard (1976) describe the process associated with the development of the game of rugby into two different forms: Rugby Union and Rugby League. Although the two have a common origin, the "bifurcation" resulted from the growth in power of the working classes in the late 1800s. This

led to increasing class consciousness and class conflict which was partly manifested in the split in the rugby game along class, regional, and amateur-profes-
sional axes. More specifically, Rugby Union is played throughout the British Isles
by middle-class amateurs, whereas Rugby League is played by both amateur and
professional working-class folk in northern England.

The appearance of class conflict in a sport milieu is further illustrated by the
occurrence of hooliganism in Great Britain during and after soccer games. This
has been hypothesized to be an expression of value differences that have arisen
because the structure and ethos of the game are no longer working-class in
orientation (Taylor, 1972). In order to express their displeasure at the increasing
professionalism and middle-class domination of soccer, working-class youth
engage in disruptive and destructive behavior such as destroying railroad cars on
the way home from games in other towns. In this context, soccer increases the
conflict between social classes in Great Britain.

A final hypothesized use of sport for social integration is the control of the
masses by the dominant social class. While historical accounts have described the
use of "bread and circuses" to appease the masses in ancient Rome, there have
been few attempts to analyze or study this phenomenon in modern times despite
the frequently made claim that sport is the opiate of the masses. One exception is
the Mexican study by Taylor (1971), who examined the use of football (soccer) by
the ruling political party to control the citizens. He argued that football is an
example of the solidarity of the Mexican people and thus public demonstrations
associated with football are acceptable, whereas similar demonstrations of a
political nature are not and are immediately quelled, often violently.

9.2.6 Sport and Social Mobility

Another question derived from the presence of a stratification system is the extent
to which mobility within the social structure is possible by individuals or groups.
Examination of this question concerning the social system of sport is relevant
since sport leaders and media representatives have argued for years that sport
provides a readily accessible avenue for upward mobility, especially for those
from a lower middle class or lower-class background.

The motivation to move upward is influenced by two factors. First, from the
societal point of view, any expansion in the number of roles available at one
rank, especially if combined with a decline in numbers at a lower rank, leads to
upward mobility. For example, the expansion of sport leagues by the addition of
franchises creates new positions and therefore opportunities to move from the
minor to the major leagues. However, if expansion in the number of ranks does
not occur, any upward mobility (to the major leagues, for example) must be
accompanied by an exchange process by which someone moves down within the
system (e.g., to a minor league team) or moves out (e.g., retires). This inter-
change is most likely to occur in a highly competitive market. A second factor,
reflecting the perspective of the individual, suggests that persons strive to protect
their ego or, as is more likely, to enhance their ego. One way to enhance the ego
is to improve one's class position, usually through occupational mobility. This

mobility can occur between generations (the son or daughter improves on the father's status) or during the career of a specific individual (from stable boy to jockey to owner).

Any movement that takes place can be the result of either "contest" or "sponsored" mobility (Turner, 1960). Contest mobility is the more prevalent North American norm whereby higher status is earned through the personal ambition, motivation, and ability of the individual who competes against others in an open contest. Sponsored mobility is a norm in aristocratic England, where high status is granted to elites on the basis of birth. In contemporary society, however, sponsored mobility refers to the status granted or opportunities attained through the efforts or assistance of others.

In sport, depending on the specific role and the specific situation, both modes of mobility may operate either independently or in combination. However, it is clear that the structure of inequality greatly limits the degree to which contest mobility actually occurs. For example, Loy and Sage (1973) conclude that a process of sponsored mobility operates with respect to the career patterns of college football and basketball coaches. Similarly, a study of minor "all-star" hockey coaches in Ontario (McPherson, 1974a) found that contest mobility operated for a few who applied for a position and were interviewed, although sponsored mobility was more common in that 65 percent of the coaches were invited by league executives to coach at the all-star level.

Although systematic evidence is lacking for most of the hypothesized mobility mechanisms, a few studies have attempted to examine the process as it operates in sport systems. First, Loy (1969) suggests that there are at least four ways in which active sport participation can facilitate upward movement: (1) the early development of sport skills (see Section 6.1) may facilitate recruitment and entrance directly into professional sport; (2) involvement in sport may lead to receiving an athletic scholarship, which may directly or indirectly enhance educational attainment; (3) participation in sport may lead to "occupational sponsorship" by which a former athlete is given preferential treatment in hiring or promotion; and (4) involvement in sport may result in learning attitudes and behavior patterns (e.g., achievement orientation, leadership traits) considered important in the occupational world (see Section 6.5).

In addition, there have been numerous journalistic "rags to riches" autobiographies describing how a star player rose from an impoverished background to attain elite status in the world of professional sport. Unfortunately most of these narratives stop at the peak of the athlete's career and fail to follow up or consider the athlete's life style and status after retirement. Furthermore, they tend to ignore the many cases in which success has not characterized the athlete's career. Some exceptions are studies of boxers (Weinberg and Arond, 1952), Brazilian soccer players (Lever, 1969), and former professional hockey players (Roy, 1974; Smith and Diamond, 1976). These analyses indicate that the social and economic gains made during the playing career are often lost soon after retirement. One reason is that most of these athletes have not completed an education that would permit them to function outside the sport system. For example, Roy (1974) found that few professional hockey players had completed high school. Furthermore,

Smith and Diamond (1976) noted that 70 percent of the former professional hockey players terminated their careers in the minor leagues on a note of downward mobility.

Most of the literature concerning the social mobility of athletes suggests that while there is some upward mobility during the playing career, the achieved status often is not permanent. This status reversal seems to occur for two reasons. First, these athletes have not attained a level of education sufficient enough to permit them to move horizontally into another career at about the same prestige level. That is, although being involved in athletics during the high school and college years may enhance mobility, unless a college degree is earned or some level of education is completed, the individual lacks the necessary skills to compete with age peers in the labor force outside sport. However, if they graduate from college they tend to be successful in their chosen careers (Loy, 1969, 1972). A second factor resulting in subsequent downward mobility may be the athlete's inability to manage his or her own financial affairs. While this situation has prevailed in the past, it may be less likely in the future as more and more professional athletes hire management consultants and lawyers to ensure that their financial gains will be intact at the end of the playing career. Furthermore, many athletes now become actively involved in the day-to-day management of their financial affairs so that they acquire business skills that can be utilized in a post-playing career.

In summary, while the myth has been perpetuated that sport provides an avenue for upward social mobility, there is still little empirical support for this hypothesis because of methodological and conceptual weaknesses. For example, longitudinal studies have not been initiated and none have used matched subjects (for example, comparing athletes on the basis of their educational and socioeconomic status with a nonathletic peer group), thereby making it impossible to determine whether mobility occurred because of sport success or because a particular cohort improved their socioeconomic status through social change. The present state of knowledge is aptly summarized by Gruneau:

> Mobility through sport for both the lowest classes and status groups may in fact stop at the comfortable level of middle class athlete. In this sense, the structure of rewards is not so much a ladder on which individuals may continue to climb but rather a tree wherein a specific limb spells the absolute extent of upper travel. (Gruneau, 1975, p. 167)

9.3 RACIAL AND ETHNIC STRATIFICATION IN SPORT

Social categories such as race and ethnicity influence the socialization process by virtue of the opportunity set that members of certain groups have available and by the prevailing behavior, values, attitudes, and norms found within specific subcultures. Moreover, these group members may encounter discrimination which has an impact on the socialization process, including the learning of sport roles and the opportunity to participate in sport systems. Since much of this discrimination has occurred in North America and South Africa, the discussion in this section is limited to racial discrimination in these two countries, plus a consideration of ethnic discrimination in Canada. In effect, the black or Francophone athlete is systematically excluded from equal opportunity to engage in full social participation in various domains within society.

9.3.1 Racial Discrimination

Discrimination is not a new phenomenon. It has been present in most societies in which one group is in a superordinate position over one or more groups that arrive later and begin to interact with the group in power. While social class, money, and education may be the basis of discrimination, it is more likely to occur and become institutionalized on the basis of race or ethnicity since these attributes are inherited and cannot be changed or removed. This institutionalization has developed in North America through social evaluation of groups and individuals on the basis of their racial or ethnic origins.

In the Republic of South Africa institutionalized discrimination results from a politically based policy known as apartheid, in which there is a systematic attempt to separate and maintain the traditions and cultures of four national groups: Europeans (whites), coloreds, Indians, and Africans (nonwhites). Each group is restricted to a geographical area, with its own educational, economic, political, and sport institutions prohibiting interaction and contests between whites and nonwhites. As a result, nonwhites have not been permitted to represent South Africa in international sporting events, thereby leading to policy conflicts with international federations, demonstrations, violence when South African athletes compete, the cancellation of sport tours to the Republic, and the exclusion of South Africa from international championships. Moreover, even if the best athlete in an objective event (e.g., a race against the clock) is a nonwhite, he or she is not permitted to compete for the Republic. This social and political environment in South Africa clearly demonstrates that democratization in sport is more myth than reality. Further information pertaining to institutionalized racism in South Africa can be found in Cheffers (1972), de Broglia (1970), Draper (1963), Grace (1974), Hain (1971), Horrell (1968), and Lapchick (1975).

In North America, members of racial and ethnic groups have been involved in sport systems since late in the nineteenth century, although none have been as involved or successful as the blacks. As a result, most of the literature on the sociology of sport has been concerned with the black athlete in professional and amateur sport. Some notable exceptions, which have examined specific sport-related phenomena using other minority groups, include: Andreano (1965), Fox (1961), Glassford (1970), Lever (1969), McKay (1975), Pooley (1976), and Zurcher and Meadow (1967), although not all of these pertain directly to minority groups in North America.

Although a detailed historical account of black involvement in sport is beyond the scope of this chapter,[5] we can state briefly that there is some evidence to suggest that many of the professional athletes imported by the Greeks were black, and that since then their involvement in institutionalized sport has been characterized by cycles of segregation and integration, depending on the value and role of sport in a society. In North America, black athletes engaged in boxing and horse racing as slaves on the southern plantations, both within a plantation for their own entertainment and against those from other plantations in contests sponsored by owners who frequently bet large sums of money on the match. For the black athletes who were successful and continued to be so, preferential treatment, status, and occasionally freedom for themselves and their families were gained. That is, social mobility through sport was an early phenomenon in American society. Throughout the late 1800s and early 1900s, black athletes were highly involved in individual sports such as boxing and racing. For example, 14 of the 15 riders in the first Kentucky Derby in 1875 were black, a black jockey named Isaac Murphy was the first to win three Kentucky Derby races, and black boxers such as Bill Richmond and Thomas Molineaux gained fame in England and the United States in the early 1800s.

In baseball, there were black teams as early as 1880, and some black baseball stars were able to "pass" into the National or American leagues before the leagues' demise in the late 1800s. However, because of increasing discrimination against blacks in the late 1800s, they were forced out of racing, and by 1898 the last black was forced out of professional baseball (Peterson, 1970). Only in boxing were they permitted to continue to participate and even then they often had to agree to lose before they could obtain a match (Boyle, 1963). Faced with institutionalized discrimination they formed their own baseball (Peterson, 1970) and basketball leagues in the 1920s.

Since 1947, when Jackie Robinson became a member of the Brooklyn Dodgers (Dodson, 1954), a number of descriptive studies have reported the degree to which blacks are involved in professional and amateur sport, including the fact that in the major professional sports 35 to 45 percent of the athletes in baseball and football are black, while over 60 percent in basketball are black. Moreover, blacks have been highly successful in terms of the number of all-star, most valuable player, and rookie of the year awards they have received. Similarly, on the amateur level and in individual sports such as golf and tennis, black athletes increasingly have gained opportunities to represent institutions and their country. For example, blacks won 24 of the 30 medals won by Americans in track and field events at the Montreal Olympics and won all the gold medals in boxing that were awarded to Americans.

In the face of this evidence, it has been stated that there is no discrimination in sport, especially when the number of black athletes in a given sport is compared to the percentage of blacks in America. In fact, it appears that blacks are overrepresented in sport and that democratization has occurred within institutionalized sport. However, black females are still underrepresented and there appears to be underrepresentation in the roles of coach, executive, manager, owner, and official. Moreover, various types of differential treatment by race are hypothesized to exist within the sport system, including the opportunity to occupy specific positions ("stacking" and "quota" systems); unequal opportunity in career progression though equal ability is present; exclusion from occupying post-playing careers as managers or executives; lower financial rewards in terms of bonuses, salaries, and endorsements; and inequity in the quality of education acquired (see Chapter 4; McPherson, 1974b).

In summary, the empirical and anecdotal or journalistic evidence suggests that differential opportunities by race remain in the sport system. Although much of this evidence pertains to professional sport, similar patterns exist at the level of elite amateur sport and among the masses who participate in institutionalized sport. In short, there is little evidence of total democratization for blacks, although the opportunity for equal involvement has improved in recent years.

9.3.2 Ethnic Discrimination

In addition to racial differences, ethnic background may also influence access to opportunities within sport. As we noted earlier in the section on social class, historically the early athletic clubs were restricted to those of acceptable social and financial standing, most of whom were white Anglo-Saxon Protestants (WASPs). Similarly, Riesman and Denney (1951) describe how the second generation of immigrants from Europe led to an ethnic shift in involvement in sport. Since then the pattern of involvement has been cyclical and sport-specific. For example, whereas the Jews dominated basketball in the early years, it is now primarily a black game, especially in urban centers in the north and east. Similarly, in Canada, lacrosse was originally an Indian game but was taken over by whites in the 1850s and became an example of discrimination and segregation between cultural groups. In fact, once professional lacrosse became popular, Indians were recruited to play on white teams, but like the black athletes, they were segregated and discriminated against away from the playing field.

In addition to the English, the other major ethnic group to settle and develop North America was the French, who are today most visible in the province of Quebec in Canada. Whereas the United States, as a pluralistic society, is dominated by black and white cultures, Canada is characterized by a dominant English culture and a minority French (with its own language) culture that defies assimilation. From the earliest contact between the French and English, there were segregated social and sport clubs, although there were contests between the two groups. In view of recent evidence, it would appear that this segregation has continued and has led to a disproportionate underrepresentation of Francophones at national and international sport events. That is, structural barriers impede equal opportunities for participation and success.

Boileau, Landry, and Trempe (1976) found that Francophones are significantly underrepresented on Canadian teams sent to the Olympic, Commonwealth, and Pan-American Games. More specifically, they averaged only 8.1 percent of the membership on these teams, despite the fact that they number an average of 30.5 percent of the Canadian population between 1908 and 1974. In no case did the degree of Francophone participation exceed 19.4 percent (in the 1950 Commonwealth Games). Similarly, Gruneau (1976a) reports that Francophones comprised only 10.6 percent of the athletes at the 1971 Canada Winter Games and were significantly underrepresented on the Quebec team, while Meisel and Lemieux (1972) found that Francophones have not been fairly represented on the executive of the Canadian Amateur Hockey Association. Even in the province of Quebec, Anglophone leaders have dominated the Quebec Amateur Hockey Association.

A further example of Francophone discrimination is illustrated by Roy's (1974) finding that although they occupy central playing positions in professional hockey about equally with Anglophones, they do not have equal opportunity to advance to the leadership positions of coach or general manager after their playing career. Moreover, with respect to hockey in particular, Marple and Pirie (1977) equated the situation of the Francophone in Canada to that of the black athlete in the United States in that although they seem to outperform Anglophones on certain skills (e.g., scoring), they continue to be underrepresented. The theme of "unequal opportunity for equal ability" appears therefore to apply to minority ethnic groups as well as minority racial groups.

While the explanation for the underrepresentation of Francophones is frequently assumed to be discrimination, some alternative explanations include the following: a disadvantaged opportunity set in the sport milieu in Quebec for the necessary early socialization into sport roles; the underdevelopment of the organization of sport in Quebec, which has recently undergone great change; a lack of interest in sport in what had traditionally been a rural and parish social life; and the lack of physical education and interschool sport programs in many parts of the province until recently. Boileau (1977) describes the many changes that have taken place in the structure and organization of sport since the Quiet Revolution in Quebec (Rocher, 1973). As a result of this period of dramatic social change, sport has become more highly valued by politicians and the general population, Francophones have taken over the leadership of a large number of sport associations within the province, and the provincial team finished first in the 1976 Canada Winter Games.

Closely related to ethnic origin is the influence that national origin may have for gaining access to positions in the sport system. Ball (1973) stated that national origin is a form of ascriptive status that operates in professional football in Canada, specifically in terms of assigning players to central positions. He found that native Canadians were less likely to occupy central positions and were also more likely to be underpaid on a position-by-position basis. He argued that this occurred first because most of the coaches are Americans who have preconceived expectations about a candidate's ability in relation to his college training; and second, because they tend to stack Canadians at defensive positions, reserving the supposedly more important and prestigeful positions to those trained at American colleges.

In summary, while the beliefs, and some evidence, suggest underrepresentation of ethnic groups within sport, there is, as yet, little concrete empirical evidence to suggest that the reason for this underrepresentation is discrimination or inequality of opportunity. Moreover, there is little empirical evidence to suggest that this pattern is widespread among all ethnic groups or in all countries. In short, this is another myth that needs further empirical investigation in a variety of social settings.

9.4 GENDER STRATIFICATION IN SPORT

Historically women have been prohibited or discouraged from participating in and/or consuming sport at some points in time and in specific communities. For example, in Greek and early Roman times they were not even permitted to attend the athletic contests. Later, once they were permitted to participate, only functional activities such as horse riding, walking, skating, and cycling were considered appropriate. Today, even though there is an increasing interest by a larger proportion of female adolescents and young adults to learn sport roles, they still encounter discouragement and perhaps discrimination in their attempts. For example, although female athletes are now able to participate in the Olympic Games, they make up less than 20 percent of the participants in the Games and can compete in only 32 percent of all Olympic events, although this is a great improvement over the situation in 1900 when only eleven women from four countries participated.[6]

At the present time, females of all ages are underrepresented in the sport system, both in terms of their frequency of participation and in terms of the number of sports in which they participate (Hall, 1976; Milton, 1975). This pattern is especially significant for married women. However, there is little analytical evidence to account for this institutionalized pattern of gender[7] stratification. Rather, similar to the early writings concerning discrimination against black athletes, this topic has been characterized by conceptual and polemic essays or rhetoric. For example, review and conceptual papers have analyzed the female role in sport (Felshin, 1974; Hart, 1976; Phillips, 1972; Willis, 1973); aggression and the female athlete (Smith, 1972); females in the competitive process (Sherif, 1972); the female spectator (Heinhold, 1972); and the socialization process for females (Ingham, Loy, and Berryman, 1972; Kenyon, 1969). These articles frequently cite case studies of sexism and discrimination against female involvement in sport and the subsequent actions, legal or political, taken to achieve equal opportunity in sport. In addition to these conceptual reviews, some empirical studies have examined the socialization process for females (Greendorfer, 1977; Hall, 1973, 1976; McPherson, 1976; Theberge, 1977a, 1977b) and the occupational world of women's professional golf (Theberge, 1977c).

There is little evidence that the explanation for underrepresentation of females can be attributed to overt discrimination. Rather, it may be related to the process of socialization and sex-role learning whereby socially induced sex-appropriated values, norms, and sanctions define what behavior is socially acceptable for the female and the male roles in society. For example, Hall (1976) notes that the most influential factors accounting for an adult woman's participation at the present time are her activity level when younger, and the interest and participation of her family, if married. She concludes that the explanation for differential participation by females may be more likely to be found in the process of socialization than in attitudinal or dispositional factors.

This suggestion has even greater validity when it is recognized that there is great variation within and between communities and across nations concerning the values, norms, and behavioral patterns for female involvement in sport. For example, in most Eastern European countries boys and girls have equal rights and access to sport activities, sport is an integral facet of the life style for both males and females, and equality of rights for women is a norm that prevails in most institutional spheres. Similarly, there is variation in the socialization process within a community in that an adolescent female may see her mother and older female siblings participating and competing in sport and thus desire to become involved. However, she may receive negative sanctions from the school or from her peer group who do not value sport highly, perhaps because they do not receive reinforcement for sport involvement from their family. In this situation, common values and norms are not present, social learning is more difficult, and role conflict may result within the individual female who happens to get interested in physical activity. In this type of socializing milieu, she is faced with the question as to whether she should behave according to what is expected of her ascribed role, or follow her interests and try to achieve and learn new roles such as that of athlete, businesswoman, politician, etc. In effect, she is in a double bind: She must worry not only about failure, but also about the outcome if she is successful.

In summary, the present status of the female in sport is a product of the socialization practices inherent within a given culture or subculture. That is, many females are socialized in an environment in which the values, norms, and expectations are not conducive to encouraging or promoting involvement in sport. Therefore, the female socialized in this milieu is deprived of the right to make her own decision as to the role of physical activity in her life style. Furthermore, although the opportunities for women in sport are improving, there still remain problems: the role conflict experienced by female athletes at all ages, but especially during the formative adolescent years; insufficient financial support for expanding programs; considerable resistance from male sport organizations with whom they must compete for facilities; and the appearance of problems similar to those in the male sport milieu such as adult domination, increasing aggression and violence, and an increasing number of dropouts on the part of those who do become involved very early in life. A full understanding of these phenomena will not be gained until there are better theoretical and empirical analyses of the early socialization process and a consideration of why so few women adopt physical activity as part of their life style.

9.5   AGE STRATIFICATION IN SPORT

9.5.1   Patterns of Involvement by Age Strata

Most social systems are age-heterogeneous and are therefore comprised of age strata with age-related norms that determine appropriate or inappropriate behavior for particular points in the life cycle. Sport is no exception: Whereas a female may be permitted to participate in sport and physical activity during her early childhood, she often receives negative sanctions if she continues this type of behavior during the adolescent years. Similarly, males in their thirties or forties often receive negative sanctions from their employer or colleagues when it is revealed that they participate or compete in "adolescent" activities such as hockey, football, or pole vaulting. On the other hand, tennis and golf are socially sanctioned activities for men at this age.

To date, there has been little theoretical or empirical work from a sociological or psychological perspective concerning physical activity patterns over the life cycle, yet a number of descriptive studies have indicated a general pattern of declining involvement in sport and physical activity with age, especially after 25 years of age. Interestingly, these patterns appear to be universal, thereby increasing the magnitude of the problem. This pattern is especially significant and problematic in light of biological, physiological, and some psychological evidence that physical activity over the life cycle is beneficial to both physical and mental health. This section presents some representative data illustrating the pattern of declining involvement in physical activity over the life cycle, and suggests explanatory mechanisms from a sociological and gerontological perspective that may account for this trend.

In a number of modern and industrialized countries, the evidence clearly demonstrates declining involvement with age in both formal sport participation and informal physical activity. The following are some selected examples of this trend. Anderson et al. (1956) found that although over 50 percent of the adults in one Danish survey read the sport pages regularly and thereby expressed an interest in sport, only a small percentage reported that they were actively involved, especially after 25 years of age (Table 9.2). There appears to be a more rapid decline in primary involvement than in secondary involvement. Thus, while interest in consuming sport remains high, active participation decreases.

In a survey of adults in the United States, Kenyon (1966) found that while vicarious participation in physical activity through television and radio broadcasts is a major life interest of a large majority of adults, active participation is inversely proportional to age. One exception to the general pattern is the greater

Table 9.2
A comparison of primary and secondary involvement
of Danish adults by age

Age	Active involvement in sport (percent)	Regular reader of the sport pages (percent)
15–25	61	71
25–35	30	66
35–50	20	59
50+	9	50

Adapted from Anderson et al. (1956).

interest in calisthenics shown by men and women in their thirties and forties. This renewed, but usually brief, rekindling of interest in fitness is a common pattern for small segments of the adult population and may reflect an attempt at midlife to get serious about weight control or cardiovascular fitness. However, seldom does it last for a long period of time or become an integrated facet of an individual's life-style.

A large-scale survey conducted in France in 1967, as cited by Dumazedier (1973), indicated that only 8 percent of French citizens over the age of 14 participated regularly in sporting activities, while an additional 14 percent participated irregularly. Furthermore, it was found that from school age to 30 years of age, participation in sporting activities declined from 80 percent to 13 percent. This decline was twice as great among women and three times as great among members of the working class, compared to members of the professions (that is, the better-educated). Finally, Dumazedier (1973) noted that "more than 75 percent of all adults over 30 participate in sport as much as if they were already 70 years of age."

Based on a secondary analysis of a national survey of over 40,000 Canadians, Milton (1975) found that regular sport activity is inversely related to age, with males being more involved than females (especially if they are married) at all age levels. Furthermore, those with higher levels of education (in other words, those who are more socialized) are more active participants at all age levels (Table 9.3).

In a more limited sample of Canadians in the province of Alberta, Hobart (1975) found trends similar to the national survey cited by Milton (1975), although the citizens of Alberta were somewhat more active in each age category. This suggests the presence of regional differences in activity patterns that may be influenced by climate, opportunity set, or local attitudes that influence life-style.

In a study of women in Canada, Hall (1976) found that active involvement in sport was explained by three variables: present family involvement, activity level when younger, and present age. She concluded that situational determinants (e.g., marriage, a young family, a husband who doesn't participate, noninvolvement in childhood and adolescence) may be more inhibiting for women than for men in determining involvement in sport during adulthood.

In addition to the national studies, there have been some attempts to compare participation rates cross-nationally. In a study of twelve countries, Robinson (1967) found little cross-national variation in the overall amount of time spent on active sport participation, but did find that the rate of participation declined with age, especially past age 30 for women and age 50 for men. On the basis of a more detailed analysis of the United States, Robinson reported that the degree of active participation declines with age, but is less rapid for males and for those with higher levels of educational attainment (Table 9.4).

More recently, cross-national data (Kenyon and McPherson, 1976) indicates that, when asked the degree of primary involvement in their favorite sport, young adults (25–34 years of age) reported that they are not highly involved as active sport participants (Fig. 9.1). Again the pattern suggests that females generally participate less than males do. Furthermore, only in Norway and

Table 9.3
Percent involved in regular seasonal sport activity by education, age, and sex
for married heads of households or their spouses

Education and age level	Males Number of sports regularly involved in			Females Number of sports regularly involved in		
	(n)	None	Two+	(n)	None	Two+
Educ. level 1 (low)						
20–34 yrs.	(785)	28.4	44.1	(909)	42.5	28.7
35–54 yrs.	(2531)	40.7	31.9	(2291)	52.9	18.2
55+	(2467)	52.9	17.5	(1598)	62.7	8.4
Educ. level 2						
20–34 yrs.	(1370)	16.7	62.4	(1906)	28.9	45.7
35–54 yrs.	(2139)	27.3	48.7	(2350)	38.9	32.9
55+	(908)	38.9	30.6	(772)	50.6	18.3
Educ. level 3						
20–34 yrs.	(839)	17.5	63.4	(1344)	24.6	49.8
35–54 yrs.	(1007)	24.5	52.2	(1251)	32.2	40.0
55+	(431)	33.6	35.3	(380)	42.9	26.6
Educ. level 4						
20–34 yrs.	(467)	14.6	65.5	(655)	18.5	55.3
35–54 yrs.	(486)	20.8	58.2	(612)	33.0	42.0
55+	(174)	33.9	32.8	(195)	44.6	27.2
Educ. level 5 (high)						
20–34 yrs.	(714)	13.9	68.2	(505)	19.2	55.8
35–54 yrs.	(725)	17.8	61.7	(383)	28.7	49.3
55+	(264)	23.5	47.0	(135)	31.9	29.6

From Milton (1975, p. 85).

Table 9.4
Approximate number of times per year that men and women in various age
and education categories participate in active sports

	Men				Women			
	<30	30–39	40–49	50+	<30	30–39	40–49	50+
College exposure	22.6	16.1	17.3	9.3	10.5	10.6	7.9	5.0
High school graduate	12.6	10.9	10.8	7.5	7.9	12.8	8.9	2.5
Non-high school graduate	18.0	15.6	6.7	8.1	8.9	5.7	4.5	1.9

From Robinson (1967, p. 81).

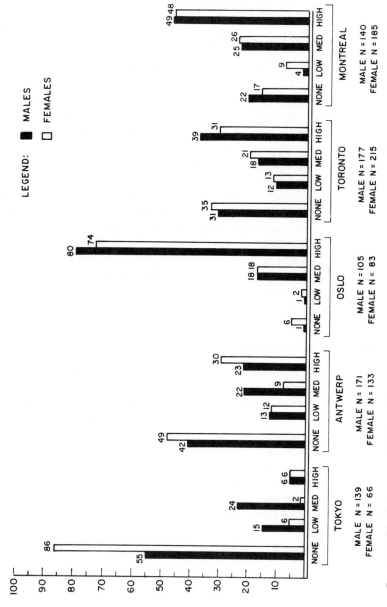

Fig. 9.1   The frequency of informal participation in one's favorite sport. (From Kenyon and McPherson, 1976)

among Francophones in Canada does there appear to be significant active involvement in sport among young adults.

A final factor that may be indirectly related to this pattern of declining primary involvement is the age of elite Olympic competitors. Chourbagi (1973) noted that there are no restrictions on the age of competitors but that at the 1968 Mexico Games 81 percent of the champions were less than 30 years of age, 13 percent were between 30 and 42 years of age, and only 4 percent were over 42 years of age. The oldest was a Swiss sailor of 66 years and the youngest a 14-year-old American swimmer. The average age of the competitors was 24. Again, there were sex differences in that 95 percent of the women champions were under 30 years of age, with the average age being 20. This finding indicates that only young elite role models are available, which indirectly suggests that sport or a specific event is for the young. Furthermore, Chourbagi (1973) noted that 15 percent of the Olympic athletes began their training before the age of ten, 45 percent began between ten and fourteen, and only 40 percent began after fourteen years of age. The average age for initiating training was thirteen. Statistics such as these facilitate the formation of age norms which imply that training for elite performance must begin early in life and that sport is for youth. Fortunately, there are many programs today such as Veterans Tennis, the Senior Olympics, the Master Track and Field and Swimming programs, and Old-Timers Hockey which demonstrate that adults of all ages can participate and compete in physical activity and that chronological or social age should not be a deterrent to participation throughout the life cycle.

9.5.2 Explaining Declining Sport Involvement by Age

Three main theories of aging and two theoretical perspectives have been used to explain both the process of aging and "successful aging" or "life satisfaction" in the later years. *Disengagement theory* (Cumming and Henry, 1961) argues that disengagement is an inevitable process whereby an individual selectively reduces the number of social roles he or she occupies in approaching the later years. Furthermore, it maintains that the process is functional for a society because it facilitates equilibrium by promoting the turnover of personnel in social roles, and that it is satisfying to the individual because it removes the pressure to perform. At the same time, disengagement reduces the frequency of interaction with others and weakens the power of norms over the individual, thereby resulting in more individual freedom.

While this theory has stimulated many empirical studies, most of which do not support the theory, it would appear to have little usefulness in explaining the process of disengagement from sport roles or physical activity. First, many individuals have never been engaged in physical activity at any point in the life cycle and therefore cannot disengage. That is, an inadequate socialization process is the problem, not disengagement. Second, disengagement from physical activity does not seem to be inevitable unless physical limitations or lack of motivation prevent continued involvement. Third, physical activity is not totally dependent on interaction with others, except for motivational reasons; some forms, such as jogging, swimming, walking, and cross-country skiiing, can be engaged in alone. Finally, the process may be functional only in professional or elite amateur sport where, for performance reasons, an individual may be voluntarily or involuntarily disengaged (retired) in order to permit a younger athlete to assume the role. However, even those who are forced to disengage at the elite level can remain involved by participating at lower levels of competition or by informal participation at a recreational level.

Activity theory (Friedman and Havighurst, 1954) argues that the norms of the later years are the same as those of the earlier years and that as people age they try to deny the existence of aging as long as possible. Thus, successful aging involves behaving like a middle-aged person and when social roles are lost (e.g., the work role at retirement), new roles are occupied in order to maintain a similar level of activity. Since the average age at which physical deterioration begins is rising, most adults in their sixties could be active and vigorous in their leisure pursuits, just as they are at work. This theory emphasizes that chronological age should not be used to define socially acceptable patterns of behavior for the adult population, and that to remain active in a variety of leisure pursuits is to age successfully.

Continuity theory (Atchley, 1977) stresses integration between phases in the life cycle. Through the socialization process, individuals develop habits, preferences, and dispositions that become integrated into their life style and as they grow older they are predisposed to maintaining continuity or consistency in this life style. This theory would seem to account for the need of older adults to remain involved in recreational or competitive forms of physical activity if it had been part of their life-style since early childhood or adolescence. That is, how one uses leisure time before 25 to 30 years of age likely determines how he or she will use it throughout the middle and later years. Furthermore, this theory stresses the importance of socializing youth early in life to incorporate physical activity into their life style. For example, Harris (1970) compared an active and a sedentary group of middle-aged males (40–59 years) and found that the active group had always participated in vigorous sports, that the parents of 70 percent of them had encouraged their involvement as a youth, and that 81 percent had participated regularly in physical activity during college. Similarly, recent cross-national evidence (Kenyon and McPherson, 1976) suggests that those who are involved in sport early in life will continue to be involved as young adults.

Two additional perspectives on aging are the *subculture of aging theory* (Rose, 1965) and the *minority group hypothesis* (Streib, 1965). The former argues that people of a certain chronological age (especially those over 65) form a readily identifiable group with their own norms and values, and as such they are forced to interact primarily with each other and therefore form a unique subculture. In terms of sport and physical activity, the norm of noninvolvement has become institutionalized in the middle and later years in many societies, and is reinforced by a lack of encouragement for those who wish to engage in physical activity in their leisure time. On the other hand, there are some exceptions, such as retirement communities in which age peers provide compatible leisure orientations and a positive reference group that legitimizes certain forms of leisure behavior, including sport. For example, there are retirement communities in which slow-pitch softball leagues and both competitive and informal tennis programs are highly institutionalized forms of sport in that particular subculture.

Closely related to this theory is the hypothesis that *older people are a minority group* and are discriminated against because they share a common biological characteristic. While this theory has more usefulness when considering the state of being old, it does have some relevance for the process of aging and involvement in physical activity and sport throughout the adult years. For example, adults are often considered a minority group by federal and local policymakers in the field of recreation, and are faced with age discrimination in terms of unequal opportunity to gain access to sport facilities and sport leaders. This is certainly evident in North America where many of the sport facilities are situated in schools and are normally reserved for youth sport programs. This is one domain in which seniority does not appear to have much influence.

In summary, involvement in physical activity and sport generally declines with age and occurs earlier and more frequently among women and among those with lower levels of educational attainment. Furthermore, the pattern varies somewhat from country to country or from generation to generation. While no definitive explanation for this pattern is available, some sociological evidence suggests that adults are sedentary and nonactive because of an inadequate socialization process that did not inculcate physical activity into their life style, because of a system of age stratification within society wherein age-based norms define socially appropriate or inappropriate behavior at specific stages in the life cycle, and because the age-based structure and opportunity set for informal participation and formal competition in sport eliminates individuals from the sport milieu when they attain a certain chronological age.

In the future, social change must occur if the present pattern is to be reversed so that physical activity throughout the life cycle becomes an integral facet of adult life styles. Continuity theory suggests that if this is to occur there must be more adequate socialization in childhood and adolescence so that physical activity becomes integrated into life styles early in life. At the same time, change in values and attitudes must take place so that the norm of being involved in physical activity through the life cycle can be inculcated. Furthermore, a structure must be created to provide adults with the opportunity to be active at all levels of ability and at all ages. For example, the use of the Master's program in swimming with the short and long courses and the use of short sets in tennis have enabled many adults to compete with age peers well into the later years of life.

9.6 SPORT AS A STRATIFICATION SYSTEM: DEMOCRATIZATION

9.6.1 Theories of Sport Stratification

Earlier in this chapter (see Section 9.1.3), the major theories of social stratification were outlined. Although less well-developed, both theoretically and empirically, there have been three attempts to develop a theory of sport stratification. First, Luschen (1969) set forth three propositions based on his analysis of the social class background of young sportsmen in the German Federal Republic. His first proposition states that the "newer a sport, the higher its social position." In support of this proposition, both Luschen (1969) and Pavia (1973) argued that basketball in the German Federal Republic and in Australia, respectively, has a high social status because it is a recent import. Similarly, Luschen (1969) indicated that the recent decrease in the social status of soccer and gymnastics in the German Federal Republic may be a reflection of the length of time that these sports have been part of the German sport culture. However, this proposition may not hold for newer sports such as skydiving or hang gliding, which are affiliated with youth or developing subcultures. That is, there may be sport differences that limit the generalizability of this proposition.

Luschen's (1969) second proposition suggests that "with increasing importance of individual achievement, the social status of a sport becomes higher." This hypothesis may partially account for the increasing status of tennis and squash, especially in North America. However, again there may be sport differences in that individual sports may reflect a pattern characterized by the inverted-U hypothesis. That is, this proposition may only be true at the upper ends of the socioeconomic scale (Gruneau, 1972). For example, amateur wrestling has not attained high status despite a high degree of individual attainment. The third proposition argues that "the higher the social status of a sport, as determined by the class to which its participants belong, the more it is dependent upon organization into clubs." From a historical perspective, we can say that sports that were originally high in status were organized within a club framework (Baltzell, 1958; Metcalfe, 1972, 1976a). However, many of these are now middle-class sports and readily available to the masses. Although many sports in North America are available on a club basis, it is only those that are restricted to the elite private clubs (such as polo and other equestrian events) that retain an image of high status.

A second theory, generated by Yiannakis (1975), suggests that the social status of a sport is influenced by four factors: the structure of the sport (i.e., individual vs. team sport), the cost of participation, the publicity it receives, and the amount of physical contact. He argues that higher-status sports are related to (1) a greater degree of autonomy in one's occupation (that is, the professions) as reflected by greater participation in individual sports; (2) the cost of participation (the upper classes can afford to participate in higher-status sports); (3) the exposure or publicity a sport receives (higher-status sports remain the privilege of the elite because the masses either do not see or hear about them, or they learn very little about the purpose or ethos of the sport); and (4) an absence of a combative element or bodily contact (the upper class uses "brains," while the lower classes emphasize physical toughness). Using original and secondary (from Loy, 1969) data, Yiannakis (1975) obtained correlations of 0.75 and 0.79, respectively, between the four predictor variables (sport structure, cost, publicity, physical contact) and the respondents' social status. The status hierarchy of sport groups, based on the prestige of the fathers' occupation, is concretely illustrated in Table 9.5 (Loy, 1972). The astute reader will no doubt have noticed that there are cross-

Table 9.5
Mean occupational status scores of fathers of former athletes
in twenty collegiate sports

Sport	n	Status score	Category
Golf	19	74	Upper-upper
Tennis	50	64	
Swimming	78	64	
Cricket	17	63	Lower-upper
Ice hockey	9	62	
Crew	64	62	
Fencing	5	60	
Gymnastics	33	58	
Basketball	91	57	Upper-middle
Volleyball	3	55	
Team managers	34	55	
Track	119	53	
Handball	6	53	
Rugby	16	52	Lower-middle
Rifle team	12	51	
Soccer	32	51	
Baseball	89	49	
Football	192	48	Upper-lower
Boxing	12	47	
Wrestling	27	43	Lower-lower

From Loy (1972, p. 9).

national differences in the prestige ranking of some sports. For example, gymnastics is low in Belgium (Renson, 1976), at the middle in Germany (Luschen, 1969), and at the upper-middle in the United States (Loy, 1972). To explain these differences requires an understanding of the historical development of the specific sport and of sport in general within each country.

These status differences across sports can be further illustrated by a third theoretical framework based on the "status symbolism" inherent in each sport. Renson (1976) analyzed the system of social stratification in Belgium and noted that the higher-class sports such as skiing, golf, field hockey, tennis, and fencing are all characterized by the use of "status sticks"; the upper-middle class sports of rowing, canoeing, horse riding, climbing, skating, hunting, and scuba diving are all "nature" sports; the lower-middle class sports such as basketball, volleyball, badminton, and table tennis require the "use of balls, nets and targets"; while the lower-class sports of gymnastics, calisthenics, track and field, boxing, soccer, and fishing are either of an "individual nature" or "involve close bodily contact."

In some respects, then, the sports played by a particular social class serve as symbols of their status and function within society. For example, Martin and

Berry (1974) argue that the adoption of motorcross racing as a sport by working-class males is a reflection of a socialization process that advocates "rugged individualism." Motocross racing serves as an accessible and popular pursuit for proving their manhood and for diffusing alienation present in the work world. In this way, stability is brought to the individual and to society through class-based participation.

9.6.2 Democratization in Sport

In recent years, North American journalists have indicated that there is a trend toward egalitarianism in society through democratization and increased opportunities for social mobility. Sport has been cited as one of the systems promoting and facilitating this process (Berryman and Ingham, 1972; Berryman and Loy, 1976). Moreover, one theme in the stratification literature has been an analysis of the extent to which there has been movement from elitism to mass involvement (i.e., democratization) in all facets of social participation, including sport. For example, Betts (1974) noted that the form of sport changed after the industrial revolution from the elite agrarian pursuits of horse racing and fox hunting to commercialized mass entertainment in the form of spectator sport. However, as we noted earlier, the masses were largely excluded from primary involvement in the sport pursuits of the upper classes through the organization of sport within highly institutionalized country clubs.

Although there has been increasing class-based interaction which has led to the "embourgeoisement"[8] (i.e., the identification of the lower and working class with the middle class) of the lower and working class in some domains, some sports are still dominated, in both the number of participants and in the background of the elite athletes, by those from specific social strata. That is, the degree of structural assimilation varies and is not a universal phenomenon.

Even though the social system of sport is no longer solely the prerogative of the elite, differential patterns of involvement suggest that inequality of opportunity persists. Furthermore, even though the importance of ascriptive criteria has declined, as reflected in greater mass secondary involvement in sport, the pursuit of elitism in primary involvement in many sports is still influenced by particularisms such as class, race, ethnicity, gender, and age. That is, ascriptive criteria serve a "gatekeeping" function in controlling access to certain institutionalized sport roles. Similarly, Gruneau (1975) argues that while there has been great democratization in consumption opportunities and some increased opportunities for mass participation, there has been little, if any, improvement in access to formal leadership positions in which the decision-making power dwells. In fact, he suggests that despite the decline of ascriptive privilege, modern sport actually contributes to the reinforcement of class distinctions. Gruneau (1976b) illustrates this point by noting the membership of the Canadian Olympic Association's "Olympic Trust," a group responsible for fund raising and allocating monies. Of the 43 members, 30 were members of Canada's corporate elite (Clement, 1975). Furthermore, these 30 individuals represent 85 dominant directorships in 113 major influential corporations in Canada. In short, access to "elite" positions in sport has not been opened to any great extent in recent years. Moreover, Gruneau (1976b) suggests that this seems "merely reflective of the 'social closure' that remains so much a part of the Canadian class structure."

The lack of democratization is also clearly revealed by an analysis of sport organized on a club basis (Baltzell, 1958; Davis, 1973; Gruneau, 1976a; Luschen, 1969; Metcalfe, 1972, 1976a, 1976b; Willis and Wettan, 1976). Rigid membership criteria (social or economic) effectively eliminate many from becoming members. More specifically, Davis (1973) analyzed the extent to which officers and members of the board of directors of two riding associations (the American Horse Shows Association and the United States Equestrian Team, Inc.) were listed in the *Social Register* from 1917 to 1973. She found that, whereas only 0.04 to 0.05 percent of the total population of the United States were listed in the *Social Register*, between 71 and 83 percent of the executives of these two associations were listed and therefore were socially prominent. In short, there has been virtually no democratization in these organizations over time.

As this chapter has indicated, particularisms concerning access to the sport world persist and, although more individuals may be involved in sport, the prestige hierarchy of each sport remains relatively stable, even though a few sports gain or lose status to some degree over time. For example, the prestige of boxing is still low and that of polo high. As a result of this prestige hierarchy, some sports remain exclusive to a specific group, while those in the middle have become more democratized. However, even in those sports in which democratization has occurred, status considerations still prevail in terms of the style of involvement.

In summary, we can state that while some democratization has occurred, it has not been universal across all sports or in all societies. In fact, there are still wide variations in terms of access to mass involvement and in the opportunity to pursue elite competition and success, especially at the amateur level. Finally, while this chapter has focused on the objective facets of social stratification in sport, Chapter 10 (see Section 10.3) concentrates on the subjective dimension. More specifically, special emphasis is placed on the subjective interpretations or evaluations of individuals that are based on perceived moral attributes pertaining to race, age, gender, religion, education, income, and occupation. That is, people are stratified on the basis of being better or more worthy if they possess certain moral attributes. This leads to a system of moral stratification of persons or groups that interacts with the more objective system discussed in this chapter.

NOTES

1. It is this evaluative component that distinguishes social stratification from the more general process of social differentiation.
2. The following account draws largely upon Tumin (1967), but differs slightly in that we typically substitute the term "role" for his use of the term "status" (see Section 2.1.1).
3. A dominant group may not necessarily be numerically the majority group. For example, in South Africa a numerical minority rules a numerical majority.

4. This is one of the few studies that has considered the class background of female athletes.

5. For historical overviews consult *Black Sports* (1972), Boulding (1957), Brown (1973), Davie (1949), Davis (1966), Govan (1971), Henderson (1968), McPherson (1974b), Orr (1969), Peterson (1970), Rust (1976), and Young (1963).

6. For a historical analysis of the role of women in the modern Olympic Games, see Simri (1976).

7. "Gender" is used rather than "sex" since, as Tresemer (1975) notes, "sex" refers to the dichotomous physiological differences between males and females, whereas "gender" refers to the psychological and cultural definitions of the dimensions of masculine and feminine. As a result, "gender" should be used when referring to learned roles.

8. See Berryman and Ingham (1972) for an analysis of six major sociohistorical trends that have led to some degree of "embourgeoisement" in North America.

REFERENCES

Anderson, H., et al. (1956). "Sports and games in Denmark in the light of sociology." *Acta Sociologica* 2: 1–28. Used with permission.

Andreano, R. (1965). "The affluent baseball player." *Transaction* (May–June): 2, 4, 10–13.

Atchley, R. (1977). *The Social Forces in Later Life*, 2nd ed. Belmont, Calif.: Wadsworth.

Ball, D. W. (1973). "Ascription and position: A comparative analysis of stacking in professional baseball." *Canadian Review of Sociology and Anthropology* 10 (May): 97–113.

Baltzell, E. D. (1958). *Philadelphia Gentlemen*. New York: The Free Press.

Beamish, M. (1976). "An analysis of the composition of the national executives of selected amateur sports: A median perspective." Unpublished B.A. thesis, Department of Sociology, Queens University.

Bendix, R., and S. Lipset (1953). "Karl Marx's theory of social class." In R. Bendix and S. Lipset (eds.), *Class, Status and Power*, pp. 26–35. New York: The Free Press.

Berryman G., and A. Ingham (1972). "The embourgeoisement of sport in America, 1869–1960." Presented at the American Sociological Association meetings, New Orleans (August).

Berryman, J., and J. W. Loy (1976). "Secondary schools and Ivy League letters: A comparative replication of Eggleston's 'Oxbridge Blues'." *The British Journal of Sociology* 27 (March): 61–77.

Betts, J. R. (1974). *America's Sporting Heritage: 1850–1950*. Reading, Mass.: Addison-Wesley.

Black Sports 2 (May/June) 1972.

Blau, P., and O. Duncan (1967). *The American Occupational Structure*. New York: John Wiley and Sons.

Blishen, B., and H. McRoberts (1976). "A revised socioeconomic index for occupations in Canada." *Canadian Review of Sociology and Anthropology* 13 (February): 71–79.

Boileau, R. (1977). "Social change, ethnicity and amateur sport involvement in Quebec: 1963–1973." M.Sc. thesis, Department of Kinesiology, University of Waterloo.

Boileau, R., F. Landry, and Y. Trempe (1976). "Les Canadiens Français et Les Grands Jeux Internationaux (1908–1974)." In R. Gruneau and J. Albinson (eds), *Canadian Sport: Sociological Perspectives*, pp. 141–169. Don Mills, Ontario: Addison-Wesley (Canada).

Boulding, D. (1957). "Participation of the Negro in selected amateur and professional athletics from 1935 to 1955." M.S. thesis, University of Wisconsin.

Boyle, R. H. (1963). "A minority group—the Negro baseball player." In R. H. Boyle (ed.), *Sport—Mirror of American Life*, pp. 100–134. Boston: Little, Brown.

Bratton, R. (1970). "Demographic characteristics of executive members of two Canadian sport associations." *Journal of the Canadian Association of Health, Physical Education and Recreation* 37 (January–February): 20–28.

Brown, R. (1973). "The black gladiator—the major force in modern American sport." In *Proceedings of the 76th Annual Meeting of the National College of Physical Education Association for Men*.

Cantril, H. (1944). "Identification with social and economic class." *Journal of Abnormal and Social Psychology* 38: 74–80.

Cheffers, J. (1972). *A Wilderness of Spite or Rhodesia Denied*. New York: Vantage Press.

Chourbagi, Z. (1973). "The age factor in competitive sport." In O. Grupe et al. (eds.), *Sport in the Modern World—Chances and Problems*, pp. 202–203. New York: Springer-Verlag.

Clark, M. (1977). "Power elites and American sport." Presented at the AAHPER National Meeting, Seattle (March).

Clement, W. (1975). *The Canadian Corporate Elite*. Toronto: McLelland and Stewart.

Collins, L. J. (1972). "Social class and the Olympic athlete." *British Journal of Physical Education* 3 (July): 25–27.

Crawford, S. (1977). "Occupational prestige rankings and the New Zealand Olympic athlete." *International Review of Sport Sociology* 12: 5–15.

Cumming, E., and W. E. Henry (1961). *Growing Old: The Process of Disengagement*. New York: Basic Books.

Davie, M. (1949). *Negroes in American Society*. New York: McGraw-Hill.

Davis, J. (1966). "The Negro in American sports." In J. Davis (ed.), *The American Negro Reference Book*, pp. 775–825. Englewood Cliffs, N.J.: Prentice-Hall.

Davis, K., and W. Moore (1945). "Some principles of stratification." *American Sociological Review* 10 (April): 242–397.

Davis, S. P. (1973). "A study of social class and the sport of riding." Unpublished paper, Department of Sport Studies, University of Massachusetts.

de Broglia, C. (1970). *South Africa: Racism in Sport*. London: Christian Action Publications.

Dodson, D. W. (1954). "The integration of Negroes in baseball." *Journal of Educational Sociology* 28 (October): 73–82.

Draper, M. (1963). *Sport and Race in South Africa*. Johannesburg: South African Institute of Race Relations.

Dumazedier, J. (1973). "Report to a symposium on sport and age." In O. Grupe et al. (ed.), *Sport in the Modern World—Chances and Problems*, pp. 198–199. New York: Springer-Verlag.

Dunning, E., and K. Sheard (1976). "The bifurcation of Rugby Union and Rugby League: A case study of organizational conflict and change." *International Review of Sport Sociology* 11: 31–68.

Eggleston, J. (1965). "Secondary schools and Oxbridge Blues." *The British Journal of Sociology* 16: 232–242.

Eichler, M. (1973). "Women as personal dependents." In M. Stephenson (ed.), *Women in Canada*, pp. 36–55. Toronto: New Press.

Elder, G. H. (1975). "Age differentiation and the life course." In A. Inkeles (ed.), *Annual Review of Sociology*, Vol. 1, pp. 165–190. Palo Alto, Calif.: Annual Reviews, Inc.

Faulkner, R. (1975). "Coming of age in organizations: A comparative study of career contingencies of musicians and hockey players." In D. W. Ball and J. W. Loy (eds.), *Sport and Social Order*, pp. 525–558. Reading, Mass.: Addison-Wesley.

Felshin, J. (1974). "The social view." In E. W. Gerber et al. (eds.), *The American Woman in Sport*, pp. 179–279. Reading, Mass.: Addison-Wesley.

Fox, J. (1961). "Pueblo baseball: New use for old witchcraft." *The Journal of American Folklore* **74**: 9–16.

Friedman, E., and R. Havighurst (1954). *The Meaning of Work and Retirement*. Chicago: University of Chicago Press.

Glassford, G. R. (1970). "Organization of games and adaptive strategies of the Canadian Eskimo." In G. Luschen (ed.), *The Cross-Cultural Analysis of Sport and Games*, pp. 70–84. Champaign, Ill.: Stipes.

Gordon, M. (1964). *Assimilation in American Life*. New York: Oxford University Press.

Govan, M. (1971). "The emergence of the black athlete in America." *The Black Scholar* **3** (November): 16–28.

Grace, M. (1974). "Origin and development of governmental sports policies in the Republic of South Africa: Sport and separate development." In U. Simri (ed.), *Proceedings of the Society for the History of Physical Education and Sport in Asia and the Pacific Area*, pp. 107–117. Netanya, Israel: The Wingate Institute for Physical Education.

Greeley, A. (1971). *Why Can't They Be Like Us?* New York: E. P. Dutton. Used with permission.

Greendorfer, S. (1977). "Socialization into sport." In C. Oglesby (ed.), *Woman Sport: From Myth to Reality*. Philadelphia: Lea and Febiger.

Gruneau, R. S. (1972). "A socio-economic analysis of the competitors of the 1971 Canada Winter Games." M. A. thesis, University of Calgary.

Gruneau, R. S. (1975). "Sport, social differentiation and social inequality." In D. W. Ball and J. W. Loy (eds.), *Sport and Social Order*, pp. 121–184. Reading, Mass.: Addison-Wesley. Used with permission.

Gruneau, R. S. (1976a). "Class or mass: Notes on the democratization of Canadian amateur sport." In R. S. Gruneau and J. G. Albinson (eds.), *Canadian Sport: Sociological Perspectives*, pp. 108–141. Don Mills, Ontario: Addison-Wesley (Canada).

Gruneau, R. S. (1976b). "Elites, class and corporate power in Canadian sport: Some preliminary findings." Presented at the International Congress of the Physical Activity Sciences, Quebec City (July).

Haerle, R. J. (1975). "Career patterns and career contingencies of professional baseball players: An occupational analysis." In D. W. Ball and J. W. Loy (eds.), *Sport and Social Order*, pp. 461–519. Reading, Mass.: Addison-Wesley.

Hain, P. (1971). *Don't Play with Apartheid*. London: Allen and Unwin.

Hall, M. A. (1973). "Women and physical recreation: A causal analysis." Presented at the Women and Sport Symposium, The University of Birmingham, Birmingham, England (September).

Hall, M. A. (1976). "Sport and physical activity in the lives of Canadian women." In R. Gruneau and J. Albinson (eds.), *Canadian Sport: Sociological Perspectives*, pp. 170–199. Don Mills, Ontario: Addison-Wesley (Canada).

Harris, D. (1970). "Physical activity attitudes of middle-aged males." In G. S. Kenyon and T. M. Grogg (eds.), *Contemporary Psychology of Sport*, pp. 419–422. Chicago: The Athletic Institute.

Hart, M. (ed.) (1976). *Sport in the Socio-Cultural Process*, 2nd ed. Dubuque, Iowa: W. C. Brown.

Heinhold, W. (1972). "The female spectator." In D. V. Harris (ed.), *Women and Sport: A National Research Conference*, pp. 307–319. University Park: Pennsylvania State University.

Henderson, E. (1968). *The Black Athlete—Emergence and Arrival*. New York: Publishers Company.

Hobart, C. W. (1975). "Active sport participation among the young, the middle-aged and the elderly." *International Review of Sport Sociology* 10: 27–40.

Horrell, M. (1968). *South Africa and the Olympic Games*. Johannesburg: South African Institute of Race Relations.

Ingham, A., J. Loy, and J. Berryman (1972). "Socialization, dialectics and sport." In D. V. Harris (ed.), *Women and Sport: A National Research Conference*, pp. 235–277. University Park: Pennsylvania State University.

Kenyon, G. S. (1966). "The significance of physical activity as a function of age, sex, education and socio-economic status of northern United States adults." *International Review of Sport Sociology* 1: 41–57.

Kenyon, G. S. (1969). "Explaining sport involvement with special reference to women." Presented at the Conference of the Eastern Association for Physical Education of College Women, Lake Placid, New York (October).

Kenyon, G. S., and B. D. McPherson (1976). "The sport role socialization process in four industrialized countries: A report from the ICSS project on leisure role socialization." Presented at the International Congress of Physical Activity Sciences, Quebec City (July).

Kinlock, G. (1974). *The Dynamics of Race Relations: A Sociological Analysis*. New York: McGraw-Hill.

Kiviaho, P. (1974a). "The regional distribution of sport organizations as a function of political cleavages." *Sportwissenschaft* 4: 72–81.

Kiviaho, P. (1974b). "Sport and class conflict in Finland." Presented at the International Sociological Association Meeting, Toronto (August).

Kiviaho, P., and M. Simola (1974). "Who leads sport in Finland?" *Sosiologia* 11: 267–274.

Krawczyk, Z. (1973). "Sport as a factor of acculturation." *International Review of Sport Sociology* 8: 63–76.

Lapchick, R. E. (1975). *The Politics of Race and International Sport: The Case of South Africa*. Westport, Conn.: Greenwood Press.

Lenski, G. (1966). *Power and Privilege: A Theory of Social Stratification*. New York: McGraw-Hill.

Lever, J. (1969). "Soccer: Opium of the Brazilian people." *Transaction* 7 (December): 2, 36–43.

Lewis, M. (1972a). "Culture and gender roles: There is no unisex in the nursery." *Psychology Today* 5 (May): 54–57.

Lewis, M. (1972b). "Sex differences in play behavior of the very young." *Journal of Health, Physical Education and Recreation* 43 (June): 38–39.

Lipman-Blumen, J., and A. R. Tickamyer (1975). "Sex roles in transition: A ten-year perspective." In A. Inkeles (ed.), *Annual Review of Sociology*, Vol. 1, pp. 297–338. Palo Alto, Calif.: Annual Reviews, Inc.

Loy, J. W. (1969). "The study of sport and social mobility." In G. S. Kenyon (ed.), *Aspects of Contemporary Sport Sociology*, pp. 101–119. Chicago: The Athletic Institute.

Loy, J. W. (1972). "Social origins and occupational mobility of a selected sample of American athletes." *International Review of Sport Sociology* 7: 5–23.

Loy, J. W., and C. H. Sage (1973). "Organizational prestige and coaching career patterns." Presented at the Annual Meeting of the Southern Sociological Society, Atlanta.

Luschen, G. (1969). "Social stratification and social mobility among young sportsmen." In J. W. Loy and G. S. Kenyon (eds.), *Sport Culture and Society*, pp. 258–276. New York: MacMillan.

Mains, D., and J. S. Williams (1975). "The role of conflict in the acculturation of minority groups." *International Review of History and Political Science* 12 (August): 59–71.

Mallea, J. R. (1975). "The Victorian sporting legacy." *McGill Journal of Education* 10: 184–196.

Marple, P., and P. Pirie (1977). "The French Canadian ice hockey player: A review of evidence and suggestions for future research." Presented at the Canadian Sociology and Anthropology Association Annual Meeting, Fredericton, New Brunswick (June).

Martin, T., and K. Berry (1974). "Competitive sport in post-industrial society: The case of the motocross racer." *Journal of Popular Culture* 8: 107–120.

Mason, K. O., and L. L. Bumpass (1975). "U. S. women's sex-role ideology, 1970." *American Journal of Sociology* 80 (March): 1212–1219.

McIntyre, T. D. (1959). "Socioeconomic background of white male athletes and four select sports at the Pennsylvania State University." M.S. thesis, Pennsylvania State University.

McKay, J. (1975). "Sport and ethnicity: Acculturation, structural assimilation, and voluntary association involvement among Italian immigrants in metropolitan Toronto." M.Sc. thesis, Department of Kinesiology, University of Waterloo.

McPherson, B. D. (1968). "Background factors of Ontario–Quebec Athletic Association hockey and tennis players." Unpublished paper.

McPherson, B. D. (1974a). "Career patterns of a voluntary role: The minor hockey coach." Presented at the Annual Meeting of the Canadian Sociology and Anthropology Association, Toronto.

McPherson, B. D. (1974b). "Minority group involvement in sport: The black athlete." In J. Wilmore (ed.), *Exercise and Sport Sciences Review*, Vol. 2, pp. 71–101. New York: Academic Press.

McPherson, B. D. (1976). "Socialization into the role of sport consumer: A theory and causal model." *The Canadian Review of Sociology and Anthropology* 13 (May): 165–177.

Meisel, J., and V. Lemieux (1972). "The Canadian Amateur Hockey Association." In J. Meisel and V. Lemieux (eds.), *Ethnic Relations in Canadian Voluntary Associations*, pp. 64–70. Ottawa: Information Canada.

Metcalfe, A. (1972). "Sport and social stratification in Toronto, Canada: 1860–1920." Presented at the American Sociological Association Meetings, New Orleans (August).

Metcalfe, A. (1976a). "Organized sport and social stratification in Montreal: 1840–1901." In R. Gruneau and J. Albinson (eds.), *Canadian Sport: Sociological Perspectives*, pp. 77–101. Don Mills, Ontario: Addison-Wesley (Canada).

Metcalfe, A. (1976b). "Working class physical recreation in Montreal, 1860–1895." Presented at the International Seminar on the History of Sport and Physical Education, Three Rivers, Quebec (July).

Milton, B. G. (1975). *Social Status and Leisure Time Activities: National Survey Findings for Adult Canadians*. Monograph 3 in the Canadian Sociology and Anthropology Association Monograph Series, B. Bernier and J. M. Rainville (eds.), Montreal. Used with permission.

Noe, F. (1974). "Leisure life styles and social class: A trend analysis, 1900–1960." *Sociology and Social Research* 58 (April): 286–294.

North, C., and P. Hatt (1953). "Jobs and occupations: A popular evaluation." In R. Bendix and S. Lipset (eds.), *Class, Status and Power*, pp. 411–426. New York: The Free Press.

Nowak, W. (1969). "Social aspects of Polish boxers and their environment in the light of questionnaires and surveys." *International Review of Sport Sociology* 4: 137–150.

Orr, J. (1969). *The Black Athlete: His Story in American History*. New York: Lion Press.

Ossowski, S. (1963). *Class Structure in the Social Consciousness*. Translated by S. Patterson. New York: The Free Press.

Park, R. (1950). *Race and Culture*. New York: The Free Press.

Pavia, G. R. (1973). "An analysis of the social class of the 1972 Australian Olympic Team." *The Australian Journal of Physical Education* 61 (September): 14–19.

Pavia, G., and T. Jaques (1976). "The socioeconomic origin, academic attainment, occupational mobility, and parental background of selected Australian athletes." Presented at the International Congress of Physical Activity Sciences, Quebec City (July).

Peterson, R. W. (1970). *Only the Ball Was White*. Englewood Cliffs, N.J.: Prentice-Hall.

Petrie, B. P. (1973). "Socioeconomic backgrounds of intercollegiate athletes of the Big Ten Conference, 1960–1965." Presented at the Canadian Congress for the Multi-Disciplinary Study of Sport and Physical Activity, Montreal (October).

Phillips, M. (1972). "Sociological considerations of the female participant." In D. Harris (ed.), *Women and Sport: A National Research Conference*, pp. 185–202. University Park: Pennsylvania State University.

Pooley, J. C. (1976). "Ethnic soccer clubs in Milwaukee: A study in assimilation." In M. Hart (ed.), *Sport in the Socio-Cultural Process*, 2nd ed., pp. 475–492. Dubuque, Iowa: W. C. Brown.

Renson, R. (1976). "Social status symbolism of sport stratification." Presented at the International Congress of the Physical Activity Sciences, Quebec City (July).

Riesman, D., and R. Denney (1951). "Football in America: A study in culture diffusion." *American Quarterly* 3: 309–319.

Riley, M., M. Johnson, and A. Foner (eds.) (1972). *Aging and Society. Volume 3: A Sociology of Age Stratification*. New York: Russell Sage Foundation.

Robinson, J. (1967). "Time expenditure on sports across ten countries." *International Review of Sport Sociology* 2: 67–84.

Rocher, G. (1973). *Le Quebec et Mutation*. Montreal: Hurtubise.

Rooney, J. (1974). *A Geography of American Sport*. Reading, Mass.: Addison-Wesley.

Rose, A. (1965). "The subculture of aging: A framework for research in social gerontology." In A. Rose and W. Peterson (eds.), *Older People and Their Social World*, pp. 3–16. Philadelphia: F. A. Davis.

Roy, G. (1974). "The relationship between centrality and mobility: The case of the National Hockey League." M.Sc. thesis, Department of Kinesiology, University of Waterloo.

Rust, A. (1976). *Get That Nigger off the Field*. New York: Delacorte Press.

Sherif, C. (1972). "Females in the competitive process." In D. V. Harris (ed.), *Women and Sport: A National Research Conference*, pp. 115–139. University Park: Pennsylvania State University.

Shibutani, T., and K. Kwan (1965). *Ethnic Stratification: A Comparative Approach*. New York: MacMillan.

Simri, U. (1976). "A historical analysis of the role of women in the modern Olympic Games." Presented at the International Seminar on the History of Sport and Physical Education, Three Rivers, Quebec (July).

Smith, M. (1972). "Aggression and the female athlete." In D. Harris (ed.), *Women and Sport: A National Research Conference*, pp. 91–114. University Park: Pennsylvania State University.

Smith, M. S., and F. Diamond (1976). "Career mobility in professional hockey." In R. S. Gruneau and J. G. Albinson (eds.), *Canadian Sport: Sociological Perspectives*, pp. 275–293. Don Mills, Ontario: Addison-Wesley (Canada).

Starosta, W. (1967). "Some data concerning social characteristics of figure skaters." *International Review of Sport Sociology* 2: 165–176.

Stone, G. P. (1957). "Some meanings of American sport." In *The Proceedings of The National College of Physical Education Association for Men, 60th Annual Meeting*.

Stone, G. P. (1969). "Some meanings of American sport: An extended view." In G. S. Kenyon (ed.), *Aspects of Contemporary Sport Sociology*, pp. 5–16. Chicago: The Athletic Institute.

Streib, G. (1965). "Are the aged a minority group?" In A. W. Gouldner and S. M. Miller (eds.), *Applied Sociology*. New York: The Free Press.

Takenoshita, K. (1967). "The social structure of the sport population in Japan." *International Review of Sport Sociology* 2: 5–16.

Taylor, I. (1971). "Social control through sport: Football in Mexico." Presented at the British Sociological Association Meeting, London.

Taylor, I. (1972). "Football mad: A speculative sociology of football hooliganism." In E. Dunning (ed.), *The Sociology of Sport*, pp. 353–377. Toronto: University of Toronto Press.

Theberge, N. (1977a). "An occupational analysis of women's professional golf." Unpublished Ph.D. dissertation, Department of Sociology, University of Massachusetts.

Theberge, N. (1977b). "Some factors associated with socialization into the role of professional woman golfer." Presented at the Ninth Annual Canadian Symposium for Psycho-Motor Learning and Sports Psychology, Banff, Alberta (September).

Theberge, N. (1977c). "The world of women's professional golf: Responses to structured uncertainty." Presented at the Annual Meeting of the Association for the Anthropological Study of Play, San Diego (April).

Tresemer, D. (1975). "Assumptions made about gender roles." In M. Millman and R. Louter (eds.), *Another Voice: Feminist Perspectives on Social Life and Social Science*. New York: Anchor Press.

Tumin, M. (1967). *Social Stratification*. Englewood Cliffs, N.J.: Prentice-Hall.

Turner, R. H. (1960). "Sponsored and contest mobility in the school system." *American Sociological Review* 25 (December): 855–867.

Ulrich, H. (1976). "The social structure of high-level sport." *International Review of Sport Sociology* 11: 139–149.

Webb, H. (1969). "Professionalization of attitudes toward play among adolescents." In G. S. Kenyon (ed.), *Aspects of Contemporary Sport Sociology*, pp. 161–178. Chicago: The Athletic Institute.

Weber, M. (1953). "Class, status and power." In R. Bendix and S. Lipset (eds.), *Class, Status and Power*, pp. 63–75. New York: The Free Press.

Weinberg, S. K., and H. Arond (1952). "The occupational culture of the boxer." *American Journal of Sociology* 57: 460–469.

Wettan, R., and J. Willis (1976). "Social stratification in the New York Athletic Club: A preliminary analysis of the impact of the club on amateur sport in late nineteenth century America." *Canadian Journal of History of Sport and Physical Education* 7 (May): 41–53.

Willis, J., and R. Wettan (1976). "Social stratification in New York City athletic clubs, 1865–1915." *Journal of Sport History* 3: 45–63.

Willis, P. (1973). "Performance and meaning: A socio-cultural view of women in sport." Presented at the Women and Sport Symposium, University of Birmingham, England.

Wohl, A. (1966). "Social aspects of the development of rural sport in Poland according to research." *International Review of Sport Sociology* 1: 109–130.

Yiannakis, A. (1975). "A theory of sport stratification." *Sport Sociology Bulletin* 4 (Spring): 22–32.

Young, A. (1963). *Negro Firsts in Sports*. Chicago: Johnson Publications.

Zurcher, L., and A. Meadow (1967). "On bull fights and baseball: An example of interaction in social institutions." *Journal of Comparative Sociology* 8: 99–117.

PART 4
CONCLUSION
The Social System
of Sport

Chapter 10
SPORT AS A
SOCIAL INSTITUTION

10.1 INTRODUCTION

We will now consider sport as a cultural system, and will examine the ways in which it has become legitimatized as a social institution. As defined by Schneider, a social institution

> . . . denotes an aspect of social life in which distinctive value-orientations and interests, centering upon large and important social concerns . . . generate or are accompanied by distinctive modes of social interaction. Its use emphasizes "important" social phenomena; relationships of "strategic structural significance." (Schneider, 1964, p. 338)

The earlier chapters of the text have illustrated the magnitude of sport in society and thus have provided some justification for its consideration as a social institution. Moreover, Chapters 6, 7, and 8 have shown how sport influences and in turn is influenced by the major institutional sectors of society.

However, the institutional status of sport is an ambivalent one, for it seemingly lacks a legitimate moral basis that is characteristic of the so-called *master* or *primary* institutions of society such as the family and kinship systems, the school and educational systems, the church and religious systems, business and economic systems, and government and political systems. These institutional orders are held to be of "strategic structural significance" because they deal with important societal maintenance problems such as ". . . (1) reproduction, (2) socialization, (3) maintenance of a sense of purpose, (4) production and distribution of goods and services, and (5) preservation of order" (Young and Mack, 1959). Therefore, it may be asked, "What large and important social concerns does sport center upon?"

10.1.1 The Paradoxical Nature of Sport

Kahn (1957) long ago observed that: "The most fascinating and least reported aspect of American sports is the silent and enduring search for a rationale." It is suggested that the ambivalent institutional status of sport and its "enduring search for a rationale" is a consequence of its inherently paradoxical nature.

On the one hand, sport is often regarded as a socially significant aspect of American culture. For example, Boyle persuasively argues that:

> Sport permeates any number of levels of contemporary society, and it touches upon and deeply influences such disparate elements as status, race relations, business life, automotive design, clothing styles, the concept of the hero, language and ethical values. For better or worse, it gives form and substance to much in America. (Boyle, 1963, pp. 3–4)

On the other hand, sport is often viewed as a trivial artifact of American culture. The essence of this viewpoint is given in Howard Cosell's pithy statement that "sport is the toy department of life." A more recent example is the retirement of Al DeRogatis as a sports commentator for the National Broadcasting Company with a year to go on his contract. When asked how he felt about kicking his habit after 35 years of involvement with professional football, DeRogatis replied: "Great, I'm playing golf on Sundays and loving it." He further stated that: "People are taking football too seriously. It's just a game." (New York Times, 1976).

Many other examples of the perceived triviality of sport could be given, but the critical question remains: "How can one account for or resolve these bipolar and conflicting views of sport in society, significant on the one hand, superficial on the other?"

An important clue for the construction of an adequate account of the paradoxical nature of sport is contained in Huizinga's classic analysis of the nature and significance of play. He states that:

> The function of play in the higher forms which concern us here can largely be derived from the two basic aspects under which we meet it: as a contest *for* something or a representation *of* something. These two functions can unite in such a way that the game "represents" a contest or else becomes a contest for the best representation of something. (Huizinga, 1955, p. 13)

On the one hand, it is suggested that the perception of sport as a shallow, nonserious activity stems from the fact that, *as a contest for something,* it is a type of *expressive behavior* producing no truly important outcomes nor resulting in any real instrumental consequences for everyday life. In short, all expressive activities originate in play and retain an underlying sense of playfulness, and all forms of play, especially playful contests, are perceived as nonserious activities within the moral framework of society.

On the other hand, it is suggested that sport is perceived as a serious social concern insofar as it *best represents* or reflects values and relationships of "strategic structural significance." Specifically, it is the general theme of this chapter that sport as a cultural system serves as a model of and for the moral framework of American culture by mirroring the dominant value system of society and by dramatizing the status concerns of individuals in society.

10.1.2 The Hegemony of the American Success Ideology

The Concept of the Dominant Value System

Before we examine how the social system of sport reflects the moral framework of society, the concept of the dominant value system is defined, and the nature of the dominant value system of American society in terms of the success ideology is described as it is reflected by the American Sports Creed. As Parkin has noted:

> The concept of a dominant value system derives from Marx's celebrated statement that "the ideas of the ruling class are, in every age, the ruling ideas." This proposition rests on the plausible assumption that those groups in society which occupy positions of the greatest power and privilege will also tend to have the greatest access to the means of legitimation. That is so to say, the social and political definitions of those in dominant positions tend to become objectified and enshrined in the major institutional orders, so providing the moral framework of the entire social system. (Parkin, 1972, pp. 82–83)

It is argued that the social institution of sport derives its legitimacy in large measure from its ideological interdependence with the major institutional sectors of society. These reflect in the clearest and most instrumental sense the "ruling ideas of the ruling class." The social system of sport both accepts and reinforces the "working ideologies" of other institutional spheres. And by virtue of the institutional backing it receives, sport acquires a degree of legitimation in its own right.

The American Sports Creed

The social significance of sport with respect to the superstructure of American society is that it reflects in highlighted form the basic ideological elements of the major institutionalized social structures of society, including the primary social institutions and the primary stratification systems. Moreover, through processes of social change and historical transformation, the sport order has combined diverse ideological elements from different institutional spheres into a coherent belief system that has been characterized as "The American Sports Creed" (Edwards, 1973).

Edwards describes this creed in terms of seven basic ideological elements: (1) character development, (2) discipline, (3) competition, (4) physical fitness, (5) mental fitness, (6) religiosity, and (7) nationalism. His analysis of the American Sports Creed suggests that it represents a value system not unlike the great success formula typified by Horatio Alger. All the elements are there—the doctrine and hard work, honesty, sincerity, perseverance, and the deserved reward of success. In brief, the American Sports Creed, like the American Dream, represents an identical model of the American success ideology.

Conformance to the Dominant Value System

Thio (1972) argues that whereas open coercion was the characteristic means of ensuring compliance with the dominant value system of society in the earlier stages of capitalism, ". . . subtle coercion through the propagation of a success ideology is more compatible with the present advanced stage of capitalism. . . ." He states that: "In classical Marxian parlance, one may say that the character- istically ideological *superstructure* has become predominant over the typically economic *infrastructure.*" Thio further notes that ". . . the various aspects of the capitalistic superstructure . . . can be encapsulated by Gramsci's concept of hege- mony:"

> [Hegemony is] an order in which a certain way of life and thought is domi-
> nant, in which one concept of reality is diffused throughout society in all its
> institutional and private manifestations, in forming with its spirit all taste,
> morality, customs, religious and political principles, and all social relations,
> particularly in their intellectual and moral connotations. (Genovese, 1970,
> p. 300)

The American success ideology represents the hegemony characteristic of modern society, and the American Dream and the American Sports Creed reflect the basic ideological elements of the dominant value system associated with this hege- mony.

Thio (1972) posits that the success ideology ensures conformance to the dominant system in two ways. First, the working ideologies of the master institu- tions propagate the value of high aspirations. Second, the institutionalized forms of social stratification in society impose ". . . the veiled threat on the subordinate strata of being stigmatized as 'lazy, worthless people' unless they accept the goal of high aspiration."

The second section of this chapter illustrates the ideological interrelation- ships between sport and other social institutions and suggests how the social system of sport supports the working ideologies of the master institutions in prop- agating the value of high aspiration. The third section of the chapter illustrates in turn the ideological interrelationships between the social system of sport and the basic systems of social stratification. It further suggests how sport influences the imposition of "the veiled threat on the subordinate strata of being stigmatized as being morally inferior unless they accept the goal of high aspiration."

10.2 SOCIAL INSTITUTIONS
AND MANIPULATIVE SOCIALIZATION

Sport is thought to serve the primary institutional order of society by propaga- ting the value of high aspiration in a four-fold manner. First, sport symbolizes the ideal expectations of adult authorities concerning proper moral conduct. It is further regarded as an influential force for mitigating deviant behavior of rebel- lious youth in the form of delinquency, radicalism, and bohemianism, whose basic tenets run counter to those of the success ideology. Second, sport provides concrete illustrations of the abstract value of high aspiration and thus ensures that the value is made readily comprehensible to youth. Third, sport presents a readily understandable interpretation of the competitive ethos underlying the success ideology and underscores the value of achievement and striving for excellence. Fourth, sport symbolically serves as a force for social integration and identification with a common life style. This life style is linked to a national character represented by a high degree of achievement motivation and competitive spirit.

In terms of these four functions, let us now examine how sport serves as a form of manipulative socialization and a reflection of the ideological schemata of the *socializing, regulative,* and *cultural* institutions of society.

10.2.1 Sport and Socializing Institutions

Within the institutional sectors of society primarily concerned with the socialization of youth (that is, the family, school, and community), sport as an agent of social control is held to be of most relevance in educational settings. As Waller perceptively observed nearly 50 years ago:

> . . . [The] use of athletics may simplify the problem of police work in the school. The group of athletes may be made to furnish a very useful extension of the faculty-controlled social order. Athletes have obtained favorable status by following out one faculty-determined culture pattern; they may be induced to adopt for themselves and to popularize other patterns of a similar nature. Athletes, too, in nearly any group of youngsters, are the natural leaders, and they are leaders who can be controlled and manipulated through the medium of athletics. (Waller, 1932, p. 116)

Sport also acts as an agent of social control by revealing in relatively concrete terms the abstract conception of aspiration. Matza states that:

> An important function of athletics is to make real the conception of aspiration. Thus, sport links aspiration to the adult social order in its functions as an agency of official social control. Athletics are the handmaiden of convention despite their harboring within them the spirit of exuberance, violence, prowess, freedom, and other attributes commonly imputed to youth. Thus, they are among the best examples of the social duplicity of which control is instituted through the illusion of autonomy. (Matza, 1964, pp. 206–207)

The degree to which athletics in educational systems in fact functions as an effective agent of social control is not an issue here. The main point to be made here is that sport has symbolic import for revealing, in a relatively concrete manner, the abstract ideological elements associated with the moral framework of society. Thus, it will suffice to say that:

> . . . athletics, and the associated codes of sportsmanship, have frequently been taken as the playground on which subsequently useful moral precepts are learned. This function can be exaggerated and idealized, but there is some correspondence between the moral demands of adult life and the particular code of sportsmanship prevalent in youthful games. A statement of correspondence or approximation need not be a mindless celebration of sports as character-building. (Matza, 1964, p. 206)

A forceful example of the correspondence between moral precepts of the play world of children and youth and the work world of adults is given in Webb's (1969) analysis of the professionalization of attitudes toward play. He describes the ideological communality of the institutional spheres of sport and the economy in terms of the value triad of success (victory), performance (skill), and equity (fairness). Webb contends that:

> . . . it is no surprise that sport, given its considerable popularity, reflects in its operation this inviolate trinity, and thus provides the rationalization and defense processes of the economy, which dominate Western society, a ready object example for illustrating its most highly touted values at work: fairness, skill, and victory. (Webb, 1969, p. 161)

More specifically, Webb theorizes that as the young progressively advance from involvement in childlike play forms, to participation in informal games, to engagement in structured sports, and finally to competition in highly organized athletics, there occur fundamental changes in attitudes toward play with respect to the attributes of equity, skill, and success. He refers to the cognitive changes in attitudes that are concomitant with the structural changes in the rationalization and formalization of play forms as the professionalization of attitude toward play—that is, the substitution of skill for fairness as the chief factor in play activity and the increasing importance of success through winning (Webb, 1969).

To test his notions about attitudes toward play, Webb developed a scale of the professionalization of play and surveyed a random sample of elementary and secondary school students attending public and parochial schools in a western Michigan community. Findings of his survey clearly showed considerable changes in attitudes toward play for both males and females as age increased. Specifically, a comparison of both sexes across grade levels revealed that an increasing importance was placed on the success factor. Females were found to rank fairness consistently higher than males at all grade levels. Moreover, differences between the sexes at each grade level were most marked for the winning or success factor, with the distance between the sexes rapidly increasing after the sixth grade.

Webb relates the differences in play attitudes between the sexes to the fact that males receive greater socialization for the future occupational world than do females. This stresses the increasing importance of achievement-based practices for males with increasing age and the relatively stable emphasis on ascriptive bases for females.

In summary, then, Webb's work shows how the secondary institution of sport supports the primary social institutions of society concerned with socialization. It further indicates how the ideological elements of sport mirror the ideological elements of the value systems of the regulative institutional sectors of society.

10.2.2 Sport and Regulative Institutions

The working ideologies of the regulative institutional sectors of society are most instrumental in ensuring the normative acceptance of the American success ideology. Each regulative institution places particular emphasis on specific sets of valued moral attributes associated with success and fulfillment of the American Dream. For example, the ideology of the *economic system* stresses the work ethic and the importance of rationality; the ideology of the *legal system* emphasizes matters of equality, justice, and fair competition; the ideology of the *military system* focuses on the value of physical fitness and mental discipline; and the ideology of the *political system* centers attention on patriotism, national character, and international supremacy.

It was demonstrated in Chapter 7 that every regulative institution uses sport metaphors to display symbolically its basic ideological creeds, and each instrumentally uses sport practices to obtain its ideological objectives. Thus, the present analysis is restricted to showing how sport serves the regulative institutional order and influences the normative acceptance of the success ideology by reflecting and reinforcing the competitive ethos shared by one and all.

Sadler has succinctly described the pervasive presence of the competitive spirit in sport and North American society as follows:

> It seems evident . . . that within the dominant institutions of American society there is a convergence of forces shaping our perception of the world so that it is seen in basically competitive terms. Added to this institutional fact is the dissipation of forces that would inhibit competition. Customs and traditions where competition made little sense have increasingly been swept away by rapid social change. In addition enduring supportive networks of relationships which inhibited competitiveness have been broken up with massive social and geographical mobility. There are few things left that Americans can rely upon to obtain acceptance and identification. The pressure to compete has therefore intensified. One has to compete not just to win a prize and to prove one's superior competence but also to win recognition and even just a place in the sun. From within this perspective Vince Lombardi was quite right: "Winning is the only thing." (Sadler, 1972, p. 12)

The competitive ethos is an inherent part of the ideology of all regulative social institutions in the United States, if not most Western nations in general. Achievement, competition, victory, and the importance of striving for success and maintaining superiority are emphasized by the economy, military, and polity alike. While typically rhetorical, such stress often has a significant function in reality in propagating the value of high aspiration for all members of society.

Furthermore, through the use of sport metaphors and sport practices, regulative institutions effectively "translate into the common language of mass spectator sports the complications and implications" of the ideology goals of regulative institutions and "make easily comprehensible to masses of people those policies which leaders" within the regulative institutional sectors of society seek to advance (Mrozek, 1974).

Many social observers and dominant societal leaders have drawn numerous parallels between the practices of sport and the functions of the regulative institutional sectors of society. Perhaps a few examples related to the economy, military, and polity will suffice to support this point.

Sport and the Economy

Numerous analogies have been made between the competitive ethos of the institutional spheres of sport and economics. For example, Huizinga points out in his discussion of the play element in contemporary civilization that:

> The statistics of trade and production could not fail to introduce a sporting element into economic life. In consequence, there is now a sporting side to almost every triumph of commerce or technology: the highest turnover, the biggest tonnage, the fastest crossing, the highest altitude, etc. (Huizinga, 1955, p. 200)

Huizinga ironically notes that in modern industrial societies "play has become business" and "business has become play."

Caillois (1961) draws similar parallels between the competitive nature of sport and the economic order. He sets forth a four-fold classification of games based on whether "the role of competition (agôn), chance (alea), simulation (mimicry), or vertigo (ilinx) is dominant." He states that:

> . . . the practice of *agôn* presupposes sustained attention, appropriate training, assiduous application, and the desire to win. It implies discipline and perseverence. (Caillois, 1961, p. 15)

Caillois contends that the principle of *agôn* is found in cultural forms such as sports at the margins of the social order, and in institutional forms such as competitive examinations and economic competition which are integrated into social life. Moreover, he holds that when "transposed from play to reality the only goal of *agôn* is success," and an obsessive concern with success corrupts the play element of *agôn* and results in violence, *will-to-power*, and trickery.

Perhaps the major way in which the competitive rhetoric of sport and economics serves to propagate the value of high aspiration is its influential impact on the process of socialization for production and consumption. High rates of productivity objectively denote successful goal attainment by economically based social systems, including society-at-large (see the annual figures for the gross national product). In a parallel manner, conspicuous consumption by members of society-at-large objectively denotes their possession of wealth, which is conventionally accepted as an index of achieved social success and as an indicator of conformity to the value of high aspiration. This was aptly illustrated by Veblen (1934) in *The Theory of The Leisure Class*, which stressed the importance of "conspicuous consumption" for displaying one's status and success.

A recent examination of socialization for consumption and production through sport involvement is Hoch's (1972) quasi-Marxist analysis of sport in North American society. The following quotation reflects the ideological ties that Hoch perceives between the institutional sectors of sport and economics:

> The mythology assumes that the Rules of the Game of life in capitalist society are perfectly neutral, so that success—whether in sport or civilian life—depends fundamentally on your attitude. If you follow the rules—or play the game—compete hard, put out to make it, and never give up, you

win the rat race. Of course, we all know that in sports, as in life, there can only be a few winners—that is the way the game is set up. This is the reason why the others must learn to be *good losers,* accepting their defeats gracefully, always imagining that we'll do better next time, but never questioning the Rules of the Game. If the system is to continue, the losers must continue to play. In fact, both the sports ethic and the Protestant ethic teach you that if you lost the game, it was basically because you didn't work hard enough.*

The ideological emphasis on competition and the value of high aspiration characteristic of the economy is also seen in the military and the polity.

Sport and the Military

The competitive ethos is particularly characteristic of the military order of society. In fact, defense programs have long used sport for both instrumental and ideological purposes. Several illustrations of the interrelationships between sport and the military are given in Mrozek's (1974) analysis of the Defense Department's use of sport between 1945 and 1950. He shows how several outstanding military leaders strongly endorsed the functional use of sport for military preparedness in terms of mental and physical discipline. He also shows how noted military and political leaders of the period rhetorically used sport metaphors in various forms of political instruction. These metaphors were used to make complex issues of the military situation clear to both members of the armed forces and members of the general public.

Mrozek (1974) records that these two uses of sport within military circles were neither antithetical nor temporally exclusive of one another. He suggests, however, that the functionalist use of sport for purposes of physical fitness and combat readiness held greater sway in the 1930s and through the early years of World War II, whereas the rhetorical use of sport gained greater prominence in the ensuing years. Mrozek concludes his analysis by stating that:

> The development of model-man or model-soldier—that is, a symbolic type suitable for a specific era—underscored that the identification with shared cultural symbols was more significant than the practical applicability of the kind of training that the symbols theoretically embodied . . . After World War II, it was less true that sport would stand as a component of the American system of political concerns. But it became more true that it would serve as a rhetorical vehicle transmitting those concerns to an increasingly accessible public. (Mrozek, 1974, p. 13)

Sport and Polity

The ideological interrelationships between sport and politics have been treated at length by Petrie (1975). Thus it may suffice for our present purposes to illustrate the rhetorical use of sport by political figures in order to underscore the importance of competition and to propagate the value of high aspiration. One of the

---

*From *Rip Off the Big Game* by Paul Hoch pp. 100–101. Copyright © 1972 by Paul Hoch. Reprinted by permission of Doubleday & Company, Inc.

best examples of the use of sport by a political figure is the many sport-related pronouncements of Gerald Ford during his tenure as Vice-President and President of the United States. For example, when serving as vice-president he wrote (in collaboration with John Underwood) an essay for *Sports Illustrated*, "In defense of the competitive urge." The essence of his essay is given in the following observations made by Ford:

> . . . outside of a national character and an educated society, there are few things more important to a country's growth and well-being than competitive athletics. If it is a cliche to say athletics build character as well as muscle, then I subscribe to that cliche. It has been said, too, that we are losing our competitive spirit in this country, the thing that made us great, the guts of the free-enterprise system. I don't agree with that; the competitive urge is deep-rooted in the American character.

> . . . being a leader, the United States has an obligation to set high standards. I don't know of a better advertisement for a nation's good health than a healthy athletic representation. Athletics happens to be an extraordinarily swift avenue of communication. The broader the achievement the greater the impact. There is much to be said for Ping-Pong diplomacy.

> With communications what they are, a sports triumph can be as uplifting to a nation's spirits as a battlefield victory.*

While serving as President of the United States in 1975, Ford was given the Theodore Roosevelt Award by the National Collegiate Athletic Association. In his acceptance speech, Ford made the following statements supporting the essential importance of the sport spirit for Americans:

> No youngster grows up today in America without participation in competitive sport. Sports not only prepares them for life, but that spirit is part of America's competitive spirit.

> As a nation, we have to be physically and mentally fit because these difficult times demand that we not only compete but that we must excel. (*New York Times*, 1975, p. 45)

In summary, we can state that the regulative institutions, like the socializing institutions, share a competitive ethos. In addition, they propagate the value of high aspiration by both direct and indirect means of economic and political socialization processes.

10.2.3 Sport and Cultural Institutions

Although not as blatantly obvious as the socializing and regulative institutions, cultural institutions also propagate the value of high aspiration and underscore the importance of achievement and competition. Cultural institutions influence

---

*Reprinted from "In Defense of the Competitive Urge," by Gerald Ford with John Underwood. *Sports Illustrated*, July 8, 1974. © 1974 Time, Inc.

coerced conformity to the dominant value system in a two-fold manner. First, through the manipulation of key symbols in creeds and ceremonies they act as a mechanism for social integration. They thus help to obtain consensus among diverse members and groups in society as to the basic standards of conventional morality. Second, through the public display of selected moral attributes, they depict a modal personality type which is regarded as representative of a society's national character, a national character that values personal achievement and natural competitiveness.

Sport as a Ceremonial Calendar

America is a pluralistic society, differentiated by a variety of social statuses and social strata based on such defining attributes as age, education, ethnicity, occupation, race, religion, sex, and wealth. Individuals of given social statuses and members of given social strata hold particular beliefs and ascribe to particular practices. Thus, and not surprisingly, individuals and groups are often in opposition to one another and their relationships are often characterized by conflict and competition.

Accordingly, the smooth functioning of social life is difficult at the best of times, and various social processes are invoked to keep social conflict at a minimum and social consensus at a maximum. One major means of ensuring social consensus is the annual construction and enactment of national ceremonies that publicly celebrate the importance of citizenship, the greatness of nationhood, and the uniqueness of national character in a society. As Warner has written about the United States:

> The ceremonial calendar of American society, (the) yearly round of holidays and holy days, partly sacred and partly secular, but more sacred than secular, is a symbol used by all Americans. Christmas and Thanksgiving, Memorial Day and Fourth of July, are days in our ceremonial calendar which allow Americans to express common sentiments about themselves and share their feelings with others on set days pre-established by the society for this very purpose. This calendar functions to draw all people together to emphasize their similarities and common heritage; to minimize their differences; and to contribute to their thinking, feeling, and acting alike.*

From a consensus perspective of society, a ceremonial calendar supports the moral basis of society by presenting a system of symbols of universally shared goals, values, and expectations. From a conflict perspective of society, a ceremonial calendar supports the value system of the dominant classes by imposing "on the lower strata a mythical system which has as its function, the moral seduction of the masses" (Kessin, 1966). Which of these interpretations has the most validity is debatable. But it is difficult to deny that ceremonial calendars in America have historically functioned as a mechanism of social integration and as

---

*From W. Lloyd Warner, Marchia Meeker, and Kenneth Eells, *Social Class in America* (New York: Harper & Row, 1960), p. 4. Copyright © 1960 by Harper & Row Publishers, Incorporated. Reprinted by permission of the publisher.

a means of ensuring some minimal degree of morale among the general population.

It may be argued, however, that as society has become increasingly less sacred and more secular the key dates on the ceremonial calendar dealing with religious and memorial occasions have been supplanted by dates denoting sporting events and spectacles. The world of sport has its own ceremonial calendar divided seasonally according to professional primary sport involvement (baseball and golf in the spring and summer, football in the fall, and basketball and hockey in the winter), and divided temporally according to major sporting events such as the NCAA National Basketball Tournament, the Indianapolis 500 car race, the World Series, and the Super Bowl.

Moreover, sport spectacles have incorporated many of the rites and sacred rituals characteristic of religious and memorial occasions such as parades, public prayers, and the singing of the national anthem. In fact, Marx's famous dictum that "religion is the opiate of the masses" has been reformulated to state that "sport is the opiate of the masses." In any event, one should not overlook the symbolic importance of sport for reinforcing existing patterns of the social order (Smith, 1976).

Sport and the Mass Media

Perhaps the clearest example of the ideological relationship between sport and cultural institutions is the connection between sport and the mass media. As Breed (1958) points out, the media are a conservative institution not prone to support or promote social causes, but more concerned with the preservation of the status quo. Breed suggests that the media function as a social control agent, not so much by what they disseminate as by what they do not present. By avoiding the spreading of stories or events incongruent with the existing normative systems, the media fulfill a function that might be labeled the "sacred cow hypothesis of social control."

In effect, the media serve as standardized ritual. Despite the social and psychological implications of media involvement, the media are a symbolic institution whose most important effect is a mythic reassertion of cultural values. At precisely this point, the functional relationship between media and sport clearly reveals itself. Sport, like the media, serves the social order through symbolic reaffirmation of prized and established norms, values, and sanctions. Moreover, sport as a set of culture patterns provides a public display of valued moral attributes held to be characteristic of national character and representative of secular correlates of values inherent in the Protestant Ethic.

The Athlete as Hero and Moral Leader

A chief way in which sport as a ceremonial calendar and as an aspect of the mass media promotes the public display of moral values is by characterizing athletes as moral leaders and depicting sport personalities as contemporary heroic figures. With respect to the institutional propagation of the value of high aspiration, Smith writes the following about the concept of the hero:

One of the hero's main functions is to raise the aspiration levels of the people in the society. Klapp (1962) argues that the hero lifts people above where they would be without the model. The essential feature of the hero from the societal vantage point is that the hero should behave in such a way as to perpetuate collective values, affirm social norms, and contribute to the solidarity of the society. (Smith, 1973, p. 61)

The ideal-typical moral traits of a hero in Western society were described in Section 5.3. These character traits were treated with reference to actual sport participants in various subcultural contexts. But one may extend the notion of moral character in sport to include secondary as well as primary forms of sport involvement. Specifically, it is suggested that through the mass media individuals may identify vicariously with the professed moral traits of sport figures and discern and lay claim to them as defining their own self-identities.' As Smith states:

Mass communication facilities have allowed images to be projected to large numbers of people simultaneously. This in turn has enabled the masses to use media celebrities for their identity voyages. (Smith, 1973, p. 62)

Smith takes care to point out, however, that the anti-hero is currently as popular in sport as in books and movies. Furthermore, he notes that: "An athletic hero normally does not have the power to take his followers outside the bounds of the social structure to produce a person with a new identity. Athletics represent stability and conservatism, the antithesis of what the transcendent hero stands for." Finally, Smith speculates that we are currently witnessing the demise of the traditional athletic hero:

What we seem to have left is a collection of incomplete or tarnished quasi-heroes. We still have the need to worship heroes, but the models that are available are becoming less and less exemplary. (Smith, 1973, pp. 67–68)

Whether there has been a demise of the sport hero is debatable. However, the issue does suggest that one must take care to distinguish different types of sport heroes and to examine historical shifts in the type of hero preferred by the public in a given society (Swetman, 1976).

One of the few efforts to examine the functions of the athlete as a "moral" leader from a historical perspective is Haerle's (1974) analysis of the success themes and basic cultural values in selected baseball autobiographies from 1900 to 1970. Haerle suggests on the basis of his analysis that a major societal function of sport is the reinforcement of the most sacred values of the culture; but notes that ". . . the culture of any society is extremely complex and full of contradictory or co-existing values which do not seem to 'hang together'."

Haerle specifically suggests in the case of professional baseball that different basic cultural values have been stressed during different periods, noting for example that "we have moved from an emphasis on teamwork in the 1870–1925 period to reaffirmation of individuals in the late 1960's." Overall, he concludes that:

To some degree, baseball, along with whatever values are dominant at the time, acts as the game of life in miniature. The players, as actors, perform their required roles, while the rest of society look on from a distance with an excellent chance for vicarious socialization experiences. Here we see fundamental human problems played out before our very eyes. Success and failure, the individual versus the group, the ultimate nature of man, the need for social order and social control—these and similar issues are constantly tested on the field of play. Whether the cultural values shift over time or not, the *process* of the morality play continues unhampered. In this manner are the basic cultural values, the so-called "sacred beliefs," constantly reinforced or challenged. (Haerle, 1974, p. 399)

Haerle's interpretation of success themes and cultural values reflected in professional baseball can be likely generalized to other sports, both amateur and professional. Moreover, it can be argued that in particular historical eras some special sports are more likely to reflect dominant cultural values than others. Thus football, rather than baseball, perhaps served as the best morality play during the cold war and vertiginous high-risk sports may best serve as the morality play of the 1970s (Donnelly, 1977).

10.2.4 Summary

From a functionalist perspective with Marxist overtones, the case has been made that the success ideology of the social institution of sport propagates the value of high aspirations and thus acts as a form of manipulative socialization that ensures acceptance of the dominant values of American culture by members of the society-at-large. Moreover, it has been contended that to the degree that the success ideology of the secondary social institution of sport supports the success ideologies of the primary social institutions of society, the social system of sport obtains legitimacy as a significant societal subsystem.

10.3 SOCIAL STRATIFICATION AND COERCED CONFORMITY

10.3.1 The Nature of Moral Stratification

This section illustrates how sport is related to another form of coerced conformity, namely, "the imposition of the veiled threat on subordinate statuses of being stigmatized as morally inferior unless they accept the goal of high aspiration." This process is discussed with reference to the moral framework of society and with respect to the phenomenon of social stratification.

The American Dream

The essence of the moral framework of our social system is contained in the collective beliefs associated with what has been called the American Dream. As Warner et al. have written:

In the bright glow and warm presence of the American Dream all men are born free and equal. Everyone in the American Dream has the right, and often the duty, to try to succeed and to do his best to reach the top. Its two fundamental themes and propositions, that all of us are equal and that each of us has the right to the chance of reaching the top, are mutually contradictory, for if all men are equal there can be no top level to aim for, no bottom one to get away from; there can be no superior or inferior positions, but only one common level into which all Americans are born and in which all of them will spend their lives. We all know such perfect equality of position and opportunity does not exist.*

The American Dream, like the American Sports Creed, provides a mythic description of the American success ideology. Furthermore, its underlying antithetical moral principles reflect the dynamic and often conflict-ridden social interaction among members of society.

From a consensus or functionalistic perspective of society, the antithetical principles of the American Dream, when in proper balance, are believed to ensure the proper functioning of society. Warner (1953) states the case as follows: "The principle of equality is necessary to provide all men with a sense of self-respect and to establish the secular essentials to the Christian belief in brotherhood"; whereas "the principle of rank and status is necessary to provide men with the motives to excel by striving for positions of higher prestige and power for themselves and for their families."

In contrast, a conflict or Marxist perspective of society suggests that the importance of the American success ideology for the superstructure of capitalistic society is that it influences institutional forms of manipulative socialization, which produces coerced conformity to the value system held by those members of society in dominant positions. Thio states the case as follows:

> Such a "normative acceptance" of the American success ideology, then, is likely to insure the perpetuation of the established dominance of the ruling groups. But there remains the inevitable self-contradiction in the making of widespread adherence to high success goals, because the established order has to account for those individuals who fail to achieve success despite their high aspirations. This task is relegated to the functions of the success ideology. It subtly coerces the subordinate strata to support the doctrine of abundant success opportunities for everyone, so that it directly legitimizes the status quo and indirectly misleads the subordinate strata to blame themselves rather than the imperfect social structure for their own lack of success. (Thio, 1972, p. 6)

Both the consensus and conflict interpretations of the moral framework outlined by the American Dream suggest that society is socially stratified. The basic tenets of these two theoretical perspectives were stated in Section 2.3.2, and the implications of these two models of society for the analysis of the relationships between sport and social stratification were discussed in Chapter 9. For the pres-

---

*From W. Lloyd Warner, Marchia Meeker, and Kenneth Eells, *Social Class in America* (New York: Harper & Row, 1960), p. 3. Copyright © 1960 by Haper & Row Publishers, Incorporated. Reprinted by permission of the publisher.

ent, notwithstanding basic differences between perspectives and purposes, both models of society share selected perceptions and conceptions about the phenomenon of social stratification.

As Kessin has pointed out, there is at least minimal agreement that:

1. "Whatever the reason, stratification is an inequality of valued symbols and/or means. (Prestige, power, or money).

2. "There is a tendency for rewards to accrue to those positions which serve "vital" functions for the society.

3. "Both schools recognize the existence of a subjective aspect of stratification. That is, there develops about the fact of inequality, a system of thought ways that serves to legitimate, support, and perpetuate the observed inequalities. This value system may become itself, the basis for the assignment of prestige and reward." (Kessin, 1966, p. 2)

In this section we wish to stress, largely from a conflict perspective, the subjective aspect of social stratification, especially a form of subjective social differentiation that is referred to as moral stratification.

Moral Stratification

Sociomoral hierarchy. As Tumin has observed: ". . .in American society one is generally considered better, superior, or more worthy if one is:

> White rather than [Black]
> Male rather than Female
> Protestant rather than Catholic or Jew
> Educated rather than Uneducated
> Rich rather than Poor
> White Collar rather than Blue Collar
> Of Good Family Background rather than
>   Undistinguished Family Origin
> Young rather than Old
> Urban or Suburban rather than Rural Dwelling
> Of Anglo-Saxon National Origin rather than Any Other
> Native Born rather than of Foreign Descent
> Employed rather than Unemployed
> Married rather than Divorced." (Tumin, 1967, p. 27)

These evaluations are based on perceived moral attributes and the ensuing stratification of persons and groups in society. This represents what Ball (1970) has termed *moral stratification.* This type of differentiation, moral stratification, appears to be a central dimension of the social psychology of social order. This order, which we create, sustain, alter, and experience, represents "a drama of social hierarchy in which we enact roles as superiors, inferiors and equals" (Duncan, 1962).

Implications of the concept. The kind of sociomoral hierarchy associated with moral stratification in society is particularly relevant to the sociological consideration of deviance and dominant-subordinate relationships such as age, class, ethnic, and sex contacts, which in this perspective become a special case of deviance considered more generally as social conflict. In short, in everyday life the term moral is generally applied to persons and groups when their character and conduct appear to be *normal* with respect to perceived standards of conventional morality.

As Garfinkel (1967) has demonstrated, for members of the mundane world, "moral," as social reality, equates with "normal." To be perceived-to-be normal is to be assumed to be conventionally situated or placed in the "natural order of persons taken for granted," that is, to be socially located in the "of course" environment of nonreflective and anyday/everyday life. Thus, to be accorded such placement is to be deemed normal, hence positioning is a moral one; to be treated as normal is to be accorded the preference due to morality.

Although Garfinkel's ethnomethodological perspective generates this equation of normality and morality, it is quite consistent with a much more conventional and longstanding tradition in social psychology and sociology, namely, research on social distance. Almost tautologically, there is least social distance between those persons or groups most nearly normal (that is, "taken-for-grantable"). Contrarily, great social distance implies the lack of normality and thus the absence of morality.

But the issue is not simply moral vs. not moral; it is moral vs. immoral. To be "not-moral" is not simply to be different. Rather, the closer one gets to the other pole of the continuum, the more the meaning implies "to be bad" or "to be contaminated." In effect, one becomes an object with whom social relationships are to be actively avoided or rigidly prescribed in their form and content. Moral and immoral are the polar opposites, then, of a continuum along which persons and groups can be and indeed are hierarchically ranked—in a word, morally stratified.

As discussed earlier (see Section 9.3.1), social stratification involves more than mere invidious ranking along some definitional dimension(s). It also involves allocation, that is, the systematic distribution of rewards and costs (or punishments) in terms of the particular criteria of a given system of social stratification. We customarily think of stratification systems as being organized around such social resources as property, power, and prestige. But it is equally as useful to view morality as a similarly pervasive basis of such systematic differentiation, the definition of which has very real consequences for very real people.

Where there is moral stratification, there are differential rewards and costs, and such a system of stratification is characterized by competition and conflict as persons and groups struggle to maximize the one and minimize the other. Moreover, such competition and conflict tend to reaffirm (if not reify) the phenomenon of moral stratification.

In the course of competition and conflict associated with moral stratification, oppositional others are characterized in a rhetoric of abuse, ranging from mild sportive slights (e.g., "the members of the opposing team are a bunch of . . "), to ethnic epithets (e.g., "that dumb . . ."), to caustic racial slurs (e.g., "'that dirty . . ."). Such rhetoric helps to increase moral stratification. Since competitors are, by definition, in conflict over the same goal objects they are, in a sense, very like one another. But a rhetoric of abuse highlights differences (real or imagined), thus increasing perceived social distance and furthering differentiation along the morality-immorality scale of social worth.

To summarize to this point, we can state that persons and groups are differentiated on the basis of perceived normality, which in turn implies morality. This differentiation assumes the form of a stratification system (i.e., an invidious hierarchy), characterized by competition and conflict among various statuses and strata since rewards and costs are systematically associated with moral rank. Furthermore, competition and conflict are associated with the rhetorical invocation of conventional (publically espoused) moral values.

10.3.2 Sport and Moral Stratification

This section explains how sport as a cultural system models systems of moral stratification, and in so doing highlights problems of status virtue and standards of conventional morality in society. Before turning to a detailed analysis of sport and moral stratification, brief mention is made of the relationship between play and equality, since the ideal-typical competition in which moral stratification might be expected to be absent is organized athletic contests (Simmel, 1955).

Play and Equality

The basic tenet of the American Dream is that "all men are created equal." But as Griffith (1974) notes, this ". . . resounding phrase, engraved on the brainpan of every American school child, has an implied religious context—meaning equal in the sight of God."

Outside of the sight of God, as Duncan (1962) has stated: "The purest form of relationships among equals exists in social play. . . ." The state of equality inherent in the social world of play is held to derive from the principle of sociability, which Simmel (see Wolff, 1964) formulated ". . . as the axiom that each individual should *offer* the maximum of sociable values (e.g., joy, relief, liveliness, etc.) that is compatible with the maximum of values he himself *receives.* "But as Simmel took care to note, ". . . this democratic character can be realized only within a given social stratum: sociability among members of very different social strata often is inconsistent and painful." Or as Duncan has more generally expressed the matter:

> We do not play with superiors, we obey them. We do not play with inferiors, we command them . . . Inferiors, like superiors, destroy social play if we cannot become equal to them, and they will not, or cannot become equal to us. (Duncan, 1962, p. 328)

As we stated in Chapter 1, in an ideal-typical game or sport contestants act as if all are equal and numerous aspects of external reality such as age, ethnicity, race, sex, and social class are excluded as relevant attributes for the duration of a given contest. But in reality, social interaction in sport situations seldom reflects this ideal state of affairs.

Although the social system of sport has been relatively successful in ensuring equality of competition between opposing contestants, it has been woefully unsuccessful in ensuring that persons of all social ranks in society can compete as social equals in sport situations. The world of sport remains morally stratified and this system of stratification in sport reflects the moral stratification of society-at-large in terms of such selected social categories as age and sex statuses, ethnic groups, and social classes.

Age Stratification: Young vs. Old

The moral order. In contemporary American society, to be young is to be healthy, attractive, and active, while to be old is to be sick, ugly, and passive. An illustration of the inferior status of aged persons and how they are perceived as sick and diseased is provided by a study conducted by Tringo (1970). He developed a modified Bogardus Social Distance Scale to measure aversion to disease, much as Bogardus measured aversion to racial and ethnic minorities. "Old age" was included as a category on the scale, itself an indication of social status. Tringo found that old age consistently scored far down the list of diseases, below serious, chronic, and even terminal diseases such as diabetes and cancer. Tringo's findings underscore the discriminatory process of *agism* and suggest why senior citizens have had their "consciousness raised" to such an extent that some have united under the banner of "Grey Power" to further their rights relative to other vested interest groups.

The social import of age stratification as regards the success ideology is that youth is valued because it represents achievement, competition, power, and success, whereas old age is devalued because it does not reflect the competitive attributes of achievement, independence, and productivity (Clark, 1967; Collette-Pratt, 1976; Cowgill and Holmes, 1972). That is to say, "in our culture with its emphasis on youth and speed, old people are expected to play a decreasingly active role in our social and industrial life" (Tuckman and Lorge, 1953). Moreover, the elderly are stigmatized and stereotypically viewed as a minority group whose perceived moral attributes undermine the active acceptance of the valued societal goal of high aspiration for one and all. In short, a specific form of social stratification in every society is age stratification, having (Riley et al., 1972) underlying moral connotations. This type of moral stratification results in patterns of social inequality based on age discrimination, including all of the prejudices associated with *agism*.

The sport order. The phenomenon of moral stratification relative to the social category of age is clearly illustrated in the context of sport. For example, Lewis (1971, 1977) offers historical interpretation of the increased popularity of sport since World War I in terms of two basic factors: youth culture and conventional morality. The import of these two factors may be gleaned from the following observations made by Lewis:

> . . . during the decade following World War I, and before many years had passed, admiration for age and what it represented had reached the point

that youth was held by all to be the most desirable period of life. One reason for holding youth in such high esteem was the conviction that success and the future belonged to it. Another favorable feature was that the age was thought to be filled with fun things and carefree hours. (Lewis, 1971, p. 3)

Important as youth culture was to the rise of sport, conventional morality was no less a factor. In fact, the role of sport in youth culture was determined to a large extent by conventional morality because the primary motivation for the promotion of sport among youth was the protection and perpetuation of conventional values. The use of sport as an instrument developed because everpresent change resulted in constant alterations in life-styles, and these modifications were invariably viewed as threats to the moral fiber of the nation. Since maintaining the status quo was not possible, efforts were directed toward finding ways to lessen the impact of incessant change. The search led first to the discovery of the potential for good in sport and later to an acceptance of the inherent goodness in sport. (Lewis, 1971, p. 7)

The original linkage of youth culture and conventional morality was based on middle-class values and was related to a masculine rather than a feminine orientation. But today the importance of youthfulness is a value shared by members of most social classes, male and female alike. The high esteem placed on youth in North American society is reflected in the numerous efforts of middle-aged adults to retain and/or regain youthful status. Just as some blacks once tried to pass as whites, many middle-agers now try to pass as young adults.

In summary, the sport order illustrates the ideological linkage between youth culture and conventional morality. Furthermore, it reveals the imposition of the veiled threat on subordinate social statuses (i.e., senior citizenship and old age) as being stigmatized as morally inferior unless they are capable of reflecting the goal of high aspiration and fullfillment of the success ideology.

Gender Stratification: Male vs. Female

The moral order. Historically, in most societies (especially Western societies), female status has long been considered inferior to male status. Even today in North America there remain residues of the Victorian ideals of womanhood in the current perceptions of the female role.

During the Victorian age, women were enveloped in a mystique that asserted their higher status, yet at the same time guaranteed their inferior status. The ideal woman was one that appeared wan, frail, delicate, passive, sensitive, and circumspect (Gerber, 1974).

Needless to say, changing cultural and social conditions have greatly attenuated many of the preferred characteristics associated with the Victorian ideal of womanhood. For example, the emergence of a youth culture in North American society has made physical attractiveness (that is, a healthy, fit, trim, and suntanned body) de rigeur for male and female alike. However, some characteristics associated with the Victorian ideal, such as the dependency and passivity of women are still ascribed to the "ideal" feminine role. A striking example of this fact is the Broverman et al. (1970) study of clinical psychologists who were asked to characterize a healthy adult male, a healthy adult female, and a healthy adult with sex unspecified. Both the healthy adult male and the healthy adult were described as independent, logical, and self-confident, whereas the healthy adult female was depicted as emotional, dependent, and passive. "Thus, for a woman to be healthy, from an adjustment viewpoint, she must adjust and accept the behavioral norms for her sex, even though these behaviors are generally less socially desirable and considered to be less healthy for the more generalized competent mature adult" (Broverman et al., 1970). Other investigations also support the notion that male roles are more valued than female roles (Dinitz, Dynes and Clarke, 1954; Goldberg, 1968; Kitay, 1940; Norman, 1974; Rosenkrantz et al., 1968).

One explanation for the fact that female status is devalued in relation to male status is that it does not reflect the highly valued attributes of achievement, aggressiveness, competitiveness, independence, and productivity. That is to say, the social category of female does not denote an emphasis of high aspiration and thus is not perceived as congruent with the success ideology. Indeed, females have been characterized as having achievement-related conflicts and as having a fear of success (Horner, 1972; Feather and Raphelson, 1974; Feather and Simon, 1975).

In summary, in spite of all the legal changes in recent years (for example, civil rights legislation), the masculine role is still valued more highly than the feminine role by a majority of both men and women. This form of social evaluation and moral judgment is closely related to the success ideology and clearly reflected in the domain of sport.

Female sport involvement. Because sport participation inherently entails achievement, aggressive actions, and the display of independence, it tends to be viewed as inconsistent with commonly accepted female stereotypes. Several studies show that it is difficult for women to be perceived as feminine while enacting active sport roles (see Brown, 1965; Griffin, 1972; Hall, 1972). For example, Brown (1965) and Griffin (1972) investigated college students' perceptions of selected women's roles using the semantic differential technique of attitude assessment and discovered that roles that were perceived as favorable on the evaluative dimension of the semantic differential were perceived as unfavorable on the activity and potency dimensions of the scale. More specifically, Brown (1965) found that college men and women rated the female roles of "sexy girl," "feminine girl," "cheerleaders," and "twirler" high on the evaluative factor, and the roles of "tennis player," "athlete," "basketball player," and "track player" low on the evaluative subscale of the semantic differential.

Similarly, Griffin (1972) found that college men and women highly evaluated the roles of "ideal women," "girl friend," and "mother," but lowly evaluated the roles of "women professor" and "women athlete," although they perceived them to be highly active and potent roles. The findings of Brown and Griffin confirm the existing stereotype of the appropriate role for a woman and its associated characteristics, and indicate that it is virtually impossible for a female to be perceived as feminine and yet be socially active and competitive.

The stereotyped perceptions of the woman's role are associated closely with the perceptions of what are appropriate and inappropriate forms of female sport involvement. Several studies indicate the most popular and most preferred participant sports for girls and women in North America. For example, studies by Metheny (1965), Petrie (1970), and Griffin (1972) indicate that there is the lingering point of view that "nice girls" don't engage in "manly sports," and that female participation should be restricted to upper-status sports such as figure skating, golf, gymnastics, skiing, and tennis, and mixed-status sports such as badminton, bowling, and swimming. These sports typically have connotations of sociability.

Male sport involvement. The socially sanctioned image of feminine sport competition is determined in large measure by the male domination of sporting life and the prevailing and persuasive norms of masculinity. David and Brannon have characterized the basic dimensions of the male sex role in terms of the following four themes:

1. "No Sissy Stuff: The stigma of all stereotyped characteristics and qualities, including openness and vulnerability."
2. "The Big Wheel: Success, status, and the need to be looked up to."
3. "The Sturdy Oak: A manly air of toughness, confidence, and self-reliance."
4. "Give 'Em Hell!: The aura of aggression, violence, and daring." (David and Brannon, 1976, p. 12)

The specific moral attributes associated with these basic dimensions of the male role were described in Section 5.3. Needless to say, it would be difficult to find a male (even a fictional male) who typifies all these characteristics. However, notwithstanding the fact that such extreme characterization of the ideal-typical male role is unrealistic, if not fantastic, the social stereotypes of the male role have significant influence on the normative expectations held for male behavior, especially the actions of adolescent males. Moreover, the normative order of sport reflects and supports these normative expectations and reinforces the extreme stereotypes of the ideal male role.

In short, for male youth, manhood and social worth are defined by the degree to which one is capable of meeting the normative expectations of masculinity. Finally, it is stressed that these normative expectations concerning masculinity emphasize the importance of high aspiration and underscore the major elements of the success ideology, namely, achievement, competition, productivity, and success.

Ethnic and Racial Stratification: Black vs. White

The moral order.   Social groups, as well as social roles, are stratified in terms of moral criteria. Some groups are regarded as superior and as having a membership of great moral and social worth, while other groups are viewed as inferior and as being composed of people of lesser moral stature and social worth. The relative ranking of ethnic groups in the United States in terms of social distance well exemplifies this type of moral stratification.

Table 10.1 shows the social distance ranks of Americans categorized by ethnicity at various points in time from 1926 to 1966. First, it is evident from the table that the relative ranking of ethnic groups has remained fairly constant over a forty-year period. Second, it is clear that the closer members of a given ethnic group are to "average white, middle-class, Protestant Americans," the more likely they are to be perceived as normal and less deviant and thus the higher their relative ranking. Third, it may be inferred from the table that ethnic groups with cultural ties to opponents of the United States in time of war are markedly' devalued. For example, the Japanese received their lowest ranking in 1946 shortly after World War II; the Koreans received their lowest ranking in 1956 shortly after the Korean War; and the Russians have ranked low in terms of relative ethnic status in America since the advent of the so-called cold war. Although comparable data are not available, one may predict that American citizens of Vietnamese heritage currently rank at the bottom of the ethnic ladder.

But it is not only in time of war that selected ethnic groups are devalued by those in the mainstream of American society. Whenever there is a large influx of members of a given ethnic group into a society as a whole or into particular regions, cities, or communities, the ethnic balance is upset and members of the immigrant subculture are typically viewed with disfavor. For example, in his analysis of immigration and public schooling at the turn of the century, Hunt (1971) states that: "Between 1880 and 1914 approximately ten million Russians, Poles, Bohemians, Hungarians, Slovaks, Greeks, and Rumanians entered the United States," and "These southern and eastern European peoples, with their poverty and 'foreign' languages and customs, aroused hostility in 'native' white American quarters . . . ." He notes that such hostility was not confined to members of the working or middle class but was expressed by professional people as well, including educators, politicians, and social scientists. For example, one senator "advocated returning to their home countries the hopeless immigrants, termed by some nativists 'sickening garbage,' 'criminals and paupers,' and 'fountains of immorality' " (Hunt, 1971).

The fear of foreigners expressed by native Americans at the turn of the century is presently portrayed by the reactions of many North Americans to what they believe to be the "menace" of the Third World. To illustrate, Kumm has written:

Today both liberals and conservatives feel threatened. The Third World, which is also the nonwhite world, looks very much like a back alley into which respectable people can be easily dragged, to be mugged, mutilated,

Table 10.1
Social distance ranks of Americans, 1926–1966

	1926	1946	1956	1966
English	1.0	3.0	3.0	2.0
Americans (U.S., white)	2.0	1.0	1.0	1.0
Canadians	3.5	2.0	2.0	3.0
Scots	3.5	5.0	7.0	9.0
Irish	5.0	4.0	5.0	5.0
French	6.0	6.0	4.0	4.0
Germans	7.0	10.0	8.0	10.5
Swedish	8.0	9.0	6.0	6.0
Hollanders	9.0	8.0	9.0	10.5
Norwegians	10.0	7.0	10.0	7.0
Spanish	11.0	15.0	14.0	14.0
Finns	12.0	11.0	11.0	12.0
Russians	13.0	13.0	24.0	24.0
Italians	14.0	16.0	12.0	8.0
Poles	15.0	14.0	13.0	16.0
Armenians	16.0	17.5	18.0	20.0
Czechs	17.0	12.0	17.0	17.0
Indians (American)	18.0	20.0	20.0	18.0
Jews	19.0	19.0	16.0	15.0
Greeks	20.0	17.5	15.0	13.0
Mexicans	21.0	24.5	28.0	28.5
Mexican Americans	—	22.0	22.0	23.0
Japanese	22.0	30.0	26.0	28.0
Japanese Americans	—	26.0	19.0	19.0
Filipinos	23.0	23.0	21.0	21.0
Negroes	24.0	29.0	27.0	28.5
Turks	25.0	25.0	23.0	26.0
Chinese	26.0	21.0	25.0	22.0
Koreans	27.0	27.0	30.0	27.0
Indians (from India)	28.0	28.0	29.0	30.0

Adapted from Bogardus (1967).

and left to bleed. Hijackings, embassy killings, bombs at airports and in planes make the world unsafe also at home. Black power has fused with oil power, creating a formidable weapon against the West. (Kumm, 1976, p. 62)

The fear of the Third World and of black power by native white North Americans is especially germane to the present analysis, for the most marked and consistent example of stratification and devaluation of ethnic status in North America, especially in the United States, has to do with the inequality between blacks and whites. As Wright succinctly stated:

Culturally the Negro represents a paradox: though he is an organic part of the nation, he is excluded by the entire tide and direction of American culture. Frankly, it is felt to be right to exclude him, and it is felt to be wrong to admit him freely. (Wright, 1977, p. 27)

The preceding observations provide strong evidence that the relative ranking of ethnic groups in terms of social distance constitutes a form of moral stratification. Devalued ethnic groups are characterized by moral attributes such as "immoral" and "lack of initiative," which run counter to the goal of high aspiration and against the grain of the success ideology. This is especially true in the case of black-Americans. The very term *black* in the white Western world has connotations of bad, dirty, evil, and immoral (as, for example, "blackballed," "black devil," "black-listed," "black dog," etc.).

We will now illustrate how the world of sport mirrors this ethnic form of moral stratification and reflects the social passage (that is, "moral" mobility) of selected ethnic groups from inferior to superior status in mainstream society.

The sport order.   One of the earliest examinations of ethnic stratification in sport is Riesman and Denney's (1951) study of football in America. They show that in broad outline there is a close correspondence between the history of major immigration patterns to the United States and the recruitment of members of given ethnic groups into the ranks of intercollegiate football. For example, the majority of the earliest non-Anglo-Saxon collegiate football players were of German, Irish, and Jewish background, which corresponds to the large number of immigrants from these groups from the Old World to America between 1790 and 1880. The next ethnic wave into collegiate football circles was largely composed of Italians, Poles, and Slavs whose parents came to the United States from eastern and southern Europe between 1880 and 1930.

Patterns of ethnic stratification found for collegiate football also seem to be characteristic of professional boxing (see Table 10.2). However, as Weinberg and Arond point out:

> The traditions of an ethnic group, as well as its temporary location at the bottom of the scale, may affect the proportion of its boys who become boxers. Many Irish, but few Scandinavians, have become boxers in this country; many Filipinos, but very few Japanese and Chinese. (Weinberg and Arond, 1952, p. 460)

Although the historical patterns of ethnic stratification in sport have been emphasized, the matter of ethnicity still poses problems for contemporary sport. Several examples are cited to illustrate this point. First, the board of the Little League Baseball Organization voted in 1974 to confine future world series to teams from the continental United States:

> The effect was to exclude Taiwan, which won the series for boys 8 to 12 years old in the last four years, causing protests in this country. Japan won the two previous years, then Monterry, Mexico, took the series in 1957 and 1958. The last United States winner was Wayne, N.J. in 1970. (*New York Times*, 1974, p. 1)

Table 10.2
Rank order of number of prominent boxers of various
ethnic groups for certain years

Year	Rank		
	1	2	3
1909	Irish	German	English
1916	Irish	German	Italian
1928	Jewish	Italian	Irish
1936	Italian	Irish	Jewish
1948	Negro	Italian	Mexican

From Weinberg and Arond (1952).

Following a great deal of protest, the ban was rescinded the following year, resulting in the domination of the series by foreign teams.

Second, the National Collegiate Athletic Association (N.C.A.A.) has in recent years been plagued with numerous difficulties concerning the eligibility of foreign athletes. Foreign athletes particularly predominate in the intercollegiate sports of ice hockey, soccer, and track and field. For example, foreign student-athletes competing in the N.C.A.A. indoor track and field championships won seven national titles in 1974, nine in 1975, five in 1976, and nine in 1977 out of fifteen individual events. Although foreign athletes have been members of college and university sport teams for nearly a century, the status of a foreign athlete was not formally defined until the N.C.A.A. adopted an alien student rule in January, 1961. This rule was instituted primarily to limit the number of Canadian hockey players on American college teams.

The extensive college recruiting in the United States of foreign athletes has resulted in the construction of "moralistic rationalizations" by both proponents and opponents of internationalism in sport. On the one hand, those who favor the recruitment of foreign athletes moralistically argue that America provides opportunity for one and all, and that participation of foreign students enhances international diplomacy and exposes students to different cultures. On more pragmatic grounds, they argue that foreign athletes introduce new coaching and training techniques, and permit middle- and small-time schools to compete on equal terms with big-time schools in selected sports.

On the other hand, those who oppose recruitment of foreign athletes argue that it deprives American students of exposure to high-level competition, forces young athletes to compete against older foreign athletes, and results in American institutions preparing foreign athletes for other national teams that may later defeat the United States in Olympic competition. The resentment, and what could be labeled American chauvinism, of those opposed to the college recruitment of foreign athletes is likely to increase in the immediate future (Van Dyne, 1976; Amdur, 1977; Kaminsky, 1974).

As previously noted in Chapters 4 and 9, ethnicity is an important factor in professional as well as amateur sport. One need only glance at the number of black athletes engaged in professional baseball, basketball, boxing, and football, the number of Latin American athletes engaged in professional baseball and horse racing, and the number of French Canadians in hockey to discern that sport is characterized by ethnic stratification.

Although the ethnic mix found in professional sport is often regarded as an index of democratization and a sign of social equality and lack of discrimination, such ethnic stratification often poses social conflict. Moreover, the ethnic social stereotyping of athletes has historically limited their participation and still affects their modes of participation in professional sport. For example, the long-lived "color line" in sport that prevented athletic competition between blacks and whites was initially established on the basis of moral superiority. Thus, just as "amateur gentlemen" would not lower themselves to compete with "professionals" of lesser moral stature, so did whites refuse to compete with blacks. Historically considered, the color line in sport is best illustrated by the sport of boxing. According to Roberts, in his account of the black heavyweight champion Jack Johnson:

> This line originated when John L. Sullivan issued his famous 1892 challenge to fight all contenders: "In this challenge, I include all fighters—first come, first served—who are white. I will not fight a Negro. I never have and never shall." And the Boston Strong Boy never did. (Roberts, 1976, p. 229)

Although Jack Johnson broke the color line by taking away the heavyweight title from Tommy Burns, a French-Canadian, in a title bout held in Sidney, Australia in 1908, the color line in other professional sports remained firm for nearly another forty years.

Moreover, even if a black athlete were successful in overcoming the color barrier of competition, he or she was still confronted with the problem of overcoming stereotypes about his or her moral character ("blacks lack endurance, intelligence, leadership ability, and don't perform well under pressure"). Although in somewhat attentuated form, many of these myths still exist in modern sport. For example, in his analysis of horse racing, Scott has the following to say about black jockeys (and the lack thereof):

> Horsemen believe—no doubt expressing a stereotypical bias—that Negroes lack the moral character necessary for being jockeys, though they are thought to possess a "sweet seat" and "strong hands." (Thus there are many Negro exercise boys but very few Negro jockeys.) By a kind of self-fulfilling hypothesis, the belief is maintained. When a Negro exercise boy is given opportunities to "don the silks" in the afternoon, he tries so hard to make a good showing that as a result he shows a lack of coolness. (Scott, 1968, p. 27)

Other illustrations could be given but the preceding observations demonstrate that both amateur sport and professional sport have a degree of ethnic stratification and that this form of stratification typically has moral connotations whereby given groups of athletes are categorized in terms of greater or lesser moral superiority. Such moral stratification in turn makes social conflict an inherent dimension of the acculturation of minority groups (Mains and Williams, 1975). Finally, we note that ethnic and racial stratification is closely related to the moral aspect of social and economic stratification, which is treated next.

Social and Economic Stratification: Rich vs. Poor

The moral order. The major form of social stratification is the hierarchical structure of social classes found in society. Social classes arranged in status hierarchies provide an example of social systems as conflicting interest groups. For example, Mayer notes:

> In general, the effect of status hierarchies seems to be the stabilization of the existing class structure; their function in this instance being the legitimation of class positions. Thus groups which have attained high economic positions usually attempt to solidify these positions by restricting status recognition and excluding others from access to the status symbols which they try to monopolize. (Mayer, 1955, p. 25)

Furthermore, Rex suggests that:

> . . . (1) the notion of a status hierarchy is something which is deeply entrenched in the ideology of the ruling class (in the sense of conflict classes) as a means of gaining recognition for the legitimacy of their position; (2) this ruling class will attempt to get the status ideology accepted by other classes, and (3) that these other classes do not all accept it, but put forward counter ideologies of their own. (Rex, 1961, p. 148)

Accordingly, status recognition, status exclusion, and efforts to legitimate status ideology are closely linked with the attribution of specific moral qualities to members of particular social classes.

A striking illustration of the moral stratification of social classes is offered by the work of W. Lloyd Warner and associates (1960) in their account of the attitudes and behavior of members of six classes in the New England community that they called Yankee City. The kinds of moral qualities that their informants used to describe members of different social classes are listed in Table 10.3. It is evident from this table that members of different social classes are ranked in terms of relative social worth. It is also clear from the table that members of the lower-lower class were the most devalued citizens in Yankee City, for they were depicted in such deprecating terms as "dirty and immoral," "those who live like pigs," and "people who scraped the bottom."

Rex (1961) has attempted to account for the findings about social classes in Warner's Yankee City study by means of a conflict model of social stratification. He contends that the key to understanding the status system reported by Warner is an analysis of the motivations and behavior associated with the claim of the lower-upper class to legitimacy. Rex's (1961) thesis is that, while in a position of economic power, the lower-upper class does not have legitimate authority. Thus:

> The lower order continually compare themselves unfavourably with the ruling classes of the past. Hence they must, if they are to gain acceptance,

abolish the distinctions between themselves and this class. At the same time they need the upper upper class and its way of life, because without it there would be no way at all of legitimating their positions. On the other hand they have to keep the lower orders in their place and the idea of an overall status hierarchy, rationalized on the lines suggested by Davis and Moore, provides them with the necessary ideology. (Rex, 1961, p. 150)

The upper-upper class does not oppose the status-seeking behavior of the lower-upper class, for the efforts of the lower-upper class to achieve upper-upper class status only serves to exalt their favored position. What seems to be at work is an Avis–Hertz principle, whereby those in second place, by trying harder, further publicize the reputation of those that they are trying to beat. Or, as Rex (1961) has stated, the upper uppers ". . . may resent the Lower Upper's trying to gate crash their tea-parties, but without the situation which the Lower Upper's have produced, the tea parties would have little excitement."

Rex further notes that:

The Upper Middle class has reasons of its own for accepting the status hierarchy. Their ambitions are limited in any case, but they can achieve them far more readily in the setting which the Lower Upper's have created. They have a delegated authority and not inconsiderable prerequisites to reward them for accepting the system. Moreover, in the immediate context of community life they do win approval for their social usefulness. (Rex, 1961, p. 151)

In brief, the "working ideology" of the upper-middle class comes closest to mirroring the success ideology held out for members of society-at-large. As Kahl has characterized the value system of the upper-middle class:

The upper-middle class believe in themselves and in the American way of life, and they are devoted to their careers. They stress planning for the future and not too much regard for the past; they stress activity, accomplishment, practical results; they stress individualistic achievement within the framework of group competition and collective responsibility. (Kahl, 1959, p. 193)

Finally, according to Rex (1961), the behavior of the members of the three lowest social strata (the LM, UL, and LL classes) may be best understood with reference to Merton's (1957) classic analysis of social structure and anomia.

In summary, the lower-upper class represents the ruling class in society and attempts to legitimate its position by ". . . offering an interpretation of the existing distribution of power and privilege in terms of a status system" (Rex, 1961). Members of the upper-upper and upper-middle classes actively accept this notion of a "just" status system, whereas members of the lower classes either passively accept the idea of a "just and necessary" status system or attempt to set forth counterideologies. Like most vested interest groups, the lower-upper class couches its ideology in moral terminology, and this dominant ideology serves to justify a system of moral stratification. This system of moral stratification, in turn, "imposes the veiled threat on subordinate social classes of being stigmatized as morally inferior unless they accept the goal of high aspiration" and actively

Table 10.3
Master list of social-class configurations

	Above the common man		Common man		Below the common man
	Class I.U.	Class II.UM	Class III.LM	Class IV.UL	Class V.LL
Carleton (Church member)	Group One—the highest / People so high up they're social history around here / People who feel secure	Group Two / People who are working to get somewhere	Third group / More religious than intelligent	The fourth group / At the bottom of the pile	
Withington (church member)	The fancy crowd / The wealthy and prominent / Federated Church people	Strictly middle-class / People a notch or two below the fancy crowd	Working people "Baptists"	Very low / People with a persecution complex	
Davis (doctor)	The 400 / The Society Class / The 398's who think they are 400's / Federated Church People	The fringe of society / The upper-middle class	The working class		The lulus / People just like animals, not worth a damn
Little (schoolgirl)	The High Class / The No. 1 Class	My class / Second highest class / Higher-middle / Middle-middle	Low-middle	Higher-lower	The lowest-class

	Upper stratum	"Upper-middle"	Lower, but middle status	Lower class	
Brown (teacher)	People with family and money				Canal renters Older Poles The people back of the tannery
Towne (politician)	The top families The Federated Church people	The solid people but don't go in for social things The Methodist Church	The plain, common people Like most of the Baptists	The little people The real poor people, but honest and fine	The poor, but not respectable
Other informants	A group founded on wealth and ancient family People who look down on everyone else in town Snobs The silk stockings The landed gentry The aristrocrats The Mainstreeters	Not in the top group but good substantial people The level just below the top group Prominent but not tops The strivers People who are in everything The community leaders Working hard to get in the 400 Above average but not tops	Average people Ordinary people Working people, but superior Top of the working people Not poor and not well off Good common people People with nice families but don't rate socially Nobodies (socially) but nice People just below the Country Club crowd Top of the common people	The Mill people The poor but honest Poor people but nothing the matter with them The little people The younger Poles Poor but hard working Poor but respectable "We're poor (UL) but not as poor as a lot of people (11)"	The poor and unfortunate The chronic rehefers Tobacco road Poor whites Hill-billies River rats Peckerwoods Dirty and immoral (Those who) live like pigs People who scrape the bottom Goddamn yellow hammers

From W. Lloyd Warner, Marchia Meeker, and Kenneth Eells, Social Class in America (New York: Harper & Row, 1960), pp. 66–67. Copyright © 1960 by Harper & Row Publishers, Incorporated. Reprinted by permission of the publisher.

support the success ideology. Let us now briefly examine how this system of moral stratification is reflected in the world of sport.

The sport order.   It appears, at least intuitively, that the sports associated with different social classes are intimately related to the value systems of those classes. For example, upper-class sports such as cricket, polo, skiing, tennis, and yachting illustrate "gracious living"—the keynote of the upper-class life (Kahl, 1959). Similarly, the emphasis on contact sports such as boxing, wrestling, and roller derby among the lower class may be symbolic of "fighting back at society" (Mott, 1965).

In any event, there seems to be a strong correlation between type of sport involvement and social class status. Specifically, survey findings indicate that primary sport involvement (that is direct participation) is greatest among members of the higher social classes, whereas secondary sport involvement (that is, vicarious participation) is greatest among members of the lower social classes. Active participation is generally viewed as being of greater moral worth than passive participation. Thus, the engagement in active athletic competition by members of the higher classes may be regarded as an index of high aspiration, whereas the emphasis on spectatorship by members of the lower classes may be assumed to denote lower aspirations and less emphasis on achievement, competition, and success.

Although evidence is not conclusive, survey data (see Clarke, 1956; Noe, 1974) suggests that the role of spectator sport is strongest among members of the lower-middle class. The stress on spectatorship among members of this class may be related to the achievement of "vicarious success" through the process of *identification*. Caillois has written:

> Everyone wants to be first and in law and justice has the right to be. However, each one knows or suspects that he will not be, for the simple reason that by definition only one may be first. He may, therefore, choose to win indirectly, through identification with someone else, which is the only way in which all can triumph simultaneously without effort or chance of failure. (Caillois, 1961, p. 120)

The process of identification in the sports context is not limited to the lower-middle class, but can be found in segments of the lower strata as well. In the former, identification seems to center on our so-called national team sports; in the latter, it seems to center on the individual combative sports of boxing and wrestling. Identification with sport stars such as championship boxers on the part of some lower-class people may express an unconscious desire to fight back at an unjust society, or it may be an emotional identification with an individual of one's own class background (and perhaps ethnic background as well) who has "made it." The latter viewpoint is given support by Olmsted's analysis of gambling among the urban proletariat. She reports:

> There is often considerable emotional identification with the actual winners on the part of other players. It is apparently reassuring to feel that one

of one's social class, with almost insuperable educational, ethnic, and social handicaps, can become *rich* without overcoming these handicaps. (Olmsted, 1962, p. 82)

Caillois also observes that "chance, like merit selects only a favored few":

> The star and the hero present fascinating images of the only great success that can befall the more lowly and poor, if lucky. An unequaled devotion is given the meteoric apotheosis of someone who succeeds only through his personal resources—muscles, voice, charm, the natural inalienable weapons of the man without social influence. (Caillois, 1961, pp. 120–121)

Interestingly, the elements of chance, fate, and luck appear to hold importance for both upper- and lower-status groups in society. As Merton (1957) states: ". . . both the eminently 'successful' and the eminently 'unsuccessful' in our society not infrequently attribute the outcome to 'luck'." Olmsted further observes:

> The very bottom ranks or outcasts in most societies and the top ranks of a hereditary aristocracy share a common faith in the importance of "fate," since they are aware that their position owes far more to accident of birth than to any characteristic of their own. (Olmsted, 1962, p. 74)

Whether the observations of Merton and Olmsted possess any real explanatory power with respect to patterns of sport participation is debatable. But there do appear to be certain affinities between patterns of sport involvement of the upper and lower strata of society not common to the large middle stratum of society. For example, various forms of involvement in "blood sports," boxing, gambling, and horse racing are perceived as more characteristic of members of the upper and lower classes than of members of the middle class. Moreover, there appear to be parallel forms of sport preferred by the top and bottom stratas that are not preferred by the middle stratum; examples are billiards and pool, roulette and craps, Grand Prix auto racing and stock car racing, equestrian events and rodeo events, foxhunting and coonhunting, falconry and pigeon racing, squash and handball.

The parallel forms of sport found for the upper and lower status groups, but not the middle status group, reflect a type of "social distancing." On the one hand, the upper classes seek to set themselves apart from the middle classes and use various means to denote their social exclusiveness, including forms of sport participation. Needless to say, due to the great social distance between the upper and lower classes, the elite are hardly concerned that members of the lower classes engage in somewhat similar forms of sport. On the other hand, the middle classes, while lacking the means to imitate the upper classes, do everything in their power to dissociate themselves from the lower classes. Lower-class sporting activities are typically viewed as immoral, sinful, deviant, and illegitimate by members of the middle classes. Thus, one means of ensuring "respectability" by the middle class is to avoid becoming involved in lower-class activities.

The relevance of class conflict and status striving for the sport sociologist is indicated in the following observations by Kahl and Mills. Kahl writes:

> Prestige tends to be bestowed through consumption behavior rather than income, for only that which can be seen can be judged. Consumption patterns and interaction networks are intimately linked; people spend their leisure time with others who share their tastes and recreational activities, and they learn new tastes from those with whom they associate. (Kahl, 1959, p. 108)

Similarly, Mills states:

> With the urban breakdown of compact groups in smaller communities, the prestige relations become impersonal; in the metropolis, when the job becomes an insecure basis or even a negative one, then the sphere of leisure and appearance become even more crucial for status. (Mills, 1956, p. 256)

Sport provides an especially relevant context for status display within the sphere of leisure.

Although numerous sports have become relatively democratized concerning patterns of participation by members of diverse social classes, sport as a leisure-time activity still provides several means of displaying one's social status. For example, Kaplan (1960) lists seven ways in which an individual can signify his or her social rank. First, people may set themselves apart from others by use of *special equipment:* The owner of a yacht is clearly differentiated from the renter of a rowboat. Second, social rank can be revealed by the *cost of participation:* The member of a golf club that charges a $15,000 membership fee is markedly set apart from the blue-collar worker participating on the public links. Third, social status is set forth by *cost of watching:* Upper-class people sit in reserved box seats, while lower-class people sit in the bleachers. Fourth, individuals may reveal their social background in terms of *time of participation:* The dentist or lawyer can play golf at midday during midweek, while the salesclerk or bankteller does well to get out on the course Sunday afternoon. Fifth, the social elite may set themselves apart from others by *special dress:* For example, a proper foxhunting habit versus blue jeans and a sweatshirt. Sixth, there is the matter of *travel costs:* The wealthy may ski abroad, while the poor must ski at home. Seventh, social status can be indicated by amount of *expendable assets:* The lower classes may have a greater proclivity for gambling, but the upper classes can afford to gamble for bigger stakes. Finally, we note that an individual can designate his or her place in the status hierarchy of society by manner or *style of involvement:* There is considerable contrast between the style of participation of the upper-class "amateur gentleman" and the working-class "semipro" in any commonly shared sport.

The social import of status striving and the display of status in sport situations is that an individual can symbolically show that he or she ascribes to the success ideology and values the importance of high aspiration. Thus, in some respects the sports played by members of a particular social class serve as symbols of their status and social worth in the structure of society.

In short, from a conflict perspective with functionalist overtones, the case has been made that the social institution of sport acts as a means of coerced conformity. It ensures acceptance of the success ideology by imposing the veiled threat on subordinate social statuses and strata of being stigmatized as morally inferior unless one accepts the goal of high aspiration. Moreover, it has been contended that to the degree that the success ideology of the secondary social institution of sport supports the dominant ideology of the ruling classes of society, the social system of sport obtains legitimacy as a significant societal subsystem.

10.4 SPORT, IDENTITY, AND IDEOLOGY

10.4.1 Sport as a Metasocial Interpretation of the American Dream

Critique of Manipulative Socialization

Drawing on the tenets of both the consensus perspective and the conflict perspective of society (with emphasis on the latter), the case was made in Sections 10.2 and 10.3 that the ideology of the social institution of sport reflects and reinforces the dominant ideology of society-at-large. Specifically, it was argued that the ideological elements of the social institution of sport (1) propagate the value of high aspiration, (2) aid the process of manipulative socialization, (3) foster coerced conformity, and thus (4) ensure acceptance of the American success ideology. A number of criticisms, however, may be leveled at the case just made.

First, it may be argued that the acceptance of the dominant ideology by diverse members of society does not necessarily result from manipulative socialization and coerced conformity, nor does it indicate a state of "false consciousness" among members of subordinate strata of society. As Parkin has stated:

> Acceptance of the dominant value system by members of the subordinate class does not necessarily promote deferential orientations. Equally consistent with such acceptance is a view of the reward structure which emphasizes the opportunities for self-advanced and social promotion. This aspirational model of reality endorses the class and status system as it stands, but also represents it as a relatively open order in which men of talent and ability can, with effort, rise above their present station. Thus, whereas the deferential version of the social world accepts the class system as a fixed, unchanging order, the aspirational version allows for the social exchange of personnel between classes, while accepting the necessity of classes as such. (Parkin, 1972, pp. 85–86)

Indeed, there is some empirical evidence which shows that individuals are more than willing to abide by the ideological edicts of various societal subsystems so long as they perceive that they are being justly rewarded for their conformance to cultural norms, values, and sanctions.

Second, it may be argued that the perceived isomorphism between the ideological elements of the American Sports Creed and the American Dream is only a simple analogy with a few meaningful consequences for everyday life. That is to say, the supposition that sport supports an ideology of domination characteristic of capitalistic corporate society may be based largely on facile rhetoric and thus have little empirical validity.

Third, it may be argued that even if it is true that sport reflects and reinforces status discriminations in society, such reflection and reinforcement is of limited influence, in that sport as a secondary institution lacks the social power of the primary or master institutions of society. That is to say, the social impact of sport as regards the acceptance of the dominant success ideology is largely symbolic, not substantive.

Fourth and finally, it may be argued that the reflection and reinforcement of status differentials is hardly necessary on the part of sport for the preservation of the social order. To paraphrase Geertz's observations on the Balinese cockfight (by substituting the term sport for cockfight):

> What sets [sport] apart from the ordinary course of life, lifts it from the realm of everyday practical affairs, and surrounds it with an aura of enlarged importance is not, as functionalist sociology would have it, that it reinforces status discriminations (such reinforcement is hardly necessary in a society where every act proclaims them), but that it provides a metasocial commentary upon the whole matter of assorting human beings into fixed hierarchical ranks and then organizing the major part of collective existence around that assortment. Its function, if you want to call it that, is interpretative. . . . (Geertz, 1973, p. 448)

The general proposition underlying the final section of this chapter is that the social significance of sport as a contest for "the best representation of something" (see Section 10.1; Huizinga, 1955) does not result from the fact that it mirrors the dominant value system of society *per se*, but rather results from the fact that from a dramaturgical perspective it provides a metasocial interpretation of the moral framework of society. Specifically, it is hypothesized that the sport order provides a meaningful metasocial interpretation of what might be termed the Marxian contradiction of the American Dream: the principle of equality on the one hand and the principle of unequal status and superior and inferior rank on the other hand (Warner, 1953).

These two antithetical moral principles influentially inform present societal concerns with social discrimination and social inequality. They are associated closely with the seemingly obsessive concern with social success, social position, and status reputation among people at all levels of society. Furthermore, and perhaps more fundamentally, they both aid and hinder the process of self-construction in mass society.

Sport as a Cultural System

What allows sport to provide a metasocial interpretation of the American Dream is the fact that the sport order of society constitutes a cultural system. As a cultural system, the sport order may be defined in the same way that Geertz (1973) has defined religion as a cultural system, namely, "(1) a system of symbols which acts to (2) establish powerful, pervasive, and long-lasting moods and motivations in men by (3) formulating conceptions of a general order of existence and (4) clothing these conceptions with such an aura of factuality that (5) the moods and motivations seem uniquely realistic."

To extend Geertz's analysis further, it is suggested that sport, like religion, as a cultural system serves as both a "model for" and a "model of" reality. The difference between these two types of models is expressed by McCready and Greeley as follows:

> A "model of" reality presents relationships in such a way as to render them apprehensible. It expresses the structure of the relationship in synoptic form. A "model for" reality is the reverse of the above; it creates relationships according to some previously attained apprehension of reality.*

Or, as Geertz (1973) has stated: "Unlike genes, and other non-symbolic information sources, which are only models *for*, not models *of*, culture patterns have an intrinsic double aspect: they give meaning, that is, objective conceptual form, to social and psychological reality both by shaping themselves to it and by shaping it to themselves."

In brief, it is argued that sport in a highly ideational sense is a dramatization of life-at-large, a type of "deep play," an art form, a social ritual. As a form of "deep play," sport has sacred overtones and ". . . is a symbol of moral import, perceived or imposed" (Geertz, 1973). To paraphrase once again Geertz's observations on the Balinese cockfight (by substituting the term sport for cockfight):

> Like any art form—for that, finally, is what we are dealing with—[sport] renders ordinary, everyday experience comprehensible by presenting it in terms of acts and objects which have had their practical consequences removed and been reduced (or, if you prefer, raised) to the level of sheer appearances, where their meaning can be more powerfully articulated and more exactly perceived. (Geertz, 1973, p. 443)

The social significance of sport as a cultural system, as an art form, and as a social ritual is indicated by the following observations of Fromm:

> Aside from art, the most significant way of breaking through the surface of routine and of getting in touch with the ultimate realities of life is to be found in what may be called by the general term of "ritual." I am referring here to ritual in the broad sense of the word, as we find it in the performance of a Greek drama, for instance, and not only to rituals in the narrower religious sense.
>
> Whether we think of the Greek drama, the medieval passion play, or an Indian dance, whether we think of Hindu, Jewish or Christian religious rituals, we are dealing with various forms of dramatization of the fundamental problems of human existence, with an *acting out* of the way the very same problems are *thought out* in philosophy and theology.

---

*Excerpted from *The Ultimate. Values of the American Population,* by William C. McCready and Andrew M. Greeley, by permission of the publisher, Sage Publications, Inc. Copyright © 1976.

What is left of such dramatization of life in modern culture? Almost nothing. Man hardly ever gets out of the realm of manmade conventions and things, and hardly ever breaks through the surface of his routine, aside from grotesque attempts to satisfy the need for a ritual as we see it practiced in lodges and fraternities. The only phenomenon approaching the meaning of a ritual, is the participation of the spectator in competitive sport. . . . (Fromm, 1965, pp. 131–132)

One of the basic problems of human existence dramatized by the cultural system of sport is the problem of self-construction. The following discussion offers speculations as to how the ritualization of experience in the course of sport involvement is related to the quest of individuals for self-identity, and suggests how the sport order provides a dramatization of status concerns among members of society.

10.4.2 Sport Involvement and Self-construction in Mass Society

Questions of Identity

The moral framework of our culture tends to legitimize certain social arrangements in our society, as, for example, the sociomoral hierarchy of statuses and strata described in Section 10.3. But because this framework contains opposing moral principles, these social arrangements and systems of moral stratification interfere with the process of self-construction ". . . by making it difficult for individuals to construct stable identities, to discern the desirable and undesirable qualities that they might develop, and indeed most crucially, ever to realize a fundamental sense of their own worth" (Hewitt, 1970).

Writing from a symbolic interactionist perspective, Hewitt states that "self-construction [may be] regarded as an attempt on the part of the person and his circle of others to establish answers to an important set of questions":

The person asks: What am I? By that he intends to discern in himself, largely but not entirely through the response of others, a set of qualities to which he can lay claim and discern as defining himself. He asks: Who am I? This is a broader question by which he lays claim not simply to qualities that may be valued, but also to identification with recognized named social statuses and groups: "I am . . . Jewish, a professor, a man." These are claims to identity. Finally, he asks: "Am I what I ought to be?" This suggests a quest for self-esteem, a desire that what-ever identities and self-images are claimed be valued by others. (Hewitt, 1970, p. 20)

We suggest that the questions raised by Hewitt are moral questions insofar as an individual's identity represents a "moral career" (Goffman, 1961). We further suggest that the moral questions concerning self-construction are related to the relationship between sport and the moral order.

Sport and moral character. When a person asks "What am I?" he or she is attempting to ascertain what set of qualities distinguish him or her as a unique human being (Hewitt, 1970). The asking of this question expresses "the need to be well thought of" (Tumin, 1967). While there are many kinds of qualities that define a social self, the most highly valued characteristics are those associated with *moral character*. Moreover, the most highly valued moral attributes are those related to the control of fateful events in action situations (Goffman, 1967).

In Section 5.3 we described how sport settings represent action situations and thus offer a context in which individuals can define and test their moral character. Such character testing is by definition, however, problematic. Outstanding performance denotes success and the establishment, at least temporarily, of "good moral character." But poor performance indicates failure and the "lack of moral character." As Ball expresses the matter in his analysis of failure in sport:

> For the person *qua* failure himself, his reaction to himself, as a self, is likely to be one of *embarrassment*: a sense of "unfulfilled expectations". . . and a concomitant discomfiture. Since failure involves the demonstration of a moral lack, to be failed is to be deemed not-to-be-normal, to be ajudged as not "fitting in". . . A failure is not normal, not moral, and thus unworthy of the deference due "respectable" persons. (Ball, 1976, pp. 727–728)

In short, the microcosm of sport mirrors the matter of moral character in the macrocosm of society; the outstanding athlete is idealized as a "moral leader," whereas the failure in sport is devalued to the point of the individual's being perceived as a "degraded deadman" or "non-person" (Ball, 1976).

Sport and moral stratification. When an individual asks "Who am I?" he or she is attempting to establish an identification with valued statuses and groups (Hewitt, 1970). The asking of this question expresses the need "to be considered as good or as worthy as others with whom one is being compared" (Tumin, 1967).

In Section 10.3 we showed that people in society are differentially evaluated in terms of social worth and accordingly ranked in a sociomoral hierarchy, and we illustrated how the sport order mirrors this system of *moral stratification*. Thus, perhaps it will suffice to note at this point that the underlying dynamics of moral stratification are founded on the efforts of individuals to achieve respectability within the framework of public morality (Ball, 1970), and to avoid being stigmatized (Goffman, 1963) and discredited as unrespectable and morally inferior. As Ball has written:

> Basically, the respectability problem involves the presentation of proper demeanor so as to be worthy of and to receive the deference from others due us by virtue of our membership in human society. Such deference is necessary in order that we may be assigned the minimal status needed for the successful pursuit of goals in social situations, as well as the creation and upkeeping of definitions of self as a morally worthy person; that is, one who is normal, who upholds social order and is deserving of the order-maintaining and sustaining gestures of worthy-acknowledgement from other like-minded persons in society. Thus, respectability becomes central to social order itself, one of the major threads of social integration. (Ball, 1970, p. 339)

The social significance of sport in the present context is that as a cultural system it serves to dramatize the problematics of respectability in society-at-large.

Sport and moral mobility.   When an individual asks "Am I what I ought to be?" he or she is expressing the desire ". . . to become better thought of than others and seek the differential rewards of such distinctions . . ." (Tumin, 1967). This desire is related closely to the marked emphasis and concern with social mobility in American society. As Goldschmidt (1955) has aptly stated: "We measure our own ability not only in terms of where we are, so to speak, but in terms of how far we have moved."

It is important to note that successful status passage from inferior to superior positions in society has moral as well as social and economic connotations. Social advancement, whether in a corporation or a community, implies acceptance of the goal of high aspiration, conformance to the success ideology, and a move upward in the sociomoral hierarchy of society. The world of sport mirrors societal concerns with social and moral mobility and symbolically supports the rags-to-riches myth. For example, the success stories of such contemporary sport figures as Muhammad Ali, Arthur Ashe, Rocky Bleier, Bob Cousy, Julius Erving, Althea Gibson, Pancho Gonzales, Mickey Mantle, Bill Russell, and Johnny Unitas have played a major role in sustaining the American Dream, for such accounts ". . . force upon the individual a recognition of both the real possibility of advancement and the personal responsibility for that advancement" (Goldschmidt, 1955). At the same time the many examples of failures and losers in the world of sport, as well as the numerous tales of athletes who went from rags to riches back to rags, dramatize the problematic nature of upward mobility in North American society.

Both the sport order and the "social order are expressed through hierarchies which differentiate men into ranks, classes and status groups, and, at the same time, resolve differentiation through appeals to principles of order which transcend those upon which differentiation is based" (Duncan, 1968). In turn, in both the sport order and the social order, "hierarchy is expressed through the symbolization of superiority, inferiority, and equality, and of passage from one to another" (Duncan, 1968). Finally, with respect to status passage in both sport and society, we note in the words of Duncan that:

> How we pass from one social position to another is as important as what we do when we get there. Every social institution must provide for transfer among equals, as well as promotion and demotion among superiors and inferiors. Successful change in status position safeguards the individual, as it does the group, by providing safe and proper ways to change status. All changes in status are moments of danger, to both the individual and his society. (Duncan, 1962, p. 257)

In short, (1) self-construction in mass society can be viewed in terms of a moral career, (2) which is problematic due to matters of moral character, moral stratification, and moral mobility, (3) whose basic dimensions are dramatized and ritualized with the sport order. As Edwards has written:

. . . the chief specific factors determining fan enthusiasm for sport are to be found within the functions of sport as an institution. As an institution having primarily socialization and value maintenance functions, sport affords the fan an opportunity to *reaffirm the established values and beliefs defining acceptable means and solution to central problems in the secular realm of everyday societal life. But this fact does not stand alone; particular patterns of values are expressed through certain intrinsic features of sports activities; in combination, the two aspects explain not only enthusiasm but sport's predominantly male following. Sports events are unrehearsed,* they involve *exceptional performances* in a situation characterized by a degree of *uncertainty* and a lack of total control, and they epitomize *competition for scarce values*—prestige, status, self-adequacy, and other socially relevant rewards. (Edwards, 1973, p. 243)

Edwards's emphasis on the socialization and value-maintenance functions of sport suggests how sport deals with important social concerns and relationships of strategic structural significance. Moreover, his thesis that "sport affords the fan an opportunity to reaffirm the established values and beliefs" indicates a critical linkage between identity and ideology, self and society.

Summary
The preceding analysis makes it clear that efforts at self-construction occur within a matrix of social interaction. Moreover, self-construction is typically a conflict-ridden and socially ambiguous process.

Self-construction is conflict-ridden because tension inevitably develops ". . . between the self the person would construct for himself and the self others would construct [for him] . . ." (Hewitt, 1970). It is ambiguous because in mass society ". . . it becomes difficult for parents and children alike to articulate their behavior with social expectations, values and norms, and with a more or less commonly shared vision of social reality" (Hewitt, 1970).

A major reason for the ambiguity associated with self-construction is that there seems to be (Douglas, 1970) an increasing incongruency between public morality (as expressed by the dominant ideology of the ruling class) and private morality (as expressed by individuals and selected subcultures). According to Douglas, there is:

. . . a growing recognition of the insincerity of public moral pronouncements, coupled with the rage for authenticity or sincerity in personal relations . . . and of the actually problematic nature of moral experience. (Douglas, 1970, p. 27)

Sentiments similar to those of Douglas have been expressed by Glasser (1972b) in *The Identity Society.* He suggests that humanity has passed through three stages (private survival society, primitive identity society, and civilized survival society) and has recently entered a fourth phase of evaluation, which he labels the "civilized identity society." Glasser characterizes this type of society as follows.

Led by the young, the half-billion people of the Western world have begun a tumultuous revolution toward a new, role-dominated society in which people concern themselves more and more with their identities and how they might express them. Of course, people still strive for goals, but increasingly these are vocational or avocational goals that their pursuers believe will reinforce the independent human role. The goals may or may not lead to economic security, but they do give people verification of themselves as humans. Not everyone can work at a job he would enjoy identity with, such as doctor, artist, or teacher; but now anyone can pursue a recreational goal (such as bowling or bridge-playing) or a volunteer goal (such as working at a hospital or fund-raising) that reinforces his identification as a worthy person. (Glasser, 1972a, p. 31)

Whether American society is evolving a new morality and moving toward a new ethic is highly debatable. Nevertheless, it is clear that in a pluralistic and constantly changing society self-construction and establishment of social worth remain a highly problematic matter.

Thus, the social significance of sport for self-construction lies in the fact that as a cultural system sport dramatizes the moral dilemmas and status concerns of individuals in society. That is, the social significance of sport is not as conflict sociologists would have it, namely, that it reflects and reinforces the dominant ideology of the ruling class and supports a sense of community, but rather that it provides a metasocial interpretation of the complexity of social reality.

Conclusion

We began this chapter with consideration of the paradoxical nature of sport, profound on the one hand and profane on the other. In the course of the chapter we have attempted to show that while "it's only a game" sport can be and has been used for instrumental purposes and does often reveal relations of strategic structural significance. Thus, the paradoxical nature of sport remains and this inherent fact characterizes both the weakness and strength of the social institution of sport.

To conclude by paraphrasing Simmel's analysis of sociability (by substituting the term sport for sociability), we note that:

Our discussion shows that people both rightly and wrongly lament the *superficiality* of [sport]. To account for this, we must remember and appreciate one of the most impressive characteristics of intellectual life. This is the fact that if certain elements are taken out of the totality of existence and united into a whole that lives by its own laws and not by those of the totality, it shows, if it is completely severed from the life of that totality, a hollow and rootless nature, in spite of all its intrinsic perfection. And yet, and often only by an imponderable change, this same whole, in its very distance from immediate reality, may more completely, consistently, and realistically reveal the deepest nature of this reality than could any attempt at grasping it more directly. Applying this consideration to the phenomenon of [sport], we understand that we may have two different reactions to it. Accordingly, the independent and self-regulated life, which the superficial aspects of social interaction attain in [sport], will strike us as formulalike and irrelevant lifelessness, or as a symbolic play whose aesthetic charms embody the finest and subtlest dynamics of broad, rich social existence. (Wolff, 1964, p. 56)

REFERENCES

Amdur, N. (1977). "Is college recruiting of foreigners excessive." *New York Times* (March 15): 46.

Ball, D. W. (1970). "The problematics of respectability." In J. D. Douglas (ed.), *Deviance and Respectability—The Social Construction of Moral Meanings*, pp. 326–371. New York: Basic Books.

Ball, D. W. (1976). "Failure in sport." *American Sociological Review* 41 (August): 726–739. Used with permission.

Bandura, A. (1969). "Social learning theory of identificatory processes." In D. A. Goslin (ed.), *Handbook of Socialization Theory and Research*. Chicago: Rand McNally.

Bogardus, E. S. (1967). *A Forty Year Racial Distance Study*. Los Angeles: University of Southern California.

Boyle, R. H. (1963). *Sport—Mirror of American Life*. Boston: Little, Brown.

Breed, W. (1958). "Mass communication and socio-cultural integration." *Social Forces* 37 (December): 109–116.

Broverman, I., et al. (1970). "Sex role stereotypes and clinical judgments of mental health." *Journal of Consulting and Clinical Psychology* 34: 1–7.

Brown, R. (1965). "A use of the semantic differential to study the feminine image of girls who participate in competitive sports and certain other school related activities." Ph.D. dissertation, Florida State University.

Caillois, R. (1961). *Man, Play and Games*. New York: The Free Press.

Clark, M. (1967). "The anthropology of aging: A new area for studies of culture and personality." *Gerontologist* 7: 55–63.

Clarke, A. C. (1956). "The use of leisure and its relation to levels of occupational prestige." *American Sociological Review* 21: 301–307.

Collette-Pratt, C. (1976). "Attitudinal predictors of devaluation of old age in a multi-generational sample." *Journal of Gerontology* 31: 193–197.

Cowgill, O., and L. C. Holmes (1972). *Aging and Modernization*. New York: Appleton-Century-Crofts.

David, D. S., and R. Brannon (1976). *The Forty-Nine Percent Majority: The Male Sex Role*. Reading, Mass.: Addison-Wesley.

Dinitz, S., R. Dynes, and A. C. Clarke (1954). "Preferences for male or female children: Traditional or affectional." *Marriage and Family Living* 16: 128–130.

Donnelly, P. (1977). "Vertigo in America: A social comment." *Quest* 27 (Winter): 106–113.

Douglas, J. D. (1970). "Deviance and respectability: The social construction of moral meanings." In J. Douglas (ed.), *Deviance and Respectability*, pp. 3–30. New York: Basic Books.

Duncan, H. D. (1962). *Communication and Social Order*. New York: Oxford University Press. Used with permission.

Duncan, H. D. (1968). *Symbols in Society*. New York: Oxford University Press.

Edwards, H. (1973). *Sociology of Sport*. Homewood, Ill.: Dorsey Press. Used with permission.

Feather, N. T., and A. C. Raphelson (1974). "Fear of success in Australian and American student groups: Motive or sex-role stereotype?" *Journal of Personality* **42** (June): 190–201.

Feather, N. T., and J. G. Simon (1975). "Reactions to male and female success and failure in sex-linked occupations: Impressions of personality, causal attributions, and perceived likelihood of different consequences." *Journal of Personality and Social Psychology* **31**: 20–31.

Ford, G. R. (with J. Underwood) (1974). "In defense of the competitive urge." *Sports Illustrated* **41** (July 8): 16–23. Used with permission.

Fromm, E. (1965). *The Sane Society.* New York: Fawcett World Library.

Garfinkel, H. (1967). *Studies in Ethnomethodology.* Englewood Cliffs, N.J.: Prentice-Hall.

Geertz, C. (1973). *The Interpretation of Cultures.* New York: Basic Books.

Genovese, E. D. (1970). "On Antonio Gramsci." In J. Weinstein and D. W. Eakins (eds.), *For a New America,* pp. 284–316. New York: Random House.

Gerber, E. W., et al. (1974). *The American Woman in Sport.* Reading, Mass.: Addison-Wesley.

Glasser, W. (1972a). "The civilized identity society." *Saturday Review* (February 9): 26–31. Used with permission.

Glasser, W. (1972b). *The Identity Society.* New York: Harper & Row.

Goffman, E. (1961). "The moral career of the mental patient." In E. Goffman, *Asylums: Essays on the Social Situation of Mental Patients and Other Inmates,* pp. 125–169. New York· Doubleday Anchor.

Goffman, E. (1963). *Stigma.* Englewood Cliffs, N.J.: Prentice-Hall.

Goffman, E. (1967). *Interaction Ritual.* Chicago: Aldine.

Goldberg, P. (1968). "Are women prejudiced against women?" *Transaction* **5**: 28–30.

Goldschmidt, W. (1955). "Social class and the dynamics of status in America." *American Anthropologist* **57**: 1209–1217.

Griffin, P. S. (1972). "Perceptions of women's roles and female sport involvement among a selected sample of college students." M.Sc. thesis, School of Physical Education, University of Massachusetts.

Griffin, P. S. (1973). "What's a nice girl like you doing in a profession like this?" *Quest* **19** (January): 96–101.

Griffith, T. (1974). "The delicate subject of inequality." *Time* (April 15): 72–73.

Haerle, R. K. (1974). "The athlete as 'moral' leader: Heroes, success themes and basic cultural values in selected baseball autobiographies, 1900–1970." *Journal of Popular Culture* **8** (Fall): 392–398, 401–407. Used with permission.

Hall, M. A. (1972). "A 'feminine woman' and an 'athletic woman' as viewed by female participants and non-participants in sport." *British Journal of Physical Education* **3** (November): xliii, xlvi.

Hewitt, J. P. (1970). "Self-construction in the mass society." Presented at the American Sociological Association Annual Meeting (August). Used with permission.

Hewitt, J. P. (1973). "Mass society, principles of organization and paradox." *International Journal of Comparative Sociology* **14**: 35–46.

Hoch, P. (1972). *Rip Off the Big Game.* Garden City, N.Y.: Doubleday.

Horner, M. S. (1972). "Toward an understanding of achievement-related conflicts in women." *Journal of Social Issues* **28**: 157–175.

Huizinga, J. (1955). *Homo Ludens.* Boston: Beacon Press. Used with permission.

Hunt, T. C. (1971). "Public schools, 'Americanism' and the immigrant at the turn of the century." *Journal of General Education* **26**: 147–155.

Kahl, J. A. (1959). *The American Class Structure.* New York: Rinehart.

Kahn, R. (1957). "Money, muscles—and myths." *Nation* **185** (July 6):9–11.

Kaminsky, A. (1974). "N.C.A.A. changes its policy governing hockey eligibility." *New York Times* (November 31): 11.

Kaplan, M. (1960). *Leisure in America.* New York: John Wiley and Sons.

Kessin, K. (1966). "The acceptance of inequality: Some problems in the social psychology of stratification." Presented at the Annual Meetings of the American Sociological Association, Miami. Used with permission.

Kitay, P. (1940). "A comparison of the sexes in their beliefs about women: A study of prestige groups." *Sociometry* **3**: 399–407.

Klapp, O. E. (1962). *Heroes, Villains, and Fools.* Englewood Cliffs, N.J.: Prentice-Hall.

Kumm, B. (1976). "Fear of foreigners." *Harper's* **253** (September): 61–71. Used with permission.

Lewis, G. (1971). "Sport, youth culture, and conventional morality, 1917–1939." Presented at the Annual Meetings of the American Historical Association, New York (December). Used with permission.

Lewis, G. (1977). "Sport, youth culture and conventionality (1920–1970)." Paper submitted to the *Journal of Sport History* (April 27). Used with permission.

Mains, D., and J. S. Williams (1975). "The role of social conflict in the acculturation of minority groups." *International Review of History and Political Science* **12** (August): 59–71.

Matza, D. (1964). "Position and behavior patterns of youth." In R. E. L. Faris (ed.), *Handbook of Modern Sociology*, pp. 191–216. Chicago: Rand McNally.

Matza, D. (1966). "The disreputable poor." In N. J. Smelser and S. M. Lipset (eds.), *Social Structure and Social Mobility in Economic Growth*, pp. 289–302. Chicago: Aldine.

Mayer, K. B. (1955). *Class and Society.* New York: Random House. Used with permission.

McCready, W., and A. M. Greeley (1976). *The Ultimate Values of the American Population*, Vol. 23. Sage Library of Social Research, Beverly Hills, Calif.: Sage Publications.

Merton, R. K. (1957). *Social Theory and Social Structure*, 2nd ed. Glencoe, Ill.: The Free Press.

Metheny, E. (1965). *Connotations of Movement in Sport and Dance.* Dubuque, Iowa: William C. Brown.

Mills, C. W. (1956). *White Collar.* New York: Oxford University Press. Used with permission.

Mott, P. E. (1965). *The Organization of Society.* Englewood Cliffs, N.J.: Prentice-Hall.

Mrozek, D. J. (1974). "Rhetoric and reality in the Defense Department's use of sport, 1945–1950." Presented at the Annual Meeting of the North American Society for Sport History (May). Used with permission.

New York Times (1974). "Little League series bars foreigners." (November 11): 1–51.

New York Times (1975). "Ford calls sport spirit essential to Americans." (January 8): 45.

New York Times (1976). "De Rogatis kicks the pro football habit." (October 3): 6.

Noe, F. P. (1974). "Leisure life-styles and social class: A trend analysis, 1900–1960." *Sociology and Social Research* **58** (April): 286–294.

Norman, R. D. (1974). "Sex differences in preferences for sex of children: A replication after 20 years." *Journal of Psychology* **88**: 229–239.

Olmsted, C. (1962). *Heads I Win, Tails You Lose.* New York: MacMillan.

Parkin, F. (1972). *Class Inequality and Political Order.* London: Paladin. Used with permission.

Petrie, B. (1970). "Physical activity, games and sport: A system of classification and an investigation of social influences among students of Michigan State University." Ph.D. dissertation, Michigan State University.

Petrie, B. M. (1975). "Sport and politics." In D. W. Ball and J. W. Loy (eds.), *Sport and Social Order*, pp. 185–237. Reading, Mass.: Addison-Wesley.

Rex, J. (1961). *Key Problems in Sociological Theory.* London: Routledge and Kegan Paul. Used with permission of Humanities Press.

Riesman, D., and R. Denney (1951). "Football in America: A study in culture diffusion." *American Quarterly* **3**: 309–325.

Riley, M. W., et al. (1972). *Aging and Society, Vol. 3: A Sociology of Age Stratification.* New York: Russell Sage Foundation.

Roberts, R. (1976). "Heavyweight champion Jack Johnson: His Omaha image, a public reaction study." *Nebraska History* **57** (Summer): 227–241. Used with permission.

Rosenkrantz, P. et al. (1968). "Sex role stereotypes and self-concepts in college students." *Journal of Consulting and Clinical Psychology* **32**: 287–295.

Roszak, T. (1968). *The Making of a Counter-Culture: Reflections on the Technocratic Society and Its Youthful Opposition.* New York: Doubleday.

Sadler, W. A. (1972). "Competition out of bounds: A sociological inquiry into the meaning of sports in America today." Presented at the Annual AAHPER Convention, Houston (March).

Sadler, W. A. (1973). "Competition out of bounds: Sport in American life." *Quest* **19** (January): 124–132.

Schneider, L. (1964). "Institution." In J. Gould and W. L. Kolb (eds.), *A Dictionary of the Social Sciences*, p. 338. New York: The Free Press.

Scott, M. B. (1968). *The Racing Game.* Chicago: Aldine.

Simmel, G. (1955). *Conflict and the web of Group Affiliations.* New York: The Free Press.

Smith, G. (1973). "The sport hero: An endangered species." *Quest* **19** (January): 59–70.

Smith, G. J. (1976). "Ritual, ceremony and sport." *Katimavik* **3** (Winter): 3–4.

Swetman, R. D. (1976). "The contemporary sport hero: A provisional investigation into the concept of heroism as it relates to contemporary sport figures." M.Sc. thesis, Department of Physical Education, University of Washington.

Thio, A. (1972). "American success ideology and coerced conformity: Toward clarifying a theoretical controversey." Presented at the Sociological Theory and Theories Section of the Ohio Valley Sociological Society, London, Ontario, Canada (May).

Thio, A. (1974). "American success ideology and coerced conformity: Toward clarifying a theoretical controversy." *International Journal of Contemporary Sociology* **11**: 12–22. Used with permission.

Tringo, J. (1970). "The hierarchy of preference toward disability groups." *Journal of Special Education* **4**: 295–306.

Tuckman, J., and I. Lorge (1953). "Attitudes toward old people." *Journal of Social Psychology* **37**: 249–260.

Tumin, M. M. (1967). *Social Stratification.* Englewood Cliffs, N.J.: Prentice-Hall. Used with permission.

Van Dyne, L. (1976). "Give me your strong, your fleet. . . ." *Chronicle of Higher Education* **12** (March 29): 1–7.

Veblen, T. (1934). *The Theory of the Leisure Class.* New York: Modern Library.

Waller, W. (1932). *The Sociology of Teaching.* New York: John Wiley and Sons. Used with permission.

Warner, W. L. (1953). *American Life (Dream and Reality).* Chicago: University of Chicago Press.

Warner, W. L., Marchia Meeker, and Kenneth Eells (1960). *Social Class in America.* New York: Harper & Row.

Webb, H. (1969). "Professionalization of attitudes toward play among adolescents." In G. S. Kenyon (ed.), *Aspects of Contemporary Sport Sociology,* pp. 161–187. Chicago: Athletic Institute.

Weinberg, S., and H. Arond (1952). "The occupational culture of the boxer." *American Journal of Sociology* 57: 460–469. Used with permission.

Wolff, K. H. (ed.) (1964). *The Sociology of Georg Simmel.* New York: The Free Press.

Wright, R. (1977). "What sets storms rolling in his soul." *New York Times* (April 8): A27.

Young, K., and R. W. Mack (1959). *Sociology and Social Life.* New York: American Book.

AUTHOR INDEX

Adams, B., 89, 222
Albaugh, G., 74
Albinson, J., 88, 240
Albrecht, M., 325
Allen, V., 20, 217
Althus, W. D., 89
Alwin, D., 231, 232
Amdur, N., 404
Amis, W., 235, 236
Anderson, H., 358
Andreano, R., 186, 299, 352
Andrew, G., 88
Andrews, G., 240
Andrud, W. E., 73
Andrus, R., 301
Angi, C. E., 230
Appenzeller, H., 283
Argyle, M., 161
Aries, P., 243
Armer, J. M., 229, 234
Arms, R., 313
Arnold, D., 181, 182, 190
Arnold, G., 106
Arond, H., 186, 190, 193, 194, 204, 344, 350, 403, 404
Ashe, A., 240
Ashour, A., 83
Asmussen, E., 88
Atchley, R., 222, 363
Auf der Maur, M., 256, 257, 279, 280, 292

Babbie, E., 40, 42

Babchuk, N., 236
Balazs, E. K., 118
Bales, R. F., 78
Ball, D., 23, 130, 137, 138, 139, 143, 151, 160, 161, 162, 245, 246, 289, 323, 355, 394, 417
Ball, J. R., 118
Baltzell, E. D., 365, 368
Bandura, A., 216, 313
Barchas, P. R., 118
Bass, B. M., 75
Bates, S., 39
Beamish, M., 345
Becker, S., 161
Beisser, A., 200, 313
Bell, J., 318
Bend, E., 229, 231, 243
Bendix, R., 40, 339
Bennett, B., 258
Berelson, B., 155
Berger, P., 51
Berkowitz, L., 111, 313
Berne, E., 23
Bernstein, J., 58, 59
Berry, K., 367
Berryman, G., 367, 369
Berryman, J., 239, 244, 343, 344, 346, 356, 367
Bertrand, A. L., 38
Betts, J., 291, 301, 305, 318, 367
Binder, R., 286
Bird, A. M., 85, 106
Birrell, S., 208, 232, 233, 306, 311, 312

427

SUBJECT INDEX

DATE